Bryn Thomas was born in Zimbabwe where he grew up on a farm. Since graduating from Durham University with a degree in anthropology, travel on five continents has included a Saharan journey in his home-built kit-car, a solo 2500km cycle ride through the Andes, more than a dozen Himalayan treks and 50,000km of rail travel.

The first edition of this book, shortlisted for the Thomas Cook Travel and Guide Book Awards, was the result of several trips on the Trans-Siberian and six months in the Reading Room of the British Library. Subsequent publications have included *Trekking in the Annapurna Region*, also published by Trailblazer, and guides to India, Goa and Britain which he co-authored for Lonely Planet.

In 1991 he set up Trailblazer, to produce the series of route guides for adventurous travellers that has now grown to over 40 titles.

Anna Cohen Kaminski updated the eighth edition of this book. She was born in Moscow, Russia, and enjoyed a thoroughly Communist childhood before her family moved to the West. Though she has travelled on five continents since earning her Bachelor's degree in Comparative American Studies at the University of Warwick, this is the first time she has properly seen the country of her birth from end to end. Anna also writes for Lonely Planet and Rough Guides, covering destinations as diverse as Chile, Peru, Jamaica and Sweden. In between travels she calls Cambridge, England, home.

Trans-Siberian Handbook
First edition 1988; this eighth edition 2011

Publisher
Trailblazer Publications
The Old Manse, Tower Rd, Hindhead, Surrey, GU26 6SU, UK
Fax (+44) 01428-607571, info@trailblazer-guides.com
www.trailblazer-guides.com

British Library Cataloguing in Publication Data
A catalogue record for this book is available from the British Library

ISBN 978-1-905864-36-2

Editor: Nicky Slade
Cartography: Nick Hill
Typesetting: Nicky Slade
Chinese text: Qing Sun
Layout: Anna Jacomb-Hood
Proofreading: Jim Manthorpe & Anna Jacomb-Hood
Cover design: Richard Mayneord
Index: Anna Jacomb-Hood and Jane Thomas

Quotations used in Part 5 are from the *Guide to the Great Siberian Railway 1900*. Background information for Vladimir, Suzdal and Nizhny Novgorod was written by Athol Yates and updated from material originally published in his *Russia by Rail* (Bradt Guides).

Important note
Every effort has been made by the author and publisher to ensure that the information contained herein is as accurate and up to date as possible. However, they are unable to accept responsibility for any inconvenience, loss or injury sustained by anyone as a result of the advice and information given in this guide.

Cover photograph: A rare picture, taken in the early 1970s, of the Trans-Siberian being hauled by a steam engine (© Ron Ziel).

Printed on chlorine-free paper by
D'Print (☎ +65-6581 3832), Singapore

Trans-Siberian HANDBOOK

BRYN THOMAS

EIGHTH EDITION RESEARCHED AND UPDATED BY

ANNA COHEN KAMINSKI

TRAILBLAZER PUBLICATIONS

Dedication

In loving memory of Patricia Major, who helped found Trailblazer and was Series Editor for 19 years

From Anna: I dedicate my research to my parents, Ellen and David, without whom none of this would have been possible, and to Nicolas, for having faith in me when my faith was unsteady.

Acknowledgements

From Anna: I would like to thank Bryn for giving me this incredible opportunity and for his help and guidance throughout, Nicky, Nick and Anna for all their hard work on the book, and Qing for doing the Chinese translations.

Thank you to everyone who assisted me at home and on the road, particularly Genie Khmelnitski and Steve Exley for sharing my journey from Moscow to Ulan-Ude and Beijing, respectively; Laila Kynningsrud and Maja-Stina Ekstedt for the tips and the airag in Ulaanbaatar; Alexander McLachlan for all his knowledge and a wonderful dinner, and Monkey Business for helping me get a bus ticket instead of the dreaded 'standing' train ticket in Beijing; Rob Hallifax for sharing his Trans-Siberian experiences with me; Neil McGowan of The Russia Experience for his insider knowledge, Paul Carter-Bowman for the Beijing tips, and Olya Belyaevskaya for opening her doors to me in Moscow; fellow CouchSurfers Zhenya Surnina and Misha Balyasin for their incredible hospitality and advice in Krasnoyarsk; the best youth hostel hosts – Vladimir at Baikal Ethnic Hostel in Ulan-Ude, 'Jack' Sheremetov at Baikaler in Irkutsk, Anya at Baikal Trail Hostel in Severobaikalsk and Katya at Meeting Point Hostel in Yekaterinburg; Yura, Valera, Andrei, Nikita and Tanya for livening up my BAM travels, and the four San Diegans – Flip, Sara, Charles and Vita – for the memorable lunches at Kungur Ice Cave and in Vladimir.

From Bryn: I am greatly indebted to the numerous people who have helped me with this project since the publication in 1988 of what became, in its second edition, the book that started Trailblazer. I'm grateful to Patricia Major, for her unwavering support right from the beginning and for setting the high editorial standards. Thanks also to Jane Thomas for her extensive work in compiling the original strip maps and town plans. Nick Hill has built on her foundations with consummate skill; I'm grateful to him for the digitised maps, his excellent line drawings and also for all his research work on earlier editions. Thanks also to Anna Cohen Kaminski for accepting the challenge and producing a very comprehensive update for this eighth edition, to Nicky Slade for her thorough editing of the text, to Anna Jacomb-Hood for laydown of the book and for help in other ways with the production, and to Jim Manthorpe for proofreading.

Thanks to James Pitkin for the seventh edition of the book; Nick Hill, John King and Neil McGowan for updating the sixth edition, Athol Yates for original text on Vladimir, Suzdal and Nizhny Novgorod, the accompanying railway text, the carriage plan and all his and Tatyana Pozar-Burgar's work on the fourth edition of the book; Athol Yates and Nicholas Zvegintzov for the railway dictionary, Dominic Streatfeild-James who updated the third edition (and whose wry comments survive); Doug Streatfeild-James for the Chinese words and phrases section; Neil Taylor (Regent Holidays); and Ron Ziel for the cover photograph. Thanks to Richard Mayneord for the cover design and also for photos.

I'm grateful to the many readers who wrote in; see p506 for their names.

A request

The author and publisher have tried to ensure that this guide is as accurate and up to date as possible but things change quickly in Russia. If you notice any changes or omissions please write to Bryn Thomas at Trailblazer (address on p2) or email him (bryn.thomas@trailblazer-guides.com). A free copy of the next edition will be sent to persons making a significant contribution.

CONTENTS

PART 3: SIBERIA AND THE RAILWAY *(cont'd)*

PART 4: CITY GUIDES AND PLANS

INTRODUCTION

After the classic film of Boris Pasternak's love story, *Dr Zhivago*, there can be few people unaware of the magic of crossing Russia and the wild forests and steppes of Siberia on the longest railway journey in the world, the Trans-Siberian. The distances spanned are immense: almost 6000 miles, a seven-day journey, between Moscow and the Pacific port of Vladivostok (for boat connections to Japan); just under 5000 miles, five days, between Moscow and Beijing.

Since a rail service linking Europe with the Far East was established at the turn of the 19th century, foreign travellers and adventurers have been drawn to it. Most of the early travellers crossed Siberia in the comfort of the carriages of the Belgian Wagon Lits company, as luxurious as those of the Venice-Simplon Orient Express of today. Things changed somewhat after the Russian Revolution in 1917 as it became increasingly difficult for foreigners to obtain permits for Siberia.

It was not until the 1960s that the situation improved and Westerners began to use the railway again for getting to Japan, taking the boat from Nakhodka (it now leaves from Vladivostok) for the last part of the journey. In the early 1980s travel restrictions for foreigners visiting China were eased and now many people have found the Trans-Siberian a fascinating and cheap way to get to or from both China and Mongolia.

Rail travel is not only far more environmentally friendly than flying but inevitably passengers absorb something of the ethos of the country through which they travel: on this train you are guaranteed to meet local people, for this is no 'tourist special' but a working service; you may find yourself draining a bottle of vodka with a Russian soldier, discussing politics with a Chinese academic, or drinking Russian champagne with a Mongolian trader.

Russia is undergoing phenomenal changes after decades of stagnation. While the ending of the Cold War has removed some of the mystique of travelling in the former USSR, Russia's increasing accessibility means that there are new travel opportunities right across the country. With foreigners no longer obliged to stay in overpriced state-run hotels, visiting the country is more affordable than ever before.

Although travel in Siberia today presents few of the dangers and difficulties encountered earlier in the last century, a journey on the Trans-Siberian still demands considerable planning and preparation. Now in its eighth edition with even more detailed information than its predecessors, this book helps you cut through the red tape when arranging the trip, gives background information on Russia and Siberia, and provides a kilometre-by-kilometre guide to the entire route of the greatest rail adventure – the Trans-Siberian.

PLANNING YOUR TRIP 1

Routes and costs

'Best of all, he would tell me of the great train that ran across half the world ... He held me enthralled then, and today, a life-time later, the spell still holds. He told me the train's history, its beginnings ... how a Tzar had said, 'Let the Railway be built!' And it was ... For me, nothing was ever the same again. I had fallen in love with the Traveller's travels. Gradually, I became possessed by love of a horizon and a train which would take me there ...'

Lesley Blanch *Journey into the Mind's Eye*

ROUTE OPTIONS

Travellers crossing Siberia have a choice of three main routes: the Trans-Siberian, Trans-Manchurian and Trans-Mongolian. The Trans-Siberian is the most expensive route as it crosses the entire length of Siberia to the Pacific terminus at Vladivostok. The Trans-Manchurian travels through most of Siberia before turning south through Manchuria and ending in Beijing. The Trans-Mongolian also terminates in Beijing but travels via Mongolia which gives you the chance to stop off in Ulaanbaatar. Out of the three, the Moscow–Beijing route is the most popular, but all three have a lot to recommend them. Another alternative to the Trans-Siberian is the road less travelled – the Baikal Amur Mainline (BAM) – that runs parallel to the former, only 600km to the north of it, between just west of Lake Baikal and the eastern coast of Russia.

If you want to travel on to Japan after your trip you have several options. From Vladivostok there are both ferries (mid-May to December) and flights. There are also cheaper ferry services from various Chinese ports including Shanghai, Tianjin and Qingdao, all of them within easy reach of Beijing.

Trans-Manchurian and Trans-Mongolian travellers can continue from Beijing by train round China, which has an extensive rail system and also direct rail links into Vietnam. You can even travel back to Europe along the Silk Road on the Turkestan–Siberia (Turksib) railway.

COSTS

Overall costs

How much you pay for a trip on the world's longest railway line depends on the level of comfort you demand, the number of stops

you wish to make along the way and the amount of time you're prepared to put into getting hold of a budget ticket. At times Russian Railways offer seriously discounted tickets for those prepared to ride in the less popular top berths. If these are on offer when you want to go, and you don't mind being in a top berth, consider it a bonus; see p14 for sample fares – from £144/US$226 – on the main routes.

Among other big costs to factor in are transport to your departure point, transport back at the end of your journey, accommodation in Moscow, Beijing and any stopover towns, and of course food. If you want to buy your own tickets en route you must budget for the extra time that this will take, though it is possible to purchase them online (see p120).

The independent package deals offered by many travel agents can be better value than they might appear. Packages on the Trans-Siberian between Moscow and Beijing, including transfers and one night's accommodation in Moscow, start at about £700/US$1145, though if you travel independently, you can get by on around £45/$73 per day if travelling *platzkart* (3rd class in an open-plan dorm carriage). If a super-luxurious two-week guided rail tour from Moscow to Vladivostok with en suite accommodation in private saloon cars pulled by a

❑ What if I don't want to do it all by train?

Of course you needn't sit in a train for a week to see Siberia or Mongolia. It's quite feasible to fly to or from an intermediate point and travel only part of the way by rail. Major airports along the Trans-Siberian which have nonstop air connections with Moscow, Beijing or other international hubs include:

- **Yekaterinburg** (Moscow daily, from US$250; Frankfurt 3/week, Prague and Cologne weekly)
- **Novosibirsk** (Moscow daily, from US$270; Frankfurt and Hanover almost daily in summer, from US$700; Beijing 3/week, from US$550; Seoul weekly, from US$700)
- **Irkutsk** (Moscow daily, from US$380; Niigata weekly, from US$800; Tianjin, Shenyang and Dalian weekly, from US$650)
- **Vladivostok** (Moscow daily, from US$700; Harbin weekly, from $350; Seoul 3/week, from US$570; Osaka weekly, from US$800; Niigata weekly, from US$490; and Hanoi weekly, from US$630)
- **Ulaanbaatar** (Moscow several times weekly, from US$620; Beijing almost daily, from US$300; Tokyo, Osaka and Seoul several times weekly, from US$590).

Outbound air tickets are generally easy to buy a few days ahead (but see the note below about the Naadam Festival).

Trans-Siberian specialist agencies such as those listed on pp27-37 can arrange rail tickets for specific segments, although buying these on arrival is quite feasible and gives you more flexibility to alter your plans. You needn't book more than a day ahead for short segments, but you may need more time for longer ones such as Irkutsk–Moscow. Sleeping berths may be scarce on services not originating in your proposed departure town. From October to April it's easy to book almost any train at short notice.

Possibilities include the 005/006 Ulaanbaatar–Moscow, No 009/010 Irkutsk–St Petersburg, No 023/024 Beijing–Ulaanbaatar, No 025/026 Novosibirsk–Moscow and No 361/362 Ulaanbaatar–Irkutsk. Certain services and times get heavily booked – eg those to and from Ulaanbaatar around Mongolia's Naadam Festival in mid-July.

Not the Trans-Siberian Express!

Travel writers often wax lyrical about the fabled 'Trans-Siberian Express' but in fact no **regular** train service of that name exists. While the British generally refer to their trains by a time (eg 'the 10:35 to Clapham'), the Russians and Chinese identify theirs by a number (eg 'Train 003' from Beijing to Moscow). As in other countries a few crack services have been singled out and given names, but 'Trans-Siberian Express' is not among them. 'Trans-Siberian', 'Trans-Mongolian' and 'Trans-Manchurian' are, however, common terms for the main **routes** across Siberia and between Moscow and Beijing.

The train which runs all the way from Moscow to Vladivostok is the 002, and going in the other direction it's the 001; both services are also called the 'Rossiya'. The 020 covers the full Trans-Manchurian route from Moscow to Beijing, while in the other direction it's the 019; these are both called the 'Vostok'. Trains on the Trans-Mongolian route between Moscow and Beijing, and most other long-distance services, are identified only by number.

There is, however, now a luxurious special tourist train that goes by the name of the 'Golden Eagle Trans-Siberian Express' (see p29).

restored steam locomotive is more your idea of travelling, be prepared to part with around £6000/US$9813 (see p29).

One-way flights from London cost around £200 to Moscow or £350 to Beijing. The cheapest fully inclusive Trans-Siberian holidays cost from around £1700 including flights to and from London.

From New York, one-way flights cost around US$650-900 to Moscow or US$650-1200 to Beijing, depending on the season. The cheapest fully inclusive Trans-Siberian holidays cost from around US$3500 per person in high season, including flights to and from New York.

From Australia, single flights cost around A$1800 to Beijing or A$2500 to Moscow, depending on the season. The cheapest fully inclusive Trans-Manchurian trip costs around A$4500 per person including two nights in Moscow. A 10-day Vladivostok to Moscow budget package costs from about A$4700 with flights.

Accommodation costs

The price and value of accommodation in Russia varies wildly. Moscow and St Petersburg are the only places with genuinely five-star hotels (US$600/£380/€450 or more per night) although a number of Trans-Siberian cities, including Khabarovsk and Vladivostok, have good four-star places. Hotel prices in Moscow and St Petersburg are higher than anywhere else in the country.

Mid-range hotels cost around US$80-140/£50-90/€60-105 for a single or US$100-200/£65-125/€75-150 for a double with attached bathroom. Independent travellers who search out basic rooms with shared bathrooms in cheaper hotels can expect to pay US$30-50/£19-30/€22-38 for a single or US$35-60/£22-38/€26-44 for a double. Breakfast is sometimes included in the price.

Youth hostels have sprung up in Moscow, St Petersburg, Irkutsk, Vladivostok, Tomsk, Suzdal and Yekaterinburg, charging about US$16-32/£10-20/€12-24 per dorm bed or US$63-95/£40-60/€47-71 for a private room. Some hostels include breakfast in the price. Homestays are an option available in most larger Trans-Siberian towns, at about US$35-60/£22-38/€26-45 per person per night including some or all meals. If travelling independently, you can cut costs by CouchSurfing. For more information on accommodation see pp61-3.

Train classes and fares

Trans-Siberian train carriages are classed as either *platzkart* (3rd class), an open-plan dorm on rails, *kupé* (coupé; also called 2nd, hard or tourist class), with four-berth closed compartments; or *spalny vagon* (SV, also called 1st or soft class), with comfortable two-berth compartments, sometimes with washbasins.

On Trans-Mongolian train Nos 003/004, however, SV compartments are four-berth and identical in layout to all other services' kupé compartments except a bit wider, so they are poor value. But these trains also have an additional '*de luxe 1st*' class, whose carpeted two-berth compartments have armchairs and attached bathrooms, and are the only ones with showers.

Compartments are not single sex. Foreigners may find themselves sharing with other foreigners if they've booked through an agency that deals mainly with non-Russians. For further details on train classes see pp120-1.

Approximate sample fares (excluding any booking fees) are shown below for a non-stop, single (one-way) journey on each of the main routes across Siberia. They are what you would pay for a ticket, were you to buy it over the counter in Moscow or Beijing; those offered by some Western travel agents may cost substantially more. Prices are also subject to increase, particularly in times of high demand. At the time of writing you could get significant discounts on upper berths in platzkart and kupé, as they are less popular than bottom ones.

The fares below which show a range of prices reflect seasonal variations, the lower ones being in the winter months.

- **Trans-Siberian route** (Moscow–Vladivostok)
  platzkart (3rd) US$226/£144/€170
  kupé (2nd) US$260-520/£165-330/€195-390
  SV (1st) US$1025-1146/£650-727/€770-860

- **Trans-Manchurian route** (Moscow–Beijing)
  platzkart (3rd) US$290/£180/€220
  kupé (2nd) US$450-700/£300-550/€350-620
  SV (1st) US$1000-1400/£670-950/€780-1200

- **Trans-Mongolian route** (Moscow–Beijing)
  platzkart (3rd) US$300/£200/€240
  kupé (2nd) US$480-800/£320-570/€370-640
  SV (1st) US$1100-1400/£750-980/€870-1200
  de luxe 1st class US$1200-1500/£800-1000/€900-1250

BREAKING YOUR JOURNEY

All major cities on the Trans-Siberian can be visited. If you're booking through an agency, plan carefully: once you have started on your trip, it's too late to change your itinerary. But if you travel independently you can just buy tickets as you go along, and stop off whenever and wherever you like.

If your trip starts in **Moscow** (see p159) you'll need several days to see the main sights. A side-trip to **St Petersburg** (p129) is highly recommended. At the other end, it's certainly worth spending several days in **Beijing** (p355).

In between there's the 'Golden Ring' city of **Nizhny Novgorod** (p222) and historically rich **Yekaterinburg** (p232). **Novosibirsk** (p253) is the sprawling capital of Western Siberia, **Tomsk** (p261) is an interesting university town and **Krasnoyarsk** (p265) is among the region's most pleasantly situated cities. **Irkutsk** (p272), capital of Eastern Siberia, is 64km from beautiful **Lake Baikal** (p283), the world's deepest freshwater lake; a stay beside the lake is highly recommended. **Ulan-Ude** (p294) is worth a stop for the Buddhist monastery nearby, and **Khabarovsk** (p307) is surprisingly pleasant. **Vladivostok** (p316), the bustling home port of Russia's Pacific Fleet, is the eastern railway terminus.

Also recommended for those headed to Beijing is a visit to **Ulaanbaatar** (p327), the capital of Mongolia. Irkutsk and Ulaanbaatar are the most popular stopovers for Trans-Siberian travellers.

When to go

The mode of life which the long dark nights of winter induce, the contrivances of man in his struggle with the climate, the dormant aspect of nature with its thick coverage of dazzling snow and its ice-bound lakes now bearing horses and the heaviest burdens where ships floated and waves rolled, perhaps only a fortnight ago: – all these scenes and peculiar phases of life render a journey to Russia very interesting in winter.

Murray's *Handbook for Travellers in Russia, Poland and Finland* (1865)

For most people 'Siberia' evokes a picture of snowy scenes from the film *Dr Zhivago*, and if they are not to be disappointed, winter is probably the best time to go. It is, after all, the most Russian of seasons, a time of fur coats, sleigh-rides and chilled vodka. In sub-zero temperatures, with the bare birch and fir trees

Winter travel

'I've just got back from a round-the-world journey that began with a trip on the Trans-Siberian Railway. We knew what to look out for, were informed about what we were seeing and, to a certain extent, had an idea of what to expect. Nothing, though, could really prepare one for the pleasure of seeing acres of snow, the tracks going seemingly nowhere, the groups of trees, the delicate reeds and huge frozen rivers and lakes'. **Elizabeth Watson** (UK)

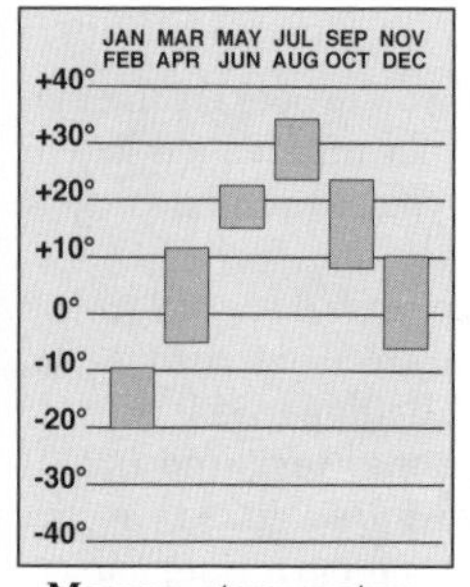

Moscow – temperature (average max/min ˚C)

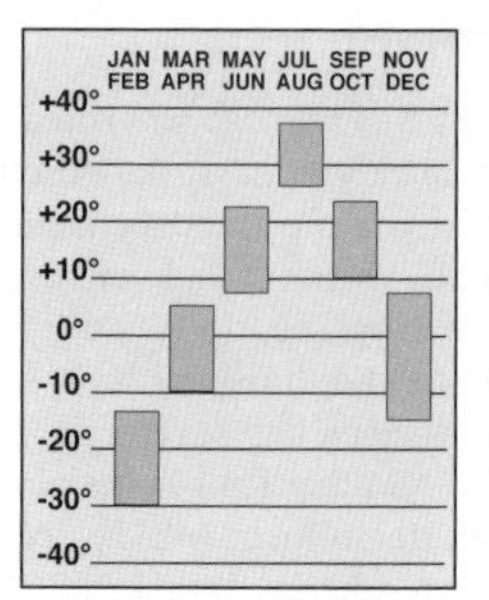

Irkutsk – temperature (average max/min ˚C)

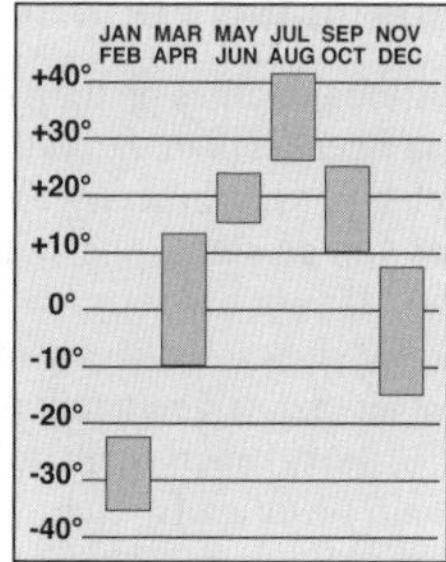

Ulaanbaatar – temperature (average max/min ˚C)

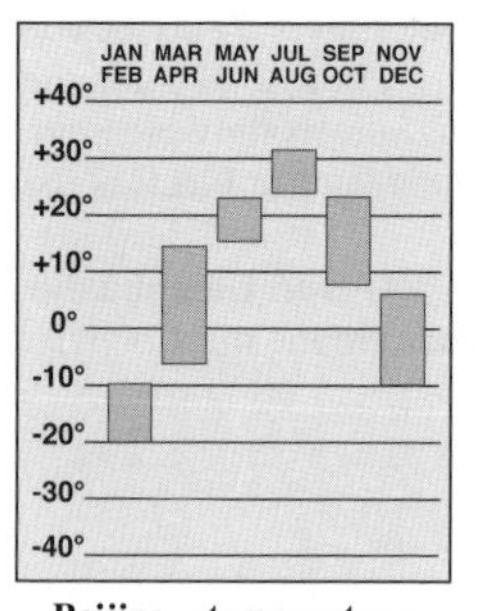

Beijing – temperature (average max/min ˚C)

encased in ice, Siberia looks as one imagines it ought to – a barren, desolate wasteland (the train, however, is well heated).

Russian cities, too, look best and feel most 'Russian' under a layer of snow. St Petersburg with its brightly painted Classical architecture is far more attractive in the winter months when the weather is crisp and skies clear. But if you want to spend time in any Siberian city you'll find it more enjoyable to go in late spring, summer or autumn, when there is more to do.

In Siberia the heaviest snowfalls and coldest temperatures – as low as minus 40°C (minus 40°F) in Krasnoyarsk and some other towns the train passes through – occur in December and January. From late January to early April the weather is generally cold and clear. Spring comes late. In July and August it is warm enough for an invigorating dip in Lake Baikal. The birch and aspen provide a beautiful autumnal display in September and October.

In Moscow the average temperature is 17°C (63°F) in summer and minus 9°C (+16°F) during the winter; there are occasional heavy summer showers.

Tourist season

The tourist season runs from May through September, peaking from mid-July to early September. In the low season (October to April) some companies offer discounts on tours; you'll also find it much easier to get a booking for the train at short notice at this time. During the summer it can be difficult to get a place on the popular Moscow–Beijing route without planning several weeks ahead.

PUBLIC HOLIDAYS AND FESTIVALS

When planning your trip it is worth taking into account national holidays (see opposite) and major festivals (see box p18) as these often have an effect on the ability to get train tickets and also to book accommodation.

Russia

If a national holiday falls on Thursday, Friday and Saturday may also be holidays. If a holiday falls on Saturday or Sunday, Monday will be a holiday.

- 1 January: New Year's Day
- 7 January: Russian Orthodox Christmas Day
- 23 February: Defenders of the Motherland Day
- 8 March: International Women's Day
- Late April/early May: Russian Orthodox Easter
- 1 May: Day of Spring and Labour (formerly May Day or International Working People's Solidarity Day). The following work day is also a holiday.
- 9 May: Victory Day, commemorating the end of WWII (known in Russia as the 1941-45 Great Patriotic War)
- 12 June: Russia Day, commemorating the 1990 declaration of Russian sovereignty
- 7-8 November: Reconciliation Day (formerly the Anniversary of the October Revolution)
- 12 December: Constitution Day

Many businesses tend to be closed the few days after New Year and many Russians have taken to celebrating Christmas on December 25 as well.

China

- 1 January: New Year's Day
- February: Chinese New Year
- 8 March: International Women's Day
- 1 May: International Labour Day
- 4 May: Youth Day
- 1 June: International Children's Day
- 1 July: Birthday of the Chinese Communist Party
- 1 August: Anniversary of the founding of the People's Liberation Army
- 1 October: National Day

It is not a good idea to travel on or around the following: 1 May, the week-long holiday following National Day or over the Chinese New Year as many places tend to close, demand outstrips supply with regard to train tickets and prices shoot up dramatically.

Mongolia

- 1 January: Shin Jil (New Year's Day)
- 13 January: Constitution Day, commemorating the adoption of the 1992 constitution
- January/February: Tsagaan Sar (Lunar New Year); Mongolian New Year, celebrated during a three-day holiday
- 8 March: International Women's Day
- 1 June: Mother and Children's Day
- 11 & 12 July: Nadaam Festival (National Day celebrations), see pp332-3
- 26 November: Mongolian Republic Day

Constitution Day, International Women's Day and Mongolian Republic Day are

❑ Festival planner

Below are the best of the festivals that you might come across during your travels:

- 5 January-15 February: **Harbin Ice Lantern Festival** – a month of other-worldly ice-lantern sculptures and competitions in Harbin, China.
- 7 January: **Russian Orthodox Christmas** – midnight church services everywhere.
- January/February: **Chinese New Year** – the biggest holiday of the year, with feasts and traffic chaos as people make their way home. It is on 23 January 2012, 10 February 2013; 31 January 2014; 19 February 2015.
- Late February/early March: ***Maslenitsa* (Pancake Week)** – the end of winter celebrated with folk shows and lots of pancake-eating before Lent.
- Mid-March: **Camel Polo Winter Festival** – involves camels and polo in Ulaanbaatar, Mongolia.
- March or April: The **birthday of Guanyin**, the Chinese Buddhist Goddess of Mercy – a good time to visit Buddhist temples. The birthday falls on the 19th day of the second moon.
- **Paskha (Easter)** – midnight church services on the Easter Sunday, followed by eating of *paskhlny keks* (Easter cake) and exchanging of painted Easter eggs.
- 9 May: **Victory Day** – military parades in Russia's big cities to celebrate the end of WWII (Great Patriotic War).
- June: **White Nights** – parties, theatre and concert performances when the sun does not set on St Petersburg.
- June: **Maitreya Buddha Festival** – held at the Ivolginsky Datsan near Ulan-Ude.
- June: **Surkharban (Buryatiya Folk Festival)** – horse-riding and wrestling at the hippodrome in Ulan-Ude.
- 11-13 July: **Naadam** – Mongolia's biggest festival (see box pp332-3) involving horse races, archery and wrestling.
- 7 November: **National Reconciliation Day** (formerly the Anniversary of the Great October Revolution) – Communist Party parades in some Russian cities.
- Late December/January: **Russian Winter Festival** – troika rides and folk performances in Moscow and Irkutsk.
- 31 December: Russian **New Year's Eve**, celebrated with raucous parties everywhere.

generally normal working days. Make your travel arrangements well in advance if travelling during the Nadaam Festival, as train tickets are often in short supply.

Bookings and visas

ORGANISED TOURS OR INDIVIDUAL ITINERARIES?

Note that regulations governing the issuing of Russian visas are particularly susceptible to change. Check the latest situation with your embassy or through the organisations listed on pp27-37.

Group tours

Many visitors come to Russia in organised groups. Going with a tour group certainly takes much of the hassle out of the experience, but it also means there isn't much room for doing your own thing. Most tours are accompanied by an English-speaking guide from the moment you set foot in the country until the moment you leave. See pp27-37 for information on tour companies.

Semi-independent travel

This is the easiest and most popular way for foreigners to travel on the Trans-Siberian. A specialist agency makes all accommodation and train bookings (with or without stops along the way), providing you in the process with the documentation needed for obtaining a Russian tourist visa. You choose departure dates and number and length of stops, in effect designing your own trip. Once in Russia you're usually on your own, although some agencies offer guides to meet you at the station and help you organise your time in stopover cities. You'll often get good-quality accommodation in Moscow as part of the deal. Numerous travel agents in the West can make these arrangements (see pp27-37), or you can deal directly with locally based Trans-Siberian specialists such as The Russia Experience (see p28) who have a member of staff in Moscow, or Monkey Business in Beijing (see p370) and Hong Kong (see p37).

Fully independent travel

Travelling independently is not difficult and is the best way to gain an insight into the 'real' Russia. Getting a tourist or business visa allows you to wander around freely. For a tourist visa, together with your visa application you must present confirmation of hotel bookings, furnished by a registered Russian tourist organisation. Various hotels and agencies can do this for you (see p22). Some will furnish documentation of accommodation for the duration of your visa, in exchange for your booking only your first night's stay with them. Once you have your visa and are registered with the organisation that's sponsoring you, or one of their affiliates, you are free to travel wherever you want, irrespective of what the documentation says.

Although few Russians outside the largest cities speak English and the tourist infrastructure is limited, this shouldn't put you off. Many Russians are friendly and generous, and learning a bit of basic Russian before you go will help communication.

ROUTE PLANNING

Main services

The table on p20 is a summary of some major Siberian train services. For timetables and other details see pp476-83, but note that timetables are subject to change. There may be occasional one-hour variations on account of differences between countries in implementing Daylight Saving Time. **Local times** are given in the table on p20 but note that official Russian timetables use **Moscow Time** only.

The trains that run across Siberia are not tourist specials but working services used by local people, and they're very popular. On most routes they run to capacity, especially in summer (when additional services may be laid on). Buying tickets as you go along shouldn't be too difficult, as many Russians usually leave it to the last minute. Barring travelling in peak season, if you book a day before you want to travel, you'll probably get what you want on the shorter sections, but you'll need more time if you want a ticket for the whole route or for a longer section such as Irkutsk–Moscow.

Train	Leaves	on	at	Arrives	on	at
001 *Rossiya*	Vladivostok	Even days	22:20	Moscow	Day 7	17:58
002 *Rossiya*	Moscow	Odd days	21:25	Vladivostok	Day 8	06:33
003 (Mongolia)	Beijing	Wed	07:45	Moscow	Day 6	14:28
004 (Mongolia)	Moscow	Tue	21:35	Beijing	Day 6	14:04
005	Ulaanbaatar	Jan-Mar Fri Jun-Dec Tue	13:50	Moscow	Fri Sat	14:28**
006	Moscow	Jan-Mar Wed Jun-Dec Thur	21:35	Ulaanbaatar	Sun Mon	06:30**
009 *Baikal*	Irkutsk	Odd days	14:20	St Petersburg	Day 5	10:00
010 *Baikal*	St Petersburg	Even days	16:22	Irkutsk	Day 5	07:39
019 *Vostok* (Manchuria)	Beijing	Sat	23:00	Moscow	Fri	18:13
020 *Vostok* (Manchuria)	Moscow	Fri	23:55	Beijing	Thur	05:32***
023*	Beijing	Tue	07:40	Ulaanbaatar	Wed	13:20
024*	Ulaanbaatar	Thur	08:05	Beijing	Fri	14:35

* *Chinese Railways (023C) will operate this route until June 2012; check after that whether Mongolian Railways (023M) will take control of the service again. Mongolian Railways may also operate an additional service in the summer months.*

** ***005**: Jan-Mar & Nov-Dec once every two weeks, weekly from June to mid-Oct and not running at all April & May; **006** as above but weekly June-Sep.*

*** *not running at all Jan-May.*

Moscow and St Petersburg to Vladivostok

There are many trains on the line between **Moscow** and Vladivostok, but the famous 001/002 *Rossiya* train is the top choice for service. There are other very good trains which cover shorter segments; these increase your options if you are making stopovers along the way. If you want to start in **St Petersburg** rather than Moscow, the 009/010 *Baikal* takes you all the way to Irkutsk, where you can change for a Vladivostok-bound service.

There are ferries from Vladivostok to Japan and Korea in the summer months (see box p35).

Moscow to Beijing: Trans-Manchurian or Trans-Mongolian?

You have two route choices between Moscow and Beijing: the Trans-Mongolian route via Ulaanbaatar in Mongolia, and the Trans-Manchurian route via Harbin in China. There are advantages and disadvantages with each.

The Trans-Manchurian train is the 019/020 *Vostok*. The 019 currently departs from Beijing at 4am local time, whereas the Trans-Mongolian leaves at a more reasonable 12:45pm. The Moscow departure is in the evening for both the Trans-Mongolian and the Trans-Manchurian.

The Trans-Mongolian Moscow–Beijing service is the 003/004, although there are additional, shorter-distance options including the 023/024 (Beijing–

The longest journey

If it's a long-distance rail-travel record you're after, begin your journey in Vila Real de Santo António in southern Portugal, cross Europe to Moscow, take the Trans-Mongolian route from there to Beijing and continue to Ho Chi Minh City (Saigon) in Vietnam – a journey of 17,852km (11,155 miles).

For an even longer journey you'll have to wait until the proposed 103km tunnel under the Bering Strait goes ahead. If it really does you'll be able to travel all the way from London to Mexico City via Moscow, Irkutsk, Magadan, Fairbanks and Vancouver – approximately 25,500km (16,000 miles).

Ulaanbaatar) and 361/362 (Irkutsk–Naushki–Ulaanbaatar). Only the 003/004 offer de luxe 1st class carriages (see pp112-13), although travellers who opt for kupé will find these carriages identical on both routes. Unless you're American, Israeli or certain other nationalities you need a Mongolian transit visa on this route, even if you do not stop along the way. The Trans-Mongolian journey takes about 12 hours less than the Trans-Manchurian.

Despite long-standing Trans-Siberian lore, there's no difference between the restaurant cars on the two routes as these are supplied by the country through which you're travelling. Both trains have weekly departures in each direction. Summer is the most difficult time to book a place on long-distance trains on either route, so make arrangements several months in advance.

Stopping off in Mongolia

If you're taking the Trans-Mongolian route, breaking your journey in Ulaanbaatar is highly recommended, particularly for stays with nomad families outside Ulaanbaatar. It's easy to organise either through a specialist agency or independently. A related option, though not in Mongolia, is a stop at Hohhot (Huhehot) in China's Inner Mongolia province, where you'll find a similar rural Mongolian Buddhist culture and similar grassland tours.

Side trips

There are numerous possibilities for side trips by rail, including on the **Siberian BAM Railway** (from Tayshet) and the **Turksib Railway** (from Novosibirsk), with links via the Turksib to the **Kazakhstan–China Railway**. See ppp108-10 for more on all these lines. From **Blagoveshchensk** (see p442), on a spur off the Moscow–Vladivostok line at Belogorsk, you can cross the Amur River by boat to Heihe in China. With onward connections via Harbin, this little-known alternative to the Trans-Manchurian line is actually the cheapest land route from Moscow to Beijing at present.

A branch line runs from Sibirtsevo, near Vladivostok, via Ussurisk to Pyongyang in **North Korea**, although at the moment it's for organised group travel only, as independent travel is not allowed in North Korea. Russia is keen to foster the extension of this line into South Korea and its deep-water port at Pusan, tying the Trans-Siberian into a potentially very profitable Asia–Europe network, though given recent events such an extension seems unlikely.

From Beijing it's easy to continue by rail into **Vietnam**; it's a three-night journey.

VISAS

Visas are required of most foreigners visiting Russia, Mongolia and China. Getting a Russian visa is not always straightforward (largely because of the need to obtain an invitation and confirmation of your accommodation, if you go for a tourist visa). It's simple to get a Chinese visa from most embassies and straightforward to get a Mongolian visa. Visa regulations change regularly; even border guards and local police officials don't always know the latest. Check with travel agents or embassies.

Whether you're starting your trip in Beijing or Moscow it's definitely best to get your onward visa for Russia or China elsewhere. The Chinese embassy in Moscow is notoriously difficult to deal with and, officially, the Russian consulate in Beijing issues tourist visas only to residents of China.

You'll always need to show your visa in Russia when staying at a hotel and whenever you buy a rail ticket.

Russia visa invitations

To get a tourist visa to Russia, you must first obtain an invitation ('visa support') or equivalent document (*podtverzhdenie* подтверждение) confirming your accommodation details while in Russia, plus one or more vouchers (*order* ордер) confirming payment for this accommodation. These documents may be issued by various travel agencies, hotels or hostels registered to do so with the Russian Ministry of the Interior. The documents must all state your passport details, itinerary and duration of stay, along with the inviting organisation's address and registration number. If you're going on a package tour, your travel agent will organise everything and you'll see very little of this paperwork.

Although an itinerary must be specified, the visa doesn't list your proposed destinations, allowing independent travellers to visit places on the spur of the moment. Most travel companies will issue an invitation/confirmation only for the days for which you have paid to stay with them, but some will confirm accommodation for the duration of your visa in exchange for your booking just your first night's stay with them, leaving you free to go where you like after that.

Costs of visa support (though not the visa itself) for a 30-day tourist visa are approximately US$30-45 for single/double entry and US$80-250 for a three-month business visa.

The following are some of the companies that can issue an invitation: **The Russia Experience** see p28; **Monkey Business** see p36; **Way to Russia** (💻 http://waytorussia.net); **Express to Russia** (💻 www.expresstorussia.com); **Visa Able** (💻 www.visaable.com); **Visa to Russia** (💻 www.visatorussia.com). All are either Russia based or have offices in Russia.

Most hostels and hotels in Moscow (see pp186-9) and St Petersburg (see pp152-4) also offer visa support, as do travel agencies (see pp27-37). Note that some companies may only offer visa support if you book a trip with them.

Russian visa

A Russian visa is a one-page form stuck directly into your passport, containing your passport information, entry and exit dates, and the name and registration of the organisation that has invited you. Application is normally made at your nearest Russian embassy or consulate. In addition to a completed visa application form you'll be asked for your passport valid for at least six months, invitation/confirmation document, accommodation voucher(s), three passport-sized photos and the visa fee. Some embassies will accept faxed copies of visa-support documents but not all, so check before you apply and don't take your 'host's' word on this.

If you're starting your trip in Beijing you must get your visa in your home country unless you are living in China, have an official residence visa **and** speak Mandarin well. The Russian Embassy in Hong Kong also requires most applicants to have a valid Hong Kong identity card or have been resident for 30 days. Other Russian consulates in China might make exceptions and accept foreigners if the consulate wasn't too busy, but only if the applicant had original copies of their invitations and other paperwork from Russia. These are either timely or costly to obtain by post. Transit visas, good for up to 10 days, were still possible to obtain at the Beijing consulate at the time of writing, but you would be required to show your train ticket and most likely onward visas and tickets as well.

Any foreigner visiting Russia for more than three months requires a doctor's certification that they are not HIV-positive, a requirement introduced to placate anti-West forces in Russia.

The visa fee depends on where you apply, your nationality, the type and duration of the visa, and how quickly you want it. For Americans a single-entry tourist visa costs from US$125, for British nationals from £50, and for EU citizens (except those from Ireland) from €34. Processing takes five working days, although you can get next-day service by paying more.

- **Tourist visa** Tourist visas are issued for up to 30 days, with single-entry and double-entry versions. A tourist visa requires an invitation and a hotel booking, but to secure the invitation this may be for as little as just one night. If you want to stay longer than 30 days you'll need to apply for a business visa or another type of visa.
- **Business visa** A business visa allows you to stay for up to a year, though not for longer than three months at a stretch without leaving the country, even if it

❑ Health insurance requirements

Citizens of countries signatory to the Schengen Convention (Austria, Belgium, Denmark, Finland, France, Germany, Greece, Iceland, Italy, Luxembourg, Netherlands, Norway, Portugal, Spain and Sweden) and from Israel, Estonia and Switzerland who apply for a Russian visa are officially required to produce proof of medical insurance valid in Russia. This is rarely enforced. Some embassies don't ask at all, while others will accept just about any insurance document. In any case, it pays to have comprehensive health insurance when travelling across Russia.

is just for a day. It requires an invitation from a registered Russian business, which is easy enough to get if you use an online visa-support service such as VisatoRussia (see p22).

Business visas are actually easier to arrange than tourist visas, because you don't need to book accommodation. They're ideal for travellers who want a longer stay in Russia and many tourists use them, but they are slightly more expensive to obtain than a tourist visa. Support for a three-month business visa costs about US$150-300/£90-200/€100-220. Costs in support of multiple-entry business visas will be higher still.

• **Private visa** This visa is for foreigners who are invited by Russian friends or relatives, but it can take three months or more to obtain. The process involves your Russian friend getting an authorisation (*izveshcheniye* извещение) from their home-town OViR/PVU (Passport & Visa Unit) office and mailing it to you. You must then take it to your Russian embassy, which confirms it with OViR/PVU back in Russia. You can get a private visa for a stay of up to three months, single-entry only. Non-Russian friends in Russia cannot invite you.

• **Transit visa** Transit visas are normally given only to those who are in transit through Russia and not staying overnight in any city. Most Russian embassies

❑ Embassies and consulates

• **Britain** **VFS Global** (🖳 http://ru.vfsglobal.co.uk; 15-27 Gee St, London EC1V 3RD and 16 Forth St, Edinburgh EH1 3LH) processes visa applications on behalf of the Russian Embassy (🖳 www.rusemb.org.uk). Applications are accepted online, by post, or in person; the process for the latter is fairly speedy (8.30am-3pm Mon-Fri; passport collection 4-5.30pm). The **Chinese Visa Service Application Centre** (🖳 www.visaforchina.org.uk; Morley House, 26 Holborn Viaduct, London EC1A; 9am-3pm Mon-Fri; passport collection 9am-4pm) is separate from the Chinese Embassy (🖳 www.chinese-embassy.org.uk). There are Chinese consulates in Manchester (🖳 http://.manchester.chinese consulate.org) and Edinburgh (☎ 0131-337 3220).

The **Mongolian Embassy** (🖳 www.embassyofmongolia.co.uk) is at 7 Kensington Court, London W8 (10am-12.30pm Mon-Fri). The **Belarus Embassy** (🖳 www.uk.belembassy.org) is at 6 Kensington Court, London W8 (Mon, Tue, Thur & Fri 9.30am-12.30pm).

• **The USA** The consular office of the **Russian Embassy** (🖳 www.russianembassy.org) is at 2641 Tunlaw Road, NW, Washington DC 20007 (9am-12.30pm Mon-Fri). There are also consulates in San Francisco (2790 Green St, CA 94123), New York (9 E 91st St, NY 10128), Seattle (2323 Westin Building, 2001 6th Ave, Seattle, WA 98121) and Houston (1333 West Loop South, Suite 1300, Houston, TX 77027).

The consular office of the **Chinese Embassy** (🖳 www.china-embassy.org) is at 2201 Wisconsin Ave NW, Rm 110, Washington DC 20007. There are consulates in New York, Chicago, Houston, Los Angeles and San Francisco.

The **Mongolian Embassy** (🖳 www.mongolianembassy.us) is at 2833 M Street NW, Washington DC 20007 (9am-noon Mon-Fri).

The **Belarus Embassy** (🖳 www.usa.belembassy.org) is at 1619 New Hampshire Avenue NW, Washington DC 20009 (9.30am-12.30pm Mon-Fri).

• **Canada** The consular department of the **Russian Embassy** (🖳 www.rusembassy.ca) is at 52 Range Rd, Ottawa, Ontario (9.30am-12.30pm). There are consulates in issue transit visas for only 72 hours; Russian embassies and consulates in China, however, will issue them for up to 10 days which allows you to travel on the Trans-Siberian, stay in Moscow for a night and then leave. You will probably have to show your Russian rail ticket, and sometimes your onward ticket, when applying for the visa. If you intend to stay anywhere other than Moscow you must get a tourist visa.

Russian visa extension In any country it's always best to arrive with a visa that is certain to cover the length of your stay, rather than having to go to the trouble of extending it.

At the time of writing, a Russian visa can only be extended in case of missing your flight, accident or serious illness, in which case you must have appropriate documents to prove your case, and the extension cost varies between £100 and £250. If you don't think that 30 days will be enough for you, seriously consider applying for a business visa.

Russian visa registration At the time of writing all visitors staying in Russia for more than seven days must register their visa with the local police or OViR/PVU (Passport & Visa Unit) within seven business days of arrival.

Montreal (🖳 www.montreal.mid.ru) and Toronto (🖳 www.toronto.mid.ru). The **Chinese Embassy** (🖳 www.chinaembassycanada.org) is at 515 St Patrick St, Ottawa, Ontario. There are consulates in Vancouver, Toronto and Calgary. The **Mongolian Embassy** (🖳 www.mongolembassy.org) is at 151 Slater St, Suite 503, Ottawa. The **Belarus Embassy** (🖳 www.canada.belembassy.org) is at 130 Albert Street, Suite 600, Ottawa.

• **Australia** The **Russian consulate** (🖳 www.sydneyrussianconsulate.com) is at 7-9 Fullerton St, Woollahra, NSW 2025 (9.30am-12.30pm Mon-Thur). There are **Chinese consulates** in: Sydney (🖳 www.sydney.chineseconsulate.org); Perth (🖳 http://perth.chineseconsulate.org); Brisbane (🖳 www.brisbane.chineseconsulate.org); and Melbourne (🖳 www.chinaconsulatemel.org). The **Mongolian Embassy** (🖳 www.canberra.mfat.gov) is at 1/44 Dalman Crescent, O'Malley, Canberra, ACT 2606.

• **New Zealand** The **Russian** consular office (🖳 www.rus.co.nz) is at 57 Messines Rd, Karori, Wellington. The **Chinese consulate** (🖳 www.chinaconsulate.org.nz) is at 630 Great South Rd, Greenlane, Auckland. **Mongolia's Honorary Consulate** (🖳 www.mongolianconsulate.com.au) is at 86 Kings Crescent, Lower Hutt 5010.

• **South Africa** The consular office of the **Russian Embassy** (🖳 http://russianembassy.org.za) is at 316 Brook St, Menle Park, Pretoria 0001. There is also a consulate in Cape Town. The **Chinese Embassy** (🖳 www.chinese-embassy.org.za) is at 965 Church St, Arcadia 0083, Pretoria. There are consulates in Durban, Cape Town and Johannesburg. There is no Mongolian embassy in South Africa.

• **Japan** The consular division of the **Russian Embassy** (🖳 www.tokyo.ruembassy.org) is at 1-1 Azabudai, 2-chome, Minato-ku, Tokyo 106. There are consulates in Osaka, Niigata and Sapporo. The **Chinese Embassy** (🖳 www.china-embassy.or.jp/chn) is at 3-4-33 Moto-Azabu, Minato-ku, Tokyo 106. The **Mongolian Embassy** (🖳 www.mnemb.go.jp) is at 21-4 Kamiyama-cho, Shibuya-ku, Tokyo 150.

Previously you had to register within 72 hours of arriving if you were staying for more than three days. Since the requirements may change again **always check** before you go. Also, you must register within three business days in any town where you stay longer than three business days. Most hostels and hotels will register you when you check in, stapling a stamped piece of paper to your passport. However, many budget hotels either can't or won't register foreigners, and with homestays it almost certainly won't be done, so you may need the services of one of the many agencies that can assist you with visa support.

If the police decide to check your papers and find that your visa is not registered but it should be, they may fine you. Border officials at your exit point can also fine you for having an unregistered visa, or for conspicuous gaps in registration. Avoid this, as stiff penalties and even jail time are allowed by law. Keep your train, bus and plane tickets, to prove when you arrived and departed from different places and how long you stayed. However, it's unclear what you should do if, for instance, you're on a rafting trip or hiking in the Altai Mountains. Many small towns and villages lack either an OViR/PVU office or a hotel that can register foreigners. Generally, if you can demonstrate that you made a good-faith effort to follow the rules, officials should be forgiving. Most border guards simply don't bother piecing together travellers' itineraries through Russia and checking it against their registrations when they leave the country.

You should certainly make every effort to register within 72 hours of entering the country. The organisation that issued your invitation is expected to handle this, but if you are travelling independently it can be taken care of by staff at your first hotel stop or by an independent agency for a small fee.

Mongolian visa

Mongolian tourist visas are issued for up to 30 days. There are single and double-entry versions; for UK citizens a single-entry visa costs around £40 and takes 2-5 working days (£60 if processed in a day); a double-entry visa costs £55/75. Transit visas are available for stays of three days and cost from £35. Embassy officials may ask to see an onward (eg Russian or Chinese) visa.

Mongolia has consular offices along the route of the Trans-Siberian, in Moscow (p184), Irkutsk (p277), Ulan-Ude (p296) and Beijing (p368). The application process is straightforward. You'll need to apply in person with a passport valid for at least six months, one or two photos and the visa fee.

Americans can stay in Mongolia up to 90 days without a visa, but if they plan to stay longer than 30 days, they must register with the authorities within seven days of arrival. Israelis can stay up to 30 days without a visa.

It may be possible to pick up a 30-day tourist visa at Ulaanbaatar's airport or at the land border if travelling by train, but it's best to get a visa in advance.

Mongolian visa extension It's possible to extend your visa for up to 30 extra days at Ulaanbaatar's Ministry of Foreign Relations (corner of Peace Ave and Olimpiin Gudamj, 9.30am-noon Mon-Fri). To extend a visa, you'll need your passport, a passport-sized photo and an application form (US$1). The processing fee is about US$4.20 and visa extensions cost US$15 for the first seven days, after which you pay US$2 per day for up to 23 additional days. You may not extend a transit visa. Some guesthouses may be able to do the visa extension for you for an additional fee. The extension takes 2-3 days to process, or you can pay an additional US$20 for same-day turnaround.

Mongolian visa registration If you intend to stay in Mongolia for more than 30 days, regardless of whether you need a visa or not, you must register within seven days of arrival at the **Office of Immigration, Naturalisation & Foreign Citizens** (INFC, on the west side of the Peace Bridge, opposite Naran Plaza, ☎ 011-315 323; 9am-1pm & 2-5pm Mon-Fri). The process is free, but you'll need a passport-sized photo and about US$0.84 for the application form. It's best to go in the morning.

Chinese visa

All foreigners require a visa to visit China. Tourist visas are generally given for up to 30 days, although if you apply for a shorter period you may only be granted a visa for the period you request. At the time of writing, prices for a single-/double-entry visa are £30/45 for UK citizens and US$130/130 for US citizens. One-month extensions are easy to arrange in most cities within China through the Foreign Office Branch of the Public Security Bureau.

The process of getting a visa is straightforward at most Chinese embassies. In addition to your passport and the application form you'll need one photo, the visa fee and the processing fee. No same-day or next-day turnaround is available. The list of places you wish to visit on the application form is merely a formality; it's not checked and doesn't limit you to those places. You must apply for your visa at the consulate under whose jurisdiction your place of residence falls and bear in mind that fees and requirements vary from place to place.

Other visas

If you are starting from Beijing and planning to continue westward through Europe after you leave Moscow or St Petersburg, depending on your own nationality you may need transit visas for some countries bordering Russia, including Belarus (see below). Try to get all your visas before you leave, as they may be extremely difficult to get while in China or Russia.

At the time of writing, nationals of most English-speaking countries needed a visa to visit or transit Belarus; however, note that for most nationalities these are very expensive. Citizens of EU countries and the US can visit Ukraine visa-free for up to 90 days.

MAKING A BOOKING IN BRITAIN

While it is relatively straightforward to organise an independent or semi-independent journey on the railway if you have the time and the inclination, many travellers benefit from an agency's expertise when it comes to drawing up an itinerary, arranging stopovers and accommodation along the way and providing advice and support. The following companies offer Trans-Siberian, Trans-Mongolian and Trans-Manchurian, as well as more general Russia, packages.

• **The Russia Experience** (☎ 0845-512 2910, 🖳 www.trans-siberian.co.uk) Recommended specialists offering a variety of packages for budget and mid-range travellers, that include innovative, off-the-beaten-track options and can incorporate local festivals and homestays into the experience.
• **Regent Holidays UK** (☎ 0845-277 3301, 🖳 www.regent-holidays.co.uk) specialise in independent travel to Russia, Eastern Europe, the Baltic States as well as China, Mongolia, Vietnam, and North and South Korea and can arrange visas (allow at least six weeks), flights, tours and accommodation.
• **Great Rail Journeys** (☎ 01904-521936, 🖳 www.greatrail.com) offer an 18-day tour including a visit to Warsaw and with travel from Moscow to Vladivostok on the Golden Eagle (see opposite); a shorter trip excluding Warsaw is also available.
• **Just Go Russia** (☎ 0203-355 7717, 🖳 www.justgorussia.co.uk) offer a variety of Trans-Siberian packages as well as a large number of adventure, eco and cultural tours, language courses and visa support. They also hold monthly seminars about Russia in London.
• **Russian National Tourist Office** (☎ 020-7495 7570, 🖳 www.visitrussia.org.uk) can help you book train tickets and arrange accommodation in Russia.
• **Intrepid Travel** (🖳 www.intrepidtravel.com) offer active adventures for all budgets, including 21-day Moscow to Beijing via Ulaanbaatar tours.
• **Sundowners Overland** (☎ 020-8877 7660 or ☎ 020-8877 9002, 🖳 www.sundownersoverland.com) and **Vodka Train** (020-8877 7650, 🖳 www.vodkatrain.com) See p33.

❑ Getting to Russia or China from Britain

There are daily **flights** to Moscow with several airlines, starting at around £170 one-way, £300 return, with Aeroflot and bmi offering the cheapest seats most often, though bmi inconveniently flies to Vnukovo airport rather than the main Sheremetyevo or Domodedovo.

Flying to Beijing is more expensive: at least £400 one way, £450 return. STA Travel (🖳 www.statravel.co.uk) and Trailfinders (🖳 www.trailfinders.co.uk) are both good travel agencies when it comes to searching for the best airfare, and by making enquiries with them, you get a good idea as to what kind of flight combinations are available. They do discounted flights for students and people under 26. Other good websites to try are Flight Centre (🖳 www.flightcentre.co.uk) and Ebookers (🖳 www.ebookers.com). You can also look through *Time Out* and *TNT* magazine for advertisements of cheap flights to Moscow.

The Man in Seat Sixty-One (🖳 www.seat61.com – see box p43) has useful information on the numerous **rail** options available, including taking the Eurostar from London to Brussels and then a direct two-day train via Berlin, Warsaw and Minsk, Belarus to Moscow. However, note that a transit visa for Belarus costs UK passport holders £100 making going through Belarus an expensive option. The Deutsche Bahn Travelservice (🖳 www.bahn.co.uk) can book a one-way ticket from London to Moscow for as little as £300 (advance purchase).

Tickets to a range of European cities (but not currently in Russia) can be booked through Rail Europe (🖳 www.raileurope.co.uk) or Eurostar (🖳 www.eurostar.com).

- **China Travel Service and Information Centre** (CTSIC; ☎ 020-7388 8838, 🖳 www.chinatravel.co.uk) The friendly staff here can help with tickets from Beijing to Moscow (this direction only) as well as tours throughout China. You're given a voucher which you exchange in Beijing for a confirmed ticket.
- **On the Go** (☎ 020-7371 1113, 🖳 www.onthegotours.com) caters for the budget traveller, offering tours in different parts of the world, including the western section of the Trans-Siberian and tailor-made tours.
- **Steppes Travel** (☎ 01285-880 980, 🖳 www.steppestravel.co.uk) offer tailor-made individual Trans-Siberian itineraries and tours, plus options for Moscow, St Petersburg and the Russian Far East.
- **Intourist** (☎ 0844-875 4026, 🖳 www.intouristuk.com) have an office in London and also in Glasgow. They can book tailor-made packages but also offer group tours. They will also arrange visas, accommodation and train tickets.
- **GW Travel Ltd/The Trans-Siberian Express Company** (☎ 0161-928 9410, 🖳 www.gwtravel.co.uk) run distinctly upmarket tours on their 'Golden Eagle Trans-Siberian Express', a fully restored private steam train with air-conditioned carriages. This is Russia's version of the Orient Express and there are en suite facilities with power showers for each sleeping compartment, flat screen DVDs, fine dining and extensive wine lists. A two-week escorted tour from Moscow via Ulaanbaatar to Vladivostok (or vice-versa), including several nights in luxury hotels, costs from £7995 to £9995 per person if travelling as a couple (£5595 with shared facilities); more pricey if travelling solo. There are regular summer departures and occasional 'Winter Wonderland' tours, plus an annual July trip to Ulaanbaatar for the Naadam festival. As of June 2011 the 'Golden Eagle' will also go to Beijing via Ulaanbaatar.

Budget travellers booking from Britain should note that they can also arrange Trans-Siberian rail tickets through specialist agencies in China (see pp35-7) and Russia (pp30-1).

MAKING A BOOKING IN CONTINENTAL EUROPE

From France

- **Espace Transsiberien** (☎ 09 70 46 18 03, 🖳 www.espace-transsiberien.com/fr) offer a range of tours.
- **Office du Tourisme de Chine** (☎ 01 56 59 10 10, 🖳 www.otchine.com) can help with tourist information as well as visas for China but not for rail travel.
- **Les Connaisseurs du Voyage** (☎ 01 53 95 27 00, 🖳 www.connaisseursvoyage.fr) specialise in tours of the world but offer Trans-Siberian and Trans-Mongolian trips as part of them.

From Germany

- **Travel Service Asia** (🖳 www.tsa-reisen.de) offers a range of independent journeys and budget tours on the Trans-Siberian, Trans-Manchurian and Trans-Mongolian routes, including in Mongolia.

> ❑ **Airline/flight information**
> The best way to find out which airlines fly into your preferred destination airport is to go direct to that airport's own website.

❑ Trains from Germany

'It comes as no surprise to those who know some geography that Deutsche Bahn, German Rail, has the best (and oldest) rail connections with Russia. There are several options:

• The old 'Est–West-Express', formerly going Paris–Moscow, still operates Cologne–Moscow as a direct service on Fridays in July and August.

• There is a daily (not Sat and in winter, Wed/Fri/Sun) train from Berlin (departure from Lichtenberg Station) to Moscow; this is the Moskva Express and sleeping cars are attached for the St Petersburg route.

• **Reservations** Ask at any German railway station or at their telesales office for tickets inside Russia and their reaction sounds like you are already in Russia: 'That's impossible!' Well, it's somehow tricky because reservations must not be sold for every train, but with insistence I got myself a ticket for the Moscow–Irkutsk train at Dusseldorf railway station. Also ask for special return offers, eg Cologne–Irkutsk–Cologne for about $350! Reservation can also be done by phone (☎ +49-1805-996633, speaking some German may be helpful but someone will speak English). You will then get a reservation number: quote this number at any German ticket counter and your reservation will be printed.

• **Information** Linked via the website of Deutsche Bundesbahn (💻 www.bahn.de), you can simply enter the time and date you want to go from and to. The server knows all European and Russian long-distance trains. English speakers can go to 💻 www.bahn.co.uk and do the same'. **Benedikt Jaeger** (Germany)

Note from updater: The Cologne–Moscow route has direct services on Fridays June-August and on Saturdays from mid-May until the end of August. There are direct trains from Berlin to Moscow (daily June-Aug; Tue/Fri/Sun the rest of the year).

• **Lernidee-Erlebnisreisen** (☎ 030-786 0000, 💻 www.lernidee.de) Siberian itineraries range from a 2nd-class ticket on the Moscow–Beijing train to stop overs in Mongolia (three nights including full board, with English-speaking guide). Other routes include Moscow to Vladivostok.

• **Die Bahn** (💻 www.reiseauskunft.bahn.de) With Deutsche Bahn's switched-on, multilingual travel service, you can make Trans-Siberian rail bookings by telephone or online.

From the Netherlands

• **Tozai Travel** (💻 www.tozai.nl) This agency, recommended by readers, concentrates on itineraries for individual travellers.

• **White Nights** (☎ 070-360 7785, 💻 www.wnights.com), with branches in the Netherlands, Germany, Switzerland, USA (see p32) and St Petersburg (see p152), can help you arrange your budget trip on the Trans-Siberian.

• **VNC Travel** (💻 www.vnc.nl) can organise Trans-Siberian trips for independent travellers as well as group tours.

From Russia

Almost all the hostels and hotels have travel desks and provide visa support and travel services as well as excursions. You could also try:

• **Star Travel** (☎ 495 797 9555, 💻 www.startravel.ru, 10am-7pm Mon-Fri, 11am-4pm Sat) See p185.

• **UniFest Travel** (☎ 495 234 6555, 💻 http://unifest.ru/eng, 9am-9pm Mon-Fri, 10am-7pm Sat & Sun) See p185.
• **Galileo-Rus** (☎ 495 256 9768, 💻 www.galileo.ru – Russian only) See p193.
• **Intourist** (☎ 495 23-400-23, 💻 www.intourist.com) based in Cosmos Hotel, pr Mira, can provide visa support, book train tickets, accommodation and tours.

If you are booking your tickets yourself in Russia or China you may find our sample booking forms on p122 (Russia) and pp126-7 (China) useful.

From Scandinavia

• **Intourist Norway** (💻 www.intourist.no) can arrange tickets for all Russia routes (in either direction) as well as visas and accommodation.

❑ Getting to Russia or China from continental Europe

All major, and several budget, **airlines** from mainland Europe fly to Moscow and Beijing. Standard return fares from major cities tend to be around €350 to Moscow and €950 to Beijing. In France, good budget flight websites to try are Anyway (💻 www.anyway.fr), Last Minute (💻 www.lastminute.fr) and Nouvelles Frontières (💻 www.nouvelles-frontieres.fr).

From Germany, there are numerous flights to Moscow and other Russian cities with Lufthansa and connections with German Wings. German cities are also served by Russian airlines, such as S7 (💻 www.s7.ru) and KMV Avia (💻 www.kmvavia.ru – in Russian). Good travel agencies include STA Travel (💻 www.statravel.de), Just Travel (💻 www.justtravel.de) and Travel Overland (💻 www.traveloverland.de). To get to Moscow or Beijing from the Netherlands, try NNVS Reisen (💻 www.nbbs.nl) or Airfair (💻 www.airfare.nl) – both in Dutch. In Spain, Barcelo Viajes (💻 www.barceloviajes.com) is a good starting point, while in Italy, CTS Viaggi (💻 www.cts.it – in Italian) does discount air fares for students.

There are also regular **train** services to Moscow and St Petersburg from Amsterdam, Berlin, Budapest, Helsinki (including the brand new high-speed Allegro), Paris, Prague, Riga, Tallinn, Vienna, Vilnius and Warsaw, continuing through Western and Eastern Europe to Moscow. From Minsk, Belarus, there are numerous daily trains to Moscow (11 hours, 20/day) and St Petersburg (15 hours, daily). You'll need a Belorussian visa. Trains from Warsaw to Moscow (18-20 hours, 2/day) and Warsaw to St Petersburg (29 hours, daily) also go through Belarus, so you'll need a transit visa.

From Estonia there are trains to Moscow (15 hours, daily) and St Petersburg (9½ hours, daily), as well as 6-7 express buses between Tallinn and St Petersburg. From Helsinki, Finland, there are trains to St Petersburg (3½-5½ hours, 3/day), including the new high-speed Allegro, as well as a daily service to Moscow (13½ hours).

There are daily overnight trains between Riga, Latvia and Moscow (16 hours) and St Petersburg (13 hours), as well as a couple of buses daily to both cities with Ecolines (💻 www.ecolines.net). From Lithuania's Vilnius, there are trains to Moscow (15 hours, 2/day) and to St Petersburg (15 hours, every other day). The Moscow-bound trains go via Minsk, Belarus, requiring you to have a Belorussian transit visa.

From Ukraine, there are frequent services to Moscow from all major cities, including: Kyiv (9½ hours, 18/day), Lviv (23 hours, daily), Odessa (23 hours via Kyiv, daily), Kharkiv (13 hours, 12/day) and Sevastopol (29 hours, daily). There are also daily trains to St Petersburg from Lviv (31 hours via Vilnius) and Kyiv (24 hours).

• **Eco Tour Production** (☎ 0498 487105, 💻 www.nomadicjourneys.com) is a Swedish partner with Nomadic Journeys, an Ulaanbaatar-based tour operator and one of the few locally based consolidators for train tickets. On offer are horse-riding, sports fishing, popular *ger* (yurt) camp stays and longer horseback expeditions. Camps are low-impact and quiet, with wind and solar power instead of generators. Eco Tour can also help with train journeys starting from Ulaanbaatar.
• **Iventus International Travel** (💻 www.iventustravel.se) is an outlet for Eco Tour/Nomadic Journeys and a specialist in travel to (and onward from) China that can organise air, train & ferry bookings; hotels & homestays; Baikal, Ulaanbaatar and China programmes; and Russia, Mongolia and China visa services.

MAKING A BOOKING IN NORTH AMERICA

From the USA

• **White Nights** (☎ 1-800-490-5008, 💻 www.wnights.com) is the US office of a Russia-based budget travel operator that offers comprehensive travel services.
• **Mir Corporation** (☎ 1-800-424-7289, 💻 www.mircorp.com) offer a range of individual and small-group escorted tours on the Trans-Siberian, with home-stay or hotel accommodation; they're also the USA agent for the Trans-Siberian Express Company (see p29). They have branch offices in Moscow, St Petersburg, Irkutsk and Ulan-Ude.
• **Go to Russia Travel** (☎ 1-888-263-0023, 💻 www.gotorussia.net) This specialist company with offices in Moscow, San Francisco and Atlanta offers both individual travel assistance (including flights and visa support) and package tours.

❑ GETTING TO RUSSIA OR CHINA FROM NORTH AMERICA

From the USA

Numerous airlines fly from the US to Russia. Aeroflot is among the cheapest, with departures from many US cities. From New York, one way/return flights to Moscow cost US$650-800 depending on the season. Aeroflot also flies direct from Seattle to Moscow every day. Korean Air has flights from several west-coast cities via Seoul to Vladivostok. One-way flights to Beijing start at about US$700 from New York or US$550 from Los Angeles.

A major budget airfare specialist is STA Travel (toll-free ☎ 1-800-781-4040, 💻 www.statravel.com), with offices all over the country. There are numerous discount travel agencies in cities such as New York, San Francisco and Los Angeles and you can find their advertisements in newspapers such as the *New York Times*, *San Francisco Examiner* and *Los Angeles Times*.

From Canada

From Vancouver, Toronto and Montreal, fares to Moscow and Beijing tend to be somewhat pricier than from major US cities. You're looking at paying around C$1600 for a return flight to Moscow from Montreal or C$2000 from Vancouver, and around C$900 from Vancouver to Beijing.

A reputable travel agency specialising in discounted student fares is Travel CUTS/ Voyages Campus (💻 www.travelcuts.com); you can also usually find flight specials to Russia and China in the travel sections of the *Vancouver Sun* and *Toronto Star*.

• **Boojum Expeditions** (☎ 800-287-0125, 💻 www.boojum.com) Through its office in Ulaanbaatar, Boojum organises horse-riding trips in Mongolia as well as jeep tours.
• **Sokol Tours** (☎ 1-724-935 5373, 💻 www.sokoltours.com) can arrange visas, train tickets and book accommodation; they also operate several tours in Russia.
• **RailsNW** (💻 www.railsnw.com) book the luxury 'Golden Eagle' tours (see p29) on the Trans-Siberian.
• **The Society of International Railway Travelers** (💻 www.irtsociety.com) is a membership organisation which organises de luxe train trips all over the world, including Siberian journeys with the 'Golden Eagle' (see p29).
• You can get information from the **Russian National Tourist Office** (💻 www.russia-travel.com). The **China National Tourist Office** (💻 www.cnto.org) has branches in New York and Los Angeles.

From Canada

• **Intours Corp** (☎ 416-766-4720, 💻 www.tourussia.com) This Intourist affiliate can organise individual or group trips on all Trans-Siberian routes, including arrangements in neighbouring countries.
• **Trek Escapes** (☎ 1-866-338-8735, 💻 www.trekescapes.com) is an agent offering a range of individual and group Trans-Siberian adventure tours, with branches in Toronto, Vancouver, Edmonton and Calgary.
• **China National Tourist Office** (💻 www.tourismchina.org) has a branch in Toronto.

MAKING A BOOKING IN AUSTRALASIA

From Australia

• **Travel Directors** (💻 www.traveldirectors.com.au) This recommended Trans-Siberian specialist agency offers high-quality tour packages strong on person-to-person contact, along with basic visa support.
• **The Russia Experience** (☎ 1300 654 861, 💻 www.trans-siberian.co.uk) See p28.
• **Sundowners Overland** (☎ 03-9672 5300, 💻 www.sundownersoverland.com) offer both independent and group Trans-Siberian, Trans-Mongolian and Trans-Manchurian trips. Under the name **Vodka Train** (💻 www.vodkatrain.com) they also offer loosely structured, unescorted group journeys for people aged 18-35, with young local guides at stopover towns.
• **Russian Travel Centre** (💻 www.eetbtravel.com) can arrange Trans-Mongolian and Trans-Manchurian trips, with options for homestay accommodation.
• **Beyond Travel** (☎ 02-9080 0400, 💻 www.beyondtravel.com.au) can arrange Trans-Siberian travel packages starting in Moscow, St Petersburg, Vladivostok or Beijing, including stopovers, transfers, accommodation, sightseeing, flights and visa support.
• The **China National Tourist Office** (☎ 02-9252 9838, 💻 www.cnto.org.au), in Sydney covers both Australia and New Zealand and can provide information about China as well as about visas.

❑ Getting to Russia or China from Australasia
From **Australia**, you can get to Moscow, Vladivostok or Khabarovsk via Seoul with Korean Air for around A$1800 return. To Beijing, flights are around A$1500 return. The best agencies for cheap air fares are STA Travel (🖳 www.statravel.com.au) and Flight Centre (🖳 www.flightcentre.com.au). From **New Zealand**, you'll find similarly priced fares to Russia and China; it's worth checking the *New Zealand Herald*'s travel section for cheap flight advertisements. Try STA Travel (🖳 www.statravel.co.nz) and Flight Centre (🖳 www.flightcentre.co.nz) for best deals on air fares.

From New Zealand

- **Adventure World** (☎ 0800-238-368, 🖳 www.adventureworld.co.nz) New Zealand's biggest adventure-travel wholesaler offers individual and group Trans-Siberian, Trans-Mongolian and Trans-Manchurian journeys.
- **Vodka Train** (☎ 0800-174073, 🖳 www.vodkatrain.com) See p33.

MAKING A BOOKING IN SOUTH AFRICA

- **STA Travel** (🖳 www.statravel.co.za) in South Africa has branches in Johannesburg, Pretoria, Bloemfontein, Durban and Cape Town, and can book the Trans-Siberian among other Russian adventures.

❑ Getting to Russia or China from South-East & Central Asia
From South-East Asia There are numerous **flights** from Singapore to Beijing; STA Travel (🖳 www.statravel.com.sg) is a good starting point when looking for discounted fares. In Bangkok, budget travellers can try STA Travel (🖳 www.statravel.co.th) or head for Khao San Rd, lined with competitive travel agencies. There are direct flights from Bangkok to Moscow and Novosibirsk with Aeroflot and S7, as well as seasonal charter flights to Vladivostok, Khabarovsk and other Siberian cities. From Vietnam, there are weekly flights between Hanoi and Vladivostok as well as flights to Beijing.

There are direct **trains** from Hanoi and Ho Chi Minh City to Beijing, taking around two days. While it's not possible to get to China by rail from Thailand, you can take a bus from Bangkok to Ho Chi Minh City via Cambodia, and from Nong Khai in the north of Thailand to Hanoi via Laos, and continue by rail from there.

From Central Asia From Ulaanbaatar, there are frequent **flights** to Moscow and Beijing with MIAT and Air China, respectively. There are numerous flights to Moscow from the capitals of various Central Asian republics, such as Almaty in Kazakhstan, Tashkent in Uzbekistan, Dushanbe in Tajikistan and Bishkek in Kyrgyzstan.

Moscow and Novosibirsk are both served by **trains** from Almaty, Kazakhstan; Bishkek, Kyrgyzstan; Tashkent, Uzbekistan and Dushanbe, Tajikistan. From Moscow, there are also train services to the currently troubled Caucasus area.

Getting to Russia from China by air There are many direct flights from Beijing to Moscow, as well as Irkutsk, Khabarovsk, Vladivostok and Novosibirsk. There are also several weekly flights from Shanghai and Hong Kong to Moscow, and from Harbin to Khabarovsk and Vladivostok. Russian airlines flying to/from China include Aeroflot, Transaero and S7. The Hong Kong to Beijing route is served by Air China and China Southern Airlines.

MAKING A BOOKING IN JAPAN

- **Euras Tours Inc** (☎ 03-5562 3381, 💻 www.euras.co.jp) is a friendly, efficient agency handling bookings for rail journeys to Europe with a choice of itineraries combining flights, ferries and trains, directly into Russia or via China. They have offices in Tokyo and Osaka.
- **Intourist** (☎ 03-3238 9117, 💻 www.intourist-jpn.co.jp; website is in Japanese only) can also book everything and offers package tours.

MAKING A BOOKING IN CHINA

From Beijing

In the summer trains fill up quickly, so if you plan to spend some time travelling around China, make Beijing your first stop and get your onward travel nailed

❑ Getting to Russia or China from Japan (and South Korea)

- **Flights** There are frequent flights from Tokyo to Moscow; expect to pay around ¥180,000, though Aeroflot does 60-day excursion fares at certain times of the year for around ¥80,000 return. There are several weekly flights from Tokyo and Osaka (Kansai) to Beijing with Japan Airlines and Air China for around ¥40,000 return. There are also flights from Niigata to Vladivostok and Khabarovsk. Reputable travel agents include STA Travel (💻 www.statravel.co.jp) and Across No 1/HIS Travel (💻 www.no1-travel.com).

There are frequent flights from Seoul to Moscow, as well as Siberian cities such as Khabarovsk and Vladivostok, and also weekly flights to Novosibirsk and Yuzhno-Sakhalinsk (for BAM-bound travellers wanting to reach Sovetskaya Gavan). There are also daily flights to Beijing with Korean Air, Air China and Asiana Airlines.

- **Ferries** In addition to flights you have several options for travel by **ferry** from Japan. You may sail to the Russian port of Vladivostok, or to Chinese ports within easy reach of Beijing: Shanghai or Tianjin.

'Eastern Dream', a new weekly ferry run by **DBS Ferries** (💻 www.dbsferry.com) operates year-round between Sakaiminato and Vladivostok via Donghae in South Korea, departing from Sakaiminato at 7pm on Sunday, and arriving in Vladivostok at noon on Tuesday. One-way tickets cost from $235 for a berth in a shared cabin, to $485 for a 2-berth private cabin, including meals and the port tax at Vladivostok. For information on the journey from Vladivostok, see box p326. The Chinese-run **Japan-China International Ferry Co** (JIFCO, 💻 www.chinajapanferry.com) runs weekly ferries to Shanghai, with departures from Osaka or Kobe on alternate weeks on Tuesdays at noon, arriving in Shanghai on Thursdays; and the **Shanghai Ferry Co** (💻 www.shanghai-ferry.co.jp) operates a weekly service from Osaka, departing on Friday at noon and arriving on Sunday at noon. One-way fares range from ¥20,000/25,000 for a berth in a shared Japanese-style room to ¥100,000 for a private room, including breakfast, with 10% discounts for students. The journey takes approximately 48 hours. From Shanghai it's a 15-hour train journey to Beijing. **China Express Line** (💻 www.celkobe.co.jp) sails weekly between Kobe and the Chinese port of Tanggu, near Tianjin, a 48-hour trip, departing on Friday at 10.30am and arriving on Sunday at 2pm. One-way fares start at ¥22,000, with a 10% discount for students, and go up to ¥79,000. From Tianjin it's a 30-minute train journey by high speed 'Hexie' train to Beijing.

Tickets for most services can also be bought from branch offices of JTB (Japan Travel Bureau) and KNT (Kinki Nippon Tourist). See also box p326.

down. Once you've made your train reservations (see pp124-8) and paid your deposit, do the rounds of the embassies and collect your visas. You'll need RMB (yuan) as well as crisp US dollar cash, and a stock of passport photos.

Alternatively you may be able to reserve a place on the train while you're in Shanghai (ask at the travel bureau in Peace Hotel). Shanghai has a Russian consulate but no Mongolian consulate.

• **Monkey Business** (☎ 010-6591 6519, 💻 www.monkeyshrine.com) Chief 'Monkey' is André and by now he and his team have put thousands of budget travellers on trains across Siberia. They'll organise everything (including visa support) and also sell some individual packages from Beijing to Moscow and a wide range of stopover options (eg Mongolia, Irkutsk, Lake Baikal and Yekaterinburg). They can even book a journey from Moscow to Beijing. See also p370.
• **CITS Beijing** (☎ 010-6512 0507, 💻 www.citsbj.com) also sell Trans-Siberian tickets. CITS is China's official tourist agency and buying tickets from them is the cheapest and quickest way besides purchasing them yourself at the railway station. Availability can be a problem in summer owing to high demand. Staff tend to be fluent in English and helpful. See also p370.
• **Beijing Tourism Group** (BTG; ☎ 010-6515 8010, 💻 www.btg.com.cn) is one of China's largest agencies, which deals with several major elements of tourism, such as accommodation, transport, tours and entertainment. While booking train tickets for onward travel is not its main function, BTG is nevertheless helpful and efficient. See also p370.

Online booking is also possible. Reliable Chinese companies dealing exclusively with train ticket bookings are 💻 www.chinatraintickets.net, 💻 www.china-train-ticket.com or 💻 www.travelchinaguide.com. While you end up paying a small mark-up fee, the tickets are conveniently delivered to your hotel or place of lodging.

Embassies in Beijing Of course you'll need a Russian visa, but you really should get this before arriving in China (see p23).

For the Trans-Mongolian route, most nationalities need a Mongolian visa as well as a Chinese one; exceptions include Americans and Israelis. However, you should get your visas before arriving in China even if you speak the relevant languages. If you're continuing through Europe after Moscow you may also need a transit visa for Belarus or Ukraine.
• **Russia** (consular department ☎ 010-6532 1267, 💻 www.russia.org.cn), 4 Dongzhimen Beizhong Jie, Beijing 100600; open for applications 9am-noon Monday to Friday, but you are strongly advised to get there before 10.30am. There are consulates in: Shanghai, Guangzhou, Shenyang and Hong Kong.

Some European nationalities need health insurance to qualify for a Russian visa (see box p23).
• **Mongolia** (☎ 010-6532 6516, 💻 www.mongolembassychina.org), 2 Xiushui Beijie, Jianguomenwai Dajie, Beijing; the consular section is open for applications 9-11am Monday to Friday.

For information on other embassies in Beijing see p368.

From Hong Kong

Hong Kong can be a good place to arrange a ticket or stopover package on the Trans-Siberian. Most visitors do not require a visa to enter Hong Kong but should have visas for their onward travel before arriving here.

Agencies here offer a range of services and booking with them from abroad is usually no problem. Several travel agencies in the Nathan Rd area can arrange tickets with a few weeks' notice. Some will sell you a voucher to exchange in Beijing for a reserved ticket. Others sell you an open ticket with a reservation voucher, leaving you to get the ticket endorsed by CITS in Beijing; don't accept an open ticket without a reservation voucher. But to visit any Russian cities apart from Moscow you'll need a tourist visa and therefore visa support.

- **Monkey Business** (💻 www.monkeyshrine.com – see opposite) is very experienced in Trans-Siberian travel and offers a full range of services. If you want to make advance plans, get in touch with their Beijing office (see p370).
- **Global Union Transportation** (☎ 852 2868 3231, 💻 www.global.com.hk) has been recommended for booking Trans-Siberian tickets and helping with Russian visa support.
- **Phoenix Travel** (💻 www.statravel.hk) Agent for STA Travel in Hong Kong.

What to take

The best advice today is to travel as light as possible. Some people recommend that you put out everything you think you'll need and then pack only half of it. Remember that unless you're going on an upmarket tour, you'll be carrying your luggage yourself.

CLOTHES

For summer in Moscow and Siberia pack thin clothes, a sweater and a raincoat. In every hotel you will be able to get laundry done, often returned the same day. Take shirts and tops of a quick-drying cotton/polyester mixture if you are going to wash them yourself.

Winter in Russia and northern China is extremely cold, although trains and most buildings are kept well-heated: inside the train you can be warm enough in a thin shirt as you watch Arctic scenes pass by your window. When you're outside, however, a thick winter overcoat is an absolute necessity, as well as gloves and a warm hat. It's easy to buy good quality overcoats/jackets in Beijing. If you're travelling in winter and plan to stop off in Siberian cities along the way you might consider taking thermal underwear. Shoes should be strong, light and comfortable; most travellers take sturdy trainers. On the train, Russians discard their shoes and wear flip flops – the type you can wear with socks. This is a good idea and you can buy them at any station or on virtually any street. Russians also wear tracksuits throughout the journey, while the Chinese might resort to pyjamas.

Luggage limits

On my first Trans-Siberian trip from Beijing we had so much luggage that several taxi-drivers refused to take us to the station. Unfortunately all thirteen bags were necessary as we were moving back from Japan. On the train we'd managed to get some of them stowed away in the compartments above the door and under the seats when we were joined by a German woman travelling home after three years in China. Her equally voluminous baggage included two full-size theatrical lanterns which were very fragile. Then the man from Yaroslavl arrived with three trunks. We solved the storage situation by covering the floor between the bottom bunks with luggage and spreading the bedding over it, making a sort of triple bed on which we all lounged comfortably – eating, drinking, reading, playing cards and sleeping for the next six days. Dragging our bags around Moscow, Berlin and Paris was no fun, however. On subsequent journeys I didn't even take a rucksack, only a light 'sausage' bag with a shoulder strap and a small day-pack. Never travel with an ounce more than you absolutely need. Nowadays a 35kg luggage limit in compartments is strictly applied in Beijing but ignored in Moscow.

LUGGAGE

If you're going on one of the more expensive tours which include baggage handling, take a suitcase. Those on individual itineraries have the choice of rucksack (comfortable to carry for long distances but bulky) or shoulder-bag (not so good for longer walks but more compact than a rucksack). A zip-up holdall with a shoulder strap or a frameless backpack is probably the best bet. It's also useful to take along a small daypack for camera, books etc. Since bedding on the train and in hotels is supplied you don't need to take a sleeping-bag even when travelling in winter, although some travellers prefer to carry their own sleeping bag liner.

GENERAL ITEMS

Essentials

A **money-belt** is essential to safeguard your documents and cash. Wear it underneath your clothing and don't take it off on the train, as compartments are very occasionally broken into. A good pair of **sunglasses** is necessary in summer as well as in winter, when the sun on the snow is particularly bright. A **water bottle** (two-litre) or flask which can take boiling water is very useful, as is a **mug** (insulated is best), and **fork/spoon/knife set**.

Useful items

The following items are also useful: a few clothes pegs, adhesive tape, ballpoint pens, business cards, camera and adequate capacity memory cards for a digital camera, torch (flashlight), folding umbrella, games (cards, chess – the Russians are very keen chess players – Scrabble etc), toilet paper, calculator (for exchange rates), notebook or diary, penknife with corkscrew and can-opener (although there's a bottle opener fixed underneath the table in each compartment on the train), photocopies of passport, visa, air tickets, etc (keep them in two separate places), sewing-kit, spare passport photographs for visas, string (to use as a washing-line), the addresses of friends and relatives (don't take your address book in case you lose it), tissues (including the wet variety), universal bath plug (Russian basins usually don't have a plug), washing powder (liquid travel soap is good) and multi-purpose travel body wash that doubles as shampoo. A compass is useful when looking at maps and out of the window of the train. Earplugs are useful on the train and in noisy Chinese hotels. Don't forget to take a good book (see pp42-5).

It's also a very good idea to bring things to show people: photos of your family and friends, your home or somewhere interesting you have been. Everyone will want to look at them, and will often get out photos of their own to show you. Looking at photographs, especially of people, is a great way to break the ice when you don't speak much of the local language.

Gifts

The Russians are great present givers (see box p73), and there's nothing more embarrassing than being entertained in a Russian home when you have nothing to offer in return. Cakes and chocolates can be bought locally, or better, bring things that are harder for Russians to get, such as postcards or souvenirs of your country. Foreign coins and badges are also good, as Russia is full of collectors.

It is essential to ensure that you have things to share while you're on the train, such as chocolate biscuits, sweets or other snacks.

Provisions

Though the menus in Russian restaurant cars are sometimes long, often they'll only have a few items on the list: soup, a meat dish and a few refrigerated salads. Beer, chocolate, crisps and biscuits are generally available. There's also a good selection of things to eat available from hawkers on station platforms along the way.

It's wise to buy some provisions before you get on the train, especially if you're going the whole way without a break. Take along fruit, cheese and sausage; you can almost always buy bread, tomatoes, boiled eggs, boiled potatoes, soft drinks and beer on the platform. If you're sharing a compartment with Russians, they'll probably insist you share their food. To refuse would be rude. You should obviously offer some of your food as well, though often it will not be accepted as they will see you as their guest.

Some travellers bring rucksacks filled with food, though it's more realistic to bring just some biscuits and tea-bags or instant coffee (with whitener and sugar if required). Other popular items include drinking chocolate, dried soups, tinned or fresh fruit, fruit-juice powder, peanut butter, Marmite or Vegemite, chocolate, crackers, pot noodles and instant porridge. If you forget to buy provisions at home there are Western-style supermarkets in both Moscow and Beijing where you can stock up with essentials.

Medical supplies

Essential items are: aspirin or paracetamol; lip salve; sunscreen lotion; insect repellent (vital if you're travelling in summer); antiseptic cream and some plasters/bandaids; an anti-AIDS kit containing sterile syringes and swabs for emergency medical treatment. Note that some Western brands of tampons and condoms are not always easily available in Russia or China, so bring your own if you favour a particular kind. Bring an extra pair of glasses or contact lenses if you wear them. You may want to take along something for an upset stomach (Arrêt, for example) but use it only in an emergency, as changes in diet often cause slight diarrhoea which stops of its own accord. Avoid rich food, alcohol and strong coffee to give your stomach time to adjust. Paradoxically, a number of travellers have suggested that it's a good idea to take along laxatives. For vaccination requirements, see pp45-6.

Mobile phones, laptops and music players

Internet cafés are available in every city along the Trans-Siberian route. The number of travellers using **laptops** in Russian trains is increasing, even in *platzkart*, so if you bring one along you won't be terribly conspicuous.

Most travellers bring **mobile phones** on the train, including Russians, and these can be charged using outlets in the carriages. If you have an unlocked tri-band phone and you are spending a lot of time in Russia, it pays to pick up a SIM card from a Russian mobile company. These are usually available for free; all you pay for are the credits. Your phone will be registered in the city where you buy it, and while local calls there are cheap, roaming charges once you leave that region can get expensive. The rates offered by different mobile companies are comparable, but the ones with the greatest coverage are Beeline and MTS.

MP3 players are commonly used, so an iPod doesn't look too out of place.

Photographic equipment

Many Russians and Chinese have digital cameras. Batteries can be charged on board from outlets in the carriages. Every city along the route has digital print shops, and in most internet cafés the staff will burn your photos onto a CD for you if you bring a USB cable. Many travellers on long journeys carry portable hard drives for storing photos.

If you shoot with film, bring more than you think you'll need. Don't forget to bring some faster film for shots from the train (400 ASA). It's wise to carry all your film in a lead-lined pouch (available from camera shops) if you are going to let them go through Russian X-ray machines at airports.

Most major brands of film are available in Russian cities, but slide or high/low ASA film may be difficult to find outside Moscow and St Petersburg. In the large cities in Siberia and China, you can have your film processed in one hour and the quality is acceptable. In Ulaanbaatar there are plenty of developers with imported machines. It is becoming more difficult to get film processed as most people have switched to digital photography.

Photography from the train The problem on the train is to find a window that isn't opaque or one that opens. They're usually locked in winter so that no warmth escapes. Opening doors and hanging out will upset the carriage attendants if they catch you; if one carriage's doors are locked try the next, and remember that the kitchen car's doors are always open. Probably the best place for undisturbed

❑ What not to photograph

Taking pictures from the train used to be forbidden but now it's OK, although it would be wise not to get trigger-happy at aerodromes, military installations or other politically sensitive areas.

Remember that in Russia, as in most other countries, it's considered rude to take pictures of strangers, their children or possessions without asking permission. Often people are keen to have their picture taken but you must always ask. This is particularly the case during political demonstrations or rallies: the updater of an earlier edition of this guide got stoned by a group of pensioners outside the White House for trying to get the next cover for *Time* magazine. Beware! If you do take photos of a person always offer to send them copies and, if they accept, make sure you follow through with your promise; ask them to write down their address for you.

Refrain from photographing touchy subjects such as drunks, queues and beggars. Photography in churches is normally discouraged, and taking a photo of someone in front of an icon is considered disrespectful. A useful phrase is 'Mozhno vas snyat?' (Можно вас снять?) meaning simply, 'Can I take a photo of you?' If travelling in winter always carry your camera inside your pocket or elsewhere near your body, as batteries get sluggish in the intense cold.

photography is right at the end of the train: 'No one seemed to mind if we opened the door in the very last carriage. We got some great shots of the tracks extending for miles behind the train'. (**Elizabeth Hehir**, The Netherlands).

MONEY

(See also pp66-7) With certain exceptions, you will have to pay for everything in local currency (roubles in Russia, RMB/yuan in China, tughrik in Mongolia). Russian hotels must accept roubles, even though some set their rates in dollars or euros.

There are abundant, well-signposted, 24-hour international ATMs in all major cities along the Trans-Siberian, and in Beijing. Most accept Visa, MasterCard and other major cards and give cash advances from your own account in local currency. This is the most convenient way to get by without carrying a huge stash of cash. Cards are also accepted by many hotels and a growing number of guesthouses, restaurants and shops.

But there are many times when cash is essential, for example when the banks are closed or there are no ATMs, for visa fees at many embassies, and in Mongolian restaurant cars on the Trans-Siberian. It's essential to have a stash of cash; by far the most useful currencies in Russia, Mongolia and China are US dollars and euros. Carry only a small amount in your pocket and the rest safely under your clothing in a moneybelt (worn in bed at night as well as during the day). Keep a second stash somewhere else for emergencies. Although cash may seem more risky than travellers' cheques many Russians carry far larger stashes around with them than you will probably have.

See pp66-7 for tips on what kind of banknotes to bring, and on places in Russia where other currencies are commonly accepted.

In Russia you'll only succeed in cashing **travellers' cheques** at selected banks, and therefore only during weekday banking hours. Few banks are interested in anything but US$ cheques. In China travellers' cheques are accepted at better hotels, though most are very fussy about signatures and will ask for your passport. The exchange rate is usually slightly better than for cash, but the difference is too small to matter. You may also be asked to show your original purchase receipts. If your cheques are lost or stolen, you're unlikely to get a swift refund or replacement.

BACKGROUND READING

A number of excellent books have been written about the Trans-Siberian railway. Several are unfortunately out of print, though they're often available through inter-library loan or second-hand on 💻 www.amazon.com. The following are well worth reading before you go:

- ***Journey Into the Mind's Eye: Fragments of an Autobiography*** by Lesley Blanch (1988) is a fascinating book: a witty, semi-autobiographical story of the author's romantic obsession with Russia and the Trans-Siberian Railway.
- ***To the Great Ocean*** by Harmon Tupper (1965, out of print) gives an entertaining account of Siberia and the building of the railway.
- ***Guide to the Great Siberian Railway 1900*** by AI Dmitriev-Mamanov (David and Charles 1971, out of print) a reprint of the guide originally published by the Tsar's government to publicise their new railway. Highly detailed but interesting to look at.
- ***Peking to Paris: A Journey across two Continents*** by Luigi Barzini (1973, out of print) tells the story of the Peking to Paris Rally in 1907. The author accompanied the Italian Prince Borghese and his chauffeur in the winning car, a 40hp Itala. Their route took them across Mongolia and Siberia and for some of the journey they actually drove along the railway tracks.
- ***The Big Red Train Ride*** by Eric Newby. This is a perceptive and entertaining account of the journey he made in the Soviet era, written in Newby's characteristically humorous style.
- ***Through Siberia by Accident***, by Dervla Murphy, is a warm and witty account of this very readable adventurer's travels in Siberia and the BAM region in 2003-4.
- ***In Siberia***, by Colin Thubron, is the best modern book for background on Siberia and certainly one you should either read before you go or take with you on the trip. Thubron's excellent earlier travelogue, ***Among the Russians***, was written after his travels in Soviet times.
- ***The Trans-Siberian Railway: A Traveller's Anthology***, edited by Deborah Manley, is well worth taking on the trip for a greater insight into the railway and the journey, through the eyes of travellers from Annette Meakin to Bob Geldof. If you can't find it in a bookshop it's available from 💻 www.trailblazer-guides.com.
- Paddy Linehan's ***Trans-Siberia*** (2001) is a warm and easily readable account of a trip made recently – the contemporary flavour shines out a-plenty. You quickly warm to the author's unpretentious style.

• ***The Princess of Siberia*** (1984) is Christine Sutherland's very readable biography of Princess Maria Volkonskaya, who followed her husband Sergei Volkonsky to Siberia after he'd been exiled for his part in the Decembrists' Uprising. Her house in Irkutsk is now a museum (see p276).
• ***As Far As My Feet Will Carry Me*** (1955, reprinted 2003) is the true story of the escape of German prisoner of war, Clemens Forell, from the Siberian Gulag where he was serving a 25-year hard-labour sentence. It's a gripping adventure tale.
• ***Into The Whirlwind*** is Eugenia Ginzburg's powerful account of how in 1937 she was arrested and falsely charged as a Trotskyite revolutionary as part of Stalin's purges, and sentenced to exile in Siberia. The sequel, ***Within the Whirlwind***, is no less moving; it describes the 18 years she spent in a Gulag, her fate shared by hundreds of thousands of Russians. Essential reading.
• ***Stalin's Nose: Travels Around the Bloc*** by Rory Maclean (1992) Maclean explores the former Eastern Bloc in a battered Trabant with his elderly aunt Zita and a pig named Winston. He recounts the histories of some of his more notorious

❏ Internet resources

Many travel agents have their own websites, some with useful links; see pp27-37.

• **CIS Railway Timetable** – 🖳 www.poezda.net The best site for timetables throughout Russia. Search by route, station or train number.
• **The Man in Seat Sixty-One...** – 🖳 www.seat61.com For information on rail travel anywhere in the world this is the best site there is. Helpful for planning rail trips to and from Russia. Includes a comprehensive section on the Trans-Siberian with lots of useful links.
• **Way to Russia** – 🖳 www.waytorussia.net Perhaps the best commercial site about travelling in Russia. The information is comprehensive and reasonably up to date.
• **Railway Ring** – 🖳 http://parovoz.com A venerable site for Russian rail fanatics, with an English version and exhaustive links to other sites on railways in Russia, the Baltic States and elsewhere in the CIS.
• **Library of Congress Russian Info** – 🖳 http://lcweb2.loc.gov/frd/cs/rutoc.html In-depth Russian history, culture, religion, politics etc: the on-line version of a book published by the LOC under its Country Studies/Area Handbook Program (1996).
• **Russian Museums directory** – 🖳 www.russianmuseums.info A useful site listing all the museums in Russia with a town by town search facility and weblinks to a number of the museums listed.
• **Russia Today** – 🖳 http://www.einnews.com/russia An excellent round-up of Russian news and analysis, though you have to be a subscriber.
• **Dazhdbog's Grandchildren** – 🖳 www.ibiblio.org/sergei Russian folklore, traditions, culture, myths; many useful links too.
• **Buryatia government page** – 🖳 http://egov-buryatia.ru Buryatia government page covering Buryatia's history, culture and more.
• **The Red Book** – 🖳 www.eki.ee/books/redbook/foreword.shtml Scholarly, sobering research (1991) on the ethnic minority communities of the ex-USSR, with lots about 'endangered' Siberian native peoples.
• **Trans-Siberian Web Encyclopedia** – 🖳 www.transsib.ru/Eng Lots of Trans-Sib memorabilia, pictures, city notes, chat and links.
• **Russian Cuisine** – 🖳 www.ruscuisine.com Russian recipes and more.

relatives, providing in the process a surreal, darkly humorous commentary on communism and its demise.

• ***Lenin's Tomb*** by David Remnick (1993) is an eyewitness account of the heady Gorbachev era by this articulate former *Washington Post* correspondent.

• ***Between the Hammer and the Sickle: Across Russia by Cycle*** by Simon Vickers (1994) is a highly entertaining account of an epic bicycle journey from St Petersburg to Vladivostok in 1990. Out of print.

• ***East of the Sun: The Conquest and Settlement of Siberia*** by Benson Bobrick (1993, reprinted 1997) A readable narrative of Russia's conquest of Siberia, a saga which in colour and drama rivals the taming of the American West.

• ***Around The Sacred Sea: Mongolia and Lake Baikal on Horseback*** by Bartle Bull (1999) In 1993 Bull and two photographers rode north from Mongolia into Siberia and around Lake Baikal, partly a Boys-Own adventure and partly to report on the growing environmental threat to the lake after the collapse of the USSR. The result is an engaging true-life adventure story.

• ***The Conquest of a Continent: Siberia and the Russians*** by American historian W Bruce Lincoln (1993) captures the ambition and cruelty of Cossacks, fur trappers and military adventurers in the region.

• ***A People's Tragedy: The Russian Revolution 1891-1924*** by British historian Orlando Figes (1997) is a scholarly work of social and political history that brings this turning point in Russia's history to life. Winner of the 1997 NCR Book Award.

• ***A History of Twentieth-Century Russia*** by Robert W Service (1997) The eminent British scholar of Russian history looks back at the entire Soviet experiment, from the rise of communism to the collapse of the USSR.

• ***Holy Russia*** by Fitzroy Maclean (1979, out of print), probably the most articulate and readable of many summaries of European Russian history, includes several topical walking tours.

However well written and accurate they may be, these books are only the impressions of foreign scholars and visitors. You will get a better idea of the Russian mind and soul from Russians' own literature, even the pre-Revolution classics. If you haven't already read them you might try some of the following:

• Dostoyevsky's thought-provoking, atmospheric ***Crime and Punishment*** (set in the Haymarket in St Petersburg).

• Tolstoy's ***War and Peace***.

• Mikhail Bulgakov's surreal masterpiece, ***The Master and Margarita***.

• ***Dr Zhivago*** by Boris Pasternak (whose grave you can visit in Moscow).

• ***Memories from the House of the Dead***, a semi-autobiographical account of Dostoyevsky's life as a convict in Omsk.

• ***A Day in the Life of Ivan Denisovitch*** by Alexander Solzhenitsyn, detailing 24 hours in the life of a Siberian convict.

• ***The Gulag Archipelago*** by Alexander Solzhenitsyn.

For information on locomotives, ***Soviet Locomotive Types: The Union Legacy*** by AJ Heywood and IDC Button is invaluable. It's co-published by Luddenden Press (UK) and Frank Stenvalls (Sweden).

Other guidebooks

Other rail guides to Russia include ***Siberian BAM Guide: Rail, Rivers and Road*** by Athol Yates (also from Trailblazer but stocks low) and ***Russia by Rail with Belarus and Ukraine*** by Athol Yates (Bradt; out of print). Trailblazer publishes guides to rail travel in several countries – see pp507-11. ***Trekking in Russia & Central Asia*** by Frith Maier (1994) covers parts of Siberia and includes a look at the history of mountaineering in Russia, although it's now a bit out of date.

Health precautions and inoculations

No vaccinations are listed as official requirements for Western tourists visiting Russia, China, Mongolia or Japan. Some may be advisable, however, for certain areas. If you plan to spend more than three months in Russia evidence of a recent negative AIDS test is required. Russia now has one of the highest incidences of AIDS infection in the world, 90% of it drug related.

Vaccination services and travel advice is available throughout the UK through **MASTA clinics** (💻 www.masta-travel-health.com) and **Nomad Travel Clinics** in London, Manchester, Bristol and Southampton (💻 www.nomadtravel.co.uk). Your GP may be able to give you some of the recommended inoculations, but you'll have to make an appointment with either of the above for the less common ones.

In the USA the **Center for Disease Control and Prevention** (💻 www.cdc.gov) in Atlanta is the best place to contact for worldwide health information.

INOCULATIONS

- **Tetanus** A booster is advisable if you haven't had one in the last 10 years: if you then cut yourself badly in Russia you won't need another.

❑ Health and travel insurance

Wherever you're travelling you should have comprehensive health insurance; most travel agents or tour operators can provide this but it is worth checking different providers to get the best level of cover for the cost. Some nationalities need **health insurance** before they can get a Russian visa (see box p23). The UK has reciprocal healthcare agreements with some countries, including Russia, but not China or Mongolia. Treatment in state hospitals in Russia is free on production of your passport (prescribed medicines need to be paid for); but given the state of most Russian hospitals you're advised to arrange proper health insurance and go to a private clinic if you get ill. EU and EEA citizens will get free or reduced cost treatment (for anything that becomes necessary during a trip) in the Czech Republic, Estonia, Finland, Germany, Hungary, Latvia, Lithuania, and Poland on production of an EHIC. However, visitors are always advised to have comprehensive travel/health insurance as well.

• **Diphtheria** Ensure that you were given the initial vaccine as a child and a booster within the last 10 years. The World Health Organisation recommends a combined diphtheria-tetanus toxoid (DTT) booster.
• **Hepatitis A** Those travelling on tight budgets and eating in cheaper restaurants run a risk of catching infectious hepatitis, a disease of the liver that drains you of energy and can last from three to eight weeks. It's spread by infected water or food, or by utensils handled by infected persons. Gamma globulin antibody injections give immediate but short-term protection (two to six months). A vaccine (trade names Havrix or Avaxim) lasts for twice that time (and up to 10 years if a booster is given within 6 to 12 months).
• **Tick-borne encephalitis** A viral infection of the central nervous system that is incurable. Those venturing into forests in Siberia and even Western Russia are strongly advised to get a vaccination against tick-borne encephalitis, as the number of cases has increased over the last few years and infected ticks have spread over a wider area.
• **Malaria** If you plan to visit rural areas of south-western China you may be at risk of malaria, a dangerous disease which is on the increase in parts of Asia. The malaria parasite (carried by the Anopheles mosquito) is now resistant to chloroquine, so you may need a complex regimen of **anti-malarial tablets** starting before you go and continuing for weeks after you leave the malarial zone; check the type you need with your travel clinic.
• **Rabies** It's also worth considering a pre-exposure **rabies** vaccination course, particularly if you're going to be dealing with animals, cycling, caving or hiking in remote areas. The injection course involves three vaccinations over 21 days minimum, so give yourself plenty of time. Bear in mind that, even after vaccination, if you've been scratched or bitten you'll still require two booster injections.
• **Other** Ensure you've had recent **typhoid**, **polio** and **tuberculosis** boosters. If you're planning to go off the beaten track it's advisable to have a vaccination against **meningococcal meningitis**. It's well worth getting vaccinated against **Japanese B Encephalitis** if you're looking to spend a month or longer in Siberia and the Russian Far East as it cannot be treated and a high percentage of cases result in brain damage or death. If you're arriving from Africa or South America you may be required to show a **yellow fever** vaccination certificate.

MEDICAL SERVICES

Those travelling with tour groups will be with guides who can contact doctors to sort out medical problems. Serious problems can be expensive, but you'll get the best treatment possible from doctors used to dealing with foreigners. If you're travelling independently and require medical assistance, contact an upmarket hotel or one of the hospitals recommended in this book.

Large hotels in China usually have a doctor in residence. In Beijing, Shanghai and Guangzhou (Canton) there are special hospitals for foreigners. Take supplies of any prescription medicine you may need. Medical facilities in Mongolia are quite limited and some medications are unavailable, so it may be better to travel to Beijing if you require serious medical treatment.

RUSSIA

2

Facts about the country

GEOGRAPHICAL BACKGROUND

The Russian Federation includes over 75% of the former USSR, but even without the other old Soviet republics it remains the largest country in the world, incorporating 17.175 million sq km (over 6.5 million square miles) and stretching from well into the Arctic Circle right down to the northern Caucasus in the south, and from the Black Sea in the west to the Bering Strait in the east, only a few kilometres from Alaska. Russia is twice as big as the USA; the UK could fit into this vast country some 69 times.

Climate

Much of the country is situated in far northern latitudes; Moscow is on the same latitude as Edinburgh, St Petersburg almost as far north as Anchorage, Alaska. Winters are bitter: the coldest inhabited place on earth, with temperatures as low as -68°C (-90°F), is Oymyakon, in Yakutia in north-eastern Siberia.

Geography is as much to blame as latitude. Most of Russia is an open plain, stretching across Siberia to the Arctic, and while there is high ground in the south, there are no northern mountains to block the cold Arctic air which blows across this plain. To the west are the Urals, the low range which divides Europe and Asia. The Himalaya and Pamir ranges beyond the southern borders stop warm tropical air from reaching the Siberian and Russian plains. Thus isolated, the plains warm rapidly in summer and become very cold in winter. Olekminsk, also in Yakutia, holds the record for the widest temperature range in the world, from -60°C (-87°F) to a breathtaking summer high of 45°C (113°F). Along the route of the Trans-Siberian, however, summers are rather milder.

Transport and communications

Railways remain the principal means of transport for both passengers and goods, and there are some 87,500km of track in Russia. The heaviest rail traffic in the world is on certain stretches of the Trans-Siberian, with trains passing every few minutes. Although the **road network** is comparatively well-developed (624,000km), few people own cars. As a result some 34% of all passengers, and 45% of all freight, go by rail.

Russia's **rivers** have historically been of vital importance as a communication network. Some of these rivers are huge, and even navigable by ocean-going ships for considerable distances. But ice precludes year-round navigation, and **air travel** is gradually taking over.

Landscape zones: flora and fauna

The main landscape zones of interest to the Trans-Siberian traveller are as follows:

- **European Russia** Flora and fauna west of the Urals are similar to those elsewhere in northern Europe. Trees include oak, elm, hazel, ash, apple, aspen, spruce, lime and maple.
- **Northern Siberia and the Arctic** The *tundra* zone (short grass, mosses and lichens) covers the treeless area in the far north. Soil is poor and much of it permanently frozen. In fact *permafrost* affects over 40% of Russia and extends down into southern Siberia, where it causes building problems for architects and engineers. Wildlife in this desolate northern zone includes reindeer, arctic fox, wolf, lemming and vole. Bird life is richer, with ptarmigan, snow-bunting, Iceland falcon and snowy owl as well as many kinds of migratory water and marsh fowl.
- **The Siberian plain** Much of this area is covered in *taiga*, a Russian word meaning thick forest. To the north the trees are stunted and windblown; in the south they form dark impenetrable forests. More than 30% of all the world's trees grow in this zone. These include larch, pine and silver fir, intermingled with birch, aspen and maple. Willow and poplar line rivers and streams. Much of the taiga forest along the route of the Trans-Siberian has been cleared and replaced with fields of wheat or sunflowers. Parts of this region are affected by permafrost, so that in places rails and roads sink, and houses, trees and telegraph poles often keel over drunkenly. Fauna includes species once common in Europe: bear, badger, wolverine, polecat, ermine, sable, squirrel, weasel, otter, wolf, fox, lynx, beaver, several types of rodent, musk deer, roebuck, reindeer and elk.
- **Eastern Siberia and Trans-Baikal** Much of the flora and fauna of this region is unique including, in Lake Baikal, such rarities as the fresh-water seal. Amongst the ubiquitous larch and pine there grows a type of birch with dark bark, *Betula daurica*. Towards the south and into China and Mongolia, the forests give way to open grassy areas known as *steppes*. The black earth (*chernozem*) of the northern steppes is quite fertile and some areas are under cultivation.
- **The Far Eastern territories: the Amur region** Along the Amur River flora and fauna are similar to those of northern China, and it is here that the rare Amur tiger (see p447) is found. European flora, including trees such as cork, walnut and acacia, make a reappearance in the Far East.

HISTORICAL OUTLINE

The first Russians

Artefacts uncovered in Siberia (see p80) suggest that human history in Russia may stretch back much further than previously believed: 500,000 or more years.

In the 13th millennium BC there were Stone Age nomads living beside Lake Baikal. By the 2nd millennium BC when fairly advanced civilisations had emerged here, European Russia was inhabited by Ural-Altaic and Indo-European peoples. In the 6th century BC the Scythians (whose magnificent goldwork may be seen in the Hermitage, see pp138-9) settled in southern Russia near the Black Sea.

Through the early centuries of the 1st millennium AD trade routes developed between Scandinavia, Russia and Byzantium, following the Dnieper River. Trading centres (including Novgorod, Kiev, Smolensk and Chernigov) grew up along the route and by the 6th century AD were populated by Slavic tribes known as *Rus* (hence 'Russian').

The year 830 saw the first of the Varangian (Viking) invasions and in 862 Novgorod fell to the Varangian chief Rurik, Russia's first sovereign.

Vladimir and Christian Russia

The great Tsar Vladimir (978-1015) ruled Russia from Kiev and was responsible for the conversion of the country to Christianity. Until then Slavs worshipped a range of pagan gods, and it is said that in his search for a state religion Vladimir invited bids from Islam, Judaism and Christianity. Islam wasn't compatible with the Slavs' love of alcohol and Judaism didn't make for a unified nation. Vladimir chose Christianity, had himself baptised at Constantinople in 988AD, and ordered the mass conversion of the Russian people, with whole towns being baptised simultaneously.

The 11th century was marked by continual feuding between his heirs. It was at this time that the northern principalities of Vladimir and Suzdal were founded.

The Mongol invasion and the rise of Muscovy

Between 1220 and 1230 the Golden Horde brought a sudden halt to economic progress in Russia, burning towns and putting the local population to the sword. By 1249 Kiev was under their control and the Russians moved north, establishing a new political centre at Muscovy (Moscow).

All Russian principalities were obliged to pay tribute to the Mongol khans but Muscovy was the first to challenge their authority. Over the next three centuries Moscow gained control of the other Russian principalities and shook off the Mongol yoke.

Ivan the Terrible (1530-84)

When Ivan the Terrible came to the throne he declared himself Tsar of All the Russians and by his successful military campaigns extended the borders of the young country. He was as wild and bloodthirsty as his name suggests: in a fit of anger in 1582 he struck his favourite son with a metal staff, fatally injuring him (a scene conjured up by Ilya Repin in one of his greatest paintings). Ivan was succeeded by his mentally retarded son Fyodor, but real power rested with the regent, Boris Godunov. Godunov himself later became Tsar, ruling from 1598 to 1605.

The early 17th century was marked by dynastic feuding which ended with the election of Michael Romanov (1613-45), first of a line that was to rule until the Revolution in 1917.

An English Tsarina for Ivan Bazilovitch?

In Elizabethan times there were diplomatic and trading links between England and Muscovy whose emissaries and merchants came to London 'dripping pearls and vermin' while Englishmen went to Moscow. Indeed the Tsar had occasion to complain of the behaviour of some of them thereby eliciting a tactful letter from the Queen.

Elizabeth's diplomatic skills brought about a peace between Ivan Bazilovitch and John, King of Sweden, and the former was so grateful to her that 'imagining she might stand his friend in a matter more interesting to his personal happiness, he made humble suit to her majesty to send him a wife out of England'. The Queen chose Anne, sister of the Earl of Huntingdon and of royal Plantagenet blood, but the lady was not willing to risk 'the barbarous laws of Muscovy which allowed the sovereign to put away his czarina as soon as he was tired of her and wanted something new in the conjugal department. The czar was dissatisfied and did not long survive his disappointment', dying in 1584. He is better known to history as Ivan the Terrible and his reputation may well have affected the Queen's thinking when she sorely tried Tsar Boris Godunov's patience with her diplomatic procrastination over his attempts to get an English bride for one of his sons.

(Sources: *The Letters of Queen Elizabeth*, ed. Harrison; *Lives of the Queens of England*, Agnes Strickland; *History of England from the Accession of James II*, Lord Macaulay; Camden's Annals).

Patricia Major

Peter the Great and the Westernisation of Russia

Peter I (1672-1725) well deserves his sobriquet, 'the Great', for it was his policy of Westernisation that helped Russia emerge from centuries of isolation and backwardness into the 18th century. He founded St Petersburg in 1703 as a 'window open on the West' and made it his capital in 1712. During his reign there were wars with Sweden and Turkey. Territorial gains included the Baltic provinces and the southern and western shores of the Caspian Sea, Russia was proclaimed an empire and recognised as a world power.

Catherine the Great and the empire's expansion

Peter's extravagant building programme in St Petersburg continued under Catherine II (1762-96). During her reign, Russia extended her territory to the west, gaining parts of Poland, and proving victorious against the Crimean khanate, thus extending her boundaries to the Black Sea. Successful in the Russo-Turkish Wars against the Ottoman Empire, by the early 19th century, Russia also made significant land gains in Transcaucasia. Catherine the Great also led a coup against her own husband and conducted extensive campaigns of a more romantic nature with a series of favourites in her elegant capital.

Alexander I and the Napoleonic Wars

In 19th-century Russia the political pendulum swung back and forth between conservatism and enlightenment. The mad Tsar Paul I came to the throne in 1796, only to be murdered five years later. He was succeeded by his son

Alexander I (1801-25) who was said to have had a hand in the sudden demise of his father. Alexander abolished the secret police, lifted the laws of censorship and would have freed the serfs had the aristocracy not objected so strongly to the idea. In 1812 Napoleon invaded Russia, and Moscow was burnt to the ground by its inhabitants before he was pushed back over the border.

Growing unrest among the peasants

Nicholas I's reign began with the first Russian Revolution, the Decembrists' uprising (see p88), and ended, after he had reversed most of Alexander's enlightened policies, with the Crimean War against the English and French in 1853-6. Nicholas was succeeded by Alexander II (1855-81) who was known as the Tsar Liberator, for it was he who finally freed the serfs. His reward was his assassination by a student in St Petersburg in 1881. He was succeeded by the paranoid and repressive Alexander III, during whose reign work began on the Trans-Siberian Railway.

Nicholas II: last of the Tsars

The dice were heavily loaded against the unfortunate Nicholas. He inherited a vast empire and a restless population that was beginning to discover its own power. In 1905 his army and navy suffered a humiliating defeat at the hands of the Japanese. Just when his country needed him most, as strikes and riots swept through the cities in the first few years of the 20th century, Nicholas's attention was drawn into his own family crisis. It was discovered that Alexis, heir to the throne, was haemophiliac. The Siberian monk, Rasputin, ingratiated his way into the court circle through his ability to exert a calming influence on the Tsarevich. His influence over other members of the royal family, including the Tsar, was said to be malevolent.

October 1917: the Russian Revolution

After the revolution in 1905, Nicholas agreed to allow the formation of a national parliament (Duma), though its elected members had no real power. Reforms came too slowly for the people and morale fell further when, during WWI, Russia suffered heavy losses.

By February 1917 the Tsar had lost control and was forced to abdicate in favour of a provisional government led by Alexander Kerensky. But the Revolution that abruptly changed the course of Russian history took place in October of that year, when the reins of government were seized by Lenin and his Communist Party. The Tsar and his family were taken to Siberia where they were murdered (see pp234-5). Civil war raged across the country, with the White pro-monarchist movement fighting against the new regime's Red Army, and it was not until 1920 that the Bolsheviks brought the lands of Russia under their control, forming the Union of Soviet Socialist Republics (USSR). Lenin created the Cheka (secret police) – a terrifying state organ that mercilessly cracked down onto any opposition, putting 'Iron Feliks' Dzerzhinsky in charge of it. The Cheka was the predecessor of the dreaded KGB and the current FSB.

The Stalin era and World War II

After Lenin's death in 1924, Joseph Stalin deftly outmanoeuvered more likely successors, such as Leon Trotsky, to become the Soviet Union's undisputed leader until his death in 1954, systematically destroying any opposition along the way. During the Great Terror in the 1930s, a climate of fear and distrust prevailed, with neighbours, family members and friends denouncing each other for crimes real or imaginary. Millions were sentenced to hard labour in the Gulags, which provided much of the workforce for ambitious building projects. Political repression came to a head in the Great Purge of 1937-38, in which thousands of dissidents were exiled or executed, including many prominent military leaders accused of plotting against Stalin. The combination of rapid social and economic changes, as well as collectivisation – major restructuring of the agricultural system whereby productive peasants were stripped of land, which was then combined to make vast collective farms – led to the famine of 1932-33. The USSR was transformed from a backward agricultural country into an industrial world power at massive cost to its own people.

In 1939, the Molotov-Ribbentrop non-aggression pact was signed with Nazi Germany, the two powers dividing Poland and the Baltic States between them. When Hitler broke the non-aggression treaty and invaded Soviet territory, the USSR rallied in spite of enormous losses and played a vital part in the defeat of the Nazis during WWII, extending its influence to the East European countries that took on Communist governments after the war.

Khrushchev, Brezhnev, Andropov and Chernenko

After Stalin died in 1953 Nikita Khrushchev became Party Secretary and attempted to ease the strict regulations which governed Soviet society, dismantling Stalin's cult of personality. Between 1957 and 1961, the USSR became the leader in space exploration, with Yuri Gagarin becoming the first man to orbit the earth.

In 1962 Khrushchev's installation of missiles in Cuba almost led to war with the USA. He was forced to resign in 1964, blamed for the failure of the country's economy and for his clumsy foreign policy. He was replaced by Brezhnev who continued the USSR's policy of adopting friendly 'buffer' states along the Iron Curtain. He ordered the invasion of Afghanistan in 1979 'at the invitation of the leaders of the country', a quagmire that the Soviet forces became stuck in for a decade.

When Leonid Brezhnev died in 1982, he was replaced by the former head of the KGB, Yuri Andropov. Andropov died in 1984 and was succeeded by the elderly Konstantin Chernenko, who managed a mere 13 months in office before becoming the chief participant in yet another state funeral.

Gorbachev and the end of the Cold War

Mikhail Gorbachev, at 54 the youngest Soviet premier since Stalin, was elected in 1985 and quickly initiated a process of change known by the terms *glasnost* (openness) and *perestroika* (restructuring). He is credited in the West with bringing about the end of the Cold War (he received the Nobel Prize in 1990) but it would be misguided to think of him as sole architect of the changes that took place in the USSR: it was widely acknowledged before he came to power that things had gone seriously wrong.

Gorbachev launched a series of bold reforms: Soviet troops were pulled out of Afghanistan, Eastern Europe and Mongolia, political dissidents were freed, laws on religion relaxed and press censorship lifted. These changes displeased many of the Soviet 'old guard,' and on 19 August 1991, a group of senior military and political figures staged a coup. Gorbachev was isolated at his Crimean villa and Vice-President Gennadi Yanayev took over, declaring a state of emergency. Other politicians, including the President of the Russian Republic, Boris Yeltsin, denounced the coup and rallied popular support. There were general strikes and, after a very limited skirmish in Moscow (three casualties), the coup committee was put to flight.

The collapse of the USSR

Because most levels of the Communist Party had been compromised in the failed coup attempt, it was soon seen as corrupt and ineffectual. Gorbachev resigned his position as Chairman in late August 1991 and the Party was abolished five days later.

The Party's collapse heralded the demise of the republic it had created, and Gorbachev began a desperate struggle to stop this happening. His reforms, however, had already sparked nationalist uprisings in the Baltic republics, Armenia and Azerbaijan. Despite his suggestions for loose 'federations' of Russian states, by the end of 1991 the USSR had split into 15 independent republics with almost no bloodshed. Having lost almost all his support, Gorbachev resigned and was relieved by Yeltsin.

Yeltsin and the 1990s

Elected in the first direct presidential election in Russian history in June 1991, Yeltsin's years in power were nothing if not turbulent. After the collapse of the Soviet Union, almost half of Russia's population was plunged into poverty practically overnight, as their life savings became worthless. Rapid privatisation followed, with control of former state enterprises going to private individuals with insider connections in the government. A massive brain drain, with many thousands of professionals emigrating, and a capital drain, with wealthy Russians investing abroad, led to an economic crisis, which in turn led to the collapse of the social services.

On 22 September 1993 Yeltsin suddenly dissolved parliament and declared presidential rule, which led to a standoff between Yeltsin and the Congress, culminating in the siege of the White House, its electricity lines cut and the building stormed by troops faithful to Yeltsin, resulting in the death of 171 people.

Besides political unrest, the 1990s saw the rise of criminal gangs and violent crime, not to mention the ongoing guerrilla war between Chechen rebel groups and the Russian military since Chechnya declared independence in the early 1990s.

Putin's Russia

His government plagued by accusations of corruption (Yeltsin's daughter became part of the presidential team) and he himself plagued by ill-health (or alcoholism), on New Year's Eve in 1999, to everyone's surprise, Yeltsin resigned and handed presidential power to his prime minister of four months, Vladimir Putin, practically an unknown. Three months later Putin won the presidential election with just 52.5% of the vote, pledging to clean up Russia and transform it into a 'rich, strong and civilised country'. He was partially true to his word, the economy growing due to high oil prices, and the overhaul of the tax system making it simpler to operate and harder to avoid, though Putin's past career as a KGB spy has clearly left him with authoritarian tendencies, and he has shown himself to be no friend of free speech, with independent newspapers hounded and their reporters killed. To date, there is only one independent newspaper left in the Russian Federation. Most worryingly, the Duma approved a law giving the president the right to declare a state of emergency and close down political parties whenever he sees fit to do so.

Continuing violence in Chechnya spilled beyond its borders, with a series of deadly apartment-block bombings in Moscow and other Russian cities blamed on Chechen terrorists, and by early 2000 much of Grozny, the Chechen capital, had been razed to the ground by Russian troops. Armed conflicts in the Northern Caucasus were brought to international attention particularly during the October 2002 Moscow theatre siege and during the Beslan school shootings in 2004, both incidents resulting in hundreds of deaths. These and the September 11 attacks in the USA gave free rein to Putin's hard-line approach in Chechnya, with no solution in sight.

Under Putin, Russia began flexing its muscles, earning international condemnation. The arrest of oil tycoon Mikhail Khodorkovsky at gunpoint on a Siberian airport runway in October 2003, later sentenced to nine years in prison for tax evasion, led to more criticism in the West, as it was an open secret that Putin had made a deal with the oligarchs: they could operate in peace as long as they didn't interfere in politics and Khodorkovsky was known to harbour political ambitions. In November 2006, former FSB (federal security service) agent and Kremlin critic Alexander Litvinenko died an excruciating death from radiation poisoning in a London hospital, in a suspected KGB hit job, souring Russian-British relations.

On 1 January 2006, the very day Russia took over chairmanship of the G8 group of industrialised nations, Russia cut its gas exports to Ukraine after that country failed to reach an agreement with Gazprom over a proposed rate hike. The cut-off negatively affected gas flow in Eastern and Western European countries as well, and tarnished Russia's image as a reliable energy and trade partner.

A law passed in January 2006 made it more difficult for foreign non-governmental organisations to operate in the country. The Kremlin has said it suspects some NGOs may harbour spies. And in December 2006, bowing to pressure from the Russian government, Shell Oil offered to hand over its controlling interest in the US$20 billion Sakhalin-2 energy project to state-owned Gazprom.

This was widely viewed in the West as a strong-armed tactic reminiscent of Russia's days as a state-controlled economy.

Medvedev and the future

As the constitution prevented Putin from running for a third consecutive presidential term, Dmitry Medvedev was elected President of Russia on 2 March 2008. Medvedev nominated Putin as Prime Minister, but there is no question either abroad or in Russia as to who actually holds the power. Many Russians see the country as a democracy in name only, but in reality a one-party state once again; only the Yedinaya Rossiya (United Russia) party to which Putin and Medvedev belong wields any real power and opposition is practically nonexistent. Putin is expected to return to power at the end of Medvedev's term in 2012. In Putin-like displays of firmness, Medvedev made the controversial decision to attack Georgia following unrest in the Caucasus that resulted in a Georgian offensive against Southern Ossetia, a Russian territory. Georgia claims to have been provoked by Russian military exercises along the border and after the signing of the peace agreement, it turned out that Russia has appropriated some of Georgia's territories.

In September 2010, Medvedev sensationally sacked Yuri Luzhkov, the mayor of Moscow for 18 years, citing 'loss of confidence', after bitter feuds erupted between the Kremlin and Luzhkov's Moscow city government. Corruption was cited as another reason for ending Luzhkov's undisputed reign of the capital, during which his wife, the third richest woman on the planet, is said to have amassed almost $3 billion, though it is widely believed that it was because Luzhkov overstepped the mark and treated the President with contempt.

Russians are quite pessimistic about the state of the country, many complaining about the lack of jobs for newly qualified professionals, which still results in a brain drain, the miserly pensions, the endemic corruption that permeates every level of government, and lack of investment in the country. Russia's wealthiest inhabitants are still investing abroad rather than at home, and Moscow is draining the wealth of the rest of the country with little investment in any other part of Russia.

Unrest continues to plague the Caucasus border areas, with small-scale terrorist acts occurring quite frequently, and the damning December 2010 Wikileaks report has accused Russia of being a 'kleptocracy' where organised crime acts under the protection of the government, bribing is rampant, the judicial system and the police are in cahoots with the mafia and the rule of law is applied very selectively indeed.

ECONOMY

Russia has vast natural resources and in this sense has the potential to be an extremely rich country. It has the world's largest reserves of natural gas as well as deposits of oil, coal, iron ore, manganese, asbestos, lead, gold, silver and copper that will continue to be extracted long after most other countries have exhausted their supplies. Russia's forested regions cover an area almost four times the size of the Amazon basin. Yet owing to gross economic mismanagement under communism and continuing corruption since the privatisation of state industries, the country has experienced severe financial hardship and had been receiving Western aid, though the high oil prices over the past few years have given a much-needed boost to the economy.

Privatisation

Mass privatisation started in the early 1990s. In an attempt to win public approval for the process, in October 1992 every citizen received vouchers worth 10,000 roubles (about US$60 at that time), which could be sold for cash or exchanged for shares in the growing number of private companies. Although the idea of buying and selling stocks caught on, confusion remained over how exactly the market works. Western economic advisers were often asked such questions as 'If I own part of the company, why can't I take the computer home?'

Over 150,000 organisations were privatised but it is now obvious that privatisation did nothing to benefit the average Russian. The country's raw materials and viable industries were mostly sold at closed auctions to officially preferred banks and tycoons, with workers left to purchase economically unviable factories and collective farms. Consequently, a relatively small number of well-connected business people pocketed most of Russia's new wealth while millions of workers were lumbered with worthless investments.

Hyperinflation in the 1990s

When once-regulated commodities markets were freed in January 1992, prices immediately soared by 300-400%. Inflation had already been stoked by a 1990 law allowing possession of hard currency, which led to a rush for dollars. Another factor fuelling inflation was an old agreement allowing former Communist Bloc countries to pay off some debts to Russia in roubles. These countries simply printed up rouble notes, further aggravating Russia's problems. In late 1993 inflation was running at around 25% per month. By the end of 1996 it had dropped to 2% but in 1997 the rouble started to dive again, and Russians sought desperately to change rouble savings into dollars before they became worthless. Foreign investment started to dry up.

In August 1998 Yeltsin took the major decision to devalue the currency: three zeros were knocked off to make the exchange rate six roubles to the dollar; new banknotes were printed and strict new rules governed access to foreign currency.

After dropping further to about 50 roubles to the dollar, the rate has more or less stabilised, wavering around 28 roubles to the dollar in 2011, with inflation running at around 9-12%.

Economic future

Russia is heavily dependent on its energy resources, mainly oil and gas, which account for about 40% of exports, and the economy is very sensitive to global energy prices. High world oil prices in 1999-2000 gave the country a revenue windfall, a jump of 8% in Gross Domestic Product (GDP) and a big boost in its recovery from the 1998 crisis, although growth has been slower since then and the outlook for the future is cloudy. In June 2002 the G8 group of industrialised countries agreed to explore the cancellation of some of Russia's Soviet-era debts.

Putin has brought in a much-needed reform of the tax system. In 1996 only 16% of Russian enterprises paid their taxes in full and on time and only 14 regions out of Russia's 75 paid their tax bills in full. For most people there's now a flat tax rate of 13% with 1% set aside for welfare; corporate taxes have been simplified, too, the idea being that if taxes are low and fair, people will pay. It is estimated that over the last decade taxes amounting to US$150 billion have not been collected.

The country's enormous backlog of wages is gradually being addressed and government coffers are slowly filling. In 2002 Russia had its first surplus budget since the fall of the Soviet Union, yet investment from abroad hasn't materialised to the extent many had hoped. In summer 2005, Putin tried to woo Rupert Murdoch and other tycoons in a private meeting. They complained that Russia's murky legal system and the presence of mafia-like power cliques make its environment too uncertain.

In many respects, things seem to be looking up for Russia. But ask anyone on the street and you'll find that for average people, real life is as tough as ever.

THE PEOPLE

Russia is the sixth most populous nation in the world with an estimated 143.1 million people (about half the population of the former USSR), but it is also one of only a few countries in the world with a declining population: Russia's is dropping by some two-thirds of a million per year, with drug use, alcoholism, sexually transmitted diseases and deteriorating medical care among suggested causes. Average life expectancy is 72 years for Russian women and just 59 years for men.

A high proportion of Russia's people (82%) are ethnic Russians. The rest belong to nearly 100 ethnic minorities, the most numerous being Tatars (4%) and Ukrainians (3%). In the former USSR it was never wise to refer to people as 'Russian' because of the many other republics they might have come from.

Russia is divided into *oblasts* (the basic administrative unit), *krays* (smaller territories) and *autonomous republics* (special territories containing ethnic minority groups such as the Buryats in Siberia). Siberia is part of the Russian Federation and exists only as a geographical, not a political, unit.

GOVERNMENT

Russia moved briskly down the political path from autocracy to 'socialist state', with a period of a few months in 1917 when it was a republic. From November 1917 until August 1991 the country was in the hands of the Communist Party, and until September 1993 it was run by the Congress of People's Deputies. This 1068-seat forum was elected from throughout the USSR. At its head sat the Supreme Soviet, the legislative body, elected from Congress. Since only Party members could stand for election in Congress, only Party members could ever run the country.

The approval of a new Russian Constitution in December 1993 means that the country is now governed by a European-style two-tier parliament – the Duma – very similar to that of France. The head of state is the Russian president, currently Dmitry Medvedev.

Despite the theory, Russia is far from democratic. The power of the country is vested in a few hundred chief executives of huge corporations who picked up enormous wealth through the corrupt privatisation of state enterprises. These so-called 'oligarchs' now monopolise the media, gas and oil, military production and banking sectors, in effect controlling the entire Russian state. Seven of these tycoons bankrolled the 1996 Yeltsin re-election and were rewarded with powerful government positions. With these monopolistic and in many cases criminal power merchants securely lodged in the Kremlin, true democracy is a long way off. Under Putin's autocratic control the situation has not changed and Medvedev's policies follow the same line as Putin's.

EDUCATION AND SOCIAL WELFARE

Education and health care are provided free for the entire population but standards for both are falling. School is compulsory between the ages of seven and seventeen, with the result that Russia has a literacy rate of 98%. Although funding for research is currently at an all-time low, until a few years ago the country ploughed some 5% of national income directly into scientific research in its 900 universities and institutes. Russia's present inability to maintain its scientists has led to a severe brain drain; certain states in the Middle East are very keen for Russian scientists to help them with their nuclear programmes.

The national health care programme is likewise suffering through lack of funds. Russia has produced some of the world's leading surgeons, yet recent outbreaks of diseases extinct in the developed world have demonstrated that health services here were never comprehensive. The most publicised epidemic in the last few years has been diphtheria, with the death of hundreds of Russians who should have been inoculated at birth. While the wealthy have access to state-of-the-art medical equipment and very high healthcare standards in private hospitals, the state hospitals tend to be grim, understaffed places, where nursing staff must be bribed to do their jobs properly.

Recent government programmes aim to stabilise living standards, gradually reduce poverty and mass unemployment, and create conditions for real growth in income. To even the most optimistic Russian, these programmes have little chance of success.

RELIGION

Russia was a pagan nation until 988 when Tsar Vladimir ordered a mass conversion to Christianity. The state religion adopted was that of the Greek Orthodox Eastern Church (Russian Orthodox) rather than Roman Catholicism. After the

Revolution religion was suppressed until the late 1930s when Stalin, recognising the importance of the Church's patriotism in time of war, restored Orthodoxy to respectability. This policy was reversed after the war and many of the country's churches, synagogues and mosques were closed down. Labour camps were filled with religious dissidents, particularly under Khrushchev.

Gorbachev's attitude towards religion was more relaxed and the 1990 Freedom of Conscience law took religion off the blacklist. In 1991 Yeltsin even legalised Christmas: Russian Christmas Day, celebrated on 7 January, is now an official public holiday again. Numerous churches have been restored to cater for the country's estimated 50 million Orthodox believers. In 1997 the Cathedral of Christ the Saviour, demolished by Stalin to make way for a public swimming-pool, was rebuilt in Moscow (see pp168-9). The new cathedral was the setting for a magnificent service on 20 August 2000 in which Tsar Nicholas II and his family, the more famous victims of communism and the Revolution, were made saints in an elaborate canonisation ceremony.

As well as Russian Orthodox Christians there are also about 1.4 million Roman Catholics. Numbers of Christian sects are growing. Sects as diverse as the so-called 'Old Believers' (who split from the Orthodox church in the 17th century), Scientology and Jehovah's Witnesses are looking for converts here. This has worried some Russians, and on 14 June 1993 the Supreme Soviet passed an amendment to the Freedom of Conscience law banning foreign organisations from recruiting by 'independent' religious activities without permission.

Although the number of Muslims has fallen with the independence of the Central Asian Republics, there are still about 11 million in Russia, who now face discrimination traditionally set aside for Jews. The Russian government has become very keen on the 'war on terror' and voiceless migrant workers, most of whom come from the impoverished Central Asian republics, are subject to horrific treatment by the police and armed gangs.

Russian Jews, historically subject to the most cruel discrimination, have been less trusting of the greater religious freedoms. Their position has been made even more uncomfortable by the recent growth of Russian neo-Nazi groups and by the canonisation of the last tsar, a confirmed anti-Semite. In 1990 more than 200,000 Jews moved to Israel, pouring in at a rate of up to 3000 per day. By 1998 over half a million had left, though there are still large Jewish communities in Moscow and St Petersburg.

In Buryatia, the centre of Russian Buddhism, many monasteries have reopened. Since all are a long way off the tourist track, they have not been kept in good repair as museums, unlike churches in European Russia.

Religious freedoms have also brought a growth in animism and Shamanism, particularly in Siberia.

Practical information for the visitor

ESSENTIAL DOCUMENTS

(Also see Part 1: Planning Your Trip) One 19th-century English traveller who left his passport and tickets behind in London still managed to travel across Siberia carrying no other document than a pass to the Reading Room at the British Library. Entry requirements for foreigners are somewhat stricter nowadays.

The essential documents are your passport, a Russian visa and, if appropriate, a visa for the countries you'll be entering after Russia. If you are travelling with an organisation which has issued you with vouchers to exchange for accommodation or train tickets, don't forget these. **Always carry a photocopy of your passport when you are in Russia**: if the police stop you and you don't have it on you, you'll be fined, and you may not wish to trust them with the actual document.

It's also worth bringing photocopies of your Russian visa. Note that **all visas must be registered within seven business days of your arrival in each Russian city**. Failure to do this will make leaving the country difficult without payment of a fine (as high as US$500 but usually less).

If you want to rent a self-drive car in Russia you'll need an international driving licence (available from your country's automobile club). International student (ISIC) cards are useful for discounts at major museums in Moscow and St Petersburg.

If you're arriving from Africa or South America you may be required to show a yellow fever vaccination certificate.

CROSSING THE BORDER

Customs allowances: entering or leaving the country

You should not have any problem bringing into Russia any items for personal use or consumption, including modest amounts of spirits or wine. Note that you need a special permit to export 'cultural treasures', a term used to include almost anything that looks old or valuable. Paintings, gold and silver items made before 1968, military medals and coins attract the attention of customs officials and may be confiscated or charged at 100% or more duty if you do not have a permit from the Ministry of Culture.

Customs declaration forms

At the Russian border you will be given a Customs Declaration Form (*tamozhennaya deklaratsiya*, таможенная декларация) on which you have to declare all the money and luggage you are carrying. These days it's largely a formality and it's unlikely that the border guards will check a foreigner's luggage.

China no longer requires visitors to fill in a separate customs form; Mongolia still does but may soon follow China's example.

Border-crossing procedures

Border-crossing procedures on the train may take anywhere from three to seven hours. The first step is for immigration and customs officers of the country you are leaving to check passports and visas and collect customs forms. They may disappear with your passport for half an hour or so, before coming back and dishing them out, and the train might even move during this time; don't worry, but of course don't forget to get it back! The compartments are then searched by border guards, though the searches usually consist just of a quick glance inside the luggage compartments. On the other side of the border the entire procedure is repeated.

As rails in Russia and Mongolia are of a wider gauge than those in China and most of Europe, bogies have to be changed at the borders. The carriages are lifted individually and the bogies rolled out and replaced. Passengers are sometimes allowed off the train during this time, in which case you can wait at the border station. If you do get off, carriage attendants won't normally let you get back on before the official boarding time, which is when the train returns to the station to pick up the passengers. Don't leave valuables behind.

Bear in mind that during the entire border-crossing procedure the train's lavatories remain locked. This is not purely for security reasons since changing the bogies requires workers to operate beneath the train.

WHERE TO STAY

There's now a wide range of places to stay in Russia: everything from B&Bs (homestays) to luxurious hotels of an international standard.

Types of accommodation

Top hotels Many are owned by large Western chains such as Marriott and Radisson, though Moscow and St Petersburg in particular boast some splendid hotels inside historical buildings restored to a very high standard.

While they look glitzy like international hotels everywhere, the service may have a touch of Soviet reticence about it. The rooms come with all mod-cons and luxurious touches, such as Jacuzzis in bathrooms. They tend to have several restaurants which are normally excellent, as well as banking facilities, room service, gym, spa, sauna and (in some cases) a swimming pool. There are often travel agencies on the premises who can help you book tickets or arrange tours. The staff are motivated and multi-lingual. These hotels are found in Moscow, St Petersburg and some of the other larger cities and prices are what you would expect in the West – US$300-800/£200-600/€250-700 per night.

Mid-range hotels These are mostly solid old Soviet-era hotels, which tend to be of gargantuan proportions and about as architecturally interesting as a multi-storey car park.

They have all the usual tourist facilities including restaurants, banks and shops. Their rooms are good and many have been fully renovated to offer features such as wi-fi, cable TV, and decent bathrooms. Rooms tend to be divided into standard single/double, 'improved' single/double, *polu-lux* and *lux* categories. The last two can be translated as 'junior suite' and 'suite'; many have extra facilities and tend to be more comfortable than the former. The 'improved' or 'business' singles/doubles tend to be more spacious than the standard rooms but may not necessarily have much more in terms of facilities. In many hotels there may be a *dezhurnaya* (floor attendant), often an elderly female busybody, who seems to spend most of her time drinking tea in a little den, gossiping with friends and keeping an eagle eye on all that happens on her floor. She usually turns very friendly when she figures out that you are a foreigner. As with *provodniks* on the trains, it's wise to keep on good terms with her. She can provide boiling water or mineral water at all hours and arrange to get laundry done.

Over the last few years, a good range of brand-new business hotels has sprung up, with modern bathrooms and good, functional rooms with all the mod cons, and often English-speaking staff. The same is true of some new mini-hotels and mid-range boutique hotels that you'll find in larger cities; these are well-run, Western-style establishments with efficient service and a good restaurant on the premises. The staff can usually help you make travel arrangements.

Most hotels have a midday check-out time, but you can usually pay for a couple of extra hours or a half-day if your train leaves in the evening.

In Moscow and St Petersburg standard hotel rooms cost US$100-300/£70-220/€80-250 and in other cities US$70-130/£50-100/€55-115.

Budget hotels These places are usually clean if basically equipped. They normally have a café or basic restaurant but no other conveniences. Rooms are simple with a TV and fridge and either an attached or shared bathroom. The best rooms are referred to as *lux* ('luxury') and most hotels have at least one such room, though unlike the mid-range hotels, here it just might mean that the room is more spacious; it won't necessarily have better facilities, though if most rooms have shared bathrooms, the lux will have an en suite. Most places now provide toilet paper, soap and a clean towel or two. Bathrooms are usually clean but may still have Soviet plumbing. Sink and bath plugs are rare, so it's wise to carry your own universal plug. Note that during the summer, your hotel and almost every other building in the city may be without hot water for up to four weeks (more in some Siberian cities), as hot water is centrally supplied and pipes must be cleaned annually. Top hotels have their own hot water systems. The staff rarely speak English, but seem more inclined to be helpful to foreigners than fellow Russians.

Basic hotel rooms range from US$30-60/£20-40/€25-45.

Train station rooms Most railway stations have rest rooms (*komnaty otdykha* комнаты отдыха) where you can stay overnight. Some require you to have an onward train ticket. These rooms are basic but clean and comfortable, some with TVs, with singles, doubles and four-bed rooms available with shared bathrooms. Solo travellers staying in anything other than a single will find that strangers will move in with them, though shared rooms are single sex. The lux singles will have ensuite bathrooms, TV and fridge. Lux rooms generally cost US$40/£25/€30, while beds in a shared room generally cost US$25/£15/€18.

Youth hostels A few cities in Russia, including Moscow, St Petersburg, Irkutsk, Yekaterinburg, Tomsk, Suzdal and Vladivostok have youth hostels. Standards are about what you would expect in the West, with the vast majority of hostels now offering free wi-fi and internet use, and many offering free breakfast. Many hostels offer a range of services – from booking your onward travel to arranging city tours, and staff tend to be bilingual, since backpacking and staying in hostels is a Western phenomenon that's only just catching on with budget Russian travellers. Dormitory beds cost about US$20-30/£15-22/€18-27 a night, while doubles may cost $60-70/£40-55/€45-60. A number of places in St Petersburg and Moscow belong to Hostelling International (HI), so it could be worthwhile investing in an HI card for the discount. Information on youth hostels can be obtained from the Russian Youth Hostel Association (💻 www.hostelling-russia.ru), Hostels.com (💻 www.hostels.com) or the similar Hostelworld.com (💻 www.hostelworld.com).

Homestays These can be organised in most cities along the Trans-Siberian for US$40-60/£30-50 /€34-55 per person per night including some or all meals, with additional charges for any tours, ticketing, transport or other services. A reliable agency is Host Families Association in St Petersburg (HOFA; 💻 www.hofa.ru); also see p153.

To minimise any misunderstandings, agree in advance on meal times, and on how much you can afford for food if this is not included. When you visit markets it's customary and polite to supplement your host's supplies with ingredients they might not otherwise have or be able to afford.

At some railway stations you may be approached by locals offering to put you up in their houses for around US$15/£10/€12 per night. Look the place over before agreeing, and don't allow yourself to be persuaded if you feel in any way uncomfortable about the arrangement.

Couchsurfing The brainchild of an American student, the free global hospitality scheme that's particularly popular with travellers in their late teens, twenties and thirties has really taken off in Russia, and in all large cities you will find numerous English-speaking hosts happy to put you up for free. Staying with a knowledgeable local can really transform your experience and give you valuable insight into today's Russia. You have to be a member of 💻 www.couchsurfing.org, and it's a good idea for you to have several positive ratings before you ask to surf someone's couch. Pick your host carefully, choosing someone with multiple positive ratings and making sure you know exactly what kind of accommodation's on offer and don't forget to be an ideal guest. The only downside to Couchsurfing is that your hosts will not be able to register your visa for you, meaning that you'll have to find a travel company that does, though this is easily arranged in larger cities.

TOURS

While guided tours allow you to cover a lot of ground quickly, you can easily get around by yourself in all the cities in this book. There are some specialised tours that are well worth going on, though, and these are mentioned in the relevant city section of this book.

LOCAL TRANSPORT

If you're booking an independent trip through an agency, you may be encouraged to purchase 'transfers' so that you will be met at the airport or station on arrival and taken to your hotel. Prices tend to be high, but transfers are more reliable than comparably priced taxis. If travelling on a budget, local public transport should be more than adequate. For information about booking rail tickets in Russia see pp120-4 and in China pp124-8.

Metro, buses, trolleybuses and trams

The **metro** is a cheap and efficient way to get around, with trains every few minutes. In Moscow it's worth using the metro just to see the stations, which are more like subterranean stately homes, with ornate ceilings, gilded statues and enormous chandeliers. Be careful boarding metro-station escalators as they move faster than Western ones. Russian metro stations are deeper underground than their Western counterparts in order to double as bomb shelters, so their escalators are long and swift. The one at St Petersburg's Ploshchad Lenina station rises 59m (194ft). At street level, metro stations are indicated by a large blue or red 'M'. Lines are named after their terminal stations, as on the Paris metro. Where two lines intersect, the transfer station may have two names, one for each line. As trains move off from the station, the next station is announced. The counter above the end of each tunnel indicates how long it's been since the last train left. Besides Moscow and St Petersburg, you'll find a metro system in Novosibirsk and Yekaterinburg.

Every major city has a comprehensive and inexpensive **bus** service (fixed-fare and often very crowded) and usually also **trolley-buses** and **trams**. Some buses have conductors, some have ticket machines and in others tickets are purchased from the driver in strips or booklets. If there's no conductor you must validate your own ticket, using one of the punches by the windows. If the bus is crowded and you can't reach, pass your ticket to someone near a punch and they'll do it for you. Occasionally, inspectors impose on-the-spot fines for those without punched tickets.

Taxis

Official taxis are safer than unofficial ones. You'll recognise the former by the green 'for hire' light. Although they have meters, not all use them. You should agree on a price before you even get in since once the driver realises you're a foreigner, he'll bump it up accordingly. Ask a local beforehand what the taxi trip should cost and don't be afraid to haggle; even if you haven't a clue, at least get the price down a bit. You'll find that taxi drivers stick together and one won't offer you a lower price than the others. You're more likely to be charged local rates if you don't pick up taxis outside big hotels or major tourist spots.

Hitchhiking

Hitchhiking *(avtostop)* is widely practised in Russia, particularly amongst young people. Drivers will readily give you a lift; if you stand in the street with your arm outstretched someone will pull over and ask where you want to go. However, if you try to hitch a ride in a city, they'll expect payment (even though it is illegal), which essentially makes them a cheaper version of the official taxis. Outside the cities, you can easily catch a lift along motorways, at truck stops and next to traffic police stations or anywhere where drivers have to slow down. Have some gifts at the ready and be prepared to be sociable. The usual precautions apply: women shouldn't hitchhike alone and if you don't like the look of the driver or the car has more than one occupant, don't get in. Don't put your luggage in the boot (trunk) or your driver could simply pull away when you get out to retrieve it.

Domestic flights

Domestic flights usually involve long delays and far too much sitting around in airports. Safety standards are not high: if you must fly use one of the larger carriers such as Aeroflot, S7 or Transaero. Many hotels have airline ticket-booking offices.

Boat

Most of the cities you will visit are built on rivers and short trips on the water are usually possible. In St Petersburg the most interesting way to reach Peterhof is by hydrofoil. Cruise boats from Moscow and St Petersburg stop at various Golden Ring cities along the way. From Irkutsk you can get to Lake Baikal by boat up the Angara River and also to various destinations on the lake's shore, though schedules are not terribly reliable. There are also some long-distance options: for example, trips up the Yenisey from Krasnoyarsk to Dudinka, or between Omsk and Tobolsk along the Ob and Irtysh rivers, from Khabarovsk to Komsomolsk-na-Amure along the Amur and from Ust-Kut to Yakutsk up the Lena.

Car rental

In many larger cities it is possible to rent a car, for which you need an international driving licence. You're not likely to want to do so, thanks to the extensive public transportation system and the poor standards of Russian driving, particularly in cities like Moscow.

ELECTRICITY

In Russian cities electricity is 220V, 50 cycle AC and the same is true in China and Mongolia. Sockets require a continental-type plug or adaptor; in Russia and Mongolia they are designed to accommodate the two European-style round prongs, whereas in China, plugs come in four designs: two round prongs, as in Europe, two flat prongs, as in the USA, three-pronged round pins as in Hong Kong and three-pronged angled pins, as in Australia. It's best to bring a universal adaptor. Sockets for electric razors are provided on trains but those are often used to charge mobile phones.

TIME

Russia spans eight time zones, and on the Trans-Siberian you will be adjusting your watch by an hour almost every day. Russian railways run entirely on Moscow Time; timetables do not list local time. It can be disconcerting to cross the border from China at breakfast-time, only to be informed by station clocks that it's just 2am.

Moscow Time (MT) is four hours ahead of Greenwich Mean Time when the country is on 'summer time': from the last Sunday in March to the last Saturday in October. Outside that period MT = GMT+3. Siberian local time zones are listed throughout the route guide; those for the main cities are: Novosibirsk (MT+3), Irkutsk (MT+5), Khabarovsk (MT+7) and Vladivostok (MT+7). Mongolia and China are both MT+5, but since Mongolia does not observe daylight savings time, in the summer it's MT+4.

MONEY

(See also pp41-2). The basic unit of Russian currency is the rouble (рубль), which is divided into 100 kopecks. There are 1, 5, 10 and 50-kopeck and 1, 2, and 5-rouble coins; banknotes come in denominations of 10, 50, 100, 500, 1000 and the rarely seen 5000 roubles.

The rouble is the only legal currency in Russia. Upmarket hotels and restaurants may quote prices in US$ or euros but will expect payment in roubles. Some Russians still change their roubles to euros or dollars for security, although as the rouble has been fairly stable over the last few years, they are gaining confidence in their own currency.

For Mongolian and Chinese currencies, see p336 and p369, respectively.

What to bring

Euros and US dollars are the easiest currencies to exchange throughout Russia. UK pounds and a few other non-EU currencies can be changed in Moscow and St Petersburg, and Swedish kronor and Finnish marks in St Petersburg. Japanese yen are easily exchanged in Khabarovsk and Vladivostok.

Foreign banknotes must be as new, crisp and clean as possible, because older ones, especially if they're torn, soiled or have writing or ink stamps on them, are likely to be rejected. US dollar notes should be dated 1996 or later, as these provide good protection against counterfeiting.

Cashing travellers' cheques is nearly impossible outside weekday banking hours, and difficult at any time outside larger cities. If you do decide to bring travellers' cheques, you will have fewer problems with American Express cheques denominated in US dollars.

Exchanging money

In 2010 there was a shake-up of currency exchange services (*obmen valyuty*). The government passed a law that stated that a currency exchange office has to offer other services as well, or be shut down; so, many have begun to offer other services also. Currently you can find them in hotels, banks, stores and kiosks in most cities. Rates at currency-exchange offices may vary according to supply and demand and whether banks are open.

You may have difficulty getting change from large denomination notes in pretty much anything that is not a large supermarket. Hoard your coins and small-denomination rouble notes for use on public transport, museums and luggage storage facilities.

❑ Exchange rates

To get the latest rates of exchange see 💻 www.xe.com/ucc

	Rouble
US$1	R28.19
UK£1	R45.21
Euro€1	R39.68
Aus$1	R29.85
Can$1	R29.37
China Y10	R43.57
Japan ¥100	R35.65
Mong T100	R2.29
NZ$1	R23.79
Sing$1	R23.15
S Africa R10	R40.37

Credit/debit cards and ATMs

Credit cards – especially Visa and MasterCard, less readily American Express and Diners Club – are now accepted in many of Russia's upmarket shops, hotels and restaurants. In most cities, including those along the Trans-Siberian, it's easy to find an ATM (банкомат) where a range of debit cards can be used for rouble cash advances. You may find, however, that some Russian banks do not accept cards from some foreign banks, regardless of whether they sport the relevant symbols or not, so keep a supply of cash on you for emergencies. Transkreditbank (Транскредитбанк) ATMs are found in all major railway stations and tend to accept all foreign Visa and MasterCards.

Tipping

You'll be seen as ostentatious if you tip at Western levels; Russians generally give up to 10% in restaurants. Guides should receive a tip of around 10% of their daily rate. In China, tipping is not done at all, unless you're tipping a porter in a high-class hotel. In Mongolia, tipping is not essential but appreciated; rounding up the bill is fine.

POST AND TELECOMMUNICATIONS

Email

Internet access is widespread in Russia, China and Mongolia. There are internet cafés in every city covered in this book (see the City Guides chapter for locations) and wi-fi is becoming increasingly common, available in most hostels and hotels (apart from the most basic hotels), and in many upmarket cafés and restaurants.

Post

Airmail to and from the UK takes about two weeks, and four weeks to the USA. Outgoing mail is generally reliable, whilst incoming mail is less reliable. To send a parcel from Russia you must have it wrapped and sealed with a wax stamp at the post office. Post offices are typically open 8am-8pm, and the larger cities have 24-hour post offices.

On international mail to and from Russia, addresses may be written in English and in standard Western format. For domestic mail the usual format is the following, and should be all in Russian:

Six-digit postal code
Name of city or town
Street name, with house number set off by a comma
Name of addressee
followed below by the return address.

On international mail it is helpful to write the country name in Cyrillic:

UK: **Великобритания**, USA: **США**
Canada: **Канада**, Germany: **Германия**
Australia: **Австралия**, New Zealand: **Новая Зеландия**

If you wish to send something urgent or valuable out of Russia you should use one of the courier companies such as DHL and FedEx that have branches around Russia, Mongolia and China.

Mail from China takes around a week to reach international destinations, and it's possible to send letters from many hotels. Post offices tend to be open 9am-5pm daily.

Mongolian post is reliable but can be very slow, and letters and postcards must be sent from the post office.

Telephone

The country code for Russia is 7. To make an international call dial 8, then wait for a second tone and dial 10 followed by the country code and number. To make a long distance call, dial 8, followed by area/city code and number. If calling abroad from a mobile phone, dial + followed by country code and phone number. Note that city codes and phone numbers in Russia often change; the numbers listed in this guide were correct at the time of writing.

Mobile phone reception is good all along the Trans-Siberian and the main mobile phone companies in Russia are MTS, Beeline and Megafon. Buying a SIM card is inexpensive (from R500) and you can top up your credit either by buying top-up cards from kiosks or by walking into any MTS/Beeline/Megafon store and using a self-service top-up machine, where you choose your network, input your number and the amount you'd like to add, and then insert cash, after which you should get a text message to notify you of a successful transaction. Roaming costs can be quite expensive, especially if you're travelling long distances. You'll find that locals may switch SIM cards when travelling across several regions.

If calling a mobile from a landline, or trying to make an international phone call from a landline, be aware that not all landlines are enabled to make anything other than local landline calls.

To call from a street telephone (*taksofon*) you need a prepaid telephone card (*kartochka dlya taksofona*); these are available from kiosks and metro station ticket windows. When placing a call from a taksofon it's important to remember that, as soon as the other party answers, you must press a button to 'start' the call; otherwise you cannot be heard! This button can be a separate button on the telephone, or a number (usually the number 3).

However, taksofon cards are only useful for local calls. For intercity and international calls you should purchase one of a variety of international cards printed with a toll-free or local-rates telephone number and a PIN number. These cards are widely available in shops and kiosks and all have similar rates. To navigate voice prompts with these cards your telephone must have '*' and '#' keys. Most Russian telephones are pulse-dial so you must switch to tone-dial after being connected, usually by pressing '*'. Some cards have a further option for English-language voice prompts.

You can also make calls from telephone offices, usually part of the post office. Leave a deposit with the cashier who will assign you a booth from which you make your call. Pay the balance after the call.

If you have your own laptop, it's a good idea to upload Skype before you go, as you'll then be able to use wi-fi sources along the way to make very cheap calls abroad.

MAGAZINES AND NEWSPAPERS

Two free, visitor-friendly, English-language newspapers worth looking out for in their respective cities are the daily *Moscow Times* and the twice-weekly *St Petersburg Times*. They're easy to find in hotels, hostels, cafés and supermarkets frequented by foreigners; for English-language publications in China see p369 and in Mongolia see p333. Western news magazines such as *Time* and *Newsweek* are sold at better hotels.

TOILETS

You may have heard frightening tales of public toilets in Russia, Mongolia and China. Some of them are very true. In Russia, Ж (zhensky) stands for 'women's' and M (muzhskoi) stands for 'men's'. Even in the larger cities, it pays to have some toilet roll on you; some public toilets will give you a miserly portion of low-grade loo roll in exchange for the entrance fee, but others may not. Many public toilets in Russia and China have old-style squatter loos, with the exception of toilets in nice shopping centres, good hotels and fast food places, which have Western-style toilets. Note that the plumbing in most Russian cities cannot cope with toilet paper, which you must deposit into the malodorous basket next to the toilet instead. If staying with nomads in rural Mongolia, you will become intimately acquainted with very basic latrine pits, where there is no toilet paper, no sink and often no door. Latrine pits are also common in rural parts of Russia and China, including Olkhon Island on Lake Baikal.

FOOD AND DRINK

There's more to Russian cuisine than borsch and chicken Kiev, but if you eat most of your meals on the train you'll have little chance to discover this. You'll probably leave with the idea that Russian cooking is of the 1950s school-dinner variety, with large hunks of meat, piles of potatoes and one vegetable (the interminable cabbage), followed by tinned fruit or ice cream. On the whole Russian cuisine is hearty and solid, but you will be surprised by the delicious food which seems to appear in the most unlikely restaurants, as well as the variety.

When Russians eat at home, the first meal of the day may include fruit juice, cheese, eggs, bread, jam, *kefir* (sour yoghurt drink), *tvorog* (cottage cheese) or *kasha* (porridge). Lunch and dinner may consist of at least three courses.

Zakuski

Russian hors d'oeuvres (*zakuski)* consist of some or all of the following: cold meat, sausages, salmon, pickled herring, paté, tomato salad, sturgeon and caviar. Large quantities of beer or vodka may be drunk with zakuski.

Soups

Soups make meals in themselves with a stack of brown bread. Best known is *borsch* (beetroot soup) which often includes other vegetables (potatoes, cabbage and onion), chopped ham and a swirl of *smetana* (sour cream). *Solyanka* is a delicious, hearty soup with meat, pickles, olives, lemon and honey, with just the right mix of salty, sweet and sour. *Shchi* (cabbage soup) is the traditional soup of the proletariat and was a favourite of Nicholas II, who is said to have enjoyed only plain peasant cooking, to the great disappointment of his French chef. *Akroshka* is a chilled soup of meat, vegetables and *kvas* (a beer-like brew made from fermented bread). *Rassolnik* is a soup of pickled vegetables.

❑ You don't eat meat?!

Vegetarian cooking isn't widely practised in much of Russia and with the exception of big cities like Moscow and St Petersburg, where you can find vegetarian restaurants, and a few Hare Krishna-style Asian restaurants throughout the country, there aren't many venues dedicated to vegetarians. Nevertheless, vegetarians can manage in Russian restaurants if they choose carefully, but they shouldn't rely on the waiter's imagination or assistance! In this book we've noted reliable vegetarian restaurants with a [V].

Amongst **appetisers**, *shchi* (cabbage soup) is often meatless; suluguni cheese is very similar to Greek halloumi and is usually served grilled; and carrot, tomato and cucumber salads are also available.

Main courses are harder; one option is to order a double portion of a starter found on almost every Russian menu: *Julienne*, also known as *griby v smetane* – wild mushrooms baked in cream sauce. Omelettes are another option, if a horribly predictable one. Perversely, you can often do better in cheap cafés than in fine restaurants because meatless food is regarded as rather down-market. Items to look for in cafés are *piroshki* (dough-pastries with fillings like onion, cabbage or carrot), *vatrushkie* (cream-cheese pastries) and *vareniki* (cheese-filled dumplings). You can almost always find *blini* or *oladi* (different kinds of Russian pancakes) served with either sour cream or jam. In Georgian restaurants *lobio* (spicy bean stew) is a vegetarian mainstay, and a few Georgian places also serve *achma* (a kind of cream-sauce lasagne) – combined with *khachapuri* cheesebreads and some salads, this is about as good as it gets.

Neil McGowan

Black gold – Russia's famous caviar

The roe of the sturgeon is becoming more expensive as the fish itself becomes rarer. Four species are acknowledged to produce the best caviar: beluga, sterlet, osetra and sevruga, all of them from the Caspian and Black Seas. To produce caviar's characteristic flavour (preferably not too 'fishy') a complicated process is involved. The female sturgeon is stunned with a mallet, her belly slit open and the roe sacs removed. The eggs are washed and strained into batches of uniform size. The master-taster then samples the roe and decides how much salt to add for preservation.

Processed caviar varies in colour (black, red or golden) and also in the size of the roe. Red caviar comes from salmon and is far cheaper than the rarer black kind. Caviar is either eaten with brown bread or served with sour cream on *blinis* (thin pancakes). You can get it in most tourist hotels, supermarkets and on the train.

A recent report from the World Wide Fund for Nature (WWF) warns that the sturgeon is on the brink of extinction because of aggressive fishing by Russia. The report says that up to 90% of caviar is now obtained illegally and that Russian authorities are doing nothing because of corruption.

Fish

Fish common in Russia include herring, halibut, salmon and sturgeon. These last two may be served with a creamy vegetable sauce. In Irkutsk you should try *omul*, the famous Lake Baikal fish, which has a delicious, delicate flavour; smoked *omul* is very good, as are other smoked fish you will come across during your journey.

Meat

The most famous Russian main course is chicken Kiev (fried breast of chicken filled with garlic and butter). Almost as famous is *boeuf Stroganov* (named after the wealthy merchant family who financed the first Siberian explorations in the 1580s), a beef stew made with sour cream and mushrooms.

Other regional specialities you're likely to encounter include *shashlyk* (mutton or pork kebabs) and *plov* (rice with mutton and spices) from Central Asia, chicken *tabaka* (with garlic sauce) from Georgia, and *salo* (pig's fat preserved with salt and spices), the Ukrainian dish said to be good for hangovers.

From Siberia comes *pelmeni*, small meat-filled dumplings which may be served in a broth, boiled and topped with soured cream or fried.

If you're expecting a rump steak when you order *bifstek* you'll be disappointed: it's just a compressed lump of minced meat, usually swimming in grease and grey in colour.

However, in supermarkets you will find a wide range of sausages as well as excellent salami and other smoked meat products.

Desserts

On many menus you'll encounter ice cream (*morozhenoye* – always good, safe and available everywhere) and fruit compote (a disappointing fruit salad of a few pieces of tinned fruit floating in a large dish of syrup). Other options may include delicious *blinis* (thin pancakes, like crêpes) with sour cream and fruit

❏ Buying your own food

A Russian supermarket (*universam* универсам) has everything you would expect a supermarket to have, though outside the big cities the choice may be limited. Supermarkets in Moscow and St Petersburg rival Western ones in terms of selection and have prices to match.

Produkty (продукты) stores sell a limited range of fresh vegetables, fruit, bread, meat, eggs and manufactured products. Because the products are kept behind a counter, you don't get much chance to inspect the merchandise, and if you don't speak Russian, all you can do is point at what you want.

A market (*rynok* рынок) can be anything from clusters of old people selling garden produce at metro exits to a large covered market with dozens of stalls offering a plethora of fruit, vegetables, dairy products, home-made honey, mushrooms, and meat.

jam; *vareniki* (dumplings filled with sweet cottage cheese or cherries) or rice pudding. Fresh fruit is readily available from street vendors.

Bread

Russian bread, the cornerstone of Russian cuisine, served with every meal, is wholesome and delicious. Over 100 different types are baked in Moscow, ranging from white to rye to black sourdough similar to German pumpernickel, not to mention sweet croissant-type creations and poppy seed rolls. If you're packing for the train, note that brown bread stays fresh much longer than white bread, which goes stale after a day or two.

Drinks

Non-alcoholic Most popular is tea, traditionally served black with a spoonful of jam or sugar. Milk is not always available so you may want to take along some powdered creamer. Russians have been brewing coffee since Peter the Great introduced it in the 17th century, but standards have dropped since then and you have to go to a decent café to find anything but instant coffee.

Bottled mineral water is available everywhere, often carbonated, the more expensive brands such as Borzhomi tasting rather strongly of all those natural minerals that are supposed to be so good for you. There are several varieties of sugary bottled fruit juice (*sok*), with Coca Cola and other soft drinks found everywhere, as well as home-grown varieties such as Takhun.

❏ Drinking water

At all costs, **avoid tap water in St Petersburg** since it may be infected with giardia, which can cause a nasty and persistent form of diarrhoea. Although tap water is safe to drink in most other Russian cities, it's wise to stick to bottled mineral water or boiled water. In Irkutsk and Listvyanka you can safely drink the tap water, which comes directly from Lake Baikal.

On the train, boiled water is always available from samovars in each carriage.

In Mongolia and China, drink only boiled or bottled water; thermos flasks of boiled water are routinely provided on trains and in hotels.

You should also try *kvas* (a beer-like, fermented mixture of stale brown bread, yeast, malt sugar and water). A popular summer cooler sold on the streets from yellow tankers, its alcohol content is so low as to be unnoticeable. A summer/autumn favourite is *mors*, a tart juice drink made from cranberries.

Alcohol

In a land synonymous with vodka, you may be surprised by the amount of **beer**-drinking that goes on. It's common to see people, young and old, nursing a bottle on the street, or even on public transport, at all hours of the day. Russian beer is cheap and readily available and the most popular brands, including Baltika, Bochka and Bochkarev, are of a high standard.

❑ RUSSIAN CUSTOMS AND ETIQUETTE

Customs

- Wine, cake, chocolate or flowers are traditional gifts if you're invited to dinner in someone's home. A small gift for any children is also appropriate. If you bring flowers be sure the number of flowers is uneven: even numbers are for funerals.
- Shaking hands or kissing across the threshold of a doorstep is considered to bring bad luck.
- Take off your gloves when shaking hands.
- Be prepared to remove your shoes upon entering a home. You will be given a pair of slippers (*tapki*) to help keep the apartment clean.
- Smoking is common and accepted in Russia.
- Be prepared to accept all alcohol and food offered when visiting friends, and this can be quite a lot. Refusing a drink or a toast is a serious breach of etiquette. An open bottle must be finished.
- Be prepared to give toasts at dinners, etc. Be careful, the vodka can catch up with you.
- Dress up for the theatre. Check in your coat and any large bags at the garderobe.
- Russian men still expect women to act in a traditional manner. It's bad form for a woman to be assertive in public, to carry heavy bags if you're walking with a man, to open doors, uncork bottles or pay your own way in social situations.
- In a Russian Orthodox church women should cover their heads with a scarf or hat and wear a skirt. Men should remove their hats.

Superstitions

Russians remain remarkably superstitious; many of the following were once also common elsewhere in Europe:

- Never light a cigarette from a candle. It will bring you bad luck.
- Do not whistle indoors or you will whistle away your money.
- Never pour wine back-handed, it means you will also pour away your money.
- A black cat crossing your path is bad luck.
- A woman who finds herself sitting at the corner of a table will be single for the next seven years.
- If you spill salt at the table you will be plagued by bad luck unless you immediately throw three pinches over your left shoulder.
- If someone offers you good wishes, or if you are discussing your good fortune, you must spit three times over your left shoulder and touch (knock on) wood to keep your good fortune.

Vodka still predominates, of course, and Russians drink it straight. The spirit originated in Poland (although some say that it was brought back from Holland by Peter the Great) and means 'little water', something of an understatement. If you tire of the original product, there's a range of flavoured vodkas to sample, including lemon, cherry, blackberry and pepper.

Be warned that the standard vodka measure in Russia is *sto gram* (100g), compared to 25g in the UK. Vodka is traditionally served ice cold and drained in one go from a shot glass. Men are expected to keep this up but a woman might be permitted to drop out after a couple of shots. It can be easy enough to drink but it will quickly catch up with you. You may be asked to give a toast and you should take this seriously – a short speech about your subject is enough.

Note that a shot of vodka ought to be followed immediately by zakuski (see p70): a popular Russian saying is that 'only drunkards drink without food'. Another goes: 'Drinking vodka without beer is like throwing money to the wind'. If someone flicks their throat with their forefinger, it usually means 'How about a drink?'. It's considered impolite to refuse.

There's also **wine**: most varieties tend to be rather sweet for the Western palate, but Georgian reds such as Saperavi are superb. **Russian champagne** can be surprisingly good if you specify that you want it dry and it's very cheap.

WHERE TO EAT

Russians who can afford to do so take great pleasure in dining out; it's not unusual to find favoured local restaurants completely booked for an entire evening by one family or party. Even in Siberia, there are restaurants as good as in any Western city. Not surprisingly, prices in top places are also a match for those in the West.

The cheapest places to eat are **self-service cafés** (*stolovaya*), where a filling but stodgy meal of salad, bread, potatoes, meat and tea costs about US$5. In many cities there are also Western **fast-food chains** such as McDonald's and Rostik's (KFC), plus Russian derivatives such as Russkoye Bistro and Teremok (serving tasty blini). In Moscow, St Petersburg and a few other large cities, **cafés** are good places for an interesting and still reasonably cheap meal.

In **restaurants**, service varies wildly: sometimes it's a struggle to get anyone to notice you, while at other times there's a friendly English-speaking waiter or waitress who can't do enough to help you. Staff give guests ample time to interpret the menu and do their best to ensure that no dish arrives too quickly. Many restaurants in larger cities have bilingual menus, though the translations can be amusing. While you await your food you might be bombarded by blaring pop radio or the occasional live band. If you get invited to join a Russian party, a visit to a restaurant can be a very entertaining, often drunken affair. Note that tsarist traditions die hard: if a man wishes to invite a woman from another table to dance he must first ask permission of the men at her table.

In some upmarket restaurants you may find cover and/or entertainment charges of up to 10% added to your bill. Sometimes they'll just round up the total by about this amount to save the bother of doing an accurate calculation.

❑ **Event tickets**

Tickets for most events can be purchased from 💻 www.innshopping.ru, with booking pages in English. They will deliver tickets for free in Moscow.

ENTERTAINMENT

Nightlife in Moscow and St Petersburg is as good as you'll get in any big Western city, as is the case in Beijing. These cities have lots of nightclubs, discos and bars, but it really helps to have Russian friends to show you the best places. In smaller towns your major options are the hotel bars and discos, which often stay open late. Most provincial cities also have a modern 'megaclub' which combines a disco, bowling alley, bar and restaurant; these places are very popular and pick up late in the evening, but they're sometimes outside the city centre. Casinos you may find difficult to get into and you may want to leave as soon as you do.

Traditional cultural activities such as opera, theatre, ballet or the circus are a better choice. Performances usually start early: between 6pm and 7pm; don't be late or ushers may not let you in until the interval.

Ballet

Many of the world's greatest dancers have been from Russia's Bolshoi and Kirov companies. Some defected to the West including the Kirov's Rudolf Nureyev, Russia's most famous ballet star, who liked to say he was 'shaken out' of his mother's womb on the Trans-Siberian as it rattled towards Lake Baikal.

Don't miss the chance of a night at the magnificent Bolshoi Theatre; the season runs from September to May. Note that many touring groups dance at the Bolshoi so it may not be the famous company you see.

Opera and theatre

In the past, opera was encouraged more than theatre as it was seen as politically neutral. Glasnost, however, encouraged playwrights to dramatise Russian life as it is, rather than as the government wanted people to see it. This has led to a number of successful new theatre groups opening in Moscow and St Petersburg. There are also several puppet theatres which are highly recommended.

Cinema

In the 1980s the Soviet film industry benefited from the greater freedoms that came with glasnost. In early 1987 one of the most successful and controversial films was *Is It Easy To Be Young?*, which was deeply critical of the Soviet war in Afghanistan. In the 1990s the pessimism of the people towards life is reflected in films made in the country.

Little Vera (1990) is the story of a provincial girl who sinks into small-time prostitution and finally drowns herself (Gorbachev walked out of it saying he disapproved of the sex scenes). In *Executioner* (1991) a female journalist takes on the mafia in St Petersburg and loses.

The 1994 film *Burnt by the Sun*, by director Nikita Mikhalkov, set in the mid-1930s just before Stalin's Great Purge, won the grand prize at the Cannes Film Festival as well as the Academy Award for best foreign-language film.

The 1997 film *Brother*, featuring a sparse crime tale reminiscent of French new wave, signalled a new era in Russian movie-making. Also notable is 2002's dreamlike *Russian Ark* by director Alexander Sokurov. Consisting of a single 90-minute camera shot moving through St Petersburg's Winter Palace, it was the world's second-ever unedited feature film.

In 2004, *Nochnoi Dozor* ('Night Watch'), part one of a fantasy horror film trilogy, directed by Timur Bekmambetov, was an international hit. Shot in Karelia, the 2006 film *Ostrov* ('The Island'), directed by Pavel Lungin, scripts the life of a fictional 20th-century sailor-turned-monk and focuses on Orthodox spirituality, while Valery Todorovsky's 2008 release, *Stilyagi* ('Hipsters'), is a musical that explores the lives of Soviet youth obsessed with fashion in the 1950s. Russia's latest offering, Alexei Popogrebski's thriller *Kak Ya Provyol Etim Letom* ('How I Ended This Summer'), set at a polar station on a remote island in the Arctic Ocean, won the Golden Bear award at the 2010 Berlin Film Festival.

Nowadays Western, and especially American, films are everywhere. Every sizeable town has a cinema, with shows starting early in the evening, though with the exception of a couple of cinemas in Moscow, all cinemas show foreign films dubbed into Russian. There is also a thriving black market in bootleg American DVDs, sold in kiosks everywhere.

Television

Despite Putin's crackdown on formerly independent television stations, Russian airwaves still carry news and current affairs programmes of quite high quality. You'll find a smattering of domestic and Western films dubbed into Russian and advertisements can be an interesting window into the local culture. Hotel TVs often have satellite channels, a welcome break from the usual round of garish game-shows.

Rock concerts and sports matches

Rock concerts and sports fixtures are invariably held in stadiums. These are usually well worth attending and very safe as the arenas swarm with police and soldiers to keep order. Football is very popular, as is ice hockey in winter. Tennis has grown in popularity following the emergence of successful Russian tennis players such as Anna Kournikova. Moscow in particular has hosted a number of big international bands and musicians.

SHOPPING

Shopping in Moscow and St Petersburg is a heady experience, as they boast some of the country's grandest and most luxurious department stores. Here you'll rub shoulders with the new Russian elite, seeking to outdo one another parading their new purchases on Nevsky prospekt and Kuznetsky Most. Outside these metropolises you'll still find a selection of quality department stores and

❑ **Museums and galleries**
All museum/gallery **opening times** refer to the peak season June-August; outside peak season, opening times are reduced. Throughout the year museums stop selling entrance tickets an hour before closing time.

a handful of fashion shops in each city. Russia takes full advantage of its position straddling Europe and Asia and you'll find no shortage of luxury items as well as cheap imitations. In the electronics section of any department store you'll find quality merchandise on a par with anything available in the West, but often pricier, too.

No visit to Moscow would be complete without a visit to GUM, Russia's largest department store. It comprises an enormous collection of arcades occupied by upmarket Western chains and boutiques, housed in an impressive glass-roofed building resembling a giant greenhouse. There is another department store chain: TsUM, which has branches in Moscow and most large cities.

Kiosks

Outdoor kiosks are shops in small booths on the sidewalks, squares, markets and around the metros and stations. They often remain open late and a few are open 24 hours. Most sell telephone cards, alcohol, drinks and cigarettes, while others specialise in newspapers, ticket sales, lotto, milk, souvenirs, fruit and vegetables, bootleg CDs and DVDs or clothing.

Opening hours

Large department stores are open from 9am to 8pm Monday to Saturday. Smaller stores have a wide range of opening times, anywhere from 8am to 11am, closing between 8pm and 11pm. Some shops are closed on Sundays.

What to buy

Handicrafts These include attractively decorated black lacquer *palekh* boxes (icon-painters started making them when religious art lost popularity after the Revolution); enamelled bowls and ornaments; embroidered blouses and tablecloths from the Ukraine; large black printed scarves; guitars and *balalaikas*; lace tablecloths and handkerchiefs; jewellery and gemstones from Siberia and the Urals, and painted wooden ornaments including the ubiquitous *matrioshka* dolls which fit one inside the other. Modern variations on the matrioshka include leaders of the former USSR, the Beatles and even South Park cartoon characters. You can also find the ubiquitous McLenin's T-shirts and other pseudo-Communist clothing.

Old Communist memorabilia have long disappeared from shops but are still sold to tourists and make interesting souvenirs. There is much military memorabilia on sale: anything from hats and hip flasks to diving suits and medals. Check what you're buying carefully as it might not be genuine, and don't declare any of it when you leave Russia. This is equally true with the old bank notes you can buy.

Beware of buying paintings, especially if they are expensive, as duty of 100% or more may be imposed on them when you leave the country. If you are going to buy one, make it a small one so that it will fit into your bag easily. If the painting looks old and potentially valuable, it may well be confiscated by customs officials unless you have a permit from the Ministry of Culture. Customs officials always make a point of looking at paintings when you leave the country.

Books You'll find few English-language books in the shops, but upmarket hotel gift shops usually have a small selection of novels. If you haven't already got one, it's well worth buying an English–Russian/Russian–English dictionary to supplement your phrasebook.

Russian-language art books are worth buying for their cheap but usually high-quality reproductions. There are branches of Dom Knigi (House of Books) in Moscow, St Petersburg and most other large cities.

CDs and DVDs Pirated Russian and Western music and movies are available everywhere; the quality is generally good, but you'll need to check that it's compatible with your part of the world.

Russian music runs the gamut from pop to metal. Pop groups with staying power over recent years include Ruki Vverkh (Hands Up), Mashina Vremeni (Time Machine), Gosti iz Budushchevo (Guests from the Future), Premier Ministr and Ivanushky International. Chai-F is a long-running rock band preferred by older fans. A popular young female vocalist is Alsu, while popular male vocalists include Philip Kirkorov, Nikolai Baskov and one-time Eurovision winner Dima Bilan. Alla Pugacheva is an older female singer with a loyal following, particularly among women over 40. Newer acts include reggae artists 5nizza, dance-club stars Dr Bronx and Natali, rockers Graydanskaya Oborona, pop artist Lyapis Trubetskoi, rapper Basta and punkers Krasnaya Plesen.

Clothes There is a huge market for fake branded sports clothes and there are now also dozens of trendy foreign fashion shops in the biggest cities. Russian or old Soviet military clothing is a popular buy for foreigners, but this should be concealed as you leave the country or it may be confiscated.

CRIME AND ANNOYANCES

Russia is generally as safe (or as dangerous) a place to travel as New York or London; the vast majority of **crime** in big cities tends to be pickpocketing, particularly on public transport and in other crowded places. Tourists are rarely singled out for muggings, though incidents have occurred in small towns as well as big cities across the country. Most of the victims have been men walking alone at night. When you go out at night, go in a group and if you are on your own, consider taking a taxi, even if the distance is short, especially if you would have to walk through a poorly lit area.

Emergency numbers Fire ☎ 01 Police ☎ 02 Ambulance ☎ 03

Be sensible about your safety. Keep a low profile and don't advertise loudly that you're a foreigner, especially in clubs or bars. Don't dress ostentatiously or wear expensive jewellery. Most hotel rooms are secure, though petty pilfering may occur in the cheaper places and youth hostels, so put any valuables in a safe if there is one. A money-belt for your passport, credit cards, travellers' cheques and foreign currency is essential. Also see the warnings on p119 for Trans-Siberian travellers.

Mafia racketeering is the crime most often associated with Russia, but the effect on tourists is minimal; mobsters deal in far more money than they could get from you.

Racism does exist in Russia, particularly in the bigger cities, so if you're non-Caucasian in appearance, you should show particular vigilance when walking around at night, as right-wing skinhead gangs have been known to pick fights with anyone who doesn't look Russian. Racial violence does occur with alarming frequency, particularly against the darker-skinned illegal immigrants from the Central Asian republics, and perpetrators are never punished by police, the police often being the guilty party themselves. Make sure you have your passport (or a photocopy of it), visa and other relevant documents on you, because the police are likely to treat you with suspicion and look for an excuse to fine you.

One of the biggest **annoyances** is that, in all three countries but particularly in China and Mongolia, people are not very good at **queuing**. This means that standing politely to one side won't get you very far, and if boarding public transport in cities you should be prepared to elbow your way into the throng.

Spitting on the street is something you'll find prevalent in China, and to a lesser degree in Russia and Mongolia. It's anything but discreet, so don't be surprised to see even pretty girls in designer gear loudly clear their throats and gob like a football player. You may also see people press down on one nostril in order to blow the contents of the other onto the pavement.

Mosquitoes abound in the summer in all three countries, so pack your DEET-infused insect repellent and a compact mosquito net, as they can be a health threat as well as an annoyance in certain parts.

❑ STREET NAMES GLOSSARY

Russian	Cyrillic	Abbreviation	English equivalent
bulvar	бульвар	бул (bul)	boulevard
gostinny dvor	гостинный двор		shopping arcade
most	мост		bridge
naberezhnaya	набережная	наб (nab)	embankment
ploshchad	площадь	пл (pl)	square
prospekt	проспект	пр (pr)	avenue
pereulok	переулок	пер (per)	lane/side street
shosse	шоссе		highway
ulitsa	улицса	ул (ul)	street

3

SIBERIA AND THE RAILWAY

Historical outline

EARLY HISTORY

Prehistory: the first Siberians

Discoveries at Dering Yuryakh, by the Lena River 100km south of Yakutsk, have indicated that man has lived in Siberia for far longer than had previously been thought. Archaeologist Yuri Mochanov, who led excavations there in the 1980s and 1990s, believes that the thousands of stone tools he found embedded in geological stratum dating back over two million years suggests human habitation stretching back this far, which would place the site on a par with Professor Leakey's discoveries in East Africa. It's a highly controversial theory as it would mean that initial human evolution also occurred outside Africa. Western archaeologists who have studied the material believe, however, that it cannot be more than 500,000 years old; that would still give the Siberians an impressively long history.

There is evidence of rather more recent human life in the Lake Baikal area. In the 13th millennium BC, Stone Age nomads roamed round the shores of the lake, hunting mammoths and carving their tusks into the tubby fertility goddesses that can be seen in the museums of Irkutsk today. Several sites dating back to this early period have been excavated in the Baikal area; the railway passes near one at the village of Malta (see pp423-40), 85km west of Irkutsk.

There is far more archaeological evidence from the Neolithic Age (12th to 5th millennia BC) and it shows that nomadic tribes had reached the Arctic Circle, with some even moving into North America via the Bering Strait (then a land bridge) and Alaska. These northern nomads trained dogs to pull their sledges, but remained technologically in the Stone Age until Russian colonists arrived in the mid-17th century.

In the south, several Bronze Age cultures emerged around the central parts of the Yenisey River. Afanassevskaya, south of Krasnoyarsk, has given its name to the culture of a people who lived in this area in the 2nd millennium BC and decorated their pottery with a characteristic herringbone pattern.

The first evidence of permanent buildings has been found near Achinsk, where the Andronovo people built huge log cabins in the 1st millennium BC. Excavations of sites of the Karassuk culture, also dated to the 1st millennium BC, have yielded Chinese artefacts, indicating trade between these two peoples.

Early civilisations

The Iron Age sites show evidence of more complex and organised societies. The clear air of the Altai Mountains has preserved the contents of numerous graves of the 2nd century BC Tagar culture. Their leaders were embalmed and buried like Egyptian pharaohs with all that they might need in the afterlife. In their burial mounds archaeologists have found perfectly preserved woollen blankets, decorated leather saddles and the complete skeletons of horses, probably buried alive when their masters died.

In the 3rd century BC the Huns moved into the region south of Lake Baikal where their descendants, the Buryats, now live. The Huns' westward progress continued for five centuries until the infamous Attila, 'The Scourge of God', having pillaged his way across Europe, reached Paris where he was defeated in 452 AD.

The ancestors of the Kyrgyz people were the Tashtyks of Western Siberia, who built large houses of clay (one found near Abakan even has an under-floor central heating system), moulded the features of their dead in clay death masks and decorated their bodies with elaborate tattoos. The tiny Central Asian republic of Kyrgyzstan, south of Kazakhstan, is all that remains of a once mighty empire that stretched from Samarkand to Manchuria in the 12th century.

In the following century the Kyrgyz were defeated by the rapidly advancing Mongols. Genghis Khan's Mongol empire grew to become history's largest land empire, including the Tartars of South Russia and the peoples of North Asia, Mongolia and China.

The first Russian expeditions to Siberia

In mediaeval times Siberia was known to Russians only as a distant land of valuable fur-bearing animals. Occasional expeditions from Novgorod in the 15th century became more frequent in the 16th century, after South Russia was released from the Mongol grip by Tsar Ivan the Terrible. Ivan's seizure of Kazan and Astrakhan opened the way to Siberia. Yediger, leader of a small Siberian kingdom just over the Urals, realised his vulnerability and sent Ivan a large tribute of furs, declaring himself a vassal of the Tsar.

Yediger's son Kuchum was of a more independent mind and, having murdered his father, he put an end to the annual tribute, proclaiming himself Tsar of Siberia. Ivan's armies were occupied on his western frontiers, so he allowed the powerful Stroganov family to raise a private army to annex the rebel lands. In 1574 Ivan granted the Stroganovs a 27-year lease on the land over the Urals as far east as the Tobol River, the centre of Kuchum's kingdom.

Yermak: the founder of Siberia

The Stroganovs' army was a wild bunch of mercenaries led by an ex-pirate named Yermak, the man now recognised as the founder of Siberia. They crossed the Urals and challenged Kuchum, gaining control of his lands after a struggle that was surprisingly long considering that Russian muskets faced only swords and arrows.

On 5 November 1581 Yermak raised the Russian flag at Isker, near modern Tobolsk, and sent the Tsar a tribute of over 2500 furs. In return Ivan pardoned him for his past crimes, sent him a fur-lined cape that had once graced the royal shoulders, and a magnificent suit of armour. Over the next few years Yermak and his men were constantly harassed by Kuchum, and on 16 August 1584 were ambushed as they slept on an island in the Irtysh. The story goes that Yermak drowned in the river, dragged under by the weight of the Tsar's armour. Yermak's name lives on as the top brand of Russian rucksack.

The quest for furs

Over the next 50 years Cossack forces moved rapidly across Siberia, establishing *ostrogs* (military outposts) as they went and gathering tributes of fur for the Tsar. Tyumen was founded in 1586, Tomsk in 1604, Krasnoyarsk in 1628 and Yakutsk in 1633. By 1639 the Cossacks had reached the east coast.

Like the Spanish Conquistadors in South America they dealt roughly with the native tribes they met, who were no match for their muskets and cannon. The prize they lusted after was not gold, as it was for the Spaniards in Peru and for later Russian adventurers in Siberia, but furs. In the days before fur farms, certain pelts were worth far more than they are today; from the proceeds of a season's trapping in Siberia a man could buy and stock a large farm with cattle and sheep. The chances of a Russian trapper finding his way into and out of the dark, swampy forests of the taiga were not very high, but quite a few did it.

Khabarov and the Amur

In 1650 a Russian fur merchant named Khabarov set out from Yakutsk to explore the Amur region in what is now the Far Eastern Territories, fertile and rich in fur-bearing animals. Khabarov found the local tribes extremely hostile, as the Russians' reputation for rape and pillage had spread before him. He and his men committed such atrocities that the news reached the ears of the Tsar, who ordered him back to the capital to explain himself. Bearing gifts of fur, he convinced the Tsar that he had won valuable new lands which would enrich his empire.

The local tribes, however, appealed to the Manchus, their southern neighbours, who sent an army to help them fight off the Russians. The Tsar's men were gradually beaten back. Periodic fighting went on until 1689, when the Russians were forced out of Manchuria and the Amur by the Treaty of Nerchinsk.

18th-century explorers

Peter the Great became Tsar in 1696 and initiated a new era of exploration in the Far East. By the following year the explorer Vladimir Atlasov had claimed Kamchatka for Russia. In 1719 the first scientific expedition set out for Siberia. Peter commissioned the Danish seaman Vitus Bering to search for a northern sea-passage to Kamchatka and the Sea of Okhotsk (unaware that such a route had been discovered by Semyon Deshnev 80 years earlier). However, the Tsar did not live to see Bering set out in 1725.

Between 1733 and 1743 another scientific expedition, comprising naval officers, topographers, geodesic surveyors, naturalists and astronomers, made detailed charts of Russian lands in the Far East. Fur traders reached the Aleutian Islands and in 1784 the first Alaskan colony was founded on Kodiak Island by Gregory Shelekhov (whose grave is in the cemetery of Znamensky Convent in Irkutsk). Russian Alaska was sold to the United States in 1868 for the bargain price of two cents an acre.

THE 19TH CENTURY

There were two developments in Siberia in the 19th century which had a tremendous effect upon its history. First, the practice of sentencing criminals to a life of exile or hard labour in Siberia was increased to provide labour for the mines and to establish communities around the military outposts.

The exile system (pp84-9), which caused a great deal of human misery, greatly increased the population in this vast and empty region. Secondly, and of far greater importance, was the building of the Trans-Siberian Railway in the 1890s (see p95).

Colonisation

By the end of the 18th century the population of Siberia was estimated to be about 1.5 million people, most of whom belonged to nomadic native tribes. The policy of populating the region through the exile system swelled the numbers of settlers, but criminals did not make the best colonists. The government therefore tried to encourage voluntary emigration from overcrowded European Russia. Peasant settlers could escape the bonds of serfdom by crossing the Urals, although Siberia's reputation as a place of exile was not much of an incentive to move.

As the railway penetrated Siberia, the transport of colonists was made easier. Tsar Alexander's emigration representatives were sent to many thickly populated regions in European Russia in the 1880s, offering prospective colonists incentives including a reduced rail fare (six roubles for the 1900km/1200-mile journey) and a free allotment of 27 acres of land. Prices in Siberia were high, and colonists could expect to get up to 100% more than in European Russia for produce grown on this land. Many peasants left Europe for Siberia after the great famine of 1890-91.

Further exploration and expansion

Throughout the 19th century scientists and explorers continued to make expeditions to Siberia. In 1829 an expedition led by the German scientist, Baron von Humboldt, already famous for his explorations in South America, investigated the geological structure of the Altai plateau in southern Siberia.

In 1840 the estuary of the Amur was discovered, and colonisation was encouraged after Count Muravyev-Amursky, Governor General of Eastern Siberia, annexed the entire Amur territory for Russia, in flagrant violation of the

1689 Russo-Chinese Treaty of Nerchinsk. But the Chinese were in no position to argue, being threatened by the French and English as well as by internal troubles in Peking. By the Treaty of Peking (1860) they ceded the territory north of the Amur to Russia, and also the land east of the Ussuri, including the valuable Pacific port of Vladivostok.

THE EXILE SYSTEM

The word 'Siberia' meant only one thing in Victorian England and 19th-century Russia: an inhospitable land of exiled murderers and other evil criminals who paid for their sins by working in its infamous salt mines. While some of the first exiles sent over the Urals did indeed work in salt mines, most of them mined gold, silver or coal.

By 1900 over a million people had been exiled and made the long march to the squalid and overcrowded prisons of Siberia.

George Kennan

In 1891 a book entitled *Siberia and the Exile System*, written by George Kennan, was published in America. It exposed the truly horrific conditions under which prisoners were kept in Siberia and aroused public opinion in both America and Britain. Kennan was a journalist working for the *New York Century Magazine*. He knew Siberia well, having previously spent two years there. At that time he had been unaware of how badly convicts were treated and in a series of lectures before the American Geographical Society had defended the Tsarist government and its exile system.

When his editor commissioned him to investigate the system more thoroughly, bureaucrats in St Petersburg were happy to give him the letters of introduction which allowed him to venture into the very worst of the prisons and to meet the governors and convicts.

The government doubtless hoped that Kennan would champion their cause. Such had been the case with the Rev Dr Henry Landsell who had travelled in Siberia in 1879. In an account of his journey, *Through Siberia*, Landsell wrote that 'on the whole, if a Russian exile behaves himself decently well, he may in Siberia be more comfortable than in many, and as comfortable as in most of the prisons of the world.' After the year he spent visiting Siberian prisons, Kennan could not agree with Landsell, and revealed the inhumanity of the exile system, the convict mines and the terrible conditions in the overcrowded prisons.

The first exiles

The earliest mention of exile in Russian legal documents was in 1648. In the 17th century exile was used as a way of banishing criminals who had already been punished. In Kennan's words: 'The Russian criminal code of that age was almost incredibly cruel and barbarous. Men were impaled on sharp stakes, hanged and beheaded by the hundred for crimes that would not now be regarded as criminal in any civilised country in the world, while lesser offenders were flogged with the knut (a whip of leather and metal thongs, which could break a man's back with a single blow) and bastinado (cane), branded with hot irons,

The Siberian Boundary Post (circa 1880) In this melancholy scene, friends and relatives bid exiled prisoners farewell beside the brick pillar that marked the western border of Siberia on the Great Post Road.

mutilated by amputation of one or more of their limbs, deprived of their tongues, and suspended in the air by hooks passed under two of their ribs until they died a lingering and miserable death.' Those who survived these ordeals were too mutilated to be of any use so they were then driven out of their villages to the lands beyond the Urals.

Exile as a punishment: the convict mines

With the discovery of valuable minerals in Siberia and in light of the shortage of labourers, the government began to use criminals to work the mines. Exile was thus developed into a form of punishment and extended to cover a range of crimes including desertion, assault with intent to kill and vagrancy (when the vagrant was of no use to the army or the community). According to Kennan, exile was also a punishment for offences that now seem nothing short of ridiculous: fortune-telling, prize-fighting, snuff-taking (the snuff-taker was not only banished to Siberia but also had the septum between his nostrils torn out) and driving with reins. Traditionally Russian drivers rode their horses or ran beside them: reins were regarded as too Western, too European.

Abolition of the death penalty

In the 18th century the demand for mine labour grew, and the list of crimes punishable by exile was extended to include drunkenness and wife-beating, the cutting down of trees by serfs, begging with a pretence to being in distress, and setting fire to property accidentally. In 1753 the death penalty was abolished (for all crimes except an attempt on the life of the Tsar) and replaced by exile with hard labour. No attention was given to the treatment of exiles en route, who were simply herded like animals over the Urals, many dying on the way. The system was chaotically corrupt and disorganised, with hardened murderers being set free in Siberia while people convicted of relatively insignificant offences perished down the mines.

Reorganisation in the 19th century

In the 19th century the system became more organised but no less corrupt. In 1817 a series of *étapes* (exile stations) was built along the way to provide overnight shelter for the marching parties. They were nothing more than crude log cabins with wooden sleeping platforms. Forwarding prisons were established at Tyumen and Tomsk from where prisoners were sent to their final place of exile. From Tyumen convicts travelled by barge in specially designed cages to Tomsk. From there some would be directed on to Krasnoyarsk or to Irkutsk, a 1670km (1040-mile), three-month march away. Prisoners were sent on to smaller prisons, penal colonies and mines. The most infamous mines were: on the island of Sakhalin, off the east coast, where convicts dug for coal; the gold mines of Kara; and the silver mines of Nerchinsk.

Records were started in 1823 and between this date and 1887, when Kennan consulted the books in Tomsk, 772,979 prisoners had passed through on their way to Siberia. They comprised *katorzhniki* (hard labour convicts), distinguishable by their half-shaved heads; *poselentsi* (penal colonists); *silni* (persons simply banished and allowed to return to European Russia after serving their sentence); and *dobrovolni* (women and children voluntarily accompanying their husbands or fathers). Until the 1850s convicts and penal colonists were branded on the cheek with a letter to indicate the nature of their crime. More than half of those who crossed the Urals had had no proper trial but were exiled by 'administrative process'. As Kennan states: 'Every village commune has the right to banish any of its members who, through bad conduct or general worthlessness, have proved themselves obnoxious to their fellow citizens.'

Life in the cells

The first prison Kennan was shown on his trip in 1887 was the Tyumen forwarding prison. He records the experience thus: 'As we entered the cell, the convicts, with a sudden jingling of chains, sprang to their feet, removed their caps and stood in a dense throng around the *nari* (wooden sleeping platforms) ... "The prison" said the warden, "is terribly overcrowded. This cell for example is only 35 feet long by 25 wide, and has air space for 35, or at most 40 men. How many men slept here last night?" he inquired, turning to the prisoners. "A hundred and sixty, your high nobility", shouted half a dozen hoarse voices ... I looked around the cell. There was practically no ventilation and the air was so poisoned and foul that I could hardly force myself to breathe it in.'

The hospital cells

None of these dreadful experiences could prepare Kennan for the hospital cells, filled with prisoners suffering from typhus, scurvy, pneumonia, smallpox, diphtheria, dysentery and syphilis. He wrote afterwards: 'Never before in my life had I seen faces so white, haggard, and ghastly as those that lay on the gray pillows in the hospital cells ... As I breathed that heavy, stifling atmosphere, poisoned with the breaths of syphilitic and fever-stricken patients, loaded and saturated with the odor of excrement, disease germs, exhalations from unclean human bodies, and foulness inconceivable, it seemed to me that over the hospital doors should be written "All hope abandon, ye who enter here".'

From the records he discovered that almost 30% of patients in the prison hospital died each year. This he compared with 3.8% for French prisons of the time, 2% for American prisons and 1.4% for English prisons.

Corruption

As well as the inhuman conditions he saw in the prisons, Kennan found that the whole exile system was riddled with corruption. Bribes were regularly accepted by warders and other officials. One provincial administrator boasted that the Governor of Tobolsk was so careless that he could get him to sign any document he was given. As a wager he wrote out The Lord's Prayer on an official form and placed it before the Governor, who duly signed it. The St Petersburg government was too far away to know what was going on in the lands beyond the Urals.

Many high-ranking officials in Siberia were so tightly bound by bureaucratic ties that change was impossible, even if they desired it. An officer in the Tomsk prison confided in Kennan: 'I would gladly resign tomorrow if I could see the (exile) system abolished. It is disastrous to Siberia, it is ruinous to the criminal, and it causes an immense amount of misery; but what can be done? If we say anything to our superiors in St Petersburg, they strike us in the face; and they strike hard – it hurts!'

Political exiles

Life for the so-called 'politicals' and 'nihilists', banished to prevent them infecting European Russians with their criticisms of the autocratic political system that was choking the country to death, was generally better than that for other prisoners. Many came from aristocratic families and, once out of prison, life for them continued in much the same way as it had west of the Urals.

The most famous political exiles were the 'Decembrists', men who took part in an unsuccessful coup in 1825. Many were accompanied into exile by their wives. Some of the houses in which they lived are now preserved as *dom* (house) museums in Irkutsk (see p276). Kennan secretly visited many of the politicals in Siberia and was convinced that they did not deserve to be exiled. He wrote later: 'If such men are in exile in a lonely Siberian village on the frontier of Mongolia, instead of being at home in the service of the state – so much the worse for the state.'

A few politicals were sentenced to exile with the native Yakuts within the Arctic Circle. Escape was impossible and life with a Stone Age tribe must have seemed unbearable for cultured aristocrats who had until recently been part of the St Petersburg court circle.

Temporary abolition of the exile system

The exile system was abolished in 1900. But however corrupt the system and inhuman the conditions in these early Siberian prisons, worse was to come only

Political exiles, many of whom came from aristocratic families, were free to adopt whatever lifestyle they could afford within the confines of Siberia, once they had completed their prison sentences.

30 years later. Under Stalin, vast concentration camps were set up, in European Russia as well as Siberia, to provide a huge slave-labour force to build roads, railways and factories in the 1930s and 1940s. Prisoners were grossly overworked and undernourished. The mortality rate in some of these camps is said to have been as high as 30%. Reports of the number of people sentenced to these slave labour camps range from 3 million to 20 million. Some researchers place the death toll up to the late 1950s as high as 18 million.

Early travellers

VICTORIAN ADVENTURERS

The Victorian era was the great age of the gentleman (and gentlewoman) adventurer. Many upper-class travellers spent the greater part of their lives exploring lesser-known regions of the world, writing long and often highly readable accounts of their adventures and their encounters with the 'natives'. Siberia attracted almost as many of this brave breed as did Africa and India. Once travel across the great Siberian plain by normal forms of transport of the time (carriage and sledge) had been tried, some resorted to such new-fangled inventions as the bicycle (RL Jefferson in 1896), the train (from 1900) and the car (the Italian Prince Borghese in an Itala in 1907). Some even crossed the country entirely on foot.

THE GREAT SIBERIAN POST ROAD

Before the railway was built there was but one route across the region for convicts, colonists or adventurers: a rough track known as the Great Siberian Post Road or *Trakt*. Posting stations, where travellers could rent horses and drivers, were set up at approximately 40km (25-mile) intervals.

Murray's 1865 *Handbook for Russia, Poland and Finland* tells travellers: 'Three kinds of conveyances are available: the *telega*, or cart without springs, which has to be changed at every station, and for which a charge of about 8d is made at every stage; the *kibitka* or cart (in winter a sledge) with a hood; and the *tarantass*, a kind of carriage on wooden springs which admits of the traveller lying down full length and which can be made very comfortable at night. The two latter vehicles have to be purchased at Perm, if the *telega*, or postal conveyance be not accepted. A *tarantass* may be bought from £12 to £15.'

❑ Travel by tarantass

Kate Marsden, a nurse travelling in 1894, recalled the agony of days spent in a tarantass in the following way: 'Your limbs ache, your muscles ache, your head aches, and, worst of all, your inside aches terribly. "Tarantass rheumatism" internal and external, chronic, or rather perpetual, is the complaint.'

(Above): Until the building of the Trans-Siberian, the Great Post Road formed the life-line for hundreds of tiny communities such as this. **(Below)**: There were few bridges on the Road – crossing frozen rivers and lakes was treacherous in early winter and spring.

George Kennan called the Imperial Russian Post System 'the most perfectly organised horse express service in the world'.

The discomforts of Siberian travel

Since a visit to Siberia could rarely be completed in a single season, most travellers had the opportunity to try the various modes of transport used in summer and winter. While most found the sledge more comfortable than the tarantass, no 19th-century travelogue would be complete without a detailed description of the tarantass.

This unique vehicle had a large boat-shaped body, and travellers stored their belongings on the floor, covering them with straw and mattresses on which they lay. This may sound comfortable, but when experienced at speed over atrocious roads and for great distances, by contemporary accounts it was not. SS Hill wrote in 1854: 'The worst of the inconveniences arose from the deep ruts which were everywhere ... and from the necessity of galloping down the declivities to force the carriage upon the bridges. And often our carriage fell with such force against the bridges that it was unsafe to retain our accustomed reclining position ...'.

The yamshchiki

The driver (*yamshchik*) of the tarantass or sledge was invariably drunk, and had to be bribed with vodka to make good time between post stations. Murray's 1865 guidebook thoughtfully includes in its Useful Russian Phrases section '*Dam na vodki*' ('I will give you drink money'). Accidents were commonplace; RL Jefferson (on a trip without his bicycle in 1895) wrote that his yamshchik became so inebriated that he fell off the sledge and died.

The same fate befell one of Kate Marsden's sledge-drivers who had gone to sleep with the reins tied around his wrists. She wrote: 'And there was the poor fellow being tossed to and fro amongst the legs of the horses, which, now terrified, tore down the hill like mad creatures ... In a few minutes there was a fearful crash. We had come into collision with another tarantass and the six horses and the two tarantasses were mixed up in a chaotic mass'.

The horses

Sledges and tarantasses were pulled by a *troika*, a group of three horses. These were small furry specimens, 'not much larger than the average English donkey', noted RL Jefferson. They were hired between post stations and usually belonged to the yamshchik.

SS Hill was shocked at the way these animals were treated by the local people. He remarked: 'The Arab is the friend of his horse. The Russian or Siberian peasant is his severe master who exacts every grain of his strength by blows accompanied with curses ... lodges him badly or not at all, cares little how he feeds him, and never cleans him or clips a hair of his body from the hour of his birth to that of his death.' Horses were worked literally until they died. RL Jefferson recalls that two of his animals dropped dead in harness and had to be cut free.

Dangers

Travel in Siberia was not only uncomfortable, it was also dangerous. Wolves and bears roamed the forests and when food was scarce would attack a horse or man (although you were safe in a tarantass). In the Amur region lived the world's largest cat, the Amur tiger. Just as wild as these animals, and probably more dangerous, were the *brodyagi*, escaped convicts in search of money and a passport to readmit them to Europe.

Dirt and disease

As well as the discomfort of the 'conveyance' and the dangers along the Trakt, travellers were warned about the dirt and disease they could encounter. RL Jefferson wrote: 'No wonder that Siberia is looked upon by the traveller with abhorrence. Apart from its inhabitants, no one can say that Siberia is not a land of beauty, plenty and promise; but it is the nature of its inhabitants which make it the terrible place it is. The independence, the filth and general want of comfort which characterise every effort of the community, serve to make a visit to any Siberian centre a thing to be remembered for many years and an experience not desirable to repeat.'

Hotel rooms were universally squalid. Kate Marsden gives the following advice to anyone entering a hotel bedroom in Siberia: 'Have your pocket handkerchief ready ... and place it close to your nostrils the moment the door is opened. The hinges creak and your first greeting is a gust of hot, foetid air.'

Insects

Especially in the summer months, travellers were plagued by flies and mosquitoes. Kate Marsden wrote: 'After a few days the body swells from their bites into a form that can neither be imagined nor described. They attack your eyes and your face, so that you would hardly be recognised by your dearest friend.'

At night, travellers who had stopped in the dirty hotels or posting stations were kept awake by lice, bedbugs and a variety of other insects with which the bedding was infested. RL Jefferson met a man who never travelled without four saucers and a can of kerosene. In the hotel room at night he would put a saucer filled with kerosene under each bed-leg, to stop the bugs reaching him in bed. However, Jefferson noted that: 'With a sagacity which one would hardly credit so small an insect, it would make a detour by getting up the wall on to the ceiling, and then, having accurately poised, drop down upon the victim – no doubt to his extreme discomfort.'

Bovril and Jaeger underwear: essential provisions

RL Jefferson (see 'Jefferson's Bicycle Jaunts', pp94-5) never travelled without a large supply of Bovril and a change of Jaeger 'cellular' underwear – 'capital stuff for lightness and durability' he wrote after one long ride on his Imperial Rover bicycle.

Kate Marsden shared his enthusiasm for Dr Jaeger's undergarments: 'without which it would have been quite impossible to go through all the changes of climate; and to remain for weeks together without changing my clothes', she wrote. On the subject of provisions for the trip, Murray's guidebook recommended taking along basic foodstuffs. Miss Marsden packed into her tarantass 'a few boxes of sardines, biscuits, some bread, tea and one or two other trifles which included 18kg (40lb) of plum pudding'.

❑ KATE MARSDEN VISITS SIBERIAN LEPERS

Miss Marsden was a nurse with a definite mission in Siberia. In the 1880s she learnt, through travellers' accounts, of the numerous leper colonies north of Yakutsk. There were rumours of a special herb found there which could alleviate the symptoms of the disease. After an audience with Queen Victoria, during which she was given useful letters of introduction, she travelled to Moscow. She arrived in mid-winter, wearing her thin cotton nurse's uniform and a white bonnet, which she immediately exchanged for thick Russian clothes.

Crossing Siberia

After meeting the Empress Maria, who gave her 1000 roubles for her relief fund, she started on her long sledge ride. It was not a dignified send-off – 'three muscular policemen attempted to lift me into the sledge; but their combined strength was futile under the load'. She got aboard eventually and was soon experiencing the extreme discomfort of Siberian travel. She said it made her feel more like 'a battered old log of mahogany than a gently nurtured Englishwoman'.

Distributing tea, sugar and copies of the Gospels to convicts in the marching parties she encountered along the Post Road, she reached Irkutsk in the summer. She boarded a leaky barge on the Lena River north of Lake Baikal, and drifted down to Yakutsk, sitting on the sacks of potatoes with which the boat was filled. Of this part of the journey she wrote: 'Fortunately we had only about 3,000 miles of this but 3,000 miles were enough'.

Her goal was still a 3200km (2000-mile) ride away when she reached Yakutsk. Although she had never been on a horse before, this brave woman arranged an escort of 15 men and rode with them through insect-infested swamps and across a fiery plain, below which the earth was in a constant state of combustion, until she reached the settlement of Viluisk.

The lepers of Viluisk

On her arrival the local priest informed her that 'On the whole of the earth you will not find men in so miserable a condition as the Smedni Viluisk lepers'. She found them dressed in rags, living in hovels and barely existing on a diet of rotten fish. This was in an area where, in winter, some of the lowest temperatures in the world have been recorded. Unfortunately she did not find the herb that was rumoured to exist there but left all the more convinced that finances must be raised for a hospital.

Although she managed to raise 25,000 roubles towards the enterprise, her task was not made any easier by several individuals who took exception to her breezy style of writing, accusing her of having undertaken the journey for her own fame and fortune. Some even suggested that the journey was a fiction invented so that Miss Marsden could collect charitable sums for her own use. In the end she was forced to sue one of her defamers who wrote a letter to *The Times* describing her journey as 'only a little pleasure trip'.

Nevertheless she achieved her aim: a hospital opened in Viluisk in 1897. It still stands and her name is still remembered in this remote corner of Russia.

SS HILL'S *TRAVELS IN SIBERIA*

This account of Hill's Siberian adventures was the result of a journey made in the early 1850s to Irkutsk and Yakutsk. Armed with a pistol loaded with goose-shot (the law forbade a foreigner to shoot at a Russian, even in self-defence), he travelled by tarantass and lived on *shchi* (soup) and tea most of the time. He makes some interesting observations upon the culinary habits of the Siberians he met along the way.

He records that on one occasion, when settling down to a bowl of shchi after a long winter's journey, 'we found the taste of our accustomed dish, however, today peculiar'. He was made aware of the main ingredient of their soup later, 'by the yamshchik pointing out to us the marks of the axe upon the frozen carcass of a horse lying within a quarter of a verst of the site of our feast'. In some places even tea and shchi were unavailable and they could find only cedar nuts ('a favourite food article with the peasants of Eastern Siberia'). He ate better in Irkutsk, where, at a dinner party, he was treated to *comba* fish, 2m (6ft) in length and served whole. 'I confess I never before saw so enormous an animal served or cooked whole save once, an ox roasted at a 'mop' in Worcestershire', he wrote later. He was shocked by the behaviour of the ladies at the table, who, when bored, displayed 'a very droll habit of rolling the damp crumb of rye bread ... into pills'. He remarks with surprise that in Siberian society 'a glass of milk terminates the dinner'.

JEFFERSON'S BICYCLE JAUNTS

RL Jefferson was an enthusiastic cyclist and made several bicycle journeys to Siberia in the 1890s. A year after cycling from London to Constantinople and back, he set out again from Kennington Oval for Moscow on his Imperial Rover bicycle. Twelve hours out of Moscow, a speeding tarantass knocked him down, squashing the back wheel of his 'machine'. Repairs took a few days but he still managed to set a cycling speed record of just under 50 days for the 6890km (4281-mile) journey from London to Moscow and back.

His next ride was to the decaying capital of the Khanate of Khiva, now in Uzbekistan. The 9700km (6000-mile) journey took him across the Kyrgyz Steppes in south-west Siberia, along the coast of the Aral Sea and over the Karakum Desert. When the bicycle's wheels sank up to their axles in the sand, he had the Rover lashed to the back of a camel for the rest of the journey. While in Central Asia he lived on a diet of boiled mutton and *koumis* (fermented mares' milk). He travelled in a camel-hair suit (Jaeger, of course) and top boots, with a white cork helmet to complete the outfit.

Across Siberia

Jefferson made two more trips to Siberia. In *Across Siberia by Bicycle* (1896), he wrote that he left Moscow and 'sleeping the night in some woodman's hut, subsisting on occasional lumps of black bread, bitten to desperation by fearful insects, and tormented out of my life during the day by swarms of mosquitoes, I arrived in Perm jaded and disgusted'. He then cycled over the Urals and through the mud of the Great Post Road to Yekaterinburg. Here he was entertained by the Yekaterinburg Cyclists' Club whom he described as 'friends of the wheel – jolly good fellows all'.

Declaring that 'from a cyclist's point of view, Russian roads cannot be recommended', he abandoned his Rover in 1897 for the adventure described in *Roughing it in Siberia*. With three chums he travelled by sledge from Krasnoyarsk up the frozen Yenisey ('jerking about like peas in a frying pan') to the gold mines in Minusinsk district, spending several weeks prospecting in the Syansk Mountains.

Building the railway

The first railway to be built in Russia was Tsar Nicholas I's private line (opened in 1836) which ran from his summer palace at Tsarkoye Selo (Pushkin) to Pavlovsk and later to St Petersburg, a distance of 23km (14 miles). The Tsar was said to have been most impressed with this new form of transport and over the next 30 years several lines were laid in European Russia, linking the main cities and towns. Siberia, however, was too far away to deserve serious consideration since most people went there only if they were forced to as exiles. As far as the Tsar was concerned traditional methods of transport kept him supplied with all the gold and furs he needed.

PLANS FOR A TRANS-SIBERIAN RAILWAY

Horse-powered Trans-Siberian Express?

The earliest plans for a long-distance railway in Siberia came from foreigners. Most books which include a history of the Trans-Siberian give passing mention to a certain English engineer, if only because of his wildly eccentric ideas and his unfortunate name. Thus it is a Mr Dull who has gone down in history as the man who first seriously suggested the building of a line from Perm across Siberia to the Pacific, with carriages being pulled by wild horses (of which there were a great many in the region at the time). He is said to have formally proposed his plan to the Ministry of Ways of Communication who, perhaps not surprisingly, turned it down.

In fact the Englishman's name was not Dull but Duff, and it's not only his name that has been distorted through time. His descendants (John Howell and William Lawrie) have requested that the story be set straight. Thomas Duff was an enterprising adventurer who went to China to seek his fortune in the 1850s. He returned to England via Siberia, spending some time in St Petersburg with wealthy aristocratic friends. Here he was introduced to the Minister of Ways of Communication and it was probably during their conversation that he remarked on the vast numbers of wild horses he had encountered on his journey. Could they not be put to some use? Perhaps they might be trained to pull the trains that people were saying would soon run across Siberia. It is unlikely that this remark was meant to be serious but it has gone down in history as a formal proposal for a horse-powered Trans-Siberian Express.

More serious proposals

At around this time the American Perry McDonough Collins was exploring the Amur River, having persuaded the US government to appoint him as commercial agent in the region. After an enthusiastic welcome by Count Muravyev-Amursky, Governor-General of Siberia, Collins set off to descend the Amur in a small boat. Collins envisaged a trade link between America and Siberia with vessels sailing up the Amur and Shilka Rivers to Chita, where a railway link would shuttle goods to and from Irkutsk. He sent his plans for the building and financing of such a line to the government but they were rejected. His next venture, a telegraph link between America and Russia, also failed but not before he had made himself a considerable fortune.

It took a further 20 years for the government to become interested enough in the idea of a Siberian railway to send surveyors to investigate its feasibility. Plans were considered for lines to link the great Siberian rivers, so that future travellers could cross Siberia in relative comfort by a combination of rail and ship. European lines were extended from Perm over the Urals, reaching Yekaterinburg in 1878.

Tsar Alexander III: the railway's founder

In 1881 Alexander III became Tsar and in 1886 gave the Trans-Siberian project his official sanction with the words: 'I have read many reports of the Governors-General of Siberia and must own with grief and shame that until now the government has done scarcely anything towards satisfying the needs of this rich, but neglected country! It is time, high time!'

He was thus able to add 'Most August Founder of The Great Siberian Railway' to his many other titles. He rightly saw the railway as both the key to developing the land beyond the Urals and also as the means to transport his troops to the Amur region which was being threatened by the Chinese. When the commission looking into the building of the new line declared that the country did not have the money to pay for it, the Tsar's reply was to dismiss it and form a new one.

THE DECISION TO BUILD

The new commission took note of petitions from Count Ignatyev and Baron Korf, the Governors-General of Irkutsk and the Amur territories, respectively. They had proposed rail links between Tomsk and Irkutsk, Lake Baikal and Sretensk (where passengers could board ships for the journey down the Shilka and Amur Rivers to the coast) and for the Ussuri line to Vladivostok. Baron Korf considered it imperative for the Ussuri line to be built as soon as possible if the valuable port of Vladivostok was not to be cut off by the advancing Chinese. The Tsar took note and declared: 'I hope the Ministry will practically prove the possibility of the quick and cheap construction of the line'.

Surveys were commissioned and detailed plans prepared. In 1891 it was announced that the Trans-Siberian Railway would indeed be built and work would start immediately. It was, however, to be constructed as cheaply as possible using thinner rails, shorter sleepers and timber (rather than stone) for the smaller bridges.

The route

The railway commission decided that the great project should be divided into several sections, on which work would commence simultaneously. The West Siberian Railway would run from Chelyabinsk (the railway over the Urals reached this town in 1892) to the Ob River where the settlement of Novo Nikolayevsk (now Novosibirsk) was being built. The Mid-Siberian Railway would link the Ob to Irkutsk, capital of Eastern Siberia. Passengers would cross Lake Baikal on ferries to Mysovaya, the start of the Transbaikal Railway to Sretensk. From there they would continue to use the Shilka and Amur River for the journey to Khabarovsk, until the Amur Railway could be built between these towns. The Ussuri Railway would link Khabarovsk with Vladivostok.

There were also plans for a shortcut from the Transbaikal area to Vladivostok, across Manchuria. This would be known as the East Chinese Railway.

Nicholas lays the foundation stone

After the decision to start work, the Tsar wrote the following letter to his son, the Tsarevich, who had just reached Vladivostok at the end of a tour around the world: 'Having given the order to build a continuous line of railway across Siberia, which is to unite the rich Siberian provinces with the railway system of the interior, I entrust you to declare My will, upon your entering the Russian dominions after your inspection of the foreign countries of the East. At the same time I desire you to lay the first stone at Vladivostok for the construction of the Ussuri line forming part of the Siberian Railway ...'.

On 31 May 1891 Nicholas carried out his father's wishes, filling a wheelbarrow with earth and emptying it onto what was to become part of the embankment for the Ussuri Railway. He then laid the foundation stone for the station.

RAILWAY CONSTRUCTION: PHASE 1 (1891-1901)

• **The Ussuri, West Siberian & Mid-Siberian railways (1891-98)** Work started on the Ussuri line (Vladivostok to Khabarovsk) some time after the inauguration ceremony and proceeded slowly. In July 1892 construction of the West Siberian line (Chelyabinsk to the Ob River) was begun. In July 1893 work started on the Mid-Siberian line (Ob River to Irkutsk).

The West Siberian reached Omsk in 1894 and was completed when the rails reached the Ob in October 1895. The Ussuri Railway was completed in 1897. In the following year the final rails of the Mid-Siberian were laid, finally linking Irkutsk to Moscow and St Petersburg.

• **Transbaikal Railway (1895-1900)** The rail link between the Lake Baikal port of Mysovaya and Sretensk on the Shilka River was begun in 1895. In spite of a flood which swept away part of the track in 1897, the line was completed by the beginning of 1900.

Passengers could now travel to Irkutsk by train, take the ferry across Lake Baikal and the train again from Mysovaya to Srtensk, where steamers would take them to Khabarovsk.

• **East Chinese Railway (1897-1901)** Surveys showed that the proposed Amur Railway between Sretensk and Khabarovsk would be expensive to build because of the mountainous terrain and the large supplies of explosives required to deal with the permafrost. In 1894 the Russian government granted China a generous loan to help pay off the latter's debts to Japan. In exchange a secret treaty was signed which allowed Russia to build and control a rail link between the Transbaikal region and Vladivostok, across the Chinese territory of Manchuria.

Every difficulty encountered in building railways in Siberia (severe winters, mountains, rivers, floods, disease and bandits) was a feature of the construction of the East Chinese Railway, begun in 1897 and opened to light traffic in 1901.

The labour force

The greater part of the Trans-Siberian Railway was built without heavy machinery, by men with nothing more than wooden shovels. They nevertheless managed to lay up to 4km (2½ miles) of rail on a good day. Most of the labour force had to be imported as local peasants were already fully employed on the land. They came not only from European Russia but from as far away as Italy and Turkey. Chinese coolies were employed on the Ussuri Railway but overseers found them unreliable and terrified of the Amur tigers with which the area was infested.

The government soon turned to the prisons to relieve the shortage of labour, and gangs of convicts were put to work on the lines. They were paid 25 kopecks (a quarter of a rouble) a day and had their sentences reduced – eight months on the railways counted for a year in prison. The 1500 convicts employed on the Mid-Siberian worked hard but those brought in from Sakhalin Island to work on the Ussuri line ran riot and terrorised the inhabitants of Vladivostok.

Shortage of materials

On many parts of the Siberian Plain engineers discovered that although there were vast forests, the trees were unsuitable for use as sleepers (ties). Timber had to be imported over great distances. Rails came from European Russia and some even from Britain. They were shipped either via the Kara Sea (a southern extension of the Arctic Ocean) and up the Yenisey River to Krasnoyarsk, or right around the continent by boat to Vladivostok (which took two months). From here, when work started on the Transbaikal line in 1895, materials were shipped up the Ussuri, Amur and Shilka Rivers to Sretensk (over 1600km/1000 miles). Horses and carts were scarce in Siberia and these, too, had to be brought in from Europe.

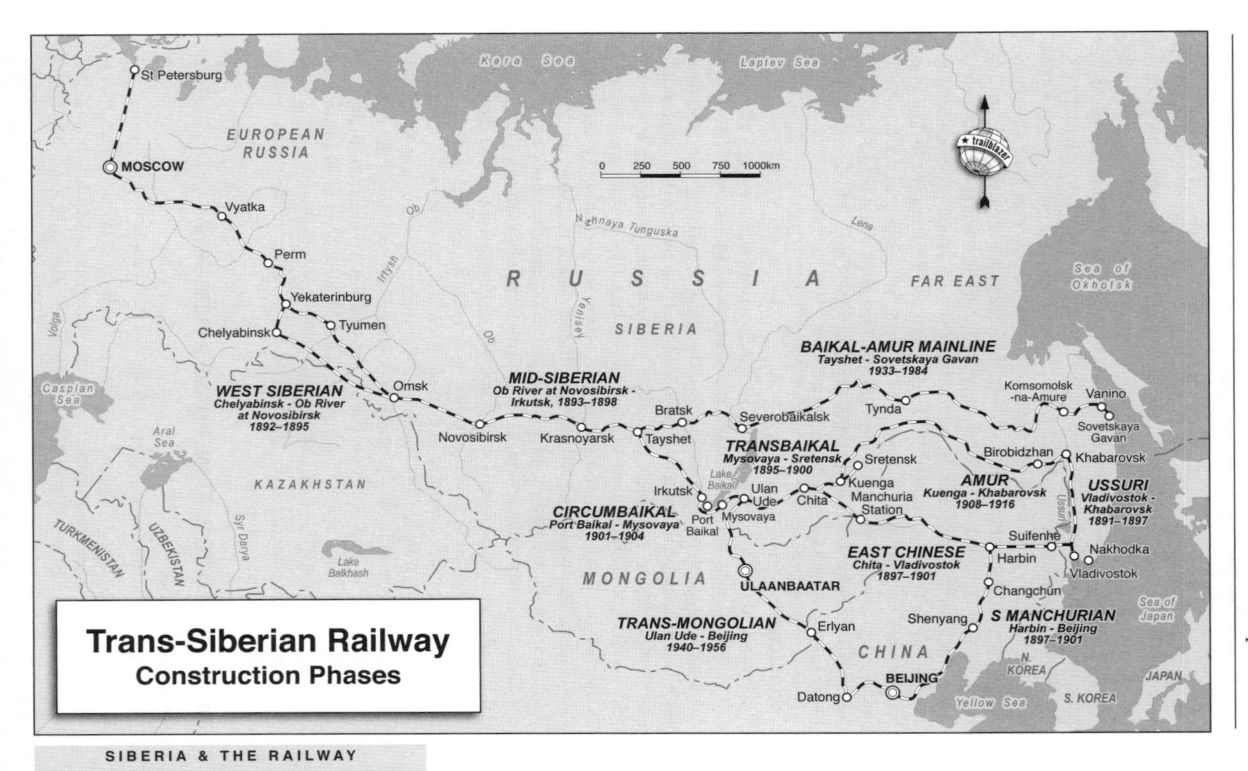
Trans-Siberian Railway
Construction Phases
WEST SIBERIAN
Chelyabinsk - Ob River at Novosibirsk
1892–1895
MID-SIBERIAN
Ob River at Novosibirsk - Irkutsk, 1893–1898
CIRCUMBAIKAL
Port Baikal - Mysovaya
1901–1904
TRANSBAIKAL
Mysovaya - Sretensk
1895–1900
AMUR
Kuenga - Khabarovsk
1908–1916
USSURI
Vladivostok - Khabarovsk
1891–1897
EAST CHINESE
Chita - Vladivostok
1897–1901
S MANCHURIAN
Harbin - Beijing
1897–1901
TRANS-MONGOLIAN
Ulan Ude - Beijing
1940–1956
BAIKAL-AMUR MAINLINE
Tayshet - Sovetskaya Gavan
1933–1984
St Petersburg
MOSCOW
Vyatka
Perm
Yekaterinburg
Tyumen
Chelyabinsk
Omsk
Novosibirsk
Krasnoyarsk
Tayshet
Bratsk
Irkutsk
Port Baikal
Mysovaya
Ulan Ude
Severobaikalsk
Chita
Kuenga
Sretensk
Manchuria Station
Tynda
Birobidzhan
Khabarovsk
Komsomolsk -na-Amure
Vanino
Sovetskaya Gavan
Nakhodka
Vladivostok
Suifenhe
Harbin
Changchun
Shenyang
BEIJING
Datong
Erlyan
ULAANBAATAR
EUROPEAN RUSSIA
R U S S I A
SIBERIA
FAR EAST
KAZAKHSTAN
MONGOLIA
CHINA
UZBEKISTAN
TURKMENISTAN
N. KOREA
S. KOREA
JAPAN
Kara Sea
Laptev Sea
Sea of Okhotsk
Sea of Japan
Yellow Sea
Caspian Sea
Aral Sea
Lake Balkhash
Lake Baikal
Volga
Ob
Irtysh
Yenisey
Nizhnaya Tunguska
Lena
Ussuri
Syr Darya
0 250 500 750 1000km
trailblazer

Difficult terrain

When the railway between St Petersburg and Moscow was being planned, the Tsar took ruler and pencil and drew a straight line between the two cities, declaring that this was the route to be followed, with almost every town bypassed. For the Trans-Siberian, Alexander ordered that it be built as cheaply as possible which is why in some places the route twists and turns so that expensive tunnelling might be avoided. There were few problems in laying foundations for the rails across the open steppeland of the Siberian Plain, but cutting through the almost impenetrable forests of the taiga proved extremely difficult. Much of this area was not only thickly forested, but swampy in summer and frozen until July. Consequently the building season lasted no more than four months in most places. Parts of the route in eastern Siberia were locked in permafrost and, even in mid-summer, had to be dynamited or warmed with fires before rails could be laid. The most difficult terrain was the short line around the southern end of Lake Baikal, the Circumbaikal Loop, which required over 200 trestles and bridges, and 33 tunnels.

Conditions

For the workers who laboured in Siberia, conditions were hardly the most enjoyable. All were far from home, living in isolated log cabins that were not much cleaner or more comfortable than Tyumen's squalid prison, graphically described by George Kennan in *Siberia and the Exile System* (see p84). Winters were very long and extremely cold. The brief summer brought relief from the cold but the added discomfort of plagues of black flies and mosquitoes in the swamps of the taiga. There were numerous outbreaks of disease. Workers on the East Chinese Railway were struck by bubonic plague in 1899 and cholera in 1902. In many places the horses were wiped out by Siberian anthrax.

There were other dangers in addition to disease. In Manchuria and the Amur and Ussuri regions, the forests were filled with Amur tigers for whom the occasional railway labourer no doubt made a pleasant snack. In Manchuria construction camps were frequently raided by *hunghutzes* (bandits) who roamed the country in gangs of up to 700. As a result the Russian government was obliged to allocate considerable money and manpower to the policing of the region.

There were several setbacks that no one could have foreseen. In July 1897 severe flooding swept away or damaged over 300km (200 miles) of track near Lake Baikal on the Transbaikal line, also destroying settlements and livestock. Damage was estimated at six million roubles. In other areas landslides were caused by torrential rainfall.

RAILWAY CONSTRUCTION: PHASE 2 (1898-1916)

Reconstruction

As the first trains began to travel over the newly laid tracks, the shortsightedness of building the railway as cheaply as possible soon became clear. Many of the materials used in its construction were either substandard or unsuitable to the conditions they were expected to withstand. The rails, less than half the weight of those used in North America and fashioned of inferior quality iron, soon bent and buckled and needed replacing. The ballast under the sleepers was far thinner than that put down on the major railways of Europe. As a result the ride in the carriages was bumpy and uncomfortable and speed had to be kept down to 13mph for passenger trains, 8mph for freight. Foreign engineers proclaimed the whole system unsafe and were proved correct by the frequent derailments which took place.

In 1895 Prince Khilkov became Minister of Ways of Communication. On a tour of inspection along the West and Mid-Siberian lines he quickly realised the need for a massive rebuilding programme. Extra trains were also needed to transport the hundreds of thousands of emigrants who were now flooding over the Urals. In 1899, 100 million roubles were allocated for repairs, work which would have been unnecessary had sufficient funds been made available from the start.

• **The Circumbaikal Loop Line (1901-1904)** In 1901 work began on the 260km (160-mile) Circumbaikal Loop Line around Lake Baikal's southern shore. The initial project had been shelved in 1893, the terrain considered too difficult. Passengers used the ferry service across the lake but it was soon found that the ships couldn't cope with the increased traffic. The situation became critical at the start of the Russo-Japanese war in 1904 when troops and machinery being sent to the East by rail were delayed at the lake. Construction of the new line continued as quickly as possible and by the end of the year the final section of the Trans-Siberian was opened. Passengers were at last able to travel from Calais to Vladivostok entirely by train.

• **The Amur Railway (1907-1916)** The original plans for a railway from Sretensk to Khabarovsk along the Shilka and Amur Rivers were abandoned because the route would entail expensive engineering work. After the Russo-Japanese war in 1904-5, the government realised there was a danger of Japan taking control of Manchuria and the East Chinese Railway. As this was the only rail link to Russia's naval base at Vladivostok, it was decided that the Amur Railway must indeed be built.

Work began at Kuenga in 1908. There were the usual problems of insects, disease and permafrost but with the rest of the railway operational, it was easier to transport labour and materials to the area. When the bridge over the Amur at Khabarovsk was finished in 1916, the Trans-Siberian Railway was at last complete. Since 1891 over 1000 million roubles had been spent on building all the sections (including the East Chinese line).

THE FIRST RAIL TRAVELLERS

Rail service begins

As each of the sectors of the Trans-Siberian was completed, a rail service was begun. To say that there were teething troubles would be a gross understatement: there was a shortage of engines and carriages, most of the system operated without a timetable and there were frequent delays and derailments along the shoddily constructed line. Nevertheless, to attract foreign travellers, luxury

The Paris Exhibition

The Russian government was keen to show off to the world the country's great engineering feat and at the Paris 'Exposition Universelle' of 1900, a comprehensive Trans-Siberian exhibit was staged. Amongst photographs and maps of Siberia, with Kyrgyz, Buryat and Goldi robes and artefacts, there were several carriages to be operated by the Belgian Wagons-Lits Company on the Great Siberian Railway. They were furnished in the most sumptuous style, with just four spacious compartments in the sleeping carriages, each with a connecting lavatory. The other carriages contained a smoking-room done up in Chinese style, a library and music-room complete with piano.

In the two restaurant cars, decorated with mahogany panelling and heavy curtains, visitors to the exhibition could dine on the luxurious fare that was promised on the journey itself. To give diners the feeling of crossing Siberia, a length of canvas on which was painted a Siberian panorama of wide steppes, dense taiga and little villages of log cabins, could be seen through the windows. To complete the illusion, the painted panorama was made to move past the windows by mechanical means.

Visitors were intrigued and impressed and more than a few soon set off on the epic trip. The reality, they were to discover, was a little different from what they experienced at the exhibition.

trains and 'Expresses' were introduced. Those run by the government were known as Russian State Expresses while another service was operated by the Belgian Compagnie Internationale des Wagons-Lits. In 1900 the Ministry of Ways of Communication published its English-language *Guide to The Great Siberian Railway*.

Early rail travellers

When RL Jefferson set out to investigate the Minusinsk gold-mining region in 1897, he was able to take the train (travelling this time without his bicycle but no doubt taking along a good supply of Bovril and Jaeger underwear) as far as Krasnoyarsk. The first Englishwoman to travel the entire length of this route was Annette Meakin, who in 1900 took her aged mother along for company. They travelled via Paris to see the Siberian display at the Paris Exhibition. Having crossed Siberia, they went by ship to Japan and then on to North America, crossing that continent by train, too. Having circumnavigated the globe by rail, Miss Meakin recorded her experiences in the book she called *A Ribbon of Iron*. Two years later Michael Myres Shoemaker took *The Great Siberian Railway from St Petersburg to Pekin* (the name of his account of the journey). He wrote enthusiastically: 'This Railway will take its place amongst the most important works of the world ... Russia is awakening at last and moving forward.'

It is interesting to compare the descriptions these travellers give of the trains they took, with the carriages displayed at the Paris Exhibition as well as with the service operated today by Russian Railways.

The carriages

In gushing prose, advertising brochures informed prospective Trans-Siberian travellers that the carriages in which they were to be conveyed would be of a standard equal to those used by European royalty. In addition to the luxurious sleeping compartments and dining cars shown at the Paris Exhibition, there would be a bathroom with marble bathtub, a gymnasium equipped with a stationary bicycle and other exercising machines, a fire-proof safe, a hairdressing salon and a darkroom equipped with all the chemicals a photographer would need. The carriages would be lit by electric lighting, individually heated in winter and cooled by under-floor ice-boxes in summer.

Although more than a few of those luxurious appointments, which they had seen in the carriages of the Siberian exhibit in Paris, were missing on their train, Annette Meakin and her mother found their accommodation entirely satisfactory. The ride was not so comfortable from Mysovaya on the Transbaikal Railway. Only fourth-class carriages were available, and the two ladies were forced to take their travelling rugs and picnic hamper to the luggage van, where they spent the next four days.

Travelling in 1902, Michael Myres Shoemaker was very impressed with the bathing arrangements on the train and wrote: 'I have just discovered that there is a fine bathroom in the restaurant car, large and tiled, with all sorts of sprays, plunges and douches. This bath has its separate attendant and all the bath towels you may demand.' He was less enthusiastic about his travelling companions, a French Consul and family whose fox terrier 'promptly domesticated itself in my compartment'.

The restaurant car

At the Paris Exhibition visitors were led to believe that a good part of the enjoyment of travelling on the Trans-Siberian would be the cordon bleu cuisine served in the restaurant car. It was claimed that the kitchens were even equipped with water tanks filled with live fish. The waiters would be multilingual and a truly international service was promised.

Travellers found this to be something of an exaggeration. Annette Meakin reported the existence of a Bechstein piano and a library of Russian novels in the restaurant car. Shoemaker wrote: 'The restaurant car is just like all those on the trains of Europe. There is a piano, generally used to hold dirty dishes. There are three very stupid waiters who speak nothing save Russian. The food is very poor.'

Travellers were warned by guidebooks that there were occasional food shortages on the trains and were advised to take a picnic hamper. The Meakins found theirs invaluable on their four-day jaunt in the luggage van. In fact during the service's first four years there were no restaurant cars. RL Jefferson wrote that at meal-times the train would stop at a convenient station and all passengers (and the engine-driver) would get off for a meal at the station.

❑ The Siberian express is a kind of "Liberty Hall", where you can shut your door and sleep all day if you prefer it, or eat and drink, smoke and play cards if you like that better. An electric bell summons a serving-man to make your bed or sweep your floor, as the case may be, while a bell on the other side summons a waiter from the buffet ... Time passes very pleasantly on such a train. **Annette Meakin** *A Ribbon of Iron*

The church car

Behind the baggage car was a peculiar carriage known as the church car. It was a Russian Orthodox church on wheels, complete with icons and candelabra inside, church bells and a cross on the roof, and a peripatetic priest who dispensed blessings along the way. This carriage was detached at stations and settlements where churches had not yet been built and services were conducted for railway workers and their families.

Transport of emigrants

While foreign visitors discussed whether or not their accommodation was all that the Paris Exhibition had led them to expect, emigrants travelled in the unenviable conditions described by RL Jefferson: 'The emigrants' train is simply one of the cattle trucks, each car being marked on the side "Forty men or eight horses". There are no seats or lights provided, and into each of these pens forty men, women and children have to herd over a dreary journey of fourteen or fifteen days ... They have to provide their own food but at every station a large samovar is kept boiling in order to provide them with hot water for their tea.' By the end of the century they were crossing the Urals to Siberia at the rate of about a quarter of a million peasants each year.

Stations

Little wooden station buildings mushroomed along the railway. Russian stations were traditionally given a class number from one to five. Of the stations listed in the official *Guide to the Great Siberian Railway*, none was of the first class and the majority were no more than fifth class. Beside most stations there towered a water-tank to supply the steam engines; many of these towers, their eaves decorated with ornate fretwork, can still be seen today. Most of the larger stations had their own churches and resident priests. If the train did not have a church car, stops would be made for lengthy services at these railside churches, especially on the eve of important saints' days.

❑ Travelling in 1901, John Foster Fraser reports, in *The Real Siberia*, that locals did good business on the platforms selling 'dumplings with hashed meat and seasoning inside ... huge loaves of new made bread, bottles of beer, pails of milk, apples, grapes, and fifty other things'. This is still true today.

RL Jefferson found that in the early years of the railways, the arrival and departure of every train at a Siberian station was quite an event, being 'attended with an amount of excitement that it is hard to associate with the usually stolid Russian. Particularly is this so in Eastern Russia where railways are new and interesting.' A man 'performs a terrific tintinabulation on a large suspended bell. All the conductors blow whistles.' Jefferson goes on to explain that none of the passengers was allowed out of the train until the engine driver had got down and shaken hands with the station-master and his staff.

Delays

Because the original line was so badly laid, the ride in the carriages was rough and uncomfortable and speed had to be kept down. There were frequent derailments and long delays. Annette Meakin complained: 'We stopped at a great many stations; indeed on some parts of the route we seemed to get into a chronic state of stopping'.

'All day long at a dog trot,' wrote Shoemaker, 'Certainly no more than ten miles an hour.' Over some sections the train went so slowly passengers could get out and pick flowers as they walked along beside it. Still, the delays did give one time to catch up on current affairs, as Miss Meakin observes when her train was delayed for four hours ('a mere nothing in Siberia') at Tayga. She writes: 'As we sat waiting in the station the good news was brought that Mafeking had been relieved.'

Bridges

Although the rails were badly laid and of poor quality, the bridges that were made of stone were built to such a high standard that many are still in use today. They were largely the work of Italian masons, who laboured throughout the winter months: the bridge-building season, since no work could be done on the snow-covered line. Many labourers succumbed to hypothermia in temperatures as low as -40°C, dropping to their death on the ice below.

In winter, where bridges had not been finished when the railway lines reached them, engineers had the brilliant idea of laying rails across the ice. The sleepers were literally frozen onto the surface of the river by large amounts of water being poured over them. When RL Jefferson's train reached the track laid across the Chulim River, passengers were made to get out and walk, in case the train proved too great a weight for the ice to bear. He wrote: 'As it passed us we felt the ice quiver, and heard innumerable cracks, like the reports of pistols in the distance, but the train got across the centre safely.'

Breakdowns

These were all too frequent. A wait of 24 hours for a new engine was not regarded as a long delay. Annette Meakin recorded the following incident: 'Outside Kainsk the train stopped. "The engine has smashed up," said a jolly Russian sailor in broken English. "She is sixty years old and was made in Glasgow. She is no use any more" ... The poor old engine was now towed to her last berth ... I had whipped out my "Kodak" and taken her photograph, thinking of Turner's "Fighting Temeraire".'

Cost of the journey

The *Guide to the Great Siberian Railway* informed its readers that, for the journey from London to Shanghai: 'The conveyance by the Siberian Railway will be over twice as quick and two and a half times cheaper than that now existing' (the sea passage via the Suez Canal). The cost of a first-class ticket for the 16-day journey was to be 319 roubles. From Moscow to Vladivostok the price was 114 roubles.

THE RAILWAY IN THE 20TH CENTURY

After the Revolution

'When the trains stop, that will be the end,' announced Lenin, and the trains, the Trans-Siberian included, continued to run throughout those troubled times.

When the new Bolshevik government pulled out of WWI in early 1918, a Czech force of 50,000 well-armed men found themselves marooned in Russia, German forces preventing them from returning to western Europe. Receiving permission to leave Russia via Vladivostok, they set off on the Trans-Siberian. Their passage was not a smooth one, for the Bolsheviks suspected that the Czechs would join the White Russian resistance while the Czechs suspected that the Bolsheviks were not going to allow them to leave. Violence erupted, several Czechs were arrested and the rest of the legion decided to shoot their way out of Russia. They took over the Trans-Siberian line from the Urals to Lake Baikal and travelled the railway in armour-plated carriages.

The Civil War in Siberia (1918-20)

At this time Siberia was divided amongst a number of forces, all fighting against the Bolsheviks but not as a combined unit. Many of the leaders were nothing more than gangsters. East Siberia and Manchuria were controlled by the evil Ataman Semenov, half-Russian, half-Buryat and supported by the Japanese. He charged around Transbaikalia murdering whole villages and, to alleviate the boredom of these mass executions, a different method of death was adopted each day. Then there was Baron General von Ungern Sternberg, a White Russian commander whose cruelty rivalled that of Semenov.

The Americans, French, English and Japanese all brought troops into Siberia to evacuate the Czech legions and to help Admiral Kolchak, the Supreme Ruler of the White Government based at Omsk. Kolchak, however, failed to win the support of the people in Siberia's towns, his troops were undisciplined and in November 1919 he lost Omsk to the Bolsheviks. He was executed in Irkutsk in early 1920 and the Allies abandoned the White Russian cause. The Japanese gave up Vladivostok in 1922, leaving all Siberia in Communist hands.

Reconstruction

After the Civil War the Soviet Union set about rebuilding its battered economy. High on the priority list was the repair of the Trans-Siberian line, so that raw materials like iron ore could be transported to European Russia. The First Five Year Plan (1928) set ambitious goals for the expansion of industry and agriculture. It also included new railway projects, the double-tracking of the Trans-Siberian and the building of the Turk-Sib, the line between Turkestan and Novosibirsk. Work began on two giant industrial complexes known as the Ural-Kuznetsk Combine. Iron ore from the Urals was taken by rail to the Kuznetsk Basin in Siberia, where it was exchanged for coal for Ural blast furnaces. For all these giant projects an enormous, controllable labour force was needed and this was to a large extent provided by prisoners from the corrective labour camps.

World War II

Siberia played an important backstage role in the 'Great Patriotic War', as Russians call WWII. Many factories were moved from European Russia to Siberia and the populations of cities such as Novosibirsk rose dramatically. The Trans-Siberian's part was a vital one and shipments of coal and food were continuously despatched over the Urals to Europe throughout the war years.

STEAM LOCOMOTIVES IN SIBERIA

In 1956 the USSR stopped producing steam engines and official policy was to phase them out by 1970. As with most official plans in the country, this one overran a little and a second official end of steam was announced for 1987, when the number of locos stood at over 6000. Some of these were sold as scrap to Germany and Korea but many were stored as a 'strategic reserve' in remote sidings and used very occasionally for shunting work; there are some to be seen along the Trans-Siberian line (see the Route Guide for locations). In 2000, however, it was decided not to retain steam engines within these strategic military reserves so numbers are now falling fast. Each of the country's 32 railway administrations is allowed to keep just 10 steam engines so now there are probably no more than 320 working steam locos in the whole of Russia. In northern China there are numerous steam engines still at work.

In 1836 Russia's first locomotive, a Hackworth 2-2-2, was delivered to St Petersburg to pull the Tsar's private carriages over the 23km (14 miles) of six-foot gauge track to his palace at Tsarskoye Selo. The Russians have always been (and still are) conservative by nature when it comes to buying or building engines. Usually large numbers of a few standard locomotives have been ordered so there's not much of a range to be seen today. They seem to be uniformly large, standing up to 5m (17ft) high, and larger than British locos, partly because the Russian gauge is almost 9cm (3½ inches) wider than that used in Britain.

They are numbered separately by classes, not in a single series and not by railway regions. If variations of the class have been built, they are given an additional letter after the main class letter. Thus, for example, the first type of 0-10-0 freight locomotive was Class E and those of this class built in Germany were Class Eg. Classes you may see in Siberia include the following (Roman alphabet class letters given in brackets; * = very rare):

- **Class O (O)** The first freight trains on the Trans-Siberian route were pulled by these long-boilered 0-8-0 locos (55 tons) which date back to 1889. The 'O' in the class name stands for *Osnovnoi Tip* meaning 'basic type'. Production ceased in 1923 but as late as 1958 there were 1500 of these locomotives still at work.
- **Class C (S)*** 2-6-2 (75 tons) A highly successful passenger engine. 'S' stands for *Sormovo*, where these locos were built from 1911. **Class Cy (Su)** ('u' for *usileny*, meaning 'strengthened') was developed from the former class and in production from 1926 to 1951.
- **Class E (Ye)** 2-10-0 1500 Ye 2-10-0s were imported from the USA in 1914.

• **Class Эу/Эм/Эр (Eu/Em/Er)*** (subclasses of the old type (E) 0-10-0, 80 tons, built in Russia from 1926 to 1952. The old type E was also produced in Germany and Sweden, as Esh and Eg subclasses.
• **Class Ea (YeA)*** 2-10-0 (90 tons) Over 2000 were built in the USA between 1944 and 1947 and shipped across the Pacific.
• **Class Л (L)** 2-10-0 (103 tons) About 4130 were built between 1945 and 1956.
• **Class П36 (P36)** 4-8-4 (133 tons) 251 were built between 1950 and 1956 – the last express passenger type built for Soviet Railways. 'Skyliner'-style, fitted with large smoke-deflectors, and painted green with a cream stripe. Preserved examples at Sharya, Tayga, Sibirtsevo, Skovorodino, Belogorsk, Mogzon and Chernyshevsk.

Classes **O**, **C/Cy**, **E (O**, **S/Su**, **Ye)** have all disappeared from the steam dumps but you will see the occasional one on a plinth.

For more information refer to the comprehensive *Soviet Locomotive Types – The Union Legacy* by AJ Heywood and IDC Button (1995, Frank Stenvalls/ Luddenden Press). There's also a good deal of information about Russian trains on the internet; a good place to start is **www.transsib.ru/Eng/** – the Trans-Siberian Railway Web Encyclopedia.

OTHER RAILWAY LINES LINKED TO THE TRANS-SIBERIAN

BAM – a second Trans-Siberian (see pp380-92 and pp467-73)

In the 1930s another Herculean undertaking was begun on the railways of Russia. The project was named the **Baikal-Amur-Mainline** (BAM): a second Trans-Siberian railway, 3140km long, running parallel but to the north of the existing line. It was to run through the rich mining districts of northern Siberia, providing an east–west communications back-up to the main line. Work began in Tayshet and the track reached Ust Kut on the Lena River before the project was officially abandoned at the end of WWI. Much of the 700km of track that had been laid was torn up to replace war-damaged lines in the west. Construction continued in secret, using slave labour until the Gulags were closed in 1954.

In 1976 it was announced that work on the BAM was recommencing. Incentives were offered to collect the 100,000 strong work-force needed for so large a project. For eight years they laboured heroically, dynamiting their way through the permafrost which covers almost half the route, across a region where temperatures fall as low as -60°C in winter. In October 1984 it was announced that the way was open from Tayshet to Komsomolsk-na-Amure. Although track-laying had been completed, only the eastern half was operational (from Komsomolsk to BAM Station, where traffic joined the old Trans-Siberian route). By 1991 the whole system was still not fully operational, the main obstacle being the Severomuysk Tunnel, bypassed by an unsatisfactory detour with an impressive 1:25 gradient. It took from 1981 to 1991 to drill 13km of the 16km of this unfinished tunnel in the most difficult of conditions. Many were already questioning the point of a railway that was beginning to look like a white elephant. Work has more or less stopped now; the main sections of the line are complete but traffic is infrequent. The BAM was built to compete with shipping routes for the transfer of freight but the cost has been tremendous:

there has been considerable ecological damage and there is little money left for the extraction of the minerals that was the other reason for the building of the railway. It is possible to travel along the BAM route starting near the north of Lake Baikal and ending up at Khabarovsk. Rail traffic on the BAM line currently remains far below capacity, with about six trains per day plying the route. According to Russian Railways, by 2009 the BAM was carrying about 12 million passengers and 12 million tons of cargo each year, though its total capacity is around 18 million. The BAM was saved from oblivion when Kremlin Chief of Staff, Dmitry Medvedev, discussed developing the Russian Far East in an April 2005 interview. However, he also mentioned the BAM as the sort of wasteful project that should be avoided. 'We do not need yet another huge construction project with an unpredictable outcome, as happened with BAM' he said. The BAM was meant to give development in Siberia a much-needed boost. But rather it has become another export route to sell Russian resources abroad. The line is now used to send crude oil from small fields near Irkutsk to China at a rate of 10,000 tons per month. Oil is loaded onto trains at Ust-Kut and sent to Komsomolsk-na-Amure and then on to the port of Vanino.

However, with the recently proposed plans to build secondary lines, connecting the BAM directly to the sources of mineral extraction, as well as plans to move all or most of the freight traffic from the main Trans-Siberian route onto the BAM, traffic on the BAM is set to treble or even quadruple in the coming years. Renovation of the Komsomolsk-na-Amure–Sovetskaya Gavan section began in 2009 to reinforce the line for the extra traffic, and is due to finish in 2016. Though plans conceived in the 1950s to build a tunnel to connect the BAM with Sakhalin Island have since been abandoned, there is now talk of building a bridge instead to connect the island to the mainland and even more ambitious talk of then connecting Sakhalin Island to the Japanese island of Hokkaido, either via a tunnel or a bridge, to allow a direct land transport link from Japan to Asia and Europe.

Through Siberia by Accident is Dervla Murphy's entertaining account of her travels in the region.

AYaM and Little BAM

The **AYaM** (Amuro-Yakutskaya Magistral) is the Amur-Yakutsk Mainline, which will eventually run from Tynda on the BAM north to Yakutsk. The project was scheduled for completion at the same time as the BAM but construction has been fraught with both engineering and financial difficulties. The Yakutiya Railway Company has, however, pushed ahead to almost reach the Lena River, 70km from Yakutsk, where it has still not been decided if the 2km-wide river is to be crossed by bridge or tunnel. They also plan to extend the line east to Magadan. The **Little BAM** is the 180km rail link between the Trans-Siberian at Bamovskaya and Tynda, start of the AYaM.

Turkestan–Siberia (Turksib) railway

The Turksib links Novosibirsk on the Trans-Siberian with Almaty in Kazakhstan, a journey of 1678km. From there it's possible to continue on into Western

China. The line was constructed in the 1930s to make it easier to transport grain from Siberia and cotton from Turkestan between these two regions.

Kazakhstan–China railway

In September 1990 a rail line was opened between Urumqi in north-west China and the border with Kazakhstan, opening a new rail route between east Asia and Europe via the Central Asian Republics. China built this link to create the shortest Eurasian rail route (2000km shorter than the Trans-Siberian) between the Pacific and the Atlantic, enabling freight to be transported faster and more cheaply than by ship. This means that it's now possible to travel along the ancient Silk Route by rail, through the old Central Asian capitals of Khiva, Bukhara and Samarkand and the Chinese cities of Dunhuang, Luoyang and Xi'an.

Kazakhstan–Iran railway

In May 1996 a 295km cross-border railway line was officially opened between Mashhad in Iran and Saraghs and Tejen in Turkmenistan. This line, it was said, was the forerunner of a network that would join land-locked Central Asia to the Persian Gulf and, via Turkey, to the Mediterranean. The potential was there for a new Silk Route between southern Europe and the Far East, cutting travel times by up to 10 days. Six years later the line had reached northwards via Turkmenabat (Turkmenistan) and Tashkent (Uzbekistan) all the way to Almaty (Kazakhstan), and southwards to Tehran (Iran). In March 2002, with great fanfare, a weekly service was inaugurated for the 3300km, 70-hour Almaty–Tehran journey. But a month later it was suspended, apparently over disagreements about right of way through Uzbekistan.

At the moment, it's possible to take the modern, efficient Trans-Asian Express that runs weekly from Istanbul to Tehran. Alternatively you could take Asseman Airlines' more-or-less weekly flight between Tehran and Ashgabat.

Sakhalin railway

The island of Sakhalin (north of Japan) is currently linked to the Russian mainland by rail ferries operating between Vanino and Kholmsk. Steam specials are occasionally run on the island's 3ft 6in-gauge rail system.

A line to Korea

Today shipments of oil, gas and other goods on the Trans-Siberian line are used to pay off Russia's staggering foreign debt. In 2001 negotiations began in earnest to extend the Trans-Siberian Railway into South Korea, forming an even more profitable link between Europe and Asia.

In 2002 North and South Korea announced they would cooperate in rebuilding the Trans-Korean Railway, with Russia bankrolling part of the project to pay off its US$1 billion debt to South Korea. Bridging Korea's DMZ (Demilitarised Zone) was the first step in extending the Trans-Siberian to the tip of the peninsula. Currently, twice-monthly trains run from Moscow to Pyongyang, consisting of extra carriages attached to the 001/002 Moscow-Vladivostok *Rossiya*; there are rumours that this service will increase in frequency in the near future.

Riding the Trans-Siberian today

THE TRAIN

Engines

If you're counting on being hauled across Siberia by a puffing steam locomotive you will be sadly disappointed. Soviet Railways (SZD), now Russian Railways (RZD), began converting the system to electricity in 1927. The work was completed in 2002 and today the Trans-Siberian line is entirely electrified (25kV 50Hz ac or in some cases 3kV dc).

Passenger engines are usually Czech Skoda ChS4T's (line voltage 25kV 50 Hz; max output 5200kW; max speed 180kph; weight 126 tonnes) or ChS2's (3kV dc; 4620kW; 160kph; 126 tonnes), or Russian-built VL10's, VL60's or VL65's. On the Moscow–St Petersburg route the latest Czech-built engines are used: the CS200 (3kV dc; 8400kW; 200kph; 157 tonnes) and the CS7 developed from it. The most common freight engines are the large VL80S and the newer VL85.

Elsewhere on the Russian system where electrification is incomplete, and for shunting duties, diesel rather than steam engines are likely to be used, typically Russian-built 2TE10L/M/V (with overhanging windscreens) or sometimes 2M62U or 3M62U twin or triple units. If you're continuing on the Trans-Mongolian or Trans-Manchurian route, it is quite likely that a steam loco will be hitched to your carriages at the China border, at least for shunting duties.

Although steam engines have been officially phased out in Russia, there are still some on the books, many of them decaying on remote sidings along the Trans-Siberian route. Their numbers are shrinking fast as they are sold off to Western Europe and China for scrap and parts. See pp107-8 for identification information and class numbers.

Carriages and carriage attendants

Many carriages in use are of East German origin, solidly built and warm in winter. Each carriage is staffed by an **attendant** (female *provodnitsa* or male *provodnik* in Russian, *fuwuyuen* in Chinese), whose 'den' is a compartment at

> **❑ Carriage keys**
>
> On our train (No 006) there were a large number of Mongolian traders who proved to be very entertaining. They had managed to obtain a carriage key so that they could unlock the loo door after it had been locked. They would always oblige us with a quick unlock when we asked. We did notice that this carriage key looked familiar and it may be worth advising British travellers to try taking their British Gas meter cupboard key with them since it looks as if it is identical. **Andrew Wingham** (UK)
>
> *Note from updater*: If the toilets have been locked because the train is travelling through a populated area, unlocking them there is not a good idea. However, the same key can be used to unlock windows on some trains, so can still be useful.

❑ **Samovar**

The coal-fired **stove-samovar** (*batchok*) provides hot water in each carriage. Savvy travellers stock up on instant pot noodles at stations.

'I'd recommend that every Trans-Siberian traveller bring, if nothing else, **porridge oats** (both plain and flavoured ones are available in Moscow). Instant porridge mixed with boiling water from the samovar makes a great warm breakfast, particularly when everyone else is tucking in to three-day-old bread'.
Jennie Wogan (UK)

the end of the carriage. Their duties include collecting your tickets, letting down the steps at stations, coming round with the vacuum-cleaner, cleaning the bathrooms and selling you tea (without milk) or instant coffee. The attendant also maintains the **samovar** (see box) which is opposite his or her compartment, and which provides a continuous supply of boiling water for drinks. The most modern samovars also have the facility to boil water and then save it to another tank to cool as safe drinking water.

There are doors at both ends of the carriages, and the only place where passengers may **smoke** is in the (unheated) area between the carriages, where the windows never open, letting stale smoke into the carriage whenever the door is opened. The smoking area rule is strictly enforced.

Carriages are heated in winter and air-conditioned in summer. The air-conditioning system works on the pressure difference between the inside and outside of the carriage and takes about an hour to get going, so all carriage windows must be kept shut. One's initial instinct (certainly that of the Russian passengers) is to throw them open, and carriage attendants wage a constant battle to keep them closed. This can be a problem as air-conditioning in cheaper carriages can be fairly ineffectual.

Radio or taped music is sometimes piped into the compartments from the attendant's den. A knob above the window controls the volume, although in some compartments you cannot turn it off completely.

Compartments

(Also see p14). Most Trans-Siberian train carriages are either *kupé* (coupé; also called 2nd, hard or tourist class), whose four-berth closed compartments are reasonably comfortable and not very expensive; or *SV* (*spalny* vagon; also called 1st or soft class), with comfortable two-berth compartments, sometimes with washbasins and a TV/video monitor. Note that in the Chinese-made car-

(Opposite) Clockwise from top: **1**. The train makes numerous stops along the way, giving you the opportunity to purchase food on the platform from local people. **2**. A young *provodnitsa* (carriage attendant); many are students doing summer work. **3**. Typical dining car in a Russian train. **4**. SV (1st class) compartment on an older train, containing two private beds. On newer trains each SV compartment has its own bathroom, some even with a shower. **5**. (Centre) Typical open-plan *platzkart* carriage, with 54 bunks arranged in groups of six.

33

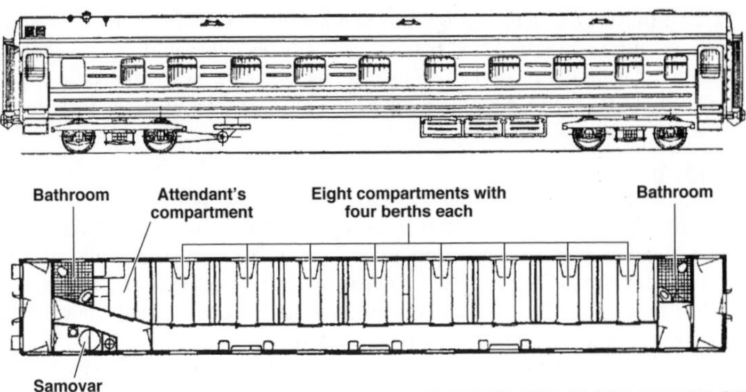

PLAN OF 2ND CLASS CARRIAGE

riages of Trans-Mongolian trains Nos 003/004, SV compartments are *four*-berth and identical to all other services' kupé compartments except 16cm wider, so they are conspicuously poor value. But these particular Trans-Mongolian trains also have an additional *de luxe 1st* class, whose two-berth, carpeted, wood-panelled compartments have wider bunks, armchair, wind-down window and attached bathroom with rudimentary hand-held shower. This is the closest you'll get to true luxury on a scheduled train service across Siberia.

The only difference between *platzkart* (3rd class) and kupé is that the former is an open-plan carriage with bunks everywhere, whereas the latter consists of four bunks in its own small compartment. Both share a bathroom at the end of the carriage. If you're travelling with friends, sharing a kupé compartment makes sense but if you're travelling solo, the question you have to ask yourself is this: would you rather share your living space with three strangers or 53 strangers, given that the facilities are comparable and that kupé costs more than double the price of a platzkart berth? The advantage of travelling platzkart is that you have more opportunity to socialise with locals, but if you happen to have a berth that runs lengthways along the carriage, people may bump into you as they're walking along. Also, platzkart carriages often have better ventilation than kupé, particularly if your kupé neighbours insist on keeping the compartment door closed at all times. Platzkart is not available on some firmenny trains.

Obshchy is the same as platzkart, only the berths are unreserved and supposed to seat three people. Some locals waste no time and climb up onto the redundant top bunks, using them as sleeping berths with no bedding. You'll only find obshchy on some slow trains.

(Opposite) Top: Russians are very sociable and when you travel on trains, particularly if you're in a *platzkart* carriage, it's common to share your food with people you meet. These four travellers, three miners and a local girl visiting her relatives, plied this author with tea and caviar. **Bottom**: Typical *kupé* compartment on a Russian train, consisting of four bunks, a table, and luggage compartments beneath the bottom bunks and above the top ones.

Bedding (two sheets, a pillowcase and a small towel) are often included in the ticket price and you'll find blankets and pillows either in the top compartments in platzkartny or in the luggage storage areas below the bunks in kupé. In newer carriages it is possible to move the lower bed up to 10cm away from the wall, giving a wider sleeping area.

Luggage

Each passenger can take up to 35kg of luggage with them for free on the Trans-Siberian, though in practice, this is only enforced in Beijing as baggage is weighed before you are allowed onto the platform. You can take additional luggage totalling up to 75kg provided you pay an excess-baggage charge. If you're leaving from Moscow, it's extremely unlikely that anyone will pay attention to how much you take, and there's no reason to pay extra.

The Trans-Siberian is a popular way for Australians and New Zealanders to return home after living in London, because baggage allowances are virtually unlimited. But if you're departing from Beijing you must box up any excess baggage, with a limit of one box per ticket, and it travels in a separate carriage. Bring only the excess to the Luggage Shipment Office (8am-noon, to the right of the main station) in Beijing at least 24 hours before departure, along with passport, ticket and customs entry declaration.

In your compartment, luggage can be stored either in the box or space under the bottom seat, in the free space beside the box, in the space above the door (kupé) or in the luggage rack above the top bunk (platzkart).

Bathroom

Sadly the marble bathtub (ingeniously designed not to overflow as the train rounded a corner) and the copious hot water and towels that Michael Myres Shoemaker (see p103) enthused over in 1902 are no more. The lack of proper bathing facilities is usually the biggest grumble from people who have done the trip although the situation is improving.

On all Russian firmenny trains there is now an extra carriage attached beside the restaurant car which not only includes accommodation for the restaurant staff (so they no longer have to sleep in the dining car) but also includes one compartment with a **shower cabinet** in it. Charges vary from train to train but are around R90; you need to tell the staff 30 mins before you wish to use it

Bathing in a Chinese spittoon

A week was a short time to go without a bath in Siberia, we were told, but this didn't make the prospect any more appealing. I read somewhere that in pre-Revolution days most Russian peasants spent the whole winter without having a bath.

Shopping for supplies on a freezing December afternoon in Beijing before we left, we resolved to find some kind of bucket or basin to facilitate washing on the train. In one shop we found weighty china buckets with bamboo handles. We settled for something smaller, an enamel spittoon (diameter 9ins/23mm) which turned out to exactly fit the basin in the train. It could be filled from the samovar in the corridor (to the astonishment of the Chinese passengers who knew the true purpose of the utensil) and it greatly simplified the process of washing, without having to queue for the shower.

so that they can turn on the water heater. The Chinese-run Trans-Mongolian (Train Nos 003 & 004) don't currently include a shower cabinet although their older-style de luxe 1st class compartments have hand-held showers.

Most passengers tend to make do with a wash in one of the 'bathrooms' at each end of every carriage. This is a small cubicle with a stainless steel basin and lavatory, with or without a seat. To flush the lavatory, fully depress and hold the foot pedal, and lean back out of the way if it's an old-style flush on the tracks job, as the contents have a nasty habit of going the wrong way if the train is moving fast. Many trains, however, have now been upgraded to bio-loos.

The taps on the basin are operated by pushing up the little lever located under the tap outlet. You should get hot water by turning the left-hand wheel above the sink (the right-hand wheel controls cold water), but the supply of hot water depends on the whim of the attendant who may not want to switch the system on. Don't forget to bring along a **universal plug** for the basin, **soap**, a **sponge** or **flannel**, and **toilet paper**.

There's a socket for an electric razor but you may need to ask the attendant to turn the power on. Charging video-camera or other batteries from these sockets may blow the fuses; use the sockets inside the main carriages instead. A good way of having a 'shower' in these bathrooms is to fill the basin with hot water from the samovar, and use a mug to scoop out water and pour it over yourself, or else buy a detachable travel shower head from an outdoor equipment store before setting out. Don't worry about splashing water around as there is a drain in the floor. The bathrooms are generally kept clean. Note that unless they contain new-style bio-loos they are often locked for up to 20 minutes before and after major station stops.

Restaurant cars

One of the myths that has sprung up amongst prospective travellers is that you get better food on the Chinese (Trans-Mongolian) train. As with most international rail travel, restaurant cars belonging to the country through which the train is travelling are attached at the border. Regardless of which train you're on, when you're passing through China you eat in a restaurant car supplied by Chinese Railways; at the border with Mongolia this is replaced by a Mongolian restaurant car; and while the train is in Russia, meals are provided by a restaurant car from Russian Railways.

Note that the Trans-Mongolian usually has no restaurant car between the Russian border and Ulaanbaatar. Regional trains such as the Irkutsk–Ulaanbaatar service may have no restaurant car at all.

• **Russian restaurant car** Russian restaurant cars are run as private franchises, so service, food quality, prices and opening hours are highly unpredictable. Staff shop en route for whatever provisions they can find, so menus are unpredictable too. On entering the car you may be presented with a menu, almost invariably in Russian and often running to 10 pages or more. The only available dishes will be indicated by a pencilled-in price or added in an indecipherable scrawl. The choice may include egg or tomato salad with sour cream, *shchi* (cabbage soup

> **❑ Getting better service**
> The only relevant information about Russian restaurant cars is that the food seems to vary much between one car and the next, as every Russian restaurant car is its own private enterprise, and I've experienced everything from excellent to disaster. A very good way to obtain a good relationship with the staff is simply to be a regular customer and learn a few Russian words. **Matz Lonnedal Risberg** (Norway)

with meat), *solyanka* (a thick meat soup), meatballs and mash or macaroni, *skumbriya* (mackerel), beef stroganov, the ever-present *bifstek*, or rice and boiled chicken. A main course will cost about R300. Payment is in roubles only.

Staff can now sell all sorts of goodies on the side. Banned for several years, alcohol is now sold on trains. In fact you may find your restaurant car offering little more than crisps, instant noodles, chocolate bars and biscuits, plus fruit juice, vodka, beer (pricier than on station platforms) or chilled Russian champagne, with no cooked food in sight. Some screen bootleg videos.

Russians think of the restaurant car as little more than a bar, and since most bring their own provisions, few eat a meal in one. You may find everything overpriced at first, but service tends to get cheaper and friendlier the more often you return. On popular tourist services the restaurant car is a good place to meet other foreigners.

• **Mongolian restaurant car** With luck you'll get a smart new Mongolian restaurant car. Generally the main differences from Russian restaurant cars are that here you're likely to get a menu in English, nearly everything comes with mutton, and you pay in US dollars or Mongolian togrogs, though Chinese yuan are accepted at bad exchange rates. Delicacies include mutton goulash or beefsteak with egg on top, priced from US$5-8. For breakfast they can do you an omelette for US$5. Tea, coffee and soft drinks are about US$2.

Some Mongolian cars have extensive stocks of duty-free goods and even souvenirs, postcards and stamps. Mongolian beer is recommended.

• **Chinese restaurant car** Travellers tend to agree that Chinese restaurant cars have the best food, the widest choice and the best service. The cars are full every evening, which is a good sign. For US$6 you can get a breakfast of eggs, bread, jam and tea. For lunch or supper (main courses about US$5-10) you can typically choose from tomato salad, cold chicken or sauté chicken with peanuts, fish, sweet and sour pork, sauté beef or eggplant with dried shrimp.

Drinks include beer (US$3), cola (US$2) and mineral water (US$2). Payment is in yuan (renminbi) and US$ are sometimes accepted.

Food at the stations

At many of the stops along the Trans-Siberian locals turn out on the station platform to sell all manner of foodstuffs: fruit, vegetables and even entire cooked meals (cabbage rolls, freshly boiled potatoes with dill, pancakes filled with goat's cheese, boiled eggs and fresh bread, smoked fish, salted cucumbers and berries). Often, the best selection of edible goodies is found at smaller stations, whereas at main stations you can pick up instant noodles, chocolate and soft drinks but little else. Some travellers have reported upset stomachs after eating platform food so you should take care with salads, cold meats and fish and anything that looks as if it has been sitting around for too long. Generally, if the food is hot you should be fine; all fruit should be washed.

❏ Platform food

What you can buy at stations very much depends upon the season and the stop. We stocked up really well in Moscow and I'm glad that we did as we only had two station stops where people were selling things. Maybe our train (No 6) went through stations such as these in the middle of the night but we had fellow travellers who had not brought much food who would have been very hungry were it not for the Mongolian traders selling pot noodles.

Angela Hollingsworth (UK)

It is worth stressing the abundance and variety of food on sale at many stations, especially rural ones, during stops. If you see something you want, buy it: the next stop might be a city, where sellers will not appear on the platforms, or rows of babushkas with prams full of raspberries might be replaced by a monotonous offering of, say, fish. Regulars knew what to expect at each stop.

Howard Dymock (UK)

LIFE ON THE TRAIN

Most people imagine they'll get bored on so long a journey but you may be surprised at how quickly the time flies. Don't overdo the number of books you bring: there are so many other things to do besides reading.

As well as looking out of the window, sleeping, exploring the train from top to bottom, trying to take photos, and getting out at each stop to see what food there is on offer, you can have monosyllabic conversations with inquisitive Russians, meet other Westerners, play cards or chess, or visit the restaurant car.

The Trans-Siberian time warp

During his trip on the Great Siberian Railway in 1902, Michael Myres Shoemaker wrote: 'There is an odd state of affairs as regards time over here. Though Irkutsk is 2,400 miles from St Petersburg, the trains all run on the time of the latter city, therefore arriving in Irkutsk at 5pm when the sun would make it 9pm. The confusion en route is amusing; one never knows when to go to bed or when to eat. Today I should make it now about 8.30 – these clocks say 10.30 and some of these people are eating their luncheon.'

You will be pleased to know that this at least has not changed. The entire system operates on Moscow Time (same as St Petersburg Time), and all timetables list Moscow Time. Crossing the border from China after breakfast, the first Russian station clock you see tells you that it's one o'clock in the morning! The restaurant car, however, runs on local time. Passing through as many as seven time-zones, things can get rather confusing. The answer is to ignore Moscow Time and reset your watch as you cross into new time zones (details in the Route Guide). A watch that shows the time in two zones would be handy; otherwise just add or subtract the appropriate number of hours every time you consult the timetable in the train corridor.

❑ How to choose your dream platzkart berth

You can't really say that you've truly adjusted to life aboard a Russian long-distance train until you find yourself in your berth, with your luggage stowed and your pyjamas already on, eating smoked fish and drinking tea while the other passengers are still boarding the train. So, which berth to go for: bottom, top, side bottom or side top?

First, let's imagine the platzkart carriage: it's basically a dormitory consisting of 54 places, and divided into lots of six, with the main entrance, the provodnitsa's 'room', a toilet and the samovar at one end, and another toilet and smoking area at the other. You have two lots of two bunks facing each other and sharing a table, and another two across the aisle, stretching along the wall. Each berth comes with its own advantages/disadvantages. The end closest to the provodnitsa is the choice end of the carriage, though if you get a berth closest to the end, your sleep may be disturbed by the light that's perpetually on by the provodnitsa's cubicle.

• **Bottom berth** The most popular and the most likely to sell out. You will have easy access to the luggage compartment underneath the bunk, a window seat and prime access to the table. However, you may also have to socialise constantly, and will have nowhere to escape to if your companions happen to be rowdy drunks.

• **Top berth** Less popular. You will be unable to sit up due to the storage shelf directly above and getting up on the bunk may be difficult for the athletically challenged. If the luggage space beneath the bottom bunk is taken, it can be a nuisance trying to get your luggage up to the top shelf.

When not sleeping you will have to perch on the bottom bunk like an unwanted guest and may be drawn into inane conversations/beer drinking/caviar consumption. However, you can crawl up to the top bunk and escape unwanted companions at any time. You will have the readiest access to the window and if you're a fresh air fiend and you get there early enough, you can open it and then pull out your top bunk so that no one will be able to close it without first dislodging you from your sleeping area. The window issue is null and void if the provodnitsa has beaten you to it and locked it.

• **Bottom side berth** Less popular than the regular bottom but perfect for those under the height of 5ft 5 inches; any taller and your legs will stick out into the aisle. Woe betide you if you get the dreaded berth No 37 at the toilet end of the carriage, where stale cigarette smoke filters through and you're repeatedly disturbed by every one on their way to the loo or to have a smoke. At least 85% of your fellow passengers are heavy smokers; you do the maths.

Since the bottom side bunks stretch along the corridor and convert into two seats and a table during the day, you have no luggage storage area of your own. However, you have easy access to the luggage compartment underneath the bottom bunk near you; rush on to the train first in order to claim it.

You also have a choice window seat. Might be a problem if the top side bunk is occupied and you have to chase the other person off the chair opposite you when you wish to turn it into a bunk.

• **Top side berth** The least popular of the lot. You don't have a view; the luggage shelf above you is almost impossible to reach unless you're really tall and strong and you feel like a pariah when you venture downstairs to perch either on a bottom bunk or a side bottom seat. You have no window access and you can't sit up; only take this as a last option if travelling overnight.

Avoid berth No 38 at the toilet/smoking area end of the carriage like the proverbial plague.

❑ Safety tips for Trans-Siberian travellers

There are many stories of crime on the railways. Most are exaggerations, distortions or complete fabrications. The most outrageous story in recent years was the so-called 'Sleeping Gas Incident', in which an entire carriage of a Moscow–St Petersburg train was supposedly put to sleep by gas and everyone robbed. After a week of international media coverage the Russian journalist who wrote the story admitted that it was fictitious, though she maintained that she did lose her purse when she was asleep!

While there is crime on the trains, a few simple precautions will substantially reduce your chances of anything untoward happening to you.

- **Lock your compartment door** from inside when you go to sleep, using both the door-handle lock and the flick-down lock; your Russian companions will do this anyway. The railways are currently installing a plastic device known as a *blokirator* to further thwart break-ins, mainly on *firmenny* trains, both kupé and SV. It immobilises the locking handle in the locked position, and is allegedly so effective that even some attendants cannot outwit it from outside. 'Best piece of information I managed to get from Russians on the train was on safety in the carriage – an explanation about the secondary door lock; the main door lock can be undone with a standard triangular UK gas meter box key (worth taking with you). I was recommended to put a cork in the second door catch to stop it being opened with a knife. Therefore worth taking a cork with you' (Will Harrison-Cripps, UK). On some *firmenny* trains electronic locks have been installed that require a swipe key to get into the compartments.
- At night, **put your bags under the sleeping bench** or in the space above the door. It is not necessary to lock them, but don't leave them lying around either.
- Always **leave someone in the compartment** to look after the luggage, or else padlock your luggage, especially if travelling solo and *platzkart*. Valuables can be left in a safe in the chief attendant's compartment but this is not recommended.
- **Dress down** and always carry your valuables on your person. Stash only non-essentials in shoulder bags, and only a few roubles and US dollars in your wallet. Money and documents should be in a **money belt** under your clothing; even sleep with it on.
- Russians tend to carry things around in tattered old carry-alls; if you do the same you'll attract much less attention than with a flashy sports rucksack.

Some tips for when you leave the train, especially in larger towns and cities:

- **Change money only at kiosks and banks**.
- Keep a **pocket torch** (flashlight) handy as many entrance halls and stairways are unlit. This is especially important in winter when it gets dark very early.
- **Never enter a taxi which is carrying anyone other than the driver**. Take a good look at the driver and the car; if you're in any doubt, wave it on. Taxis ordered by telephone or through organised services at hotels are often a better bet.
- A very **common scam** is for someone to drop a roll of cash and then to act as if they are searching for it. If you pick it up and return it, you may then be treated with mock suspicion and asked to show your own cash. A nimble-fingered thief can then slip notes out of your own wad of cash.
- **Street urchins** can be the most visible and aggressive thieves. If you don't ignore them they'll swarm around you like bees, begging and even grabbing your legs or arms to distract you, and before you realise it they'll have opened your bag or pulled out your wallet. Their 'controller' is often a dishevelled-looking woman with an infant in her arms. If you're approached, don't look at them but walk away quickly. If you fear you're becoming a victim, go into a shop or towards a group of Russians, who will usually send them packing.

Stops

Getting enough exercise on so long a journey can be a problem and most people make full use of the brief stops:

'We even managed to persuade our carriage attendant to take part in our efforts to keep fit on the platforms. However, if your attendant indicates that you shouldn't get off at a stop, take her advice. At some stops another train pulls in between the platform and yours, making it almost impossible for you to get back on board' (Jane Bull, UK). Always carry your passport and valuables with you in case you miss your train.

> ❑ **Stopping off**
> At station stops, before you alight, check with the provodnitsas the time allotted at the particular station. If the train is late stops will be curtailed. If the attendant says 15 minutes (normally signalled in sign language) make it 10. And take your passport with you in case you get left behind on the platform!
> **John Gothard** (UK)

BUYING A TRAIN TICKET IN RUSSIA

Within Russia you will probably want a ticket for travel either the same day or within a couple of days. In either case it's usually possible to go to the station or ticket office, find the correct window, buy your ticket and be out again fairly quickly. If you don't speak Russian you can use the form on p122. Payment is in rouble cash only.

If you can read Cyrillic, you can buy your ticket online directly from the Russian Rail website (💻 www.rzd.ru), which means avoiding any markup that's inevitable when buying tickets through a third party, and which can be up to 30%. Bear in mind that 💻 www.rzd.ru does not accept Barclaycards. If you purchase a ticket online, you have to print out the voucher with the barcode and reference number. At some of the larger cities, such as Moscow, St Petersburg and Irkutsk, there are self-service machines that allow you to print out those tickets (these are usually located in ticketing halls); you'll need to either scan the barcode or input your reference number, as well as scanning the passport that you used to book the ticket. Otherwise, you can present your printed voucher at a ticket window along with your passport, and they will print out your ticket.

Classes of service

There are four main classes of service on Russian trains. ***Obshchy*** (meaning general) signifies carriages with unreserved seating only, available on limited services. ***Platzkartny*** (3rd class) is the most basic of sleeping carriages, an open-plan arrangement of doorless compartments, each with four bunks in tiers of two plus another bunk beside the corridor. ***Kupé*** (coupé; also called 2nd class) refers to carriages with four-berth closed compartments. ***SV*** (*spalny vagon*, literally 'sleeping car'; also called 1st class) has comfortable, two-berth compartments which sometimes have washbasins; on newer, firmenny trains each SV compartment may have its own shower. Some Trans-Siberian trains have an additional ***de luxe 1st class*** (see pp112-113).

Ticket buying for non-Russian speakers

If you can't speak enough Russian to buy a ticket write what you need on a piece of paper as shown below. The clerk will usually write down a suggested train number and departure time and hand it back to you. Say *Da* (Yes) and you'll get the ticket. Check that the time the clerk writes down is Moscow Time by pointing to it and saying *Moskovskoye vremya*?

For more complex enquiries use the form on p122. If there's a long queue, however, it would be better to transcribe the question you need answered from the form on p122 onto a piece of paper rather than trying to get the clerk to look through the whole page.

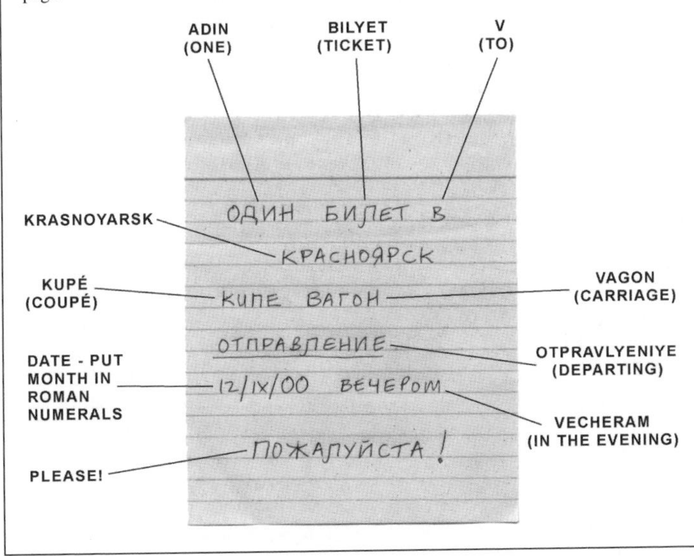

The term *firmenny* refers not to carriages but to certain train services, including all international trains and many domestic ones. On *firmenny* trains you can expect extra attention to detail and comfort in all classes. Finally, there are the *premium* trains – six *firmenny* trains which are distinguished by particular levels of comfort – and two of which you'll find along the Trans-Siberian: 'Yarmarka', the Nizhny Novgorod–Moscow and the 015/016 'Ural', between Yekaterinburg and Moscow.

Fares

Overnight rail tickets in Russia are considerably cheaper than in the West; a kupé ticket for a 24-hour journey costs about US$80/£60/€65. Supply varies and the official response appears to be to raise prices when demand seems to be exceeding supply. The ticket price comprises a booking fee (US$15-40 depending on where you buy the ticket) plus a charge depending upon the class of service and

TRAIN INFORMATION AND TICKET-BUYING FORM

Please help me.
I don't speak Russian.
Please read the question I point to and write the answer or...
* = circle your answer.
Q = question / A = answer
MT = Moscow Time

Information

Q. When is the next train with available SV* kupé* platzkartny* spaces to ....?
A. The train No is ....
It departs at .... : .... (MT).

Q. Are there SV* kupé* platzkartny* tickets to ....
on train No ....?
A. Yes / No

Q. When does the train depart and arrive?
A. It departs at .... : .... and arrives at .... : .... (MT).

Q. How much does a SV* kupé* platzkartny* ticket cost?
A. It costs .... roubles.

Q. Which ticket window should I go to?
A. Ticket window No ....

Q. What platform does train No .... leave from?
A. Platform No ....

Buying tickets

Q. May I buy .... SV* kupé* platzkartny* tickets to ....
on train No ..... leaving on ....?
(DD/MM/YY format, eg 31/12/00.)
A. Yes, it costs .... roubles.
A. No.

Q. Why can't I buy a ticket?
A. There is no train.
A. The train is fully booked.
A. You must buy your ticket at window No ....
A. You can only buy a ticket .... hours before the train arrives.

Thank you for your help.

Будте любезны, помогите мне.
Я не говорю по-русски.
Прочтите вопросы на которые я укажу, и напишите ответ, или
* = обведите свой ответ.
Воп. = вопрос / Отв. = ответ
МВ = Московское Время

Информация

Воп. Когда следующий поезд со свободными местами (СВ* купе* плацкарт*) до ....?
Отв. Номер поезда ....
Отправляется в .... : ....(МВ).

Воп. Есть ли свободные места (СВ* купе* плацкарт*) до ....
в поезде номер ....?
Отв. Да / Нет

Воп. Когда поезд отправляется и прибывает?
Отв. Отправляется в .... : ....
и прибывает в .... : .... (МВ).

Воп. Сколько стоит билет в СВ* купе* плацкарт*?
Отв. Билет стоит .... рублей.

Воп. К какой кассе мне подойти?
Отв. Касса номер ....

Воп. С какой платформы отправляется поезд номер ....?
Отв. Платформа номер ....

Покупка билетов

Воп. Можно ли купить ... (СВ* купе* плацкарт*) билет до ....
на поезд номер .... который отправляется до ....?
Отв. Да. Билет стоит .... рублей.
Отв. Нет.

Воп. Почему я не могу купить билет?
Отв. Нет поезда.
Отв. Нет мест.
Отв. Вы должны купить билет в кассе номер.............
Отв. Вы можете купить билет за .... часов до прибытия поезда.

Большое спасибо за помощь.

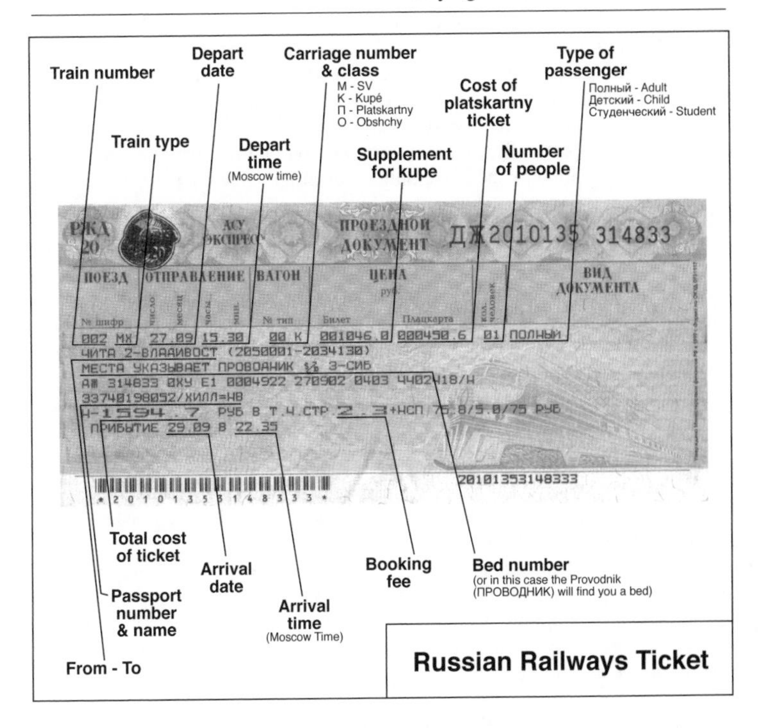

the distance travelled. Most popular for overnight journeys is the four-berth kupé ticket, though platzkart is very popular with budget travellers, and tends to cost less than half the price of a kupé ticket. At the time of writing, the Russian railway cut prices for top berths in both kupé and platzkart, as those are far less popular than bottom berths, though this promotion may not last. A two-berth *SV* ticket is generally 1½-2 times the cost of kupé; tickets for firmenny trains cost about 1¼ to 1½ times non-firmenny tickets.

Stations in Moscow or St Petersburg issue domestic tickets up to 45 days in advance and international tickets up to 40 days ahead. Larger stations elsewhere may only allow 30 days' advance purchase. Locals can hold reservations without paying until 10 days before departure, at which point unsold tickets are released and resold.

Which train?

The timetable displayed in the booking hall states the train's number, the time of departure and the days on which it travels.

- The train number indicates its direction, with even numbers indicating generally eastbound or northbound travel, and odd numbers westbound or southbound.

• Timetables invariably use Moscow Time. Across a network covering eight time zones this is the only way the system could work. The clock in the booking hall is normally set to Moscow Time. Some station clocks have two hour-hands, black for local time and red for Moscow Time.
• Most trains depart daily, but some run only on odd-numbered days of each month (1st, 3rd, 5th etc) and some only on even-numbered days.

Which ticket window?

There are usually several ticket windows (*kassa* касса) depending on your destination and possibly on whether you want a same-day or advance-purchase ticket. Staff may not always be very helpful. If the choice is not obvious, go to the administrator's window (Администртор) where you'll either be sold a ticket or told where to get one. If there's a queue and you want to return later, take note of the window's closing times.

Stations in most major cities have 'service centres' with staff who speak a little English. At these centres you must pay an extra service fee of up to US$7.

Which ticket?

At the window you'll need to tell them your destination, train number, date of departure and compartment class: Л (L = two-berth *SV*), M (M = four-berth *SV*), K (K = *kupé*), П (P = *platzkartny*), O (O = *obshchy*), either verbally or in writing (see p120). There are several types of long-distance tickets but the most common is a long computer-printed one (see p123). It contains not only information about the train but also your name and passport number, which will be checked when you board the train. If you're buying for someone else you have to present their passport.

BUYING A TRAIN TICKET IN CHINA

If you're planning on travelling by train in China and if your travels include the Beijing (via Harbin) to Chita route or any long-distance route to a popular destination it's best to reserve ahead, particularly if travelling during the Spring Festival, around May 1st, October 1st, or at the end of August when students are going back to university and all the desirable tickets – soft sleeper, hard sleeper and soft seats – are sold out way in advance.

If you don't speak any Mandarin you can use the form on pp126-7 to help; alternatively book your ticket through an agency (see pp35-7). Payment at railway stations is in cash only, whereas agencies accept credit cards as well.

Tickets for most long-distance journeys go on sale 5-10 days in advance at railway stations and designated ticket offices, though a proportion is made available from travel agencies a day before they go on sale elsewhere. D and Z train tickets (see p125) go on sale 10-20 days before the travel date. In big cities, such as Beijing and Shanghai, ticket windows at railway stations are open 24 hours.

If you're looking to do the Trans-Siberian route with Beijing as your starting point, it's actually easier to get Beijing–Moscow tickets than Moscow–Beijing, though tickets for trains passing through Ulaanbaatar and Chita still sell out quickly in summer, and it may be easier to buy tickets for trains going via Manchuria. If your travel dates are fairly flexible you can book the tickets in person at the international train booking office on the ground floor of Beijing International Hotel, about five minutes' walk north of Beijing Zhan station on Jianguo Men Nei Dajie. If you need to travel on specific dates, you have to book in advance via one of the travel agencies (see p370) and have the tickets delivered to your hotel. International tickets may be purchased up to 40 days before travel.

Classes of service

On Chinese trains, there are five classes of tickets: **soft sleeper** (ruan wo 软卧), **hard sleeper** (ying wo 硬卧), **soft seat** (ruan zuo 软座), **hard seat** (ying zuo 硬座) and **standing** (zhan piao 站票). Soft sleepers are bunks in lockable compartments of four; they are the priciest but also the easiest to book due to relative lack of demand.

Bedding is provided both for soft and hard sleepers, the latter consisting of lots of three bunks, which are half the cost of soft sleeper bunks. The middle bunk is best, as the top ones are cramped and people sit on the bottom bunks.

Hard and soft seats are fine for a short journey but not recommended for overnighters as you won't get much sleep due to the clamour, the light, the smoke (though smoking is officially forbidden in carriages, it's not always strictly enforced), and the scores of souls unlucky or desperate enough to possess standing tickets, otherwise known as 'hell on rails'. If you find yourself among their number, and you're fast enough, you may manoeuver yourself into a free luggage rack or try sleeping on top of your luggage on the floor, though you may wake up covered with a blanket of sunflower seed shells. If you don't book your ticket in advance during national holidays and peak season, this may be your only option.

Fares

Sample one-way ticket prices for the Beijing to Moscow trains are roughly US$610-710 for hard sleeper, US$880 for soft sleeper, and US$960-1085 for de luxe soft sleeper. Between Beijing and Harbin one-way tickets cost roughly US$115-135 for soft sleeper, US$105 for hard sleeper and US$65 for hard seat. Between Shanghai and Beijing one-way ticket prices are around US$125 for soft sleeper, US$93 for hard sleeper and US$72 for hard seat.

Which train?

Chinese trains are divided into roughly three categories:

- **Bullet trains** **G** High-Speed Electric Multiple Units (EMU) Train, Gaotie (高铁), the fastest train available; **C** – Intercity EMU Train, Chengji Lie Che (城际列车); and **D** – Electric Multiple Units (EMU) Train, Dongche (动车).
- **Express trains** **Z** – Direct Express Train, Zhida (直达), no stops and lightning fast; **T** – Express Train, Tekuai (特快), few stops and very fast; and **K** – Fast Train, Kuaiche (快车), few stops and fast.
- **Slower trains** These have few facilities and stop at all the stations so are best avoided – Pukuai (普快) and Puke (普客).

All trains, apart from international ones, depart daily.

TICKET BUYING FOR NON-CHINESE SPEAKERS

If you don't speak Mandarin, you can use the form below for train departure-related queries. However, if there's a long queue, you're better off going to the ticket office that deals with foreigners as your fellow Chinese travellers may not be terribly patient with you, or else book your (marked-up) ticket via an agency on p370.

NOTE: **soft sleeper** (软卧) **hard sleeper** (硬卧)
soft seat (软座) **hard seat** (硬座)

Train information and ticket-buying form

Please help me.	我需要您的帮助
I don't speak Mandarin.	我不会讲中文
Please read the question I point to and write the answer or…. * = circle your choice.	请您查看我所指向的问题，写下您的回答或者… 圈出您的回答

Q = question 问题 / A = answer 回答

Information

Q. When is the next train with available soft sleeper* / hard sleeper*/ soft seat* / hard seat* spaces to ....?	请问下一班通往 …………… 的并且有 软卧* / 硬卧*/ 软座* / 硬座* 车票出售的旅客列车什么时候发车
A. The train No is .... It departs at .... :	车次是 …........…................... 发车时间是 ….......: ….......
Q. Are there soft sleeper*/ hard sleeper*/ soft seat* / hard seat* tickets to (A) .... on train No (B) ....?	请问通往 (A)…................…. 的 (B)…...................... 次旅客列车有没有 软卧* / 硬卧*/ 软座* / 硬座* 车票出售

(A) ……….......................... is for destination (B) ......… is for train number

A. Yes 有 / No 没有

Q. When does the train depart and arrive?	请问该次列车的发车时间和到达时间是
A. It departs at .... : .... and arrives at .... :	该次列车的发车时间是 …… : ……. 到达时间是 .... : ....

Q. How much does one soft sleeper* / hard sleeper* / soft seat*/hard seat* cost?	请问一张 软卧* / 硬卧*/ 软座* / 硬座* 的票价是
A. It costs .... yuan.	票价是 …............ 元
Q. Which ticket window should I go to?	请问我应该在哪个售票窗口买票
A. Ticket window No	售票窗口…….......号
Q. What platform does train No .... leave from?	请问........... 次旅客列车从哪个站台发车
A. Platform No	站台...........号

Buying tickets

Q. May I buy *A*........ soft sleeper*/ hard sleeper* / soft seat* / hard seat* tickets to *D*........................ on train No *C*............... leaving on *B* ....?	请问我可不可以买 *B*….................... 年 *B* ....… 月 *B*.......................... 日 *A* .... 张 *C* ....… 次通往 *D*….................................. 的 软卧* / 硬卧* / 软座* / 硬座车票

(*A* is for the number of tickets wanted; *B* is for the date in the order of YYYY/MM/DD; *C* is for the train number; *D* is for the destination)

A. Yes, it costs .... yuan A. No.	可以，总票价是…..........…元 不可以
Q. Why can't I buy a ticket?	请问为什么我不能买票
A. There is no train.	没有你想搭乘的车次
A. The train is fully booked.	车票已售完
A. You must buy your ticket at window No	你需要在第….….... 号售票窗口买票
A. You can only buy a ticket .... hours before the train arrives.	你只能在列车到站前提前 …….…... 小时买票.
Thank you for your help.	谢谢您的帮助

Which ticket window?

At **Beijing's** main railway station you'll find the English-speaking ticket office for foreigners in the north-west corner of the 1st floor, accessed via the soft seat waiting room. You may only purchase domestic Chinese tickets here. At Beijing West station, you'll find one 24-hour ticket window in the main hall is marked 'English speaking'.

If you're buying a train ticket in **Shanghai**, at the main railway station, the English-speaking ticket window is No 10 on the ground floor of the main ticket office to the south-east of the main station. At the new Hongqiao station, the departure point for most fast trains to Beijing, the ticket office is signposted in the departures area on the 2nd floor.

Which ticket?

At the window you'll need to tell them your destination, train number, date of departure and compartment class (see p125) either verbally or in writing (see pp126-7). There are several types of long-distance tickets but the most common is a short computer-printed one. It contains information such as the train number, time of departure, carriage and seat number.

Colour section (following pages)

• **C1 (Opposite) China** – **Top**: a particularly steep section of the Great Wall of China, between Jinshanling and Simatai (see p379). **Bottom**: The Forbidden City palace complex in Beijing, seen from a viewpoint in Jingshan Park (p358).

• **C2** (Clockwise from top left): **1**. The Red Square in Moscow (p162), particularly popular on summer nights. **2**. Suzdal is famous for its *medovukha* (honey mead, see p218). **3**. Vladivostok promenade, alongside the popular Sportivnaya Gavan beach just to the west of the city centre. **4**. Tobolsk kremlin (p245) is the most beautiful in Siberia and worth the detour.

• **C3** (Clockwise from left): **1**. There are still some traditional, ornately-decorated wooden buildings to be seen in Siberian cities such as Novosibirsk (see pp253-9; photo © Nick Hill). **2**. A stall at Beijing's Donghuamen Night Market (see p373) offering skewers of grasshoppers and scorpions, as well as more traditional fare. **3**. The dramatic statue of Lenin in Novosibirsk stands in the main square in front of the vast Opera House. **4**. A poster in Tynda celebrating the 35th birthday of the BAM (see p108-9): 'The railway built with love.' The BAM was built largely using forced labour, at a cost of thousands of lives.

• **C4** (Clockwise from top left): **1**. One of the most sacred sites for the local Buryat people is Shaman Rock on Olkhon Island (see p292), Lake Baikal. **2**. Hikers on a ridge overlooking Lake Baikal towards the northern end of Olkhon Island. **3**. The main temple building at the Ivolginsky Datsan (see p300) near Ulan-Ude, Russia's largest and most splendid Buddhist temple complex. **4**. *Obo* (sacred place) near Shaman Rock, Olkhon Island; lengths of cloth are attached as offerings and can be any colour other than black, the colour of death. **5**. A ship dwarfed by the great expanse of Lake Baikal, seen from Port Baikal.

• **C5** (Clockwise from top left): **1**. The old and the new: a modern skyscraper overlooking the Choijin Lama Temple Museum, Ulaanbaatar (see p330). **2**. Outside the Mongolian capital, many Mongolians still lead a semi-nomadic existence, herding cattle and living in yurts. **3**. A modern yurt with a generator inside it and a motorcycle replacing the more traditional horse. **4**. The head of the family at a nomad camp, leading a baby camel; many camps offer camel rides as one of the attractions. **5**. Though the Lama Temple in Beijing (see p360) is popular with tourists, it is very much a working temple, with scores of the devout praying and burning incense as an offering.

Весёлый
мёд
ядрёный
ВЕСЁЛЫЙ
МЁД
ядрёный
12.5

БАМ
35
ЛЕТ
Дорога, построенная с любовью...

雍和宫

CITY GUIDES & PLANS 4

St Petersburg
Санкт Петербург

'It is in Russia – but it is not Russian!' exclaimed Tsar Nicholas I to his visitor, the Marquis de Custine. The remark speaks volumes: the city was conceived as one to rival any European city. Russia has always wanted to be seen as an equal, first by European powers, and then by other world powers – a statement that is as true today as it has been for the past three centuries.

St Petersburg, more Western in appearance and with a more relaxed feel to it than the uncompromisingly Russian Moscow, is named after the patron saint of its founder, Tsar Peter I 'the Great', a man who had toured Europe, who wrote fluently in eight languages and who felt his illiterate, unwashed forebears were a shaming heritage. The city was created as a 'window to the West', a face Russia could proudly show the world, and remained the capital until the Soviet era. It can hardly be coincidence that Vladimir Putin, architect of post-Soviet Russia's rediscovered pride in its image abroad, is a St Petersburg lad.

Though not officially part of the Trans-Siberian railway, St Petersburg is an excellent place to either start or finish your journey, if only to experience a part of Russia that's markedly different from the rest of the country. Built on multiple waterways, with opulent palaces – former residences of nobles and former rulers – St Petersburg has a wealth of world-class museums, a lively art and music scene and nightlife to rival the capital. This city, which has played a pivotal role in Russia's history, particularly in the 20th century, which suffered unimaginably during WWII but managed to recover, epitomises for many Russians that key quality of the 'Russian character': stoicism.

'The Northern Capital'

Petersburgers persistently refer to their city as the 'Northern Capital' (or more conversationally as 'Peter', while to the older generation it remains 'Leningrad'). The criteria for its location were strategic rather than climatic. At the same latitude as the

---

(Opposite) St Petersburg: Clockwise from top: **1**. Peter and Paul Cathedral, (see p143) **2**. The Hermitage museum is housed in the Winter Palace (see p138). **3**. Gilded statues on the Grand Cascade at Peterhof (p147). (Photos 2&3 © BT).

Orkney Islands or North Dakota, winter photos taken before about 10am or after 2pm will show the city in half-darkness, while summertime darkens for only a few hours of twilight – down to about 45 minutes during June's 'White Nights' celebrations. Biting winter gales off the Gulf of Finland give way in summer to armies of hungry (but non-malarial) mosquitoes.

St Petersburg was Russia's first paved city. These paving-stones were a legacy of Catherine the Great; it is said that they were swept clean each day by prostitutes arrested the previous night. Their modern-day successors escape such duties, and with Soviet potholes to add topographic interest, sturdy footwear is recommended. Winter ice isn't removed but crushed, turning the city into an unofficial skating-rink from October until April. Bring ridge-soled boots.

HISTORY

Imperial glories

At the turn of the 18th century Peter the Great finally defeated Sweden in the Great Northern Wars campaign inherited from his father. Sweden's navy had once sailed unopposed down Russia's rivers and Peter, determined never to be thus humiliated again, in 1703 ordered construction of a defensive garrison, the St Peter and Paul Fortress, on the banks of the River Neva. Russia had no navy, so shipyards were needed too. Peter detested Moscow and he made the decision to simply abandon Russia's backward, shambling capital and move the title here. Swedish PoW labour and bottomless reserves of cash saw a complete new city rise in just nine years. By 1712 this was the new Russian capital, and Peter was styling himself not merely 'Tsar' but 'Imperator'.

Falconet's riverside Bronze Horseman statue, the city's virtual trademark, bears the legend *Petrus Primus – Katerina Secunda*, a Latin double-entendre which not only translates their titles but reminds us that 'Peter was first – and Catherine followed through'. The glory-days of the Russian Empire were under a woman born in Germany as Princess Sophie of Anhalt-Zerbst, now known to the world as Catherine the Great. St Petersburg flourished during her reign, benefiting from her skills at empire-building and statesmanship, and her private passions for architecture, the arts, fine conversation, the Russian language, cavalry officers and horsemanship.

Once clear of the threat of Napoleonic France, Catherine's successors ruled over Europe's wealthiest empire, from a capital barely a century old. The fortunes to be made here attracted Europe's highest achievers. The city showcased the neoclassical architecture of Rossi, Rastrelli and Karl Ton. Home-grown writers like Pushkin, Gogol, and Dostoyevsky vied with visitors like Balzac, and Anton Chekhov wrote *Uncle Vanya* and *The Seagull*. The Imperial Opera commissioned Verdi to write 'Don Carlos'. Mikhail Lomonosov, the poet and scientist considered the father of modern Russian literature, was made rector of a new University, and Dmitri Mendeleev conceived his Periodic Table of Elements. Yet in most of Russia, serfs worked the land in conditions bordering on slavery to pay for all this. Change was inevitable, but was resisted until it took control of events by itself.

St Petersburg to Leningrad and back again

It was not only the working classes who envied the wealth and privilege of St Petersburg. Any Russian not of noble birth or military inclination found himself excluded from the capital, and even a century before the Revolution of 1917 Gogol was satirising the capital's wealth and social iniquities in his surreal tales *The Nose* and *The Overcoat*. Most of Dostoyevsky's writing depicts St Petersburg as a force wrecking the lives of its inhabitants. In 1881 Tsar Alexander II was blown to pieces by anarchists in the very centre of the city.

A bungled attempt to quash a protest over the price of bread in January 1905 led to the 'Bloody Sunday' massacre in Palace Square. In February 1917 Tsar Nicholas II retired to private life, with effective power transferred to a provisional government. Armed attempts by aristocratic cavalry officers to return Nicholas to the throne created an atmosphere of panic and havoc. This played into the hands of Trotsky's Bolsheviks, who in October 1917 arrested the provisional government and declared Soviet Power, under a leader freshly returned from exile in Switzerland, Vladimir Ilyich Ulyanov, better known under his adopted name: Lenin.

Lenin returned all governmental functions to Moscow – and left them there, making the change of capital official in 1918. Between 1914 and 1924, the city was briefly known as Petrograd. The Imperial capital was left to fall into genteel decay. Gentility descended into barbarity during WWII: for 900 days the city – renamed Leningrad in 1924 after Lenin's death – was besieged, and nearly a quarter of the population died of hunger, disease or bombardment.

Yet the Communists, resentful of their own Imperial past, starved the city of resources after the war, preferring to develop new industrial centres in Russia's interior. Perversely, this policy – and boggy terrain unconducive to high-rise building – saved it from the excesses of Soviet planning, but left it in a state of disrepair. Little time was wasted, however, in renaming the city St Petersburg within a year of the fall of communism.

St Petersburg today

Millions of roubles were invested in the country's second wealthiest city in time for its tricentenary celebrations in 2003, and some investment has continued, thanks to the efforts of the two local lads: former president and current prime minister Vladimir Putin and President Dmitrii Medvedev. Though one may argue that it was an insufficient effort given the decades of neglect, few visitors will fail to be impressed by the city's somewhat tarnished grandeur, which served as inspiration to some of Russia's leading literary figures. St Petersburg – now with a population of some 4.8 million – gives the impression of a lively, growing city, though the older buildings in the historical centre are still under threat, many already demolished to give way to new building projects.

A particularly wonderful time to be in St Petersburg is during the White Nights in the summer, when the sun never sets and the city seems to be in a permanent state of celebration, though every season holds its own attractions.

(continued on p138)

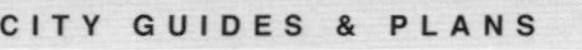
CITY GUIDES & PLANS

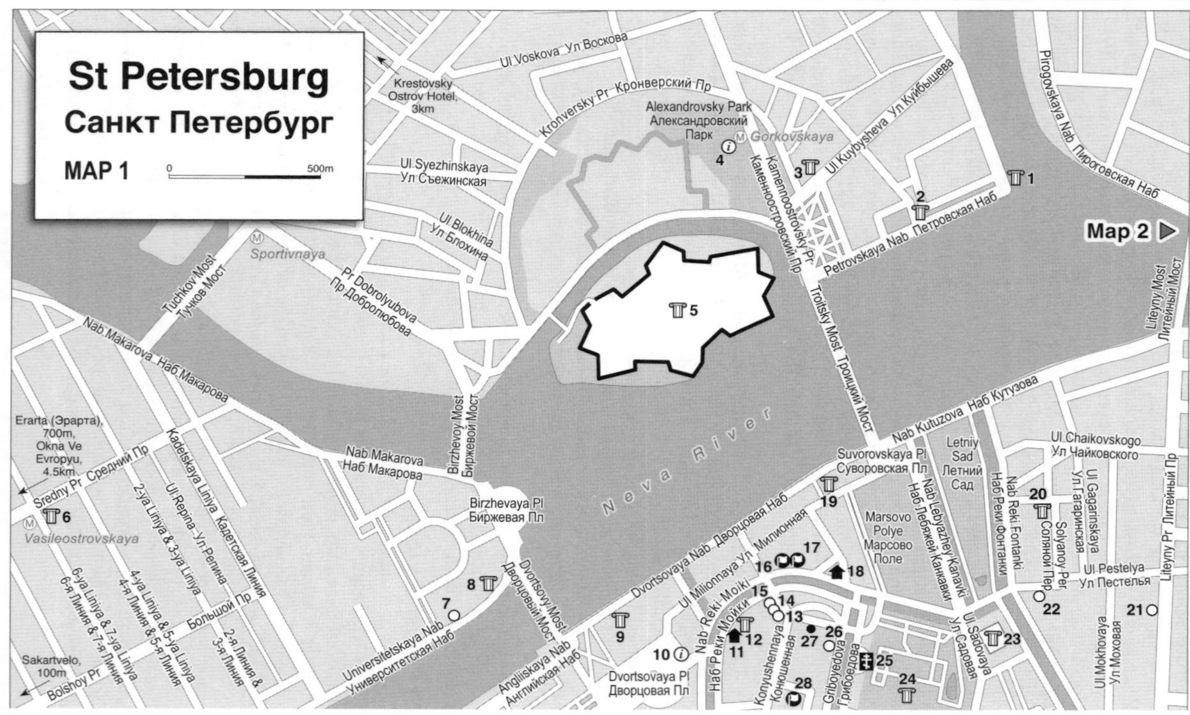
St Petersburg
Санкт Петербург
MAP 1
0
500m
Map 2
Pirogovskaya Nab Пироговская Наб
Liteyny Most Литейный Мост
Liteyny Pr Литейный Пр
Ul Mokhovaya Ул Моховая
Ul Pestelya Ул Пестеля
Ul Chaikovskogo Ул Чайковского
Ul Gagarinskaya Ул Гагаринская
Solyanoy Per Соляной Пер
Nab Reki Fontanki Наб Реки Фонтанки
Letniy Sad Летний Сад
Ul Sadovaya Ул Садовая
Nab Lebyazhey Kanavki Наб Лебяжей Канавки
Marsovo Polye Марсово Поле
Suvorovskaya Pl Суворовская Пл
Nab Kutuzova Наб Кутузова
Petrovskaya Nab Петровская Наб
Ul Kuybysheva Ул Куйбышева
Troitsky Most Троицкий Мост
Kamennoostrovsky Pr Каменноостровский Пр
Gorkovskaya
Alexandrovsky Park Александровский Парк
Kronversky Pr Кронверский Пр
Ul Voskova Ул Воскова
Neva River
Griboyedova Грибоедова
Konyushennaya Конюшенная
Nab Reki Moiki Наб Реки Мойки
Ul Millionaya Ул Милионная
Dvortsovaya Nab Дворцовая Наб
Dvortsovaya Pl Дворцовая Пл
Angliiskaya Nab Английская Наб
Dvortsovy Most Дворцовый Мост
Birzhevaya Pl Биржевая Пл
Birzhevoy Most Биржевой Мост
Universitetskaya Nab Университетская Наб
Nab Makarova Наб Макарова
Ul Blokhina Ул Блохина
Ul Syezhinskaya Ул Съежинская
Krestovsky Ostrov Hotel, 3km
Pr Dobrolyubova Пр Добролюбова
Sportivnaya
Tuchkov Most Тучков Мост
Kadetskaya Liniya Кадетская Линия
Ul Repina Ул Репина
2-ya Liniya & 3-ya Liniya
2-я Линия & 3-я Линия
Bolshoy Pr Большой Пр
4-ya Liniya & 5-ya Liniya
4-я Линия & 5-я Линия
6-ya Liniya & 7-ya Liniya
6-я Линия & 7-я Линия
Sredny Pr Средний Пр
Vasileostrovskaya
Erarta (Эрарта), 700m, Okna Ve Evropyu, 4.5km
Sakartvelo, 100m
1 2 3 4 5 6 7 8 9 10 11 12 13 14 15 16 17 18 19 20 21 22 23 24 25 26 27 28

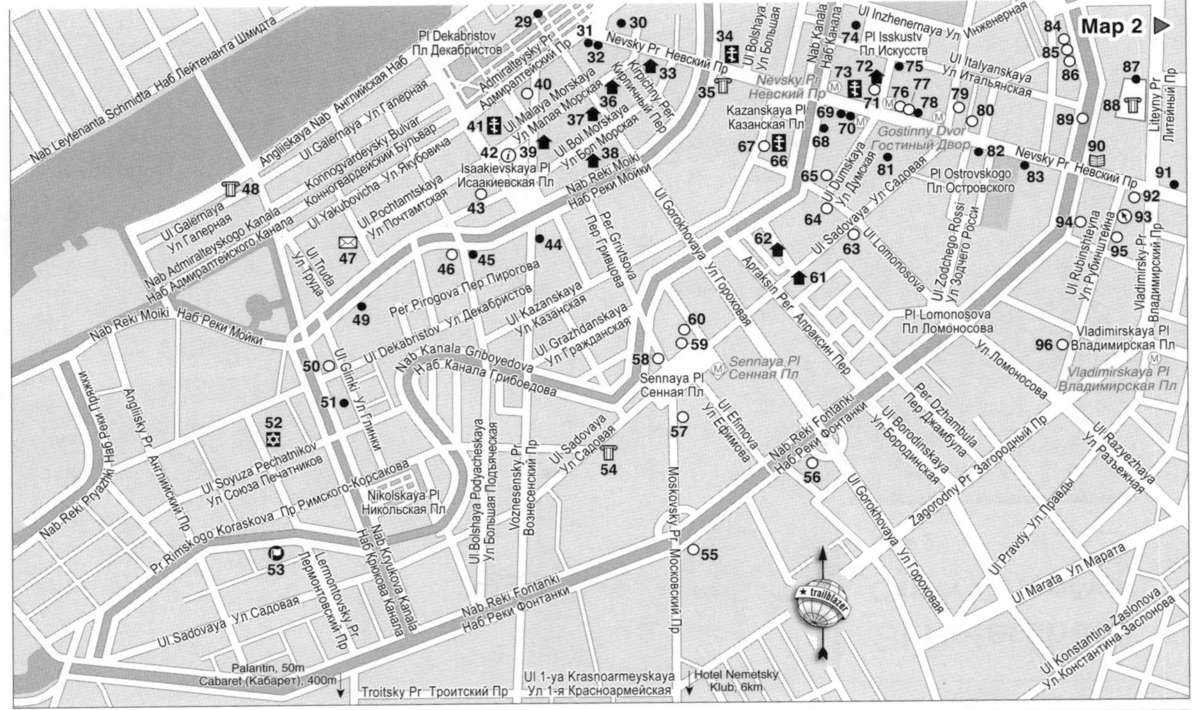

CITY GUIDES & PLANS

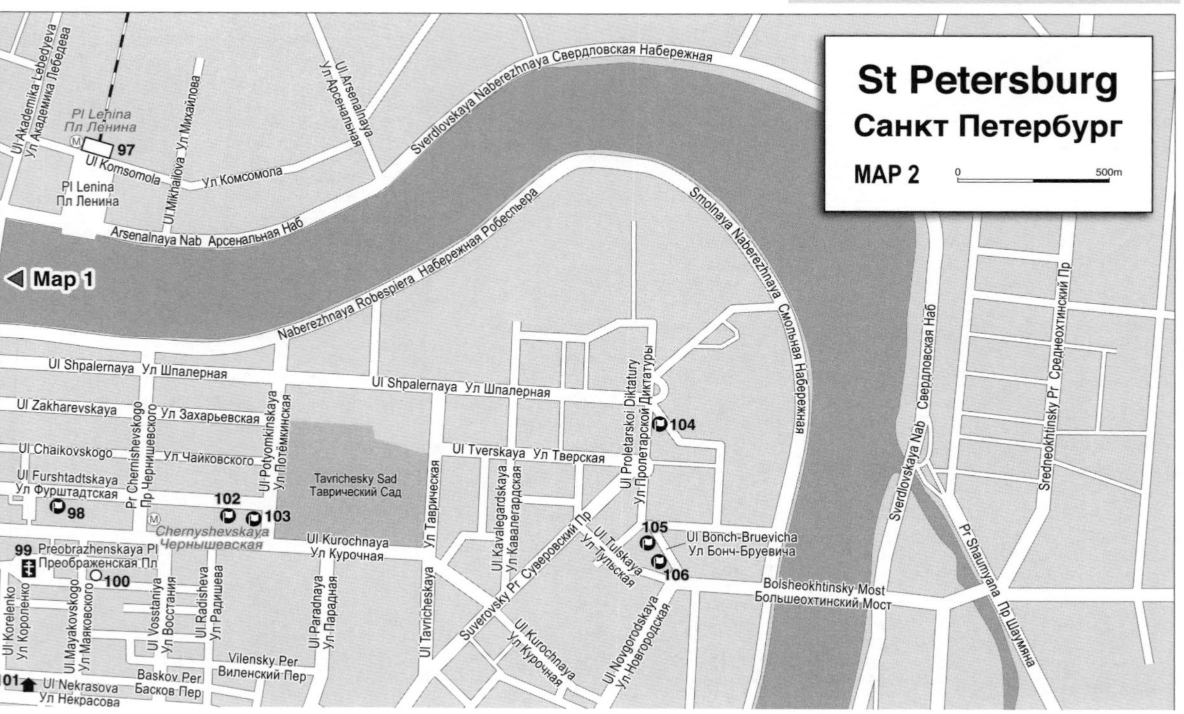
St Petersburg
Санкт Петербург
MAP 2
0
500m
Map 1
Ul Akademika Lebedyeva
Ул Академика Лебедева
Pl Lenina
Пл Ленина
97
Ul Komsomola
Ул Комсомола
Ul Mikhailova
Ул Михайлова
Pl Lenina
Пл Ленина
Ul Arsenalnaya
Ул Арсенальная
Arsenalnaya Nab Арсенальная Наб
Sverdlovskaya Naberezhnaya Свердловская Набережная
Naberezhnaya Robespiera Набережная Робеспьера
Smolnaya Naberezhnaya Смольная Набережная
Sverdlovskaya Nab Свердловская Наб
Sredneokhtinsky Pr Среднеохтинский Пр
Pr Shaumyana Пр Шаумяна
Ul Shpalernaya Ул Шпалерная
Ul Shpalernaya Ул Шпалерная
Ul Zakharevskaya
Ул Захарьевская
Pr Chernishevskogo
Пр Чернишевского
Ul Potyomkinskaya
Ул Потёмкинская
Ul Chaikovskogo
Ул Чайковского
Ul Furshtadtskaya
Ул Фурштадтская
98
102
103
Chernyshevskaya
Чернышевская
Tavrichesky Sad
Таврический Сад
Ul Tverskaya Ул Тверская
Ul Proletarskoi Diktatury
Ул Пролетарской Диктатуры
104
Ul Kavalegardskaya
Ул Кавалегардская
Suverovsky Pr Суверовский Пр
Ul Tulskaya
Ул Тульская
105
106
Ul Bonch-Bruevicha
Ул Бонч-Бруевича
Bolsheokhtinsky Most
Большеохтинский Мост
Ul Kurochnaya
Ул Курочная
Ul Tavricheskaya
Ул Таврическая
Ul Novgorodskaya
Ул Новгородская
Ul Kurochnaya
Ул Курочная
99
Preobrazhenskaya Pl
Преображенская Пл
100
Ul Korelenko
Ул Короленко
Ul Mayakovskogo
Ул Маяковского
Ul Vosstaniya
Ул Восстания
Ul Radisheva
Ул Радишева
Ul Paradnaya
Ул Парадная
Vilensky Per
Виленский Пер
Baskov Per
Басков Пер
101
Ul Nekrasova
Ул Некрасова

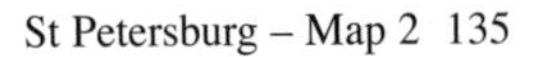

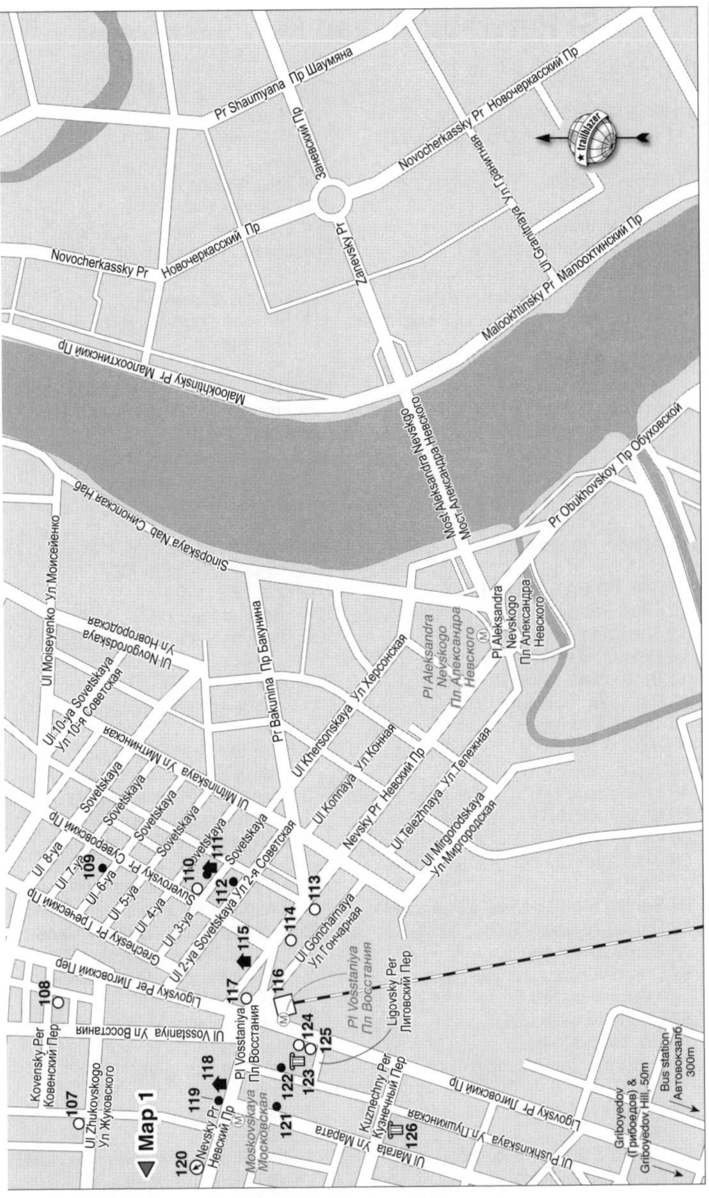
Pr Shaumyana Пр Шаумяна
Novocherkassky Pr Новочеркасский Пр
Novocherkassky Pr Новочеркасский Пр
Zanevsky Pr Заневский Пр
Ul Granitnaya Ул Гранитная
Malookhtinsky Pr Малоохтинский Пр
Malookhtinsky Pr Малоохтинский Пр
Most Aleksandra Nevskgo
Мост Александра Невского
Sinopskaya Nab Синопская Наб
Pr Obukhovskoy Пр Обуховской
Ul Moiseyenko Ул Моисейенко
Ul Novgorodskaya Ул Новгородская
Pr Bakunina Пр Бакунина
Ul Khersonskaya Ул Херсонская
Pl Aleksandra Nevskogo Пл Александра Невского
Pl Aleksandra Nevskogo Пл Александра Невского
Ul 10-ya Sovetskaya Ул 10-я Советская
Ul Mitinskaya Ул Митинская
Ul Konnaya Ул Конная
Nevsky Pr Невский Пр
Ul Telezhnaya Ул Тележная
Ul Mirgorodskaya Ул Миргородская
Sovetskaya
Ul 8-ya
Ul 7-ya
Ul 6-ya
Ul 5-ya
Ul 4-ya
Ul 3-ya
Suvorovsky Pr Суворовский Пр
Grechesky Pr Греческий Пр
Ul 2-ya Sovetskaya Ул 2-я Советская
Ligovsky Per Лиговский Пер
Ul Goncharnaya Ул Гончарная
Pl Vosstaniya Пл Восстания
Ul Vosstaniya Ул Восстания
Pl Vosstaniya Пл Восстания
Ligovsky Per Лиговский Пер
Kovensky Per Ковенский Пер
Ul Zhukovskogo Ул Жуковского
Map 1
Nevsky Pr Невский Пр
Moskovskaya Московская
Kuznechny Per Кузнечный Пер
Ul Marata Ул Марата
Ul Pushkinskaya Ул Пушкинская
Ligovsky Pr Лиговский Пр
Griboyedov (Грибоедов) & Griboyedov Hill, 50m
Bus station Автовокзал 300m
trailblazer
107
108
109
110
111
112
113
114
115
116
117
118
119
120
121
122
123
124
125
126

St Petersburg map key Санкт-Петербург

(M1) = Map 1, (M2) = Map 2

WHERE TO STAY

11 Pushka Inn Hotel Отель Пушка Инн (M1)
18 Hotel 3 Mosta Гостиница 3 Моста (M1)
33 Nevsky Inn (M1)
36 Marmalade Hostel (M1)
37 Herzen House Герцен Хаус (M1)
38 Casa Leto Каса Лето (M1)
39 Hotel Astoria Гостиница Астория (M1)
61 B&B Assembly Мини-отель Ассамблея (M1)
62 Friends Hostel (M1)
72 Grand Hotel Europe Гранд Отель Европа (M1)
101 St Petersburg Puppet Hostel (M2)
111 St Petersburg International Hostel
115 Soul Kitchen Hostel (M2)
118 Apricot Hostel (M2)

WHERE TO EAT AND DRINK

7 Grad Petrov Град Петров (M1)
13 The Other Side (M1)
14 Daiquiri Bar (M1)
15 Stolle Café Кафе Штолле (M1)
22 Botanika Ботаника (M1)
40 Tandoor Indian Restaurant Тандур (M1)
43 Teplo Тепло (M1)
46 Idiot Идиот (M1)
50 Shamrock (M1)
55 Dickens (M1)
56 Russkaya Charka Русская Чарка (M1)
57 Sennoi Market Сенной Рынок (M1)
58 Bardak Бардак (M1)
59 Carl's Junior (M1)
64 Cherdak Khudozhnika Чердак Художника (M1)
67 Charlotte Café (M1)
71 Chopsticks (M1)
76 Supermarket Passazh Пассаж (M1)
77 Chaynaya Lozhka Чайная Ложка (M1)
79 Coffee Shop Company (M1)
80 Carl's Junior (M1)
84 Aragvi Арагви (M1)
92 Palkin Палкин (M1)
94 Palermo Палермо (M1)
95 Mops Мопс (M1)
96 Tres Amigos (M1)
100 Pickwick Pub (M2)
107 Liverpool Ливерпуль (M2)
108 Mechta Molokhovets Мечта Молоховец (M2)
113 Garcon Гарсон (M2)
114 Teremok Теремок (M2)
117 Al-Shark (M2)

NIGHTCLUBS AND LIVE MUSIC

21 Jimi Hendrix Blues Club (M1)
26 Marstall (M1)
60 Dali Café Дали Кафе (M1)
63 Money Honey (M1)
65 Dacha Дача (M1)
85 Purga I Пурга 1 (M1)
86 Purga II Пурга 2 (M1)
89 Purga Party Boat (M1)
110 XXXX Bar (M2)
124 Fish Fabrique (M2)
125 Fish Fabrique Nouvelle (M2)

PLACES OF INTEREST

1 Cruiser Aurora Крейсер Аврора (M1)
2 Peter the Great's Log Cabin Домик Петра Великого (M1)
3 Museum of Political History Музей Политической Истории России (M1)
5 Peter and Paul Fortress Петропавловская Крепость (M1)
6 Novy Muzey Новый Музей (M1)
8 Kunstkamera Кунсткамера (M1)
9 State Hermitage/Winter Palace Эрмитаж/Зимний Дворец (M1)
12 Pushkin House Дом Пушкина (M1)
19 Marble Palace Мраморный Дворец (M1)
20 Blockade Museum Музей Блокады Ленинграда (M1)
23 St Michael's Castle Михайловский Замок (M1)
24 State Russian Museum Русский Государственый Музей (M1)

PLACES OF INTEREST ***(cont'd)***

25 Church of the Resurrection Церковь Воскресения Христова (M1)
29 Admiralty Адмиралтейство (M1)
30 Former General Staff Building Здание Главного Штаба (M1)
34 Dutch Church (M1)
35 Stroganov Palace Строгановский Дворец (M1)
41 St Isaac's Cathedral Иссакиевский Собор (M1)
44 Mariinsky Palace Мариинский Дворец (M1)
48 Rumyantsev Mansion Особняк Румянцева (M1)
49 Yusupov Palace Юсуповский Дворец (M1)
51 Mariinsky Theatre Мариинский Театр (M1)
52 Great Choir Synagogue Большая Хоральная Синагога (M1)
54 Central Railway Museum Музей Железной Дороги (M1)
66 Kazan Cathedral Казанский Собор (M1)
69 Former City Duma Бывшая Городская Дума (M1)
73 Church of St Catherine (M1)
74 Mussorgsky (Maly) Theatre Театр Мусоргского (Малый Театр) (M1)
75 St Petersburg State Philharmonia Филармония (M1)
81 Gostinny Dvor Универмаг Гостинный Двор (M1)
83 Anichkov Palace Аничков Дворец (M1)
87 Sheremetyevsky Palace Шереметьевский Дворец (M1)
88 Anna Akhmatova Museum Музей Анны Ахматовой (M1)
99 Cathedral of the Transfiguration Преображенский Собор (M2)
123 Museum of Non-Conformist Art Музей Нонконформистского Искусства (M2)
126 Dostoyevsky House-Museum Дом-музей ФМ Достоевского (M2)

EMBASSIES AND CONSULATES

16 French Consulate Французское Консульство (M1)
17 Dutch Consulate Консульство Нидерландов (M1)
28 Swedish Consulate Шведское Консульство (M1)
53 Chinese Consulate Китайское Консульство (M1)
98 US Consulate Консульство США (M2)
102 German Consulate Консульство Германии (M2)
103 Swiss Embassy (M2)
104 British Consulate Британское Консульство (M2)
105 Ukrainian Consulate Украинское Консульство
106 Belarus Consulate Беларусское Консульство (M2)

OTHER

4 Tourist Office (M1)
10 Tourist Office (M1)
27 Rentabike (M1)
31 Nevsky Souvenir (M1)
32 Central Air Ticket Office Центральная Авиакасса (M1)
42 Tourist Office (M2)
45 American Medical Clinic (M1)
47 Central Post Office Почтамт (M1)
68 Central Train Ticket Office Центральная Железнодорожная Касса (M1)
70 Histours (M1)
78 Theatre Ticket Kiosk Театральная Касса (M1)
82 City Bus Tour (M1)
90 Anglia Book Shop Книжный магазин Англия (M1)
91 Westpost (M1)
93 A-Club Internet Café (M1)
97 Finlyandsky Station Финляндский Вокзал (M2)
109 White Nights (M2)
111 Peter's Walking Tours (M2)
112 Sindbad Travel (M2)
116 Moskovsky Station Московский Вокзал (M2)
119 Ost-West Kontaktservice (M2)
120 Café Max Internet Café (M2)
121 MEDEM International Clinic & Hospital (M2)
122 Your Visa To Russia (M2)

WHAT TO SEE AND DO

The State Hermitage Museum Эрмитаж

The director of the Hermitage once said: 'I can't say that the Hermitage is the number one museum in the world, but it's certainly not the second.' No visit to St Petersburg should omit the **Hermitage** (Dvortsovaya pl 2, **M** Nevsky Prospekt, 🖳 www.hermitagemuseum.org, 10.30am-6pm Tue-Sat, until 5pm Sun; adults/students with valid ISIC card R400/free, free admission for all visitors first Thur of month; photos/video R200), combining the city's two must-see attractions. Most famously, this is one of the world's biggest and most splendid collections of fine art. As a bonus, it is housed in the grandest rooms of the former **Winter Palace** (Зимний Дворец) of the Tsars, Europe's wealthiest royal family.

The collection began with 225 paintings presented to Catherine the Great by a Berlin-based Russian banker named Gotskovsky, the first of many to gain Imperial promotion by sending artworks home to Her Majesty. Catherine displayed them in her Hermitage, a purpose-built annexe of the Winter Palace added by the Italian architect Rastrelli in his 1762 remodelling of the complex.

The collection swelled with gifts from foreign rulers seeking favour or trade agreements, and officers and civil servants looking for a quick promotion. Some pieces were eventually shifted to the Russian Museum. But the greatest, and most controversial, of the Hermitage's acquisitions came after 1917 with the 'nationalisation' of the private collections of Russia's aristocracy and bourgeoisie.

The massive collection now numbers more than three million catalogued works housed in five interconnected buildings. All the state rooms, private chambers and servants' quarters of the Winter Palace, plus the Old and New Hermitage buildings, cannot display more than half the items at one time. This is also a research centre, with priceless works from ancient Rome, Greece, and Egypt amongst many others, and experts on archaeology and ancient cultures in residence.

Indeed there is so much to see here that a single visit can only scratch the surface. Many visitors make several visits, following themed routes. The museum comprises the following main departments:

- **Prehistoric Art**, including the exquisite Scythian gold collection
- **Antiquity**, including Ancient Greece and Rome
- **Western European Art**, which draws the biggest crowds
- **Oriental Art**, including the Middle East, China, Japan and Central Asia
- **Russian Culture**.

There are also special sections including armaments, numismatics and jewellery; and, of course, the extraordinary 'collection' represented by the setting itself, including grand marble halls with gilded columns, mosaic floors and immense crystal chandeliers.

Most casual visitors follow a well-trodden path combining Western European Art and the most impressive of the Palace State Rooms. The goal of many is the superb French Impressionist collection, which is on the top floor on the Dvortsovaya pl (Palace Sq) side. The museum is so vast that it's easiest to navigate by looking out of the windows and using the river and Palace Square as landmarks.

You enter via the splendid **Jordan Staircase**. Of the **State Rooms**, don't miss the Malachite Hall, designed by Brullov, and the adjacent Small Dining Room, where the 1917 revolutionaries arrested the Provisional Government (who had made the Palace their headquarters). Perhaps most impressive are three adjacent rooms: the Royal Throne Room, the Great Banquet Hall and the Gallery of Heroes of 1812, the last decorated with over 1000 portraits of officers who served in the Napoleonic campaign. Various stories are told about the missing canvases – that their subjects died before the portraits were finished or, more credibly, that they were subsequently disgraced by their involvement in the 1825 Decembrist plot to depose Nicholas I.

For guided tours, call ☎ 571 8446. To avoid the queues you can buy tickets online for US$17.95 (one-day ticket), valid for the Hermitage complex only or US$25.95 (two-day ticket), valid for exhibitions at the General Staff Building (Здание Главного Штаба), the Menshikov Palace, the Winter Palace of Peter the Great and the Porcelain Museum. See the Hermitage's excellent website for details.

The State Russian Museum Русский Государственый Музей

Given the size of the Hermitage collection, it seems almost impossible that there could be another art museum of similar scope anywhere in the world – but there is, just halfway down Nevsky pr. The State Russian Museum (ul Inzhenernaya 4/2, **M** Nevsky Prospekt or Gostinny Dvor, 💻 www.rusmuseum.ru, 10am-5pm, until 4pm Mon, closed Tue, entrance to Mikhailovsky Palace only adult/student R350/150; entrance to other branches adult/student R300/150, joint ticket, valid for 24 hours, adult/student R600/300; photos R100), the country's **first public art gallery**, has four branches, the main one being the former Mikhailovsky Palace, with its maze of beautifully decorated rooms. While the Hermitage contains almost uniquely non-Russian works, the Russian Museum is home to the finest of the country's own Old Masters.

The original collection, which opened in 1895, is displayed in chronological order around the palace, while work from the turn of the 20th century is in the adjacent **Benois Wing**. You begin with icons and applied art from as early as the 12th century, including those by legendary 14th-century master Andrei Rublyov. The heart of the collection, however, is the work of Russian painters of the 18th to mid-19th centuries, rarely exhibited abroad. Don't miss the chance to see Brullov's *The Last Days of Pompeii*, Vasnetsov's over-the-top medieval heroes, or Aivazovsky's boiling seascapes. Perhaps the finest of all are the portraits of Ilya Repin, whose monumental *The State Parliament* fills a whole room and depicts the last Tsar, Nicholas II, with his ministers.

Other branches, which host excellent temporary exhibitions, are found at the **Marble Palace** Мраморный Дворец (ul Milionnaya 5/1, **M** Nevsky Prospekt), the nearby **St Michael's Castle** Михайловский Замок (ul Sadovaya 2, **M** Nevsky Prospekt or Gostinny Dvor) and **Stroganov Palace** Строгановский Дворец (Nevsky pr 17, **M** Nevsky Prospekt).

❑ **A walk down Nevsky prospekt Невский проспект**

Nevsky prospekt (pr) has been the main shopping street and the most fashionable place to be seen in St Petersburg since the city's founding. A walk along this grand street, past palaces and churches, over canals and beside faded buildings is a walk through the history of the city itself. Nevsky pr starts near the **Admiralty Building** Адмиралтейство and, as you walk south-east from here, you can identify the buildings by the numbers beside the doors.

No 7 Gogol wrote *The Government Inspector* here in the 1830s.

No 9 This building was modelled on the Doges' Palace in Venice, for the Swedish banker Wawelberg.

No 14 A blue and white sign here, dating from the WWII Siege of Leningrad, advises pedestrians to walk on the other side of the street during shelling.

No 17 This impressive building, designed by Rastrelli and completed in 1754, was once the palace of the wealthy Stroganov family (see pp81-2). Although they are more famous for the beef stew named after them, it was the Stroganovs who initiated the conquest and colonisation of Siberia by sending their private army to the Urals in the 1570s.

No 18 The **Literaturnoye Kafe** was Pushkin's favourite. It's worth seeing but tends to be packed with tourists. The entry fee covers high-class entertainment such as violin concerts.

No 20 The former **Dutch Church**, built in 1837.

No 24 Once the showrooms of the court jewellers Fabergé (creators of the golden Easter eggs now on display in the Kremlin).

No 28 The former showrooms of the Singer Sewing Machine Company with their trademark (a glass globe) still on the roof.

On the southern side of Nevsky pr stands **Kazan Cathedral** Казанский Собор (Kazanskaya pl 2, **M** Nevsky Prospekt, 10am-7pm, services 10am & 6pm) designed by Voronikhin and completed in 1811. Prince Peter Kropotkin, writing in 1911, called it 'an ugly imitation on a smaller scale of St Peter's in Rome'. The large, domed cathedral is approached via a semi-circular colonnade with statues at either end. The one on the left is Mikhail Kutuzov, who prayed here before leading an army to fight Napoleon. After the 1812 victory over the French the cathedral became a monument to Russia's military glory. In an act of supreme tastelessness the Soviets turned it into a Museum of Atheism. Part of the cathedral still houses exhibits on the history of religion, while the rest has been returned to the Orthodox Church.

KAZAN CATHEDRAL

Looking north along Griboyedov Canal you'll see the pseudo-Old Russian style **Church of the Resurrection** Церковь Воскресения Христова, whose multicoloured onion domes are reminiscent of St Basil's in Moscow. It's also called the Church of the Resurrection Built on Spilt Blood as it's erected on the spot where Alexander II was assassinated in 1881.

No 31 This building housed the **City Duma** Бывшая Городская Дума (Municipal Council) in Tsarist times. The tower was used as a fire lookout.

Opposite the Duma is Mikhailovskaya ul, running north into pl Iskusstv (Arts Square). In the former Mikhailovsky Palace on the square is the **State Russian Museum** (see p139), home to over 300,000 paintings, drawings and sculptures.

The **Mussorgsky Opera and Ballet Theatre** Театр Мусоргского (Малый Театр; the former Maly Theatre) and the **St Petersburg State Philharmonia** Филармония are near the museum.

The **Grand Hotel Europe** Гранд Отель Европа is a short distance away at Mikhailovskaya ul 32.

No 32 In the **Church of St Catherine** is the grave of Stanislaw Poniatowski, the last King of Poland and one of Catherine the Great's lovers. Local artists sell their sketches and watercolours outside.

Gostinny Dvor Универмаг Гостиный Двор, the city's largest department store, fills the entire block between Sadovaya ul and Dumskaya ul. This is the place to splurge on upmarket items alongside fashion-conscious New Russians. **Passazh**, across the street, was the city's first privately owned department store and has a range of goods similar to any large Western department store. There is a large supermarket (see pp155-6) in the basement.

From the street you can see a **statue of Catherine the Great**, surrounded by her lovers (or 'associates' as some guides coyly put it) in the middle of **pl Ostrovskogo**, referred to as Catherine Gardens. In the park behind this is **Pushkin Theatre** and on the western side of the square you'll find the **National Library of Russia**, filled with over 31 million books.

No 56 Eliseyevsky Gastronom was a delicatessen rivalling the Food Halls at Harrods in Tsarist times. After the Revolution it became Gastronom No 1 and the ornate showcases of its sumptuous interior were heaped with jars of boiled vegetables. It is a wonderful example of classic St Petersburg interior design. Western delicacies are now on offer.

The building on the south side of the street beside the Fontanka 'Canal' (properly River Fontanka) is known as **Anichkov Palace** Аничков Дворец, after the nearby **Anichkov Bridge** with its famous equestrian statues.

No 82 Art Gallery of the Masters' Guild (Gildiya Masterov) offers a good range of contemporary art, tapestries, ceramics, batik, jewellery and glassware by well-known artists.

It's 1km from here to pl Vosstaniya where **Moskovsky station** (for trains to Moscow) is situated.

From pl Vosstaniya it's 700m to the end of the avenue at pl Aleksandra Nevskogo where you will find **Alexander Nevsky Monastery**, with seven churches in its grounds.

MOSKOVSKY RAILWAY STATION

St Petersburg by boat

Peter the Great imagined his city as the 'Venice of the North', and many of its finest buildings are meant to be approached by water. A boat ride along the city's canals and rivers can be an excellent way of seeing the sights, although you'll need to make sure to take an English-language tour.

Sights on most routes include **St Isaac's Cathedral**; the **Church of the Resurrection**; **Mariinsky Theatre** Мариинский Театр, the blue-and-white home of top-rated opera and ballet; **Mariinsky Palace** Мариинский Дворец, built without stairs for the invalid Princess Marie, and now the City Hall; **Kazan Cathedral**; and **Yusupov Palace**. Some trips also go out onto the Neva.

Don't miss a **night boat tour** in summer: the sight of the city's many lit-up bridges being raised (see box below) is spectacular. Locals claim that if you make a wish just as a bridge is raised, it will come true.

Recommended tour operators include **Neptun Boat Tour** (day tour R500, night tour R600), which leaves from nab Reki Moiki 26, near the junction of Nevsky pr with the Moika Canal, several times in the afternoon and at 00.45 for the night tour (book in advance ☎ 971 8439). You're provided with audio guides in several languages so you can enjoy the scenery without having to listen to the drone from the boat's speakers. Another recommended operator, **Astra Marine** (tours R300-800), leaves from nab Admiraltiyskaya 2, the 'Lion's Pier'. They specialise in daytime audio-guide trips along the Neva and the Gulf of Finland, with some of their boats going as far as Peterhof (see p147).

St Isaac's Cathedral **Иссакиевский Собор**

St Isaac's Cathedral (Isaakievskaya pl 4, **M** Nevsky Prospekt, 10am-10.30pm; closed Wed; colonnade 11am-7pm, closed 2nd Wed of each month; museum inside the cathedral R320, colonnade R160, after 6pm R300; photography costs extra), its interior decorated with mosaics, paintings and gold trim, is one of the largest cathedrals in the world and its colossal bronze dome dominates the city skyline. Its 40-year construction, completed in 1859, was the life's work of French architect Nicholas Montferrand (whose petition to the Empress to be buried there was refused on the grounds that he was Roman Catholic). It's well worth climbing the 262 steps up the colonnade for the wonderful view of the city.

Near the cathedral is **Decembrists' Square** Площадь Декабристов, scene of the ill-fated 'patriotic rebellion' of 14 December 1825. It's now dominated by Etienne-Maurice Falconet's **Bronze Horseman**, an equestrian monument to Peter the Great erected in 1782 by order of Catherine the Great.

❑ Bridge raising

St Petersburg is a working port and shipping must pass. It does so at night from May to September when the waterways aren't frozen; **all** the city's bridges are raised from approximately 2am until 5am. There is no alternative way home if you are caught out; you just have to wait. There are no commuter boat services even in daylight hours and the metro shuts down at midnight.

Great Choir Synagogue Большая Хоральная Синагога

The second largest synagogue (Lermontovsky pr 2, **M** Sennaya Ploshchad, Sun-Fri 9am-6pm, daily services 9am) in Europe, its splendid Great Hall accommodating up to 1200 worshippers, remains an important focal point for the city's Jewish community. On the premises you'll also find a ***kosher restaurant*** and a shop where you can purchase unique rabbi *matryoshkas*.

Yusupov Palace Юсуповский Дворец

This stately building (nab Reki Moiki 94, **M** Sadovaya/Sennaya Ploshchad, 11am-5pm; closed Wed; adult/student R500/380, including audioguide in English) is famous as the place where in 1916 the ersatz monk Rasputin was poisoned by his dinner host, young Viscount Felix Yusupov, stabbed and shot by Yusupov's cronies and thrown through the ice of the Moika Canal. Rasputin proved to be remarkably resilient; the cause of death was drowning, but not before he managed to claw through a substantial chunk of the ice. The palace is an opulent, splendidly decorated building inside, especially its private theatre, and in the cellar you'll find wax figures of Rasputin and the plotters. Tours in English must be reserved in advance (☎ 314 8893).

Peter and Paul Fortress Петропавловская Крепость

Begun in 1703, the city's first stone structure (**M** Gorkovskaya; fortress open 6am-11pm in summer, except Wed and last Tue of month; shorter hours the rest of the year; museums 11am-6pm, until 5pm Tue; entrance to fortress is free; entrance to all attractions R350, valid for two days) was built to keep Swedish invaders out and was subsequently used to keep prisoners in. Its Trubetskoy Bastion served as a Tsarist political prison, with a roster of inmates including Dostoyevsky and Gorky (who survived) and Lenin's elder brother Alexander (who did not). After the revolution the fortress was turned into a museum.

Time your visit to see the noon-day cannon fired from the ramparts. The highlight of the fortress is **SS Peter and Paul Cathedral**, where most of Russia's rulers from Peter the Great to Nicholas II (see box p144) are buried. Also on offer are reconstructions of the **Trubetskoy dungeons** and a **Cosmonaut Museum**, as well as temporary exhibitions along the Nevskaya panorama roof walk. If you take a walk around the outside of the fortress wall, you will spot intrepid locals swimming in the Neva year-round. Join them if you dare.

The cabin of Peter the Great Домик Петра Великого

A short stroll from the Peter and Paul fortress, this cabin (Petrovskaya naberezhnaya 6, **M** Gorkovskaya, 11am-9pm; closed Tue, adult/student R200/100), built in just two days in 1703, was Peter the Great's first residence in his new city. The only surviving original wooden building in St Petersburg, it's a surprisingly small and humble dwelling, given both the man's status and stature (Peter was said to have stood almost seven feet tall). Visitors can see the original furniture and tiled stove, some of Peter's collection of Dutch Masters, and even a boat built by the emperor himself.

The Romanov Reburial

Despite considerable controversy, July 1998 saw the remains of the Romanov Royal Family transferred for reburial in SS Peter and Paul Cathedral from the abandoned mineshaft near Yekaterinburg where they had been hidden after the murder in 1918.

The list of those who had much to lose from this event was numerous. Hardline Communists feared the backlash that the story would cause. The City of Yekaterinburg fought long and hard to hold on to the relics (and the tourist trade they brought in). The City of Moscow argued they should be buried in the Kremlin with the earliest Tsars. President Boris Yeltsin felt a lump in his throat – 30 years previously the Communists had razed the holding-place in Yekaterinburg where the murders took place, and as Yekaterinburg's mayor he'd signed the orders himself. Even the Russian Orthodox Church winced: in their haste to damn the Communists for the murders, they'd rushed in in the 1920s to authenticate a set of remains in Paris (purchased for a tidy sum) which had been worshipped as holy relics for nearly 50 years, and were now shown up as fakes.

Then there were the embarrassed relatives of the late 'Anna Anderson', the woman who'd hoodwinked even close intimates of the Royal Family that she was the escaped Princess Anastasia, rightful Tsarina (her body was subsequently DNA-tested at the behest of greedy relations and shown to be Franziska Schanzkova, a Polish refugee). Last but not least, Fox Motion Pictures had just released a full-length animation, *Anastasia*, showing her not only escaping but marrying the sensitive young soldier who'd pulled her not-quite-dead body from the corpses, and finding happiness in America…

As you enter the Cathedral take a sharp right before the inner doors, to an anteroom where an official plaque declares that you are surrounded by the complete, authenticated and indubitable remains of those killed in Yekaterinburg on 16 July 1918. Even with such a definitive statement (which sidesteps a short tally of bones, and the whereabouts of the Royal valet, chambermaid and physician who also fell in the hail of bullets), this was to be a burial that refused to go easily to the grave. Opening the catacombs to inter Nicholas with his forebears, workmen found a 'last laugh' from the Communists, who had piped concrete into the foundations to prevent any further burials. Ceremonies were delayed whilst digging equipment blasted enough space for the funeral urns.

With a date set and foreign dignitaries invited (including the British Royal Family, cousins of the Romanovs), Yeltsin's Vice-President Boris Nemtsov went to the Finance Ministry with his budget for the rites, commemorative stones, VIP reception – in all, around US$10m. 'What?', he was told, 'Don't you know the economy's going down the tubes? We can let you have US$1m, but don't hang around, the country will be bust in a month!' Thus, at least most of the Romanovs were finally united with their ancestors – in a hurry, and on the cheap. **Neil McGowan** (Russia)

Cruiser Aurora Крейсер Аврора

Further along the Neva lies the battleship (Petrogradskaya nab, **M** Gorkovskaya, 10.30am-5pm, closed Mon, Fri; admission free; tour R200) famous for firing the shot that signalled the beginning of the 1917 revolution. Since the collapse of the Soviet Union, rumours have been circulating that this may be a replica. Either way, it's an impressive ship.

Rumyantsev Mansion Особняк Румянцева
The first privately owned museum (Angliiskaya nab 44, **M** Sadovaya, 11am-6pm, until 5pm Tue, closed Wed, R110) in Russia, this splendid neoclassical building was refurbished for the 200th anniversary of the city; several of its rooms reflect its former glory and feature the original belongings of its former owners. Other exhibitions focus on life in St Petersburg in the 1930s, while the most powerful display, 'Leningrad during the Great Patriotic War', focuses on the suffering of the city during the Siege of Leningrad during which 700,000 people perished. A particularly poignant exhibit is the siege diary kept by 11-year-old Tanya Savicheva, who continued going to school while her whole family died one by one. Some displays are in English; there are very worthwhile temporary art and photography exhibitions as well.

Blockade Museum Музей Блокады Ленинграда
Looking at St Petersburg today, a flourishing modern city, it's difficult to imagine its intense suffering during WWII, when the city was cut off by the Nazi forces and starved for 2½ years. This extremely moving museum (Solyanoy per 9, **M** Chernyshevskaya, 10am-5pm; closed Wed and last Thur of month, R150) chronicles the 900-day Blockade of Leningrad, focusing on the military and civilian aspects of it: the advance of the combined German-Finnish force and its eventual repulsion by the Red Army; and the famine that ravaged the city in spite of the 'Road of Life' – the heroic Allied effort to get provisions across the frozen Lake Ladoga during the winter months. Most of the exhibits are provided by survivors of the blockade.

In spite of the lack of English translations, visitors won't have much trouble following most of the exhibits; the enthusiastic staff, many of whom were children of the blockade, know enough basic English to explain the main points.

Museum of Political History Музей Политической Истории России
An art nouveau mansion built for Matilda Kshesinskaya, a prima ballerina at the Mariinsky and Nicholas II's mistress, the museum building (ul Kuibysheva 2-4, **M** Gorkovskaya, 🖳 www.polithistory.ru, 10am-6pm, closed Thur and last Mon of month, adult/student R200/100, cameras R100) was also the Bolshevik headquarters during 1917, and Lenin's office has been restored to its original state. The huge exhibition, spanning the whole of the Soviet period, is based on the original collection of artifacts collected by the key players in the Revolution, such as documents, posters and personal effects of Lenin, Gorbachev and others, and provides a fascinating insight into the period of collectivisation and the daily struggle for survival among others.

From the beginning of the 1990s, the displays of this former Museum of the Revolution were drastically reworked to reflect the museum's new goal: to dispassionately reveal the truth about the Soviet Union, including its most recent history. A particularly powerful display is dedicated to the GULAG prisoners, with its heartbreaking collection of items made by political prisoners. Contemporary exhibits include the camera used by Gorbachev to record his message to the nation in 1991, and a piece of the Berlin Wall.

Kunstkamera Кунсткамера

Founded by Peter the Great in 1714 and known also as the **Peter the Great Museum of Anthropology and Ethnography** (Universitetskaya nab 3, **M** Vasileostrovskaya, 🖳 www.kunstkamera.ru, 11am-7pm, closed Mon and last Tue of month, R250), the city's oldest museum is also the most bizarre. Besides the anthropological and archaeological collections from cultures around the world, exhibits comprise miscellaneous curios picked up by Peter during his travels. The most popular exhibit is still Peter's Anatomical Collection, featuring two-headed babies in jars and other grotesquery. Not for those with weak stomachs.

Railway museums

For Trans-Siberian travellers, the **Central Railway Museum** Музей Железной Дороги (ul Sadovaya 50, **M** Sadovaya or Sennaya Ploshchad, 11am-5.30pm Sun-Thur except last Thur of every month, adult/student R150/80) offers first-hand insight into the building of the railway and the trains that have served it. The exhibition charts the development of Russian railways from the first steam locomotive and includes incredibly detailed models and dioramas as well as a superb collection of scale locomotives going uphill and railway bridges, and an original 1903 Trans-Siberian wagon fitted with a piano salon and bathtub. However, the displays are labelled in Russian only.

The open-air branch of the above, the **Locomotive Museum** Паровозный Музей (Liteyny pr 62, Mon-Thur 11am-5pm; admission R100; tours in English US$10) is a short suburban train ride from the city and includes 30 locomotives and 22 steam engines among other exhibits. To get there, take a suburban train from Vitebsky station to the Paravozny Muzey stop. To book a tour in English, call ☎ 272 4477 in advance.

Contemporary art galleries

Besides boasting one of the world's richest collections of fine arts, St Petersburg also nurtures a thriving contemporary art scene. Some of the best examples of the post-WWII alternative art are found at the **Museum of Non-conformist Art** Музей Нонконформистского Искусства (ul Pushkinskaya 10, entrance from Ligovsky pr 53, **M** Ploshchad Vosstaniya, Wed-Sun 3-7pm), a ramshackle gallery with most of the works donated by local artists.

The newly opened **Erarta** Эрарта (29-ya linya 2, Vasilyevsky Ostrov, **M** Vasileostrovskaya, 🖳 www.erarta.com, 10am-8pm, closed Wed, adult/student R300/150) is Russia's biggest non-governmental contemporary museum. Housed in a spectacularly restored gallery, it features a monumental collection of Russian modern art from the last 60 years. Some of the installations are staggering due to their size alone and the curators regularly update the collection by travelling to the furthest reaches of Russia to seek out new and exciting work. A must. Take tram 6 or 40 from **M** Vasileostrovskaya or tram 6, buses 6 or 1, or trolleybus 10 from **M** Primorskaya to get here. For non-conformist art of the later Soviet period to the present day, head to **Novy Muzey** Новый Музей (6-ya lineya 29, Vasilyevsky Ostrov, **M** Vasileostrovskaya, 11am-7pm Wed-Fri, noon-8pm Sat & Sun, adult/student R200/100), its collection ranging from massive abstract paintings to satirical works and thought-provoking photography.

Literary Museums

St Petersburg has always been at the centre of events, so it's little surprise that it has been home to Russia's biggest literary figures. At nab Reki Moiki 12 you can visit **Pushkin House** Дом Пушкина (**M** Nevsky Prospekt or Gostinny Dvor, Wed-Mon 10.40am-5pm), the apartment where the poet lived and later died from duel-inflicted wounds.

Housed in a wing of **Sheremetyevsky Palace** Шереметьевский Дворец (Liteyny pr 53), **Anna Akhmatova Museum** Музей Анны Ахматовой (**M** Mayakovskaya, Tue-Sun 10.30am-6.30pm, R200, audioguide R150, camera R100) traces the life of Russia's most famous poetess through photographs, personal effects and letters from her imprisoned lover.

Those interested in Dostoyevsky's turbulent life can stop by **Dostoyevsky House** Дом-музей ФМ Достоевского (Kuznechny per 5/2, **M** Vladimirskaya, 11am-6pm, closed Mon, adult/student R150/70). The displays in the author's well-worn apartment give you an insight into his arrest and exile and the inspiration behind his works. An audioguide enhances the experience.

EXCURSIONS FROM ST PETERSBURG

Scorching heat and reeking rivers (the waterways doubled as open sewers) drove St Petersburg's aristocrats into the countryside in the summer, to residences no less grand than their *pied-à-terres* in town. Day-trips to these magnificent mansions make a rewarding change from yet another walk down Nevsky pr.

Thirty kilometres west of the city lies **Peterhof** Петергоф (💻 www.peterhofmuseum.ru, park 9am-8pm daily, adult/student R350/180, palace 10.30am-6pm daily except Mon, last Tue of month and in the winter, adult/student R520/250, audioguide R500), built by Peter the Great as his Versailles-by-the-sea, with each subsequent ruler adding their own palace or fountain to the complex. Its great attractions are the Ornamental Gardens and the Cascades (fountains) whose gilded figures appear in every tourist brochure; the grounds look particularly splendid mid-May to mid-October, when all 147 fountains are turned on. In summer the nicest way to arrive is by a Meteor speedboat (10am-4pm, every 30 mins, R500), departing from Dvortsovaya nab 39 (Palace Pier) outside the Hermitage's main entrance; discounts available for students and return journeys. From Baltiisky station (**M** Baltiiskaya), take a suburban train or alternatively, buses 350, 351, 352, 356 or marshrutka 404.

Set in beautiful parklands at **Pushkin** Пушкин (formerly Tsarskoye Selo, the 'royal village'), 25km south of St Petersburg, is the vast Catherine Palace (park 9am-10pm in summer, adult/student R180/90, palace noon-2pm & 4-5pm, closed Tue and last Mon of month, adult/student R550/280), completed in 1756. The palace was looted by German soldiers in WWII. Its famous Amber Room (whose original amber panels disappeared during the German retreat and have never been found) has been called the largest piece of jewellery in the world. The adjoining estate, 4km further south at **Pavlovsk** Павловск (park 8am-8pm, adult/student R150/80, palace 10am-5pm, adult/student R500/300), was built by Catherine the Great for her son, 'mad' Tsar Paul I. Pavlovsk Palace, with its stunning neoclassical interior, is surrounded by an astounding 1500 acres of park, criss-crossed by streams and endless paths for strolling. Pavlovsk and Pushkin are joined by a country path and make a practical full-day's outing.

To get to Pushkin take a train from Vitebsky station (**M** Pushkinskaya), to Detskoye Selo Детское Село, from where you can either walk to the palace or take buses 371 or 382. Alternatively, take marshrutka 286, 287, 342, 347 or 545 from **M** Moskovskaya.

PRACTICAL INFORMATION

Arriving in St Petersburg

By air There are two airports, sharing one runway, 17km south of the city. **Pulkovo 2** (☎ 704 3444, 💻 www.pulkovoairport.ru/eng) is for international flights. Buses N113, N213 (R19) and minibuses K13 and T113 (R28) run frequently between **M** Moskovskaya and the airport (5.30am until the last flight). Alternatively, take minibuses K3 or K213 from the more central Sennaya Ploshchad. Taxis going to and from the airport cost around R800 depending on your bargaining power; you get a better deal if you order a taxi in advance. Reputable taxi companies include Taxi Million (☎ 700 0000) and Ladybird (☎ 900 0504), a women-only taxi service.

Most domestic flights use **Pulkovo 1** (☎ 704 3822), a charmless Soviet heap 15 minutes further south. Hang on to your baggage-reclaim tag on domestic flights as you may have trouble retrieving your bag without it. Minibus N39 goes to **M** Moskovskaya (R19).

By train Direct express trains from Helsinki, the *Repin* and the *Sibelius*, arrive at **Finlyandsky station** Финляндский Вокзал (**M** Ploshchad Lenina), while the *Leo Tolstoy* arrives at **Ladozhsky station** (**M** Ladozhskaya). The arrival point from almost anywhere in Eastern and Western Europe, including the Baltic States, Poland, Ukraine and Belarus, is **Vitebsky station** (**M** Pushkinskaya).

Baltiisky station handles mostly domestic routes and suburban trains to Peterhof (see p147), Krasnoye Selo and Gatchina.

Trains from Moscow and Siberia come into **Moskovsky station**, Московский Вокзал, the grandest and most central, on Nevsky pr (**M** Ploshchad Vosstaniya or Mayakovskaya).

By bus All national and international buses arrive at the city's only bus station (**Avtovokzal No 2**, nab Obvodnogo Kanala 36, ☎ 766 5777, 💻 www.avokzal.ru, in Russian only). **M** Ligovsky Prospekt is a 15-minute hike away or you can take a short taxi ride (around R150) to the centre (north of the bus station).

Comfortable international services run by Eurolines (nab Obvodnogo Kanala 118, **M** Baltiiskaya, ☎ 441 3757, 💻 www.eurolines.ru) and Ecolines (Podezdnoy per 3, **M** Pushkinskaya, ☎ 325 2152, 💻 www.ecolines.net) arrive at **M** Baltiiskaya and the Avtovokzal respectively.

By boat Ocean-going cruisers anchor on the Neva. River cruises use the river terminal (*rechnoy vokzal*) at pr Obukhovskoy Oborony 195 (take tram No 24 or 29 from **M** Proletarskaya).

Local transport

St Petersburg's **metro** is quick, cheap and efficient, and is open from 6am to midnight.

A ticket to anywhere on the system costs R22; old-style tokens (*zhetoni*) are still used as well as magnetic cards (valid for 10, 20 or more rides). Unlike the 'Stalin-wedding-cake' style of Moscow's stations, many of those in St Petersburg, notably Mayakovskaya station, feature bold Soviet Constructivist designs.

But the metro network has great gaps where waterways prevent tunnelling (including vast swathes of the city centre); for these areas you must square up to the **buses**, **trams**, **trolley-buses** or **minibuses**.

Пр Просвещения
Pr Prosveshcheniya
Озёрки
Ozyorki
Удельная
Udelnaya
Пионерская
Pionerskaya
Чёрная Речка
Chyornaya Rechka
Петроградская
Petrogradskaya
Горьковская
Gorkovskaya
Девяткино
Devyatkino
Гражданский Пр
Grazhdansky Pr
Академическая
Akademicheskaya
Политехническая
Politekhnicheskaya
Пл Мужества
Pl Muzhestva
Лесная
Lesnaya
Выборгская
Vyborgskaya
Пл Ленина Pl Lenina
Финляндский Вокзал
Finlyandsky station
Чернышевская
Chernyshevskaya
Комендантский Пр
Komendantsky Pr
Старая Деревня
Staraya Derevnya
Крестовский Остров
Krestovsky Ostrov
Чкаловская
Chkalovskaya
Спортивная
Sportivnaya
Адмиралтейская
Admiralteyskaya
Приморская
Primorskaya
Василеостровская
Vasileostrovskaya
Невский Пр
Nevsky Pr
Гостиный Двор
Gostinny Dvor
Пл Восстания Pl Vosstaniya
Московский Вокзал
Moskovsky station
Маяковская
Mayakovskaya
Сенная Пл
Sennaya Pl
Спасская
Spasskaya
Садовая
Sadovaya
Достоевская
Dostoyevskaya
Владимирская
Vladimirskaya
Лиговский Пр
Ligovsky Pr
Технологический Институт
Tekhnologichesky Institut
Пл Александра Невского
Pl Aleksandra Nevskogo
Балтийская Baltiiskaya
Валтийский Вокзал
Baltiisky station
Пушкинская
Pushkinskaya
Звенигорская
Zvenigorskaya
Витебский Вокзал
Vitebsky station
Новочеркасская
Novocherkasskaya
Ладожская Ladozhskaya
Ладожский Вокзал
Ladozhsky station
Фрунзенская
Frunzenskaya
Нарвская
Narvskaya
Московские Ворота
Moskovskie Vorota
Елизаровская
Yelizarovskaya
Пр Большевиков
Pr Bolshevikov
Электросила
Elektrosila
Кировский Завод
Kirovsky Zavod
Ломоносовская
Lomonosovskaya
Ул Дыбенко
Ul Dybenko
Парк Победы
Park Pobedy
Автово
Avtovo
Obvodny Kanal
Обводный Канал
Московская
Moskovskaya
Volkovskaya
Волковская
Пролетарская
Proletarskaya
Ленинский Пр
Leninsky Pr
Звёздная
Zvyozdnaya
Bukharestskaya
Бухарестская
Обухово
Obukhovo
Пр Ветеранов
Pr Veteranov
Купчино
Kupchino
Mezhdunarodnaya
Международная
Рыбацкое
Rybatskoye
Line 1
Line 2
Line 3
Line 4
Line 5
Метро Санкт Петербурга
Saint Petersburg Metro

Buy your ticket from the conductor on board (R19 for any distance). Minibuses with the same numbers, on the same routes, provide a faster, more frequent service but are marginally pricier.

Orientation and services

St Petersburg stands at the mouth of the Neva, in a web of channels and islands (33 main ones and countless small ones) where the river meets the Baltic Sea's Gulf of Finland. The main axis is 4km-long Nevsky pr, with Dvortsovaya pl (Palace Sq) and the Hermitage at its north-western end. This square is the ceremonial centre, although the city's heart beats from the block of Nevsky pr between **M** Nevsky Prospekt and **M** Gostinny Dvor.

Across the Neva are the city's other main areas: Vasilevsky ostrov (St Basil's Island), Petrograd side (beyond Peter and Paul Fortress) and Vyborg side to the north-east.

Diplomatic representation **China** (nab Kanala Griboyedova 134, **M** Sennaya Ploshchad, ☎ 714 7670); **Belarus** (ul Bonch-Bruevicha 3A, **M** Chernyshevskaya, ☎ 273 4018); **France** (nab Reki Moiki 15, **M** Nevsky Prospekt, ☎ 332 2270); **Germany** (ul Furshtadskaya 39, **M** Chernyshevskaya, ☎ 320 2400); **Netherlands** (nab Reki Moiki 11, **M** Nevsky Prospekt, ☎ 334 0200); **Sweden** (ul Malaya Konyushennaya 1/3, **M** Nevsky Prospekt, ☎ 329 1430); **Switzerland** (pr Chernyshevskogo 17, **M** Chernyshevskaya, ☎ 327 1430); **UK** (pl Proletarskoy Diktatury 5, **M** Chernyshevskaya, ☎ 320 3200); **Ukraine** (ul Bonch-Bruevicha 1V, **M** Chernyshevskaya, ☎ 271 1402); **USA** (ul Furshtadtskaya 15, **M** Chernyshevskaya, ☎ 331 2600).

Internet cafés Internet cafés and wi-fi are easy to come by. Internet cafés include **A-Club** (ul Rubinshteyna 8, **M** Vladimirskaya, 10am-6am) and **Café Max** (Nevsky pr 90-92, **M** Mayakovskaya, 24 hours, wi-fi access also).

For those with their own laptops, pre-paid internet cards may be purchased from computer shops and kiosks.

Local publications You can find the following free English-language publications in bars, hotels, hostels and restaurants. *In Your Pocket* (💻 www.inyourpocket.com/russia/st-petersburg) is an extremely useful bi-monthly listings booklet with irreverent reviews, useful practical info and short features. The slick and glossy colour monthly *Pulse* (💻 www.pulse.ru) also has reviews and features. *The St Petersburg Times* (💻 www.sptimes.ru) is a bi-weekly source for local news, with an excellent listings and arts review section on Fridays.

Medical For 24-hour medical, dental or emergency services, contact **American Medical Clinic** (nab Reki Moiki 78, **M** Sadovaya, ☎ 740 2090, 💻 www.amclinic.ru) or **MEDEM International Clinic & Hospital** (ul Marata 6, **M** Mayakovskaya, ☎ 336 3333, 💻 www.medem.ru).

Money Access to cash is not a problem in St Petersburg as ATMs and currency exchange bureaux are ubiquitous, with a particularly high concentration along the main tourist thoroughfares such as Nevsky pr. American Express travellers' cheques can be cashed at most banks. Though many establishments accept credit cards, have some cash on you just in case.

Russian visas and extensions Remember, if you plan to stay in St Petersburg (or any Russian town) for longer than seven days, you need to register your visa within those seven days. Hotel (and

❑ Emergency numbers

If you have been robbed, or hassled by the police, and you don't speak Russian, call the English-language Tourist Helpline: ☎ 300 3333.

Other useful numbers are: Fire ☎ 01; Police ☎ 02; Ambulance ☎ 03 usually hostel) guests are automatically registered at check-in.

Alternatively, most travel agencies will register any visa when you drop off your immigration card at their office. **Ost-West Kontaktservice** (see p152) or **Your Visa To Russia** (☎ 812 309 4770; ul Pushkinskaya 8A-10H, **M** Ploshchad Vosstaniya, open 24 hours) are efficient.

Telephone The green street telephones (*taksofony*) use pre-paid cards available from kiosks and metro station ticket windows and are good for local calls. For cheap long-distance and international calls you should purchase an IP phonecard *telefonnaya karta* (international phone card) available in shops, kiosks, post offices and metro ticket desks. Using a call centre makes it even cheaper; alternatively, if you have a Skype account set up you can make the cheapest calls of all through your own laptop. It's relatively inexpensive to purchase a SIM card for your mobile phone from any major provider, such as MTS, Megafon or Beeline – their shops abound in the city.

Post The city's **central post office** Почтамт (and Russia's first!) is at ul Pochtamtskaya 9, **M** Nevsky Prospekt, and is open 24 hours. Russian post is slow but pretty reliable. If you need a package sent abroad in a hurry, **Westpost** (☎ 336 3652), at Nevsky pr 86, **M** Mayakovskaya, sends packages through the Finnish postal service. They can also arrange couriers, including an overnight service to Moscow. Customers can have packages and mail delivered here as well. Staff are helpful and speak English.

Tourist information During the summer, you'll find multilingual 'tourist angels' wandering around Nevsky pr, offering help and advice to tourists. There are several tourist offices in the city (10am-7pm in summer, reduced hours for the rest of the year), the most useful branches being at Dvortsovaya pl, **M** Nevsky Prospekt; Aleksandrovsky Park, **M** Gorkovskaya, and Isaakievskaya pl, **M** Sadovaya.

For information on the city, try the excellent 🖳 www.saint-petersburg.com which focuses on sights and current events, has a virtual city tour, and a message board used by other travellers. Run by the city tourist board, 🖳 www.visit-petersburg.com is another comprehensive website, the downloadable walking tours being its best feature. See also Local publications.

Tours Independent sightseeing is easy but if it's a tour you want, **Peter's Walking Tours** (🖳 www.peterswalk.com) is highly recommended for knowledgeable, innovative tours. Their daily walk (R600) starts at 10.30am at St Petersburg International Hostel, 3-ya Sovetskaya 28, **M** Ploshchad Vosstaniya, with other walks also available.

Cycling is a great way of exploring this completely flat city; **Rentabike** (Konyushennaya pl 2, **M** Nevsky Prospekt, 9am-11pm, from €15/day) can provide you with bicycles, helmets and maps. It's better to rent bikes at weekends, when the traffic is quieter, and in the summer; on Fridays at midnight you can join the local bikers and skaters at Dvortsovaya pl for White Nights bike rides.

The hop-on, hop-off **City Bus Tour** (R450) traces a route around the city's most popular sights and leaves every two hours from pl Ostrovskogo, **M** Gostinny Dvor, from 10am to 6pm.

Though not cheap, those who wish to properly delve into St Petersburg's military and political history may wish to join one of the excellent **Histours** (☎ 904 630 4403, 🖳 http://histours.ru, May-Sep, adult/student R2100/1900), such as the day-long Siege of Leningrad Battlefield Bus tour, as well as themed walks available on request. The meeting point is café 'Mocco Club'at Nevsky pr 29.

Travel services **White Nights** (ul 5th Sovetskaya 6A, ☎ 715 6433, 🖳 www.wnights.com) offers comprehensive services geared for independent travellers, including visa support, accommodation and homestays, air and train tickets, and tours in St Petersburg and many cities along the Trans-Siberian.

Sindbad Travel (ul 2-ya Sovetskaya 12, **M** Ploshchad Vosstaniya, ☎ 244 1000, 🖳 www.sindbad.ru, 9am-10pm Mon-Fri, 10am-6pm Sat & Sun) specialises in discount air tickets. It can book train tickets and youth hostel accommodation and sells ISIC/ITIC/IYTC cards. The multilingual staff at **Ost-West Kontaktservice** (Nevsky pr 100, 1st floor, **M** Mayakovskaya, ☎ 327 3416, 🖳 www.ostwest.com, 10am-6pm Mon-Fri) can book tickets and tours for you and do visa registrations.

Where to stay

St Petersburg has a chronic shortage of accommodation at every level so you should make arrangements early, especially in the spring and summer.

Budget accommodation There are more and more state-of-the-art hostels with free internet, wi-fi access and even free phone calls abroad. Breakfast is not included (unless stated otherwise).

A friendly new hostel that really caters to the needs of backpackers, ***Soul Kitchen Hostel*** (ул 1-я Советская 12 кв 1, ul 1-ya Sovetskaya 12 apt 1, **M** Ploshchad Vosstaniya, ☎ 964 378 9445, 🖳 www.soulkitchenhostel.com, dorm/dbl R800/2900) has brightly decorated, clean rooms, free breakfast in a fully equipped kitchen, free internet and wi-fi and even unlimited free international calls! The staff organise a plethora of activities – from Russian-pancake tasting on Friday nights to weekend flea-market tours on retro bicycles. Nearby ***St Petersburg International Hostel*** (ул 3-я Советская 128, ul 3-ya Sovetskaya 128, **M** Ploshchad Vosstaniya, ☎ 717-0569, 🖳 www.ryh.ru, dorm/dbl R500-700/R600-800) was Russia's first accredited youth hostel. They offer visa support and internet access but also have wi-fi. Peter's Walking Tours (see p151) start from here.

Offering similar facilities and perks (including free international phone calls) to Soul Kitchen and inspired by the American sitcom of the same name, ***Friends Hostel*** (Банковский пер 3, Bankovsky per 3, **M** Sennaya Ploshchad, ☎ 310 4955, 🖳 http://eng.friendsplace.ru; dorm/dbl/trpl R900/2300/3000) is another great addition to the budget scene, drawing an international backpacker crowd. The rooms are bright, the shower facilities ample, the common room has a giant plasma TV and a classic table football set, and the friendly, helpful staff make this a very enjoyable place to stay.

The small, slick ***St Petersburg Puppet Hostel*** (ул Некрасова 12, ul Nekrasova 12, **M** Ploshchad Vosstaniya, ☎ 272 5401, 🖳 www.hostel-puppet.ru, dorm/dbl R600/R1400) offers budget accommodation with no strings attached on the top floor of the Puppet Theatre. There is no common room or kitchen, but the rooms are spacious and welcoming and the knowledgeable staff are happy to help with visa registration and sightseeing tips. ISIC discount available.

Squeaky clean and brightly coloured, ***Apricot Hostel*** (Невский пр 106 5-й этаж кв 7, Nevsky pr 106 5th floor apt 7, **M** Nevsky Prospekt, ☎ 272 7178, 🖳 http://en.abrikos-hotel.ru, dorm/sgl/dbl R800/R1600/2200) attracts a sociable crowd of international travellers with its winning combination of multiple facilities (including a large kitchen) and young, well-travelled staff who can help you arrange onward travel. A second branch (ул Чехова 11 4-й этаж кв 5, ul Chehova 11 4th floor apt 5, **M** Mayakovskaya) is a mini hotel with nine airy doubles for the same rates.

Within easy walking distance of the main attractions, ***Marmalade Hostel*** (ул Малая Морская 8 кв 7, ul Malaya Morskaya 8 apt 7, **M** Nevsky Prospekt, ☎ 315 5489, 🖳 www.marmaladeru.com, dorm/sgl/dbl R800/2450-3050/2600-3200), a cosy place with comfortable rooms and the best showers in town, is sociable without being party central.

Homestays with a Russian family can be organised through Host Families Association (HOFA; 🖳 www.hofa.ru). You are matched to your host according to the language you speak. Singles in a B&B start from €30 per night; services including visa support are available at additional cost.

Mid-range hotels All rooms in this category have attached bathrooms. Many hotels offer weekend discounts (Friday and Saturday nights) of up to 30%, if you ask.

Catering to German-speaking guests but open to all is ***Hotel Nemetsky Klub*** **Гостиница Немецкий Клуб** (ул Гастелло 20, ul Gastello 20, **M** Moskovskaya, ☎ 371 5104, 💻 www.hotel germanclub.com, sgl/dbl R4000/4500), a slightly wacky place in a Stalin-era building with furnishings in hilariously bad taste. It's 6km south of the city centre.

Herzen House **Герцен Хаус** (ул Большая Морская 25, ul Bolshaya Morskaya 25, **M** Nevsky Prospekt; ☎ 315 5550, 💻 www.herzen-hotel.com, sgl/dbl from R4800/5800) has 20 simple, modern, air-conditioned rooms and a good hot breakfast. There's free wi-fi and internet access and you can peruse the DVD selection.

If you want to stay in a historical building in a super-central location you can do little better than the delightful ***Pushka Inn Hotel*** **Отель Пушка Инн** (наб Реки Мойки 14, nab Reki Moiki 14, **M** Nevsky Prospekt, ☎ 571 9557, 💻 www.pushka-inn.com, sgl/dbl from R4500/7500). The staff are very professional and you can rent a laptop (R200/hour) to make use of the free wi-fi.

An attractive, centrally located mini-hotel, ***Nevsky Inn*** (Кирпичный пер 2 кв 19, Kirpichny per 2 apt 19, code 19B, **M** Nevsky Prospekt, ☎ 972 6873, 💻 www.nevskyinn.com, sgl/twin R3300/3900) has seven light, bright en suite twin rooms. A good breakfast is included in the price and there's a guest kitchen. The second branch, on Malaya Morskaya, has four twin rooms plus shared kitchen for the same price, but with the additional bonus of air-conditioning.

Just a few minutes' walk from the Hermitage and with views of the River Moika, ***Hotel 3 Mosta*** **Гостиница 3 Моста** (наб Реки Мойки 3a, nab Reki Moiki 3a, ☎ 332 3470, 💻 http://3mosta.com, doubles R3000-8000) has several elegant, comfortable rooms with large-screen plasma TVs, free wi-fi and air-conditioning. Fresh flowers are a nice touch.

Palantin **Палантин** (Рижский пр 4-6, Rizhskiy pr 4-6, **M** Baltiiskaya, ☎ 607 7763, 💻 www.palantinhotel.ru, sgl/dbl/suite R2700/3300/3700), 50m to the south, distinguishes itself with its quiet yet convenient location, excellent beds, and pretty little balconies in most rooms, while the superior rooms boast Jacuzzis. The rate includes a good buffet breakfast and wi-fi.

B&B Assembly **Мини-отель Ассамблея** (ул Садовая 32/1 кв 170, ul Sadovaya 32/1 apt 170, **M** Sadovaya, ☎ 571 8311, 💻 nata204@hotmail.com, room with shared bathroom/en suite R1525/2070) has a homey atmosphere and only four rooms.All the rooms are comfortable; three of them share a bathroom. The effusive English-speaking owner, Natalia, can assist with your travel/sightseeing needs. The paintings in the living rooms are all by local artists and are for sale; the fully equipped guest kitchen is perfect for impromptu group dinners.

Upmarket hotels The rates quoted here are for the high season and include 18% VAT, but confirm this whenever you're quoted a price.

Anyone who was anyone in the 19th century stayed either at the Astoria or the Yevropeyskaya (now Grand Hotel Europe). The guestbook at the Rocco Forte-owned ***Hotel Astoria*** **Гостиница Астория** (ул Большая Морская 39, ul Bolshaya Morskaya 39, **M** Nevsky Prospekt, ☎ 494 5757, 💻 www.thehotelastoria.com) features writers, artists and actors in endless streams of great names. All natural materials are used in the design of the fully equipped bedrooms, facilities include a superb spa and the interior boasts stunning original marble work, such as the Winter Garden. It's a thoroughly excellent five-star hotel with dbls/suites from R36,000/51,000.

Grand Hotel Europe **Гранд Отель Европа** (ул Михайловская 1/7, ul Mikhailovskaya 1/7, **M** Nevsky Prospekt, ☎ 329 6000, 💻 www.grandhoteleurope.com; dbls/suites cost from R19,000/39,000)

The St Petersburg area code is ☎ 812. From outside Russia dial ☎ +7-812.

lives up to its name. Housed in a palatial building, this ultra-elegant hotel features original art deco detailing, extremely comfortable beds, and no fewer than five top-notch restaurants on the premises, including the bustling Caviar Bar. The guest list has included heads of state and the crowned heads of Europe; the service is so good it's almost worth the breathtaking prices.

Close to St Isaac's and the Hermitage, ***Casa Leto*** **Каса Лето** (ул Большая Морская 34, ul Bolshaya Morkaya 34, **M** Nevsky Prospekt, ☎ 600 1096, 💻 www.casaleto.com; sgl/dbl R8500/11,000) is a stylish boutique hotel run by an English-Italian couple, with amenities such as internet, international calls and refreshments included in the rate. There are five large, comfortable rooms and the personalised service adds to the luxurious experience.

Where to eat and drink

St Petersburg boasts a dining scene to rival that of any cosmopolitan European city.

Restaurants At the upper end of the spectrum for quality and price is ***Palkin*** **Палкин** (Невский пр 47, Nevsky pr 47, **M** Gostinny Dvor, ☎ 703 5371, mains R1500), putting a contemporary spin on the 'aristocratic cuisine' that melded French influences with traditional Russian recipes in the 18th and 19th centuries. The seasonally changing five-course special menu makes for a superb splurge. At ***Russkaya Charka*** **Русская Чарка** (наб Реки Фонтанки 92, nab Reki Fontanki 92, **M** Pushkinskaya, mains R300) you can enjoy Russian peasant fare such as hearty soups, blini, pies and meat dishes, washed down with an unusual horseradish vodka.

For upmarket 19th-century Russian cuisine head to ***Mechta Molokhovets*** **Мечта Молоховец** (ул Радищева 10, ul Radisheva 10, **M** Ploshchad Vosstaniya, ☎ 579 2247, mains R1000, [V]), where baronial dishes are prepared according to Elena Molokhovets's famous cookbook. Only the freshest ingredients are used and the fish dishes, such as the sturgeon, are particularly superb. ***Teplo*** **Тепло** (which means 'warmth', ул Большая Морская 45, ul Bolshaya Morskaya 45, **M** Sennaya Ploshchad, mains R350) has a warm atmosphere to match its name, wonderful service, and delicious pies, breads and meat dishes.

Named after the hero of Dostoyevsky's novel, ***Idiot*** **Идиот** (наб Реки Мойки 82, nab Reki Moiki 82, **M** Sadovaya, mains R500, [V]) serves a selection of traditional Russian and vegetarian dishes in a cosy, jokey Bohemian-intellectual basement with antique furniture.

For superb Georgian food go to ***Sakartvelo*** **Сакартвело** (100m to the west, 12-я Линия 13, 12-ya Liniya 13, **M** Vasileostrovskaya, mains R350, [V]) where the shashlyk is truly superb, there are 12 kinds of *khachapuri* (bread with cheese and other toppings) and the homemade wine is served in bowls. Also wonderful is ***Aragvi*** **Арагви** (наб Реки Фонтанки, nab Reki Fontanki 9, **M** Gostinny Dvor, mains R400, [V]), with its outstanding *lobio* (bean salad), tasty *satsivi* (chicken in walnut sauce), pork shashlyk and – for the more adventurous – sheep's brains braised with tomato and coriander.

Mops **Мопс** (ул Рубинштейна 12, ul Rubinsteina 12, **M** Mayakovskaya, mains R600, [V]) should not be missed by anyone who appreciates great Thai food; all dishes, including the spring rolls, dumplings and soups, are exquisitely flavoured, there's a great selection of rice, noodle and curry dishes and the toilets resemble a spa.

Tandoor **Тандур** (Вознесенский пр 2/10, Voznesensky pr 2/10, **M** Sadovaya, mains R500, [V]), the recipient of multiple 'best restaurant' prizes, serves authentic, spicy Indian food. If you're after quality Chinese food, ***Chopsticks*** (ул Михаиловская 1/7, ul Mikhailovskaya 1/7, **M** Nevsky Prospekt, mains R800) serves beautifully prepared, authentic dishes amidst elegant surroundings. The service is equally superb.

The Mexican-themed ***Tres Amigos*** (ул Рубинштейна 25, ul Rubinsteina 25, **M** Dostoyevskaya, mains R450) has an extensive list of cocktails and tequila, the dishes are properly spicy and the fresh guacamole particularly tasty, though the service can be hit-and-miss. ***Palermo*** **Палермо** (наб Реки Фонтанки 50, nab Reki Fontanki 50,

M Gostinny Dvor, mains R600) is an intimate, upmarket Italian restaurant serving excellent seafood and meat dishes, homemade pasta and salads – all made from the freshest ingredients.

Despite its not-so-central location, ***Botanika*** **Ботаника** (ул Пестелья 7, ul Pestelya 7, **M** Chernishevskaya, mains R300, [V]) is well worth seeking out for its great vegetarian food: fresh salads (including tabouleh), hearty soups and delicious homemade pasta.

Cafés and snacks Nevsky pr is lined with **fast-food** outlets – Pizza Hut, KFC, Subway and the rest. The American chain ***Carl's Junior*** (ул Малая Садовая 8, ul Malaya Sadovaya 8, **M** Nevsky Prospekt, Литейный пр 47, Liteyny pr 47, **M** Mayakovskaya, and Сенная пл 9, Sennaya pl 9, **M** Sadovaya, meal R150) stands out for the size and quality of its burgers.

Teremok **Теремок** (Невский пр 93, Nevsky pr 93, **M** Nevsky Prospekt, meal R100, [V]) serves blini with a myriad of sweet and savoury fillings, as well as porridge dishes, fish soup and beer on tap. In all it has 35 locations around the city. Also known for its blini, the ***Chaynaya Lozhka*** **Чайная Ложка** chain (Невский пр 44, Nevsky pr 44, **M** Nevsky Prospekt, meal R100, [V]) has good salads and an extensive selection of teas. Also at ул Восстания 13, ul Vosstaniya 13, **M** Ploshchad Vosstaniya, and other locations. ***Garcon*** **Гарсон** (Невский пр 103, Nevsky pr 103, **M** Ploshchad Vosstaniya, [V]) is a delightful French-style bakery serving good coffee along with its sublime bread creations. The almond croissants are particularly good.

Cherdak Khudozhnika **Чердак Художника** (Artist's Attic, ул Ломлносова 1/28, ul Lomonosova 1/28, **M** Nevsky Prospekt) is a minuscule roof terrace with funky furniture, particularly great for milkshakes and cocktails in summer. Walk through the glass design shop to find it. Particularly known for its sandwiches, ***Charlotte Café*** (ул Казанская 2, ul Kazanskaya 2, **M** Nevsky Prospekt, [V]) is a chilled-out spot that doubles as a deli where you can enjoy the salads and cakes on the lovely covered terrace or get a takeaway.

With several branches around the city, ***Stolle Café*** **Кафе Штолле** (Конюшенный пер 1/6, Konyushenny per 1/6, **M** Nevsky Prospekt, [V]) is justifiably popular for its pies, with fillings as varied as fruit, mushrooms, meat and fish, as well as good coffee, served in a Viennese café ambience. Another great spot for coffee is ***Coffee Shop Company*** (ул Малая Садовая 3, ul Malaya Sadovaya 3, **M** Nevsky Prospekt, [V]) with its bright interior and expensive but good milkshake and cake selection.

Self-catering Self-caterers shouldn't miss **Sennoi Market Сенной Рынок** (Московский пр 4a, Moskovsky pr 4a, **M** Sennaya Ploshchad, 8am-8pm in summer), an excellent place where you can buy anything from fresh fruit to half a cow at a reasonable price. More expensive, but well-stocked, is the basement **Supermarket Passazh Пассаж** (Невский пр 48, Nevsky pr 48, **M** Nevsky Prospekt, 10am-10pm), which has a lot of Western products and an extensive alcohol section.

Bars and nightlife

Shamrock (ул Декабристов 27, ul Dekabristov 27, **M** Sadovaya) is popular with Russians and expats alike thanks to its beer selection and excellent pub food. It is particularly lively during football matches and there's live music nightly. The German food at ***Grad Petrov*** **Град Петров**

> **❑ Don't drink the water!**
> Avoid St Petersburg's tap water at all costs (including ice in your drinks and for brushing your teeth) as it may be infected with *giardia*, a particularly nasty parasite which can cause stomach cramps, nausea and an unpleasant and persistent form of diarrhoea. Buy bottled water and stick to fresh fruit that you can peel.

(Университетская наб 5, Universitetskaya nab 5, **M** Vasileostrovskaya) is as good as its beer; it brews Hefe-Weizen, Dunkel, Lager and Pilsner in-house to classic Bavarian methods and it's even possible to arrange a tour with the brewmaster.

Catering to Beatles' fans, ***Liverpool* Ливерпуль** (ул Маяковского 16, ul Mayakovskogo 16, **M** Ploshchad Vosstaniya) hosts nightly live bands, and though the beer isn't the cheapest, the lively crowd of regulars adds to the atmosphere.

One of the best drinking venues in town, the English ***Pickwick Pub*** (ул Рулеева 6, ul Ryleeva 6, **M** Chernyshevskaya) draws the punters with its attractive, cosy interior with a fireplace, 20 beers on tap, premiership football on TV and friendly service. A great place to linger over a drink is the welcoming American-owned ***The Other Side*** (ул Большая Конюшенная 1, ul Bolshaya Konyushennaya 1, **M** Nevsky Prospekt), its menu offering a more exotic blend of Thai, Chinese and Mexican than your average bar menu.

With its authentic pub atmosphere, ***Dickens*** (наб Реки Фонтанки 108, nab Reki Fontanki 108, **M** Sennaya Ploshchad) serves beer from all over the world as well as a superb selection of whiskies. The restaurant on the 2nd floor serves large portions of excellent pub food amidst candlelit tables and massive oil paintings.

Hide in one of the nooks and crannies to sip your cocktail at ***Bardak* Бардак** (ул Гривцова 11, ul Grivtsova 11, **M** Sennaya Ploshchad), or join the well-heeled clientele at the more upmarket *Sex and the City*-esque ***Daiquiri Bar*** (ул Большая Конюшенная 1, ul Bolshaya Konyushennaya 1, **M** Nevsky Prospekt), where friendly staff serve over 250 cocktails (the daiquiris are best).

Clubs ***Dacha* Дача** (ул Думская 9, ul Dumskaya 9, **M** Gostinny Dvor, R100) is a café by day and raucous, smoky nightspot by night, with people dancing in what little space there is. Open until 6am.

The punk, ska and hardcore scene thrives at gritty ***Fish Fabrique*** (Лиговский пер 53, Ligovsky per 53, **M** Ploshchad Vosstaniya, R100-500), while the new branch next door, ***Fish Fabrique Nouvelle***, hosts rock and alternative concerts within a peachy interior.

Nearby ***Griboyedov*** (50m to the south, ул Воронежская 2a, ul Voronezhskaya 2a, **M** Ploshchad Vosstaniya, R300 after 8pm), a converted bomb shelter, plays electronica, drum'n'bass, house and alternative, and there is nightly live music at ***Griboyedov Hill***, its café-bar extension with a lovely terrace.

Purga I* Пурга 1** (наб Реки Фонтанки 11, nab Reki Fontanki 11, **M** Mayakovskaya, R100-300) is kitsch fun, with the Soviet New Year celebrated nightly, complete with countdown and mock TV addresses by Soviet leaders, while ***Purga II* Пурга 2**, next door, holds mock weddings where you can dress up as brides and grooms. The two attractions are combined on the ***Purga Party Boat in summer, the boat departing from nab Reki Fontanki 21 at 11.20pm (R500).

***Dali Café* Дали Кафе** (Спасский пер 11, Spassky per 11, **M** Sennaya Ploshchad, R400) is a gay-friendly chillout lounge with interestingly named dishes, cabaret shows Mon-Wed and drag shows the rest of the week.

Inside the former Soviet Culture Palace, ***Cabaret*** (400m to the south, наб Обводного Канала 181, nab Obvodnogo Kanala 181, **M** Baltiiskaya, R100-400) hosts lively transvestite shows at 2.30am; women are welcome here Fri-Sun only. ***XXXX Bar*** (3-я ул Советская 34, 3-ya Sovetskaya 34, **M** Ploshchad Vosstaniya) gets particularly lively at weekends where

❏ Face control

Though by no means an unknown concept in European and American nightclubs, this practice is particularly prevalent in Moscow and St Petersburg. 'Face control' means: 'If you're not dressed right and/or you're not good-looking enough, you're not coming in.'

you might encounter impromptu dancing on the bar and strip competitions. Face control (see box opposite) and dress code apply and there may be an entry charge.

Nightly rockabilly music attracts a young, rowdy crowd to ***Money Honey*** (Апраскин Двор 13, Apraskin Dvor 13, **M** Sennaya Ploshchad, R100-250), including regulars dressed as cowboys, while ***Marstall*** (наб Канала Грибоедова 5, nab Kanala Griboyedova 5, **M** Nevsky Prospekt) is particularly popular with expats and international students, attracted by a mix of dance, house and erotic shows. Show your passport to get a discount.

The ***Jimi Hendrix Blues Club*** (Литейный пр 33, Liteyny pr 33, **M** Mayakovskaya, ☎ 579 8813, R200-250) hosts excellent nightly blues by local musicians; it's well worth booking a table here to enjoy the freshly prepared Russian and Georgian dishes.

Cultural life

The classical season is from September until the end of June; in July and August all of St Petersburg's main companies go on holiday or on tour, though some performances are still staged by lesser ensembles.

Mariinsky Opera and Ballet Theatre (Teatralnaya pl 1, **M** Sadovaya, ☎ 326 4141, 💻 www.mariinsky.ru), with its sublime interior, is where the world-famous Kirov Ballet and Opera company perform. You can purchase tickets on their website for performances here and at the new concert hall on ul Pisareva 20, known for its superb acoustics. Performances at **Mikhailovsky Opera and Ballet Theatre** (pl Isskusktv 1, **M** Nevsky Prospekt, ☎ 595 4319, 💻 www.mikhailovsky.ru), a splendidly restored imperial theatre, rival those at the Mariinsky. You can hear the renowned St Petersburg Philharmonic Symphony Orchestra either at the large concert hall at **St Petersburg State Philharmonia** (ul Mikhailovskaya 2, **M** Gostinny Dvor, ☎ 710 4257, 💻 www.philharmonia.spb.ru), or the smaller Maly Zal imeni Glinki (Nevsky pr 30, **M** Nevsky Prospekt, ☎ 571 8333) – two venues where ticket prices put world-class music within reach of even the budget traveller.

Tickets for most concerts and theatres (though not the Mariinsky) can be bought at the central **Teatralnaya Kassa** Театральная Касса (theatre tickets kiosk), Nevsky pr 42. See also box p75.

Shopping

Try **Anglia Book Shop** Книжный магазин Англия (nab Reki Fontanki 38, **M** Nevsky Prospekt) for the widest range of English-language books in the city, as well as five other European languages. It also stocks a variety of books on Russian history and culture.

For nifty souvenirs, head for **Nevsky Souvenir** (Nevsky pr 3, **M** Nevsky Prospekt), where you can pick up Fabergé-style eggs, lacquered boxes, Russian string instruments and chess boards. The helpful English-speaking staff are happy to assist.

Moving on

By air St Petersburg is served by most major European airlines as well as local carrier Pulkovo Aviation; there are daily flights to London, Berlin, Helsinki, Prague and Warsaw and regular weekly flights to most other European capitals. Most international flights land at Pulkovo 2 while domestic flights use Pulkovo 1 (see p148).

Tickets for most airlines can be purchased at the **Central Air Ticket Office** Центральная Авиакасса (Nevsky pr 7/9, **M** Nevsky Prospekt, 8am-8pm Mon-Fri, to 6pm Sat & Sun), where you can also purchase train and international bus tickets.

By train Intercity train timetables are available at all stations and you can check timetables at 💻 www.poezda.net, and 💻 www.rzd.ru (in Russian only). Tickets for same-day departure can only be purchased at the station of departure, at the 'same-day' window (*sutochnaya* суточная) or service centre. Buying last-minute tickets from speculators is risky because of the name-on-ticket/passport rule. Advance-purchase long-distance and international tickets can be bought from the departure station or from the **Central Train Ticket Office** Центральная Железнодорожная Касса (nab Kanala Griboyedova 24, **M** Nevsky

❑ TRAIN SERVICES FROM ST PETERSBURG

St Petersburg to other Russian cities

Destination	Train name & No	Journey time	Dep time & station	Arrival time
Irkutsk	*Baikal* 009/010	35hrs 44mins	16:22, Ladozhsky	04:06*
Kaliningrad	079	26hrs 12mins	18:15, Vitebsky	20:27
Nizhny Novgorod	*Sapsan* 175/176	8hrs 05mins	15:15, Moskovsky	23:20
Yekaterinburg	072	37hrs 31mins	17:04, Ladozhsky	06:35

*= odd-numbered days only

St Petersburg to other European cities

***Note**: The arrival time indicated is Local Time rather than Moscow Time.*

Destin-ation	Train name & No	Journey time	Dep time & station	Arr time	Frequency
Berlin	019	30hrs 10mins	23:59, Vitebsky	09:09	Mon-Thur & Sat, June-Sep
Brest	049	18hrs 21mins	15:03, Vitebsky	08:24	daily
Helsinki	*Allegro* 151/30	3hrs 36mins	06:40, Finlyandsky	09:16	
Helsinki	*Allegro* 155/36	3hrs 36mins	15:25, Finlyandsky	18:01	
Helsinki	*Repin* 033	5hrs 18mins	07:17, Finlyandsky	12:35	
Helsinki	*Sibelius* 035	5hrs 18mins	16:30, Finlyandsky	21:48	
Kyiv	001	7hrs 42mins	23:17	06:59	
Odessa	019	35hrs 17mins	23:59	10:16	Mon, Wed, Fri
Prague	049	40hrs 02mins	15:03	05:05	daily except Sun
Riga	037	12hrs 05mins	20:55	09:00	daily
Vilnius	091	13hrs 20mins	20:55	09:15	daily
Warsaw	019	28hrs 01mins	23:59	06:00	Mon-Thur & Sat June-Sept, less frequently Oct-Dec

Prospekt, 8am-8pm Mon-Sat, to 4pm Sun). You'll need your passport; your name and passport number will printed on the ticket. To avoid the crowds there is a little-used window in the Central Air Ticket Office (see 'Moving on by air') that sells rail tickets.

If you plan to return to Europe you may pass through Belarus or Ukraine. **Belarus** requires visas from almost every visitor and it can take three days to get one, so check your proposed route carefully.

Check your ticket to see which station you depart from. Trains are usually available for boarding 30 minutes before leaving. They rarely depart late and have been known to roll out of the station a few minutes ahead of schedule. Don't underestimate the time it takes to walk the length of a 16-carriage train!

By bus Both the fairly rundown domestic buses and the plusher international coaches depart from the main bus station, Avtovokzal No 2 (see p148; nab Obvodnogo kanala 36, **M** Ligovsky Pr), though some Eurolines buses may leave from their office at **M** Baltiiskaya, where you can also buy tickets. Sample departures from Avtovokzal include: Moscow (several daily, 12hrs, R1500), Tallinn (6/day, 7½hrs, R1300), Helsinki (2/day, 8hrs, R2200) and Riga (2/day, 11hrs, R1200). Tickets for all departures can be purchased from Avtovokzal or the Central Air Ticket Office (see p157).

❑ TRAIN SERVICES BETWEEN ST PETERSBURG AND MOSCOW

The arrow-straight 650km railway between Moscow and St Petersburg is Russia's busiest and most prestigious line, and high standards are maintained in terms of both facilities and service. When it was opened in 1851 the average travel time was 25 hours, whereas now, the high-speed *Sapsan* (at least 6/day) takes around four hours.

There are about two dozen trains a day in each direction. Many travellers prefer an overnight journey as it saves accommodation costs and leaves more time for sight-seeing, though few can resist the *Sapsan*. The firmenny *Smena A Bentakur, Severnaya Palmira* and *Ekspress* have an all-night restaurant service. First-class passengers get a packed lunch (daytime trains) or breakfast (overnight trains).

If you buy a ticket yourself, a berth in a two-berth cabin (*SV*) on an overnight firmenny train costs R4279-6039; in a four-berth cabin (*kupé*) it's R1897-3200, and third class (*platzkartny*) is R1250. Non-firmenny train tickets cost a little less. *Sapsan* fares are typically from R2612 for *kupé* and from R5058 for *SV*; prices go up on Fridays but are cheaper on Sundays.

See box p193 for services from Moscow to St Petersburg.

St Petersburg to Moscow

Train name	No	Journey time	Departure time	Arrival time
Severnaya Palmira	027	9hrs	22:40	07:40*
Ekspress	003	8hrs 01mins	23:59	08:00
Smena A Bentakur	025	8hrs 17mins	22:55	07:12
Krasnaya Strela	001	8hrs	23:55	07:55
Dve Stolitsy	063	7hrs	23:35	06:35
Sapsan	151	3hrs 45mins	06:45	10:30
Sapsan	153	3hrs 55mins	07:00	10:55
Sapsan	157	4hrs 15mins	13:30	17:45
Sapsan	175	4hrs	15:30	19:25
Sapsan	165	3hrs 54mins	19:55	23:19

**= even-numbered days only*

***= arrives at Kursky vokzal in Moscow instead of Leningradsky*

Moscow
Москва

This will either be the start or the end of your journey. All railway lines in Russia lead to the capital so you'll be spending some time here, even if it's just a quick visit to Red Square as you change stations. Moscow is so much more than that, however. It's a vast, overwhelming, cosmopolitan city that never seems to sleep and which has boundless energy. Almost all the resounding changes that have taken place in the country have been initiated here. If you're looking for the pulse of the new Russia, this is where you'll find it. Moscow is perhaps more uncompromisingly Russian than any other city, and if you're heading east, you might be exhausted by it after a few days, and relieved to be departing after getting your fill of the sights and sounds, and if you're arriving from the east, you may well be drawn to the glitz, the food, the pulsing nightlife and the rich cultural life.

Moscow's historic sights alone make it a fascinating place to explore; bank on a minimum of three days to see the main attractions. Besides the revered historical locations, such as the Kremlin and the Tretyakov Gallery, these days, Moscow boasts cutting-edge modern art galleries and other attractions that would have been inconceivable in Soviet times, such as the Gulag History Museum that sheds light on Russia's troubled 20th-century history.

Long gone are the queues for basic essentials and food staples; Moscow is now brimming with sushi bars, restaurants serving every cuisine imaginable and shopping centres stocked full of international goods – all for those who can afford it. At night, there are innumerable clubs, blues bars, arts cafés and bare-bones drinking dives clamouring for your attention.

Finding a place to stay, whatever your budget, is not a problem and the metro makes getting around easy. Take your time exploring Moscow, for Russia is famous for its rapid changes and you may not find the same city the next time you're here.

HISTORY

The archaeological record shows that the Moscow area has been inhabited since Neolithic times. However, the first written mention of the city was not until 1147, when Prince Yuri Dolgoruki founded the city by building a wooden fort beside the Moskva River, in the principality of Vladimir. The settlement which grew up around the fort soon developed into a major trading centre.

The Mongols

Disaster struck the Russian principalities in the early 13th century in the form of the Mongol invasion. Moscow was razed to the ground in 1238 and for the next 250 years was obliged to pay an annual tribute to the Mongol Khan. But in 1326 Moscow was made seat of the Russian Orthodox Church, a role carrying with it the title of capital of Russia. Prince Dmitry Donskoi strengthened the city's defences, built a stone wall around the Kremlin and in 1380 defeated a Mongol-Tatar army at Kulikovo. But it was not until 1476 that tributes to the Khan ceased.

The years of growth

The reign of Ivan III 'The Great' (1462-1505) was a period of intensive construction in the city. Italian architects were commissioned to redesign the Kremlin, and many cathedrals and churches date from this period. Prosperity continued into the 16th century under Ivan IV 'The Terrible'; it was at this time that St Basil's Cathedral was built.

The early 17th century was a time of civil disorder, and a peasant uprising culminated in the invasion of Moscow by Polish and Lithuanian forces. When they were driven out in 1612 the city was again burnt to the ground. Rebuilt in stone, by the end of the 17th century Moscow became Russia's most important trading city. It remained a major economic and cultural centre even after Peter the Great transferred the capital to St Petersburg in 1712.

The last sacking of the city occurred in 1812 when Napoleon invaded Russia. Muscovites, seeing the invasion as inevitable, torched their own city rather than let Napoleon have it (Tolstoy describes Count Bezukhkov being arrested as an arsonist in *War and Peace,* his semi-fictionalised account of the campaign). But recovery was swift and trade increased after the abolition of serfdom in 1861.

Revolution

Towards the end of the 19th century Moscow became a revolutionary centre, its factories hit by a series of strikes and riots. Michael Myres Shoemaker, who was here in 1903, wrote in *The Great Siberian Railway from St Petersburg to Peking*: 'Up to the present day the dissatisfaction has arisen from the middle classes especially the students, but now for the first time in Russia's history it is spreading downward to the peasants... but it will be a century at least before that vast inert mass awakens to life.' But in 1905 there was an armed uprising, and 12 years later 'that vast inert mass' stormed the Kremlin and established Soviet power in the city. The subsequent civil war saw terrible food shortages and great loss of life.

The capital once more

In March 1918 Lenin transferred the government back to Moscow. In the years between the two world wars the city embarked on an ambitious programme of industrial development, and by 1939 the population had doubled to four million. During WWII many factories in the European part of the USSR were relocated across the Urals, a wise move in retrospect. By October 1941 the German army had surrounded the city (getting as close as the present-day site of Sheremetyevo airport) and the two-month Siege of Moscow began.

Moscow was rebuilt following the war, growing in size, grandeur and power. But by the late 1980s services had started to collapse under Gorbachev's reforms and the breakdown of Communist power. The years following the 1991 disintegration of the Soviet Union was a time when little worked in the city and roads, buildings and public utilities were continually on the verge of collapse.

Moscow today

The USSR has gone but the Soviet habit of centralised decision-making and financial control remains intact, and has made Moscow vastly wealthier than any other city in Russia. Average wages are six to twenty times higher than those in even moderate Siberian cities, which is a source of resentment elsewhere in Russia, as the capital is seen to be bleeding the country dry. But even here remnants of the past coexist incongruously with the elegant shops, restaurants and offices of the 'new Russians'. Lenin's description of 19th-century London as 'two nations living in one city' has become true of Moscow itself.

But the city's pugnacious former mayor, Yury Luzhkov, ensured that those who can afford to pay were made to (while he and his wife – Russia's wealthiest woman – reaped huge financial benefits themselves) and enormous infrastructure projects have gone ahead with little help from the central government. On September 28, 2010, after 18 years in office, Luzhkov was finally sacked by Medvedev with Putin's blessing after Luzhkov had overstepped himself, repeatedly criticising Medvedev in print and believing himself to be more important that the president.

The recent boost to Russia's economy from record-high oil prices has yet to trickle down to everyday people, and many blame the city itself for the country's continuing economic malaise, complaining of a 'robber baron' state in which compliance with impossible regulations can only be achieved by paying off the city officials who uphold them. Yeltsin-era Prime Minister Yevgeny Primakov once noted glumly that 'any new business wishing to open must obtain 57 different authorisations – and we all know that not one of them can be had for the official fee'.

Your Trans-Siberian co-passengers will doubtless include some of Russia's luckless thousands taking a trip to the capital to pay a fortune in bribes for permission to build a Scout hut in Bryansk or lease horses to tourists in the Altai Mountains. Yet many Russians dream of relocating to the capital's bright lights and high incomes. Fewer than half its residents were actually born here.

Visitors, happily, can only benefit from Moscow's luck. No other Russian city offers the enormous range of cultural heritage, entertainment, hotels, dining, nightlife and shopping that Moscow has pilfered from the rest of the country since the 13th century.

WHAT TO SEE AND DO

The Kremlin area (see map p165)

Red Square (Krasnaya ploshchad, Красная Площадь) This grand cobbled square, the heart of the city, extends across the area beside the north-eastern wall of the Kremlin. On most days, you'll find it teeming with crowds of sightseers, and rightly so: it's surrounded by some of the city's top attractions: St Basil's Cathedral, the State History Museum, Lenin's Mausoleum, the GUM shopping arcade and the Kremlin. The square has always been the venue for military parades, celebrations and executions. The name derives from the red cobblestones first laid when the stinking city market was cleared away from the Kremlin's walls in the 16th century. The name has nothing to do with Communism or the colour 'red'; in old Russian, 'krasny' meant 'beautiful' and has only come to mean 'red' fairly recently.

Lenin's Mausoleum Мавзолей В И Ленина Built onto the side of the Kremlin in 1930, the red granite mausoleum (**M** Ploshchad Revolutsii or Okhotny Ryad, Tue-Thur and Sat & Sun 10am-1pm) and its mummified occupant were the centre of a personality cult that flourished for almost 70 years. Nowadays Lenin and his mausoleum continues to draw the crowds, with tourists queueing up to file past the embalmed body, laid out in dark suit and tie. The **body** is the real thing and not a waxwork, contrary to rumours. Talking is not allowed and guards will move you along if you dawdle. The one-way route,

Mummification for the masses

A few years ago the Centre for Biological Researches, responsible for the preservation of Lenin's body, announced the offer of full mummification services to anyone for a mere US$300,000. Previous clients are a testimony to their skill. An independent team of embalmers recently inspected Lenin's corpse and declared it to be in perfect condition.

After Lenin's death from a massive stroke on 21 January 1924, at the age of 53, an autopsy was carried out and a full report published in *Pravda*, treating the public to the weights and measurements of their dead leader's internal organs. Then the embalmers began their work. Boris Zbarsky, a biochemist, and Vladimir Vorobyov, an anatomist, were given the task of preserving the Communist leader's body as a sacred relic and they managed to find a way to stop the decaying process. The embalming process was kept secret until the fall of Communism, when Zbarsky's son, who took over from his father, admitted that the body is 'spruced up' every 18 months by being submerged in a tub of chemicals.

Lenin's brain (1340g, far larger than average, of course) was removed and placed in a specially founded Institute of Lenin's Brain, where scientists analysed deep-frozen micro-slices in an attempt to discover the secret of his greatness. The Institute was quietly closed in the 1960s and any discoveries it had made went unpublished.

The debate over what to do with Lenin continues, with liberal politicians suggesting that Russia should bury its past and allow Lenin's body to rest beside his mother's in St Petersburg, as was his wish, and Communists arguing that to move him now would be a denial of the country's history. Putin left this poisoned chalice to his successor when he announced a moratorium on any decision until 2012.

which also features the Tombs of Soviet Heroes (including Yury Gagarin) in the Kremlin walls, emerges at St Basil's Cathedral.

The mausoleum was Stalin's idea, and the deceased Stalin lay beside Lenin until his legacy was reassessed by Khrushchev. The tomb's design is the work of one AV Shchusev, who saw the cube, like the pyramid, as a symbol of eternity and envisaged every Soviet home having its own little cube to the memory of the dead leader.

The long queue moves along quickly, but make sure you leave your bags and cameras in the storage lockers provided before going through the metal detector.

St Basil's Cathedral **Собор Василия Блаженного** Also known as the Church of the Saviour (11am-5.30pm, closed Tue, adult/student R200/100, camera R100), the most recognised building in Russia is as much a symbol of Moscow as Tower Bridge is of London. It was commissioned by Ivan the Terrible to celebrate his victory over the Tatars, and completed in 1561. So pleased was Ivan with the result that, according to legend, he had the architect's eyes put out so that he could never produce anything to equal or surpass it.

The cathedral is named after a holy hermit known as Basil the Simpleton, who dressed year-round in a loincloth, begging and sleeping in the street outside. Basil proved less of a simpleton when he denounced Tsar Boris Godunov as the murderer of the rightful ruler, Ivan the Terrible's weakling son Dmitry.

St Basil's is a quite incredible building, with its nine brightly painted, dissimilar domes and stonework decorated with intricate patterns more usually found on the wooden buildings of the time. Its painted interiors were burnt off when Napoleon used it as a stable. The domes' paintwork dates from the 18th century. Outside the cathedral is a statue of Kuzma Minin and Prince Dmitry Pozharsky, who saved Russia from the Polish-Lithuanian invasion in the early 17th century. Inside, the cathedral is a warren of tiny chapels and spiral staircases – a shock after seeing the grand open spaces of Russia's other cathedrals.

GUM The remarkable glass-roofed GUM shopping arcade (pronounced 'goom', an acronym for *Generalny Universalny Magazin*) was constructed in 1894 on the site of a covered market which was torn down as a health hazard. It was nationalised after the Revolution and turned into a huge department store, a monument to Soviet shortages. Now the Western chains have moved in and turned it into a shopping mall for the wealthy.

State History Museum Государственный Исторический Музей This museum (**M** Teatralnaya, 10am-6pm Tue-Sat, 11am-7pm Sun, closed Mon, adult/student R250/130, audioguide R300) is at the north end of Red Square. Extensive collections – from relics from the Middle Ages to a grand portrait gallery educating you as to who is who in Russian aristocracy – cover the history of the country up to 1917. The red palatial building, each of its rooms decorated in the style of a different period, is worth seeing in itself. It now houses the contents from the former Lenin Museum and you can get a joint admission ticket that takes in St Basil's Cathedral at either location. There's a lack of English information on the second floor, so an audioguide enhances the experience.

Tomb of the Unknown Soldier Могила Неизвестного Солдата It is traditional for newlyweds to visit this monument in the Aleksandrovsky Gardens (the former Kremlin moat) to be photographed beside its eternal flame. Beneath the marble lies the body of one of the soldiers who helped to stop the German advance on Moscow in 1941. The blood-red marble caskets beside the flame contain soil from Soviet 'Hero-Cities' (those with the greatest number of WWII dead). The honour guard which once stood watch at Lenin's Mausoleum now stands here, with a goose-stepping Changing of the Guard every hour.

The Kremlin Кремль The heart of Moscow, the seat of the Russian government, and formerly the centre of the Orthodox Church, the Kremlin (**M** Aleksandrovsky Sad, 💻 www.kreml.ru, 10am-6pm May-Sept, until 5pm rest of the year, closed Thur), is in fact a large walled citadel with the golden domes of the churches peeking from above the red brick walls. Although the site has been continuously occupied for at least eight centuries, the present walls and many of the cathedrals inside date from the 15th century. There are 20 towers, the most famous being the **Saviour (Spassky) Clock-Tower** above Red Square, and assorted buildings ranging from Romanov imperial classicism to 1960s Soviet modernism in style. Though parts of the Kremlin are out of bounds for

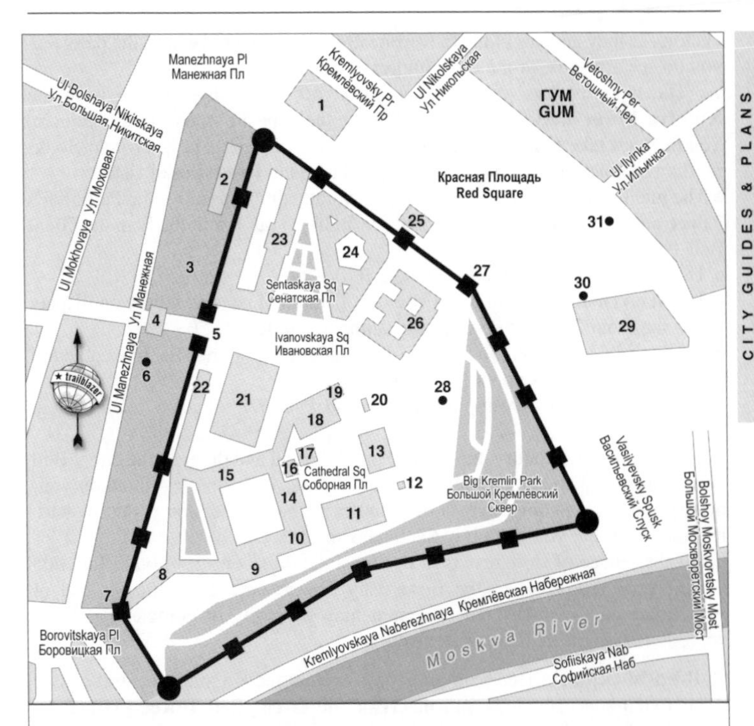

Moscow Kremlin Московский Кремль

1 State History Museum Государтвенный Исторический Музей
2 Tomb of the Unknown Soldier Могила Неизвестного Солдата
3 Aleksandrovsky Gardens Александровский Сад
4 Kutafya Tower Башня Кутафья
5 Trinity Tower Троицкая Башня
6 Ticket Office Кассы
7 Borovitskaya Tower Entrance Боровицкая Башня
8 Armoury Chamber Оружейная Палата
9 Great Kremlin Palace Большой Кремлёвский Дворец
10 Cathedral of the Annunciation Благовещенский Собор
11 Cathedral of the Archangel Michael Архангельский Собор
12 Tsar Bell Царь Колокол
13 Bell Tower of Ivan the Great Колокольня Ивана Великого
14 Facetted Chamber Грановитая Палата
15 Teremnoy Palace Теремной Дворец
16 Church of the Deposition of the Robe Черковь Ризоположения
17 Cathedral of the Assumption Успенский Собор
18 Patriach's Palace Патриарший Дворец
19 Church of the Twelve Apostles Церковь Двенадцати Апостолов
20 Tsar Cannon Царь Пушка
21 Palace of Congress Конгресс Дворец
22 Poteshny Palace Потешный Дворец
23 Arsenal Арсенал
24 Senate Сенат
25 Lenin's Mausoleum Мавзолей В И Ленина
26 Supreme Soviet Верхвный Совет
27 Spasskaya Tower Спасская Башня
28 Lenin Memorial Памятник Ленину
29 St Basil's Cathedral Собор Василия Блаженного
30 Minin & Pozharsky Memorial Памятник Минину и Пожарскому
31 Place of Executions Лобное Место

visitors, as they are part of the Government and Presidential estate, the parts that you do see are some of the most impressive in Russia.

The main visitors' entrance and ticket office for the Kremlin is in the **Kutafya Tower** in Aleksandrovsky Park, on the opposite side from Red Square. You may not take large bags or rucksacks inside (there is a pay-per-item cloak-room in the basement of Kutafya Tower). There are **five types of ticket**:

- The main grounds, Cathedral Square, five cathedral-museums, the Patriarch's Palace and exhibitions in the Assumption Belfry – but not in the Ivan the Great Bell Tower – adult/student R350/100
- The Armoury Chamber, adult/student R700/200
- The State Diamond Fund – a priceless collection of state jewellery on display in the same building as the Armoury, adult/student R500/250
- The Ivan the Great Bell Tower (which includes admission to the five cathedral museums also) adult/student R500/250
- Exhibitions in the Assumption Belfry and Patriarch's Palace, adult/student R300/150.

Note that the Armoury, the State Diamond Fund and the Ivan the Great Bell Tower may only be entered during timed sessions (the time is printed on your ticket), the tickets going on sale 45 minutes before the session is due to start. It's annoying, but you can't buy the tickets in advance.

If the Palace of Congress is in use for a daytime concert or other function you may be redirected to the Borovitsky Tower entrance at the far end of Aleksandrovsky Gardens. The Kremlin may be partly or completely closed without warning if there are VIP visitors.

Cathedral Square (see map on p165) Around the Kremlin's central square stand four main cathedrals and the **Ivan the Great Bell Tower** (81m/263ft high) which Napoleon attempted to blow up in 1812 and which houses exhibitions on the ground level. You can also ascend the tower for some great views. Beneath the tower stands the enormous **Tsar Bell**, at 200 tons the heaviest in the world; the piece that stands beside it broke off during the fire of 1737. Nearby is **Tsar Cannon**, the largest-calibre cannon in the world. The cannon-balls don't fit the cannon, which never fired a shot.

The **Cathedral of the Assumption**, the work of Italian architect Aristotle Fiorovanti and his sons, was completed in 1479 and was the traditional place of coronation for Russia's tsars. The last coronation, on 26 May 1896, saw what many considered a bad omen: as Nicholas II climbed the steps to the altar the chain of the Order of St Anthony fell from his shoulders. The interior is one of the most richly decorated in Russia. There are three thrones; the wooden one to the right as you enter belonged to Ivan the Terrible.

The **Cathedral of the Archangel Michael** (1505-9) looks classically Russian from the outside but the hand of its Italian architect, Alevisio Novi, can be seen in the light interior. Forty-six tsars (including Ivan the Great and Ivan the Terrible) are buried here. The smaller **Cathedral of the Annunciation** (1484-89), the tsars' private chapel, was the work of Russian architects and contains icons by the great master, Andrei Rublyov.

The **Church of the Deposition of the Robe** (1484-5) was designed as a private chapel for the clergy. The Patriarch worshipped in the **Church of the Twelve Apostles** next door to his residence.

The Armoury The **Armoury Chamber** Оружейная Палата is an incredible treasure house containing a dazzling display of tsars' jewellery and regalia, weapons and armour. Of special interest to Trans-Siberian passengers is the ornate Great Siberian Easter Egg (probably the finest of the 56 famous Imperial Easter Eggs made by Carl Fabergé), containing a tiny clockwork model of the train, complete with gold and platinum engine, five gold coaches and a church-car. Besides the ornate royal carriages, highlights include a huge collection of gold and silverware and the diamond-encrusted throne of Tsar Alexey Mikhailovich. Visits to the Armoury are by sessions: 10am, noon, 2.30pm and 4.30pm; purchase tickets 45 minutes before the beginning of a session at the main ticket office.

Speaking of diamonds, the collection of jewels in the adjoining **State Diamond Fund** is not to be missed. Peter the Great started the trend of jewellery collecting, specifying that his successors must each leave a number of jewels to the Russian state. Originally housed in St Petersburg's Winter Palace, the collection was hidden in the Kremlin's vaults during WWI and though two-thirds of it were sold off at Christie's in London in 1927 to raise funds for the Soviet Union's economy, the remains are vastly impressive, glittering in the semi-dark of the display halls. They include not just the world's largest sapphire but also the famous Orlov Diamond, thought to be the re-cut Great Mogul that was stolen from the Mogul treasury in the 17th century. The Orlov Diamond was presented to Catherine the Great as a gift by Count Gregory Orlov, who was trying to reignite a former flame. He was unsuccessful but Catherine the Great kept the diamond's original Indian rose cut.

Other buildings in the Kremlin The **Great Kremlin Palace**, now a government building, is only open to guests of State and other VIPs. A total renovation, to restore the palace to its pre-Communist finery, was completed in 1999. 'Put it back as it was before', said Yeltsin, and they did, for a mere US$800 million. Also VIP-only is the sole secular building on Cathedral Square, the Italian-designed **Facetted Chamber**, so-called because of its façade of pointed stone blocks. The **Golden Tsarina Palace**, or Terem Palace, has a striking red and white tiled roof.

The modern building facing the Kremlin's main entrance is the **Palace of Congress**, formerly the seat of the Parliament of the USSR. It was designed also to do duty as a theatre in the evenings; now that Parliament meets elsewhere (at the former State Planning Ministry on ul Okhotny Ryad), this building is the full-time home of the Moscow Kremlin Ballet as well as hosting some big international musicians, such as Leonard Cohen. Ticketholders get special entrance to the Kremlin in the evenings, but you can't sightsee before the show.

Tretyakov Gallery **Третьяковская Галерея** **[see Map 3]**
The best collection of Russian paintings, icons and sculpture is housed at this gallery (Lavrushinsky per 10, **M** Tretyakovskaya, 🖳 www.tretyakovgallery.ru,

10am-7.30pm, closed Mon, adult/student R300/180). Highlights include: icons by Andrei Rublyov; two halls devoted to the great Russian masters Ilya Repin and Vasily Surikov, including Repin's boozy, vodka-stricken portrait of the composer Mussorgsky; *Christ's First Appearance to the People* which took Alexander Ivanov 20 years to complete; and Ge's *Peter the Great Interrogates His Own Son* and *Ivan the Terrible, Having Murdered His Own Son*.

New Tretyakov Gallery Новая Третьяковская Галерея [see Map 3]
An excellent addition to the Tretyakov Gallery (Krymsky Val 10, **M** Park Kultury, 10am-7.30pm, closed Mon, adult/student R300/180), this wing, 1km away from the original, houses the best of **20th-century Soviet art**, including numerous socialist realism works. The works are extremely well presented, with plenty of information in English, and the visitor comes away with a real understanding of the complexities and different stages of the development of modern Russian art.

Behind the museum you'll find **Muzeon sculpture park** Парк Музеон (9am-9pm, R100), the final resting place of the many Soviet statues which were torn from their pedestals in the aftermath of the Soviet Union's collapse. Wander amongst the Lenins, Red Army monuments and cute worker statues. Overlooking the park is the **controversial nautical sculpture** by Zurab Tsereteli which allegedly features Peter the Great, though rumour has it that it was originally supposed to be Columbus. Now that Luzhkov, Moscow's former mayor, has been sacked in disgrace (see p55), the statue – which was his idea – might be removed.

Pushkin Museum of Fine Arts [see Map 4]
Музей Изобразительных Искусств имени А С Пушкина This excellent museum of non-Russian art (ul Volkhonka 12, **M** Kropotkinskaya, 10am-7pm, until 9pm Thur, closed Mon, adult/student R300/150, temperamental audioguide R200) boasts a large collection of European works, including numerous works from the 19th century, Greek and Roman sculptures in the Ancient Civilisation section, and also galleries of Egyptian antiquities and works by the Old Masters.

In a separate wing next door, at ul Volkhonka 14 (additional admission charge), you'll find a superb collection of Impressionist and post-Impressionist art, including works by Renoir, Pissarro, Monet, Manet, Picasso and Van Gogh. The Gaugin section is particularly splendid. At the same address is the **Museum of Private Collections** (10am-6pm Wed-Sun, adult/student R300/150) displaying the best of many works 'liberated' from wealthy Muscovites during the Revolution. Fans of the Georgian sculptor **Zurab Tsereteli** will want to visit the nearby **Tsereteli Gallery** Галерея Церетели (Map 3, ul Prechistenka 19, noon-7pm Tue-Sat, R200).

Cathedral of Christ the Saviour Храм Христа Спасителя [see Map 4]
Moscow's central cathedral was bulldozed by Stalin to make way for an ambitious Palace of the Soviets, planned as the world's largest building. But expert opinion concluded that the riverside location, directly opposite the Pushkin

❑ **Sandunovskiye Baths Сандуновская Баня** [see Map 4]
If you've just stepped off a Trans-Siberian train, a traditional Russian bath in the oldest and most luxurious public *banya* in the city is an invigorating and interesting experience. The Sandunovskiye baths (ul Neglinnaya 14, **M** Chekhovskaya, 8am-10pm daily; R700-900 for two hours' general admission, or else you can get a private room from R1700/hour) are beautifully decorated in classical style.

Museum, wouldn't support the weight and after an embarrassing hiatus a rather good swimming pool was built there instead. In 1997 a replica (ul Volkhonka 15, **M** Kropotkinskaya, 10am-5pm, services at 8am and 5pm, 9am Sat, 10am Sun) of the original cathedral with an enormous golden dome, financed with public and corporate contributions, was opened by then Mayor Luzhkov. The view from the dome is worth the climb.

'The Arbat' [see Map 2]

Pedestrianised ul Arbat is one of Moscow's most famous and well-loved streets. It may now be a popular tourist-trap, swarming with buskers, street artists and hawkers of everything from *matrioshka* dolls to McLenin T-shirts, but the 19th-century buildings which line it hint at former grandeur. Bargain hard and watch out for pickpockets.

The best known of the 1960s singer-songwriter 'bards', **Bulat Okudjava**, lived here at Plotnikov per 43 – his statue stands on the corner – and wrote *Arbat*, his best-loved song. Banned from recording in Soviet times, his funeral drew 60,000 people. The 'Viktor we still love you' graffiti along Krivoarbatsky per refers to Viktor Tsoy, a cult-status underground rock star killed in a 1990 car crash. Spot the individually painted tiles that make up the **Wall of Peace** at Arbat's eastern end.

Novodevichy Convent and cemetery Новодевичий Монастырь [Map 3]

This beautiful 16th-century walled **convent** (**M** Sportivnaya, 10am-5.30pm, closed Tue and last Mon of month, R150) has also served as a fortress (holding out against a Polish siege in 1610) and a prison.

Peter the Great imprisoned his half-sister Sofia here for taking part in the Streltsy rebellion, in which the plotters intended to dethrone him and put Sofia in his place. Sofia's supporters were beheaded in Red Square (see p162). Many of the nuns here were daughters of noble families who had brought shame upon family honour in the days before contraception. Napoleon tried unsuccessfully to blow it up in 1812: one brave nun rushed in and extinguished the fuses to the powder kegs at the last minute.

The white, imposing **Smolensky Cathedral**, at Novodevichy Convent, is famous for its frescoes and highly ornate, multi-tiered iconostasis (the backdrop to the altar). The convent's private **cemetery** was a safe location for graves which might otherwise become unwanted shrines, including those of many Decembrist officers. Adjacent to the convent is a more public cemetery with some outlandish gravestones (one soldier lies under a model tank) plus the graves of many an influential Russian, including Chekhov, Prokofiev, Khrushchev, Brezhnev and, as of 2007, Yeltsin.

All-Russia Exhibition Centre/VDNKh ВДНХ [see Map 1]

The initials stand for Vystavka Dostizheny Narodnogo Khozyaystva SSSR – USSR Economic Achievements Exhibition, and this sprawling complex of pavilions and wide pedestrian avenues (pr Mira 119, **M** VDNKh, 9am-7pm), often teeming with two-legged and two-wheeled traffic, was built in the 1930s to showcase the triumph of the Soviet economic system. There are monuments to every imaginable aspect of it – technology, science, agriculture, education and health, which will appeal to lovers of socialist realism, the most impressive being Friendship Fountain with dancing maidens, each representing a Soviet Republic, and the 100m titanium obelisk celebrating the Soviet Union's race to the stars.

Next to the obelisk is **Memorial Museum of Cosmonauts** Музей Космонавтики (10am-7pm, R100), a must for space fanatics. Its collection includes original Soviet and American space suits, satellite models, photos and documents relating to Yuri Gagarin and other famous astronauts and the stuffed bodies of the first two dogs in space – Belka and Strelka.

You can catch a ride on the **tourist train** (R35) to help you cover the whole exhibition or rent bikes and rollerblades just outside the entrance.

Park Pobedy Парк Победы [see Map 1]

This park was designed to celebrate Russia's victory in the Great Patriotic War, with its great promenade surrounded by fountains and the centrepiece 142m obelisk covered with representations of images from the war.

Behind the obelisk lies the **Museum of the Great Patriotic War** Музей Великой Отечественной Войны (**M** Park Pobedy, 10am-7pm, closed Mon and last Thur of month, R100), its exhibits including dioramas of every major WWII battle with excellent English captioning. The Hall of Glory commemorates Soviet war heroes and contains weaponry, photos and other war memorabilia.

At the eastern end of the park, the **Memorial synagogue** Мемориальная Синагога, at Poklonnaya Mountain, houses the **Museum of Jewish Legacy, History & Holocaust** Музей Истории Еврейского Наследия, Истории и Холокоста (ul Minskaya, 10am-6pm Mon-Thur, 11am-7pm Sun, admission with guide only; free entry). It's set to be replaced in late 2011 with the **Russian-Jewish Museum of Tolerance**, the world's largest Jewish Museum, currently under construction in a historic building at the Jewish community centre.

Vorobyovy Gory Воробьёвы Горы [see Map 1]

For an all-encompassing panoramic view of the capital, head to Vorobyovy Gory (Sparrow Hills), formerly known as Leninskiye Gory (Lenin Hills). From the Moscow State University site, Moscow stretches out before you; the view cannot be described as beautiful, but it is certainly impressive.

The Moscow metro and the secret metro [Metro map opp p512]

Construction of the metro began in the early 1930s, and it was planned that the first line would open on May Day 1935. In late April that year Stalin was invited to inspect the system but his tour came to an unexpected 30-minute halt following a signal failure. Expecting imprisonment or worse, engineers nearly collapsed with relief when Stalin suggested that it might be better to fix all the problems and delay the opening until 15 May. The honour of driving the first train, which consisted of local copies of 1932 New York carriages, went to the alliteratively named Ivan Ivanovich Ivanov.

As well as transporting passengers, the metro served as a bomb shelter in 1941-42. Male Muscovites slept on wooden platforms assembled every evening in the tunnels while women and children slept on camp stretchers on the platforms. During the Cold War the metro was modified to contain fallout shelters, and evidence of both the WWII and Cold War preparations can still be seen today. These include large recessed blast doors at ground-level entrances, collapsible platform edges which become steps, and large storerooms on the platforms for medical supplies.

A second, 'secret' metro was finished in 1967 which would enable government leaders to flee Moscow in the face of a nuclear attack. This 30km line runs from the former Central Communist Headquarters building on Staraya pl (near **M** Kitay-Gorod) via the government's underground bunker complex in the Ramenky region (near **M** Universitet) to Vnukovo-2 airport. Closed to the public, the line is said to be still operational.

New N5 metro carriages from Moscow's Mytishchi railway factory have been phased in. They are significantly quieter, smoother and safer, with automatic fire quenchers and extensive use of fireproof material.

While women drive many of Moscow's buses and trams, until recently only men were train drivers. The reason for this is the belief that men are better at handling the stress of suicidal passengers jumping in front of oncoming trains.

Moscow Metro Museum Музей Московского Метрополитена (Map 3; ul Khamovnichesky Val 36, 3rd floor, 11am-6pm Mon, 9am-4pm Tue-Fri), attached to the southern exit of **M** Sportivnaya, contains maps, models and documents about the history of Moscow's public transport system from the early 19th century; you can even sit in a full-size driver's cab and play with the equipment. Bear in mind that the displays relating to the building of the first metro lines play up the role of Komsomol volunteers in their creation and downplay the role of forced labour used alongside.

Other museums and galleries

Moscow has far too many attractions to describe in just one chapter, but if you have some spare time, the museums below are well worth your while.

- **Andrei Rublyov Ancient Russian Culture and Art Museum** Древнерусской Культуры и Искусства имени Андрея Рублёва (Map 1; pl Andronyevskaya 10, **M** Ploshchad Ilyicha, 11am-6pm, closed Wed and last Fri of month, R300) is dedicated to the art of the Russian icon through the ages.
- **Borodino Battlefield Panorama** Музей-Панорама «Бородинская Битва» (Map 1; Kutuzovsky pr 38, **M** Kutuzovskaya, 10am-6pm except Fri and last Thur of month, R300) focuses on one of the most famous battles in Russian history, and besides the munitions collection, the centrepiece is an enormous painting of the battle.

(continued on p180)

Moscow Москва
MAP 1
0
3km
See map 2
See map 4
Losiny Ostrov Park
Парк Лосиный Остров
Sokolniki Park
Парк Сокольники
Izmaylovsky Park
Измайловский Парк
Kuskovo Park
Парк Кусково
Botanical Garden
Ботанический Сад
Timiryazev Academy Park
Парк Академии имени Тимирязева
Dinamo Stadium
Стадион Динамо
Stadium of Young Pioneers
Стадион Юных Пионеров
Pokrovsko-Streshnevo Park Лесопарк Покровско-Стрешнево
Filyovsky Park
Филёвский Парк
Rizhsky Station
Рижский Вокзал
Savyolovsky Station
Савиоловский Вокзал
Leningradsky Station
Ленинградский Вокзал
Yaroslavsky Station
Ярославский Вокзал
Kazansky Station
Казанский Вокзал
Kursky Station
Курский Вокзал
Belorussky Station
Белорусский Вокзал
Kievsky Station
Киевский Вокзал
Paveletsky Station
Павелецкий Вокзал
Leningradskoye Shosse Ленинградское Шоссе
Leningradsky Pr Ленинградский Пр
Ul Tverskaya Ул Тверская
Pr Mira Пр Мира
Ul Botanicheskaya Ул Ботаническая
Ul Ak Koroleva Ул Ак Королёва
Ul Vilgelma Pika Ул Вильгельма Пика
Ul B Galushkina Ул Б Галушкина
Ul Argunovskaya Ул Аргуновская
Shchyolkovskoye Shosse Щёлковское Шоссе
Shosse Entuziastov Шоссе Энтузиастов
Kutuzovsky Pr Кутузовский Пр
Ul Bol Filyovskaya Ул Бол Филёвская
Volgogradsky Pr
Ulitsa Podbelskogo
Shchyolkovskaya
Pervomayskaya
Partizanskaya
Izmaylovsky Park
Novogireyevo
Perovo
Cherkizovskaya
Preobrazhenskaya Pl
Sokolniki
Semyonovskaya
Elektrozavodskaya
Shosse Entuziastov
Aviamotornaya
Baumanskaya
Krasnoselskaya
Kurskaya
Pl Ilyicha/Rimskaya
Proletarskaya/Krestyanskaya Zastava
Marxistskaya/Taganskaya
Rizhskaya
Alexeyevskaya
VDNKh
Botanichesky Sad
Sviblovo
Ul S Eizenshteina
Vladykino
Ul Ak Koroleva
Teletsentr
Ul Milashenkova
Timiryazevskaya
Dmitrovskaya
Savelovskaya
Dinamo
Petrovsko-Razumovskaya
Aeroport
Sokol
Voykovskaya
Vodny Stadion
Belorusskaya
Barrikadnaya
Krasnopresnenskaya
Ulitsa 1905 Goda
Begovaya
Polyezhayevskaya
Oktyabrskoye Polye
Shchukinskaya
Kievskaya
Studencheskaya
Kutuzovskaya
Fili
Bagrationovskaya
Filyovsky Park
Park Pobedy
Pionerskaya
Varsh
1
2
3
4
5
6
7
8
9
10
11
12

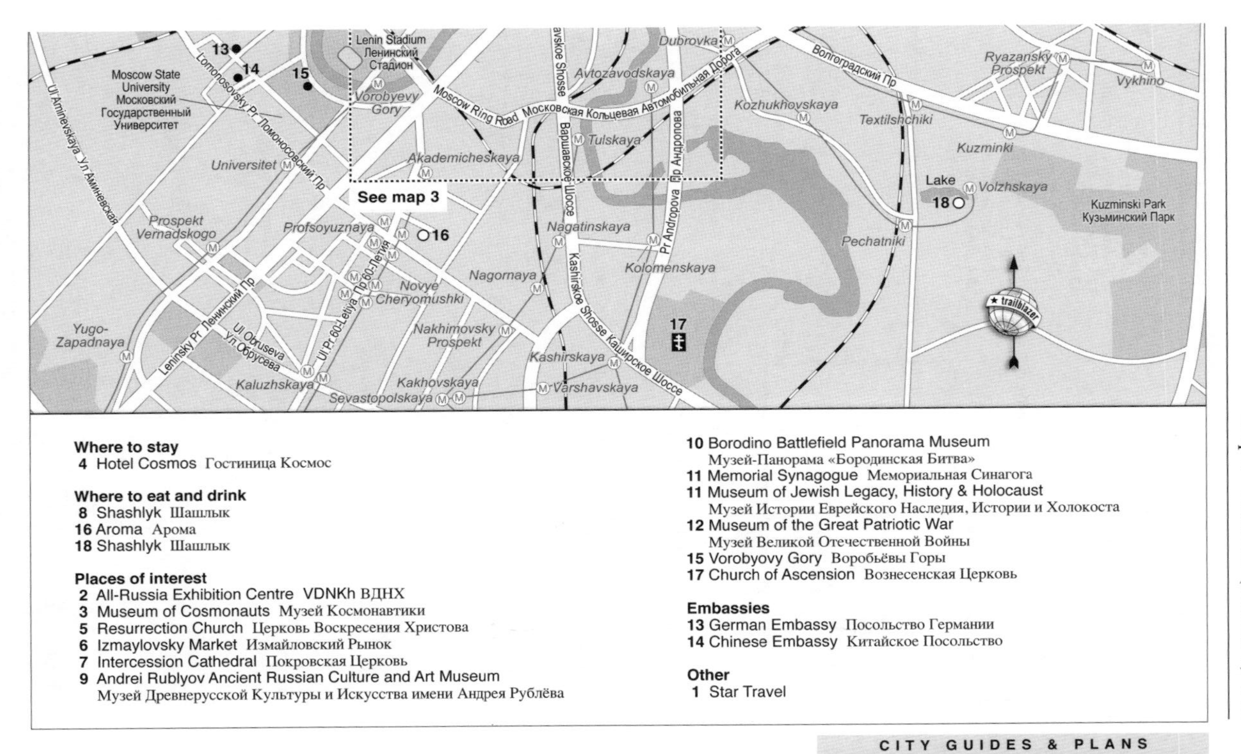

Where to stay
4 Hotel Cosmos Гостиница Космос

Where to eat and drink
8 Shashlyk Шашлык
16 Aroma Арома
18 Shashlyk Шашлык

Places of interest
2 All-Russia Exhibition Centre VDNKh ВДНХ
3 Museum of Cosmonauts Музей Космонавтики
5 Resurrection Church Церковь Воскресения Христова
6 Izmaylovsky Market Измайловский Рынок
7 Intercession Cathedral Покровская Церковь
9 Andrei Rublyov Ancient Russian Culture and Art Museum
Музей Древнерусской Культуры и Искусства имени Андрея Рублёва
10 Borodino Battlefield Panorama Museum
Музей-Панорама «Бородинская Битва»
11 Memorial Synagogue Мемориальная Синагога
11 Museum of Jewish Legacy, History & Holocaust
Музей Истории Еврейского Наследия, Истории и Холокоста
12 Museum of the Great Patriotic War
Музей Великой Отечественной Войны
15 Vorobyovy Gory Воробьёвы Горы
17 Church of Ascension Вознесенская Церковь

Embassies
13 German Embassy Посольство Германии
14 Chinese Embassy Китайское Посольство

Other
1 Star Travel

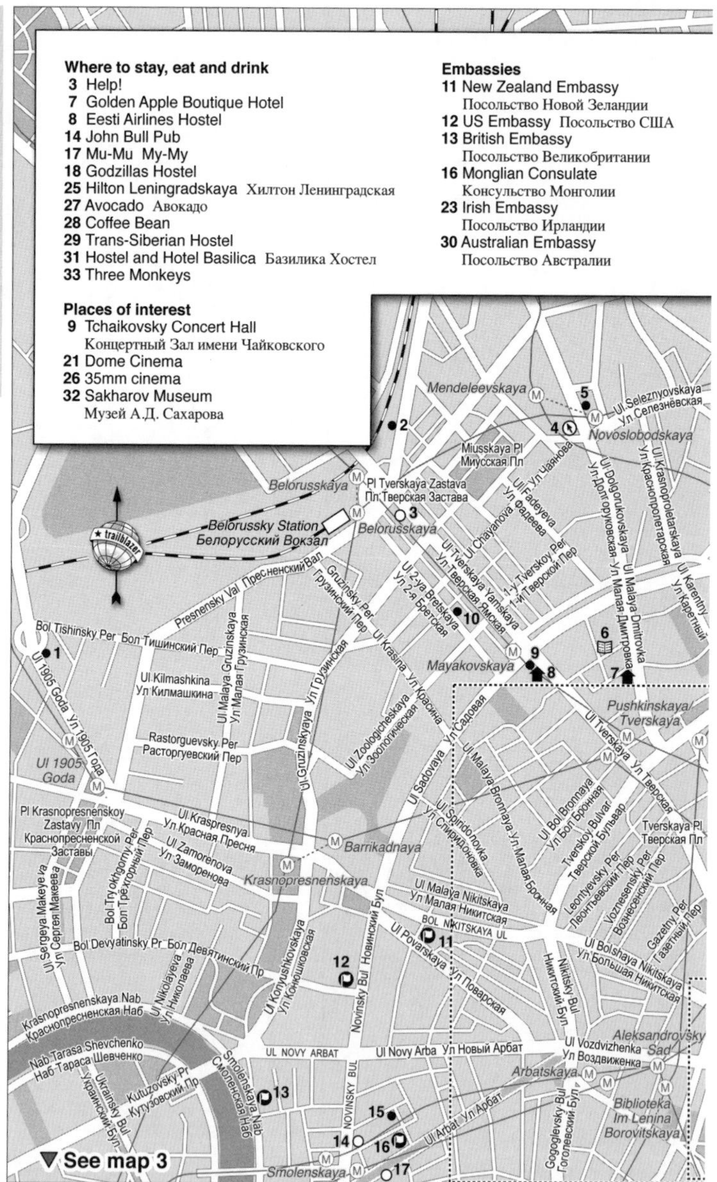
Where to stay, eat and drink
3 Help!
7 Golden Apple Boutique Hotel
8 Eesti Airlines Hostel
14 John Bull Pub
17 Mu-Mu My-My
18 Godzillas Hostel
25 Hilton Leningradskaya Хилтон Ленинградская
27 Avocado Авокадо
28 Coffee Bean
29 Trans-Siberian Hostel
31 Hostel and Hotel Basilica Базилика Хостел
33 Three Monkeys
Places of interest
9 Tchaikovsky Concert Hall Концертный Зал имени Чайковского
21 Dome Cinema
26 35mm cinema
32 Sakharov Museum Музей А.Д. Сахарова
Embassies
11 New Zealand Embassy Посольство Новой Зеландии
12 US Embassy Посольство США
13 British Embassy Посольство Великобритании
16 Monglian Consulate Консульство Монголии
23 Irish Embassy Посольство Ирландии
30 Australian Embassy Посольство Австралии
Mendeleevskaya
Novoslobodskaya
Ul Seleznyovskaya Ул Селезнёвская
Miusskaya Pl Миусская Пл
Belorusskaya
Pl Tverskaya Zastava Пл Тверская Застава
Belorussky Station Белорусский Вокзал
Presnensky Val Пресненский Вал
Gruzinsky Per Грузинский Пер
Ul 2-ya Bretskaya Ул 2-я Брестская
Ul Tverskaya Yamskaya Ул Тверская Ямская
1-y Tverskoy Per 1-й Тверской Пер
Ul Chayanova Ул Чаянова
Ul Fadeyeva Ул Фадеева
Ul Dolgorukovskaya Ул Долгоруковская
Ul Malaya Dmitrovka Ул Малая Дмитровка
Ul Krasnoproletarskaya Ул Краснопролетарская
Ul Karetnyy Ул Каретный
Mayakovskaya
Bol Tishinsky Per Бол Тишинский Пер
Ul 1905 Goda Ул 1905 Года
Ul Kilmashkina Ул Килмашкина
Ul Malaya Gruzinskaya Ул Малая Грузинская
Ul Gruzinskaya Ул Грузинская
Ul Krasina Ул Красина
Ul Zoologicheskaya Ул Зоологическая
Ul Sadovaya Ул Садовая
Pushkinskaya/ Tverskaya
Ul Tverskaya Ул Тверская
Rastorguevsky Per Расторгуевский Пер
Ul 1905 Goda
Ul Malaya Bronnaya Ул Малая Бронная
Ul Bol Bronnaya Ул Бол Бронная
Tverskoy Bulvar Тверской Бульвар
Ul Spiridonovka Ул Спиридоновка
Tverskaya Pl Тверская Пл
Pl Krasnopresnenskoy Zastavy Пл Краснопресненской Заставы
Ul Kraspresnya Ул Красная Пресня
Ul Zamorenova Ул Заморенова
Barrikadnaya
Krasnopresnenskaya
Leontyevsky Per Леонтьевский Пер
Voznesensky Per Вознесенский Пер
Bol Tryokhgorny Per Бол Трёхгорный Пер
Ul Sergeya Makeyeva Ул Сергея Макеева
Ul Malaya Nikitskaya Ул Малая Никитская
Bol Nikitskaya Ul
Gazetny Per Газетный Пер
Bol Devyatinsky Pr Бол Девятинский Пр
Ul Konyushkovskaya Ул Конюшковская
Novinsky Bul Новинский Бул
Ul Povarskaya Ул Поварская
Ul Bolshaya Nikitskaya Ул Большая Никитская
Ul Nikolayeva Ул Николаева
Nikitsky Bul Никитский Бул
Krasnopresnenskaya Nab Краснопресненская Наб
Aleksandrovsky Sad
Nab Tarasa Shevchenko Наб Тараса Шевченко
Ul Novy Arbat
Ul Novy Arba Ул Новый Арбат
Ul Vozdvizhenka Ул Воздвиженка
Arbatskaya
Ukrainsky Bul Украинский Бул
Kutuzovsky Pr Кутузовский Пр
Smolenskaya Nab Смоленская Наб
Novinsky Bul
Ul Arbat Ул Арбат
Gogolevsky Bul Гоголевский Бул
Biblioteka Im Lenina Borovitskaya
Smolenskaya
trailblazer
See map 3

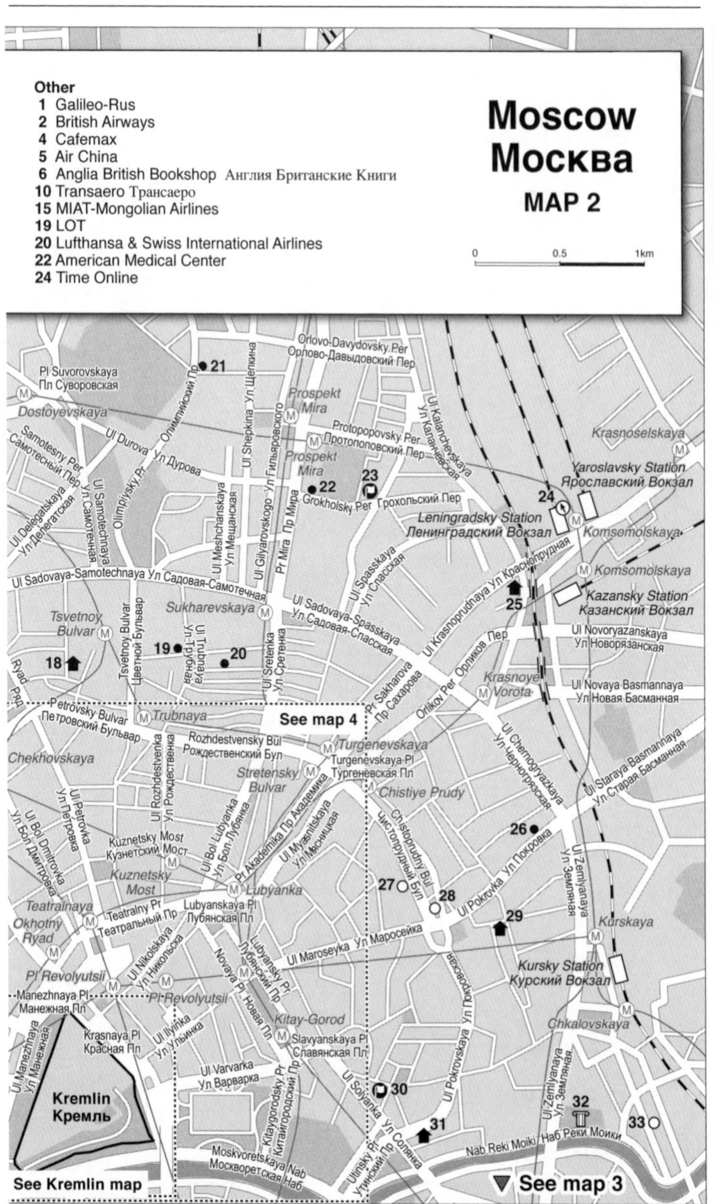
Other
1 Galileo-Rus
2 British Airways
4 Cafemax
5 Air China
6 Anglia British Bookshop Англия Британские Книги
10 Transaero Трансаеро
15 MIAT-Mongolian Airlines
19 LOT
20 Lufthansa & Swiss International Airlines
22 American Medical Center
24 Time Online
Moscow
Москва
MAP 2
0 0.5 1km
Orlovo-Davydovsky Per
Орлово-Давыдовский Пер
Pl Suvorovskaya
Пл Суворовская
Dostoyevskaya
Prospekt Mira
Protopopovsky Per
Протопоповский Пер
Krasnoselskaya
Yaroslavsky Station
Ярославский Вокзал
Leningradsky Station
Ленинградский Вокзал
Komsomolskaya
Kazansky Station
Казанский Вокзал
Grokholsky Per Грохольский Пер
Ul Sadovaya-Samotechnaya Ул Садовая-Самотечная
Sukharevskaya
Tsvetnoy Bulvar
Ul Sadovaya-Spasskaya
Ул Садовая-Спасская
Ul Novoryazanskaya
Ул Новорязанская
Ul Novaya Basmannaya
Ул Новая Басманная
Krasnoye Vorota
Petrovsky Bulvar
Петровский Бульвар
Trubnaya
See map 4
Rozhdestvensky Bul
Рождественский Бул
Turgenevskaya
Turgenevskaya Pl
Тургеневская Пл
Chekhovskaya
Stretensky Bulvar
Chistiye Prudy
Kuznetsky Most
Кузнетский Мост
Lubyanka
Lubyanskaya Pl
Лубянская Пл
Teatralnaya
Teatralny Pr
Театральный Пр
Okhotny Ryad
Ul Maroseyka Ул Маросейка
Kurskaya
Kursky Station
Курский Вокзал
Pl Revolyutsii
Manezhnaya Pl
Манежная Пл
Kitay-Gorod
Slavyanskaya Pl
Славянская Пл
Chkalovskaya
Krasnaya Pl
Красная Пл
Ul Varvarka
Ул Варварка
Kremlin
Кремль
Nab Reki Moiki Наб Реки Моики
Moskvoretskaya Nab
Москворетская Наб
See Kremlin map
See map 3

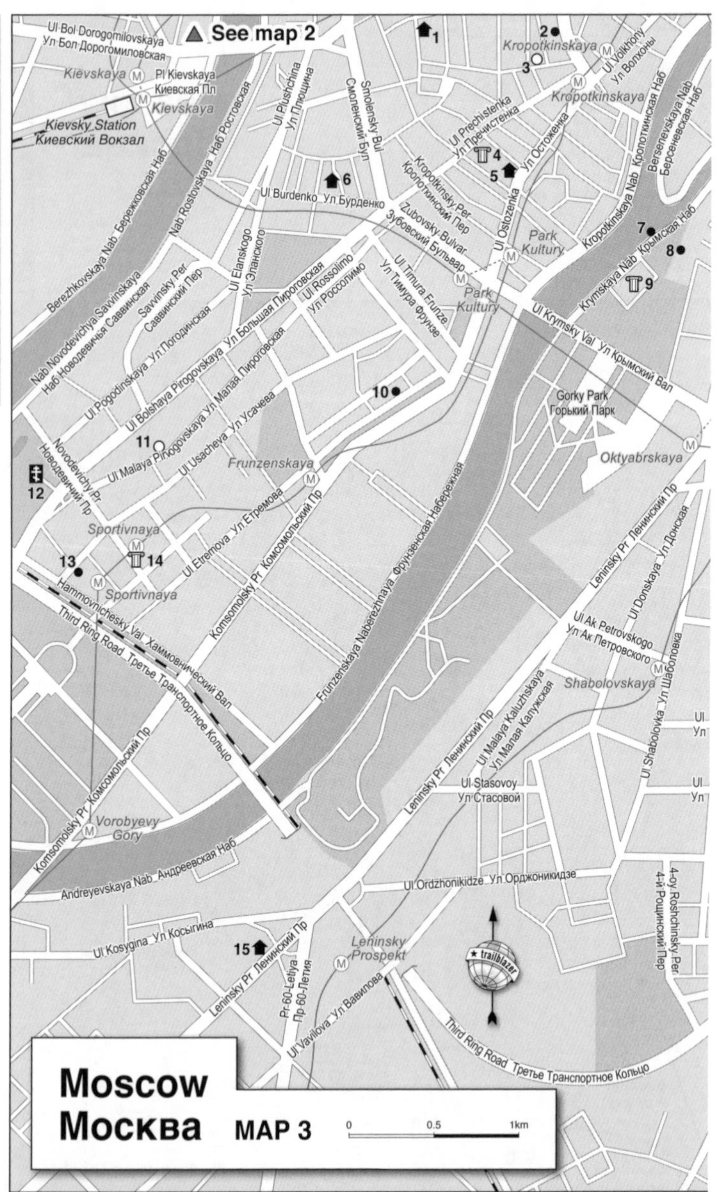

See map 2
Ul Bol Dorogomilovskaya
Ул Бол Дорогомиловская
Kievskaya
Pl Kievskaya
Киевская Пл
Kievskaya
Kievsky Station
Киевский Вокзал
Nab Rostovskaya Наб Ростовская
Berezhkovskaya Nab Бережковская Наб
Ul Plushchina
Ул Плющина
Smolensky Bul
Смоленский Бул
Kropotkinskaya
Ul Volkhony
Ул Волхоны
Kropotkinskaya
Ul Prechistenka
Ул Пречистенка
Ул Остоженка
Kropotkinskaya Nab Кропоткинская Наб
Bersenevskaya Nab
Берсеневская Наб
Ul Burdenko Ул Бурденко
Kropotkinsky Per
Кропоткинский Пер
Zubovsky Bulvar
Зубовский Бульвар
Ul Ostozhenka
Park Kultury
Park Kultury
Krymskaya Nab Крымская Наб
Ul Elanskogo
Ул Эланского
Savvinsky Per
Саввинский Пер
Nab Novodevichya Savvinskaya
Наб Новодевичья Саввинская
Ul Rossolimo
Ул Россолимо
Ul Timura Frunze
Ул Тимура Фрунзе
Ul Krymsky Val Ул Крымский Вал
Ul Pogodinskaya Ул Погодинская
Ul Bolshaya Pirogovskaya Ул Большая Пироговская
Ul Malaya Pirogovskaya Ул Малая Пироговская
Ul Usacheva Ул Усачева
Gorky Park
Горький Парк
Oktyabrskaya
Novodevichy Pr
Новодевичий Пр
Frunzenskaya
Sportivnaya
Ul Etremova Ул Етремова
Komsomolsky Pr Комсомольский Пр
Frunzenskaya Naberezhnaya Фрунзенская Набережная
Leninsky Pr Ленинский Пр
Ul Donskaya Ул Донская
Sportivnaya
Hammovnichesky Val Хаммовнический Вал
Third Ring Road Третье Транспортное Кольцо
Ul Ak Petrovskogo
Ул Ак Петровского
Shabolovskaya
Ul Shabolovka Ул Шаболовка
Ul Malaya Kaluzhskaya
Ул Малая Калужская
Leninsky Pr Ленинский Пр
Ul Stasovoy
Ул Стасовой
Komsomolsky Pr Комсомольский Пр
Vorobyevy Gory
Andreyevskaya Nab Андреевская Наб
Ul Ordzhonikidze Ул Орджоникидзе
4-oy Roshchinsky Per
4-й Рощинский Пер
Ul Kosygina Ул Косыгина
Leninsky Prospekt
Leninsky Pr Ленинский Пр
Pr 60-Letiya
Пр 60-Летия
Ul Vavilova Ул Вавилова
trailblazer
Third Ring Road Третье Транспортное Кольцо
1
2
3
4
5
6
7
8
9
10
11
12
13
14
15
Moscow
Москва
MAP 3
0
0.5
1km

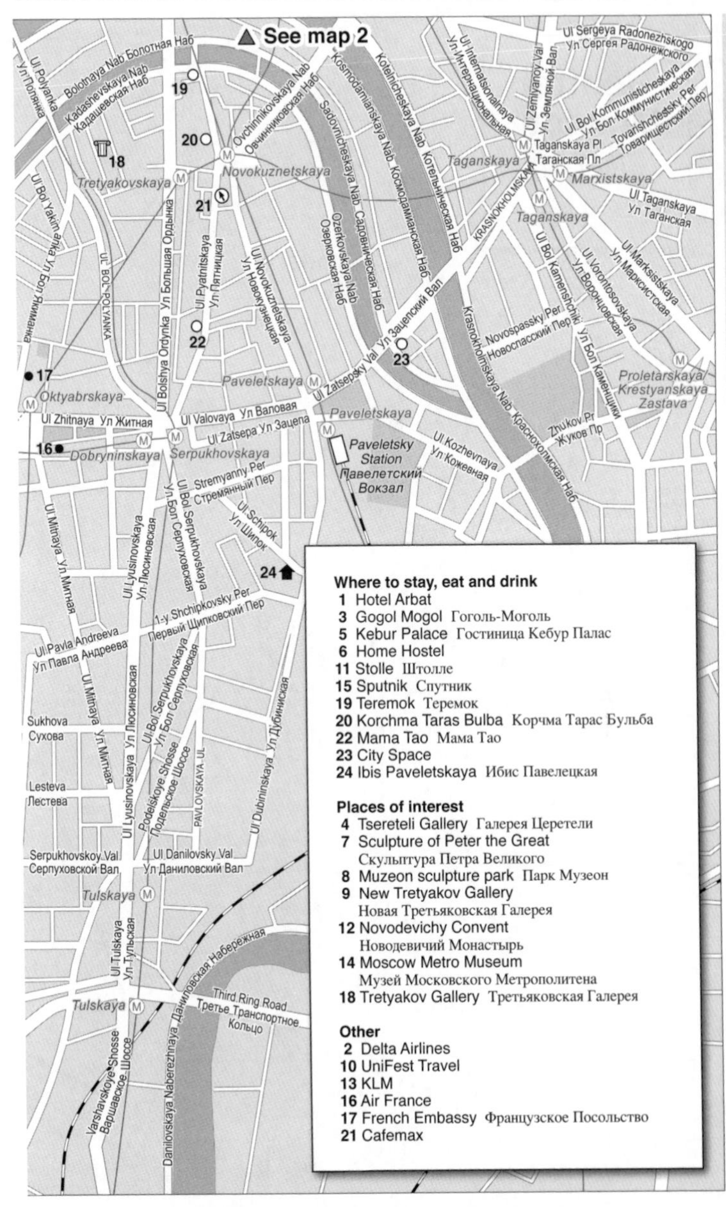
See map 2
Where to stay, eat and drink
1 Hotel Arbat
3 Gogol Mogol Гоголь-Моголь
5 Kebur Palace Гостиница Кебур Палас
6 Home Hostel
11 Stolle Штолле
15 Sputnik Спутник
19 Teremok Теремок
20 Korchma Taras Bulba Корчма Тарас Бульба
22 Mama Tao Мама Тао
23 City Space
24 Ibis Paveletskaya Ибис Павелецкая
Places of interest
4 Tsereteli Gallery Галерея Церетели
7 Sculpture of Peter the Great Скульптура Петра Великого
8 Muzeon sculpture park Парк Музеон
9 New Tretyakov Gallery Новая Третьяковская Галерея
12 Novodevichy Convent Новодевичий Монастырь
14 Moscow Metro Museum Музей Московского Метрополитена
18 Tretyakov Gallery Третьяковская Галерея
Other
2 Delta Airlines
10 UniFest Travel
13 KLM
16 Air France
17 French Embassy Французское Посольство
21 Cafemax
Tretyakovskaya
Novokuznetskaya
Taganskaya
Marxistskaya
Oktyabrskaya
Dobryninskaya
Serpukhovskaya
Paveletskaya
Proletarskaya/Krestyanskaya Zastava
Tulskaya
Paveletsky Station Павелецкий Вокзал
Third Ring Road Третье Транспортное Кольцо
Ul Zhitnaya Ул Житная
Ul Valovaya Ул Валовая
Ul Zatsepa Ул Зацепа
Ul Zatsepsky Val Ул Зацепский Вал
Stremyanny Per Стремянный Пер
Ul Schipok Ул Шипок
1-y Shchipkovsky Per Первый Щипковский Пер
Ul Pavla Andreeva Ул Павла Андреева
Serpukhovskoy Val Серпуховской Вал
Ul Danilovsky Val Ул Даниловский Вал
Ul Kozhevnaya Ул Кожевная
Zhukov Pr Жуков Пр
Novospassky Per Новоспасский Пер
Ul Taganskaya Ул Таганская
Taganskaya Pl Таганская Пл
Bolotnaya Nab Болотная Наб
Kadashevskaya Nab Кадашевская Наб
Ovchinnikovskaya Nab Овчинниковская Наб
Kosmodamianskaya Nab Космодамианская Наб
Kotelnicheskaya Nab Котельническая Наб
Krasnokholmskaya Nab Краснохолмская Наб
Danilovskaya Naberezhnaya Даниловская Набережная
Varshavskoye Shosse Варшавское Шоссе
Podolskoye Shosse Подольское Шоссе

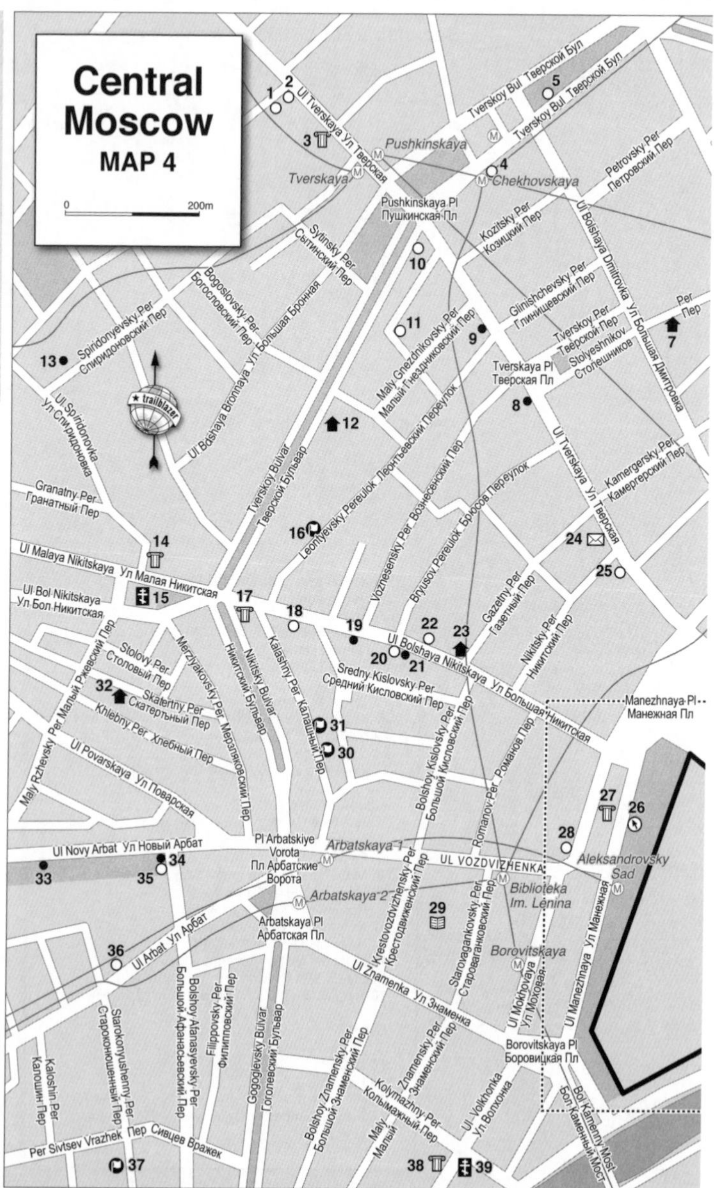
Central Moscow
MAP 4
0
200m
trailblazer
Pushkinskaya
Tverskaya
Chekhovskaya
Tverskoy Bul Тверской Бул
Ul Tverskaya Ул Тверская
Pushkinskaya Pl
Пушкинская Пл
Petrovsky Per
Петровский Пер
Kozitsky Per
Козицкий Пер
Sytinsky Per
Сытинский Пер
Bogoslovsky Per
Богословский Пер
Ul Bolshaya Bronnaya Ул Большая Бронная
Spiridonyevsky Per
Спиридоновский Пер
Ul Spiridonovka
Ул Спиридоновка
Maly Gnezdnikovsky Per
Малый Гнездниковский Пер
Glinishchevsky Per
Глинищевский Пер
Tverskoy Per
Тверской Пер
Stolyeshnikov
Столешников
Ul Bolshaya Dmitrovka Ул Большая Дмитровка
Tverskaya Pl
Тверская Пл
Tverskoy Bulvar
Тверской Бульвар
Leontyevsky Pereulok Леонтьевский Переулок
Voznesensky Per Вознесенский Пер
Bryusov Pereulok Брюсов Переулок
Kamergersky Per
Камергерский Пер
Granatny Per
Гранатный Пер
Ul Malaya Nikitskaya Ул Малая Никитская
Ul Bol Nikitskaya
Ул Бол Никитская
Gazetny Per
Газетный Пер
Nikitsky Per
Никитский Пер
Ul Bolshaya Nikitskaya Ул Большая Никитская
Stolovy Per
Столовый Пер
Merzlyakovsky Per Мерзляковский Пер
Nikitsky Bulvar
Никитский Бульвар
Kalashny Per Калашный Пер
Sredny Kislovsky Per
Средний Кисловский Пер
Skaterny Per
Скатертный Пер
Khlebny Per Хлебный Пер
Maly Rzhevsky Per Малый Ржевский Пер
Ul Povarskaya Ул Поварская
Bolshoy Kislovsky Per
Большой Кисловский Пер
Romanov Per Романов Пер
Manezhnaya Pl
Манежная Пл
Ul Novy Arbat Ул Новый Арбат
Pl Arbatskiye Vorota
Пл Арбатские Ворота
Arbatskaya 1
Arbatskaya 2
UL VOZDVIZHENKA
Aleksandrovsky Sad
Biblioteka Im. Lenina
Borovitskaya
Krestovozdvizhensky Per
Крестовоздвиженский Пер
Starovagankovsky Per
Староваганковский Пер
Arbatskaya Pl
Арбатская Пл
Ul Arbat Ул Арбат
Ul Znamenka Ул Знаменка
Ul Mokhovaya
Ул Моховая
Ul Manezhnaya Ул Манежная
Borovitskaya Pl
Боровицкая Пл
Starokonyushenny Per
Староконюшенный Пер
Kaloshin Per
Калошин Пер
Bolshoy Afanasyevsky Per
Большой Афанасьевский Пер
Filippovsky Per
Филипповский Пер
Gogolevsky Bulvar
Гоголевский Бульвар
Bolshoy Znamensky Per
Большой Знаменский Пер
Znamensky Per
Знаменский Пер
Kolymazhny Per
Колымажный Пер
Maly
Малый
Ul Volkhonka
Ул Волхонка
Bol Kamenny Most
Бол Каменный Мост
Per Sivtsev Vrazhek Пер Сивцев Вражек
1
2
3
4
5
7
8
9
10
11
12
13
14
15
16
17
18
19
20
21
22
23
24
25
26
27
28
29
30
31
32
33
34
35
36
37
38
39

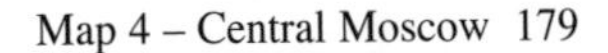

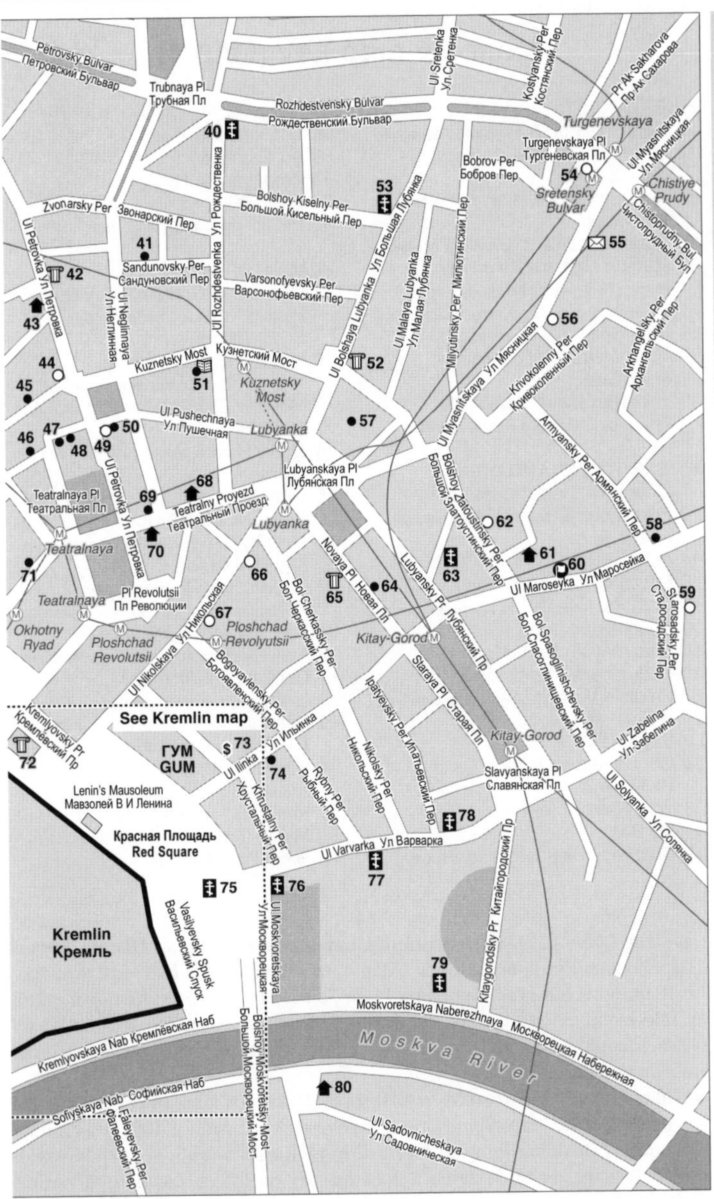

CITY GUIDES & PLANS
Petrovsky Bulvar
Петровский Бульвар
Trubnaya Pl
Трубная Пл
Rozhdestvensky Bulvar
Рождественский Бульвар
Ul Sretenka
Ул Сретенка
Kostyansky Per
Костянский Пер
Pr Ak Sakharova
Пр Ак Сахарова
Turgenevskaya
Turgenevskaya Pl
Тургеневская Пл
Ul Myasnitskaya
Ул Мясницкая
Bobrov Per
Бобров Пер
Sretensky Bulvar
Chistiye Prudy
Chistoprudny Bul
Чистопрудный Бул
Zvonarsky Per
Звонарский Пер
Ul Rozhdestvenka
Ул Рождественка
Bolshoy Kiselny Per
Большой Кисельный Пер
Ul Bolshaya Lubyanka
Ул Большая Лубянка
Milyutinsky Per
Милютинский Пер
Ul Petrovka
Ул Петровка
Sandunovsky Per
Сандуновский Пер
Varsonofyevsky Per
Варсонофьевский Пер
Ul Malaya Lubyanka
Ул Малая Лубянка
Ul Neglinnaya
Ул Неглинная
Kuznetsky Most
Кузнетский Мост
Kuznetsky Most
Krivokolenny Per
Кривоколенный Пер
Arkhangelsky Per
Архангельский Пер
Ul Pushechnaya
Ул Пушечная
Lubyanka
Lubyanskaya Pl
Лубянская Пл
Armyansky Per
Армянский Пер
Bolshoy Zlatoustinsky Per
Большой Златоустинский Пер
Teatralnaya Pl
Театральная Пл
Teatralny Proyezd
Театральный Проезд
Lubyanka
Teatralnaya
Novaya Pl
Новая Пл
Lubyansky Pr
Лубянский Пр
Ul Maroseyka
Ул Маросейка
Starosadsky Per
Старосадский Пер
Pl Revolutsii
Пл Революции
Teatralnaya
Okhotny Ryad
Ploshchad Revolutsii
Ploshchad Revolyutsii
Ul Nikolskaya
Ул Никольская
Bol Cherkassky Per
Бол Черкасский Пер
Kitay-Gorod
Staraya Pl
Старая Пл
Bol Spasoglinishchevsky Per
Бол Спасоглинищевский Пер
Bogoyavlensky Per
Богоявленский Пер
Ipatyevsky Per
Ипатьевский Пер
Kremlyovsky Pr
Кремлёвский Пр
See Kremlin map
ГУМ
GUM
Ul Ilinka
Ул Ильинка
Nikolsky Per
Никольский Пер
Rybny Per
Рыбный Пер
Khrustalny Per
Хрустальный Пер
Kitay-Gorod
Ul Zabelina
Ул Забелина
Slavyanskaya Pl
Славянская Пл
Ul Solyanka
Ул Солянка
Lenin's Mausoleum
Мавзолей В И Ленина
Красная Площадь
Red Square
Ul Varvarka
Ул Варварка
Kitaygorodsky Pr
Китайгородский Пр
Ul Moskvoretskaya
Ул Москворецкая
Vasilyevsky Spusk
Васильевский Спуск
Kremlin
Кремль
Moskvoretskaya Naberezhnaya
Москворецкая Набережная
Kremlyovskaya Nab
Кремлёвская Наб
Moskva River
Bolshoy Moskvoretsky Most
Большой Москворецкий Мост
Sofiyskaya Nab
Софийская Наб
Faleyevsky Per
Фалеевский Пер
Ul Sadovnicheskaya
Ул Садовническая
40
41
42
43
44
45
46
47
48
49
50
51
52
53
54
55
56
57
58
59
60
61
62
63
64
65
66
67
68
69
70
71
72
73
74
75
76
77
78
79
80

Moscow map key (Map 4)

WHERE TO STAY
7 Hotel Akvarel Гостиница Акварель
12 Hotel East-West Гостиница Восток-Запад
23 Assambleya Nikitskaya Ассамблея Никитская
32 Hotel Melodiya Гостиница Мелодия
43 Marriott Moscow Royal Aurora Hotel Марриотт Москва Аврора
61 Napoleon Hostel Хостел Наполеон
68 Artel Hotel Артель Отель
70 Hotel Metropol Гостиница Метрополь
79 Hotel Baltschug-Kempinski Гостиница Балчуг-Кемпинский

WHERE TO EAT AND DRINK
1 Goodman Steak House
2 Filimonova & Yankel Филимонова & Янкель
4 Purga Пурга
5 Bocconcino Бокകончино
10 Café Pushkin Кафе Пушкин
11 Khacha-puri Хача-Пури
18 Club Mayak Клуб Маяк
20 Coffeemania Кофемания
22 Prostiye Veshchi Простые Вещи
25 Silvers
28 Eat & Talk
35 Genatsvale na Arbate Генатсвале На Арбате
36 Yolki-Palki Ёлки-Палки
44 My Bar
49 Russkoye Bistro Русское Бистро
54 Pasta i Basta Паста и Баста
56 Bochonok Бочонок
59 Art Garbage
62 Propaganda Пропаганда
66 Club Che Клуб Че
67 Pelmeshka Пельмешка

PLACES OF INTEREST
3 Museum of Contemporary Russian History Музей Современной Русской Истории
8 Moscow Drama Theatre Московский Драматический Театр
9 Moscow City Government Building Мэрия
14 Gorky House Museum Дом-Музей Горького
15 Grand Ascension Church Большая Вознесенская Церковь
17 Mayakovsky House-Museum Дом-Музей Маяковского
19 Tchaikovsky Conservatory Консерватория имени Чайковского
21 Rakhmaninov Conservatory Консерватория имени Рахманинова
27 Central Exhibition Hall Центральный Выставочный Зал
29 Russian State Library Российская Государственная Библиотека
34 Helikon Opera Театр Геликон-опера
38 Pushkin Museum of Fine Arts Музей Изобразительных Искусств имени А С Пушкина

(continued from p171) • **Museum of Contemporary Russian History** Музей Современной Русской Истории (Map 4; ul Tverskaya 21, **M** Tverskaya, Tue-Fri 10am-6pm, Sat 11am-7pm, Sun 11am-5pm, R100) is a must for anyone with an interest in Soviet history. Its engaging displays cover the Revolutionary phase, life under Communism, the Space Race and there's even a who's who of Russian popular music.

• **Gulag History Museum** Музей Истории Гулага (Map 4; ul Petrovka 16, **M** Kuznetsky Most, 11am-7pm, Thur noon-9pm, closed Mon, R100) is a chilling eye-opener, shedding light on the history of Russia's millions of 'repressed' persons. There are three parts: a documentary on the persecution of various

❑ **MOSCOW METRO – see colour map at back of book (opp p512)**

PLACES OF INTEREST ***(cont'd)***

39 Cathedral of Christ the Saviour Храм Христа Спасителя
40 Nativity of Our Lady Cathedral Рождественскый Собор
41 Sandunovskiye Baths Сандуновская Баня
42 Gulag History Museum Музей Истории Гулага
46 Operetta Theatre Театр Оперетты
47 Youth Theatre Театр Юного Зрителя
48 Bolshoi Theatre Большой Театр
50 TsUM Department Store ЦУМ
52 KGB Museum Музей КГБ
53 Church of Vladimir Mother of God Церковь Владимирской Богоматери
57 Lubyanka (former KGB Headquarters) Лубянка
63 St Nicholas Church Никольская церковь
65 Moscow City History Museum Музей Истории Города Москвы)
69 Maly Theatre Малый Театр
71 State Duma House Государственная Дума
72 State History Museum Государственный Исторический Музей
74 St Basil's Cathedral Собор Василия Блаженного
75 St Barbara's Church Церковь Святой Варвары
76 Monastery of the Sign Belltower Колокольня Знаменского Монастыря
77 St George's Church Церковь Святого Георгия
78 Church of St Anne's Conception Церковь Зачатия Святой Анны

EMBASSIES

16 Ukraine Embassy Посольство Украины
30 Netherlands Embassy Посольство Нидерландов
31 Japanese Embassy Японское Посольство
37 Canadian Embassy Канадское Посольство
60 Belarus Embassy Посольство Белоруссии

OTHER

13 European Medical Centre
24 Central Post & Telegraph Office Центральная Почта и Телеграф
26 Time Online
33 36.6 Pharmacy
45 Aeroflot Airlines Аэрофлот
51 36.6 Pharmacy
51 Dom Inostrannoi Knigi Дом Иностранной Книги
55 Post Office Почтамт
58 36.6 Pharmacy
64 S7 Airline Office
73 Capital Tours

social groups; art by ex-Gulag prisoners; and a reproduction of a punishment cell and Gulag barracks. Don't let the lack of Russian captioning put you off.

• **Sakharov Museum** Музей А Д Сахарова (Map 2; Zemlianoy Val 57/6, **M** Kurskaya, 11am-7pm, closed Mon, free admission) charts the life of the Nobel Peace Prize-winning physicist, and focuses on the creation of the Soviet regime, dissent and its repercussions.

There are other museums devoted to Gorky, Tolstoy, Dostoyevsky, Pushkin, Chekhov, Gogol, Glinka, Bulgakov and Lermontov. For details of these and other museums in Moscow see 💻 www.russianmuseums.info.

PRACTICAL INFORMATION

Arriving in Moscow

By air Moscow has five airports. **Sheremetyevo 2** (SVO; ☎ 232 6565, 🖳 www.sheremetyevo-airport.ru), 35km from the city centre, is used only for international flights. Many foreign airlines currently use this inadequate, worn-out airport, built for the 1980 Olympics, while others use Domodedovo (see below). The arrivals hall has an information desk whose multilingual staff will at least direct you to the public transport. A kiosk in the hall sells city maps. **Sheremetyevo 1** has mainly domestic flights plus some international ones to Mongolia and former-USSR destinations.

Getting to and from Sheremetyevo 2 has become much easier since the introduction of the Aeroexpress train (every hour, 5am-11.30pm, R300) that runs to Belorussky Train Station, right next to **M** Belorusskaya, in just 35 minutes. Otherwise, marshrutka (minibus) 949 runs to **M** Rechnoy Vokzal (last stop on green line 2), which is also served by the slower bus No 851 (every half an hour, 6am-11pm, R25), which runs between the two airports and takes around 90 minutes to get to the metro station. A free shuttle also runs between the two airports.

Change a bit of foreign currency into low-denomination rouble notes before boarding as drivers won't accept anything else. You may be charged a nominal extra fare on the bus if you have a lot of baggage. Given the abundance and quality of public transport, taking a taxi into town would be one of the longest and most expensive options, and is best avoided.

City-run **Domodedovo** (DME, ☎ 933 6666, 🖳 www.domodedovo.ru) airport has metamorphosed into an efficient, modern facility, handling domestic connections to Siberian destinations plus international charter flights. Many international carriers (including Transaero, British Airways, Swissair, Lufthansa and Egyptair) are now opting for its modern facilities. Hang onto your baggage reclaim ticket as you may be unable to retrieve your bags without it. The quickest way to and from Moscow city centre is the Aeroexpress train (every half an hour, 6am-midnight, R300), which takes 45 minutes to get to Paveletsky Vokzal and the adjacent **M** Paveletskaya. Alternatively, take one of the bright blue Scania buses (every 15 mins, R80), which take an hour on a good day to reach **M** Paveletskaya.

You're advised to avoid taxis into the city centre from Domodedovo, as they can take at least two hours and could cost R2500.

The other two airports are **Vnukovo**, a small airport which is served by a few international flights, and **Sheremetyevo 3**, exclusively for private jets.

By train Moscow has nine railway stations (see Map 1), which are all handily connected to the Metro. The stations are:

- **Belorussky vokzal** (**M** Belorusskaya) Serves Berlin, Warsaw, Minsk, Vilnius, Kaliningrad and Prague.
- **Kazansky vokzal** (**M** Komsomolskaya) Trains to Kazan, Tashkent, Samara, Ulan-Ude, Yekaterinburg (Sverdlovsk on the timetables), some to Vladimir and Nizhny Novgorod.
- **Kievsky vokzal** (**M** Kievskaya) Trains to Kiev, Odessa, Budapest and Bucharest, plus the Aeroexpress to Vnukovo Airport for mostly domestic flights.
- **Kursky vokzal** (**M** Kurskaya) Trains to the Caucasus, Eastern Ukraine, Crimea, Azerbaijan and Georgia. Some trains to Vladimir, Nizhny Novgorod and Perm.
- **Leningradsky vokzal** (**M** Komsomolskaya) Serves Helsinki, St Petersburg, Tallinn, and the north of Russia.
- **Paveletsky vokzal** (**M** Paveletskaya) Aeroexpress to/from Domodedovo Airport.
- **Rizhsky vokzal** (**M** Rizhskaya) Serves Riga.
- **Savyolovsky vokzal** (**M** Savyolovskaya) Aeroexpress train to/from Sheremetyevo-2 airport.
- **Yaroslavsky vokzal** (**M** Komsomolskaya) The departure point for most Trans-Siberian trains, serving Vladivostok, Mongolia and China. Note that it's opposite Leningradsky vokzal, so make sure you're in the correct railway station.

> ❑ **STREET TERMINOLOGY**

bulvar (bul) бульвар (бул)	boulevard
gostinny dvor гостинный двор	shopping arcade
most мост	bridge
naberezhnaya (nab) набережная (наб)	embankment
ploshchad (pl) площадь (пл)	square
prospekt (pr) проспект (пр)	avenue
pereulok (per) переулок (пер)	lane/side street
shosse шоссе	highway
ulitsa (ul) улицса (ул)	street

Local transport

Metro The palatial metro system (**see map opposite p512**), a tourist attraction in itself, is the most efficient way to travel around Moscow. The metro uses magnetic cards available in denominations of 1, 2, 5, 10 and 20 rides; it's worth buying a multiple-ride ticket to avoid queueing. A ride to anywhere on the system costs R26. Buy tickets inside the metro station building at windows marked касса.

The metro runs daily 6am-1am. During peak hours, trains arrive every one or two minutes and you're unlikely to wait more than five minutes even at midnight. Peak-hour trains are very crowded. Metro stations are marked with **large red 'M' signs outside** and stations names are displayed in Russian and English.

Useful Cyrillic signs to recognise are вход (entrance), выход (exit), переход (crossover between stations) and выход в город (way out or exit to street level).

Buses, trams and trolleybuses All of these function under the same ticketing system. Services are comprehensive but can be overcrowded. Tickets cost R24 from kiosks, R28 from the driver. Virtually any Russian car can be a **taxi** (see pp64-5) but for your own safety don't get in if there are already passengers. Recommended taxi companies include Accord Logistic (☎ 8 800) with English-speaking drivers.

Moscow's only **monorail** runs between **M** VDNKha on the orange line to **M** Timiryazevskaya on the grey line.

Orientation and services

At the very centre of the city are the Kremlin, Red Square and St Basil's Cathedral. Moscow is not unlike a spider's web, with main roads branching out from the centre and consecutive circles of ring roads. The most conveniently placed (and generally expensive) hotels are in this area. The metro system is efficient, however, so it's not vital to stay at a hotel right on Red Square.

Money Banks and **ATMs** are everywhere in Moscow. Currency exchanges are also easy to find, though at the time of writing, the Russian government had passed a law stating that all currency exchanges must do something else as well as change money, or face closure, so the system is currently undergoing restructuring.

US dollars and euros can be exchanged at almost any bank or currency exchange; with other currencies you must go to larger bank branches. Credit cards are widely accepted in big cities, Visa and MasterCard in particular. It's a good idea to hoard your small change for your travels because many shops and businesses find it difficult to break large denomination notes.

Travellers' cheques are accepted at major banks but hardly anywhere else and are tedious to cash (you must show your passport and often your purchase receipts).

American Express (Vetoshny per 17, **M** Teatralnaya, 10am-7pm) accept only their own cheques. There's an ATM for American Express cards.

Diplomatic representation **Australia** Map 2; Podkolokolny per 10A/2, **M** Kitay-Gorod, ☎ 956 6070; **Belarus** Map 4; ul Maroseyka 17/6, **M** Chistiye Prudy, ☎ 921 3071; **Canada** Map 4; Starokonyushenny per 23, **M** Smolenskaya, ☎ 956 666; **China** Map 1; ul Druzhby 6, **M** Universitet, ☎ 938 2006; **France** Map 3; ul Bolshaya Yakimanka, **M** Oktyabyrskaya, ☎ 937 1500; **Germany** Map 1; ul Mosfilmovskaya 56, **M** Universitet, ☎ 937 9500; **Ireland** Map 2; Grokholsky per 5, **M** Prospekt Mira, ☎ 937 5911; **Japan** Map 4; Kalashny per 12, **M** Arbatskaya, ☎ 202 8303; **Mongolia** Map 2; Borisogrebsky per 11, **M** Arbatskaya, ☎ 290 6792; **Netherlands** Map 4; Kalashny per 6, **M** Arbatskaya, ☎ 797 2900; **New Zealand** Map 2; ul Povarskaya 44, **M** Barrikadnaya, ☎ 956 3579; **UK** Map 2; Smolenskaya nab 10, **M** Smolenskaya, ☎ 956 7200; **Ukraine** Map 4; Leontyevsky per 18, **M** Tverskaya, ☎ 629 0681; **USA** Map 2; Novinsky bul 19/23, **M** Smolenskaya, ☎ 956 4227.

Local publications English-language freesheets, available in the lobbies of larger hotels, theatres, etc, include the worthy *Moscow Times* (💻 www.themoscowtimes.com), whose weekend edition has good listings and travel sections, while *The Moscow News* (💻 www.mnweekly.ru) covers domestic and international politics. The St Petersburg listings magazine *Pulse* has an excellent Moscow edition too.

Fun and foul-mouthed, *The eXile* (💻 www.exile.ru) discards political correctness but is worth it for the ruthlessly honest listings.

Element (💻 www.elementmoscow.ru) is a weekly featuring restaurant reviews and concert listings.

Finally, *In Your Pocket* guides (💻 www.inyourpocket.com) print the excellent *Moscow In Your Pocket* listings guide several times a year, though it can be quite difficult to find; the website features all the listings, plus up-to-date concert listings.

Medical The **European Medical Centre** (Map 4; Spiridonyevsky per 5/1, **M** Pushkinskaya, ☎ 933 6655, 💻 www.emcmos.ru) offers 24-hour medical and dental services; also at Orlovsky per 7, **M** Prospekt Mira. Doctor on call ☎ 933 6645.

The **American Medical Center** (Map 2; Grokholsky per 1 (**M** Prospekt Mira, ☎ 933 7700, 💻 www.amcenter.ru) also offers 24-hour emergency medical and dental services and has an on-site pharmacy with English-speaking staff.

Pharmacies are easy to come by: **36.6** is a good, reliable chain that's open 24 hours. Branches are located at ul Novy Arbat 15 (Map 4), **M** Arbatskaya; Kuznetsky Most 18/7, **M** Kuznetsky Most; and ul Pokrovka 1/13 (Map 2), **M** Kitay-Gorod/ Lubyanka.

Russian visas and extensions The situation with visa extensions is ever-changing. At the time of writing, tourist visas were not eligible for an extension, so if you're not sure how long you'll be travelling for, get a visa for a longer time period than you think you'll need.

In heading west, bear in mind that many trains from Russia into Eastern Europe cross the border after midnight, so make sure your visa is still valid (see Russian visas, pp22-6).

Telecommunications The **main post office** Почтамт (Map 4; ul Myasnitskaya 26, **M** Chistiye Prudy) and the **Central Telegraph Office** Центральная Почта и Телеграф (Map 4; ul Tverskaya 7, **M** Tverskaya) are both good places for phone calls and all your postal needs. Rates are listed in English and there are some English-speaking staff. They also sell discount phonecards – their own Tsentel as well as rival brands – which offer much cheaper international calls from domestic or hotel telephones.

Street telephones (*taksofon*) for local calls use cards sold at some kiosks, though they are increasingly difficult to find with the proliferation of mobile phones. For more on telephone cards and on making local and long-distance calls see pp68-9.

There are numerous places to access the **internet** in Moscow: Cafemax (open 24 hours) is at ul Pyatnintskaya 25/1 (Map 3), **M** Novokuznetskaya; also at Moscow State University, ul Leninskiye Gory 1/54, **M** Universitet, and at ul Novoslobodskaya 3 (Map 2) **M** Novoslobodskaya). Time Online (Map 4; on the bottom level of the Manezh shopping complex, **M** Okhotny Ryad, and also at pl Komsomolskaya 3, Map 2, **M** Komsomolskaya) is also open 24 hours and has English-speaking staff. English-language browsers are available on request; access costs R70 per hour.

More and more hotels, hostels and cafés now offer **wi-fi**; see pp186-9 for more details.

Tours **Capital Tours** (Map 4; ul Ilyinka 4, entrance 6, office 21, **M** Kitay-Gorod, ☎ 232 2442, 💻 www.capitaltours.ru) offer a walking tour of the Kremlin, a Moscow Metro/Secret Bunker tour, and 'Moscow All Around' – a bus tour that takes in the city's main sights. The bus doesn't run frequently enough to be a hop-on, hop-off bus, but it does give you around 20 minutes at each site to take photos.

Patriarshy Dom Tours (☎ 795 0927, 💻 http://russiatravel-pdtours.netfirms.com, 9am-6pm Mon-Fri) run highly rated English-language excursions – both obvious ones, such as tours of the Kremlin, and more specialised ones, such as Jewish Moscow and tours around famous writers' houses – that are popular with the hostel crowd as well as upmarket travellers.

It's worth enquiring about the KGB tour that they occasionally offer, which includes demonstrations of miniature cameras, micro-dots, bugging techniques and more at the Federal Counterintelligence Service (KGB) Museum, plus a great deal of whitewash about the darker side of the KGB's history. You cannot visit this museum except on a tour.

Moscow Mania (☎ 916 992 4644, 💻 www.mosmania.com, 9am-9pm) is a team of young, energetic female guides who can put together anything, from classic Red Square/Kremlin jaunts to themed Soviet tours and 'Moscow mysteries' tours which titillate visitors with the more salacious tidbits from the city's history. Walking tours cost from R350.

There's a pleasant **river trip** (R200) which leaves from outside Evropeisky Shopping Centre, **M** Kievskaya every 15 minutes (May-Oct) and stops at different sightseeing spots – Sparrow Hills, Gorky Park and Neskuchny Gardens – on its way towards the Kremlin. The 1½ hour trip ends at the Novospassky Bridge terminal, about 2km past the Kremlin. R400 one way, or R800 unlimited day pass.

Travel agencies General travel agencies are convenient sources for rail tickets, plane tickets and visa support and accept at least some credit cards.

For those who know exactly what they want, the service bureaux at railway stations are cheaper and just as competent; if your itinerary is simple you can go right to the source and avoid any mark-up. For details see Moving on, pp192-3.

Almost all the hostels and hotels have travel desks and provide visa support and travel services as well as excursions. You could also try:

- **Star Travel** (Map 1; ul Baltiiskaya 9, 3rd floor, **M** Sokol, ☎ 797 9555, 💻 www.star travel.ru, 10am-7pm Mon-Fri, 11am-4pm Sat). This student-friendly agency does hotel bookings and air ticketing, and sells international youth and student cards.
- **UniFest Travel** (Map 3; Komsomolsky pr 16/2, **M** Park Kultury, ☎ 234 6555, 💻 http://unifest.ru/eng, 9am-9pm Mon-Fri, 10am-7pm Sat & Sun) concentrates on outbound air and rail tickets and visa support.

Useful websites

- 💻 **www.inyourpocket.com/russia/Moscow** Extensive independent reviews of accommodation, clubs and restaurants, as well as a plethora of practical advice.
- 💻 **www.redtape.ru** Expat forum where you can find answers to almost any question about the country.
- 💻 **www.moscow-taxi.com** Extensive descriptions of sites in and around Moscow provided by Victor the virtual taxi driver.
- 💻 **www.moscowmaximum.blogspot.com** Anonymous blog bringing you the best of Moscow's nightlife.
- 💻 **www.maps-moscow.com** Moscow Architecture Preservation Society focuses on historical buildings under threat in the capital.

Where to stay

All prices given below are for high season and include 18% VAT where applicable. In upmarket hotels you may be quoted a price without tax so it's worth checking. Note that some places set their prices in US dollars or euros and then charge in roubles according to that day's rate or a rate set by the hostel or hotel.

Budget accommodation Moscow has numerous hostels, with more and more opening each year. They have English-speaking staff and facilities to satisfy most budget travellers, including internet or wi-fi access (unless stated otherwise), and offer services such as transfers to/from the airport or railway station and visa support.

British-run ***Godzillas Hostel*** (Map 2; Большой Каретный пер 6 1-й этаж кв 5, Bolshoi Karetny per 6 apt 5 1st floor, **M** Tsetnoy Bulvar, ☎ 699 4223, 🖳 www.godzillashostel.com, dorm/dbl/trpl R910/2260/3100) is a large, lively hostel a short distance from the centre in a quiet area. Perks include helpful staff, free internet access, three kitchens and satellite TV in the lounge. They also organise tours and book train tickets.

Given the excellent central location of the ***Trans-Siberian Hostel*** (Map 2; Барашевский пер 12, Barashevskiy per 12, **M** Kurskaya, ☎ 916 2030, 🖳 www.transsiberianhostel.com, dorm/dbl R625-750/2200), the cost of a double room is an absolute bargain. There's a communal kitchen and the staff can help you plan your Trans-Siberian trip and direct you to the many nearby attractions. From **M** Kurskaya take the underpass to get to the west side of ul Zemlyanoy. Walk north and take the second street, Bolshoi Kazonny per which leads into Barashevskiy per; the hostel is at No 12.

***Napoleon Hostel* Хостел Наполеон** (Map 4; Малый Златоустинский пер 2, 4-й этаж, Maly Zlatoustinskiy per 2, 4th floor, **M** Kitay-Gorod, ☎ 624 5978, 🖳 www.napoleonhostel.com, dorm R500-800) is in a superb location only a few minutes' walk from Red Square. Popular backpacker haunt with large, comfortable bunk beds and a custom-built ventilation system that's a blessing in summer. The comfy lounge has a plasma TV and there is a nightly happy hour at the on-site small bar. Two bathrooms for 47 guests is the only drawback. Breakfast R99 extra. Take the Maroseyka exit from **M** Kitay-Gorod.

Not quite so central but still an excellent choice since it's well-equipped (with several bathrooms) is ***Home Hostel*** (Map 3; 2-й Неопалимовский пер 1/12, 2-oy Neopalimovsky per 1/12, **M** Park Kultury, ☎ 778 2445, 🖳 www.moshostel.com, dorm/dbl/en suite dbl R490-865/ 2250/3200). Clean, spacious rooms on two floors range from the 14-person dorm for the budget-conscious to private en suite facilities, the common room is a great place to meet fellow travellers and the multilingual staff are on hand to assist with buying train tickets or giving tips on the best of Moscow's nightlife. From **M** Park Kultury take the exit to Zubovsky bul and follow this busy street in the opposite direction to the river. Turn down ul Burdenko, the fourth street on the left, and then take the second street on the right to reach the hostel.

On one of Moscow's most popular streets, ***Eesti Airlines Hostel*** (Map 2; ул Тверская 27/2 кв 83, ul Tverskaya 27/2 apt 83, **M** Tverskaya, ☎ 926 060 6000, 🖳 6460005@mail.ru, dorm/dbl R600/1800) is a new hostel in a converted apartment. It does not have a common room, so all socialising is done in the dorms or in the small kitchen, and there is only one computer for guest use (though it does have wi-fi). On the upside, the young owner is helpful, all rooms have air-con, which you'll appreciate in the summer, and not only are you a 20-minute walk from Red Square, but there are plenty of places to eat along Tverskaya. To reach the hostel, walk through the archway just before the blue Pepsi shop and take the first entrance on the left.

In the grounds of the 18th-century Silver Trinity church on the bank of the Moskva River, ***Hostel and Hotel Basilica* Базилика Хостел** (Map 2; Серебрянический пер 1a, Serebryanichesky per 1a, **M** Kitay-Gorod, ☎ 669 8645, 🖳 www.sweetmoscow.com, dorm/hostel dbl/

hotel dbl R700/2500-2700/3500-4500) is a unique place to stay. The spacious, luxurious rooms – once inhabited by monks – are complimented by clean, colourful bathrooms, kitchen and lounge, and guests even get a free tour of the church's bell tower, which is closed to the public. There is no computer, but the hostel offers free wi-fi and the location couldn't be better – just a 10-minute walk from the Kremlin and with great views to boot. Take the ul Solyanka exit from **M** Kitay-Gorod, follow ul Solyanka for 500m until you reach the church bell tower, take the stairs down to Serebryanichesky per and the hostel is the first building on the left.

A five-minute walk from the Kremlin, ***Artel Hotel*** **Артель Отель** (Map 4; Театральный проезд 3/3, Teatralny proezd 3/3, **M** Kuznetsky Most, ☎ 626 9008, 🖳 www.artelhotel.ru, sgl/dbl R3100-5200/3400-5700) couldn't be more different from the above. An art concept hotel, each of its rooms is uniquely decorated in a bold style; even the bathrooms haven't escaped the same treatment. Very popular among night owls (it's on the 3rd floor above the Barbarello bar and the bohemian Masterskaya night club), this is not the place for an early night due to the live music downstairs several times a week. There is no kitchen, but Masterskaya downstairs does good business lunches, there's good wi-fi access in all the rooms and the travel desk can assist you with journey planning. All rooms have fans, but note that the economy singles/doubles have no windows and are like ovens in summer.

Homestays are possible from about R1000 per day. Contact Host Families Association (HOFA; see p153).

Mid-range accommodation ***Sputnik*** **Спутник** (Map 3; Ленинский пр 38, Leninsky pr 38, **M** Leninsky Prospekt, ☎ 930 2287, 🖳 www.hotelsputnik.ru, sgl/dbl/suite R4400/4960/8040), a multi-storey Soviet relic, is a little out of the centre, but the rooms are comfortable (though the singles are on the small side) and there's a good Indian restaurant on the 16th floor. Breakfast costs R370 extra.

Hotel Melodiya **Гостиница Мелодия** (Map 4; Скатерный пер 13, Skaterny per 13, **M** Arbatskaya, ☎ 643 1910, 🖳 www.melody-hotel.com, sgl/dbl/suite R5500/5900/8400), located in a quiet street just off the popular Arbat area, belongs to the Soviet record company Melodiya (hence the lilting tunes when you enter). There's still a Soviet feel to the rooms, which are comfortable though lack oomph. The singles are particularly spacious and the hotel does 'deal of the day' discounts.

Nearby, ***Hotel Arbat*** **Гостиница Арбат** (Map 3; Плотников пер 12, Plotnikov per 12, **M** Smolenskaya, ☎ 499 271 2801, 🖳 www.president-hotel.ru/arbat/index, sgl/dbl/suite R10,500/13,500/16,000) is modern and stylish, with large rooms equipped with flat-screen TVs and fridges. The winter garden is particularly pleasant.

North of the centre, the renovated Soviet giant ***Hotel Cosmos*** **Гостиница Космос** (Map 1; пр Мира 150, pr Mira 150, **M** VDNKHa, ☎ 234 1000, 🖳 www.hotelcosmos.ru, dbl/suite R8150/10,500) features clean, basic rooms and grand views of the VDNKHa monuments across the street, as well as the Ostankino tower.

The small, friendly business ***Hotel Akvarel*** **Гостиница Акварель** (Map 4; Столешников пер 12/3, Stoleshnikov per 12/3, **M** Teatralnaya, ☎ 502 9430, 🖳 www.hotelakvarel.ru, dbl/suite R10,150/13,000) distinguishes itself by its excellent service and its rooms, where the beds are separated from the main room by an alcove, giving them a touch of personality. The décor features watercolours – a nod to the hotel's name.

The beautiful boutique ***Assambleya Nikitskaya*** **Ассамблея Никитская** (Map 4; ул Большая Никитская 12/2, ul Bolshaya Nikitskaya 12/2, **M** Okhotny Ryad, ☎ 933 5001, 🖳 www.assambleya-

The Moscow area code is ☎ 495. From outside Russia dial ☎ +7-495.

hotels.ru, sgl/dbl/suite R8900/10,900/13,700) should be particularly commended for its ultra-comfortable rooms, with even the singles having sumptuous beds large enough for two people. Other nice touches include heated floors in the bathrooms, wi-fi access and helpful staff who can book all manner of tickets for you.

An upmarket hotel at a budget price, ***Ibis Paveletskaya*** **Ибис Павелетская** (Map 3; ул Щипок 22/1, ul Shchipok 22/1, **M** Paveletskaya, ☎ 661 8500, 🖳 www.ibishotel.com, sgl/dbl R5900/7100), housed in a brand-new building, features bright, fully equipped rooms, with the ones facing north being particularly spacious. Breakfast is R800 extra. Disabled travellers welcome.

Hotel Kebur Palace **Гостиница Кебур Палас** (Map 3; ул Остоженка 32, ul Ostozhenka 32, **M** Kropotkinskaya, ☎ 733 9070, 🖳 www.keburpalace.ru, sgl/dbl/suite R11,000/12,000/20,665), in the shadow of the Church of the Saviour, is an elegant hotel with walnut and mahogany detailing, a superb indoor swimming pool and a libraryesque feel to its long dark corridors. The upmarket restaurant next door, Tiflisskiy Dvorik, serves delicious Georgian and European dishes.

Hotel East-West **Гостиница Восток-Запад** (Map 4; Тверской Бул 14/4, Tverskoy bul 14/4, **M** Pushkinskaya, ☎ 690 0404, 🖳 www.eastwesthotel.ru, sgl/dbl/suite R8200/11,000/14,400) is a four-star boutique hotel in a charming 19th-century mansion (part of the former Governor's residence) on an historic central street. The décor inside matches the building's history, with each room individually decorated, and there's an intimate restaurant on-site.

Upmarket hotels These prices include 18% VAT, but it's always worth checking when you're quoted a price.

Marriott Moscow Royal Aurora Hotel **Марриотт Москва Аврора** (Map 4; ул Петровка 11/20, ul Petrovka 11/20, **M** Kuznetsky Most, ☎ 937 1000, 🖳 www.marriott.com, dbl/suite from R35,000/R45,000) is a bastion of refinement. Expect classically styled rooms, enormous, luxurious beds, well-trained butlers catering to your every need and white-gloved waiters serving you at the Polo Club Steakhouse, reminiscent of a British gentlemen's club.

In contrast, ***Golden Apple Boutique Hotel*** (Map 2; ул Малая Дмитровка 11, ul Malaya Dmitrovka 11, **M** Tverskaya, ☎ 980 7000, 🖳 www.goldenapple.ru, dbl/suite R18,000/35,000) is ultra-modern, with a combination of luxurious minimalism and avant-garde features. Rooms are stylishly decorated with marble, stone and natural wood, the Apple Restaurant boasts skillfully prepared international dishes and, faithful to the hotel name, apples abound – including the giant golden apple that you can sit in, in the lobby.

The city's first hotel, the ***Hilton Leningradskaya*** Хилтон Ленинградская (Map 2; ул Каланчевская 21/40, ul Kalanchevskaya 21/40, **M** Krasniye Vorota, ☎ 627 5550, 🖳 www1.hilton.com, dbl/suite R17,000/20,000-74,000) is now one of the grandest, housed inside one of the seven Stalinist skyscrapers, yet oozing elegance. Its six-storey chandelier is in the *Guinness Book of Records*, each room boasts panoramic views of Moscow and offers the ultimate in comfort. The icing on the cake is the luxurious spa, swimming pool and a superb gourmet restaurant. Breakfast costs R1260 extra.

As much an historic monument as a place to stay, it was at ***Hotel Metropol*** **Гостиница Метрополь** (Map 4; Театральный проезд 2, Teatralny Proezd 2, **M** Teatralnaya, ☎ 499 501 7848, 🖳 www.metropol-moscow.ru, sgl/dbl/suite R14,000/16,000/20,000-65,000), close to Red Square, where Rasputin is said to have dined and Lenin to have made several speeches. Its beautiful Art Nouveau interior has remained unchanged since the 1917 revolution and it also featured in the film *Dr Zhivago*. Besides the princely rooms, there is a sumptuous banquet hall and a large indoor swimming pool.

It's difficult to get any closer to the Kremlin than in the ***Hotel Baltschug Kempinski*** **Гостиница Балчуг-Кемпинский** (Map 4; ул Балчуг 1, ul Balchug 1, **M** Novokuznetskaya, ☎ 287

2000, 🖳 www.kempinski.com/ru/moscow, dbl/suite R38,000/47,000). The service is impeccable and the riverside location affords superb views of some of Moscow's top sights. The facilities are all you would expect in a hotel of this class, with marble bathtubs in the most incredible of bathrooms, and satellite telephones. Some of the rooms have even been designed by minor members of the British royal family. On-site eating options include the highly recommended Baltchug and the Japanese restaurant Shogun. High-profile guests have included Helmut Kohl, Tina Turner and Sting.

Where to eat and drink

You can find just about anything you want to eat in Moscow and it is an immensely rewarding city for a diner with means. Your budget will stretch furthest if you take advantage of the weekday 'business lunch' deals.

The **Arbat** (see p169) is lined with restaurants largely aimed at tourists, so prices can be accordingly high. Other streets with a fair number of reasonable eateries are **Myasnitskaya**, starting from **M** Lyubyanka, ul Tverskaya (**M** Tverskaya) and **Maroseyka** (**M** Kitay-Gorod).

Fast food and cafés You can get hot dogs, burgers, shwarma-kebab, pancakes and snacks of all kinds at kiosks gathered around most metro stations, for very low prices. Fast-food chains abound – particularly McDonald's and Rostik's (KFC). 'Summer cafés', serving beer, pizza and snacks at rock-bottom prices, spring up on any spare patch of ground.

For cheap, ultra-convenient fast food close to Red Square, the multi-concession **Food Court** on the bottom level of the Manezh Shopping Complex (Map 4; **M** Okhotny Ryad) has everything from Russian to Italian to Korean food, plus clean lavatories.

For super-cheap Russian café food – pies, pastries, soups etc – ***Russkoye Bistro*** **Русское Бистро** (Map 4) has branches all over Moscow, notably on ул Покровка, ul Petrovka, behind the TsUM department store and Bolshoi Theatre, where you can sit outside in summer.

Coffee Bean (Map 2; ул Покровка 19, ul Pokrovka 19, **M** Chistiye Prudy) may be the opposite of intimate, being inside a giant hall, but its coffee is superb and the staff efficient and attentive.

Gogol Mogol **Гоголь-Моголь** (Map 3; Гагаринский пер 6, Gagarinsky per 6, **M** Kropotkinskaya, [V]), on the other hand, is an attractive little café with a red silk interior, equally good coffee and a most tempting array of cakes and homemade ice cream.

Stolle **Штолле** (Map 3; ул Малая Пироговская 16, ul Malaya Pirogovskaya 16, **M** Sportivnaya, [V]) serves pies and only pies – meat pies, fish pies and berry pies, and it executes them beyond reproach. Gobble them there or take them away.

Mu-Mu **Му-Му** (Map 2; ул Арбат 45/24, ul Arbat 45/24, **M** Smolenskaya, [V]) appeals to locals and visitors alike. Grab a tray and shuffle past the counters displaying an array of salads, soups, meat and fish dishes and desserts, pointing at what you want. Look for the gormless black-and-white plastic cow outside.

More kitschy than Mu-Mu, the ***Yolki-Palki*** **Ёлки-Палки** (Map 4; ул Арбат 16/2, ul Arbat 16/2, **M** Arbatskaya, R550, [V]) rustic-style theme restaurant features an all-you-can-eat buffet and a wide selection of main courses and drinks. The name, a favourite cuss of Russian villagers, roughly translates as 'bleedin' 'ell!'

For tasty blini with a myriad of fillings, great fish soup and beer on tap head for ***Teremok*** **Теремок** (Map 3; ул Пятницкая 2/38, ul Pyatnitskaya 2/38, **M** Kuznetsky Most, [V]). Also at Okhotny Ryad shopping centre opposite the Kremlin.

In summer, some of the best **shashlyk Шашлык** in the city is found in Izmailovsky Park, Измайловский Парк, (**M** Izmailovsky Park) though some people have been told one price upon ordering and a different price at the end. For even better shashlyk, look for the gazebo run by the friendly Armenians at Lublino Palace.

A stone's throw from Red Square, ***Pelmeshka*** **Пельмешка** (Map 4; ул Никольская 8/1, ul Nikolskaya 8/1, **M**

Ploshchad Revolutsii, mains R180) is a cheap lunch spot where you point to the buffet-style array of pelmeni and crêpes. Look for the sign of the dancing dumpling.

Directly opposite the Kremlin, ***Eat & Talk*** (Map 4; ул Моховая 7, ul Mokhovaya 7, **M** Aleksandrovsky Sad, [V]) is perfect for just that. It's not the easiest to find, being inside a nondescript building, but once you do, you can partake of their selection of coffees, smoothies, salads and desserts while simultaneously checking your email; there's wi-fi access and they even rent laptops by the hour!

Restaurants ***Genatsvale na Arbate*** **Генатсвале На Арбате** (Map 4; ул Новый Арбат 11/2, ul Novy Arbat 11/2, **M** Arbatskaya, mains R450, [V]) may sport ultra-kitschy décor, but the Georgian dishes it serves are wonderfully flavourful. Don't miss the *satsivi* (chicken with walnut sauce), the ultra-cheesy khachapuri, the exquisite grilled meats or the *lobio* (bean paste with herbs). Slightly more upscale is the original restaurant (ул Остоженка 121, ul Ostozhenka 121, **M** Kropotkinskaya), with excellent service and live music; it's considered one of the best in the city.

With its light interior and minimalist décor, ***Khacha-puri*** **Хача-Пури** (Map 4; Большой Грездниковский пер 12, Bolshoy Gnezdnikovsky per 12, **M** Tverskaya, mains R350) offers good Georgian food without the pomp and ceremony. The *khinkali* (large meat dumplings) are particularly tasty, but the selection of dishes doesn't match Genatsvale.

For hearty Ukrainian dishes at wallet-friendly prices, try ***Korchma Taras Bulba*** **Корчма Тарас Бульба** (Map 3; ул Пятницкая 14, ul Pyatnitskaya 14, **M** Novokuznetskaya, mains R550), with a cutesy-folksy interior, good service and a Bible-sized menu of hearty favourites. There are branches at 13 other locations around the city.

For Russian dishes, as enjoyed by the nobles of old, within stylish cellar surroundings, head to ***Bochonok*** **Бочонок** (Map 4; ул Мясницкая 24/3, ul Myasnitskaya 24/3, **M** Chistiye Prudy, mains R500). The stews, soups and grilled meats are well prepared and the service is remarkably friendly.

Goodman Steak House (Map 4; ул Тверская 23, ul Tverskaya 23, **M** Tverskaya, mains R500-1500) is particularly popular with the local business set. Chic interior, great service, and decent (though expensive) steaks make this a good lunch or dinner spot. The business lunch (R400) is a good deal. Next to Goodman, ***Filimonova & Yankel*** **Филимонова & Янкель** (Map 4) is a busy upscale spot specialising in excellent fish and seafood dishes at reasonable prices. The grilled seafood platter (R740) is a meal in itself, but your bill can grow considerably if you pick from their extensive wine selection.

For great pizza and pasta, head to ***Pasta i Basta*** **Паста и Баста** ('Pasta and that's it!', Map 4; Сретенский бул 4, Sretensky bul 4, **M** Turgenevskaya, [V]), open until 5am at weekends for the post-party set. Even better pizza is found at the classy ***Bocconcino*** **Бок514кончино** (Map 4; Страстной бул 7/1, Strastnoy bul 7/1, **M** Tverskaya, [V]), the light and crispy base complemented by numerous toppings. The drawback is the extortionate drink prices.

Once you get past the kitschy gold-and-red décor at ***Mama Tao*** **Мама Тао** (Map 3; ул Пятницкая 56/1, ul Pyatnitskaya 56/1, **M** Dobryninskaya, mains R350, [V]), you can enjoy the light, fragrant dim sum, noodle soups and an array of other inexpensive Chinese dishes.

An expat favourite, ***Aroma*** **Арома** (Map 1; ул Крижизановская 20/30, ul Krizhizanovskaya 20/30, **M** Profosoyuznaya, mains R4500, [V]) serves authentic Indian dishes courtesy of its six Indian chefs. The tandoori and the South Indian dishes are particularly good.

Prostiye Veshchi **Простые Вещи** (Map 4; ул Большая Никитская 14/2, ul Bolshaya Nikitskaya 14/2, **M** Okhotny Ryad) means 'simple things' but it's anything but. This bohemian wine bar offers attentive service and lovingly prepared Eurocentric dishes that are popular with the dancers and musicians from the Conservatoire across the street. Adjacent to the Conservatoire, ***Coffeemania*** **Кофемания** (Map 4; mains R550, [V]) is an upscale restaurant serving imaginative dishes such as buckwheat noodles with prawns, pappardelle with rabbit ragout, an array of lovely salads and soups and some very expensive drinks. Great service.

If you feel like pushing the boat out for Moscow's top Russian food, ***Café Pushkin*** **Кафе Пушкин** (Map 4; Тверской бул 26а, Tverskoy bul 26a, **M** Pushkinskaya, ☎ 229 5590), is the place to see and be seen, a favourite of government ministers and film stars alike. The interior is in the style of a 19th-century gentleman's study, complete with globes, telescope and leather-bound books. Immaculate cuisine runs at R1000 and above for dinner.

Avocado **Авокадо** (Map 2; Чистопрудный бул 12/2, Chistoprudny bul 12/2, **M** Chistiye Prudy, [V]) is a popular vegetarian eatery; though its interior is a bit spartan, the dishes featuring mushrooms, tofu and spinach come highly recommended and there's also an extensive choice of teas to wash them down with.

Boasting a French-Italian menu, ***Club Mayak*** **Клуб Маяк** (Map 4; ул Большая Никитская 19, ul Bolshaya Nikitskaya 19, mains R350) is the favourite hangout place of journalists, artists and intellectuals. Despite the name and the atmosphere, it's not actually a club and you don't have to be a member to go in. The interesting toilets deserve a mention.

Bars and nightclubs

Moscow has great nightlife. You can have as wild a time as in any Western city, or wilder, but be prepared to wake up with a throbbing head and an empty wallet.

Among the **bars**, one of the most popular expat places is ***Silvers*** (Map 4; ул Тверская 5, ul Tverskaya 5, **M** Okhotny Ryad), a perpetually packed, thimble-sized sports bar with two TV screens tuned into the football/cricket/rugby match of the day.

John Bull Pub (Map 2; Карманицкий пер 9, Karmanitsky per 9, **M** Smolenskaya), part of the Europe-wide chain, is popular with locals and expats alike, thanks to its easy-going atmosphere, great range of beers and a Russian take on pub grub. In an area dominated by 'elitny' clubs blighted by 'face control' (see box p156), the expat-owned ***My Bar*** (Map 4; ул Кузнецкий Мост 3/2, ul Kuznetsky Most 3/2, **M** Teatralnaya) is refreshingly down-to-earth, playing a selection of rock music while serving reasonably priced drinks into the wee hours. Inside the Swissoten Krasniye Holmy, the chic ***City Space*** (Map 3; Космодамьянская наб 52/6, Kosmodamianskaya nab 52/6, 34th floor, **M** Paveletskaya) offers unparalleled views of the city as well as an extensive cocktail menu with innovative twists.

With its polished wooden floors and brick walls, the award-winning ***Help*** (Map 2; ул 1-я Тверская-Ямская 27, ul 1-ya Tverskaya-Yamskaya 27, **M** Belorusskaya) is a cosy cocktail bar serving very affordable concoctions. Open 24 hours. Despite the silly name, ***Art Garbage*** (Map 4; Старогрaдский пер 5, Starogradsky per 5, **M** Kitay-Gorod) has a great set-up, with an attractive terrace for outdoor drinks in summer, a bar and DJs spinning tunes in the basement club at the weekend. Popular with students.

Open 24 hours, ***Club Che*** **Клуб Че** (Map 4; ул Никольская 10/2, ul Nikolskaya 10/2, **M** Lubyanka) is another expat favourite – laidback, with salsa music playing, constantly packed and hosting live music shows nightly at 10.30pm.

Like its sister club in St Petersburg, ***Purga*** **Пурга** (Map 4; Страстной бул 4/3, Strastnoy bul 4/3, **M** Chekhovskaya) is the place to celebrate Soviet New Year and mock weddings, complete with associated drunken revelry. Enter through bar Poslednyaya Kaplya in the courtyard.

Other reliable club favourites include ***Propaganda*** **Пропаганда** (Map 4; Большой Златоустинский пер 7, Bolshoy Zlatustinsky per 7), formerly a top dance club with notoriously vicious face-control; its popularity is now waning but it's still good on Thursday nights,

Friendly triple-level gay club ***Three Monkeys*** (Map 2; Наставический пер 11/1, Nastavichesky per 11/1, **M** Chkalovskaya, R200/500 men/women after midnight) hosts flamboyant transvestite shows. Face control (see box p156) applies.

Cultural life

Tickets for many of the city's theatres and other live performances can be obtained at ticket offices such as **Teatralnaya Kassa** at ul Novy Arbat 21 or in the **M** Teatralnaya.

The world-famous **Bolshoi Theatre Большой Театр** (Map 4; Teatralnaya pl 1, **M** Teatralnaya, ☎ 250 7317, 💻 www.bolshoi.ru), the sacred home of Russian opera and ballet, is closed until October 2011 for renovations. Meantime, you can catch performances by the world-famous ballet company at the adjacent **Bolshoi New Stage**. Tickets are easy to come by for around R400-2500, and can be purchased either from the box office or online (to be collected from the box office before the performance). During the summer there's a quality ballet festival at the **Youth Theatre** Театр Юного Зрителя (Map 4; RAMT Theatre) next door to the Bolshoi.

For ballet or opera on a budget, there are equally good performances at **Kremlin Palace of Congress** (see map p167; ☎ 620 7831, 💻 www.gkd-kremlin.ru, tickets R200-1000). Both venues close in the summer as both the Bolshoi Ballet and Kremlin Ballet go on tour abroad. The *Moscow Times* has what's-on listings, as does 💻 www.expat.ru.

Moscow is also home to the **Helikon Opera** Театр Хеликон-опера (Map 4; ul Novy Arbat 11/2, **M** Arbatskaya, ☎ 695 6584, 💻 www.helikon.ru) with extremely avant-garde productions.

Splendid classical-music concerts can be heard at the **Tchaikovsky Concert Hall** Консерватория имени Чайковского (Map 2; 4/31 Triumfalnaya pl, **M** Mayakovskaya, ☎ 232 0400, 💻 www.meloman.ru) and the **Rakhmaninov Conservatory** Консерватория имени Рахманинова (Map 4; ul Bolshaya Nikitskaya, **M** Okhotny Ryad) for R350-1000.

35mm cinema (Map 2; ul Pokrovka 47/24, **M** Krasnye Vorota, 💻 www.kino35mm.ru) screens undubbed mainstream and art films in the original languages. For undubbed blockbusters in English, check out **Dome Cinema** (Map 2; Olymiysky pr 18/1, **M** Prospekt Mira, 💻 www.domecinema.ru).

What to buy

Moscow's main shopping streets are ul Arbat and ul Tverskaya. Most foreigners end up buying their *matrioshkas*, ceramic boxes and furry hats from street sellers, although you should check quality first and bargain hard.

The best place for **Soviet kitsch** souvenirs is at the **flea market** at Ismaylovsky Park Измайловский Рынок (Map 1; **M** Ismaylovsky Park, 8am-8pm), where you'll find everything from Soviet posters and badges to nesting dolls and lacquer boxes. From **M** Ismaylovsky Park just follow the crowds to the market, a five-minute walk away. Get there early as some vendors leave around noon.

To stock up on books for your Trans-Siberian trip, Moscow's best selection of English-language publications is at **Dom Inostrannoi Knigi** Дом Иностранной Книги (Map 4; Kuznetsky Most 18/7, **M** Kuznetsky Most, 10am-9pm), where you can find both novels and Russian guidebooks.

Moving on

By air For tickets go to one of the travel agents on p185 or to the airlines. Domestic airlines include **Aeroflot** Аэрофлот (Map 4; ul Kuznetsky Most **M** Okhotny Ryad, ☎ 223 5555, 💻 www.aeroflot.ru), **Transaero** (Map 2; ul Bretskaya 8, **M** Mayakovskaya, ☎ 937 8459, 💻 www.transaero.com) and **S7** (Map 4; Novaya pl 3/4, **M** Kitay-Gorod, ☎ 777 9999, 💻 www.s7.ru).

Other major carriers with Moscow services include: **Air China** (Map 2; ul Novoslobodskaya 4, **M** Novoslobodskaya, ☎ 980 5768, 💻 www.airchina.com); **Air France** (Map 3; ul Korovy Val 7, **M** Dobryninskaya, ☎ 937 3839, 💻 www.airfrance.com); **British Airways** (Map 2; 4th Lesnoy per 4, **M** Belorusskaya, ☎ 363 2525, 💻 www.britishairways.com); **Delta** (Map 3; Gogolevsky bul 11, **M** Arbatskaya, ☎ 937 9090, 💻 www.delta.com); **KLM** (Map 3; ul Usacheva 33, **M** Sportivnaya, ☎ 258 3600, 💻 www.klm.com); **LOT** (Map 2; ul Trubnaya 21/11, **M** Trubnaya, ☎ 775 7737, www.lot.com); **Lufthansa** (Map 2; Posledniy per 17, **M** Sukharevskaya, ☎ 980 9999, www.lufthansa.com); **MIAT-Mongolian Airlines** (Map 2; Spasopeskovsky per 7/1, ☎ 241 0752, www.miat.com); and **Swiss International Airlines** (Map 2; Posledniy per 17, **M** Sukharevskaya, ☎ 937 7767, www.swiss.com).

There are frequent daily flights to St Petersburg from Sheremetyevo 2, plus daily flights from Domodedovo airport to many Siberian cities including Yekaterinburg, Irkutsk, Khabarovsk, Novosibirsk, Ulan-Ude and Vladivostok.

By train Trains to Siberia use either Yaroslavsky or Kazansky station (both at Komsomolskaya pl). For details of these and other connections see box p194.

If you're unsure of your plans the easiest source of tickets is one of the **travel agencies** listed on p185. Those with a straightforward itinerary can save a bit at one of the **service centres** in the stations: Yaroslavsky, Kazansky, Leningradsky, Belorussky (in the building across the tracks behind the station, at the end nearest the station), Paveletsky or Kievsky. Service is quick, some English is spoken and the price includes a mark-up of about R150 **for each ticketed segment**. Take your passport with you for ID when buying a ticket.

If you know exactly what you want, you'll do even better with a rail ticket consolidator such as **Galileo-Rus** (Map 2; ul 1905 Goda 5, **M** Ulitsa 1905 Goda, ☎ 256 9768, www.galileo.ru – Russian only).

To avoid a markup altogether, if you can read Cyrillic, you can purchase tickets directly at the **Russian railway website** www.rzd.ru, though you'll have to register first. The site accepts foreign cards (apart from any issued by Barclays), and even lets you see how many places are left on a particular train and whether they are upper or lower bunks. Upon purchase, you can print out the receipt with the barcode, which you can then use, in conjunction with your passport, at special ticket machines at the bigger railway stations (not to be confused with the machines that let you browse train timetables). Alternatively, you can note down the reference number given and then present it at any long-distance ticket office at the railway station, along with your passport, to have the tickets printed for you; allow plenty of time before departure.

Payment at Central Railway Agency offices and stations is with rouble cash only. Domestic tickets are sold for departures up to 45 days ahead, and international tickets up to 40 days ahead. Timetables (*raspisanie*) for all Moscow arrivals and departures are on sale at ticket offices.

❑ Train services from Moscow to St Petersburg

Train name	No	Journey time	Depart	Arrive
Severnaya Palmira	028	7hrs 58mins	21:30	05:28*
Ekspress	004	8hrs 01mins	23:59	08:00
Smena A Bentakur	026	7hrs 45mins	23:00	06:45
Krasnaya Strela	002	8hrs	23:55	07:55
Dve Stolitsy	064	7hrs 56mins	22:10	06:06
Sapsan	152	3hrs 45mins	06:45	10:30
Sapsan	158	3hrs 55mins	13:30	17:45
Sapsan	162	3hrs 55mins	16:30	20:25
Sapsan	164	3hrs 58mins	16:45	20:43
Sapsan	166	3hrs 45mins	19:45	23:30
Sapsan	173/174	4hrs 10mins	19:20	23:30**

**= even-numbered days only*

***= departs from Kursky vokzal rather than Leningradsky*

See box p159 for services from St Petersburg to Moscow.

❑ TRAIN SERVICES FROM MOSCOW

Moscow is Russia's biggest train hub, with numerous departures to all major cities, both in Russia and abroad. The routes listed below are the best routes to each city in question.

Moscow to other Russian cities

Destination	Train name & No	Journey time	Dep time	Arr time	Frequency
From Yaroslavsky station					
Irkutsk	044	86hrs 17mins	00:35	14:52	odd days
Novosibirsk	*Sibiryak* 026	46hrs 55mins	16:20	15:15	even days, Jun-Sep
Krasnoyarsk	*Yenisey* 056	59hrs 41mins	16:20	04:01	odd days
Tomsk	*Tomich* 038	56hrs 55mins	22:40	07:45	odd days, Jun-Sep
Ulan-Ude	*Rossiya* 002	83hrs 07mins	21:25	08:32	odd days
Khabarovsk	044	147hrs 26mins	00:35	04:01	odd days
Vladivostok	*Rossiya* 002	146hrs 08mins	21:25	23:33	odd days
Nizhny Novgorod	*Sapsan* 172	3hrs 55mins	06:45	10:40	daily
From Kazansky station					
Yekaterinburg	*Premium* 016	25hrs 33mins	16:50	18:17	daily
From Kursky station					
Vladimir	*Sapsan* 172	1hr 46mins	06:45	08:31	daily

Moscow to other international cities

Destination	Train name & No	Journey time	Dep time	Arr time	Frequency
From Yaroslavsky station					
Beijing	*Vostok* 020	144hrs 37mins	23:55	05:32	Fridays
Beijing	043	131hrs 29mins	21:35	14:04	Tuesdays
Ulaanbaatar	006	99hrs 55mins	21:35	06:30	Wed, Thur
From Belorussky station					
Berlin	013	26hrs 52mins	08:00	08:52	Sat-Tue, Thur*
Nice	017	50hrs 23mins	17:21	17:44	Thursdays*
Prague	021	33hrs 09mins	23:44	06:53	daily*
Vienna	025	8hrs	23:00	07:00	daily*
Vilnius	005	4hrs 30mins	18:55	08:00	daily*
Warsaw	009	18hrs 04mins	16:50	08:54	daily*
From Kievsky station					
Budapest	015	39hrs 07mins	22:13	11:20	daily
Kyiv	*Stolichny Ekspress* 001	9hrs 20mins	23:23	07:43	odd days
Odessa	023	21hrs 49mins	21:20	19:09	daily
From Leningradsky station					
Helsinki	*Lev Tolstoy*	14hrs 10mins	22:50	12:00	daily
Tallinn	034	15hrs	18:25	08:25	daily
From Rizhsky station					
Riga	001	16hrs 06mins	18:59	10:05	daily

**=frequency of departure in peak season (June-Aug), less frequent at other times of year*

❑ **Luggage storage**

All railway stations have luggage storage facilities, be they storage rooms or luggage lockers. Using one of the *avtomaticheskie kamery khranenia* (combination-lock luggage lockers) is quite straightforward. Put your bag in the locker, deposit the amount of money required (exact change is sometimes necessary), and firmly close the locker door. Collect the receipt with the code that you'll later need to input to open the door. Note down your locker number and don't lose the code!

You may also come across some old-fashioned lockers; to use one, buy a token from the luggage room attendant. On the inside of the locker door is a set of four dials, on which you select your own combination of three numbers and a Cyrillic character. **Before you shut the locker, write down the locker number and your chosen combination**. Then insert the token, close the door and twirl the knobs on the outside.

To get your bags out, set the combination on the knobs and wait two seconds until you hear the electric lock click back (some lockers require you to put in a second token before this happens). Alternatively, pay a set fee according to the size of your luggage, valid for up to 12 hours (until midnight), and leave your bag in the storage room; most places will require you to produce an onward ticket. Don't lose your luggage tag and if possible, carry exact change: the luggage room attendant will love you for it.

Although most storage rooms function 24 hours a day, they're often closed several times a day for breaks of up to 30 minutes, so you should find out when these breaks are.

Sergiev Posad

Сергиев Посад

[Moscow Time] Sergiev Posad is one of the most popular tourist attractions in the Golden Ring (see box p398) and a must even for those who are 'all churched out'. Known as Zagorsk in the Communist period, the town (pop: 114,000) contains Russia's religious capital, the Exalted Trinity Monastery of St Sergius (Troitse-Sergiyeva Lavra). Entering the white-walled, six-century-old monastery is like taking a step back into mediaeval Russia, with long-bearded monks in traditional black robes and tall klobuki hats, and continuous chanting emanating from lamp-lit, incense-filled churches.

HISTORY

The monastery was founded in 1340 by Sergius of Radonezh (1321-91), who was later to become Russia's patron saint. The power of his monastery grew quickly because he was closely allied to Moscow's princes, and actively worked for the unification of Russian lands by building a ring of 23 similar monastery-fortresses around Moscow. His friendship with Moscow's ruler, Grand Prince Dmitry Donskoi, was so strong that when Dmitry asked for the church's blessing in 1380 before leaving to fight the Tatar-Mongols at Kulikovo, Sergius himself delivered the service. While the resultant victory had already indicated to Sergius's followers that he had God's ear, 17 years after his death it became obvious that he also had divine protection: in 1408, after the Tatar-Mongols levelled the monastery, the only thing to survive unscathed was Sergius's corpse.

WHERE TO STAY, EAT AND DRINK

25 Monastyrskaya Trapeza Монастырская Трапеза
28 Restaurant Russky Dvorik Ресторан Русский Дворик
29 Hotel Russky Dvorik Гостиница Русский Дворик
34 Gnyozdishko Гнёздышко

PLACES OF INTEREST

1 Duck Tower Утиная Башня
2 Pilgrim Gate Tower Каличья Воротная Башня
3 Bathhouse Баня
4 Tsar's Palace Царский Дворец
5 Church of Our Lady of Smolensk Смоленская Церковь
6 Bell Tower Колокольня
7 History Museum in Church of SS Zosima & Savvaty Исторический Музей и Церковь Зосимы и Савватия
8 Former Treasurer's Wing Казначейский Корпус
10 Former Hospital of the Trinity Monastery of St Sergei Больница-Богодельня Троице-Сергиевой Лавры
11 Museum of Ancient Russian Art, in vestry Музей Древнерусского Прикладного Искусства (Ризница)
12 Trinity Cathedral Троицкий Собор
13 Chapel over the Well Надкладезная Часовня
14 Assumption Cathedral Успенский Собор
15 Red Gate, Holy Gates & John the Baptist Gate Church Красные Ворота, Святые Ворота и Надвратная Церковь Иоанна Предтечи
16 Descent of the Holy Spirit Church Духовная Церковь
17 St Micah's Church Михеевская Церковь
18 Refectory & St Sergius's Church Трапезная Палата и Церковь Святого Сергия
19 Metropolitan's Chambers Палаты Метрополитена
20 Water Gate/Tower Водяные Ворота/Башня
21 Elijah the Prophet's Church Ильинская Церковь
22 Church of St Paraskeva Pyatnitsa Пятницкая Церковь
23 Presentation of the Mother of God Church Веденская Церковь
24 Krasnogorskaya Chapel Красногорская Часовня
26 Lenin Bust Бюст Ленина
30 Pyatnitsa Well Chapel Часовня Пятницкого Колодца
31 War Memorial Памятник Великой Отечественной Войне
32 Ascension Church Вознесенская Церковь
33 Dormition Church Успенская Церковь

OTHER

9 Museum Ticket Kiosk Музейная Касса
27 Sberbank Сбербанк
35 Bus Station Автовокзал
36 Railway Station Железнодорожный Вокзал

TRINITY CATHEDRAL

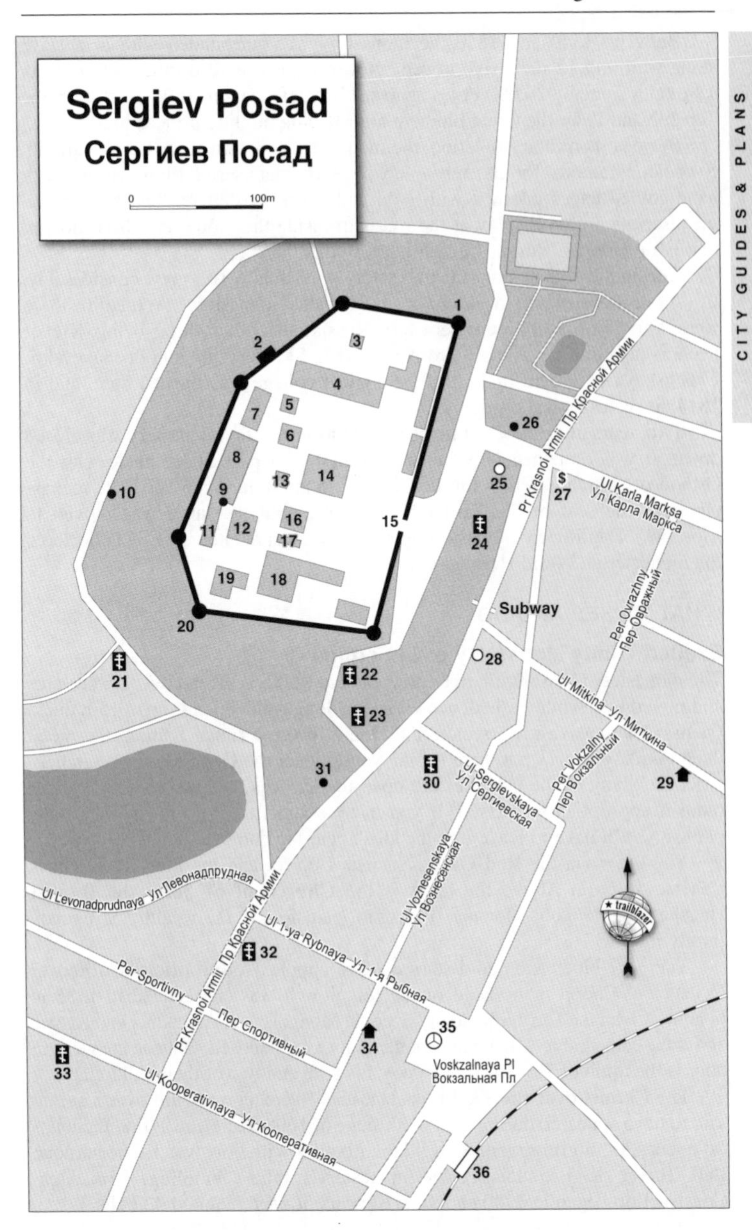
Sergiev Posad
Сергиев Посад
0
100m
Subway
Ul Karla Marksa
Ул Карла Маркса
Pr Krasnoi Armii Пр Красной Армии
Per Ovrazhny
Пер Овражный
Ul Mitkina Ул Миткина
Per Vokzalny
Пер Вокзальный
Ul Sergievskaya
Ул Сергиевская
Ul Levonadprudnaya Ул Левонадпрудная
Ul Voznesenskaya
Ул Вознесенская
Ul 1-ya Rybnaya Ул 1-я Рыбная
Per Sportivny
Пер Спортивный
Ul Kooperativnaya Ул Кооперативная
Voskzalnaya Pl
Вокзальная Пл
trailblazer
1 2 3 4 5 6 7 8 9 10 11 12 13 14 15 16 17 18 19 20 21 22 23 24 25 26 27 28 29 30 31 32 33 34 35 36

Between 1540 and 1550 the monastery was surrounded with a massive stone wall and 12 defensive towers. Never again was it to fall, even after an 18-month siege by 20,000 Poles against 1500 defenders in 1608. Both Ivan the Terrible and Peter the Great hid here after fleeing plotting princes in Moscow.

Besides its military function, the monastery was a great centre of learning. It became famous for its *Sergievsky*-style of manuscript illumination, with hand-copied pages adorned with gold and vermilion letters. Several of these manuscripts are on display at the museum inside the monastery. It is thought that Ivan Fedorov, Russia's first printer, studied here.

During the 18th century the monastery's spiritual power grew considerably. In 1744 it was elevated to a *lavra* or 'most exalted monastery'. At the time there were only four such monasteries in Russia, the other three being Kievo-Pechorskaya in Kiev, Aleksandro-Nevskaya in St Petersburg and Pochayevsko-Uspenskaya in Volyn. In 1749 a theological college was opened here, and in 1814 an ecclesiastical academy.

Two years after the Communists came to power the monastery was closed down. It was reopened only in 1946 as part of a pact Stalin made with the Orthodox Church in return for the Church's support during WWII. The monastery was the seat of the Patriarch of Russia until the latter was moved to Moscow's Danilovsky monastery in 1988. Five years later UNESCO declared the monastery a World Heritage Site.

WHAT TO SEE AND DO

Exalted Trinity Monastery of St Sergius

The monastery (10am-6pm, free entry, camera R200) is spread over six hectares and ringed by a whitewashed, one kilometre-long wall which is up to 15m thick. Of its 12 defensive towers, note the **Duck Tower** Утиная Башня: the metal duck on its spire was put there for the young Peter the Great to use for archery practice. Many of the churches are open for services, but you may only enter them if appropriately dressed. If you have a camera but do not wish to take photos, you'll have to leave it at the kiosk near the entrance.

You enter via the **Red Gate** Красные Ворота and the inner Holy Gates Святые Ворота. Above the latter is the **Church of St John the Baptist** Надвратная Церковь Иоанна Предтечи, paid for by the wealthy Stroganov family in 1693.

The sky-blue and gold-starred, five-cupola **Assumption Cathedral** Успенский Собор is the heart of the complex. It was consecrated in 1585 in honour of Ivan the Terrible's victory over the Mongols near Astrakhan and Kazan, and is the cathedral in which many of the Tsars were baptised. Outside the western door is the tomb of Tsar Boris Godunov, his wife and two of their children.

The **Chapel over the Well** Надкладезная Часовня was built over a spring said to have appeared during the Polish siege of 1608. Here you'll find the longest queues, of pilgrims waiting to fill their bottles with holy water. The baroque **Bell Tower** Колокольня is the monastery's tallest building, 93m high. Construction began in 1740 and took 30 years; it once featured 42 bells.

The **Refectory** Трапезная Палата, completed in 1693, served as a dining hall for pilgrims. You can't miss this red, blue, green and yellow chequered building with its carved columns. Outside it is the squat **Church of St Sergius** Церковь Святого Сергия, crowned with a single golden dome. The **Church of the Descent of the Holy Spirit** Духовная Церковь contains the grave of the first Bishop of Russian Alaska.

Trinity Cathedral Троицкий Собор is the monastery's most sacred place, being the site of St Sergius's original wooden church. It contains Sergius's corpse in a dull silver sarcophagus donated by Ivan the Terrible. Built in 1422 in honour of Sergius's canonisation, the cathedral contains 42 icons by Andrei Rublyov, Russia's most revered icon painter. The **Church of Our Lady of Smolensk** Смоленская Церковь was built to house the icon of the same name in 1745. Decorated in baroque style, it resembles a rotunda. The **Tsar's Palace** Царский Дворец was built at the end of the 17th century to house Tsar Alexei and his entourage of over 500 people when they visited. It now houses the theological college and ecclesiastical academy.

The monastery's **vestry** ризница (*riznitsa*, 10am-5pm Wed-Sun, R300) contains the Museum of Ancient Russian Art, one of Russia's richest collections of ancient religious art (14th-17th centuries), plus gifts presented to the monastery over the centuries. The gifts are displayed in the order they were given, and it is interesting to see how tastes changed over the centuries. Tickets can be used only at the time printed on them; at peak times you may have to wait several hours so it's best to buy your ticket on arrival.

English-language tours can be arranged at the respective ticket offices.

PRACTICAL INFORMATION

Orientation and services

The main street is pr Krasnoy Armii пр Красной Армии, while the bus and railway stations are located at the opposite corners of Vokzalnaya pl, east of the main street.

You can **change money** or visit the **ATM** during normal business hours at Sberbank Сбербанк on the corner of ul Karla Marksa and pr Krasnoy Armii.

Where to stay and eat

The best overnight option is ***Russky Dvorik*** **Русский Дворик** (ул Миткина 14/2, ul Mitkina 14/2, ☎ 096 547 3571, sgl/dbl from R2700/3100, more expensive at weekends), a small hotel with views of the monastery's onion domes from some of its rooms. Service is excellent and the rustic atmosphere and large courtyard garden are pleasant. The nearby ***Restaurant Russky Dvorik*** **Ресторан Русский Дворик** serves tasty Russian classics – from soups to *pelmeni* to meat dishes – amidst kitschy rustic décor (meals R300-1000), while ***Monastyrskaya Trapeza*** **Монастырская Трапеза**, opposite the monastery entrance, is a good spot for *blini* and other light meals (R160-300).

If Russky Dvorik is full, ***Gnyozdishko*** **Гнёздышко** (ул Вознесенская 53a, ul Voznesenskaya 53a, ☎ 48534 540 4214, rooms R2700-3800), a cosy inn with just eight rooms, is a clean, quiet and convenient place to stay.

Getting there

Around two trains per hour run to Sergiev Posad from suburban (*prigorodnie*, пригородние) platforms behind Moscow's Yaroslavsky station; take any train bound for Sergiev Posad or Aleksandrov. It's about R130 for the 95-minute trip. The slightly pricier 8.20am *Yaroslavl Express* or the suburban 8.24am train also stop at Sergiev Posad, taking one hour.

The monastery is a 20-minute walk from the station.

Rostov-Yaroslavski (Rostov-Veliki)

Ростов-Ярославский (Ростов-Великий)

[Moscow Time] Rostov-Yaroslavski (to differentiate from Russia's other Rostov – Rostov-na-Donu), 225km north-east of Moscow, is one of the most attractive Golden Ring cities to visit. Although it's no longer on the main Trans-Siberian route, if you're travelling via Yaroslavl, Rostov is a worthwhile stopover. It's a small city in a beautiful location beside scenic Lake Nero with a wonderfully sleepy atmosphere and the added attraction of being able to spend the night inside the Kremlin itself.

Founded in 862, Rostov-Yaroslavski played a major role in the formation of Russia and at one time was as big as the mighty capitals of Kiev and Novgorod. Yuri Dolgoruky, who founded Moscow in 1147, gave Rostov the honourable and rare title of *veliki,* meaning 'great'. Rostov-Veliki soon became an independent principality. Rebuilt after the Tatar-Mongol sacking, it continued to have political importance for two more centuries until the local prince sold the remainder of his hereditary domain to Moscow's Grand Prince Ivan III in 1474. The city remained an important ecclesiastical centre as it was the religious capital of northern Russia and home to the senior religious leader called the Metropolitan.

In the 17th century, however, the Metropolitan was moved to the larger city of Yaroslavl. No longer called Rostov the Great, the city became known as Rostov-Yaroslavski. It rapidly became a backwater and now maintains an air of genteel decay. The modern part of the town is drab and uninspiring, but the historical centre makes for a pleasant day's ramble.

WHAT TO SEE AND DO

Cathedral of the Assumption Успенский Собор

The cathedral, just north of the Kremlin, is an impressive 16th-century, 60m-high, five-domed building with white stone friezes decorating the outside. The cathedral contains the tomb of the canonised Bishop Leontius who was martyred by Rostov's pagans in 1071 during his Christianity drive. The Metropolitan Ioan is also buried here. The **bell-tower** contains superb examples of 17th-century Russian bells, the largest, Sysoi, weighing 32 tons. There are 15 in all, and most of them have their own names; they're rung at 1pm on Saturday and Sunday and can be heard up to 20km away. To attend one of the fantastic bell-ringing concerts, contact the excursions office in the west gate.

CATHEDRAL OF THE ASSUMPTION

The Rostov Kremlin Ростовский Кремль

The white-walled Rostov Kremlin (10am-5pm, grounds R45, exhibits R40-60 each, all-inclusive ticket R250) is one of the most photogenic in the country. It is spread over two hectares, has six churches and is ringed by eleven towers. The Kremlin was founded in 1162 by Prince Andrei Bogolybusky, son of Yuri Dolgoruky, though all traces of the original buildings disappeared in the 17th century when the Kremlin was rebuilt.

Despite its mighty 12m high and 2m thick walls and towers, this reconstructed Kremlin is actually an imitation fortress. All the elements of real fortifications are missing. The ambitious 17th-century Metropolitan, Ioan Sisoyevich, wanted a residence to reflect his importance. After the 17th century, when the Metropolitan was moved to nearby Yaroslavl, the Kremlin became derelict. Today most of the buildings have been restored to their 16th- and 17th-century condition, though work still continues.

The central part of the Kremlin contains five churches. The religious part of each church occupies only the second floor as the ground floor was left for animal husbandry, storage and accommodation.

The Kremlin's **main entrance** and ticket office is on its western side through the **St John the Divine Gateway Church**, built in 1683, which has a richly decorated façade. The entrance to the Kremlin's northern part from the central part is through the **Resurrection of Christ Gate Church** built in 1670. This church has a stone iconostasis instead of the traditional wooden one.

The **Transfiguration of the Saviour above the Cellars Church**, the tallest in the Kremlin, was the private church of the Metropolitan. It is quite austere from the outside but its interior is lavish. The **White Chamber** next door was designed as a sumptuous dining hall; it now houses a museum featuring religious antiquities while other Kremlin buildings display Russian 18th- to 20th-century art and *finift* enamelware (see box below). The **Church of the Virgin Hodegitria** was erected 20 years after the death of Metropolitan Ioan and has a Moscow baroque interior. It now contains an exhibition of church vestments.

Finift

Rostov-Yaroslavski's most famous handicraft is *finift*, multi-coloured enamel work. This craft originated in Byzantium: the name derives from the Greek *fingitis* meaning colourful and shiny. Finift was used to decorate icons, sacred utensils and bible covers, as well as in portraits of people. The enamel's greatest advantages are that it cannot be damaged by water and does not fade with time.

The process of making the enamel is extremely complex and involves oxidising various metals to produce different colours. Iron produces yellow, orange-red and brown, copper produces green and blue, tin produces a non-transparent white, and gold with tin produces a cold ruby red.

Finift has been produced here since the 12th century and the Rostov Finift Factory has been operating since the 18th century. You can see unusual works of art involving enamel in combination with wood, metal and stone at **Khors House of Art** Хорс (see p204; ul Podozerka 31, www.khors.org, noon-8pm), a small gallery between the Kremlin and the lake, in the home of artist Mikhail Selishchev.

The building housing the **Prince's Chambers** is the oldest here, dating from the 16th century. It's claustrophobic with small dark passages, narrow doors and slit windows filled with slivers of mica. This is a good place to get an impression of the daily life of 16th-century Russian nobility.

The **Metropolitan's House** is now a museum and has a large collection of stone carvings, wooden sculptures, and 14th- and 15th-century doors from local churches. The servants' quarters of the **Rostov Kremlin** (Red Chamber), built as a residence for visiting tsars and their large retinue, are now a hotel (see Where to Stay p204).

Other places of interest

In front of the eastern entrance of the Kremlin is the **Saviour on the Market Place Church** Церковь Спаса на Торгу. It was built in the late 1600s and is now a library. The name comes from the rows of shops and stalls around the church that have stood there for centuries. Beside the church is the Arcade built in the 1830s and on the opposite side of the street is the Traders' Row.

The neoclassical **St Nicholas in the Field Church** Церковь Святово Николая (on ul Gogola) was built in 1813 and has been well restored. It has a golden iconostasis with *finift* enamel decorations and icons from the 15th to 19th centuries. This was one of two main churches in Rostov that conducted services during the Communist era (the other was the **Church of the Tolg Virgin** Церковь Толгской Богоматери).

The single-domed **Church of St Isidore the Blessed** Церковь Исидора Блаженного (ul Karla Marksa) dates from the 16th century and was originally called Ascension Church. It is hidden partly by the old Kremlin walls.

WHERE TO STAY, EAT AND DRINK

- 6 Restaurant Slavyansky Ресторан Славянский
- 7 Hotel Russkoye Podvorie Гостиница Русское Подворье
- 8 Restaurant Russkoye Podvorie Ресторан Русское Подворье
- 11 Dom na Pogrebakh Дом на Погребах
- 11 Trapeznaya Трапезная
- 12 Khors House of Art Хорс

PLACES OF INTEREST

- 2 Church of St Nicholas in the Field Церковь Святово Николая
- 3 Lenin statue Памятник Ленину
- 4 Church of St Isidore the Blessed Церковь Исидора Блаженного
- 5 Church of the Virgin Birth Церковь Рождества Богородицы
- 9 Church of the Saviour on the Market Place Церковь Спаса на Торгу
- 10 Cathedral of the Assumption Успенский Собор
- 11 Rostov Kremlin Ростовский Кремль
- 12 Khors House of Art Хорс
- 13 Metropolitan's Horse Stables Конный двор
- 14 Church of the Tolg Virgin Церковь Толгской Богоматери
- 16 St Jacob Monastery Яковлевский Монастырь

OTHER

- 1 Railway, Bus Station & ATM Железнодорожный Вокзал, Автовокзал и Банк
- 15 Market Рынок

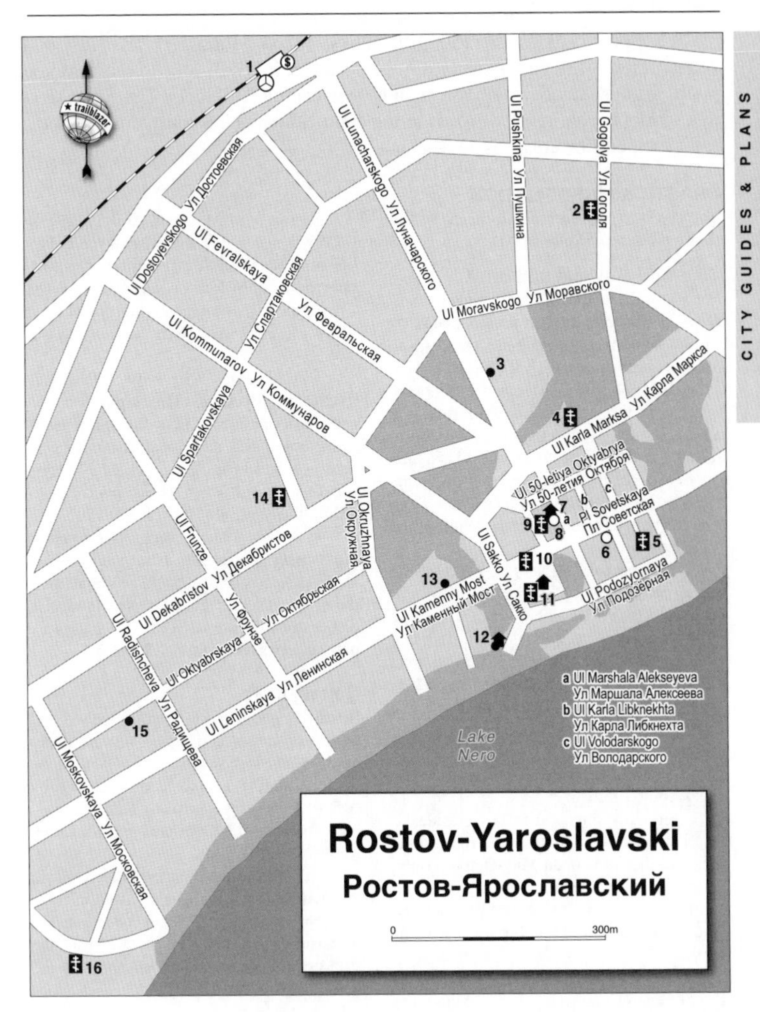

In front of the Kremlin's main gate on the western side, ul Kamenny Most, are the **Metropolitan's Horse Stables** Конный двор. It was planned to demolish this nondescript two-storey building but after the plaster was knocked off the walls it was discovered that the building was part of a 300-year-old complex which included stables, rooms for tack, sledges and carriages, and quarters for grooms, coachmen and watchmen.

It's worth walking the 1500m to the **St Jacob Monastery** Яковлевский Монастырь. Although it seems almost deserted, it is still functioning and you might glimpse a monk walking silently between the buildings. There is a shop that stocks a wide range of icons in the main church and a courtyard of beautifully scented flowers.

PRACTICAL INFORMATION

You can hire rowing boats at the **river station** near Khors House of Art.

Where to stay, eat and drink

For atmosphere, the most appealing place is ***Dom na Pogrebakh*** **Дом на Погребах** (☎ 61244, 🖳 dom_na_pogrebah@mail.ru, sgl/dbl/trpl with shared bath R700/1100/1500, suite R2400-3000), the former servants' quarters of the Rostov Kremlin turned into a basic hotel. All rooms have large, comfortable beds and heavy medieval wooden doors. To get there during business hours use the main Kremlin entrance. After 5pm, ring the bell at the door just to the left of the main entrance.

Trapeznaya **Трапезная** (also inside the Kremlin's Red Chamber) is a formal-looking dining hall where you can sample solid Russian dishes (mains R200-350).

Another interesting place to stay is ***Khors House of Art*** **Хорс** (see box p201; ул Подозёрка 31, ul Podozerka 31, ☎ 624 83 or 962 209 0605, 🖳 www.khors.org, sgl/dbl/quad R500/700/1500), in the lakeside home of an outgoing married couple who speak some English.

Originally intended to be a residence for visiting artists, this small 12-room summer guesthouse is open May-October only. There's a guest kitchen, a rowing boat you can borrow and the views from the terrace of the lake and the Kremlin are just wonderful.

Hotel Russkoye Podvorie **Гостиница Русское Подворье** (ул Маршала Алексеева 9, ul Marshala Alekseeva 9, ☎ 64255, single with shared bathroom/double/suite R800/1800/3100) offers comfortable rooms in an 18th-century building. The singles are rather compact, but the location – two minutes' walk from the Kremlin – is very good.

Restaurant Russkoye Podvorie **Ресторан Русское Подворье** on the ground floor allows you to dine like a medieval noble, with traditional dishes such as pike poached in milk, as well as *blini* and superb *solyanka*. Wash it down with a tankard of honey mead. Mains R300-1200.

In the same vein, ***Restaurant Slavyansky*** **Ресторан Славянский** (пл Советская 8, pl Sovetskaya 8) maintains a rather formal air, but the meat and fish dishes are well-prepared and the salads are particularly good. Mains R250-600.

Getting there

Rostov is about 60km from Yaroslavl and there are trains and buses almost every hour. From Moscow, Rostov is 4½ hours by train, including a change at Aleksandrov (R320). Or take the *Yaroslav Express*, leaving Moscow at 8.20am and 4.35pm (3hrs, R500).

To get from the railway station or from the main bus station to the Kremlin, take bus No 6 (R12). To get to St Jacob Monastery, take bus Nos 1 or 2 from the stop on ul Sakko, one block north of the Kremlin.

The Rostov-Yaroslavski area code is ☎ 48536. From outside Russia dial ☎ +7-48536.

Yaroslavl
Ярославль

[Moscow Time] Yaroslavl's old central section and the tree-lined streets and squares make this one of the most attractive cities in Russia. In many ways the buildings in this old section surpass those of Moscow as they have not suffered as much from the ravages of war and rapid industrialisation. With most Trans-Siberian trains now going via Vladimir, however, Yaroslavl, 260km away from Moscow, sees fewer Siberian-bound travellers than it used to – a shame, because it's a very pleasant city, with golden-domed churches lining the Volga promenade.

Yaroslavl is the Volga River's oldest city, founded in 1010 by Grand Prince Yaroslav the Wise. With the expansion of river trade from the 16th century, Yaroslavl became the second most populous city after Moscow. Until the opening of the Moscow–Volga River Canal in 1937, which gave Moscow direct access to the Volga, Yaroslavl was Moscow's main port.

WHAT TO SEE AND DO

Transfiguration of Our Saviour Monastery
Спасо-Преображенский Монастырь

This attractive white monastery was founded in the 12th century but the oldest building to be seen today dates from 1516 when the wooden walls were replaced with stone and brick. As it was considered impregnable, part of the tsar's treasury was stored here, protected by a garrison.

Transfiguration of Our Saviour Cathedral occupies central place in the monastery. This three-domed cathedral was built in 1516 after the original building was destroyed in a fire in 1501. Sixteenth-century frescoes include depictions of John the Baptist on the eastern wall, Christ Pantokrator on the cupola in the central dome, and the Last Judgement on the western wall.

The **Refectory** was built in the 16th century. On the second floor a single mighty pillar supports the vaults, creating a large open dining area. It's now a history museum. Climb the **bell tower** for a panoramic view of the city (R90). There are four flights of stairs, each getting narrower, and you'll end up standing on the wooden roof. Directly above you is the main bell which was cast in 1738. The bell-tower's clock was installed in 1624 after being brought from the Saviour (Spassky) Tower in the Moscow Kremlin.

The **Monks' Cell Block** consists of four buildings and was built at the end of the 17th century. It now contains a large museum of Old Russia which includes icons, handicrafts, weapons, armour and books.

Entry into the grounds (8am-8pm) is R20; entry to each museum and exhibition (10am-5.30pm Tue-Sun) costs R40-80.

Around the monastery

This area is rich in churches and other historic buildings. Directly opposite the monastery on the Moscow Highway is the **Epiphany Church** Церковь Богоявления. The five-domed church was completed in 1693 and has nine large windows which make the interior extraordinarily light. It is an excellent example of the Yaroslavl school of architecture (see box opposite) with its glazed tiles and festive decorations. Most of the church has been restored save for the dangerously leaning tower near the entrance.

EPIPHANY CHURCH TOWER

House of Ivanov Дом Иванова (ul Chaikovskovo 4) is a typical two-storey residence of a well-to-do town dweller built at the end of the 17th century. The ground floor was used for storage and the sleeping and living rooms are upstairs.

The **Church of St Nicholas on the Waters** Церковь Святого Николы (ul Chaikovskovo 1) was built from 1665 to 1672 in red brick and has marvellous glazed bands around the altar windows. The five green onion-domes complement the red brick and make for an impressive sight.

The white **Church of the Tikhvin Virgin** Церковь Тихвинской Богоматери next door is a small church dwarfed by its neighbour but specially designed for winter worship as it can be heated. It has extensive glazed tilework on its exterior.

Volga River Embankment

A stroll down the landscaped high right bank of the Volga River from the river station to the Metropolitan's Chambers is an enjoyable way of exploring this area. At the end of ul Pervomaiskaya is the **river station**: one section is for long-distance hydrofoils and, slightly downstream, there's another for local passenger ferries.

The tent-roofed **Nativity Church** Церковь Рождества Христова (ul Kedrova 1), built over nine years starting in 1635, consists of two buildings and is famous as being the first church to use glazed tiles for external decoration. This practice was soon adopted everywhere and led to the development of the Yaroslavl architecture style. The names of those involved in the building of the church have been inscribed on the tiles and, if you look closely, you can still see them. Unfortunately, this church is in desperate need of restoration and much of the tilework is disappearing.

The **Art Museum** Художественный Музей (nab Volzhskaya 23, 🖳 http://artmuseum.yar.ru, 10am-5.30pm Tue-Sun, exhibitions R70) is housed in the former governor's residence and it contains European works of art and furniture from the 15th to 19th centuries. Its other branch, the **Metropolitan's Chamber**

Палаты Метрополита (nab Volzhskaya 1, 10am-5pm, closed Fri, R50) was built in the 1680s for the Metropolitan of the nearby city of Rostov-Yaroslavski. The two-storey building is now one of the country's richest museums of Old Russian Art. While Yaroslavl's most revered icon, *The Sign of the Virgin,* painted in about 1218, now sits in Moscow's Tretyakov Gallery, the museum contains a number of other notable icons. Particularly interesting are the 13th- and 14th-century Mongolian icons.

The newest museum in the city, the worthwhile **History Museum of Yaroslavl** Музей Истории Ярославля (nab Volzhskaya 17/1, 💻 http://museum.city-yar.ru, 10am-6pm, closed Tue, R12, tours in English R300) traces the city's thousand-year history in a series of well-presented exhibits.

Volga Tower Волжская Башня, also known as the Arsenal Tower, sits on the river bank at nab Volzhskaya 7. It is one of two towers which remain from the former Yaroslavl Kremlin. This citadel consisted of earth ramparts with wooden fortress walls and stone towers. This tower was finished in 1668 and is now a naval club.

Further along is the extremely photogenic, golden-domed **Church of Patriarch Tikhon** Церковь Патриарха Тихона, with a collection of bells outside it, while beyond lies the attractively landscaped **memorial park** Мемориальный Пар, created on the banks of the Volga in celebration of the 1000-year anniversary of the founding of Yaroslavl, and filled with strolling pedestrians.

Yaroslavl centre

The centre of the city is Soviet Square (pl Sovetskaya). On the east side of the square is the Church of St Elijah the Prophet and on the north side is a government office building of circa 1780. The imposing **Church of St Elijah the Prophet** Церковь Ильи Пророка stands out in a city full of beautiful churches due to its superb 17th-century frescoes, still in excellent condition. The church was commissioned by one of the richest and most influential Russian merchant dynasties, the Shripins.

Vlasyevskaya Tower Власьевская Башня (ul Pervomaiskaya 21) is the second of the two towers that remain from Yaroslavl's original Kremlin. It's also known as the Sign (Znamenskaya) Tower and flower sellers gather underneath it every day.

Yaroslavl style

The Yaroslavl school of architecture dates from the second half of the 16th century and is epitomised by tall, pointed tent roofs, free-standing bell-towers, large airy churches with side chapels, external glazed tiles, and large interior frescoes and mosaics. Yaroslavl has many buildings in this style as its evolution coincided with a massive reconstruction drive after the great fire in 1658. The city had developed a rich merchant class which commissioned churches to its own taste. As this style also appealed to hereditary nobles and peasants, it became widespread throughout Russia, much to the chagrin of the conservative clergy.

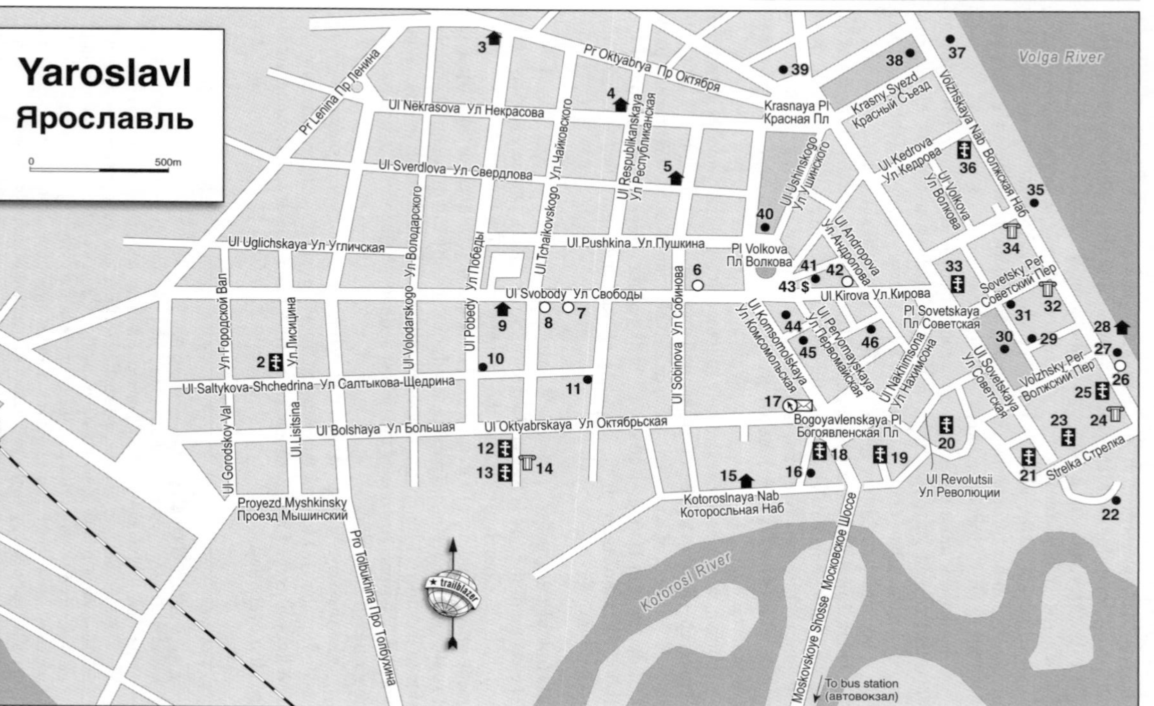

Yaroslavl
Ярославль
0
500m
Volga River
Kotorosl River
Volzhskaya Nab Волжская Наб
Ul Volkova Ул Волкова
Ul Kedrova Ул Кедрова
Krasny Syezd Красный Съезд
Krasnaya Pl Красная Пл
Pr Oktyabrya Пр Октября
Ul Ushinskogo Ул Ушинского
Pl Volkova Пл Волкова
Ul Andropova Ул Андропова
Ul Kirova Ул Кирова
Pl Sovetskaya Пл Советская
Sovetsky Per Советский Пер
Volzhsky Per Волжский Пер
Ul Sovetskaya Ул Советская
Strelka Стрелка
Ul Revolutsii Ул Революции
Ul Nakhimsona Ул Нахимсона
Ul Pervomayskaya Ул Первомайская
Ul Komsomolskaya Ул Комсомольская
Bogoyavlenskaya Pl Богоявленская Пл
Moskovskoye Shosse Московское Шоссе
To bus station (автовокзал)
Kotoroslnaya Nab Которосльная Наб
Ul Sobinova Ул Собинова
Ul Respublikanskaya Ул Республиканская
Ul Pushkina Ул Пушкина
Ul Svobody Ул Свободы
Ul Tchaikovskogo Ул Чайковского
Ul Oktyabrskaya Ул Октябрьская
Ul Nekrasova Ул Некрасова
Ul Sverdlova Ул Свердлова
Ul Pobedy Ул Победы
Ul Volodarskogo Ул Володарского
Ul Saltykova-Shchedrina Ул Салтыкова-Щедрина
Ul Bolshaya Ул Большая
Ul Uglichskaya Ул Угличская
Pro Tolbukhina Про Толбухина
Pr Lenina Пр Ленина
Ul Lisitsina Ул Лисицина
Ul Gorodskoy Val Ул Городской Вал
Proyezd Myshkinsky Проезд Мышинский
trailblazer
1 2 3 4 5 6 7 8 9 10 11 12 13 14 15 16 17 18 19 20 21 22 23 24 25 26 27 28 29 30 31 32 33 34 35 36 37 38 39 40 41 42 43 44 45 46
$

WHERE TO STAY

3 Mini-hotel Zvyozdny Мини-отель Звёздный
4 Gostevoi Dom Гостевой Дом
5 Medvezhy Ugol Медвежий Угол
9 Ring Premier Hotel Гостиница Ринг Премиер
15 Hotel Yubileynaya Гостиница Юбилейная
28 Volzhskaya Zhemchuzhina Волжская Жемчужина

WHERE TO EAT AND DRINK

6 CCCP Sovnarpit СССР Совнарпит
7 Sushi-bar Sakura Суши-бар Сакура
8 Restaurant Vlasyevsky Ресторан Власьевский
26 Café Dacha Кафе Дача
42 Restaurant and Café Bristol Ресторан и кафе Бристоль

PLACES OF INTEREST

2 Church of Vladimir Mother of God Церковь Владимирской Богоматери
10 Bell-tower of St Nicholas Колокольня Святого Николы
11 Seminary Духовная Семинария
12 Church of St Nicholas on the Waters Церковь Святого Николы
13 Church of Tikhvin Virgin Церковь Тихвинской Богоматери
14 House of Ivanov Дом Иванова
16 Descent of Holy Spirit Consistorium Духовная Консистория
18 Epiphany Church Церковь Богоявления
19 Transfiguration of Our Saviour Monastery Спасо-Преображенский Монастырь
20 Church of St Michael the Archangel Церковь Михаила Архангела
21 Church of Saviour in the Town Спасская Церковь
22 Memorial Park Мемориальный Парк
23 Church of St Nicholas in Log Town Церковь Святого Николы
24 Metropolitan's Chamber Палаты Метрополита
25 Church of Patriarch Tikhon Церковь Патриарха Тихона
27 Volga Tower Волжская Башня
29 House of the Vakhrameyevs Дом Вахрамеевых
30 Chelyuskintsev Park Парк Челюськинцев
31 House of Matreev Дом Матреева
32 Yaroslavl History Museum Музей Истории Ярославля
33 Church of St Elijah the Prophet Церковь Ильи Пророка
34 Art Museum Художественный Музей
35 Provincial Governor's Rotunda-Pavilion Павильон
36 Church of the Nativity Церковь Рождества Христова
38 Nekrasov Monument Памятник Некрасову
40 Volkov Drama Theatre Драматический Театр имени Волкова
41 Philharmonic Hall Филармония
44 Vlasyevskaya Tower Власьевская Башня
45 Gostinny Dvor (Traders' Arcade) Гостинный Двор

OTHER

1 Yaroslavl-Glavny (main station) Вокзал Ярославль-Главный
17 Central Post Office & Internet Почтамт и интернет
37 River Station Речной Вокзал
39 University Универсиет
43 Sberbank Сбербанк
46 Market Рынок

Volkov Drama Theatre Драматический Театр имени Волкова (pl Volkova) was built in 1911 and is named after Fedor Volkov (1729-63) who is considered the founder of Russian national theatre. He inherited his stepfather's factories in Yaroslavl which enabled him to organise his own private theatre company before moving on to bigger and better things. Amongst his claims to fame was that he organised the first staging of *Hamlet* in Russia. The theatre is currently being restored and the finished parts look beautiful.

Church of St John the Baptist **Церковь Иоанна Крестителя**

In the Tolchkovski district, once famous for its leather work, this impressive 15-domed church (10am-6pm, closed Tue), built between 1671 and 1687, is considered the architectural pinnacle of Yaroslavl. From a distance it looks as if it is trimmed in lace and carved of wood but this deception is created by carved and patterned bricks. It consists of two side chapels, unusual in that they are practically as tall as the church and each is crowned with five domes. Inside is a mass of frescoes – reputedly more than in any other church in Russia.

You can see this church from the train as you cross over the Kotorosl River.

PRACTICAL INFORMATION

Orientation and services

There are two railway stations: **Yaroslavl-Glavny** Ярославль-Главный (Yaroslavl-Main) is on the northern side of the Kotorosl River and **Yaroslavl-Moskovski** is on the southern side. All trains to Yaroslavl go through Yaroslavl-Glavny while only those trains travelling along the east and west line (such as from Ivanovo and St Petersburg) go through Yaroslavl-Moskovski.

The main thoroughfare is ul Svobody ул Свободы. Most attractions are found either along or near the Volga embankment, while numerous places to stay and eat are found within easy walking distance of pl Volkova, the main square. To get from the station to pl Volkova, catch trolleybus No 1. Buses 8, 9, 11 and 20 run up and down ul Svobody.

You'll find several ATMs around pl Kirova and you can change money and travellers' cheques at **Sberbank** Сбербанк, which is on the pedestrianised section of ul Kirova. There's **internet** access at the **Central Post Office** Почтамт (ul Volodarskogo 10, 8.30am-8pm).

In the summer there are various **river trips** leaving from the river station.

Where to stay

Centrally located, quiet ***Mini-hotel Zvyozdny*** **Мини-отель Звёздный** (ул Победы 37, ul Pobedy 37, ☎ 585 884, 💻 www.yarstars.ru, sgl/dbl from R2800/3000) entices with its 17 spotless, well-appointed rooms with wi-fi.

Medvezhy Ugol **Медвежий Угол** (ул Свердлова 16, ul Sverdlova 16, ☎ 329 749, sgl/dbl from R1500/2500) may not have terribly imaginative décor but the rooms are clean and functional and only a few minutes' walk from the main attractions. Internet access is available.

In a historical 19th-century building, ***Gostevoi Dom*** **Гостевой Дом** (ул Республиканская 42/24, ul Respublikanskaya 42/24, ☎ 738 998, 💻 www.gapm.ru/ru/hostel, doubles from R2800) boasts just 22 attractive en suites with a colour scheme to match the exterior and wi-fi throughout.

The four-star ***Ring Premier Hotel*** (ул Свободы 55, ul Svobody 55, ☎ 580 858,

The Yaroslavl area code is ☎ 4852. From outside Russia dial ☎ +7-4852.

🖳 http://ringhotel.ru, dbl/suite from R4500/ R7500, cheaper rates at weekends) boasts spacious, comfortable rooms as well as a sauna, pool, Jacuzzis, fitness centre, and Irish pub. On-site Restaurant Sobinov serves excellent Russian and European dishes.

Literally right on the water by the Volga Tower, the hotel-boat ***Volzhskaya Zhemchuzhina*** **Волжская Жемчужина** (Волжская наб, Volzhskaya nab, ☎ 727 717, 🖳 www.riverhotel-vp.ru, sgl/dbl/suite from R2700/4300/6900) offers compact, modern wi-fi enabled rooms with air-con. The boat itself has a sauna and the on-board restaurant offers 24-hour room service.

Rooms at the revamped ***Hotel Yubileynaya*** **Гостиница Юбилейная** (наб Которосльная 26, nab Kotorosolnaya 26, ☎ 726 565, 🖳 www.yubil.yar.ru, sgl/dbl R2500/3200) range from cosy singles and doubles to grand apartments with parquet floors. Internet throughout and buffet breakfast included.

Where to eat and drink

The main restaurant strip is along ul Svobody ул Свободы, with cafés and pizzerias sprinkled around the tourist attractions.

The upmarket ***Restaurant Bristol*** **Ресторан Бристоль** is at the end of the pedestrianised section of ul Kirova ул Кирова and serves traditional Russian food. There's a much cheaper version, ***Café Bristol*** **кафе Бристоль**, on the ground floor, with lunch deals as low as R150.

At ***Restaurant Vlasyevksy*** **Ресторан Власьевский** (ул Свободы и ул Чайковского, corner of ul Svobody and ul Tchaikovskogo), you'll find a café and beer garden downstairs, while upstairs is the restaurant serving a variety of Russian standards for around R400. The food is tasty and the portions are generous.

CCCP Sovnarpit **СССР Совнарпит** (ул Свободы 2, ul Svobody 2) is a bright, Communist-themed basement café where you can get some inexpensive lunch deals consisting of 'area' (soup and salad) 'region' (soup and main) and 'republic' (soup, main and dessert) combos for around R150-250.

Sushi-bar Sakura **Суши-бар Сакура** (ул Свободы 27, ul Svobody 27) offers well-presented Japanese food with an emphasis on sushi which is more than passable in quality. The R240 business lunch is a bargain.

Café Dacha **Кафе Дача** (Волжская наб, Volzhskaya nab, next to the Volga Tower) is a good lunchtime spot for Russian favourites. Business lunches from R230.

Moving on

There are about 14 trains a day to Moscow (5hrs, R500), including two particularly handy express trains, No 811 and 813, leaving at 7.15am and 4.30pm respectively (3¾hrs, R527-811).

The bus station is about 2km south of the city. There are buses to many destinations, including about 12 a day to Rostov-Yaroslavski (R70, 1½hrs) and three to Vladimir (R270, 4hrs).

In the summer from the river station it's possible to get a boat along the Volga to Moscow. The trip takes 40 hours.

Vladimir

Владимир

[Moscow Time] Vladimir, 180km from Moscow, is a rewarding place to visit as part of a day trip, or even as a Trans-Siberian stopover. One of Russia's oldest cities, and part of the Golden Ring (the cities that shaped early Russian history),Vladimir is a now a busy modern place with some architectural gems.

HISTORY

Vladimir was officially founded in 1108, although there was a village here as early as 500BC. During the great migration of Slavs from the disintegrating Kievian Rus empire in the late 10th and early 11th centuries the Vladimir region was settled and its ancient inhabitants evicted.

In 1108 Grand Prince Vladimir Monomakh of Kiev, after whom the town is named, built a fortress here to protect his eastern lands. Vladimir's grandson, Andrei Bogolyubsky, stormed and pillaged Kiev in 1157 and took its master craftsmen away to build a new Russian capital at Vladimir. By the time of Andrei's murder at Bogolyubovo in 1174, Vladimir surpassed Kiev in grandeur and had become the centre of a powerful principality. Unfortunately Andrei's brother and successor, Vsevolod III, was unable to hold the principality together and it was soon divided amongst family members.

Despite its defeat by Tatar-Mongols in 1238 the town remained the political centre of north-eastern Russia. It became the religious centre of the entire country in 1300 when the seat of the Metropolitan of All Rus was moved here from Kiev, but this power disappeared too when the seat was shifted to Moscow 20 years later. Vladimir's glory came to an end in 1392 with its absorption into the Moscow Principality. It rapidly became a backwater and by 1668 its population numbered just 990.

Vladimir slowly recovered from this low point (its current population is about 350,000) but it played no role in the revolutionary turmoil at the turn of the 20th century. However, it has since become an industrial centre.

WHAT TO SEE AND DO

The Golden Gate Золотые Ворота

Vladimir was once ringed by several kilometres of earth ramparts topped with oaken walls. Traditionally, a city Kremlin consisted of a small, heavily fortified citadel with an unprotected settlement beyond its walls. With a defensive wall around the entire city, the town's population swelled as settlers arrived seeking security. The only surviving remnants of these defences is the so-called Golden Gate. Built by Andrei Bogolyubsky in 1158, it was modelled on that of Kiev, which in turn was based on the Golden Gates of Constantinople.

To emphasise further Vladimir's inherited majesty, the heavy oaken outer doors were covered in gilded copper. Adorning the gate is a copy of the Byzantine icon of Our Lady of Vladimir (the original went to Moscow when the Metropolitan's seat was moved there in 1320). In 1785 two ornamental towers were added as buttresses and most earth ramparts removed to make way for increased traffic.

Above the gate is the golden-domed Gate-Church of the Deposition of the Robe. This now houses the **Military Exposition** (10am-6pm, closed Tue and last Fri of month, R60), centred on a diorama of the storming of Vladimir by the Tatar-Mongols, and the **Gallery of Vladimir Heroes**. Remnants of the earthen walls can be seen beside the gate.

In front of the gate is the **Crystal Museum** Музей Хрусталя (ul Dvoryanskaya 2, 11am-7pm, closed Tue and last Wed of month, R65), featuring crafts from nearby towns. The red-brick building was formerly the Old Believers' Trinity Church, built in 1913.

Just to the south of the gate is the **Exhibition of 'Old Vladimir'** Выставка 'Старый Владимир' (ul Kozlov Val, 10am-5pm, Wed & Fri 10am-4pm, closed Mon and last Thur of month, R60) housed in a 19th-century **water tower**. On the top floor is an observation deck offering panoramic views of Vladimir.

Assumption Cathedral Успенский Собор

The city is justifiably proud of its gleaming white, golden-domed cathedral (Sobornaya pl, 1.30-4.45pm, R110) built by Andrei Bogolyubsky in 1160 to rival Kiev's St Sophia Cathedral. At the time this was the tallest building in all of Russia. Following a fire in 1185 it was enlarged to hold 4000 worshippers. All of Russia's rulers from Andrei Bogolyubsky to Ivan III (the Great) were crowned here. This served in turn as the 15th-century model for its namesake in Moscow's Kremlin. The cathedral's 25m-high iconostasis contains 100 icons. These once included works by Andrei Rublyov, now held in Moscow's Tretyakov Gallery and St Petersburg's State Russian Museum. But Rublyov's work can still be seen in the form of frescoes done in 1408.

Adjacent to the cathedral are the **Chapel of St George**, a 'winter church' (meaning it could be heated) built in 1862, and a three-storey **bell tower** built in 1810 after the original tent-roofed tower was destroyed by lightning.

Cathedral of St Demetrius of Salonica Дмитриевский Собор

The unusual, single-domed, square Cathedral of St Demetrius of Salonica nearby was completed in 1197 as Vsevolod III's court church. It is built from white limestone blocks and its exterior walls have over 1300 bas-relief carvings showing a range of people, events, animals and plants. The cathedral is permanently closed, but it's the exterior that's of real interest.

CATHEDRAL OF ST DEMETRIUS OF SALONICA

Other attractions

The **House of Officers** Дом Офицеров (ul Bolshaya Moskovskaya 33), formerly the Noblemen's Assembly Club, was built in 1826. The building, opposite the Assumption Cathedral, played an interesting role in the anti-religion campaign of the 1970s and 1980s. Every time a major service was held in the cathedral, loudspeakers in the House of Officers blared out (rarely heard) Western rock music. The decision to use decadent music to destroy insidious religion must have been full of anguish for the local Soviet leadership.

The **Monument to the 850th Anniversary of Vladimir** Монумент в честь 850-летия города Владимир, unveiled in 1958, symbolises, with its bronze figures of an architect, a soldier and a worker, the Communist theory that ordinary people are the makers of history. **Traders' Row Arcade**, completed in 1792, is being renovated into a retailing district and many of the shops are now open again.

The **History Museum** Исторический Музей (ul Bolshaya Moskovskaya 64, 10am-5pm, until 4pm Mon & Wed, closed Tue and last Thur of month, R60) contains archaeological finds, coins, weapons and rare books. Its most interesting exhibits are the so-called Vladimir Mother of God icon, attributed to Andrei Rublyov, and the white stone sarcophagus of the great Russian hero Alexander Nevsky.

The **Nativity Monastery** Богородице-Рождественский Монастырь (ul Bolshaya Moskovskaya 68) was completed in 1196 and was the city's most important monastery until the end of the 16th century. Alexander Nevsky was buried here in 1262, until Peter the Great had him reinterred in St Petersburg in 1724. **Frunze Monument** (Памятник Фрунзе; 600m to the east) honours Communist hero Mikhail Frunze, who carried out revolutionary work in this region. Just 300m away is the maximum-security prison where Frunze was incarcerated in 1907. The walls around this part of the city followed the Lybed River which now flows through large pipes under the road.

PRACTICAL INFORMATION

Orientation and services

The long-distance **bus station** and the **railway station** are opposite one another on ul Vokzalnaya. Trolleybus No 5 runs from the railway station to the Golden Gate along ul Bolshaya Moskovskaya. Bus No 14 also travels along the main street but does not go to the station.

There's a good **internet** spot (Mon-Fri 8am-8pm, Sat 9am-3pm, R40/hour) on the third floor at ul Gagarina 2, just off pl Svobody. Look for the sign on the street that says Интернет (Internet). For more information on the city visit 💻 www.vladimir-russia.info.

There's a Sberbank at ul Bolshaya Moskovskaya 27 with an **ATM** and exchange facilities.

Where to stay and eat

The closest hotel to the station is ***Hotel Vladimir*** **Гостиница Владимир** (ул Большая Московская 74, ul Bolshaya Moskovskaya 74, ☎ 327 201, 💻 www.hotel-vladimir.ru, sgl/dbl/suite R2050/R2700/3900), with renovated, comfortable en suite rooms. There is free wi-fi access in the restaurant and a travel agency on-site.

Near the Golden Gate, the appropriately named ***U Zolotykh Vorot*** **У Золотых Ворот** (ул Большая Московская 15-17, ul Boshaya Moskovskaya 15-17, ☎ 420 823, sgl/dbl from R2000/2800) is a small and cosy hotel with just 14 attractive rooms. The on-site restaurant serves a good selection of traditional Russian and European dishes.

Also with some English-speaking staff, the bright, modern ***Hotel Orion*** **Гостиница Орион** (ул 2-я Никольская 3, ul 2-ya Nikolskaya 3, ☎ 420 002, 💻 www.orionhotel.ru, sgl/dbl/suite from R1900/2800/3900) has well-appointed rooms, an internet café in the lobby and a decent restaurant.

There are numerous places to eat at along ul Bolshaya Moskovskaya, ул Большая Московская, including ***Stariy Gorod*** **Старый Город** at No 41, which

The Vladimir area code is ☎ 4922. From outside Russia dial ☎ +7-4922.

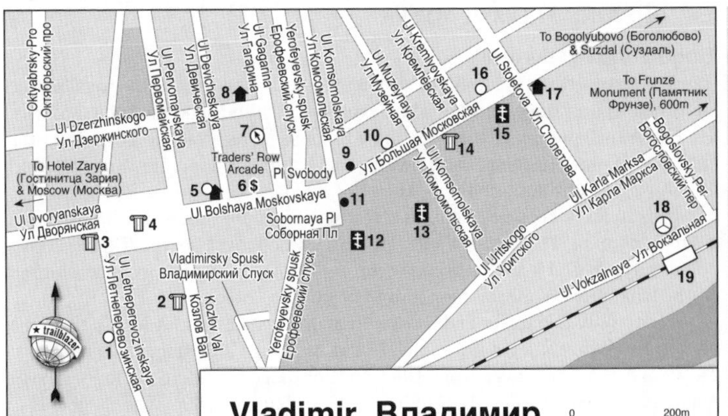

WHERE TO STAY, EAT & DRINK

1 Traktir Трактир
5 Hotel/Restaurant U Zolotykh Vorot Гостиница/Ресторан У Золотых Ворот
8 Hotel Orion Гостиница Орион
10 Stariy Gorod Старый Город
16 Shashlichnaya VAN Шашлычная ВАН
17 Hotel Vladimir Гостиница Владимир

PLACES OF INTEREST

2 Exhibition of 'Old Vladimir' Выставка 'Старый Владимир'
3 Crystal Museum Музей Хрусталя
4 Golden Gate Золотые Ворота
9 House of Officers Дом Офицеров
11 Monument to 850th Anniversary of Vladimir Монумент в честь 850-летия города Владимир
12 Assumption Cathedral Успенский Собор
13 Cathedral of St Demetrius of Salonica Дмитриевский Собор
14 History Museum Исторический Музей
15 Nativity Monastery Богородице-Рождественский Монастырь

OTHER

6 Sberbank Сбербанк
7 Internet Интернет
18 Bus Station Автовокзал
19 Railway Station Железнодорожный вокзал

serves Russian and European dishes and has English-speaking staff, and at 61a, ***Shashlichnaya VAN*** **Шашлычная ВАН**, a Georgian/Armenian place that does a mean *shashlyk* (grilled meat skewer).

Traktir Трактир (ул Летнеперевозинская 19, ul Letneperevozinskaya 19) in a cute wooden cottage, serves inexpensive Russian dishes and its summer terrace is a great spot for *shashlyk* and beer.

Moving on

There are rail services from Vladimir to Moscow (12-14/day, 1¾-3½hrs), the fastest and the most expensive being the 153 and 171 from Nizhny Novgorod, departing at 11.40am and 8.52am, respectively, and to Nizhny Novgorod (14/day, 2-4½hrs), the most convenient option being the high-speed 172, departing at 8.33am.

There are numerous buses to Suzdal (R48; 60 mins).

EXCURSIONS FROM VLADIMIR

Bogolyubovo (Боголюбово)

Ten kilometres from Vladimir, this ancient town was the site of the royal palace of Prince Andrei Bogolyubsky, who developed Vladimir into the capital of Rus. He chose this site rather than Vladimir because of its strategic position at the junction of the Klyazma River, which runs through Vladimir, and the Nerl River, which runs through the rival city of Suzdal.

This quickly became Vladimir's real power centre but, following Andrei's murder here in 1174, the whole lot was turned over to the Bogolyubovo Monastery. Andrei's assassins, powerful *boyars* from Suzdal, wounded him in his bedchamber before stabbing him to death on a staircase.

Today only one tower and a covered archway date from Andrei's time, the rest from 19th-century renovations. Major buildings still standing include the Holy Gates, a bell tower from 1841 and the huge five-domed Bogolyubovo Cathedral of the Icon of the Mother of God, built in 1866. The cathedral is slowly being renovated but is open for services.

Getting there To get to Bogolyubovo, take a suburban train from Vladimir (11/day, 14 mins). The station is about 400m from the walled Bogolyubovo Monastery. You can also catch one of the numerous buses from Vladimir's central bus station, opposite the railway station, to Bogolyubovo.

Suzdal

Суздаль

[Moscow Time] Of all the Golden Ring towns, Suzdal is the true gem. It must hold the record for the largest number of churches per capita in Russia: incredibly, at one time there was a church for every 12 of its citizens, along with 15 monasteries (more than any other Russian city except Moscow) and over 100 major architectural monuments, all in the space of just 8 square kilometres.

Aside from its historic draw, Suzdal delights visitors by presenting an idyllic picture of Russian village life without even trying. It's the sort of town where goats and chickens roam the streets, cattle graze in the meadows, and children fish from wooden bridges. Wander the rutted streets along the river in the afternoon, or watch the mist rise to shroud the placid River Kamenka at night, and you'll find yourself wanting to stay long after you've seen the sights.

Over 40 old religious buildings survive in Suzdal. The explanation for this is that in medieval times just about every street in every town had its own small, invariably wooden, church. This tradition was effectively sustained as a result of Suzdal's shrinking population, even as it was forgotten elsewhere, and taken a step further with the gradual replacement of wooden churches with durable stone ones. Two other events contributed to this unprecedented degree of historical preservation. In 1788 a new town plan limiting building heights to two storeys forced urban growth outwards instead of upwards, leaving many older, central buildings still standing instead of being replaced. Then in 1862 the railway from Moscow to Nizhny Novgorod bypassed Suzdal by 30km, reducing the town to an underdeveloped backwater until its renaissance in the last years of the Communist era – as a tourist attraction.

HISTORY

The first recorded mention of Suzdal was in 1024 when many townsfolk were put to the sword by the local prince after a peasant rebellion. By the end of that century the town's first major fortification had been built and in 1152 Yuri Dolgoruky, son of Prince Vladimir Monomakh, transferred the seat of princely power here. Within a few years Suzdal had more people than London at that time.

Despite the shift of power by Dolgoruky's son, Andrei Bogolyubsky, to Vladimir, Suzdal continued to grow until 1238, when it was devastated by the Tatar-Mongols. The town tried to rebuild itself as a trading and political centre but its dreams were shattered after another rebellion was put down by Moscow in the mid-15th century. Although most of its people eventually moved elsewhere, Suzdal remained a strong religious centre. At one point there were seven churches and cathedrals in the Kremlin, 14 within the city ramparts and 27 more scattered around various local monasteries.

In 1573 the town had just 400 households, and disasters over the next few centuries ensured that the number didn't rise much. Between 1608 and 1610 the town was raided several times by Polish and Lithuanian forces; in 1634 it was devastated by Crimean Tatars; in 1644 most of its wooden buildings were burnt down; in 1654 the plague wiped out almost half the population; and in a huge fire in 1719 every remaining wooden building in the centre was destroyed.

WHAT TO SEE AND DO

Kremlin Кремль

The **Suzdal Kremlin** (10am-6pm, closed Tue and last Fri of month, all-inclusive ticket R300) of the 11th century was ringed by 1400m of earth embankments topped with log walls and towers. These fortifications survived until the 18th century but the only sections left today are the small earth walls dotted around the city.

The enormous **Cathedral of the Birth of the Mother of God** Собор Рождества Богородицы, its five blue onion domes dotted with golden stars, is the most striking building within the Kremlin and one of the oldest cathedrals in Russia. It was begun in 1222 and completed in just two years; the upper tier was rebuilt in 1530. The octagonal **bell tower**, added in 1635, was once fitted with bells that chimed not only hourly but on the minute. Attached to the bell tower by a gallery is the 15th- to 18th-century Archbishop's Chambers, which now houses **Suzdal History Museum** Суздальский Исторический Музей. The museum traces the history of the town through Iron Age artefacts, medieval costumes and weaponry and exhibits dealing with the Soviet destruction of Suzdal's wealth and its subsequent restoration. Nearby is the Cross Chamber, a vast ceremonial reception hall built in the 18th century.

Also within the old walls are two **churches** dedicated to St Nicholas: a stone one to the south-east, completed in 1739 and considered one of Suzdal's finest 18th-century buildings, and a wooden one to the south-west, brought here from the nearby village of Glotovo.

Torgovaya ploshchad Торговая пл Trading Sq

On one side of Torgovaya pl are the Torgoviye Ryady, **Gostinny Dvor** Гостинный Двор built at the turn of the 19th century, now containing tourist shops, bars and restaurants. Originally there was a second arcade facing the Kamenka River. Nearby are several more 18th-century churches, including the **Church of the Resurrection** Воскресенская Церковь. On the square and along the adjoining ul Kremlyovskaya ул Кремлёвская, you'll usually find a number of stalls selling *medovukha*, the traditional mead made by mixing distilled honey and water together. It may go down smoothly, but it is rather potent!

Monastery of the Saviour and St Euthimius Спасо-Евфимеевский Монастырь

This fortified monastery (10am-6pm, closed Mon and last Thur of month, R60-100 per museum, or R400 all-inclusive, camera R100) was founded in the mid-14th century to protect Suzdal's northern approaches, and is now home to several museums.

You enter the monastery via a 22m-high tower gate and beneath the **Gate-Church of the Annunciation**. In the church is an exhibition on a local prince, Dmitry Pozharsky, who with Kuzma Minin, a village elder in Nizhny Novgorod, raised the volunteer army which liberated Moscow from Polish-Lithuanian forces in 1612.

Pozharsky's grave is by the eastern wall of the **Cathedral of the Transfiguration of the Saviour**. The 17th-century frescoes here are particularly impressive. Some mornings a choir gives a short but beautiful recital in the cathedral and you can hear the bells being rung on the hour, every hour. In a side chapel is the grave of St Euthimius, who founded the monastery in 1352.

Beside the 17th-century Church of St Nicholas is the **Infirmary**, where a museum called the **Golden Treasury** features Russian decorative art of the 13th-20th centuries.

The long, single-storey building nearby was the monastery **prison**, used until 1905 for those who had committed crimes against the faith. Now it's become the **Convicts of the Monastery Prison Museum**. In Stalinist times, political prisoners were kept here before being sent to Siberia, and exhibits include heartbreaking letters to their loved ones (in Russian only). The same prison was used to house Italian and German prisoners of war after WWII.

The **Monks' Cells** now house an exhibition showing the history of the town's convents and monasteries, and their restoration. The only drawback is the lack of English labelling.

Convent of the Intercession Покровский Монастырь

This convent (Thur-Mon 9.30am-4.30pm), founded in 1364, offers an insight into the patriarchal nature of traditional Russian society. Euphemistically referred to as a retreat for high-spirited women, it was in fact a place of banishment for infertile wives, victims of dynastic squabbles and women who broke any of the harsh customs of medieval society.

First to use it in this way, in 1525, was Moscow's Grand Prince Vasily, whose wife Solomonia Saburova bore him no heirs. Solomonia, whose revenge was to outlive Vasily and his second wife, is buried in the **Intercession Cathedral**, completed in 1518. Other famous women forced into the habit here were Praskovya Solovaya, second wife of Ivan the Great; Anna Vasilchikova, Ivan the Terrible's fourth wife; and Evdokya Lopukhina, Peter the Great's first wife.

The three-domed **Gateway Church of the Annunciation** sits above the Holy Gates. The two-storey **Refectory Church of the Conception of St Anna** was built in 1551 on the orders of Ivan the Great. Since this is a working convent and not a museum, you may not enter the buildings on the premises, but that doesn't detract from the pleasure of wandering through the grounds.

Museum of Wooden Architecture Музей Деревянного Зодчества

This open-air museum (ul Pushkarskaya, 9am-7pm, until 4pm in the winter season, closed last Wed of month, all-inclusive ticket R200) comprises around twenty examples of a vanishing regional wooden architecture, including churches, peasant houses, windmills, barns and granaries. Among the most striking buildings are the **Church of the Transfiguration**, erected in 1756, and the **Church of the Resurrection**, built in 1776. Though you may only enter three of the above buildings you can imagine what life was like for Russian peasants, thanks to museum staff in traditional costumes who can demonstrate the workings of a weaving loom and other equipment.

Monastery of the Deposition of the Robe Ризоположенский Монастырь

Founded in 1207, this is Suzdal's oldest monastery, although only a few of its original buildings remain: the asymmetrical, double-arched **Holy Gates** (1688), topped with tiny onion domes; the plain **Cathedral of the Deposition of the Robe**, dating from the first half of the 16th century; and a 72m-high **bell tower** visible from all over town and thought to have been erected in honour of Napoleon's defeat in 1812.

PRACTICAL INFORMATION

Orientation and services

Ul Lenina ул Ленина is the town's main street, running north–south. Virtually everything to see is within walking distance of the centre of town and there's a **Sberbank** Сбербанк with an **ATM** along the main street.

There's a **post office** Почта (8am-8pm Mon-Sat) on Krasnaya pl. At the time of research, internet access wasn't available anywhere in Suzdal though it may be when you are here so check on arrival.

To get to and from the **bus station** автовокзал, either take one of the frequent buses along ul Vasilyevskaya ул Васильевская (or pay the driver an additional R10 if coming from out of town to get you to the centre of Suzdal) or walk for around 40 minutes.

Where to stay, eat and drink

Backpackers make straight for the busy and popular ***Godzillas Suzdal*** (ул Набережная 32, ul Naberezhnaya 32, ☎ 25146 or ☎ 495 699 4223, 💻 www.godzillashostel.com, dorm bed R750). This branch of the popular Moscow hostel is a large, well-furnished wooden house with spacious en suite dorms. The friendly woman who runs it doesn't speak much English, but she goes out of her way to make you feel welcome. For an English speaker call the Moscow office.

Budget travellers may also want to keep an eye out for '**гостевой дом**' ('gostevoi dom' – guest house) signs, as many locals rent out their cottages or rooms in their homes to visitors. Prices start from around R1000 per night.

Elena Surikova and her family (☎ 213 90) have converted their house (Surikov Home, **Дом Суриковых**, ул Красноармейская 53, ul Krasnoarmeyskaya 53) into a small hotel. They charge R1000-1500pp including a blini breakfast.

Hotel Rizopolozhenskaya **Гостиница Ризоположенская** (☎ 24 314; sgl/dbl/trpl/quad R1100/2800/2550/2800) is in the Monastery of the Deposition of the Robe (see p219) and it still retains that Soviet Intourist flavour. Room quality varies widely but the location is interesting and the rate is cheap.

Also central, ***Pushkarskaya Sloboda*** **Пушкарская Слобода** (ул Ленина 45, ul Lenina 45, ☎ 233 03, sgl/dbl from R3000/3300-10,900) is a family-friendly

---

WHERE TO STAY, EAT AND DRINK

1 Surikov home Дом Суриковых
3 Traktir Kuchkova Трактир Кучкова
5 Hotel Pokrovskaya Гостиница Покровская
6 Restaurant Trapeznaya (in convent) Ресторан Трапезная
12 Hotel Rizopolozhenskaya Гостиница Ризоположенская
13 Likhoninsky House Лихонинский Дом
14 Godzillas Suzdal
16 Kharchevnya Харчевня
18 Mead-Tasting Hall Дегустационный зал Суздальского медоваренного завода
19 Losos I Kofe Лосось и Кофе
22 Hotel Sokol Гостиница Сокол
23 Restaurant Pogrebok Ресторан Погребок
26 Restaurant Trapeznaya (in the Kremlin) Ресторан Трапезная
32 Pushkarskaya Sloboda Пушкарская Слобода

PLACES OF INTEREST

2 Monastery of the Saviour & St Euthimius Спасо-Евфимеевский Монастырь
4 Convent of the Intercession Покровский Монастырь
7 Church of SS Peter & Paul Петропавловская Церковь
8 Church of St Nicholas Никольская Церковь
9 St Aleksandr Nevsky Monastery Александровский Монастырь
11 Monastery of the Deposition of the Robe Ризоположенский Монастырь
17 Gostinny Dvor (Traders' Arcade) Гостинный Двор
20 Resurrection Church Воскресенская Церковь
24 Church of St Nicholas Никольская Церковь
25 Cathedral of the Birth of the Mother of God Собор Рождества Богородицы
27 Suzdal History Museum Суздальский Исторический Музей
28 Wooden church of St Nicholas Церковь Святого Николы
29 Church of the Transfiguration Преображенская Церковь
30 Resurrection Church Воскресенская Церковь
31 Museum of Wooden Architecture Музей Деревянного Зодчества
33 Church of the Deposition of the Robe Ризоположенская церковь

OTHER

10 Post Office Почта
15 Sberbank Сбербанк
21 ATM Банк

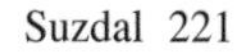

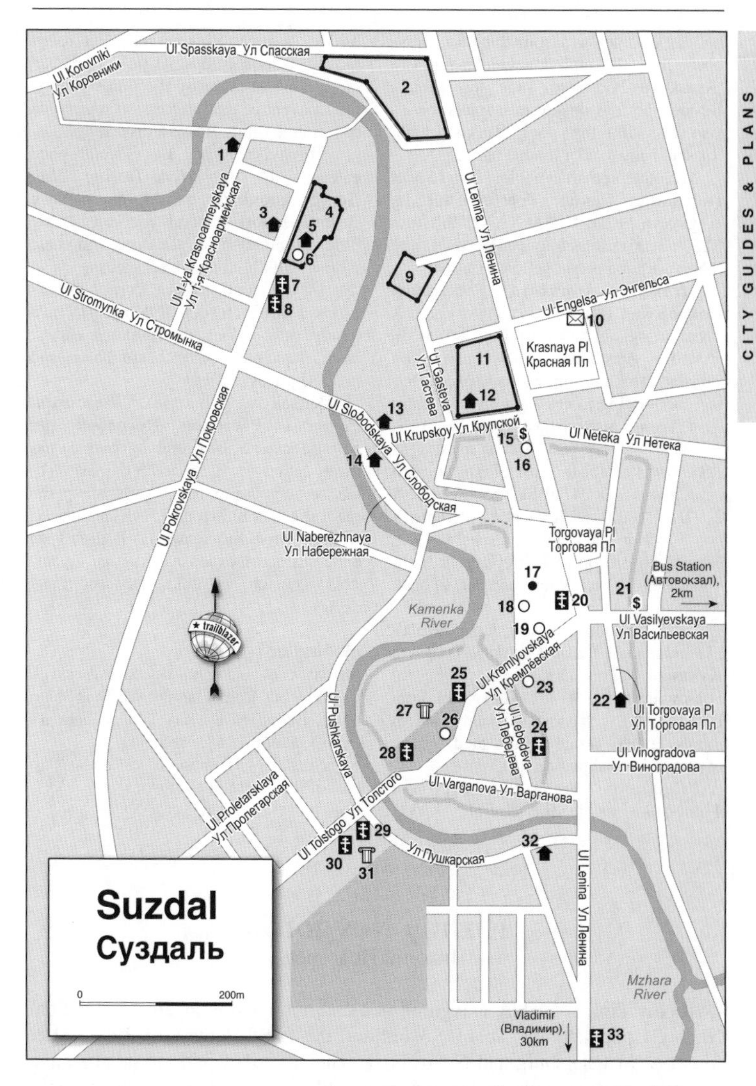

The Suzdal area code is ☎ 49231. From outside Russia dial ☎ +7-49231.

holiday complex with something for everyone – from romantic honeymoon suites to 'Russkoye Podvorye' pine log cabins. Besides the four on-site restaurants there's also a swimming pool, Turkish bath, Russian banya and a fondue bar.

Another upmarket choice, ***Hotel Sokol*** **Гостиница Сокол** (Торговая пл 2а, Torgovaya pl 2a, ☎ 209 87, sgl/dbl from R2200/2800) offers fully equipped en suite rooms within a bright yellow exterior.

Hotel Pokrovskaya **Гостиница Покровская** (☎ 250 77, 🖳 www.na-pokrovke.ru, sgl/dbl from R1800/2300) is an attractive guesthouse at the Intercession Convent (Покровский Монастырь), offering comfortable rooms with a rustic ambience. There's also a banya on the premises.

One of the best places to stay is ***Likhoninsky House*** **Дом Лихонинский** (ул Слободская 34, ul Slobodskaya 34, ☎ 219 01, R1000), a 17th-century merchant's house with just seven cosy rooms; you can even sleep on top of a fireplace in traditional Russian style! Very popular, so book weeks in advance.

Also popular but with a non-Suzdal-like ambience is ***Traktir Kuchkova*** **Трактир Кучкова** (ул Покровская 35, ul Pokrovskaya 35, ☎ 202 52, sgl/dbl from R3000/3200), with garish but comfy modern rooms. There is a sauna and a good, though overpriced, restaurant on the premises.

Restaurant Trapeznaya **Ресторан Трапезная** inside the Kremlin serves pricey, classical Russian food but caters mostly to tour groups. There's a smaller, more intimate place by the same name in the Convent of the Intercession where you can sample filling Russian dishes.

Torgoviye Ryady has several good eateries. In the ***Mead-Tasting Hall*** **Дегустационный зал Суздальского медоваренного завода** you can sample different variations on the drink and chase it down with blini and other snacks.

In the south-eastern corner there's ***Losos I Kofe*** **Лосось и Кофе** ([V]), a trendy café serving tasty salmon dishes, sushi, Japanese noodle bento boxes and good, if pricey, coffee.

Kitschy pub-style ***Restaurant Pogrebok*** **Ресторан Погребок** (ул Кремлёвская 5, ul Kremlyovskaya 5) has meaty mains for R250 and a dungeon-like bar serving cheap beer, while along the main street, at ul Lenina 73, ул Ленина 73, ***Kharchevnya*** **Харчевня** ([V]) dishes up delicious and inexpensive Russian favourites – borsch, solyanka, fish and meat dishes.

Moving on

Suzdal is not on any railway but it is easy to get to by bus from Vladimir which is 35km away. Buses leave every half an hour to/from Vladimir (R48, one hour).

Suzdal's bus station is just under 2km east of the centre of the town.

Nizhny Novgorod

Нижний Новгород

[Moscow Time] Nizhny Novgorod is a charming and enjoyable destination. Nizhny's population is about 1.3 million, the fourth largest in Russia after Moscow, St Petersburg and Novosibirsk. The city takes pride in its attractive riverside location, with locals promenading till late at night along the embankment and on the pedestrianised ul Bolshaya Pokrovskaya.

Still listed as Gorky on railway timetables, Nizhny Novgorod was founded in 1221 by Prince Vladimir Monomakh at the junction of the Oka and Volga rivers. This strategic location on two central shipping routes virtually guaranteed its growth and prosperity, and its importance as a major trading centre was consolidated with the opening in 1817 of the Nizhny Novgorod Fair. By the 1870s this fair had a turnover of some 300 million gold roubles. To put this into perspective, the entire Trans-Siberian railway cost about 1000 million roubles to build.

In the 1930s Nizhny Novgorod was turned into a major Soviet military-industrial centre, closed to foreigners and renamed Gorky, after the Russian novelist and playwright Maxim Gorky (1868-1936), who was born here. In the 1980s it was best known outside the USSR as a place of internal exile for dissidents, most famously the nuclear physicist and Nobel Peace Prize winner Andrei Sakharov.

Following the collapse of communism the city was reopened in 1991 and given back its old name, and its fair was reborn in the fabulously renovated 1800s Empire-style Fair Building. Nizhny Novgorod's history as a proud part of the old Rus, its attractive old centre with ramshackle old wooden buildings, killer views of the Volga, and a laidback atmosphere have turned it into a tourist destination.

WHAT TO SEE AND DO

Kremlin Кремль

The well-preserved Kremlin, with its 12 impressive towers, dating back to the 16th century, sits on a hill dominating the area. The sweeping views of the Volga and Oka rivers from the memorial park more than justify the steep walk up inside the Kremlin, and there's another attractive walk around its walls. Inside are the City Hall, the **Cathedral of the Archangel Michael** Собор Михаила Архангела, an eternal flame dedicated to the memory of the unknown soldier, and **Nizhegorodsky State Art Museum** Нижегородский Художественный Музей (11am-6pm Wed-Mon R80) in the former Governor's House, featuring icons and paintings by Russian masters.

The **Arsenal** (noon-8pm Tue-Sun) is the local centre of modern art which doubles as a workspace for artists and an art gallery with temporary exhibitions.

Old Nizhny Novgorod

The old town has two interesting pedestrian-only streets. The one-kilometre long **ul Bolshaya Pokrovskaya** runs from pl Gorkogo to pl Minina i Pozharskogo (in front of the Kremlin), past one of the city's biggest food markets, the Drama Theatre, the impressive art nouveau State Bank building and the Duma parliamentary building.

Typical of Russian cobbled streets of the late 18th century is **ul Rozhdestvenskaya**, the most appealing section of which is from the river station to the northern gate of the Kremlin.

SS PETER & PAUL CHURCH

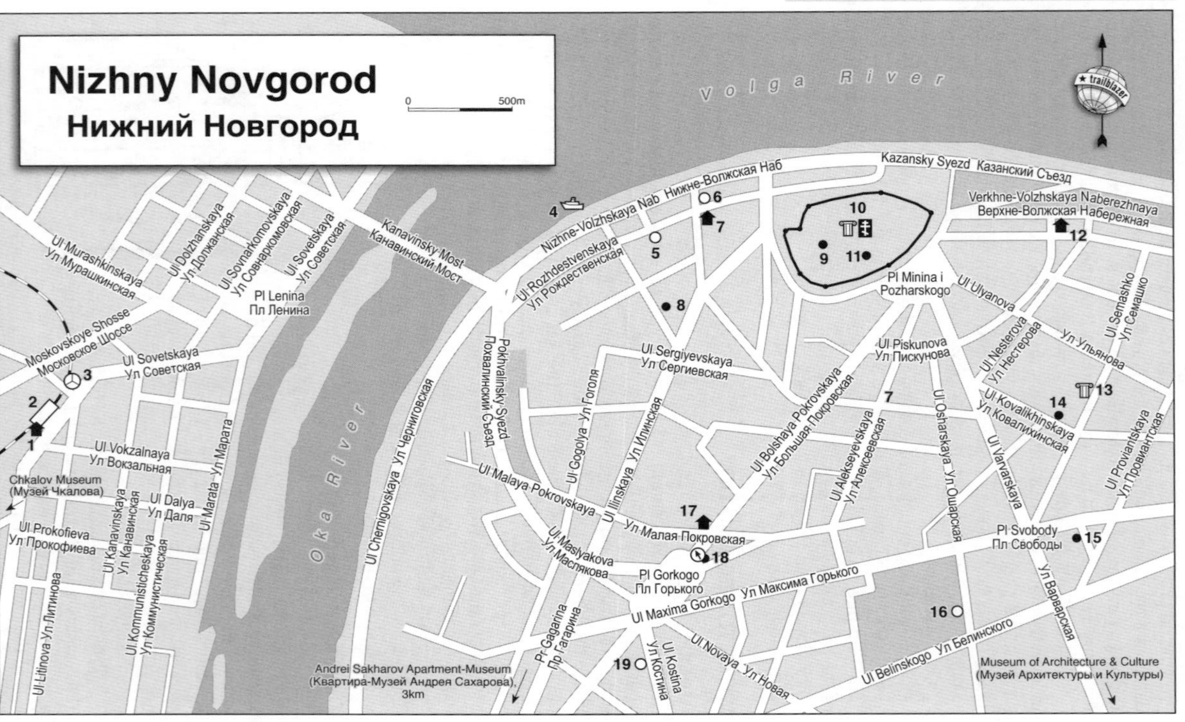
Nizhny Novgorod
Нижний Новгород
0
500m
trailblazer
Volga River
Oka River
Kazansky Syezd Казанский Съезд
Verkhne-Volzhskaya Naberezhnaya
Верхне-Волжская Набережная
Nizhne-Volzhskaya Nab Нижне-Волжская Наб
Ul Rozhdestvenskaya Ул Рождественская
Kanavinsky Most Канавинский Мост
Ul Murashkinskaya Ул Мурашкинская
Ul Dolzhanskaya Ул Должанская
Ul Sovnarkomovskaya Ул Совнаркомовская
Ul Sovetskaya Ул Советская
Pl Lenina Пл Ленина
Moskovskoye Shosse Московское Шоссе
Ul Sovetskaya Ул Советская
Ul Vokzalnaya Ул Вокзальная
Ul Marata Ул Марата
Chkalov Museum (Музей Чкалова)
Ul Dalya Ул Даля
Ul Prokofieva Ул Прокофиева
Ul Kanavinskaya Ул Канавинская
Ul Kommunisticheskaya Ул Коммунистическая
Ul Litinova Ул Литинова
Ul Chernigovskaya Ул Черниговская
Pokhvalinsky Syezd Похвалинский Съезд
Ul Gogolya Ул Гоголя
Ul Ilinskaya Ул Ильинская
Ul Sergiyevskaya Ул Сергиевская
Ul Malaya Pokrovskaya Ул Малая Покровская
Ul Maslyakova Ул Маслякова
Pl Gorkogo Пл Горького
Ul Maxima Gorkogo Ул Максима Горького
Pr Gagarina Пр Гагарина
Ul Kostina Ул Костина
Ul Novaya Ул Новая
Andrei Sakharov Apartment-Museum
(Квартира-Музей Андрея Сахарова),
3km
Ul Bolshaya Pokrovskaya Ул Большая Покровская
Pl Minina i Pozharskogo
Ul Piskunova Ул Пискунова
Ul Alekseyevskaya Ул Алексеевская
Ul Osharskaya Ул Ошарская
Ul Ulyanova Ул Ульянова
Ul Nesterova Ул Нестерова
Ul Kovalikhinskaya Ул Ковалихинская
Ul Varvarskaya Ул Варварская
Ul Semashko Ул Семашко
Ul Proviantskaya Ул Провиантская
Pl Svobody Пл Свободы
Ul Belinskogo Ул Белинского
Museum of Architecture & Culture
(Музей Архитектуры и Культуры)
1
2
3
4
5
6
7
8
9
10
11
12
13
14
15
16
17
18
19

The **Ostrog** (Острог) is where prisoners exiled to Siberia were kept overnight on their forced march to the east. Its most famous prisoner was the USSR's first prime minister, Mikhail Sverdlov. The building is now a museum (pl Svobody 2, 10am-5pm Tue-Sun; tours in Russian R150) where you can inspect the cells of the incarcerated.

Museums

Maxim Gorky, born here in 1868, wrote of the cruelty and injustice of rural Tsarist Russia, making his books compulsory reading for Soviet children. Gorky historical sites include his **birthplace** Место Рождения Горького (ul Kovalikhinskaya 33); **Domik Kashirina**, his grandfather's house on Pochtovy syezd, where he and his mother moved in 1870; and **Gorky Apartment-Museum** Музей Горького (ul Semashko 19, 9am-5pm, closed Mon and Thur, R45) where he lived from 1902 to 1904. There's also a statue commemorating the man on pl Gorkogo.

The dissident nuclear physicist Andrei Sakharov was exiled to Gorky from January 1981 to December 1986. His old flat at pr Gagarina 214 has been turned into the **Andrei Sakharov Apartment-Museum** Квартира-Музей Андрея Сахарова (10am-5pm, R45); the exhibition includes the telephone which Gorbachev called to tell Sakharov that he was free. It's 3km south of the centre; marshrutka 4 or 104 runs there from pl Minina i Pozharskogo.

Another well-known regional son is air pioneer Valery Chkalov; his fame comes from circumnavigating the USSR in June 1936 and flying non-stop from Moscow via the North Pole to Vancouver in June 1937. In a hangar at the **Chkalov Museum** Музей Чкалова (ul Chkalova 5, to the west of the city, 💻 www.vchkalov.ru, 10am-5pm, closed Mon), are several well-preserved planes,

WHERE TO STAY, EAT & DRINK
1 Resting rooms Комнаты отдыха
5 Papasha Billy Папаша Билли
6 Pyatkin Пяткинъ
7 Hotel Troitskaya Гостиница Троицкая
12 Hotel Oktyabrskaya Гостиница Октябрьская
16 Ali Baba Али Баба
17 Hotel Jouk Jacque Гостиница Жук-Жак
19 Vesyolaya Kuma Весёлая Кума

PLACES OF INTEREST
8 Domik Kashirina Домик Каширина
9 Arsenal
10 Kremlin Кремль
10 Cathedral of the Archangel Michael
Собор Михаила Архангела
10 Nizhegorodsky State Art Museum
Нижегородский Художественный Музей
11 Monument to Heroes of WWII
Памятник Героям Великой Отечественной Войны
13 Gorky Apartment-Museum Музей Горького
14 Gorky's Birthplace
Место Рождения Горького
15 Ostrog Острог

OTHER
2 Railway Station Железнодорожный Вокзал
3 Bus Station Автовокзал
4 River Station Речной Вокзал
18 Volga Telecom Волга Телеком

including the ANT-25 Chkalov flew to North America. Chkalov's **statue** stands by the Aleksandrovsky Gardens.

The **Museum of Architecture and Culture** Музей Архитектуры и Культуры (ul Gorbatovskaya 41; 10am-4pm Sat-Thur, R40) is set in the park area known as Shcholokovsky Khutor, south-east of the city centre and at the end of bus route No 28. There's an interesting collection of traditional wooden buildings including an Old Believers' Church and the five main village holidays per year are celebrated here.

PRACTICAL INFORMATION

Orientation and services

The central part of Nizhny Novgorod and the Kremlin lie at the junction of the Volga and Oka rivers. The **railway station** Железнодорожный Вокзал is across the river from the centre. Pedestrianised ul Bolshaya Pokrovskaya ул Большая Покровская is the main shopping street.

Nizhny Novgorod's **metro** is still not extensive enough to be much use to the visitor. There's a good network of **trams** and **buses**. Tram No 1 is a slow way of getting to the Kremlin (R12); it runs south from the railway station before crossing a bridge and running along ul Ilinskaya, which runs parallel to the main ul Bolshaya Pokrovskaya. Alternatively, take any bus with пл Минина и Пожарского (pl Minina i Pozharskogo) as its destination.

Komanda Gorkiy (Team Gorky, ul 40 let Oktyabrya 1a, ☎ 465 1919, 🖳 www.teamgorky.ru) organises weekend rafting in the Nizhny Novgorod region on the Kerzenets River, trekking, fishing and white-water rafting in Siberia, and bicycling around the Golden Ring. Their website has an English-language section.

Internet is available 24 hours at the VolgaTelecom office at pl Gorkogo for R65 per hour.

Where to stay

The ***Resting rooms*** **комнаты отдыха** (*komnaty otdykha*, sgl/quad R1100/550) at the railway station are found in a separate building on your right as you come out of the main exit. There are no frills but the rooms are perfectly clean and adequate.

Right near the Kremlin, ***Hotel Troitskaya*** **Гостиница Троицкая** (пер Вахитова 8, per Vakhitova 8, ☎ 433 0555, 🖳 www.hotel-troickaya.ru (in Russian), rooms R2200-4000) has air-conditioned cosy rooms with internet access, and an excellent sauna with Jacuzzi. Breakfast costs R200 extra. ***Hotel Oktyabrskaya*** **Гостиница Октябрьская** (наб Верхне-Волжская 9a, nab Verkhne-Volzhskaya 9a, ☎ 432 8080, 🖳 www.oktyabrskaya.ru, doubles from R5000) has a prime location overlooking the Volga and its cheerful, renovated rooms are wi-fi enabled. Discounts on weekends. Allegedly one of Russia's top 50 hotels, ***Hotel Jouk Jacque*** **Гостиница Жук-Жак** (ул Большая Покровская 57, ul Bolshaya Pokrovskaya 57, ☎ 433 0462, 🖳 www.jak-hotel.ru, dbl/suite from R3750/5250) impresses with its professional service and its modern, spacious rooms with satellite TV and wi-fi. The central location is superb, too.

Where to eat and drink

There's a good range of places on ul Bolshaya Pokrovskaya (ул Большая Покровская) and ul Rozhdestvenskaya (ул Рождественская).

Pyatkin **Пяткинъ** (ул Рождественская 23, ul Rozhdestvenskaya 23, mains R400), in mansion-like surroundings, is a favourite with well-heeled visitors thanks to its excellent service and imaginative menu of meat

The Nizhny Novgorod area code is ☎ 831. From outside Russia dial ☎ +7-831.

and fish dishes. Cowboy saloon-like ***Papasha Billy* Папаша Билли** (ул Рождественская 22, ul Rozhdestvenskaya 22, mains R500-1900) is a Tex-Mex place serving up palatable fajitas and decent (though pricey) steaks. Offering a flavourful mixture of Georgian, Uzbek and Armenian cuisine, ***Ali Baba* Али Баба** (ул Белинского 61, ul Belinskogo 61, mains R500) is a great spot for shashlyk, *manti* (giant meat dumplings) and grilled meats in general. Good business lunch for R300.

For hearty Ukrainian dishes, such as borsch and *vareniki* (cherry dumplings) within cheerful, kitschy surroundings, head for ***Vesyolaya Kuma* Весёлая Кума** (ул Костина 3, ul Kostina 3, mains R450, [V]).

Moving on

By air There are daily flights to and from Moscow, St Petersburg, and other major Russian cities from Nizhny Novgorod International Airport, as well as direct flights from Frankfurt with Lufthansa (4/week, 3½hrs).

By rail There are over a dozen daily trains between Nizhny Novgorod and Moscow, both suburban and long-distance (5½-7hrs), the fastest being the high-speed Sapsan (6.45am and 3.15pm, 4hrs).

Other departures include Vladimir (13/day, 2-4½hrs), Perm (7/day, 15hrs) and Yekaterinburg (5/day, 19-21hrs).

EXCURSIONS FROM NIZHNY NOVGOROD

Gorodets Городец

The village of Gorodets, home of folk artists, is famous for its hand-painted toys. You can see them being made at the Gorodetskaya Rospis handicraft factory (closed weekends). It's also known for *pryaniki* (the hard honey cakes that Russians eat with tea). On the way you pass the Gorkovsky hydro-electric station with its 15km-long dam. Ferries travel regularly between Nizhny Novgorod and Gorodets.

Makariev Макарьев

A small, quiet village 60km east along the Volga, Makariev's main attraction is Makariev Monastery, whose walls and domes loom over the town. The monastery was founded in the 15th century and the town grew up around it as a river trading post. Today there's a small museum in the village schoolhouse and several rustic wooden homes. Locals come to take a dip or sunbathe on the sandy beach. Bring your own food, as shops are in short supply in this village of around 200 people. Boats leave from Nizhny Novgorod's river station (💻 www.vftour.ru – in Russian) several times daily in summer.

Perm
Пермь

[Moscow Time +2] The city of Perm, Pasternak's Yuryatin in *Dr Zhivago*, is the gateway to Siberia. Lying in the foothills of the Ural Mountains it's an industrial city of just over a million people, and the focus of the region. The surrounding area is good for hiking and skiing, and some operators offer white-water rafting trips.

Perm dates back to 1723 and the construction of the Yegoshikhinsky copper foundry, established by VN Tatichev, a close associate of Peter the Great. Its location on two major trading rivers ensured that Perm grew as both an industrial and a trading city. Salt caravans arrived along the Kama River while wheat, honey and metal products from the Urals travelled along the Chusovoy River. The arrival of the railway in 1878, the discovery of oil in the region and the transfer of factories from European Russia during WWII all boosted the local economy further.

The city's most familiar product is the Kama bicycle which, while rarely seen on the streets of Russian cities, is still widely used in the country. Perm's most specialised products are the first-stage engines for Proton Heavy-Lift rockets.

Despite its industrial history Perm has a tradition of culture and scholarship, thanks largely to the revolutionaries, intellectuals and political prisoners exiled here in the 19th century. Perm had the Urals' first university, whose most famous student was Alexander Popov (1859-1905), a local boy (born in nearby Krasnoturinsk) and, according to Russian historians, the inventor of the wireless. Popov is said to have demonstrated his invention in 1895, the same year that Marconi proved his concept. From 1940 to 1957 Perm was called Molotov, after the subsequently disgraced Soviet Foreign Minister who signed the 1939 Ribbentrop-Molotov Pact, dividing up Poland with the Nazis.

Today Perm remains a major centre for culture, administration and business in the region. Its main industries include processing wood from the surrounding forests as well as producing 3% of Russia's oil output and it also boasts one of Russia's top ballet schools. Its sister city is Oxford, England.

WHAT TO SEE AND DO

The most interesting part of town is the old quarter around Perm 1 railway station. Old churches here include the baroque **Cathedral of SS Peter and Paul** (1757-65, with a 19th-century belfry) and the Empire-style **Cathedral of the Saviour**, part of the **Transfiguration Monastery** (1798-1832). There are also numerous examples of eclectic and art nouveau architectural styles, of which the old building of Perm 2 station is one. The river station is near Perm 1.

Perm Art Gallery Пермская Галерея Изобразительных Искусств (Komsomolsky pr 4, Tue-Sat 10am-6pm, Sun 11am-6pm, adult/student R100/50) is one of the largest galleries in Russia, with a collection of wooden sculptures carved by the native Finno-Ugric population following their conversion to Christianity. The sculptures include a figure of Jesus with Mongolian features and saints with the blood of sacrificial animals on their faces as a nod back to the ancient Finno-Ugric deities.

Inside the splendid **Meshkov Mansion** Дом Мешкова, the thorough **Museum of Local Studies** (ul Ordzhonikidze 11, 10am-7pm Tue-Sun, R100) has well-presented exhibits charting the region's history from the earliest human settlement to the 20th century. Of particular interest are the metal castings of the 'Perm animal style', as practised by the ancient Finno-Ugric tribes, as well as the exhibit dedicated to the impact of the civil war and WWII on the

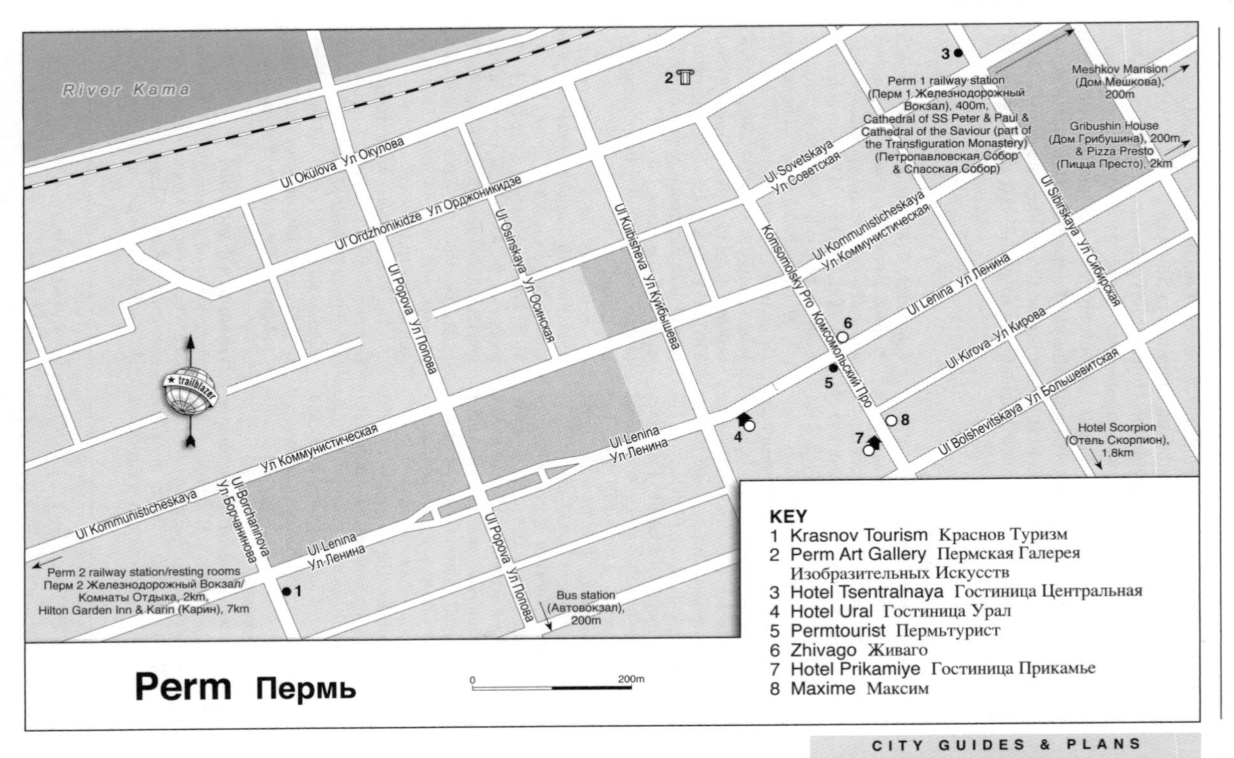
Perm Пермь
River Kama
Ul Okulova Ул Окулова
Ul Ordzhonikidze Ул Орджоникидзе
Ul Popova Ул Попова
Ul Osinskaya Ул Осинская
Ul Kuibisheva Ул Куйбышева
Ul Sovetskaya Ул Советская
Komsomolsky Pro Комсомольский Про
Ul Kommunisticheskaya Ул Коммунистическая
Ul Lenina Ул Ленина
Ul Kirova Ул Кирова
Ul Bolshevitskaya Ул Большевитская
Ul Sibirskaya Ул Сибирская
Ul Borchaninova Ул Борчанинова
Perm 1 railway station (Перм 1 Железнодорожный Вокзал), 400m, Cathedral of SS Peter & Paul & Cathedral of the Saviour (part of the Transfiguration Monastery) (Петропавловская Собор & Спасская Собор)
Meshkov Mansion (Дом Мешкова), 200m
Gribushin House (Дом Грибушина), 200m & Pizza Presto (Пицца Престо), 2km
Hotel Scorpion (Отель Скорпион), 1.8km
Perm 2 railway station/resting rooms Перм 2 Железнодорожный Вокзал/ Комнаты Отдыха, 2km, Hilton Garden Inn & Karin (Карин), 7km
Bus station (Автовокзал), 200m
0 200m
trailblazer
KEY
1 Krasnov Tourism Краснов Туризм
2 Perm Art Gallery Пермская Галерея Изобразительных Искусств
3 Hotel Tsentralnaya Гостиница Центральная
4 Hotel Ural Гостиница Урал
5 Permtourist Пермьтурист
6 Zhivago Живаго
7 Hotel Prikamiye Гостиница Прикамье
8 Maxime Максим

Perm area. Other exhibits include the fauna and flora of the region and a section dedicated to prominent manufacturer families in Siberia.

Other sights include **Gribushin House** Дом Грибушина (ul Lenina 13) on which Dr Zhivago's 'house with figures' was based. At ul Osinskaya 5 you'll find an attractive mosque, while those with an interest in macabre facts may wish to wander past **Hotel Tsentralnaya** Гостиница Центральная (ul Sibirskaya 5), where the man next in line for the throne after the demise of the Romanov family, Grand Prince Mikhail, stayed on his last night before the Bolsheviks dispatched him.

PRACTICAL INFORMATION

Orientation and services

The town is spread along the Kama River with its centre around Perm 1 station, on the left (eastern) bank. At the southern end of Perm, also on the left bank, is Perm 2 station where Trans-Siberian trains stop. Suburban trains run the 5km between Perm 2 and Perm 1.

The city has two airports: Bolshoye Savino, 20km to the west, which handles most traffic, and the older Bakharevka airport, 10km south in the suburb of Balatovo. You can buy plane tickets for destinations such as Moscow (several daily, 2hrs) and Frankfurt (4/week, 6hrs) from the ticket office in the lobby of Hotel Ural.

Krasnov Tourism Краснов Туризм (ul Borchaninova 4, ☎ 238 3520, 🖳 www.uraltourism.com, 10am-6pm Mon-Fri) is a recommended agency that does all manner of tours, ranging from multi-day wilderness excursions to Perm city tours and trips to Kungur Ice Cave (see opposite).

Permtourist Пермьтурист (☎ 290 6237, 🖳 www.permtourist.ru – in Russian only) at Hotel Ural can arrange boat trips along the Kama and Chusovoy rivers and also does day trips to Kungur Ice Cave.

Where to stay

At the big, plush ***Hotel Ural*** **Гостиница Урал** (ул Ленина 58, ul Lenina 58, ☎ 218 6262, 🖳 www.hotel-ural.com, sgl/dbl from R2000/2300), the rooms fail to match the glamorous lobby, though they are perfectly comfortable. There's also a fitness hall, business centre, Permtourist travel agency, and the Stroganovskaya Votchina restaurant serves European and old Russian dishes that would've been enjoyed by the nobility.

Hotel Prikamiye **Гостиница Прикамье** (Комсомольский пр 27, Komsomolsky pr 27, ☎ 237 7607, 🖳 www.prikamie-hotel.ru, sgl/dbl from R2300/3100) is another good mid-range option, each of its en suite rooms equipped with TV and fridge. Take tram No 4 or 7 from the railway station to the 'Tsentralny Univermag' stop.

For something a bit more modern, head for oddly named ***Hotel Scorpion*** Отель Скорпион (ул Полины Осипенко 57, ul Poliny Osipyenko 57, 1.8km to the south-east, ☎ 245 6622, 🖳 www.scorpion-hotel.ru, double from R3200), with its 10 rooms, decorated in warm colours, each equipped with wi-fi, TV, fridge and fan, as well as excellent showers.

The ***Resting rooms*** **комнаты отдыха** (*komnaty otdykha*) at Perm 2 (sgl/twin/5-person room R1500/1000/600 for 24 hours) are basic but perfectly adequate for a night's stay. The rooms for three or more people can be rented for a minimum of one hour.

Where to eat and drink

There are good restaurants in Hotel Ural (see Where to stay). Another recommended restaurant is ***Karin*** **Карин** (mains R550, [V]), in Hilton Garden Inn (ул Мира 456),

The Perm area code is ☎ 342. From outside Russia dial ☎ +7-342.

ul Mira 456, 7km south-west of the town centre. It features international fusion cuisine; its Chilean sea bass is very good.

Pizza Presto (ул Белинского 57, ul Belinskogo 57, 2km south-east of town centre, mains from R160, [V]) has over 30 different pizzas and very good lasagne. ***Zhivago*** **Живаго** (ул Ленина 37, ul Lenina 37, mains R500 upwards) is a plush restaurant serving some wonderfully experimental meat and seafood medleys, though such experimentation can come at quite a price.

Maxime **Максим** (Комсомольский пр 24, Komsomolsky pr 24) is a great spot for smoothies, milkshakes and good coffee.

Outside Perm 2 station there are several hole-in-the-wall places selling meat-filled pastries and other snacks.

Moving on

By air Aeroflot flies daily to Moscow, and Lufthansa has two weekly flights between Perm and Frankfurt.

By train By rail from Perm 2, eastbound departures include Moscow (8/day, 21-25hrs), while westbound departures include Novosibirsk (5/day, 25-30hrs) and Yekaterinburg (12/day, 5¼-6½hrs) – the most convenient and fastest being the 836, departing at 4.45am (Moscow Time).

By bus From the bus station at ul Revolutsii 68, there are numerous departures to or via Kungur (at least once hourly, 2hrs) and to Khokhlovka (3/day, 1½hrs).

EXCURSIONS FROM PERM

Khokhlovka Хохловка

About 45km out of town near the village of Khokhlovka is a year-round, open-air **Museum of Architecture and Ethnography** (10am-6pm, R100) with a collection of 16th- to 20th-century buildings, including a traditional *izba* (peasant dwelling), two attractive 18th-century wooden churches, and a firehouse. To get here, catch one of the frequent buses from Perm's bus station (1½hrs).

Kungur Ice Cave Кунгурская Ледяная Пещера

About 100km from Perm and 6km away from the town of Kungur is the fabulous Kungur Ice Cave (☎ 34271 62 610), among the biggest in the Urals, and an estimated 10-12,000 years old. It is 5.7km long including 48 grottos, underground lakes and hundreds of stalactites and stalagmites. Only some 1.5km of the cave is open to the public and fitted with electric lights. Most of the year, the tour takes place along the central route, whereas in spring, you might have to take the shorter route as sections of the main route are prone to flooding.

Highlights include the **Diamond Cave**, the snow and ice crystals glittering like precious stones, ice sculptures such as **The Bat**, the **Underwater Cave**, its rock formations reminiscent of coral formations, two underwater lakes (where people are baptised in winter), and a series of uneven rock steps called '**Ladies' Tears**'. When two British royal ladies went on a tour of the cave in the 1930s, they were inappropriately dressed in long dresses and high heels, and naturally tripped and fell on the steps. They both married princes afterwards and the local story goes that if you're an unmarried woman and you fall on those steps, you have a chance to marry royalty.

All tours are guided (in Russian) and take place at set times: 10am, noon, 2pm and 4pm – up to 20 people at a time (R600). There are also laser shows inside the cave at 11am, 1pm and 3pm (request in advance; R700). Take warm clothes, as even in summer the temperature inside the cave can be down to -5° Celsius.

Tours to Kungur Ice Cave from Perm are far pricier than doing it solo, though they may include an invaluable interpreter and transport there and back. There are several direct trains a day from Perm to Kungur, both suburban and long-distance (2hrs); to get to the cave, you either take the bus that runs past the station to Hotel Stalagmit (Гостиница Сталагмит; R12) or take a taxi (R200).

You can stay at the friendly ***Hotel Stalagmit*** (☎ 34271 62 610, 💻 www.kungurcave.ru – in Russian, sgl/twin from R800/1400) with clean, basic rooms and a restaurant serving standard Russian dishes. There's another café next to the Ice Cave ticket booth, which serves tasty solyanka and salads.

Yekaterinburg
Екатеринбург

Yekaterinburg's role in shaping Russian history has been both immense and paradoxical: ushering in the Socialist era in 1918 with the murder of the Romanov family, providing the setting for the 1960s 'U2 Affair' (effectively a caricature of the Cold War itself) and giving the country Boris Yeltsin, who played a key role in dismantling the Soviet myth. The city seems to act as Russia's litmus paper: as a harbinger of what is to come.

Its historical significance alone justifies a visit and the wealth of pre-Stalinist architecture makes a change from other Siberian cities, harking back to the days before the Revolution when Yekaterinburg was already the centre of a rich mining region, a region that gave rise to related tales of the supernatural, such as the 'Queen of Copper Mountain' and 'Malachite Box'. From 1924 to 1992 the city was known as Sverdlovsk, the name still used on railway timetables.

Today, it's a very pleasant, eminently walkable city with an attractive riverside promenade and it makes a good base for exploring the Urals area.

HISTORY

The earliest settlers in the area were 'Old Believers', religious dissidents fleeing the reforms of the Russian Orthodox Church in 1672. They created the *Shartash* township here and were the first to discover that the area was rich in iron ore. This discovery was the key to later development: Peter the Great, embroiled in the Great Northern War against Sweden, gave instructions for new sources of iron to be sought, and the first ironworks were established here just as the war ended in 1721. A fortress was built a year later and in 1723 the town of Yekaterinburg was founded, in honour of Peter's new wife, Catherine. The railway arrived in 1888 bringing foreign travellers on their way to Siberia.

The murder of the Romanovs

The Romanov family was moved from Tobolsk to Yekaterinburg in April 1918 and imprisoned in a house belonging to a rich merchant named Ipatyev. Here they spent the last two months of their lives being tormented by the guards, who

The road to Romanov sainthood

The story behind the discovery of the Romanov remains is almost as bizarre as that of their 'disappearance'. In July 1991 it was announced that parts of nine bodies had been found and that these were almost certainly those of the Imperial Family. Perhaps the most intriguing aspect of the discovery was that three of the skulls, including that of the Tsar himself, had been placed in a wooden box. In fact the bodies had been discovered some 20 years before by a local detective-novel writer named Geli Ryabov. He deduced from the skulls' immaculate dental work that these were indeed the bodies of the Royal Family, but reburied them for fear of persecution by the secret police. In December 1992, DNA testing at the Forensic Science Service laboratory in Aldermaston (UK) matched samples from the bodies with those from a blood sample provided by Prince Philip, Duke of Edinburgh (Tsarina Alexandra's sister was Philip's maternal grandmother).

The state burial of the royal remains was delayed for several years following a disagreement between the government, which favoured burial of the bones in St Petersburg, and surviving members of the Romanov family who wanted them returned to Yekaterinburg as a memorial to the millions killed by the Communists. On 19 August 1998 the remains were finally interred in the Romanov vault in St Petersburg's Peter and Paul Cathedral. At the service, then President Boris Yeltsin made the first official apology: 'The massacre of the Tsar was one of the most shameful pages of our history ... We are all guilty. It is impossible to lie to ourselves by justifying the senseless cruelty on political grounds'.

On 20 August 2000, at a special ceremony in Moscow's Cathedral of Christ the Saviour, Patriarch Alexi II canonised the Tsar, the royal family and hundreds of priests who died as 'zealots of faith and piety' during the Communist era.

openly referred to Nicholas as the 'Blood Drinker' and scrawled lewd pictures on the walls depicting the Tsarina with Rasputin.

Several attempts were made to save the royal family, and eventually the Bolshevik government, deciding that the Tsar was too great a threat to its security, ordered his elimination. Shortly before midnight on 16 July, Nicholas, Alexandra, their four daughters and their haemophiliac son Alexis, were taken to the cellar where they were shot and bayoneted to death. The bodies were then taken to the Four Brothers Mine, 40km outside the city, where guards spent three days destroying the evidence. The corpses were dismembered, doused with petrol and burned.

A week later the White Army took Yekaterinburg, and their suspicions were immediately aroused by the sight of the cellar's blood-spattered walls. In the garden they found the Tsarevich's spaniel, Joy, neglected and half starved. However, it was not until the following January that investigators were led to the mineshaft, where they found fragments of bone and pieces of jewellery that had once belonged to members of the Imperial Family. They also found the body of Jimmy, Anastasia's dog, which the murderers had callously flung down the mineshaft without bothering to kill it first. All the evidence was identified by the Tsarevich's tutor, Pierre Gilliard. At first the Bolsheviks would not admit to more than the 'execution' of Nicholas, accusing a group of counter-revolutionaries of the murders of his family. Five of them were tried, 'found guilty' and executed. However, in 1919 after the death of Party official Yacob Sverdlov, it was acknowledged that it was in fact he who had arranged the massacre. In his honour the town was renamed Sverdlovsk.

The U2 Affair

The next time the town became the focus of world attention was in May 1960 when the American U2 pilot, Gary Powers, was shot down in this area (see box p406). He survived the crash, parachuting into the arms of the Soviets and confirming that he had been spying. The ensuing confrontation led to the collapse of the Summit conference in Paris.

The city today

With a population of 1.5 million Yekaterinburg is Russia's fifth-largest city (after Moscow, St Petersburg, Novosibirsk and Nizhny Novgorod), a major transportation hub, with seven radiating railway lines, and one of the country's most important industrial centres, ever since hundreds of factories were relocated here during WWII. The city once specialised in armaments research and production but munitions factories, including the vast 'Pentagon' building in the eastern part of town, are being closed down. Because of its strategic importance, the city was off-limits to foreigners until 1990. In 1991, Sverdlovsk became Yekaterinburg again and the city now shows few signs of the Mafia troubles of the early '90s. The city's most famous son is, of course, Boris Yeltsin: coup-buster, economic reformer, referendum winner, dissolver of parliament and former Russian President.

Today, Yekaterinburg is a modern, lively city with an attractive riverside promenade, a host of good museums and the home of the Romanov cult.

WHAT TO SEE AND DO

The Romanov Memorial Памятник Романовым

Yeltsin had the original building in the basement of which the Imperial family was murdered (Ipatyev House Бывший Дом Ипатьева) demolished in 1976; now the Byzantine-style **Church of the Blood** (10am-6pm) forms an expensive memorial to the 'Tsar martyrs', as the Romanovs were declared when they were canonised by the Russian Orthodox Church; rumour has it that the icon inside the church is the most expensive ever to be commissioned.

Not everyone reveres the Romanovs; many believe that sainthood is incompatible with virulent anti-Semitism and poor military leadership – two prominent qualities displayed by Tsar Nicholas II. It seems that the Russian Orthodox Church is trying to instil a sense of guilt in the population over the royal deaths, much more so than over the deaths of any others who were executed in far more horrific fashion during Communist times.

The church contains several monuments to the Romanovs, including icons of the royal family and memorabilia from their last days in Yekaterinburg. Upstairs, the main sanctuary is a soaring and brightly lit affair. By the main entrance, there are metal sculptures of the royal family and sellers doing a brisk trade in Romanov-related souvenirs.

Also here is the far more attractive wooden **chapel**, built in the late 1980s and repeatedly burnt down by anti-monarchists. It's dedicated to St Elizabeth (Grand Princess Yelizaveta Fyodorovna), Alexander II's sister-in-law who, following the Romanov murders, was thrown down a mineshaft and left to die. Local villagers claimed to have heard her miserable wailings for two days as she prayed for the souls of her attackers who, when they realised that she was still alive, piped poisonous gas into the well and filled the hole with earth. When they came to collect her body, it was allegedly found in sitting position, looking as though she were merely asleep, with no signs of decomposition. She and her faithful maidservant have since been canonised as well.

Military Museum Музей «Боевая Слава Урала»

There is a small exhibit on the U2 incident (see opposite and box p406) in the Military Museum at the **House of Officers** Доме Офицеров (Dom Ofitserov, ul Pervomayskaya 27, 9am-4pm Tue-Sat, R70) near the city centre.

On display upstairs are a few pieces of the aircraft, photos of the wreckage and of Gary Powers in court, plus items from his survival kit. The House of Officers is easily recognisable by the massive armoury outside; around the back is a collection of Soviet military hardware.

Museum of Fine Arts Музей Изобразительных Искусст

Housed in two separate buildings, this is one of the most important museums in the area (ul Voyevodina 5 and ul Vaynera 11, 11am-7pm Tue-Sun, until 8pm Wed & Thur, adult/student R150/70). Here you'll find a fine collection of 19th-century iron sculpture, a gallery of Russian paintings including works by Ivanov and Tarakanova, a portrait of PA Stroganov (of beef Stroganov fame) and a famous painting of Christ by Polenov. Pride of place goes to the iron pavilion, which won first prize in the Paris Exhibition in 1900 and which is now a UNESCO treasure.

Urals Mineralogical Museum Уральский Минералогический Музей

Don't miss this incredible private collection of crystals, minerals and semi-precious stones belonging to Vladimir Pelepenko – the perfect introduction to the mineral wealth of the Urals.

The displays in the large hall range from mammoth-sized chunks of amethyst to beautiful stones you may never have heard of, such as the pink-and-black zmeyevik. There are also some incredibly skilful creations, like malachite boxes, intricate jewellery and more.

The museum is located in Bolshoy Ural Hotel (ul Krasnoarmeyskaya 1a, 10am-8pm Mon-Fri, 10am-6pm Sat & Sun, R70). You can obtain some remarkable souvenirs at the gift shop.

Other attractions

The **Museum of Local History** Краеведческий Музей (ul Malysheva 46, 10am-5pm Tue-Sat, R60) has interesting displays on 19th-century Yekaterinburg, the Revolution, the murder of the Romanovs and the discovery of their remains.

The **Railway History Museum** Железнодорожный Музей (ul Chelyuskintsev, in the old railway station, opposite **M** Uralskaya, noon-6pm Tue-Sat) traces the history of the railroad in the region.

Inside the Urals Mining University, **Urals Geology Museum** Уральский Геологический Музей (ul Kuybysheva 39, 11am-5pm Mon-Fri, R120) has an extensive, meticulously catalogued mineral collection from all over the region, as well as meteorites.

Metenkov House Museum of Photography Дом Метенькова/Музей Фотографии (ul Karla Libknekhta 36, 10am-6pm, R100) has some great early 20th-century photos of Yekaterinburg and its inhabitants.

WHERE TO STAY
3 Hotel Kristall Гостиница Кристалл
25 Atrium Palace Hotel Гостиница Атриум Дворец
28 Hotel Tsentralnaya Гостиница Центральная
31 Hotel Antey Гостиница Антей
32 Park Inn Отель Парк Инн

WHERE TO EAT AND DRINK
13 Dudki Дудки
15 Mamma's Big House
16 Old Dublin Irish Pub Паб Старый Дублин
17 Paul Bakery Поль Бейкери
20 Doctor Scotch Pub Паб Доктор Скотч
24 Ben Hall
30 Tinkoff Тинкофф
36 Pozharka Пожарка
37 Uralskiye Pelmeni Уральские Пельмени

PLACES OF INTEREST
1 Railway History Museum Железнодорожный Музей
4 Mining Office and former Rastorguiev-Kharitonov Estate Бывшая Усадьба Расторгуева-Харитонова
5 Church of the Blood Церковь на Крови
6 Chapel of the Revered Martyr Princess Yelizaveta Fyodorovna Часовня Великомученницы Княгини Елизаветы Фёдоровны
7 Romanov Memorial (former Ipatyev House) Памятник Романовым (Бывший Дом Ипатьева)
8 Monument to Urals Young Communists Памятник Комсомолу Урала
9 Ascension Cathedral Церковь Вознесения
10 Military Museum (in the House of Officers) Музей «Боевая Слава Урала» (в Доме Офицеров)
11 Afghan War Memorial Памятник Войне в Афганистане
12 Metenkov House Museum of Photography Дом Метенькова/Музей Фотографии
19 Museum of Fine Arts Музей Изобразительных Искусств
21 Museum of Local History Краеведческий Музей
22 Urals Geology Museum Уральский Геологический Музей
33 Urals Mineralogical Museum Уральский Минералогический Музей
34 Opera & Ballet Theatre Театр Оперы и Балета
35 Sverdlov Statue Памятник Свердлову

OTHER
2 Railway Station Железнодорожный Вокзал
14 Central Post Office & Internet Почтамт и Интернет
18 Railway and Air Tickets Железнодорожные билеты и Авиакасса
23 Pyatachok Пятачок
26 US Consulate Консульство США
27 British Consulate Британское Консульство
29 German Consulate Консульство Германии

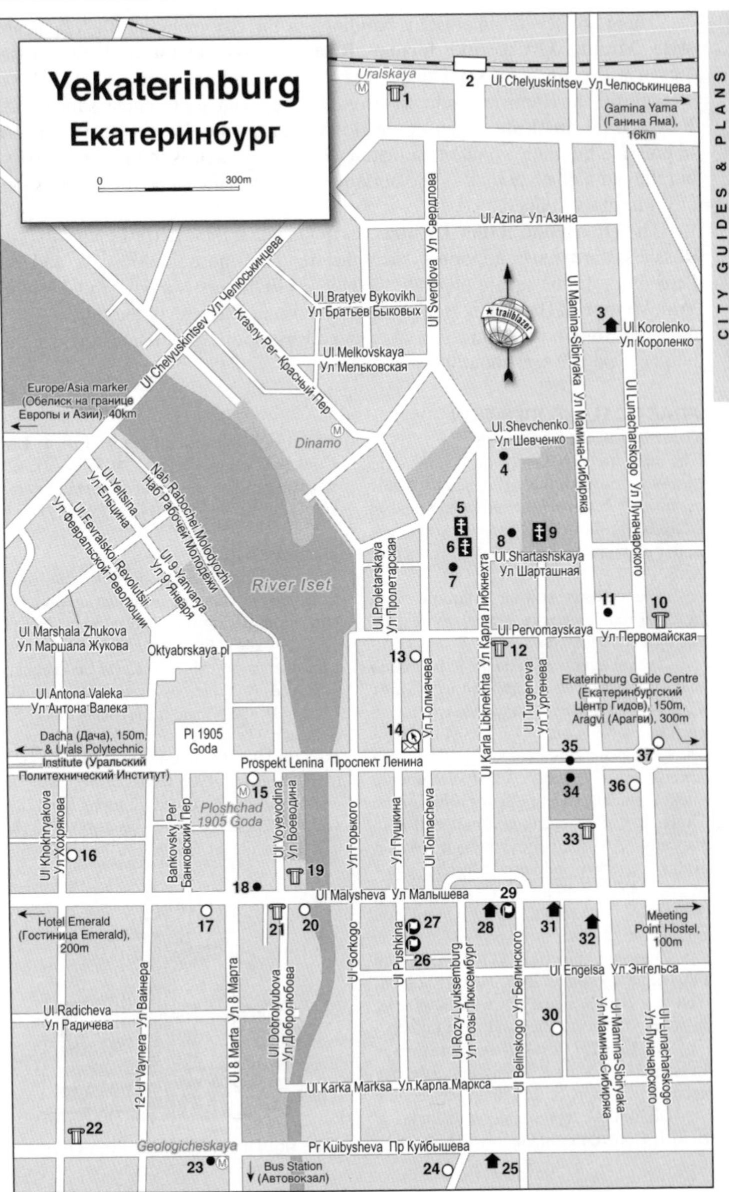
Yekaterinburg
Екатеринбург
0
300m
Uralskaya
2
Ul Chelyuskintsev Ул Челюскинцева
Gamina Yama (Ганина Яма), 16km
Ul Azina Ул Азина
Ul Sverdlova Ул Свердлова
Ul Chelyuskintsev Ул Челюскинцева
Krasny Per Красный Пер
Ul Bratyev Bykovikh Ул Братьев Быковых
Ul Melkovskaya Ул Мельковская
trailblazer
Ul Mamina-Sibiryaka Ул Мамина-Сибиряка
Ul Korolenko Ул Короленко
Ul Lunacharskogo Ул Луначарского
Europe/Asia marker (Обелиск на границе Европы и Азии), 40km
Dinamo
Ul Shevchenko Ул Шевченко
Ul Yeltsina Ул Ельцина
Nab Rabochei Molodyozhi Наб Рабочей Молодёжи
Ul Fevralskoi Revolutsii Ул Февральской Революции
Ul 9 Yanvarya Ул 9 Января
River Iset
Ul Proletarskaya Ул Пролетарская
Ul Shartashskaya Ул Шарташная
Ul Karla Libknekhta Ул Карла Либкнехта
Ul Marshala Zhukova Ул Маршала Жукова
Oktyabrskaya pl
Ul Pervomayskaya Ул Первомайская
Ул Толмачева
Ul Turgeneva Ул Тургенева
Ekaterinburg Guide Centre (Екатеринбургский Центр Гидов), 150m, Aragvi (Арагви), 300m
Ul Antona Valeka Ул Антона Валека
Dacha (Дача), 150m, & Urals Polytechnic Institute (Уральский Политехнический Институт)
Pl 1905 Goda
Prospekt Lenina Проспект Ленина
Ul Khokhryakova Ул Хохрякова
Ploshchad 1905 Goda
Bankovsky Per Банковский Пер
Ul Voyevodina Ул Воеводина
Ул Горького
Ул Пушкина
Ul Tolmacheva
Ul Malysheva Ул Малышева
Hotel Emerald (Гостиница Emerald), 200m
Meeting Point Hostel, 100m
Ul Gorkogo
Ul Pushkina
Ul Rozy Lyuksemburg Ул Розы Люксембург
Ul Belinskogo Ул Белинского
Ul Engelsa Ул Энгельса
Ul Radicheva Ул Радичева
12-Ul Vaynera Ул Вайнера
Ul 8 Marta Ул 8 Марта
Ul Dobrolyubova Ул Добролюбова
Ul Karka Marksa Ул Карла Маркса
Ul Mamina-Sibiryaka Ул Мамина-Сибиряка
Ul Lunacharskogo Ул Луначарского
Geologicheskaya
Pr Kuibysheva Пр Куйбышева
Bus Station (Автовокзал)
1 3 4 5 6 7 8 9 10 11 12 13 14 15 16 17 18 19 20 21 22 23 24 25 26 27 28 29 30 31 32 33 34 35 36 37

There are several interesting buildings in the city including the classical-style **Mining Office and former Rastorguiev-Kharitonov Estate** Быв Усадьба Расторгуева-Харитонова (1794-1824), both at ul Karla Libknehkta 44 opposite the Romanov memorial. At the eastern end of pr Lenina is the **Urals Polytechnic Institute** Уральский Политехнический Институт (UPI), an impressive building which often features on postcards (it is in fact a university but the old name has stuck). The building beside it with cannons outside is the city's military college.

The **Opera and Ballet Theatre** Театр Оперы и Балета (pr Lenina 46a) is Russia's third most important such theatre after those in Moscow and St Petersburg. In the square opposite the House of Officers is a powerful **Afghan War Memorial** Памятник Войне в Афганистане. The pose of the soldier, very different from most such memorials around Russia, offers an interesting insight into how people feel about the war.

PRACTICAL INFORMATION

Orientation and services

The main street, pr Lenina пр Ленина, runs east–west through the city. The city centre is more or less between pr Lenina and ul Malysheva; most of the hotels, restaurants and sights are within walking distance of here.

The **railway station** is around 2km north of the city centre, and easily reachable by public transport.

Travel agents include the experienced and recommended **Ekaterinburg Guide Centre** Екатеринбургский Центр Гидов (pr Lenina 52/1, office 12, ☎ 384 0048, 🖳 www.ekaterinburgguide.com). They can arrange tours of the city and surrounding sites, including trekking and rafting in the Urals, as well as cheap accommodation in the city. Alternatively, you can contact Katia, a friendly and knowledgeable guide at the Meeting Point Youth Hostel (see Where to stay), who can also help you organise all manner of tours.

There are numerous **ATMs** around the city centre as well as at the railway station. You can change money at various places, including the post office and most hotels.

The **Central Post Office** Почтамт (pr Lenina 51, 7.30am-8.30pm) has **internet access** Интернет for R80/hour.

Diplomatic representation includes a **British Consulate** (ul Gogolya 15, ☎ 379 4931, 🖳 www.britainінrussia.ru), a **US Consulate** (ul Gogolya 15, ☎ 379 4691, 🖳 www.uscgyekat.ur.ru) and a **German consulate** (ul Kuybysheva 44, ☎ 359 6399).

Local transport

Yekaterinburg has a good bus, tram and trolleybus system and a limited metro system. From the railway station, trams No 3, 14, 21 and 32 run south along ul Lunacharskogo, while ul Karla Libknekhta is served by numerous buses, including 1, 13, 23, 31 and 57 and trolleybuses No 1, 5, 6, 9, and 11. To get to the city centre you can also take the metro from **M** Uralskaya to **M** Ploshchad 1905 Goda.

Pr Lenina is served by trams No 4, 8, 13, 15, 22 and 26 and buses No 5, 10, 18 and 36, while ul Malysheva is served by

THE MODERNIST CENTRAL POST OFFICE

trolleybuses No 6, 7, 8, 19 and 20 and buses No 13, 14, 18, 25 and 61.

To get to the airport, take bus No 1 from the railway station or else marshrutka No 26 from **M** Ploshchad 1905 Goda.

Where to stay

The best place for budget travellers is ***Meeting Point Hostel*** (ул Малышева 87 кв 73, ul Malysheva 87 apt 73, ☎ 922 607 0033, 💻 www.meetingpoint.hostel.com, dorm R450), consisting of a two-bedroom apartment with guest kitchen and wi-fi, which can accommodate 8 people maximum. The hostel is run by the bilingual, knowledgeable local guide, Katia, who goes out of her way to make you feel welcome and help you organise your stay.

A few blocks from the railway station, budget ***Hotel Kristall*** **Гостиница Кристалл** (ул Короленко 5, ul Korolenko 5, ☎ 370 6203, 💻 www.kristall-ekb.ru – in Russian, sgl/dbl from R550/1100) has plain, pristine rooms with shared bathrooms. Each room is equipped with a fridge and kettle.

Just west of the centre, the brand-new ***Hotel Emerald*** **Отель Эмеральд** (ул Сакко и Вансетти 38, ul Sakko i Vansetti 38, ☎ 253 0797, 💻 www.emeraldhotel.ru, sgl/dbl from R3000/4500) dazzles with its colour scheme, but the spacious rooms come with air-con, wi-fi and satellite TV. Buffet breakfast included.

Hotel Antey **Гостиница Антей** (ул Красноармейская 10, ul Krasnoarmeyskaya 10, ☎ 378 4114, 💻 www.antey-e.ru, sgl/dbl from R3600/7000), inside the Antey skyscraper, has 12 modern rooms. It offers access to the viewing deck with great views of the city below. You can combine your stay with shopping and clubbing, all in the same building.

Part of the Radisson chain, the centrally located ***Park Inn*** **Отель Парк Инн** (ул Мамина-Сибиряка 98, ul Mamina-Sibiryaka 98, ☎ 216 3606, 💻 www.ekaterinburg.parkinn.com.ru, double from R6500) is as you'd expect: spotless, efficient, and popular with the business set. Its rooms come equipped with mod-cons such as wi-fi and satellite TV and its Magellan Restaurant serves a good four-course business lunch for R350.

In a historical art nouveau building, ***Hotel Tsentralnaya*** **Гостиница Центральная** (ул Малышева 74, ul Malysheva 74, ☎ 350 0505, 💻 www.hotelcentr.ru, sgl/dbl/suite R3500/4500/7000), has simple but luxurious rooms with wi-fi, popular with business travellers. Its Restaurant Savoy once entertained the likes of Fidel Castro; it now serves exemplary European dishes and has an extensive wine list.

The top place to stay is the five-star ***Atrium Palace Hotel*** **Атриум Палас Отель** (ул Куйбышева 44, ul Kuibysheva 44, ☎ 359 6000, 💻 www.atriumhotel.ru, sgl/dbl/suite from R8100/12,500/42,000), with its ultra-plush rooms, exemplary service, central location and the excellent restaurant 'La Ronde' on-site, serving an upmarket take on Russian and European cuisine.

Homestays can be organised by Ekaterinburg Guide Centre (see Orientation and services).

Where to eat

Uralskiye Pelmeni **Уральские Пельмени** (пр Ленина 69/1, pr Lenina 69/1, meals R300) is a popular self-serve canteen-style eatery with kitsch decor, where you can pick up a variety of salads, soups, meat dishes, and, of course, the signature pelmeni. Open until 2am at weekends.

Mamma's Big House (пр Ленина 26, pr Lenina 26, meals R350, [V]) is a busy café-restaurant, popular with young people and families, serving good salads, pizzas, coffee and desserts. Decked out like a fire station, popular ***Pozharka*** **Пожарка** (ул Луначарского 128, ul Lunacharskogo 128, meals R300) attracts locals and visitors alike with its large helpings of solid Russian dishes and good beer.

The Yekaterinburg area code is ☎ 343. From outside Russia dial ☎ +7-343.

Paul Bakery **Поль Бейкери** (ул Малышева 36, ul Malysheva 36, [V]) excels at creating baked goodies and is a great spot for coffee in elegant surroundings.

For innovative takes on Ukrainian food, head to ***Dudki*** **Дудки** (ул Толмачева 23, ul Tolmacheva 23, mains R450). The service is efficient, the homemade *kvas* is great and their version of *golubtsy* (meat and rice wrapped in cabbage leaves) is delicate and uses pork ribs.

Dacha **Дача** (пр Ленина 20a, pr Lenina 20a, ☎ 379 3569) is a place for special occasions, each of its rooms decorated as if it's part of a wealthy merchant's house. The Russian dishes are not cheap, but they are exquisitely prepared. Reservations recommended at weekends.

Aragvi **Арагви** (пр Ленина 103, pr Lenina 103, [V]) is a Georgian restaurant where you'd go for excellent grilled meats and tasty lobio.

Bars and nightlife

Right near the river, ***Doctor Scotch Pub*** **Паб Доктор Скотч** (ул Малышева 56a, ul Malysheva 56a) attracts a good mix of locals and expats. Also popular, ***Tinkoff*** **Тинкофф** (ул Красноармейская 64, ul Krasnoarmeyskaya 64) is a microbrewery serving seven home brews and has a meaty menu full of bar snacks.

West of the river, ***Old Dublin Irish Pub*** **Паб Старый Дублин** (ул Малышева 23, ul Malysheva 23) is the only authentic Irish pub in the region. Popular with homesick expats, it serves Guinness on tap and has a lively atmosphere.

For local rock music, check out ***Ben Hall*** (ул Народной Воли 65, ul Narodnoi Voli 65) at the weekend.

Shopping

For some unusual local souvenirs, such as boxes made of malachite and busts of Lenin, head to **Pyatachok**, the local outdoor market on the corner of ul Kuibysheva and ul 8 Marta, open at the weekend (10am-5pm) – as good for its atmosphere as it is for the shopping.

Moving on

By rail Yekaterinburg (Sverdlovsk on timetables) is a major train hub. Westbound destinations include Moscow (16/day, 26-46hrs, the fastest and most comfortable being the firmenny 015), while heading east, you reach Tobolsk (9/day, 9-10½hrs, the best being the overnight 310 and the firmenny 060 departures), Omsk (11/day, 12½-15½hrs, the best overnighters being the 082, 080 and the firmenny 026), Novosibirsk (10/day, 20-24hrs, the most comfortable being the firmenny 026), and Irkutsk (3/day, 51-56hrs, the most convenient being the firmenny 010).

If you are waiting for a train, or arrive late at night, there is a comfortable VIP hall with soft seats, toilets and a bar. The entrance is to the left of the main station entrance and it costs R120/hour, with showers an extra R180).

At the **railway station** Железнодорожный Вокзал, domestic rail tickets are sold downstairs, international tickets upstairs; or for better service but with a small fee, try the service centre on the west side of the station's ground floor.

By air Airport Koltsovo (💻 www.koltsovo.ru), the largest airport in the Urals, is 16km south of the city and served by Czech Airlines, Air China, Lufthansa, Finnair and Turkish Airlines, as well as Aeroflot, Vladivostok Avia, S7 and Transaero, among others. There are frequent flights to Moscow, St Petersburg, Irkutsk, Krasnoyarsk, Khabarovsk, Yakutsk and Vladivostok.

There are numerous **air-ticket offices** (*Aviakassa*) in the city; all offer flights on major and minor carriers; many sell rail tickets as well. Particularly convenient is the **Railway and Air Kassa** Железнодорожные билеты и Авиакасса (ул Малышева 31, ul Malysheva 31).

EXCURSIONS FROM YEKATERINBURG

Ganina Yama Ганина Яма

Located in a lovely wooded area 16km north-east of Yekaterinburg is the Monastery of the Holy Martyrs, built around the spot where the Romanovs' bodies were originally disposed of in an abandoned mine. The monastery consists of several attractive wooden churches, a holy pool which you may enter only if previously blessed, and a horseshoe-shaped covered walk that skirts the remnants of the pit where the bodies were dumped. The covered walk is decorated with endearing family photographs of the royal family, though the Tsarevich looks perpetually unhappy in the photos, with a scowl and weak chin. The monastery is considered sacred ground by the Russian Orthodox Church, even though the royal bodies have now been reburied in St Petersburg (see box p144), so women have to don headscarves and wraparound skirts; these are provided at the entrance.

The easiest way to get here is to take bus No 17 (R30) from the bus stop to the left of the railway station entrance along the main street, getting off at the final Monastyr/'Монастырь' stop. If you speak Russian you can ask one of the priests for a guided tour. Otherwise, your best bet is to join an English-speaking tour organised by Ekaterinburg Guide Centre (see p238) or to go with Katia from the Meeting Point Hostel (see p239).

Europe/Asia marker Обелиск на границе Европы и Азии

About 40km to the west along the main road to Moscow (Novy Moscovsky Trakt) is the point which the German scientists Humboldt and Roze designated as the border between Europe and Asia while doing barometric surveys in 1829. The original marker was destroyed in the 1920s and replaced with a concrete obelisk faced with granite. Trips can be arranged through Ekaterinburg Guide Centre (see p238). There's another marker beside the railway line, 36km west of Yekaterinburg at Vershina (Вершина).

Tyumen
Тюмень

[Moscow Time +2] Tyumen is the booming oil capital of Western Siberia and certainly feels more affluent than many other Siberian cities. It's a pleasant-enough place and its pedestrianised City Park and tree-lined streets make for enjoyable strolling in good weather.

Founded in 1586, Tyumen's location on a major trading river, the Tura, made it an important transit point for goods between Siberia and China. It was also a major transit point for settlers and convicts destined for Siberia and the Russian Far East. By 1900 over a million convicts had tramped through the town.

During WWII, many of European Russia's people, treasures and factories were relocated to Siberia. The greatest treasure to be transferred from Moscow to Tyumen during this time was Lenin's corpse. For years he rested secretly in a building of the Agricultural Institute, tended by a team of specialists.

Prior to the drilling of the region's first oil well in 1960, Tyumen was just a dusty backwater of 150,000 inhabitants. Since then its population has grown to an estimated 508,000.

WHAT TO SEE AND DO

Tyumen's museums generally leave something to be desired, but one gem is the **Fine Arts Museum** Музей Изобразительных Искусств (ul Ordzhonikidze 47, 10am-5pm Tue-Sun, R70). Pride of place goes to the small but excellent collection of 18th-, 19th- and 20th-century Russian art, including a lone Kandinsky. Upstairs there is everything from icons to photos, some fine bone carvings, and interesting Soviet and American propaganda posters, as well as challenging temporary modern art exhibits. On nearby Tsentralnaya pl, you'll find a large Lenin statue.

Architecturally, the most interesting sites are just north of the city centre at Kommunisticheskaya 10, where you'll find a cluster of religious buildings including the **Church of SS Peter and Paul** Петропавловская Церковь and the **Cathedral of Trinity Monastery** Троицкий Собор inside the monastery's walls. Admission to the grounds (9am-5pm daily) is free. A small chapel in the cathedral is open to worshippers.

The **Historical Home Museum** (ul Respubliki 18) is a wooden house built in 1804 and owned at one time by the town's 1830s mayor, Ikonikov. **Masharov House-Museum** Дом-музей Машарова (ul Lenina 24, 9.30am-12.30pm & 1.30-4.30pm Wed-Sun, R50) provides an insight into the life and times of a wealthy 19th-century factory owner.

In the city centre, the **City Park** (Парк) is good for strolling amidst the fairgrounds; the covered **Central Market** Центральный рынок at its eastern end is the best place for fresh produce. Further east, along ul Melnikayte, there is a giant candle-shaped **war memorial** Мемориал Великой Отечественной Войны.

Near the railway station, along ul Pervomayskaya, you'll spy an **FD-class locomotive** through the greenery.

PRACTICAL INFORMATION

Orientation and services

The railway station is 1.5km south of the city centre. From there all buses and trolley-buses take you up ul Pervomayskaya either to ul Lenina or ul Respubliki. Bus No 25 goes to Hotel Vostok, while bus No 30 runs west towards the Trinity Monastery.

There's **internet access** at the main **post office** Почтамт (ул Республики 56, ul Respubliki 56) and several **ATMs** in the centre, particularly along ul Respubliki.

Where to stay, eat and drink

The cheapest accommodation is in one of the station's spartan ***resting rooms*** **комнаты отдыха** *(komnata otdykha;* sgl/dbl/trpl costs from R1500/1200/600pp) on the 8th floor; the bathrooms are in the

WHERE TO STAY, EAT AND DRINK

10 Yermolayevo Ермолаево
16 Pizza Mia Пицца Миа
18 Hotel Tyumen Гостиница Тюмень; Vremena Goda Времена Года; Café Vienna Кафе Вена
20 Central Market Центральный рынок
21 Restaurant Schultz Ресторан Шультс
24 Hotel Vostok Гостиница Восток

PLACES OF INTEREST

1 History Museum Complex (SS Peter & Paul Church & Cathedral of Trinity Monastery) Музей Истории Города (Петропавловская Церковь и Троицкий Собор)
2 Elevation of the Cross Church Крестовоздвиженская Церковь
3 Remains of the Kremlin Walls Остатки Земляных Валов бывшего Кремля
4 Church of Mikhaila Maleina Церковь Михаила Малеина
5 Masharov House-Museum Дом-музей Машарова
6 Historical Home Museum
7 Cathedral of the Holy Cross Знаменский Собор
8 Church of the Saviour Спасская Церковь
9 Philharmonic Hall Филармония
11 Drama Theatre Драматический Театр
12 City Park Парк
13 Parliament House Дом Советов
19 Fine Arts Museum Музей Изобразительных Искусств
23 War Memorial Мемориал Великой Отечественной Войны

OTHER

14 Central Stadium Центральный Стадион
15 Central Post Office Почтамт
17 Central Square Центральная Площадь
22 Old Cemetery Старое Кладбише

The Tyumen area code is ☎ 3452.
From outside Russia dial ☎ +7-3452.

corridor. The entrance is to the left of the main station entrance.

Hotel Vostok **Гостиница Восток** (ул Республики 159, ul Respubliki 159, ☎ 3452 205 350, 💻 www.vostok-tmn.ru – in Russian only, sgl/dbl from R1500/2300) is a huge Soviet place with clean but drab en suite rooms. The service is surprisingly helpful and friendly.

Brand-new ***Hotel Filton*** **Гостиница Фильтон** (ул Привокзальная 30, ul Privokzalnaya 30, ☎ 3452 523 740, 💻 www.filton.ru, sgl/dbl from R3200/4200) has bright, attractive rooms, all with TV, fridge and wi-fi, there's an excellent sauna on the premises (R700/hour) and the hotel bar serves inexpensive salads, soups, pelmeni, sandwiches and meaty mains.

The 230-room ***Hotel Tyumen*** **Гостиница Тюмень** (ул Орджоникидзе 46, ul Ordzhonikidze 46, ☎ 3452 494 040, 💻 www.hoteltyumen.ru, sgl/dbl/suite from R6500/7000/12,500) is the town's top hotel and its rooms have all the mod cons you'd expect. The price includes an excellent buffet breakfast and among the on-site restaurants, ***Vremena Goda*** **Времена Года** stands out with its imaginative takes on Russian dishes and ***Café Vienna*** **Кафе Вена** [V] has an extensive menu of salads, blini, soups and sandwiches.

Pizza Mia **Пицца Миа** (ул Мельникайте 103, ul Melnikayte 103, [V]) serves pizza by the slice as well as soups and salads. Nearby, at ul Melnikayte 100, ***Telega*** **Телега** is the place to come for well-prepared Ukrainian dishes in a semi-formal setting.

The rustic décor at ***Yermolayevo*** **Ермолаево** (ул Кирова 37, ul Kirova 37) belies the quality of its cooking, with large portions of traditional Russian dishes served to a discerning local crowd. The homemade kvas is particularly good.

The rustic tavern-themed ***Restaurant Shultz*** **Ресторан Шультс** (ул Республики 81, ul Respubliki 81) specialises in traditional German dishes, washed down with some excellent Bavarian beers.

Self-caterers shouldn't miss the **central market** (see p242).

Moving on

Tyumen is about halfway between Moscow and Irkutsk, with numerous trains to all Trans-Siberian destinations. Departures include Moscow (12/day, 33-56hrs), Omsk (11/day, 7½-9hrs), Yekaterinburg (over 20/day, 4½-7hrs) and Tobolsk (12/day, 3½-4½hrs).

Tobolsk
Тобольск

[Moscow Time +2] Though it's 250km from Tyumen and the Trans-Siberian line, the old Siberian capital of Tobolsk, population 110,000, boasts a stunning Kremlin and a crumbling, atmospheric Old Town. Poverty and monolithic Soviet housing blocks have a strong grip here, but locals take pride in the city's once-great history and in the skill of its craftsmen, who specialise in intricate bone carvings.

Lying at the confluence of the Tobol and Irtysh rivers, Tobolsk is famed as the site where Yermak Timofeevich and his Cossack forces defeated a Tatar army in 1582. Though the Russian victors were soon driven out, they declared their 'conquest' of Siberia and a fort was founded here in 1587. The outpost grew into the administrative, financial and religious centre of the region; home of Siberia's first bishopric and seat of the governor-general, who ruled from the Urals to the Far East.

The city was sidestepped by the Great Siberian Trakt road, which cut further south, and later by the Trans-Siberian Railway. Its influence waned, but Tobolsk remained a cultural centre until the end of the 19th century, aided by the arrival of educated Decembrist exiles, who founded a school for women and treated the sick free of charge. Dostoyevsky was jailed here for a short time in 1850 on his way to exile in Omsk, and Tobolsk was the Romanovs' last stop before their fatal visit to Yekaterinburg in 1918.

Today, Tobolsk's residents make their living mainly at a large petrochemical plant, built in 1974 along with the vast housing complex on the north side of the city. There's also a famous bone-carving factory here and a thriving community of artists.

WHAT TO SEE AND DO

The Kremlin and around

Most of the main attractions are centred around the handsome white **Kremlin** with a cluster of golden domes, perched on a hill above the plain where Yermak won his victory. Originally the site of a wooden fort, its stone walls were built starting in 1700. The perimeter wall is 620 metres long and contains nine towers — don't miss the view from the hilltop behind.

Inside the Kremlin is the large **St Sophia Cathedral** Собор Святой Софии, with a splendid ceiling mural inside. Built from 1686 to 1700, before the defensive walls, it's the oldest original stone building in Siberia. Just south is the 75-metre-tall **bell tower**, built in 1799, and next to it, the small but lovely **Cathedral of the Intercession** Покровский Собор (1746), where services are held in the evenings. Immediately north of the Kremlin is **Gostinny Dvor** Гостинный Двор trading arcade, once the centre of local commerce but now abandoned by all but visiting school children.

The Kremlin also contains Arkhereisky Dom, formerly the bishop's residence and now home to the interesting **Tobolsk State Museum of History and Architecture** Тобольский Музей Истории и Архитектуры (10am-5pm Wed-Sun, R40) with displays about the Tatar, Khanti and Mansi peoples, maps made by the first Russian settlers, weaponry from the 16th-18th centuries and an exhibition on the chemist **Mendeleyev**, one of the city's famous sons. The museum also contains a replica of the **Uglich bell**. When the original bell was used to call for an insurrection in 1581, it was exiled to Tobolsk by Tsar Boris Gudonov, after he had had its tongue ripped out and it received twelve lashes. The bell was housed in the Kremlin courtyard but has since been returned to Uglich.

Just west of the Kremlin is a **former prison** Тюремный Замок (Krasnaya pl 5, 10am-5pm Wed-Sun, R40, camera R50) where tsarist exiles were held while awaiting their final place of banishment. Built in 1855 and closed in 1989, it's now open to visitors, who can wander through its dark halls and into the small, depressing cells.

On the southern side of the Kremlin, a cobbled ramp leads to 189 wooden steps descending to the Old Town. This was originally just a muddy slope where merchants dragged their wares from the town up to Gostinny Dvor. Looming over the path is the **Swedish House** Шведский Дом, built by Swedish exiles and formerly home to the government treasury.

The Old Town

If you take the stairs leading down from the Kremlin you reach the **Old Town**. Its many churches and wooden homes are mostly in a run-down condition, creating a sad and haunting atmosphere. The **Church of Michael Archangel** Церковь Михаила Архангела, built 1745-54, has been restored, but the larger **Church of Zacharias and Elizabeth** Церковь Захария и Елизаветы has been left to crumble. Also here are the Catholic **Church of the Holy Trinity** Церковь Святой Троицы, built by Polish exiles, and a small **mosque** мечеть still used by a handful of local Tatars.

The preserved office of Tsar Nicholas II, who stayed here with his family from August 1917 to April 1918, is now a one-room **museum** Кабинет-Музей Императора Николая II with some original furniture and photos of the royal family, but no English captioning and the guide speaks Russian only. Enter from the back of the large administrative building on ul Kirova. Across the street, at ul Mira 9, is **Mendeleyev House** Дом Менделеева, the former home of the famous chemist. Also in the Old Town is the **Siberian-Tatar Cultural Centre** Сибирско-Татарский Культурный Центр (upstairs at ul Yershova 30) housing Tatar clothing, tools and other items.

Local art

Art lovers should stop in at the **Art Salon** (ul Oktyabrskaya 2, 10am-5pm), across from Hotel Sibir, where visitors can see how an antler is turned into an intricate bone carving in the Tatar master's studio and purchase work by him and other local craftsmen.

Next door is the **Fine Arts Museum** Музей Изобразительных Искусств (ul Oktyabrskaya 1, 10am-5pm Wed-Sun, R50) with a collection of icons, 18th-century renderings of the city, 19th- and 20th-century painting, and artefacts from various Siberian peoples, such as traditional hunting equipment and shaman drums. The bone-carving display is particularly worthwhile.

PRACTICAL INFORMATION

Orientation and services

The city centre is divided into two parts: the dilapidated wooden Old Town to the south on the plain below, and a giant 1970s Soviet housing complex above it to the north. Between them is a cluster of older apartment blocks and the Kremlin.

The **railway station** is 10km north-east of the city centre. Bus No 4 runs from the station past Hotel Slavyanskaya to the Kremlin (every half an hour; 30 mins, R30), while buses 1, 3 and 10 connect Old Town with the bus stop on ul Remezova.

There are **ATMs** in the lobby of Hotel Slavyanskaya and in Hotel Sibir.

Where to stay and eat

The **resting rooms комнаты отдыха** (*komnaty otdykha*) at the railway station (dorm/sgl R200/450) are clean but basic. The showers are not always in operation owing to the lack of hot water.

Even though Tobolsk railway station is the most basic of all Trans-Siberian stations (not even a café on-site), on the platform you'll find numerous **stalls** selling all kinds

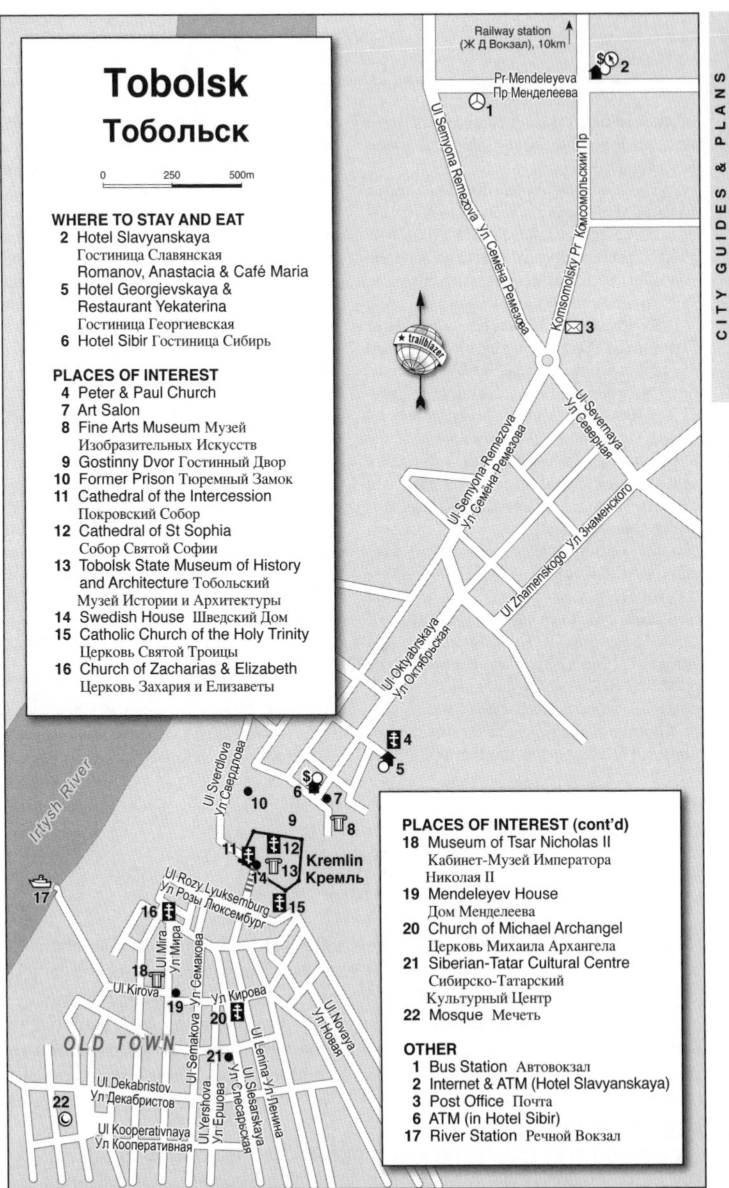

Tobolsk
Тобольск
0 250 500m
WHERE TO STAY AND EAT
2 Hotel Slavyanskaya Гостиница Славянская
Romanov, Anastacia & Café Maria
5 Hotel Georgievskaya & Restaurant Yekaterina Гостиница Георгиевская
6 Hotel Sibir Гостиница Сибирь
PLACES OF INTEREST
4 Peter & Paul Church
7 Art Salon
8 Fine Arts Museum Музей Изобразительных Искусств
9 Gostinny Dvor Гостинный Двор
10 Former Prison Тюремный Замок
11 Cathedral of the Intercession Покровский Собор
12 Cathedral of St Sophia Собор Святой Софии
13 Tobolsk State Museum of History and Architecture Тобольский Музей Истории и Архитектуры
14 Swedish House Шведский Дом
15 Catholic Church of the Holy Trinity Церковь Святой Троицы
16 Church of Zacharias & Elizabeth Церковь Захария и Елизаветы
PLACES OF INTEREST (cont'd)
18 Museum of Tsar Nicholas II Кабинет-Музей Императора Николая II
19 Mendeleyev House Дом Менделеева
20 Church of Michael Archangel Церковь Михаила Архангела
21 Siberian-Tatar Cultural Centre Сибирско-Татарский Культурный Центр
22 Mosque Мечеть
OTHER
1 Bus Station Автовокзал
2 Internet & ATM (Hotel Slavyanskaya)
3 Post Office Почта
6 ATM (in Hotel Sibir)
17 River Station Речной Вокзал
Railway station (Ж Д Вокзал), 10km
Pr Mendeleyeva Пр Менделеева
Ul Semyona Remezova Ул Семёна Ремезова
Komsomolsky Pr Комсомольский Пр
Ul Severnaya Ул Северная
Ul Znamenskogo Ул Знаменского
Ul Oktyabrskaya Ул Октябрьская
Ul Sverdlova Ул Свердлова
Irtysh River
Kremlin Кремль
Ul Rozy Lyuksemburg Ул Розы Люксембург
Ul Mira Ул Мира
Ul Semakova Ул Семакова
Ul Kirova Ул Кирова
Ul Novaya Ул Новая
OLD TOWN
Ul Lenina Ул Ленина
Ul Dekabristov Ул Декабристов
Ul Kooperativnaya Ул Кооперативная
Ul Yershova Ул Ершова
Ul Slesarskaya Ул Слесарьская
trailblazer

The Tobolsk area code is ☎ 3456. From outside Russia dial ☎ +7-3456.

of smoked fish, salted cucumbers and other homemade food to fortify you for the journey ahead.

The renovated ***Hotel Sibir* Гостиница Сибирь** (Ремизова пл 1, Remizova pl 1, ☎ 251 353, sgl/dbl/suite R1300-1700/2800/3200) is centrally located next to the Kremlin and offers comfortable beige-and-brown en suite rooms with TVs and fridges.

A better choice is ***Hotel Georgievskaya* Гостиница Георгиевская** (ул Ленская 35, ul Lenskaya 35, ☎ 220 909, 🖳 www.hotel-georgievskaya.ru, sgl/dbl R2300-2700/2700-4100), a perky, brand-new hotel by the Peter and Paul church, north of the Kremlin. The well-appointed rooms are spacious and warm, the young staff are helpful and the on-site ***Restaurant Yekaterina*** serves all manner of Russian classics – filling soups, salads, blini, meat and fish dishes (mains R150-320).

Siberia's first five-star hotel, ***Hotel Slavyanskaya* Гостиница Славянская** (пр Менделеева и Комсомольский пр, corner of pr Mendeleeva and Komsomolsky pr, ☎ 399 101, 🖳 www.slavjanskaja.ru, sgl/dbl/suite from R2200/4200/6300), 3km north of the Kremlin, is not near the attractions but it is right on the bus route. The grand complex, which hosted President Medvedev during his 2010 visit, boasts two top **restaurants** – ***Romanov*** and ***Anastacia*** – serving Russian and European cuisine, Rasputin **nightclub** if you want to let your hair down, ***Café Maria*** for light meals, and a full-size swimming pool and spa. The rooms are suitably plush; there's even an **internet centre** in the lobby that's open to non-guests as well. Note that the cheapest rooms are located under the nightclub.

Moving on

By rail From Tobolsk there are no particularly convenient departures for Omsk; the 363 leaves on odd days at 10.40am but arrives at 2.10am (Moscow Time, or 5.10am Local Time; 15hrs), while the firmenny 395 arrives in Omsk at a reasonable 12.34pm (Moscow Time) but departs at 00.21am on even days; 12hrs. Other departures include Yekaterinburg (9/day, 9½-11½hrs, the most convenient being the 109 with its 7.51pm overnight departure) and Tyumen (12/day, 3½-5hrs).

By boat Three-day cruises to Omsk leave from Tobolsk's river station Речной Вокзал (☎ 296 617) when the river is navigable.

Omsk
Омск

[Moscow Time +3] With friendly locals and a laid-back atmosphere accentuated by a wealth of parks and public sculptures, Omsk, now Siberia's second-largest city, is a pleasant and slightly offbeat place to break your Trans-Siberian trip.

The city was founded in 1719 as a small fortress on the west bank of the River Om, to be used as the military headquarters of the Cossack regiments in Siberia. It had been considerably enlarged and included a large *ostrog* (prison) by the time Fyodor Dostoyevsky arrived in 1849 to begin four years of hard labour for political crimes.

His unenviable experiences were recorded in *Buried Alive in Siberia*. He was twice flogged, once for complaining about a lump of dirt in his soup; the second time he saved the life of a drowning prisoner, ignoring a guard who ordered that the man be left to drown. Dostoyevsky received so severe a flogging for this charitable act that he almost died and had to spend six weeks in the hospital.

During the Civil War Omsk was the capital of the White Russian government of Admiral Kolchak, until November 1919 when the Red Army entered and took the city. The population grew fast after the war and now an estimated 1.3 million people live here. Textiles, food, agricultural machinery and timber products are the main industries. There is also an important petrochemical complex here, supplied by a pipeline from the Ural-Volga oil region.

WHAT TO SEE AND DO

The revamped **Omsk State Museum of History and Regional Studies** Омский Государственный Историческо-Краеведческий Музей (ul Lenina 23a, 10am-6pm Tue-Sun, R100) has extensive exhibits charting the first human settlement in the area through archaeological remains, as well as exhibits telling the story of eastern Siberia and how it came to be linked to the Russian empire.

Exhibits concerning the impact of WWII on the Omsk area are particularly moving; out of every two men who went to the front, one perished. The ethnographic displays show traditional dwellings of the peoples who've populated Siberia, and the national costumes of Tatars, Cossacks, Russians and Ukrainians are colourful and varied. An extensive flora and fauna section shows off the taxidermied representatives of the Siberian animal and bird kingdom. There are also interesting temporary exhibitions on the ground floor.

In front of the museum a **WWII memorial** Мемориал Великой Отечественной Войне states: 'We sing our praise to the madness of the brave,' and there's a small **Lenin statue** Памятник Ленину nearby.

On pl Lenina there's a long overdue **memorial to the victims of Stalinist repression** Памятник Жертвам Сталинских Репрессий.

Inside the grand former Siberian governor's palace, **Vrubel Fine Arts Museum** Художественный Музей имени Врубеля (ul Lenina 23, 💻 www.vrubel.ru, 10am-7pm, adult/student R50/30) is home to decorative arts by Russian and Western artists from the 16th to the early 20th century. The building itself has an interesting history as it was the home of White Army Admiral Kolchak between 1918 and 1919 before the Red Army overran the city. There's a separate wing of the museum at ul Lenina 3 (adult/student R100/50) showcasing an extensive collection of Russian art from the 18th to the 20th centuries, as well as icons and a smaller collection of Western art.

SERAFIMO-ALEKSIEVSKAYA CHAPEL

You'll recognise the **Military Museum** Военный Музей (ul Taube 7, 10am-5pm, R100) by the collection of tanks and other military apparel in the fenced-off area outside it. Inside there are displays on WWI, the Afghan and Chechnya conflicts and a particularly extensive WWII section, created in time for the 65th anniversary of the end of the war. Omsk State **Literature Museum** Литературный Музей (ul Dostoyevskogo 1, 💻 www.litmuseum.ru, Tue-Fri 10am-4pm, R100 entry, R400 tour) has changing literary exhibits and a section on Dostoyevsky. It is said that all his great works were written after his four years in the city 'in penal servitude' and that they contain echoes of Omsk.

Near the junction of the Om and Irtysh rivers are the ramparts and **Tobolsk Gate** Тобольские Ворота of the old Omsk fortress. By the Om River is the distinctive **Serafimo-Aleksievskaya Chapel**, built to commemorate the birth of the Tsarevich Alexis in 1904 and restored in the 1990s. On the northern part of ul Lenina you'll find a **monument to slacker workers**, consisting of a jolly upper body of a man sticking out of a manhole.

River trips

There are two river stations in Omsk. Long-distance vessels, such as those for Tobolsk, leave from the **River Station** Речной Вокзал. Timetables and the ticket office are in the large station building.

Tourist trips along the Irtysh depart from a separate **Excursion River Station**, with tickets and timetables available from a kiosk just west of Yubileyny Bridge. The river is navigable from late May to September.

In the summer months people sunbathe, swim and fish on the sandy bank of the Irtysh south of the long-distance river station.

WHERE TO STAY

14 Hotel Mayak Гостиница Маяк
16 Hotel Turist Гостиница Турист
17 Hotel Ibis Sibir Omsk

WHERE TO EAT AND DRINK

6 Bevitore Бевиторе
7 Terra Sushi Терра-Суши
8 Pertsy Перцы
9 Vilka-Lozkha Вилка-Ложка
15 Irish Pub
20 Café Berlin Кафе Берлин
26 Restaurant Journalist Ресторан Журналистъ

PLACES OF INTEREST

2 Drama Theatre Драматический Театр
3 Military Museum Военный Музей
4 Literature Museum Литературный Музей
5 Slacker Workman Statue
10 Serafimo-Aleksievskaya Chapel
12 Tobolsk Gate Тобольские Ворота
18 Vrubel Fine Arts Museum Художественный Музей имени Врубеля
19 Omsk State Museum of History and Regional Studies Омский Государственный Историческо-Краеведческий Музей
21 WWII Memorial Мемориал Великой Отечественной Войне
22 Lenin Statue Памятник Ленину
23 Memorial to the Victims of Stalinist Repression Памятник Жертвам Сталинских Репрессий
24 Musical Theatre Музыкальный Театр
25 St Nicholas Cathedral Никольский Собор

OTHER

1 Central Post Office Почтамт
11 Excursion River Station
13 River Station Речной Вокзал

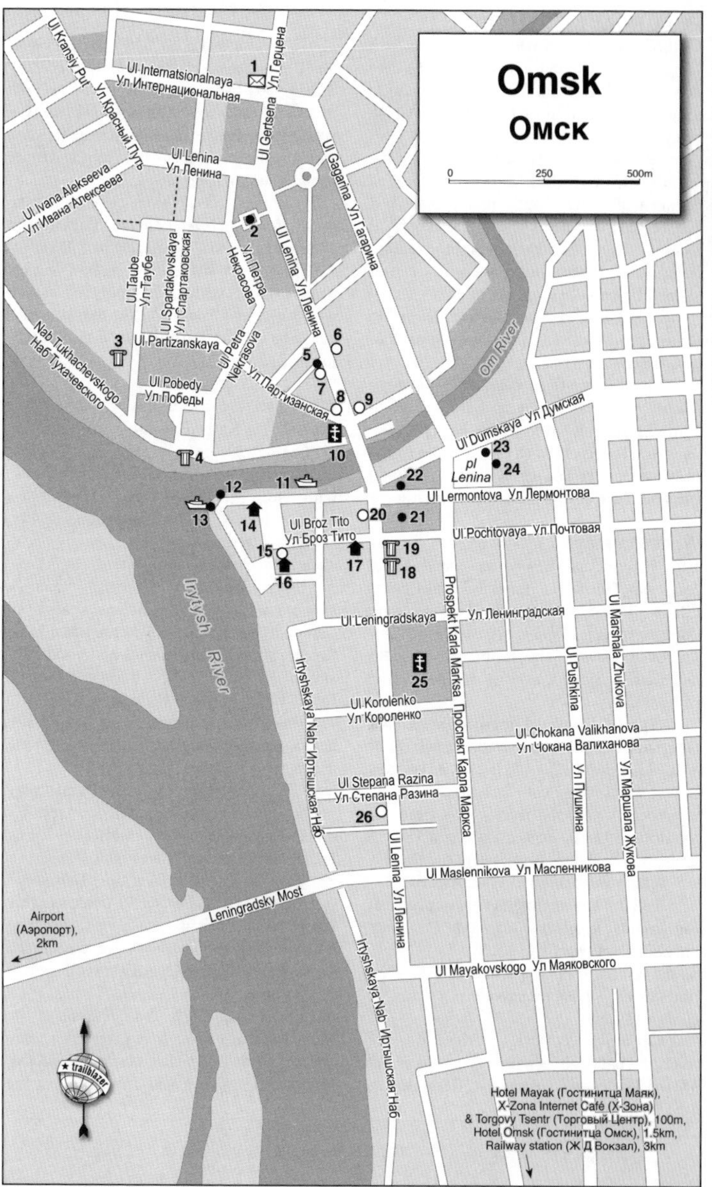
Omsk
Омск
0
250
500m
Ul Internatsionalnaya
Ул Интернациональная
Ul Krasniy Put
Ул Красный Путь
Ul Gertsena
Ул Герцена
Ul Lenina
Ул Ленина
Ul Ivana Alekseeva
Ул Ивана Алексеева
Ul Gagarina
Ул Гагарина
Ul Taube
Ул Таубе
Ul Spartakovskaya
Ул Спартаковская
Ul Petra Nekrasova
Ул Петра Некрасова
Ul Partizanskaya
Ул Партизанская
Ul Pobedy
Ул Победы
Nab Tukhachevskogo
Наб Тухачевского
Om River
Ul Dumskaya
Ул Думская
pl Lenina
Ul Lermontova
Ул Лермонтова
Ul Broz Tito
Ул Броз Тито
Ul Pochtovaya
Ул Почтовая
Irytysh River
Ul Leningradskaya
Ул Ленинградская
Prospekt Karla Marksa
Проспект Карла Маркса
Irtyshskaya Nab
Иртышская Наб
Ul Korolenko
Ул Короленко
Ul Pushkina
Ул Пушкина
Ul Marshala Zhukova
Ул Маршала Жукова
Ul Chokana Valikhanova
Ул Чокана Валиханова
Ul Stepana Razina
Ул Степана Разина
Ul Maslennikova
Ул Масленникова
Leningradsky Most
Airport
(Аэропорт),
2km
Ul Mayakovskogo
Ул Маяковского
trailblazer
Hotel Mayak (Гостинитца Маяк),
X-Zona Internet Café (Х-Зона)
& Torgovy Tsentr (Торговый Центр), 100m,
Hotel Omsk (Гостинитца Омск), 1.5km,
Railway station (Ж Д Вокзал), 3km
CITY GUIDES & PLANS

PRACTICAL INFORMATION

Orientation and services

Most hotels and museums are in the city centre which is about 6km from the station around the junction of the Om and Irtysh rivers.

Several buses and trolleybuses run the length of pr Karla Marksa пр Карла Маркса, the most handy being trolleybus No 4 (R15) that takes you to the central pl Lenina, its most distinguishing feature being the theatre building with a roof shaped like an Olympic ski jump.

The **Central Post Office** Почтамт (8am-7pm Mon-Sat, 10am-5pm Sun) is at ul Gertsena 1.

There is **wi-fi** access at the **Torgovy Tsentr** Торговый Центр (corner of ul Karla Marksa and ul Tsiolkovskaya) as well as inside the Rostik's (KFC) in front of the railway station, and an **X-Zona** (X-Зона) **internet café** across the street from it.

Where to stay

Ultra-central and newly renovated ***Hotel Ibis Sibir Omsk*** (ул Ленина 22, ul Lenina 22, ☎ 311 551, 🖳 www.ibishotel.com, doubles from R2499) is popular with visiting businessmen. The rooms are modern and wi-fi equipped; ask for one not facing ul Lenina.

Hotel Omsk **Гостиница Омск** (Иртышская наб 30, Irtyshskaya nab 30, ☎ 310 721, sgl/dbl R1800/3100) is a concrete Soviet monstrosity with basic rooms, some upgraded, with good river views from the top floors. Take any bus up pr Karla Marksa to the 'Circus' stop, from where the hotel is a 5-minute walk through Park Pobedy.

The railway station has revamped ***resting rooms*** **комнаты отдыха** (*komnaty otdykha*; sgl/twin/trpl R2500/850/750pp) on the left as you exit the station. The luxurious single is best, though all the rooms are clean and cosy.

Centrally located overlooking the river, the nautically themed four-star ***Hotel Mayak*** **Гостиница Маяк** (ул Лермонтова 2, ul Lermonotva 2, ☎ 315 431, 🖳 www.hotel-mayak.ru, sgl/dbl/suite from R2860/3220/6590) has smart, stylish rooms with excellent modern bathrooms. There is a very good restaurant on-site serving Russian and European dishes and the staff are friendly and helpful.

Another good choice would be the multi-storey ***Hotel Turist*** **Гостиница Турист** (ул Броз Тито 2, ul Broz Tito 2, ☎ 316 414, 🖳 www.tourist-omsk.ru, rooms from R6200) with fully upgraded rooms with satellite TV and a good buffet breakfast. The on-site ***Restaurant Globus*** serves fusion cuisine.

Where to eat and drink

Café Berlin **Кафе Берлин** (ул Ленина 20, ul Lenina 20) is a trendy and popular hangout for locals and foreigners alike, with their menu of salads, sandwiches, good coffee and delicious homemade *mors*, as well as free wi-fi access. The only drawback is the smokey atmosphere.

Pertsy **Перцы** (ул Партизанская и ул Ленина, corner of ul Partizanskaya and ul Lenina, mains R350, [V]) is the place to go for inexpensive pasta dishes and good thin-and-crispy pizzas. Across the street, the 2nd floor ***Vilka-Lozhka*** **Вилка-Ложка** is a self-service canteen-type place, where you help yourself to the array of soups, pelmeni and other hot dishes (mains R150).

The **Irish pub** next to Hotel Turist may not be authentic, but it's still a good spot for a beer or two, and you can also get filling Uzbek dishes there for around R250.

Restaurant-café ***Bevitore*** **Бевиторе** (ул Ленина 9, ul Lenina 9) comes highly recommended for its shashlyk dishes and has intermittent free wi-fi for customers. ***Terra-Sushi*** **Терра-Суши** across the street (ул Ленина 14, ul Lenina 14) has good lunchtime sushi deals, though some of the sushi rolls are a bit heavy on the cream cheese. With a dim but charming interior filled with antiques and mementos of the

> The Omsk area code is ☎ 3812. From outside Russia dial ☎ +7-3812.

newsman's trade, ***Restaurant Journalist*** **Ресторан Журналистъ** (ул Ленина 34, ul Lenina 34, mains R300) is the kind of place you want to sit all day. The Russian cuisine is creative and excellent, including several healthy 'fitness' options, there's a good business lunch and this is one of the few places you'll find wine from Abkhazia.

Almost directly in front of the railway station there are several fast-food options, including **Rostik's**.

Moving on

By rail Destinations include Novosibirsk (18/day, 7-9hrs, the most convenient overnighters being the firmenny 088, and also the 140 and 073), Tobolsk (1-2/day, 12-14hrs, with the 395 and 397 arriving inconveniently at 3.25am local time, the 363 on even days arriving at a more sensible 10.40pm), Tomsk (1/day, 14hrs, 038 on odd days and 211 on even days – both convenient overnighters), Yekaterinburg (12/day, 11-18hrs, the 067 being the most convenient overnighter) and Moscow (up to 11/day, 39-68hrs, the fastest being the 001 and the 055).

By air Head to the airport (☎ 517 570), 5km away on the west bank of the Irtysh. Destinations include Moscow (5/day), St Petersburg (3/week), Irkutsk and other cities. Several buses go there from downtown.

Novosibirsk
Новосибирск

[Moscow Time +3] With a population of just under 1.5 million, this is Siberia's largest city and Russia's third most populous city after Moscow and St Petersburg. But among the Trans-Siberian cities that foreigners usually visit, Novosibirsk is a relatively young city and has few buildings of historic interest, though it does boast an excellent railway museum in nearby Seyatel and the vast scale of parts of the centre is amazing. As Colin Thubron, author of *In Siberia,* writes: 'Space, in the end, may be all you remember of Novosibirsk'.

You can also visit the enormous opera house, the museums and the nearby town of Akademgorodok (see box p260), the 'City of Scientists' where hundreds of researchers live in a purpose-built, lakeside town. Winters here are particularly harsh, with temperatures falling as low as -35°C.

Novosibirsk is the jumping-off point for trips to the gorgeous Altai Mountains to the south. It's also the terminus of the Turksib railway (see pp109-10). Travellers can catch a train from here to Almaty in Kazakhstan and then continue east into China.

HISTORY

Novosibirsk didn't exist before the Trans-Siberian was built. Its spectacular growth in the 20th century is largely due to the railway. In 1891 it was decided that a railway bridge over the Ob should be built here, and two years later a small settlement sprang up on the river bank to house the bridge builders. The town was named Novo-Nikolayevsk in honour of the accession of the new Tsar.

By 1900 over 15,000 people lived here and the numbers grew as railway and water-borne trade developed. As far as tourists were concerned there was only one reason to get off the Trans-Siberian here, as Baedeker's 1914 *Guide to Russia* points out: 'It is a favourite starting point for sportsmen in pursuit of the wapiti, mountain sheep, ibex and other big game on the north slopes of the Altai'.

The town suffered badly during the Civil War when 30,000 people lost their lives. During the first four months of 1920 a further 60,000 died of typhus. In 1925 Novo-Nikolayevsk was re-christened Novosibirsk ('New Siberia').

Between 1926 and 1939 the population mushroomed as smelting furnaces were built and fed with coal from the nearby Kuznetsk Basin and iron ore from the Urals. The early 1930s saw the laying of the final sections of the Turksib Railway (a project begun in the years just before WWI), completing a 2600km line from Novosibirsk across Kazakhstan via Semey (Semipalatinsk) and Almaty to Arys in the fertile valley of the Syr-Darya river in Central Asia. Grain from the lands around Novosibirsk could now be exchanged for cotton, which grew best in Central Asia. A film of the final stages of construction of this line, the jewel in the new government's first Five Year Plan, provides a fascinating early example of documentary cinema.

During WWII many civilians and complete factories were shifted to Novosibirsk from European Russia, and the city has been growing ever since. It's now the area's busiest river port and Siberia's major industrial centre, with many people employed in engineering and metallurgy factories.

WHAT TO SEE AND DO

Lenin Square and the Opera House

Pl Lenina (Lenin Sq) is the heart of the city. It's dominated by the vast **Opera and Ballet Theatre** Театр Оперы и Балета (Krasny pr 36, 💻 www.opera-novosibirsk.ru) one of the largest in the world, with its silver dome and gigantic portico. The theatre was completed in 1945 after most able-bodied young men had been sent off to war. The effort was seen as all the more heroic in that many of the city's women and children helped the few builders who remained behind.

You can get tickets from the kiosk on the left side of the theatre. The cheapest performances are in the morning, with seats costing as little as R170, and if the theatre isn't full you can move to more expensive seats for free.

In the middle of the square is the most dramatic-looking **statue of Lenin** along the Trans-Siberian, his coat blowing behind him in the cold Siberian wind. He is flanked by three soldiers on his right and by two 'Peace' figures on his left, who look as if they are directing the traffic that flows around the great square.

In the winter there are troika rides here, and people build ice-sculptures. Come summer, the square and the adjacent park are the venue for a thriving local promenade scene.

The low building above **M** Ploshchad Lenina is the oldest stone structure in the city.

NOVOSIBIRSK RAILWAY STATION – SIBERIA'S LARGEST

Museum of Local Studies

The Museum of Local Studies consists of **three sections**: the History Museum, the Natural History Museum which shares the building with the Siberian Centre of Modern Art, and Kirov House-Museum.

The **History Museum** Исторический Музей (Krasny pr 23, 10am-6pm Wed-Fri, 11am-7pm Sat & Sun, adult/student R200/120) traces the history of the region from its earliest settlement through to Soviet Siberia and the Novosibirsk area's participation in WWII. Ethnographic displays covering the Altai, Evenk, Yakut, Siberian Tatar and other native people of Siberia are particularly interesting, featuring traditional dress, tools and ceremonial objects, though there's a lack of English captioning.

The **Natural History Museum** Музей Природы (Vokzalnaya Magistral 11; under renovation at the time of writing) contains an extensive display of Siberian flora and fauna including some of the 50 species of mammals, 30 species of fish and 30 species of birds that are found only in Novosibirsk Oblast. There's also a collection of Siberian trees and grasses, a geological display and the skeleton of a mammoth. The labels on the natural history exhibits are in Latin as well as Russian: for translations see pp484-5.

Its neighbour, **Siberian Centre of Modern Art** Сибирский Центр Современного Искусства (10am-6pm Wed-Fri, 11am-7pm Sat & Sun) hosts innovative temporary exhibitions by Russian artists and features the Laboratory of Improvised Music (adult/student R100/50); bring your own musical instrument and join in.

Kirov House-Museum Дом-Музей Кирова (ul Lenina 23, Mon-Fri 10am-6pm, free entry) is devoted to Sergey Kirov, a rising Communist Party leader who was assassinated in 1934 on Stalin's orders, and who lived here for a relatively short while in 1908. It's an attractive log cabin, one of the few to have survived here, with original furniture in place.

Other sights

Near the main railway station, the **History Museum of the Western Siberian Railway** Музей Истории Западно-Сибирской Железной Дороги (ul Shamshurina 39, 9am-5pm Tue-Fri; free entry but with guide only), true to its name, covers the history of the Western Siberian railway through a series of railway-related artefacts, such as uniforms through the ages, photographs, train furniture, and scale models of freight and passenger locomotives, as well as a delightful model railway (though unfortunately, visitors are not allowed to play with it).

The 1898 red-brick **Aleksander Nevsky Cathedral** Собор Александра Невского (at the southern end of Krasny pr Красный пр near the river) has been fully restored and features colourful new murals. Just south of pl Lenina is the tiny **Chapel of St Nicholas** Часовня Святителя Николая, in the middle of the road and reached from beneath via the pedestrian subway. It was built on the spot said to mark the geographic centre of Russia, and opened during the city's centenary celebrations in 1993. The original church here was destroyed after the Revolution.

On ul Sovetskaya ул Советская, the **Cathedral of the Ascension** Вознесенский Собор with its blue dome was built just 100 years ago.

The **State Art Museum** Государственный Художествнный Музей (Krasny pr 5, 10am-5pm Tue-Fri, from 11am Sat & Sun, adult/student R200/120) features interesting temporary art and photography exhibitions by local and international artists, while its permanent collection includes landscapes by Nikolai Rerikh and other Siberian art.

PRACTICAL INFORMATION

Orientation and services

Novosibirsk was designed on a grand scale. Krasny pr Красный пр, its main street, extends for over 10km. The mighty River Ob bisects the city, leaving the main hotels, sights and railway station on the east bank.

You can buy **city maps** from the many newspaper kiosks outside the main railway station; just ask for a '*karta goroda*'.

Recommended local travel agents include the adventure travel company **Altair** (☎ 212 5115, 🖳 www.altairtour.ru), who offer extreme outdoor adventures in the nearby Altai region and beyond.

You can access the **internet** at the **main post office** Почтамт (ul Lenina 5, 8am-9pm Mon-Fri, to 7pm Sat & Sun, R40/hour); there are several **ATMs** along Krasny pr.

Local transport

On foot, pl Lenina пл Ленина is about 20 minutes from the railway station, straight

WHERE TO STAY, EAT AND DRINK
- 2 Resting rooms Комнаты Отдыха
- 5 Hotel Sibir Гостиница Сибирь
- 9 Matryoshka Матрёшка
- 10 Shultz Шультс
- 12 Vilka-Lozhka Вилка-Ложка
- 13 Vogue Café Дождь
- 14 Kroshka-Kartoshka Крошка-Картошка
- 17 Murakami Мураками
- 18 Grill Master Гриль Мастер
- 19 5'nizza
- 20 Perchini Перчини
- 24 Goodman Steakhouse Гудман Стейкхаус
- 27 People's Grill-Bar
- 28 Beerman & Pelmeni
- 33 Hotel Naberezhnaya Гостиница Набережная
- 35 Hostel Dostoyevsky

PLACES OF INTEREST
- 3 History Museum of the Western Siberian Railway
- 4 Kirov House-Museum Дом-Музей Кирова
- 6 Natural History Museum/Siberian Centre of Modern Art Музей Природы/ Сибирский Центр Современного Искусства
- 7 Cathedral of the Ascension Вознесенский Собор
- 15 Opera & Ballet Theatre Театр Оперы и Балета
- 16 Lenin Statue Памятник Ленину
- 22 FD-21 Steam Engine Паровоз ФД-21
- 23 Synagogue Синагога
- 25 History Museum Исторический Музей
- 26 Chapel of St Nicholas Часовня Святителя Николая
- 29 Philharmonia Филармония
- 30 State Art Museum Государственный Художествнный Музей
- 31 Aleksander Nevsky Cathedral Собор Александра Невского Музей Истории Западно-Сибирской Железной Дороги

OTHER
- 1 Central Railway Station Железнодорожный Вокзал
- 8 Air Ticket Office Авиакасса
- 11 Market Рынок
- 21 Central Post Office Почтамт
- 32 Bus Station Автовокзал
- 34 River Station Речной Вокзал

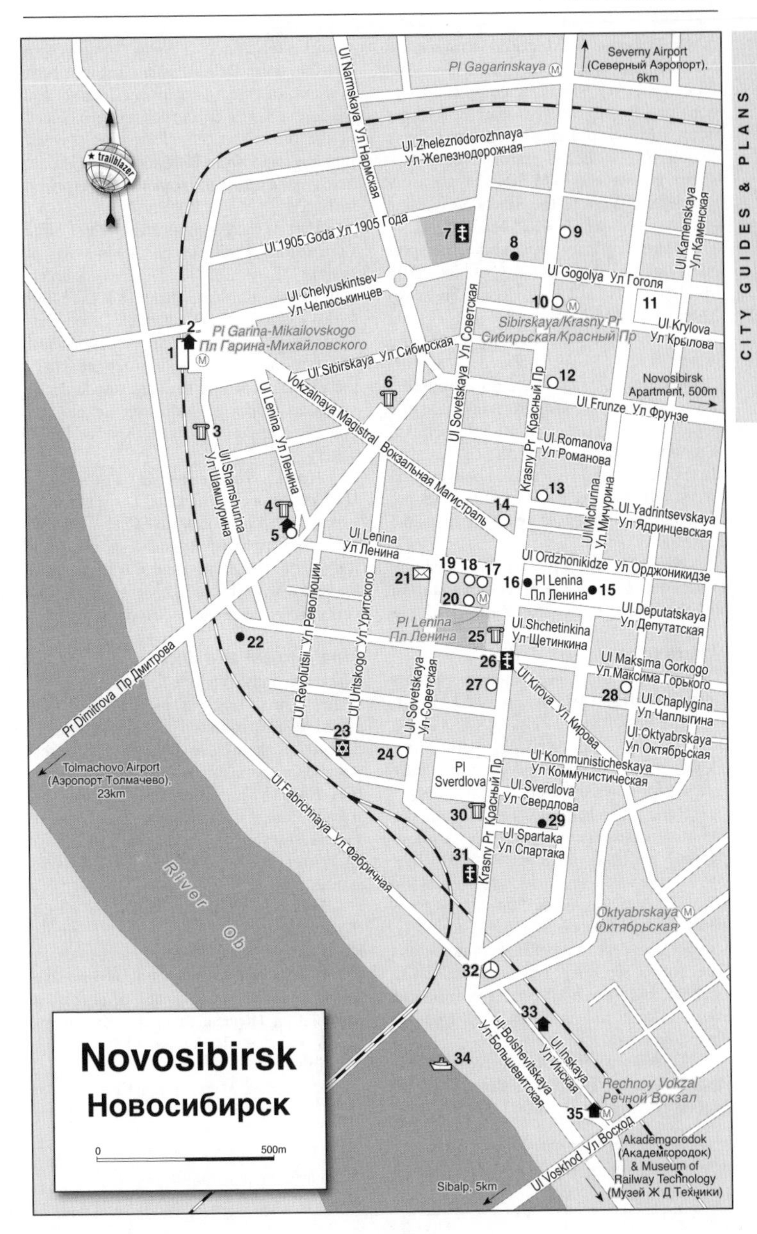
CITY GUIDES & PLANS
Novosibirsk
Новосибирск
0
500m
Severny Airport (Северный Аэропорт), 6km
Pl Gagarinskaya
Ul Narmskaya Ул Нармская
Ul Zheleznodorozhnaya Ул Железнодорожная
Ul 1905 Goda Ул 1905 Года
Ul Gogolya Ул Гоголя
Ul Kamenskaya Ул Каменская
Ul Chelyuskintsev Ул Челюськинцев
Pl Garina-Mikailovskogo Пл Гарина-Михайловского
Sibirskaya/Krasny Pr Сибирская/Красный Пр
Ul Krylova Ул Крылова
Ul Sibirskaya Ул Сибирская
Ul Sovetskaya Ул Советская
Krasny Pr Красный Пр
Novosibirsk Apartment, 500m
Ul Frunze Ул Фрунзе
Vokzalnaya Magistral Вокзальная Магистраль
Ul Lenina Ул Ленина
Ul Shamshurina Ул Шамшурина
Ul Romanova Ул Романова
Ul Michurina Ул Мичурина
Ul Yadrintsevskaya Ул Ядринцевская
Ul Ordzhonikidze Ул Орджоникидзе
Pl Lenina Пл Ленина
Ul Deputatskaya Ул Депутатская
Ul Revolutsii Ул Революции
Ul Uritskogo Ул Урицкого
Ul Shchetinkina Ул Щетинкина
Ul Maksima Gorkogo Ул Максима Горького
Ul Kirova Ул Кирова
Ul Chaplygina Ул Чаплыгина
Pr Dimitrova Пр Дмитрова
Ul Oktyabrskaya Ул Октябрьская
Ul Kommunisticheskaya Ул Коммунистическая
Pl Sverdlova
Ul Sverdlova Ул Свердлова
Ul Spartaka Ул Спартака
Tolmachovo Airport (Аэропорт Толмачево), 23km
Ul Fabrichnaya Ул Фабричная
River Ob
Oktyabrskaya Октябрьская
Ul Bolshevitskaya Ул Большевитская
Ul Inskaya Ул Инская
Rechnoy Vokzal Речной Вокзал
Ul Voskhod Ул Восход
Akademgorodok (Академгородок) & Museum of Railway Technology (Музей Ж Д Техники)
Sibalp, 5km
trailblazer

down Vokzalnaya Magistral Вокзальная Магистраль. Novosibirsk has a good but limited **metro** system (including some stations panelled in Siberian marble; R16 per ride). To reach pl Lenina from the railway station (**M** Ploshchad Garina-Mikhailovskogo), go one stop to **M** Sibirskaya/Krasny Prospekt, change to the Studentskaya line and go one stop to **M** Ploshchad Lenina.

There's plenty of public transport going up and down Krasny pr, including trolleybuses No 5, 13 and 36 and buses No 21 and No 122 (R11).

Novosibirsk has two **airports**: the international Tolmachevo airport (Аэропорт Толмачево), 23km from the city centre on the western bank, and the domestic Severny airport (Северный Аэропорт), 6km to the north of the centre. Buses No 111 and No 122 run between the two via the railway station and bus station, although the minibuses covering the same routes are quicker.

Near **M** Rechnoy Vokzal (meaning 'river station') are the **river-boat station** and the **long-distance bus station**.

Where to stay

The railway station has spacious ***rest rooms*** **комнаты отдыха** (*komnaty otdykha*, sgl/twin/trpl R1500/900/750pp, or R3500/4500 for sgl/dbl with private bathroom). However, it's often full and you must show a ticket for onward travel.

Run by two helpful young women, the brand-new ***Hostel Dostoyevsky*** (ул Инская 56 кв 8, ul Inskaya 56 apt 8, ☎ 913 399 5690 or 913 450 0512, 💻 http://hosteldostoyevsky.com, dorms R500-600) is good news for backpackers in a city notoriously short of decent budget accommodation. The dorms are cosy, spacious, and wi-fi enabled, and there are river views from the rooms. The hostel is a short walk from **M** Rechnoy Vokzal.

A more central hostel, ***Novosibirsk Apartment*** (ул Ипподромская 21/41, ul Ippodromskaya 21/41, ☎ 903 900 6741, 💻 www.hostels.com as it doesn't have its own website, dorm R1000) offers just four beds in a spacious studio apartment. Internet and a good self-service breakfast are included in the price; the central location, several minutes' walk from **M** Marshal Pokrishkin, helps make up for the somewhat overpriced beds.

Part of the Azimut chain, ***Hotel Sibir*** **Гостиница Сибирь** (ул Ленина 21, ul Lenina 21, ☎ 223 1215, 💻 www.hotel-sibir.ru, sgl/dbl/suite from R3000/3700/6900) has modern, comfortable, wi-fi enabled rooms, decorated in pastel shades. The rate includes a good buffet breakfast, the service is of international standard, the staff can help you with train tickets and you can sate your sweet tooth in the lobby bakery.

Hotel Naberezhnaya **Гостиница Набережная** (ул Инская 39, 4-й этаж, ul Inskaya 39, 4th floor, ☎ 264 4711, 💻 www.nabergnaja.ru – in Russian, sgl/dbl from R2500/2900), a few minutes' walk from **M** Rechnoy Vokzal, has colourful décor and perks include a sauna and river views.

Where to eat and drink

There are numerous fast-food places in the centre including ***Kroshka-Kartoshka*** **Крошка-Картошка** (ул Орджоникидзе 23, ul Ordzhonikidze 23), serving baked potatoes with numerous fillings, the ubiquitous ***Rostik's***, up Krasny pr Красный пр from pl Lenina пл Ленина and ***Grill Master*** **Гриль Мастер** (ул Ленина 25/1, ul Lenina 25/1), serving large burgers and Russian staples.

Vilka-Lozhka **Вилка-Ложка** (Красный пр 50, Krasny pr 50, meals R200) is a popular self-serve canteen chain where you can load up on inexpensive salads, soups and meat dishes. ***Matryoshka*** **Матрёшка** (Красный пр 81, Krasny pr 81, [V]) serves similar food but also has tasty blini.

Murakami **Мураками** (Красный пр 25, Krasny pr 25, meals R550) is a stylish

The Novosibirsk area code is ☎ 383. From outside Russia dial ☎ +7-383.

Japanese restaurant with oriental décor and private booths. The service can be somewhat snooty, but the sushi sets are superb. Directly opposite, ***Perchini*** **Перчини** (Красный пр 25, Krasny pr 25, mains R350, [V]) is part of a smart chain of Italian restaurants, serving veal carpaccio alongside excellent thin-and-crispy pizzas and homemade pasta dishes. The cocktail section is good and the service is friendly and helpful, though it can be slow when busy. Wi-fi access.

For a meat fix head to ***Goodman Steakhouse*** **Гудман Стейкхаус** (ул Советская 5, ul Sovetskaya 5, mains R500-1500), a popular contemporary chain specialising in, erm, steak. Their fusion dishes are good as well and the service is very efficient.

You can probably guess the speciality at ***Beerman & Pelmeni*** (ул Каменская 7, ul Kamenskaya 7, meals R300), with numerous beers on tap and the widest selection of the beloved pelmeni in the Urals. There's another branch at Вокзальная Магистраль 1, Vokzalnaya Magistral 1.

Good places for a drink and live music in the evening are ***Shultz*** **Шультс** (Красный пр 66, Krasny pr 66), a German-style beer house with Blagbacher, Kellers and Bierbach on tap, among others, accompanied by meaty German dishes.

People's Grill-Bar (Вокзальная Магистраль 16 и Красный пр 17, Vokzalnaya Magistral 16 and Krasny pr 17) is a trendy spot for a beer and the grilled items on the menu aren't bad. ***5'nizza*** (Красный пр 25, Krasny pr 25) is another trendy, lively bar.

Vogue Café Дождь (Красный пр 42a, Krasny pr 42a) is a chilled-out lounge with an extensive wine list and very good salads.

Entertainment

Novosibirsk boasts the grand **Opera and Ballet Theatre** Театр Оперы и Балета (Красный пр 36, Krasny pr 36, ☎ 227 1537, 💻 www.opera-novosibirsk.ru, tickets R200-3000), which opera and ballet devotees shouldn't miss, as its sumptuous interior and excellent acoustics make for a wonderful experience.

The **Philharmonia** Филармония (ул Спартака 11, ul Spartaka 11, ☎ 222 1511, 💻 www.philharmonia-nsk.ru) is the prime venue for classical symphony concerts.

Moving on

By rail On the ground floor of the station at the northern end there is a Service Centre where some staff speak English. Novosibirsk is a major train hub with numerous departures east, west and south.

Eastbound departures include Moscow via Omsk, Yekaterinburg, and other major cities (6-12/day, 47-70hrs, the most comfortable being the firmenny 025 on even days or the 055 on odd days). For Omsk, (up to 20/day, 7-9½hrs) the 087 is a convenient overnighter. For Yekaterinburg (12/day, 20-22hrs), the 139 is usefully timed.

Westbound departures include Krasnoyarsk (9/day, 11-13hrs, the 080 and 012 are convenient overnighters), Irkutsk (6/day, 30-31hrs, the best being the firmenny 010 with its morning arrival), Severobaikalsk (1/day, 40-42hrs), Vladivostok (1-2/day, 100-106hrs, the plushest being the firmenny 002 on odd days, and the equally fast 008 on even days). To Tomsk, there are two overnight trains on even days only (6hrs), with the 211 departure being marginally earlier.

On the **Turksib railway**, there are departures to Almaty, Kazakhstan (1-2/day, 39-40hrs) and Tashkent, Uzbekistan (Wed 1.53pm local time, 64hrs).

By air Most international and long-distance domestic flights use **Tolmachevo airport** (💻 www.tolmachevo.ru has a timetable) while the much smaller **Severny airport** handles a decreasing amount of domestic air traffic.

You can buy plane tickets at the large **air-ticket office** Авиакасса (Aviakassa) at ul Gogolya 3 in the city centre (daily 9am-6pm).

There are several daily flights to Moscow (4hrs) with Transaero and Siberian Airlines. Other well-served destinations include St Petersburg, Vladivostok, Yekaterinburg, Beijing, Frankfurt (on Saturdays) and Tashkent.

EXCURSIONS FROM NOVOSIBIRSK

Museum of Railway Technology

This large open-air **museum** (Музей Железнодорожной Техники; 💻 www.parovoz.com, 11am-5pm Tue-Sun, entry R250, camera R70) contains an impressive display of locomotives, most of which have worked on the Western Siberian railway, and carriages, including some of the first used on the Trans-Siberian Railway. This is one of just three such museums in Russia (the other two being in St Petersburg and Rostov-na-Donu) and there are over 100 exhibits, including 12 locomotives, sitting there, spruced up and proud. You can take a peek inside some of the exhibits, though most can only be viewed from the outside.

The museum is at **Seyatel Сеятель**, 25km from Novosibirsk on the road to Akademgorodok; take any Akademgorodok-bound bus (No 36, 38, 52, 65, 121, 1129, R30) and get off at the Klinika Meshalkina (Клиника Мешалкина) stop; you can't miss the museum on your left. An easier way is to take one of 11 suburban trains daily to/from Seyatel (R40), though not many run between 10am and 2pm.

❑ Akademgorodok (Академгородок)

Akademgorodok, 30km from Novosibirsk, was established in the 1950s as a university and research centre for scientists. The forested, lakeside setting offers a relaxing opportunity to get away from polluted Novosibirsk, and the town, with its badly maintained buildings and a rather melancholic atmosphere, is a Soviet relic which hints at the old Soviet utopian dream.

Soon after its foundation it grew into an élite township of over 30,000 of the Soviet Union's top intellectuals and their families. In this pleasant sylvan setting researchers and students grappled with scientific problems with a two-fold aim: to push ahead of the West in the arms race and to harness the wealth of Siberia for the good of the USSR. As with its Olympic athletes, the Soviet Union believed in training its academics from a very early age, spiriting them away from home to attend special boarding schools for the gifted in Akademgorodok. Compared to the ordinary citizen they were well looked after here, the shops stocked with little luxuries hard to find elsewhere.

As government funding slowed to a trickle in the early 1990s the utopian dream ended and many scientists were lured abroad. The university still has a good reputation and since 1988 funding has been on the rise. With its high concentration of brain power, Akademgorodok, also known as the 'silicon taiga', is becoming an important centre of Russia's burgeoning software and IT sector.

South of Akademgorodok through the birch forest and over the railway track lie the **beaches** of the **Obskoye Morye** ('Ob Sea'), the vast reservoir created by the construction of the Novosibirskaya power station, Siberia's first large hydroelectric project.

Should you wish to visit either, many Akademgorodok-bound buses run either from the main bus station (Avtovokzal) or from the **M** Rechnoy Vokzal. Alternatively, several suburban trains per day stop at 'Obskoye Morye'.

Tomsk
Томск

[Moscow Time +3] A university town with some finely preserved wooden 'lace' architecture, Tomsk is 270km north-east of Novosibirsk and easily reached by overnight trains from Omsk and Krasnoyarsk from the main Trans-Siberian line.

Founded in 1604 on the River Tom, Tomsk developed into a large administrative, trading and gold-smelting centre on the Great Siberian Post Road. For a time it was the most important place in Siberia, visited by almost every 19th-century traveller. The city was an important exile centre and had a large forwarding prison. Having almost succumbed to the stench from the overcrowded cells in 1887, Kennan wrote: 'If you visit the prison my advice to you is to breakfast heartily before starting, and to keep out of the hospital wards.'

Tomsk was bypassed by the original Trans-Siberian railway, and began to lose out to stations along the main line. But it remains a robust city of 480,000 people, administrative capital of Tomskaya Oblast and a centre for industrial engineering. There's an intellectual and open atmosphere that's hard to find elsewhere in Siberia, and while it's very laid back, Tomsk will surprise you with the sophistication of its restaurants and nightlife.

WHAT TO SEE AND DO

It's rewarding to simply wander and check out the fine old wooden homes, especially along ul Krasnoarmenskaya, though it's sad to see so many that are burnt out or buckling over. At No 71 is the vivid blue **Russian-German House** Российско-Немецкий Дом, with elaborate white ornamentation. Down the street at No 68 is **Dragon House** Дом Дракона, with stylised dragons over the door and more sprouting from the roof. At No 67a is another beauty, **Peacock House** Дом Павлина, though it's not as well preserved. No 51 looks as if it's being restored one window-frame at a time. There are also some stately homes along ul Gagarina and ul Tatarskaya, as well as **Shushkin House** Дом Шушкина at ul Shishkova 10.

The city's **World War II Memorial** Памятник/Лагерный Сад in the attractive Lagerny Gardens at the southern end of pr Lenina is truly impressive, including music piped from endless rows of eerie beech trees. Don't miss the view over the river at the back.

Walking up pr Lenina from Lagerny Gardens you pass the **University Grounds** Университет, well worth a stroll, with a handsome white colonnaded building as their centrepiece. Opposite Troitsky skver, where you find the world's largest rouble made of wood, is the **Memorial Museum** Мемориальный Музей (2-6pm Mon-Fri, R40), housed in a former KGB office at pr Lenina 44 (enter

WHERE TO STAY
- 3 Magistrat Hotel Гостиница Магистрат
- 4 Hotel Toyan Гостиница Тоян
- 12 Hotel Sibir Гостиница Сибирь
- 19 Hotel Sputnik Гостиница Спутник

WHERE TO EAT AND DRINK
- 1 Traktir Zolotaya Dolina Трактир Золотая Долина
- 3 Restaurant Parmesan Ресторан Пармезан
- 4 Stonebridge
- 7 Osh Ош
- 8 Café Bulanzhe Кафе Буланже
- 9 Restaurant Stariy Zamok Ресторан Старый Замок
- 13 Perchini Перчини
- 15 Jazz Café Джаз Кафе
- 18 Sibirsky Pub Сибирский Паб

PLACES OF INTEREST
- 2 Epiphany Cathedral Богоявленский Собор
- 5 Tomsk History Museum Томский Исторический Музей
- 6 Shushkin House Дом Шушкина
- 10 Art Museum Художественный Музей
- 14 Atashev Palace & Regional Museum Дворец Аташева & Краеведческий Музей
- 16 Memorial Museum Мемориальный Музей
- 17 Monument to Victims of Stalinist Repressions Памятник Жертвам Сталинских Репрессий
- 20 Dragon House Дом Дракона
- 21 Peacock House Дом Павлина
- 22 Russian-German House Российско-Немецкий Дом
- 24 University Университет
- 26 World War II Memorial/Lagerny Gardens Памятник/Лагерный Сад

OTHER
- 11 Post Office/internet Почта/Интернет
- 23 Tomsk Tourist Томск Турист
- 25 Netcafé

around the back), and dedicated to the victims of the Communist regime. It includes actual interrogation chambers, a model of a prison camp, maps of the Gulag system, a slew of documents and many haunting photos. Unfortunately there's no English captioning and tours are in Russian only. By the museum you'll find two **Monuments to Victims of Stalinist Repressions** Памятник Жертвам Сталинских Репрессий – the larger one to Russians and the smaller to Poles.

Nearby **Atashev Palace & Regional Museum** Дворец Аташева & Краеведческий Музей (pr Lenina 75, 10am-6pm Wed-Sun, R40) features interesting local history exhibits as well as separately priced temporary ones, the most recent one being the extremely worthwhile microminiature exhibition.

Further along, at per Nakhanovicha 5, is the **Art Museum** Художественный Музей (10am-5.30pm Tue-Sun, R75), featuring works by local artists.

Passing the messy, shapeless pl Lenina, presided over by a Lenin statue that seems to be directing the traffic, you reach **Tomsk History Museum** Томский Исторический Музей (ul Bakunina 3, 11am-5pm Tue-Sun, R25). It has some fairly interesting local history exhibits, but actually the view from the top of the wooden tower alone is worth the price of admission.

PRACTICAL INFORMATION

Orientation and services

Tomsk's railway and bus stations are next to each other about 2km south-east of the centre. Running north–south near the Tom River, pr Lenina is the city's main artery. Pick up a bus route map from the kiosk in front of the station.

The **post office** Почта is in the centre of town at pr Lenina 95 (9am-7.30pm Mon-

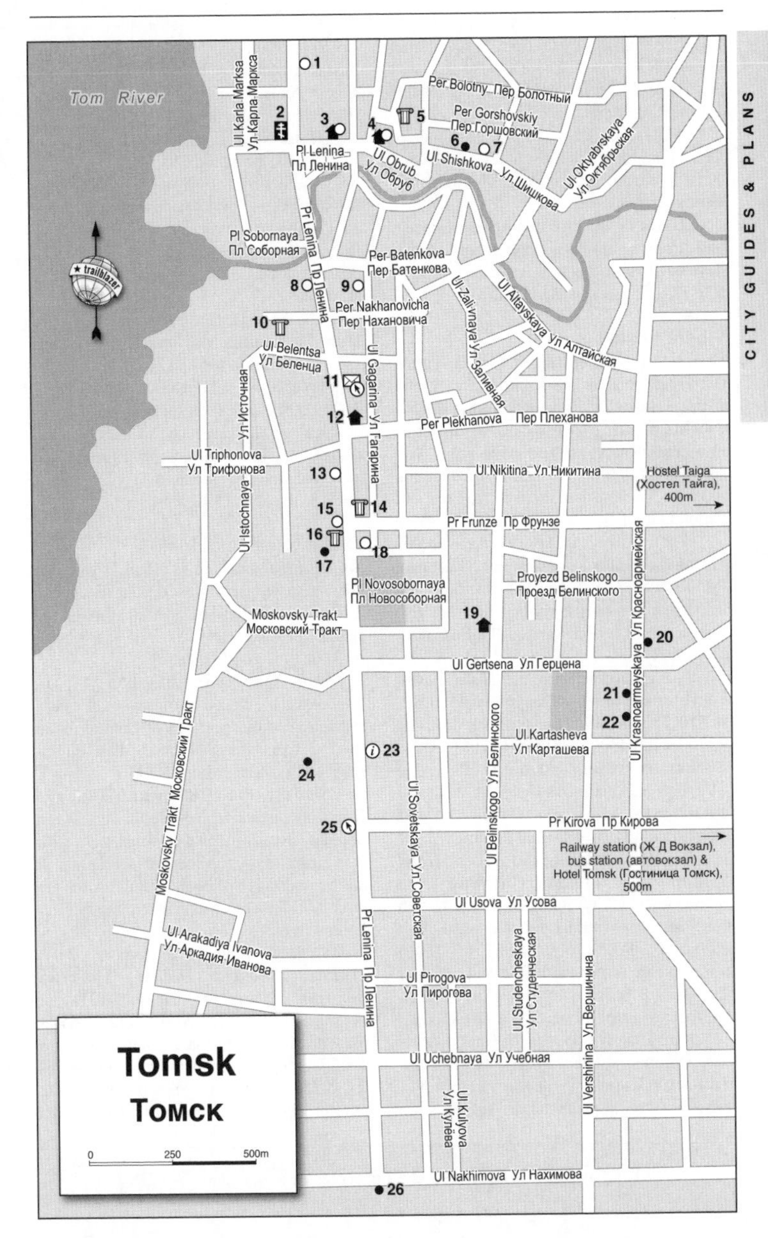
Tomsk
Томск
0
250
500m
Tom River
Ul Karla Marksa
Ул Карла Маркса
Per Bolotny Пер Болотный
Per Gorshovskiy
Пер Горшовский
Pl Lenina
Пл Ленина
Ul Obrub
Ул Обруб
Ul Shishkova Ул Шишкова
Ul Oktyabrskaya
Ул Октябрьская
Pl Sobornaya
Пл Соборная
Pr Lenina Пр Ленина
Per Batenkova
Пер Батенкова
Ul Zalivnaya Ул Заливная
Ul Altayskaya Ул Алтайская
Per Nakhanovicha
Пер Нахановича
Ul Belentsa
Ул Беленца
Ul Gagarina Ул Гагарина
Per Plekhanova Пер Плеханова
Ul Triphonova
Ул Трифонова
Ul Istochnaya Ул Источная
Ul Nikitina Ул Никитина
Hostel Taiga
(Хостел Тайга),
400m
Pr Frunze Пр Фрунзе
Proyezd Belinskogo
Проезд Белинского
Pl Novosobornaya
Пл Новособорная
Moskovsky Trakt
Московский Тракт
Ul Gertsena Ул Герцена
Ul Krasnoarmeyskaya Ул Красноармейская
Ul Kartasheva
Ул Карташева
Ul Belinskogo Ул Белинского
Ul Sovetskaya Ул Советская
Moskovsky Trakt Московский Тракт
Pr Kirova Пр Кирова
Railway station (Ж Д Вокзал),
bus station (автовокзал) &
Hotel Tomsk (Гостиница Томск),
500m
Ul Usova Ул Усова
Ul Arakadiya Ivanova
Ул Аркадия Иванова
Ul Pirogova
Ул Пирогова
Ul Studencheskaya
Ул Студенческая
Ul Vershinina Ул Вершинина
Ul Uchebnaya Ул Учебная
Ul Kulyova
Ул Кулёва
Ul Nakhimova Ул Нахимова
trailblazer
1 2 3 4 5 6 7 8 9 10 11 12 13 14 15 16 17 18 19 20 21 22 23 24 25 26

Fri, 8am-5pm Sat, 9am-5pm Sun; internet access R30/hour) There's also internet access at **Netcafé**, pr Lenina 32 (9am-11pm; R30/hour).

ATMs are easy to find around pr Lenina, including in most hotels and banks. Most banks cash **travellers' cheques**, and **change money**.

Tours of the city in English, German and French are available from **Tomsk Tourist** Томск Турист (pr Lenina 59, ☎ 531 723, 💻 www.tomskturist.ru).

Where to stay

Bright little ***Hostel Taiga*** **Хостел Тайга** (ул Никитина 56, ul Nikitina 56, ☎ 504 218, 💻 hostel@vtomske.ru, dorm R450) consists of just two spick-and-span dorms in a central location, and a reception with super-helpful bilingual staff. No common room or kitchen, but there is free tea and coffee and wi-fi.

The railway station ***resting rooms*** **комнаты отдыха** (*komnaty otdykha*) cost R450 for a bed in a four-person room and R560 in a two-person room. There are also 'lux' doubles for R2200 and 'halflux' doubles for R1600.

Plush, modern business ***Hotel Toyan*** **Гостиница Тоян** (ул Обруб 2, ul Obrub 2, ☎ 510 151, 💻 www.toyan.ru, sgl/dbl/suite R3700-4700/4300-5500/6700-8700) boasts spacious rooms with dark brick walls, cable TV, wi-fi and luxurious baths, as well as a gastropub (Stonebridge) next door. The staff are particularly friendly and helpful.

Popular with business travellers, ***Hotel Sputnik*** **Гостиница Спутник** (ул Белинского 15, ul Belinskogo 15, ☎ 526 660, 💻 http://sputnik.tomskturist.ru, sgl/dbl/suite R920-1600/2400/2700-3500) offers clean rooms with TV and internet access. Full board is available on request; cheaper twin/trpl rooms cost R920/850pp.

Immediately opposite the bus and railway stations is ***Hotel Tomsk*** **Гостиница Томск** (пр Кирова 65, pr Kirova 65, ☎ 544 115, 💻 www.tomskhotel.ru, sgl/dbl/suite from R3200/3600/5000), a comfortable business option with sauna, solarium and fitness centre, though it's a bus ride away from all the attractions.

Hotel Sibir **Гостиница Сибирь** (пр Ленина 91, pr Lenina 91, ☎ 527 225, 💻 www.hotelsibir.tomsk.ru, sgl/dbl/suite R2500/2500/4200-4500) is centrally located and has a sauna and swimming pool. Rooms are wi-fi enabled. Ask for a room that doesn't face the street, which is noisy at night.

The top choice is the four-star ***Magistrat Hotel*** **Гостиница Магистрат** (пл Ленина 15, pl Lenina 15, ☎ 511 111, 💻 www.magistrathotel.com, sgl/dbl/suite R4900/5900/7100-8900), in a fully renovated neo-classical building with one of the city's top restaurants. The staff are professional and bilingual and the spacious, stylish rooms come with cable TV and internet.

Where to eat and drink

Stonebridge, attached to Hotel Toyan (see Where to stay), serves decent European dishes in an English pub setting, though the steaks get mixed reviews. The R200 business lunch is good value.

Osh **Ош** (ул Шишкова 14, ul Shishkova 14, closed Sun) is a small eatery serving generous portions of Central Asian food. Expect massive meat-filled dumplings and pastries. Mains R200.

Sibirsky Pub **Сибирский Паб** (ул Новособорная 2, ul Novosobornaya 2) is a popular, British-themed establishment with live music that's too loud on weekends. It has a good range of beers, though some are pricey (Guinness costs R300); happy hour noon-4.30pm.

Serving hungry customers 24/7, ***Traktir Zolotaya Dolina*** **Трактир Золотая Долина** (пр Ленина 121a, pr Lenina 121a, next to TSUM) serves shashlik with rice, soups, salads and more in a rustic setting. Order at the counter. Mains R150-250. With its chrome-and-white interior, ***Perchini*** **Перчини** (пр Ленина

The Tomsk area code is ☎ 3822. From outside Russia dial +7-3822.

54a, pr Lenina 54a) attracts the trendy with its selection of delicious pizza and pasta as well as Russian dishes. Service can be hit-and-miss but the cocktails are good. Mains R250-350.

Excellent Georgian, Armenian and Turkish dishes are on offer at ***Restaurant Stariy Zamok*** **Ресторан Старый Замок** (ул Гагарина 11a, ul Gagarina 11a). The 'rustic' interior is cosy, there's attractive courtyard seating in summer and the shashlyk is among the best in the city. Mains from R380.

Jazz Café Underground **Джаз Кафе** (пр Ленина 46, pr Lenina 46) is a stylish underground venue with good live music, mute black-and-white films and excellent service. There's an extensive food and drink menu; mains R350.

Ever-popular ***Café Bulanzhe*** **Кафе Буланже** (пр Ленина 80, pr Lenina 80) is an excellent spot for coffee and cakes. The blini (from R55) are particularly tasty and there are two more branches in town, including at ul Krasnoarmeyskaya 107.

For excellent service within elegant surroundings, and the best Italian food in the city, head for ***Restaurant Parmesan*** **Ресторан Пармезан** (inside Magistrat Hotel). Unless you go for the pizza (R550), count on at least R1500 per person for a full meal with antipasto.

Moving on

By rail There are departures to Moscow (firmenny 037 *Tomich*, odd days only, departing at 11.11am local time, 56½hrs), Novosibirsk (1/day, 5-6hrs), Krasnoyarsk (1/day, 13½-14hrs) and Omsk (1/day, 14½-15½hrs).

By bus There are numerous buses to Novosibirsk (R450, 5½hrs), which are a more flexible option than the train, leaving every hour. Minibuses also ply the same route for R900 or so (3½-4hrs).

By air There are three daily flights from Tomsk to Moscow, two flights a week to Yekaterinburg and three to Novosibirsk and Omsk from Tomsk's Bopgashevo Airport (💻 www.airport.tomsk.ru – in Russian). Tickets are available at the Central Air Ticket Office beside the Passazh Department Store at ul Lenina 46.

Krasnoyarsk
Красноярск

[Moscow Time +4] Nestled among commanding hills and cliffs along the Yenisey River, Krasnoyarsk is certainly more pleasantly located than many Siberian cities. While its architecture isn't its distinguishing feature, the city does boast some of the best cultural life in the region and the nearby natural attraction of the Stolby Nature Reserve (see pp271-2) makes Krasnoyarsk an excellent place for a stopover.

Russian settlement dates back to the construction of Krasny Yar fort on a hill overlooking the River Yenisey in 1628. By 1900 the population was 27,000 and the town boasted 20 churches and two cathedrals, a synagogue, 26 schools, a railway technical college and a botanical garden reputed to be the finest in Siberia.

RL Jefferson (see pp94-5) visited Krasnoyarsk in 1897 and was impressed: 'Its situation cannot fail to elicit admiration – the tall mountains rear up around it.' Most of the townsfolk he met here were ex-convicts. So used were they to their own kind that they were particularly suspicious of anyone who lacked a criminal record. He was told of a certain merchant in the city who found it difficult to do business, never having been behind bars. To remedy the situation this merchant is said to have travelled back to St Petersburg and deliberately committed a crime punishable by exile to Siberia. After a short sentence in Irkutsk he returned to his business in Krasnoyarsk and 'got on famously' thereafter.

During WWII many factories were relocated here from European Russia. The city grew as a trading centre and in the course of the Soviet Union's early five-year plans underwent massive industrialisation to become Siberia's third largest city, now with a population of about 910,000.

General Alexander Lebed, the late army hardliner, was a local governor. In the 1996 presidential elections Lebed challenged Boris Yeltsin but finally stood down and supported him, earning Yeltsin's backing for his own election campaign in Krasnoyarsk.

WHAT TO SEE AND DO

Housed rather oddly in a building resembling an Egyptian temple, the large **Museum of Regional Studies** Краеведческий Музей (ul Dubrovinskogo 84, Tue-Sun 10am-6pm, until 7pm in summer, adult/student R100/40) is a must-see for its excellent ethnographic exhibits, with shamanic ritual dress and objects. Also here are interactive displays of Siberian fauna, where you can press a button by each one to listen to the distinctive bird calls and animal cries. Other displays include Christian and Buddhist relics, and a full-size replica of a Cossack riverboat; there are several multi-lingual interactive points within the museum where you can learn more about the history and culture of the region. There's a good gift shop selling tsarist coins and medals.

Born in Krasnoyarsk, Vasily Surikov (1848-1916) is the best-known painter of grand Russian historical subjects (such as the *Conquest of Siberia by Yermak*, now in St Petersburg). **Surikov Estate Museum** Музей Сурикова (Tue-Sat 10am-5.30pm, R70) is in the 19th-century wooden house at ul Lenina 98 alongside a peaceful garden. The worthwhile **Krasnoyarsk VI Surikov Art Museum** has two branches: one at ul Karla Marksa 36 (10am-6pm Tue-Sun, R70), where you can see Surokov's works, and the other at pr Mira 12 (10am-6pm Tue-Sun, R50), with changing exhibitions by 20th-century artists.

By the waterfront you'll find the excellent **Krasnoyarsk Museum of Culture and History** Красноярский Музей Культуры и Истории (pl Mira 1, 💻 www.mira1.ru, 11am-7pm Tue-Sun, adult/student R100/50), which hosts exciting temporary exhibitions by cutting-edge young artists. The permanent exhibitions include Lenin's personal effects (since the building formerly housed the Lenin Museum), 'The War Diaries' focusing on the involvement of Russian troops in the Afghan and Chechen conflicts, and 'The Communist Guide to New York'. In front of the museum, moored on the Yenisey, is ***SS Nikolay*** Пароход «Св Николай», the steamship on which Lenin sailed to exile in Shushenkoye, which is now a museum itself (10am-8pm daily, R50).

The terraced hill around the old part of town is an interesting place for a walk. The restored **Annunciation Cathedral** Благовещенский Собор, on ul

Lenina, is worth visiting. The old **Catholic Church** Католическая Церковь, which contains an organ, is near the Central Park.

The tiny **Chapel of St Paraskeva Pyatnitsa** Часовня Святой Великомученницы Параскевы Пятницы – well known throughout the country as it appears on the R10 note – stands above the city and there are good views from here. It takes about 40 minutes to reach it from Hotel Krasnoyarsk (see p270).

PRACTICAL INFORMATION

Orientation and services

Krasnoyarsk has two parts, separated by the Yenisey River. The northern bank is a mass of terraces and is bounded on the north by a steep hill known as Karaulnaya Mountain and on the west by the forested Gremyachinskaya Ridge. The railway station, museums and hotels are on this side. Just south of the station is the academic area (another Akademgorodok). The southern bank is relatively flat and is mostly factories and multi-storey apartment blocks.

Going strong since 1996, **Sib Tour Guide** (☎ 251 2654, 🖳 www.sibtourguide.com) is run by the knowledgeable, English-speaking Anatoliy Brewhanov, who can also arrange homestays. It's recommended for city tours, tours to Stolby (see p271), the hydroelectric dam and Yenisey discovery tours on the river.

There's an **ATM** in Hotel Krasnoyarsk (see p270), along ul Karla Marksa, and at the railway station.

Internet is available on the 1st floor of the central library (10am-7pm Mon-Fri, until 6pm Sat) for R70/hour.

Local transport

For the airport catch bus No 135 from the **bus station** (R60) or take a taxi (R1500). From the railway station, buses No 1, 37, 55 and 56 go along ul Karla Marksa, while ul Lenina is served by buses No 77 and 81, as well as trolleybus No 7. Public transport tickets cost R14 per ride.

Where to stay

HOFA (see p153) and **Sib Tour Guide** (see Orientation and services) offer **homestays**.

The railway station ***resting rooms*** **комнаты отдыха** (*komnaty otdykha*, sgl 'lux'/4-person R2672/543 for 24hrs) are a good overnight option.

Aimed at business travellers, efficient ***Dom Hotel*** **Дом Отель** (ул Красной Армии 16а, ul Krasnoi Armii 16a, ☎ 290 6666, 🖳 www.dom-hotel24.ru, sgl/dbl from R4000/4500) has modern rooms with orthopaedic mattresses, internet access and cable TV. The on-site gastropub has an extensive array of dishes for meat lovers; the buffet breakfast costs extra.

North of the railway station, ***MiniOtel 24*** **МиниОтель 24** (ул Куйбышева 97, ul Kuybysheva 97, ☎ 226 8899, 🖳 www.miniotel24.ru, dbl R1700-3800, apartment for four R3200) has something for everyone – from clean basic rooms with shared bathroom to an apartment with its own kitchen. Breakfast costs extra but there's free wi-fi on the ground floor.

A good budget option in the centre, ***Hotel Sever*** **Гостиница Север** (ул Ленина 121, ul Lenina 121, ☎ 266 2266, 🖳 www.sever.krasland.ru, single with shared bathroom R700/en suite double from R1700) has clean, basic rooms, the pricier ones come with their own bathroom, whereas the budget range have sinks and fridges but you must pay extra for breakfast. If travelling with a group of friends, it might be worth getting the 5-person room for R2000 or the 6-person room for R2220.

The Krasnoyarsk area code is ☎ 391. From outside Russia dial +7-391.

Krasnoyarsk
Красноярск
0
750m
trailblazer
River Yenisey
Ul Ostrovnaya Ул Островная
Ul Karatanova Ул Каратанова
Ul Dubrovinskogo Ул Дубровинского
Ul 9 Yanvarya Ул 9 Января
Ul Parizhskoi Komunny Ул Парижской Комунны
Ul Surikova Ул Сурикова
Ul Veynbauma Ул Вейнбаума
Ul Perensona Ул Перенсона
Ul Kirova Ул Кирова
Ul Diktatury Proletariya Ул Диктатуры Пролетариата
Ul Dzerzhinskogo Ул Дзержинского
Ul Lebedevoy Ул Лебедевой
Ul Krasnoi Armii Ул Красной Армии
Ul Gorkogo Ул Горкого
Ul Dekabristov Ул Декабристов
Ul Robespyera Ул Робеспьера
Ul Respubliki Ул Республики
Ul Lenina Ул Ленина
Prospect Mira Проспект Мира
Ul Karla Marksa Ул Карла Маркса
Ul Uritskogo Ул Урицкого
Ul Bograda Ул Бограда
Ul Oborony Ул Обороны
Ul Bryanskaya Ул Брянская
Ul Igarskaya Ул Игарская
Ul Konstitutsii Ул Конституции
Ul Zheleznodorozhnikov Ул Железнодорожников
Ul Profsoyuzov Ул Профсоюзов
Bus station (Автовокзал), 2km
MiniOtel24 (МиниОтель24), 300m
People's Grill Bar & Madagascar, 200m, Stolby Nature Reserve (Заповедник Столбы) & Divnogorsk (Дивногорск)
Pl Revolutsii Пл Революции
Pl Teatralnaya Пл Театральная
Central Park Центральный Парк
Krasnaya Pl
1 2 3 4 5 6 7 8 9 10 11 12 13 14 15 16 17 18 19 20 21 22 23 24 25 26 27 28 29 30 31 32 33 34 35 36 37 38 39 40
$

WHERE TO STAY
4 Dom Hotel Дом Отель
8 Hotel Sever Гостиница Север
16 Resting rooms Комнаты Отдыха
21 Hotel Krasnoyarsk Гостиница Красноярск
32 Hotel Oktyabrskaya Гостиница Октябрьская
33 Hotel Metelitsa Отель Метелица

WHERE TO EAT AND DRINK
3 Central Market Центральный Рынок
5 Syem Slona Съем Слона
6 Chemodan Чемодан
10 Shkvarok Шкварок
12 James Shark Pub
14 Che Guevara Че Гевара
17 Traveller's Coffee
19 Matryoshka Матрёшка
20 Santa Fe Санта Фе
22 Munchen Pub Мюнхен Паб
27 Wasabi Васаби
30 Kabinet Кабинетъ
35 Pertsy Перцы
36 Burzhuy Pelmen Bar Буржуй Пельмень-бар

PLACES OF INTEREST
1 Chapel of St Paraskeva Pyatnitsa Часовня Святой Великомученницы Параскевы Пятницы
2 Trinity Church Троицкая Церковь
7 Surikov Estate Museum Музей Сурикова
11 Lenin Statue Памятник Ленину
13 Catholic Church Католическая Церковь
15 Palace of Culture of the Combine Harvester Builders Дворец Культуры Комбайностроителей
23 Opera & Ballet Theatre Театр Оперы и Балета
24 Museum of Regional Studies Краеведческий Музей
29 Intercession Church Покровская Церковь
31 Krasnoyarsk V I Surikov Art Museum Красноярский Художественый Музей имени В И Сурикова
34 Annunciation Cathedral Благовещенский Собор
37 Krasnoyarsk V I Surikov Art Museum Красноярский Художественый Музей имени В И Сурикова
38 Main Concert Hall Большой Концертный Зал
39 Krasnoyarsk Museum of Culture and History Красноярский Музей Культуры и Истории
40 *SS Nikolay* Пароход «Св. Николай»

OTHER
9 Bilet Market Билетный киоск
16 Railway Station Железнодорожный Вокзал
18 Central Library & Internet Центральная библиотека и Интернет
21 ATM (in Hotel Krasnoyarsk)
25 Boats to Divnogorsk
26 River Station Речной Вокзал
28 Central Post Office Почтамт

STALINIST-GOTHIC
RIVER STATION
KRASNOYARSK

Centrally located ***Hotel Krasnoyarsk*** **Гостиница Красноярск** (ул Уритского 94, ul Uritskogo 94, ☎ 274 9420, 💻 www.hotelkrs.ru, sgl/dbl/suite from R3460/4940/6300) may not immediately sway you with the Soviet charm of its exterior, but all the rooms are fully renovated and come with all mod cons, including wi-fi, though only the priciest have air-con. The sauna and swimming pool are bonuses.

The most luxurious hotel in the city centre, ***Hotel Metelitsa*** **Гостиница Метелица** (пр Мира 14/1, pr Mira 14/1, ☎ 227 6060, 💻 www.hotel-metelica.ru, sgl/dbl/suite from R3585/4585/7985) has plush, tastefully decorated rooms with plasma satellite TV, wi-fi and fresh fruit brought daily. Guests have use of the excellent sauna and the price includes a good breakfast. The on-site restaurant serves a plethora of European dishes and has a separate sushi menu.

One of the best hotels in town, the three-star ***Hotel Oktyabrskaya*** **Гостиница Октябрьская** (пр Мира 15, pr Mira 15, ☎ 227 3780, 💻 www.hoteloctober.ru, sgl/dbl from R3900/4400) has modern rooms with satellite TV and helpful, professional staff, some of whom speak English.

Where to eat and drink

The square in front of Hotel Krasnoyarsk (see above) has many cafés and is a lively place on summer evenings. You can also pick up fresh produce and all kinds of snacks at the large **central market Центральный Рынок**.

Matryoshka **Матрёшка** (ул Карла Маркса 95, ul Karla Marksa 95, mains R200) is a bright, cheerful eatery decorated in rustic style, serving tasty blini, good soups and nicely presented mains.

Burzhuy Pelmen Bar **Буржуй Пельмень-бар** (пр Мира 10, 2-й этаж, pr Mira 10, 2nd floor, mains R150) is an inexpensive eatery where you can fill up on tasty pelmeni and other Russian favourites.

Nearby, ***Pertsy*** **Перцы** (пр Мира 10, pr Mira 10, mains R350) serves good thin-and-crispy pizza and homemade pasta dishes in a stylish setting.

For good sushi and sashimi head for ***Wasabi*** **Васаби** (пр Мира 45, pr Mira 45). Their business lunch is good value and they sometimes have an all-you-can-eat-sushi special.

Syem Slona **Съем Слона** ('I Can Eat an Elephant'; ул Красной Армии 14, ul Krasnoi Armii 14, mains R250) is a good cafeteria-type chain where you can gorge yourself on inexpensive Russian dishes.

Traveller's Coffee (ул Карла Маркса 135, ul Karla Marksa 135) is the Russian equivalent of Starbucks, with prices to match. Expect light, comfortable surroundings, good cakes, excellent coffee, and slow, relaxed service. There's another branch at pr Mira 54.

Kabinet **Кабинетъ** (пр Мира 19, pr Mira 19) is an upscale restaurant specialising in quality Russian dishes.

Shkvarok **Шкварок** (пр Мира 102, pr Mira 102, mains R300) serves tasty Ukrainian cuisine; don't miss their *vareniki* (cherry-filled dumplings) or the *golubtsy* (cabbage leaves stuffed with meat and rice).

For quality steak, head for ***Santa Fe*** **Санта Фе** (ул Уритского 94, ul Uritskogo 94), an Argentinian joint specialising in grilled meats.

There's a classy watering hole at ***Chemodan*** **Чемодан** (ул Ленина 116, ul Lenina 116), serving Guinness and other Irish brews, as well as a dark Czech beer, in a 1940s atmosphere. Their food is delicious but pricey at about R650 per main course.

Munchen Pub **Мюнхен Паб** (ул Уритского 93, ul Uritskogo 93) is a good spot for a variety of German beers and pub grub, while ***James Shark Pub*** (ул Карла Маркса 155a, ul Karla Marksa 155a) is an excellent English pub with another branch in London. It has five types of own brew on tap, an extensive whisky and liqueur list and an imaginative menu, which includes smoked venison as a beer snack.

Che Guevara **Че Гевара** (ул Бограда, ul Bograda) has a fun Communist Cuban theme and live music, popular with the student crowd.

Directly across the river from the centre via Kommunalny Bridge you'll find a cluster of trendy bars including ***People's Grill-Bar*** and ***Madagascar Bar***.

Moving on

By rail Krasnoyarsk is served by all major Trans-Siberian and China-bound trains.

Westbound destinations include Novosibirsk (12/day, 12-16hrs, the best one being the overnight firmenny 085), Omsk (12/day, 20-29hrs, the 079 is a good option, originating in Krasnoyarsk), Yekaterinburg (6/day, 34-36hrs, the 349 being the only train that doesn't arrive in the middle of the night) and Moscow (6-7/day, 60-96hrs, the quickest option is the firmenny 055, even days only).

Eastbound destinations include Severobaikalsk (1-3/day, 26-33hrs), Tynda (up to 3/day, 53-65hrs) and Irkutsk (6/day, 18-26hrs, the best being the firmenny 010 on even days). For Tomsk, you can either take a long-distance train (1-2/day, 13-17hrs, the slower 481 is the better overnight option), or if there are no tickets available for direct trains, take any westbound train to Taiga and then catch a suburban train up to Tomsk (several daily, 2½hrs).

Tickets are available from **Bilet Market** Билетный киоск (ul Lenina 115; 8am-8pm Mon-Fri, until 7pm Sat & Sun).

By river Yenisey River is a major communications link and passenger ferries sail nearly 2000km along it from Krasnoyarsk. For three months in the summer boats go north to Dudinka or on to Dickson on the Arctic Ocean, a four- or five-day trip northbound and about a week coming back. However, at the time of writing, Dudinka and neighbouring Norilsk were closed to foreigners; even Russians needed to have a good reason to go there, so you could only go as far as Igarka. Tickets are available on the ground floor of the **river station** Речной Вокзал (☎ 227 4446, 8am-7pm). It's not usually necessary to book more than a few days in advance if you don't mind which class you travel in.

See box p272 for details about hydrofoil services to Divornogorsk.

By air Krasnoyarsk's Yemelyanovo-1 airport is 40km north of the railway station. There are daily flights to Moscow (5hrs) and several flights a week to Novosibirsk, Yekaterinburg, Khabarovsk and Yakutsk. There are also occasional charter flights to Hanover in Germany.

Tickets are available from Bilet Market (see By rail).

EXCURSIONS AROUND KRASNOYARSK

Stolby Nature Reserve Заповедник Столбы

Krasnoyarsk is particularly well-known for its vast 17,000-hectare recreational area, covered in forest and dotted with giant boulder formations known as **stolby** (pillars). There are over 100 formations in total, some of them up to 100m high, but the most popular walking route is the loop that takes in the 1st Stolb, Babka (Grandma), Ded (Grandpa), Perya (Feathers), Lviniye Vorota (Lion's Gates) and 4th Stolb formations. The park is very popular with locals who come here to picnic, stroll and go rock-climbing on the rock formations.

To get to the main part of the park it's a 7km gentle uphill walk from the main road; you can't miss it thanks to all the locals who are heading there. Halfway up the trail is an information booth where you can purchase a map of the park; it's a good idea unless you're here with knowledgeable locals as the park is criss-crossed with many (largely unmarked) trails and it's easy to get lost unless you stick to the main ones.

Take buses No 19, 50 78 or 106a from the Teatr Opery i Baleta (Театр Оперы и Балета) stop to the Turbaza (Турбаза) stop. Alternatively, if you don't want to do all that walking and still wish to see some of the Stolby, you can take bus No 37 to **Bobrovy Log Funpark** Фанпарк Бобровый Лог, which is a ski and snowboard resort in winter and a centre for zorbing and other extreme sports in summer. From here you can take the chairlift up to a viewpoint which gives you an expansive view of the rock formations and then you can walk to the impressive cluster of Takmak formations. Another option is to take a tour (see p267).

Divnogorsk Дивногорск

About 30km away on the railway past Stolby Nature Reserve is the town of Divnogorsk and the Yenisey Hydroelectric Dam. The 100m-high dam has a huge 'escalator', a kind of mobile basin mounted on a cog railway, to lift ships right over the dam. From a distance you can observe this unusual system operating until late October, when the river freezes over, as entry to the turbine rooms themselves is forbidden. **Hydrofoils** travel between Krasnoyarsk's river station and Divnogorsk from May to September, departing every two hours. The trip takes about 45 minutes and costs R300 return; buy your ticket on board. It's a 5km cab ride from the jetty to the dam itself.

To get to Divnogorsk, you can take marshrutka No 106a from the Opera and Ballet Theatre (Театр Оперы и Балета), a suburban train (3/day) to Divnogorsk (Дивногорск) station or else take a tour (see p267).

Irkutsk
Иркутск

[Moscow Time +5] Irkutsk is one of the most popular stops for Trans-Siberian travellers due to its proximity to Lake Baikal. In this city, which was once known as the 'Paris of Siberia', you'll find people rather more friendly and relaxed than those in European Russia. Along many of the streets you can still see the cosy-looking log cabins (eaves and windows decorated with intricate fretwork) which are typical of the Siberian style of domestic architecture.

Some 64km from Irkutsk is the incredible natural phenomenon of Lake Baikal, set within some of the world's most beautiful countryside. Trekking, camping, boat excursions, diving and riding are just a few of the pursuits available in this outdoor paradise.

HISTORY

Military outpost

Irkutsk was founded as a military outpost in 1652 by Ivan Pakhobov, a tax collector who had come to encourage the local Buryat tribesmen to pay their fur tribute. By 1686 a church had been built and a small town established on the banks of the Angara. Tea caravans from China passed through Irkutsk, fur-traders sold their pelts here and the town quickly developed into a centre for trade in Siberia.

By the beginning of the 19th-century Irkutsk was recognised as Siberia's administrative capital. The Governor, who lived in the elegant white building that still stands by the river (opposite the statue of Alexander III), presided over an area 20 times the size of France. Being the capital it was the destination of many exiled nobles from Western Russia. The most celebrated exiles were the Decembrists, who had attempted a coup against the tsar in St Petersburg in 1825.

Boom town

With the discovery of gold in the area in the early 19th century, 'Gold Fever' hit Irkutsk. Fortunes were made in a day and lost overnight in its gambling dens. In spite of a great fire in 1879 which destroyed 75% of its houses, the city had by the end of the century become the financial and cultural centre of Siberia. Its cosmopolitan population included fur traders, tea merchants, gold prospectors, exiles and ex-convicts. A few lucky prospectors became exceedingly rich, amassing personal fortunes equivalent to £70-80 million today. Often no more than illiterate adventurers, they spent their money on lavish houses, French tutors for their children and Parisian clothes for their wives.

By far the most exciting occasion in the Irkutskian social calendar for 1891 was the visit of the Tsarevich (later Nicholas II), who stayed only a day but had time to visit the museum, a gold-smelting laboratory and the monastery, to consecrate and open a pontoon bridge over the Angara (replaced only in 1936), to review the troops and to attend a ball.

The first rail travellers arrive

On 16 August 1898 Irkutsk was linked by rail to Europe with the arrival of the first Trans-Siberian train. The railway brought more European tourists than had dared venture into Siberia in the days when travelling meant weeks of discomfort bumping along the Trakt (the Post Road) in a wooden tarantass (carriage).

Their guidebooks warned them of the dangers awaiting them in Irkutsk. Bradshaw's *Through Routes to the Capitals of the World* (1903) had this to

How to get on in society

Travelling along the Trans-Siberian at the end of the 19th century, John Foster Fraser spent several days in Irkutsk. Recording his observations on the city's social order he wrote, 'To do things in the proper way and be correct and Western is, of course, the ambition of Irkutsk. So there is quite a social code. The old millionaires, who for forty years found Irkutsk society – such as it was before the coming of the railway – quite satisfied with a red shirt and a pair of greased top boots, are now 'out of it'. A millionaire only becomes a gentleman when he tucks in his shirt and wears his trousers outside and not inside his boots. It is etiquette to put on a black coat between the hours of ten in the morning and noon. No matter how sultry the evening is, if you go for the usual promenade and do not wear a black overcoat you proclaim you are unacquainted with the ways of good society. As to wealth, there is but one standard in Irkutsk. A man is known by his furs, and his wife by her furs and pearls'.

In Irkutsk Fraser was unimpressed by the standards of hygiene exhibited by all classes of society and declared that 'certainly the Russian is as sparing with water as though it were holy oil from Jerusalem'. **John Foster Fraser**, *The Real Siberia* (1902)

say: 'The streets are not paved or lighted; the sidewalks are merely boards on crosspieces over the open sewers. In summer it is almost impassable owing to the mud, or unbearable owing to the dust. The police are few, escaped criminals and ticket-of-leave criminals many. In Irkutsk and all towns east of it, the stranger should not walk after dark; if a carriage cannot be got as is often the case, the only way is to walk noisily along the planked walk; be careful in making crossings, and do not stop, or the immense mongrel mastiffs turned loose into the streets as guards will attack. To walk in the middle of the road is to court attack from the garrotters with which Siberian towns abound.' The dangers that Bradshaw warned his travellers against were no exaggeration for at the time the average number of reported murders per year in Irkutsk was over 400, out of a population of barely 50,000.

Irkutsk today

A city of about 594,500, Irkutsk is still one of the largest suppliers of furs to world markets, although engineering is now the main industry.

In the 2000 elections Putin polled just over 50% of votes in Irkutsk oblast. On a campaign visit to Irkutsk in February 2000 he highlighted the problems of the region: 'The economic successes of the oblast are modest... More than four million people live in extreme poverty'. He added that he wanted to encourage the creation of large companies able not only to extract the region's mineral resources but also to develop and sell them on Russian and world markets.

As of 2010, the aluminium plants and the oil pipeline to the north border of China have been completed, bringing new jobs to the region. It's now two

Shamanism

Shamanism is a primitive religion centred around the shaman, a medium and healer. Although the concept of the shaman is fairly common throughout the world, the word itself comes from the language of the Tungus tribes of Siberia.

Wearing spectacular robes, the shaman beats a drum and goes into a trance in order to communicate with the spirits. From them the shaman discovers the cause of an illness, the reason for the failure of the crops, a warning of some approaching disaster. Commonly, spirits are thought to select their shamans before they are born and brand them with distinguishing features: an extra finger or toe or a large birthmark. During their adolescence they may be 'tortured' by the spirits with an illness of some kind until they agree to act as shaman. Some shamans may be physically weak, epileptic, mentally disordered, but through their spiritual power they gain authority and perform rituals.

'Shamanism played an extremely negative role in the history of the Siberian peoples... In status, activity and interests, the shamans were hand in glove with the ruling cliques of the indigenous populations', wrote the Marxist anthropologists MG Levin and LP Potapov in *The Peoples of Siberia*. Other anthropologists have been less severe, noting that shamanism gave those with mental and physical disorders a place in society at a time when most other societies shunned the handicapped.

In the spirit of freedom of religious expression in Russia today shamanism is undergoing something of a revival, though it is difficult to find a high-ranking shaman, as they had all been executed during Stalinist times. The Republic of Tuva, west of Irkutsk, is the modern centre of Shamanism.

decades since the dawn of the market economy, and at least for some Irkutsk residents, the Siberian dream is coming true.

WHAT TO SEE AND DO

Cathedral of the Epiphany and around

Irkutsk in 1900 had two cathedrals. The splendid Cathedral of Our Lady of Kazan, bigger than Kazan Cathedral in St Petersburg, was damaged during the Civil War. It was demolished and now the ugly bulk of the **Central Government Headquarters** Дом Правительства stands in its place, opposite the **WWII Memorial**. Behind it, however, the 1706 boat-shaped **Church of our Saviour** Спасская Церковь features some interesting exterior frescoes which depict, from left to right, Buryats being baptised, Christ being baptised and the local bishop, Innocent, being canonised. The interior is rather plain, having housed a museum until a few years ago.

CHURCH OF OUR SAVIOUR (1706)

On the riverfront across the road, the restored **Cathedral of the Epiphany** Богоявленский Собор (1724) with its attractive green, white and pink towers is much more colourful by comparison. In the great fire of 1879 it was badly damaged and the heat was so intense that it melted one of the 12-ton bells. It served for a time as a museum of icons but is now a practising church again; the icons have been relocated to the Art Museum.

Polish Catholic Church Польский Костёл

Opposite the Church of Our Saviour is a Catholic church with a tall steeple. It is Siberia's only neo-Gothic church, built in 1883 by exiled Poles, and services are held on Sundays for their descendants.

During summer there are usually organ concerts on Sundays and Wednesdays, starting around 7.30pm.

Regional Museum Краеведческий Музей

This museum of local history (ul Karla Marksa 2, 10am-6pm Tue-Sun, R120) features a 'local achievements' gallery including a model of part of the BAM railway. Above the stairs is a panorama showing the Great Irkutsk Fire of 1879.

Ethnographic galleries downstairs include flints and bones from an archaeological site at nearby Malta, where evidence of human habitation has been found dating back 24,000 years; the inside of an early 20th-century settler's house with a carved wooden sideboard; a shaman's robes, antlers and drum; old photographs; and a most peculiar article of clothing: a suit made completely of fish skins, standard summer attire of the Goldi tribe who lived in the Far Eastern Territories.

Other places of worship

At the start of the 20th century Irkutsk boasted 58 places of worship. This fell to only three or four after the Revolution but many are now reopening.

Znamensky Monastery Знаменский Монастырь (Apparition of the Virgin), with its turquoise domes, lies north-east of the city. The frescoes inside are impressive but restoration left the interior looking rather modern. The casket containing the body of **St Innokent**, a Siberian missionary who died here in 1731, was returned to Irkutsk in the 1990s and may be moved to the cathedral when restoration there is complete. It is said that his body is incorruptible and has been the source of many miracles.

Beside the church are the graves of Yekaterina Trubetskaya (see below) and Gregory Shelekhov who founded the colony of Alaska in 1784 (sold to the USA in 1868). Shelekhov's grave is marked by an obelisk decorated with cartographic instruments. By the gate stands a controversial statue commemorating the White Russian Admiral Kolchak, erected in 2004. To get here, take trolleybus No 3 from the south end of pl Kirova.

It's also interesting to visit the old **synagogue** синагога, a large blue building at ul Karla Libknekhta 23, the lower storey of which has been converted into a factory. Enter through the door on the left with the three stars above it.

Art Museum Художественный Музей

Comprising works by 18th- and 19th-century Russian, German, Flemish, French, Italian and English painters, this collection (ul Lenina 5, 10am-5.30pm Tue-Sun, R120) was begun by Vladimir Sukachev in the 1870s and 'donated' to the city after the Revolution. There are Mongolian thangkas (Buddhist scroll paintings) and the inevitable modern Soviet masterpieces, such as AA Plastov's *Supper of Tractor Operators* and AV Moravov's *Calculating of Working Days*. The gallery devoted to 19th-century local scenes is particularly interesting; in the gallery of Western Art (15th-19th centuries) you'll find a small canvas labelled 'Landsir 1802-73' which is *The Family of Dogs* by Sir Edwin Landseer, who designed the lions in Trafalgar Square. Its extension gallery (ul Karla Marksa 23, 10am-6pm Tue-Sun, R120) has an interesting collection of 17th-century icons as well as Siberian landscapes.

Volkonsky House Museum Музей-усадьба Волконского

The large, attractive house of this famous Decembrist, whose wife Maria followed him into Siberian exile, is open to the public (per Volkonskogo 10, 10am-6pm Tue-Sun, R110). If you've read Caroline Sutherland's *The Princess of Siberia* then you must visit the house, a grand old building but sparsely furnished and without the lived-in feel of other house-museums. Displays include Maria's clothes, letters and furniture, beadwork, church robes of the 18th and 19th centuries and a very unusual piano.

Trubetskoy House Музей-усадьба Трубецкого

The wooden house (ul Dzerzhinskogo 64) once occupied by Sergey Trubetskoy and Yekaterina Trubetskaya and other nobles involved in the unsuccessful coup of 1825 was preserved as a museum, kept as it was when the exiles lived here. It was dismantled in 2007 in order to be renovated and though it was supposed to have reopened in 2009; a 2011, or even 2012, opening is looking more likely.

Trans-Siberian Builders' Monument
Памятник Строителям Транссибирской Магистрали

In 1900 the city duma commissioned a monument to commemorate the construction of the Trans-Siberian Railway. Designed by PP Bakh, it was made of Finnish red granite, topped by a statue of Tsar Alexander III, and included Yermak and Count Muravyev-Amursky on its sides and the double-headed Imperial eagle on the railings surrounding it.

In 1920 the statue of the tsar was removed and destroyed and it was not until 1964 that his replacement, a drab obelisk, was installed. In 2004, however, a reconstruction of the statue was returned to the plinth. Alexander looks north in the direction of the great railway line he founded in 1886.

Angara steamship Пароход «Ангара»

Moored near the Raketa hydrofoil terminal, the *Angara* (daily 9am-9pm, R45) commissioned in 1899, was partially assembled in England and then sent to Irkutsk in pieces by train. Until the completion of the Circumbaikal line she ferried rail passengers across the lake together with her bigger sister, the *Baikal*. Following the line's completion in 1904 the *Angara* performed a series of menial tasks before being abandoned, partially submerged, in 1958. She was later restored as a Museum of Nautical Navigation.

To get here, take trolleybus No 1, 5, 7, 8 or 10 which cross the river via the Angara dam.

River cruises

Rivers are navigable from mid-May to September. There are three river stations in Irkutsk, each for a different destination. For boats to Lake Baikal see p283.

PRACTICAL INFORMATION

Orientation and services

Irkutsk railway station is on the west bank of the river; the city centre and tourist hotels are on the east. The city centre is along two intersecting arteries, ul Lenina and the shopping and museum street, ul Karla Marksa; ul Lenina runs north-west from the administrative and public transport centre of pl Kirova.

Any bus or tram heading north from the railway station should take you over the bridge; from here all the main hotels are within walking distance.

A good starting place for **information** is 🖳 www.irkutsk.org, which has links to numerous other Irkutsk-related sites including internet cafés. You can get good **maps** of Irkutsk and the Baikal region from Hotel Baikal, or from **Knigomir bookshop** (ul Karla Marksa 28), where they also sell wall maps of Lake Baikal.

The **Mongolian Consulate** (ul Lapina 11, ☎ 3952 342 145, 9.30am-noon & 2.30-5pm Mon, Tue, Thur and Fri) issues both transit visas and 30-day visas; turnaround time is two business days. Bring a passport photo and your ticket out of Mongolia.

Communications The **Central Post Office** is at ul Karla Marksa 28. For long-distance calls, Sibir Telecom office is best. Most hotels and hostels offer **internet** and wi-fi, but you could also go to **Epicentr** (ul Bogdana Khmelnitskogo 1, 9am-10pm), a modern internet café that may be open 24/7 by the time you are here.

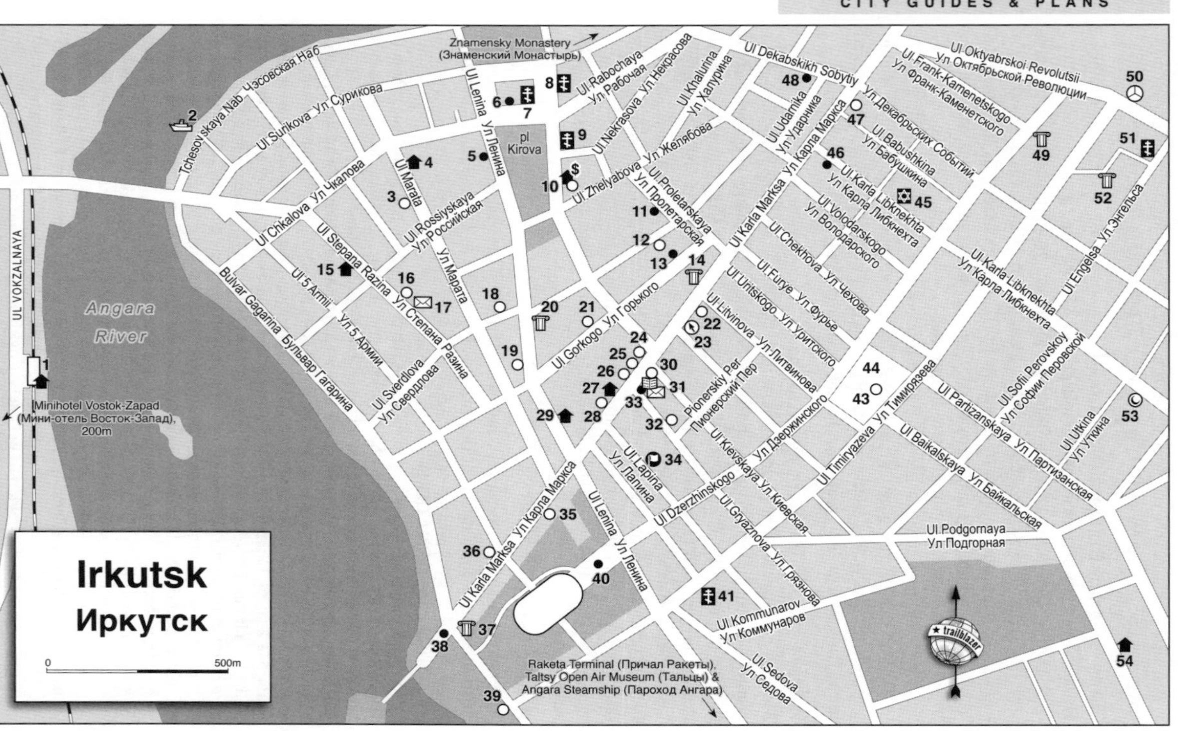
Irkutsk
Иркутск
0
500m
Angara River
Minihotel Vostok-Zapad (Мини-отель Восток-Запад), 200m
UL VOKZALNAYA
Tchesovskaya Nab Чусовская Наб
Ul Surikova Ул Сурикова
Ul Chkalova Ул Чкалова
Bulvar Gagarina Бульвар Гагарина
Ul 5 Armii Ул 5 Армии
Ul Stepana Razina Ул Степана Разина
Ul Sverdlova Ул Свердлова
Ul Marata Ул Марата
Ul Rossiyskaya Ул Российская
Ul Lenina Ул Ленина
Ul Karla Marksa Ул Карла Маркса
Ul Gorkogo Ул Горкого
Znamensky Monastery (Знаменский Монастырь)
pl Kirova
Ul Rabochaya Ул Рабочая
Ul Nekrasova Ул Некрасова
Ul Zhelyabova Ул Желябова
Ul Khalurina Ул Халурина
Ul Proletarskaya Ул Пролетарская
Ul Udarnika Ул Ударника
Ul Dekabskikh Sobytiy Ул Декабрьских Событий
Ul Chekhova Ул Чехова
Ul Furye Ул Фурье
Ul Uritskogo Ул Уритского
Ul Litvinova Ул Литвинова
Pionerskiy Per Пионерский Пер
Ul Dzerzhinskogo Ул Дзержинского
Ul Lapina Ул Лапина
Ul Kievskaya Ул Киевская
Ul Gryaznova Ул Грязнова
Ul Kommunarov Ул Коммунаров
Ul Sedova Ул Седова
Ul Timiryazeva Ул Тимирязева
Ul Volodarskogo Ул Володарского
Ul Karla Libknekhta Ул Карла Либкнехта
Ul Babushkina Ул Бабушкина
Ul Frank-Kamenetskogo Ул Франк-Каменецкого
Ul Oktyabrskoi Revolutsii Ул Октябрьской Революции
Ul Engelsa Ул Энгельса
Ul Sofii Perovskoy Ул Софии Перовской
Ul Partizanskaya Ул Партизанская
Ul Baikalskaya Ул Байкальская
Ul Utkina Ул Уткина
Ul Podgornaya Ул Подгорная
Raketa Terminal (Причал Ракеты), Taltsy Open Air Museum (Тальцы) & Angara Steamship (Пароход Ангара)
trailblazer

WHERE TO STAY
1 Resting Rooms Комнаты Отдыха
4 Baikal Explorer Hostel
10 Hotel Angara Гостиница Ангара
15 Irkutsk Downtown Hostel
27 Sayen International Hotel
29 Baikaler Hostel Байкалер
54 Hotel Yevropa Гостиница Европа

WHERE TO EAT AND DRINK
3 Bonjour
16 Wiener Café Венское Кафе
18 Double Coffee
19 Papa Johns
21 Kochevnik Кочевник
22 Café Snezhinka Кафе Снежинка
24 WasabiKo ВасабиКо
25 Supermarket Супермаркет
26 Marciano Restaurant Ресторан Марциано
28 Kyoto Киото
30 Supermarket Супермаркет
32 Krendel Креньдель
35 Ca:fe Ка:фе
36 Yefimych Ефимич
43 Chudo-Blyudo Чудо-Блюдо
44 Central Market Центральнный Рынок

BARS AND NIGHTCLUBS
10 London Pub
12 Liverpool Ливерпуль
26 Stratosfera Стратосфера
33 Bier Haus
39 Akula Акула
47 U Shveyka У Швейка

PLACES OF INTEREST
6 Central Government Headquarters Дом Правительства
7 Church of Our Saviour Спасская Церковь
8 Cathedral of the Epiphany Богоявленский Собор
9 Polish Catholic Church Польский Костёл
14 Art Museum extension
20 Art Museum Художественный Музей
37 Regional Museum Краеведческий Музей
38 Trans-Siberian Builders' Monument Памятник Строителям Транссибирской Магистрали
40 Philharmonic Hall Филармония
41 Church of the Elevation of the Cross Крестовоздвиженская Церковь
45 Synagogue Синагога
49 Trubetskoy House-Museum Музей-усадьба Трубецкого
51 Church of the Transfiguration Преображенская Церковь
52 Volkonsky House-Museum Музей-усадьба Волконского
53 Mosque Мечеть

OTHER
1 Railway Station Железнодорожный Вокзал
2 River Station Речной Вокзал
5 Ploshchad Kirova Bus Stop Остановка «Пл Кирова»
10 ATM
11 Sibir Telecom Office Сибирь Телеком
13 Central Air Agency Центральная Авиакасса
17 Post Office Почтамт
23 Epicentr Internet Café Интернет Кафе 'Эпицентр'
31 Knigomir (bookshop) Книгомир & Central Post Office Почтамт
34 Mongolian Consulate Консульство Монголии
46 AquaEco АкваЭко
48 Green Express Преображенская Церковь
50 Bus Station Автовокзал

Banks There are numerous **ATMs** in the city centre, particularly along ul Karla Marksa, ul Stepana Razina and bulvar Gagarina, as well as at Hotel Angara (see Where to stay). **Travellers' cheques** can be cashed at Sberbank (ul Uritskogo 19). You can exchange currency at most banks, or at Hotel Baikal.

Travel agents and tours

The travel agents listed here run city tours, day trips and **adventure tours** such as hiking, skiing and trekking. They also offer trips along the **Circumbaikal Railway Line** (see p287) and excursions to **Olkhon Island**. Also on offer are **scuba-diving** and **horse-riding**.

Baikaler (☎ 3952 336 240, 🖳 www.baikaler.com), run by bilingual Yevgeny 'Jack' Sheremetoff, is an excellent choice for budget travellers. Imaginative group and personalised tours abound; the hostel (see Where to stay) can organise your onward travel as well. A recommended budget agency is **Baikal Complex** (☎ 3952 461 557, 🖳 www.baikalcomplex.com), run by the friendly Yuri Nemirovsky, which organises homestays and excursions into the surrounding area. Call ahead for directions to the office (it's not in the town centre) or for a visit by staff.

Another helpful tour operator is Andrey Berenovsky whose company, **AquaEco** (ul Karla Libknekhta 12, ☎ 3952 334 290, 🖳 www.aquaeco.eu.org), specialises in diving and sailing on Baikal.

Green Express (ul Dekabrskikh Sobyty 24, ☎ 3952 734 400, 🖳 www.greenexpress.ru) is another recommended outfit that runs a hotel in Listvyanka and can organise a variety of activities on Olkhon Island.

Local transport

Since most sights, restaurants and shops are close to the hotels, walking is the most pleasant and interesting way to get around. However, ***marshrutka*** No 20 runs between the railway station and the airport down ul Lenina.

Trams No 1 and 2 go from the station over the bridge and into the centre of town. Trolleybus No 4 goes out to the airport from Skver im Kirova. Tickets cost R14.

Where to stay

HOFA (see p153) can arrange **homestays** in Irkutsk, Listvyanka, Bolshie Koty and Olkhon Island.

If you're just in town for a night, the ***railway station resting rooms*** **комнаты отдыха** (*komnaty otdykha*, R80/hour) are a good choice as you can pay only for the time you need. Showers cost R100 extra. If all the rooms are full, which is frequently the case, and you need to while away a few hours waiting for your train, or have arrived preposterously early, you can snooze on the sofas in the secure waiting room next to the komnaty otdykha (R60 for the first hour, then R35 per hour after).

Another budget option is ***Minihotel Vostok-Zapad*** **Миниотель Восток-Запад** (ул Пушкина 34, ul Pushkina 34, ☎ 3952 642 122, 🖳 www.irk-vostzap.narod.ru, rooms from R500) near the railway station. The rooms are basic but clean; there is a guest kitchen with microwave and shared bathrooms. They register visas.

Irkutsk Downtown Hostel (ул Грязнова 15 ul Gryaznova 15 , ☎ 9025 164 248, 🖳 www.hostel.irkutsk.ru, dorm/family room for 5/dbl R550/3000/1400) has friendly English-speaking staff. They offer internet access and wi-fi, visa registration, kitchen, videos, laundry service and tours. The place is clean and homey but a bit crowded.

To get there, ride four stops on a city centre-bound tram (No 1 or 2) from the railway station, then follow the tram line until it crosses ul Gryaznova and turn left.

Baikal Explorer Hostel (ул Марата 13 кв 3, ul Marata 13 apt 3, ☎ 8950 089 0255 or 8902 577 8432, 🖳 http://baikalexplorerhostel.ru, dorm/dbl R500/1400) is a central apartment hostel with room for 6-10 people, with a guest kitchen, wi-fi and free pickup available. The owners can arrange tours of Lake Baikal as well as stays at their rustic hostel in the tiny Baklan village along the Circumbaikal Railway.

German-run ***Baikal Hostel*** (ул Лермонтова 136 кв 1, ul Lermontova 136 apt 1, ☎ 3952 525 742, 💻 www.baikalinfo.com, dorm/dbl R550/800) is a good place for travellers interested in Lake Baikal's ecology, as Irkutsk's first hostel has played a big part in the creation of the Great Baikal Trail (see box p284). It's a few kilometres south of the station, with buses No 1, 3, 7, 10, 24, 72 and 84 running along ul Lermontova; get off at the 'Microchirurgia Glaza' stop. Free transfers are offered and staff speak English and German.

Baikaler Hostel **Байкалер** (ул Ленина 9 кв 11, ul Lenina 9 apt 11, ☎ 3952 336 240, 💻 www.baikaler.com, dorms R650) is centrally located and very popular so you must book in advance as they only have nine beds. The cheerful apartment has a guest kitchen, wi-fi and internet and very helpful staff. 'Jack', the owner, is a treasure trove of local knowledge and can arrange all manner of tours in the area (see Travel agents). If they're full they offer alternative accommodation nearby.

The monolithic ***Hotel Angara*** **Гостиница Ангара** (ул Сухе Батора 7, ul Sukhe Batora 7, ☎ 3952 255 107, 💻 www.hotel-angara.ru, sgl/dbl/suite from R1900/3000/5800) is central and used to dealing with tour groups. The cheapest rooms are en suite but basic, whereas the suites on the top floor are of Western standards and come with Jacuzzis. There are five restaurants on the premises and the staff can assist with booking onward travel. A good buffet breakfast is included.

One of the best hotels in the city but out of the centre, ***Hotel Yevropa*** **Гостиница Европа** (ул Байкальская 69, ul Baiklaskaya 69, ☎ 3952 291 515, 💻 www.europehotel.ru, sgl/dbl/suite from R2700/3500/12,100) has comfortable rooms with wi-fi and buffet breakfast included. The suites have Jacuzzis and guests have use of the hotel gym. Staff can help book train and plane tickets.

Japanese-designed ***Sayen International Hotel*** (ул Карла Маркса 136, ul Karla Marksa 136, ☎ 3952 500 000, 💻 www.sayen.ru, dbl R6700-12,500) distinguishes itself with its minimalist design and the ultimate in creature comforts. All rooms have balconies, climate control, plasma TVs and wi-fi; the Japanese-style spa offers numerous relaxation options and the hotel sports three excellent restaurants – including the Japanese 'Kyoto', as well as a genuine Irish pub. A sister hotel is currently being built in Ulan-Ude.

Where to eat and drink

One local delicacy worth looking out for on menus and at the produce market is smoked *omul*, a delicious fish native to Lake Baikal. There are plenty of quick places to eat at in the centre including ***Papa Johns*** pizza (ул Марата 48, ul Marata 48) and ***Chudo-Blyudo*** **Чудо-Блюдо** (ул Литвинова 17 ul Litvinova 17, 2nd floor, inside the shopping centre) which does cheap Russian dishes.

Wiener Café **Венское Кафе** (ул Степна Разина 19, ul Stepana Razina 19, meals R450) is the Russian approximation of a Viennese café. Picture unsmiling waitresses in jolly Austrian barmaid-style outfits, and a mostly Russian menu of soups, salad, good meat dishes. The pricey dessert selection does include strudel, though.

Krendel **Креньдель** (ул Грязнова 1, ul Gryazova 1, mains R300) is a basement café-restaurant with ultra-kitsch faux-rustic interior, though the food is very good – from the salads to the baked omul to the liver pelmeni. The service is on the leisurely side.

A good *stolovaya* is at the branch of the ***Bonjour*** chain (ул Марата 14, ul Marata 14, meals R250), with a wide range of tasty and inexpensive Russian staples.

Double Coffee (ул Свердлова 19, ul Sverdolova 19) is part of a popular coffee chain and the coffee here is good, if not cheap, while ***Ca:fe*** **Ка:фе** (ул Карла Маркса 18, ul Karla Marksa 18) is a trendy spot for coffee and inexpensive business lunches. Wi-fi access is available.

Other good cheap cafés include the highly recommended ***Café Snezhinka*** **Кафе Снежинка** (ул Литвинова 2, ul Litvinova 2, mains R250), with its elegant, airy interior, friendly service and nicely presented Russian dishes.

Kyoto **Киото** (ул Карла Маркса 13, ul Karla Marksa 13, mains R350), with its attractive minimalist interior in Japanese style, serves very good Japanese food, including buckwheat soba with seafood and a large variety of sushi sets. ***WasabiKo* ВасабиКо** (ул Сухе Батора 18, ul Sukhe Batora 18) is part of a sushi chain that does good daily specials. ***Yefimych* Ефимич** (ул Карла Маркса 3, ul Karla Marksa 3, mains R300) has a nice summer beer terrace and serves tasty Czech brew. The Russian dishes are very good, in spite of the amusing mistranslations; try the 'salmon poorly salty', the blini with different fillings, and *syrniki* (fried sweet cottage cheese patties) for dessert.

For Italian cuisine head to upmarket ***Marciano Restaurant* Ресторан Марциано** (ул Карла Маркса 15, ul Karla Marksa 15). Count on at least R900 for a full meal, without wine.

Very popular with Trans-Siberian visitors is ***Kochevnik* Кочевник** (ул Горького 19, ul Gorkogo 19, meals R800), sister restaurant of Ulan-Ude's Modern Nomads, and allegedly specialising in Mongolian food, though there is far more variety here than in your average Mongolian eatery. The service is excellent as are the meat dishes, *buuzy* (meat-filled dumplings) and large salads.

Self-caterers should visit the ***central market* центральный рынок**, brimming with all kinds of fresh produce. To stock up on food for the Trans-Siberian trip, there are two good **supermarkets супермаркеты** opposite one another on ul Karla Marksa, near the intersection with ul Kievskaya.

Bars and nightlife

For drinking spots, try ***Bar Yefimych*** (see above), the ***U Shveyka*** У Швейка chain (ул Карла Маркса 34, ul Karla Marksa 34), with its excellent beer, or the mock-Bavarian beer hall that is ***Bier Haus*** (ул Грязнова 1, ul Gryaznova 1), where jolly barmaids in Alpine dress present you with excellent German beers at London prices and platters of sausages.

London Pub in Hotel Angara has good but pricey beer and steaks that can be hit-and-miss in quality.

Liverpool Ливерпуль (ул Свердлова 28, ul Sverdlova 28) is a Beatles-themed pub, popular with locals and tourists, with an international (and overpriced) beer menu and dishes named after Beatles' songs.

There are several nightclubs, including the local hot-spot ***Stratosfera*** Стратосфера (ул Карла Маркса 15, ul Karla Marksa 15), with a large dance club, bar, casino, restaurant and bowling alley on the premises. A dress code applies. Another lively place is ***Akula*** Акула ('Shark'; бульв Гагарина 9, bul Gagarina 9), an entertainment centre that includes 24-hour bowling, and hosts decent DJs as well as '80s nostalgia nights.

Entertainment

Concerts are given at the **Philharmonic Hall** Филармония (ул Дзержинского 2, ul Dzerzhinskogo 2, ☎ 3952 241 100) and there are organ recitals at the Polish Church.

The local promenade behind the Okhlopkov Drama Theatre that runs along the Angara is popular with strollers on summer evenings.

Moving on

By rail There are three sections at the Irkutsk railway station for buying tickets. Area one sells same-day domestic tickets; area two sells advance purchase domestic tickets, the Service Centre on the second floor (area three, 8am-7pm) sells international tickets, and downstairs from the Service Centre you can buy tickets for suburban trains. The VIP hall next to the Service Centre has air conditioning and soft seats (R60/hour). You can also purchase train tickets from the Central Air Agency (see By air), with the help of Baikaler Hostel, or at Hotel Baikal.

Heading west, departures include Moscow (up to 3/day, 75½-86hrs), St Petersburg (the 009 departs on odd days; 91hrs), and all the major cities in between. Heading east, there are departures to Vladivostok on alternate days with the 002 (60hrs) and the 032 (72hrs) via Khabarovsk. The 019 Trans-Manchurian via Chita (60hrs) passes through on Tuesday mornings, while the Trans-Mongolian 004 (31hrs) passes through early on Saturday mornings. The fast 006 to Ulaanbaatar passes through on Sundays and Mondays (31hrs), as does the daily 361.

By bus From the bus station, buses and minibuses depart for Listvyanka (at least 6/day in summer, 50-75mins), Olkhon Island (around 4/day in summer, all departing before noon, 5½-7hrs). Buses for Bratsk (8pm, 11hrs) depart from the ticket booth opposite the main bus station, while minibuses to Ulan-Ude (around 4/day in summer, departures before noon, 7hrs) leave from the railway station forecourt.

By river Boats for **Lake Baikal** depart from Raketa Terminal above Angara Dam; the dam is 5km upstream (south) of Irkutsk. Minibus No 16 (but don't take 16M or 16K) runs to the terminal from pl Kirova (20min; get off at the Raketa (Ракета) stop. Check the timetable online at 🖳 http://kbzd.irk.ru.

From Raketa Terminal there are hydrofoils to **Listvyanka** (60 mins, R220) and **Bolshie Koty** (1½hrs, R280) one to three times daily (only one service on Monday at 9am), with one departure on Wednesdays and Saturdays stopping at Port Baikal. These boats fill up, so book two days in advance.

Services to **Nizhneangarsk** (12hrs, R1400) and **Severobaikalsk** via Olkhon Island (5hrs, R1800) go on Tuesday and Friday mornings, returning Wednesday and Saturday.

Hydrofoils for **Bratsk** (12hrs, R1450) via **Angarsk** depart from the River Station, near the bridge from the railway station, on Tuesday, Thursday and Saturday (June-Sept). Buy your ticket two days in advance. All hydrofoil services are subject to weather-induced delays and cancellations.

By air There are direct international flights from Irkutsk airport (🖳 www.iktport.ru) to Bangkok, Phuket, Beijing (2/week), Seoul (2/week) and Tashkent (1/week). Domestic flights include Moscow (several daily), as well as several weekly flights to Vladivostok, Khabarovsk, Novosibirsk, Yekaterinburg, Krasnoyarsk, Ulan-Ude, Nizhneangarsk and Yakutsk.

Flight tickets can be purchased from the Central Air Agency (ul Gorkogo 29, ☎ 3952 341 596, 8am-8pm).

Lake Baikal
Озеро Байкал

The world's deepest lake

Lake Baikal, 64km (40 miles) south-east of Irkutsk, is 1637m (5371ft) deep and estimated to contain more than 20,000 cubic kilometres of water, roughly 20% of the world's freshwater supplies. If all the rest of the world's drinking water ran out tomorrow, Lake Baikal could supply the entire population of the planet for the next 40 years.

Known as the 'Blue Eye of Siberia,' it is the world's oldest lake, formed almost 50 million years ago. It is also among the planet's largest lakes; about 400 miles long and between 20 and 40 miles wide. The water is incredibly clear and, except around Baikalsk and the Selenga delta, completely safe to drink, owing to the filtering action of numerous types of sponge which live in its depths, along with hundreds of other species found nowhere else on earth.

Holy Sea

Russian colonists called Baikal the 'Holy Sea' since there were so many local myths and legends surrounding it. The Buryats believed that the evil spirit

The Great Baikal Trail

In 2003 some enthusiastic locals began work on a sustainable tourism initiative, grandly entitled the Great Baikal Trail (GBT), or Bolshaya Baikalskaya Tropa. The original plan was to create a continuous hiking trail that may eventually encircle Lake Baikal, not unlike the Tahoe Rim Trail in California, though that goal seems quite far-fetched at the moment. This trail is the first of its kind in Russia. In 2008 the GBT gained international prominence when it was nominated as a finalist in National Geographic's Geotourism Challenge.

For the moment, efforts are being made to improve on ancient trails that have been used by the indigenous tribes in the area before Baikal was 'civilised' by the Soviets. Every year volunteers come from all over the world to take part in trail construction, helping with building footbridges, clearing and marking existing trails, or even planting trees or acting as interpreters for other volunteers who don't speak Russian. Current trail sections include Listvyanka to Bolshoye Golustnoye via Bolshiye Koty, two trails along the Holy Nose on the eastern side of Lake Baikal, accessed from Ust-Barguzin and the Mount Poroshisty climb.

For further information on the trails, or if you wish to volunteer, visit www.greatbaikaltrail.org.

Begdozi lived on Olkhon Island in the middle of the lake, though Evenki shamans held that this was the home of the sea god Dianda. It is hardly surprising that these primitive tribes were impressed by the strange power of the lake for at times sudden violent storms spring up, lashing the coast with waves two metres high or more. It freezes to a depth of three metres for four months of the year, from late December. The Angara is the only river that flows **out** of the lake. Since a dam and hydroelectric power station were built on the Angara in 1959 the level of the lake has been slowly rising.

Environmental threats

The lake's remoteness kept it safe from environmental damage until the building of the Trans-Siberian railway at the end of the 19th century. The risk of damage has further increased with the construction of new towns on the northern shores for the construction of the BAM line, and because of industrial waste from Ulan-Ude (the Selenga River flows past this city into the lake via one of the world's last large wetlands, the Selenga delta).

The most famous campaigner for the protection of the lake is author Valentin Rasputin. Demonstrations in Irkutsk in 1987 resulted in filtration equipment being installed in the wood pulp mill at Baikalsk on the edge of the lake but reports suggest that it is inefficient and that pollution is continuing. A coastal protection zone was established around the entire lake in 1987 but campaigners bemoan the fact that government anti-pollution laws have no teeth.

Baikal became a UNESCO World Heritage Site in 1996 and is ringed by nature reserves, but this hasn't stopped environmental threats to the lake. Today the main concerns stem from numerous gas and oil pipelines – some proposed and some already built – that pass near the shore on their way to China and the Sea of Japan. Activists worry that a pipeline rupture in this earthquake-prone

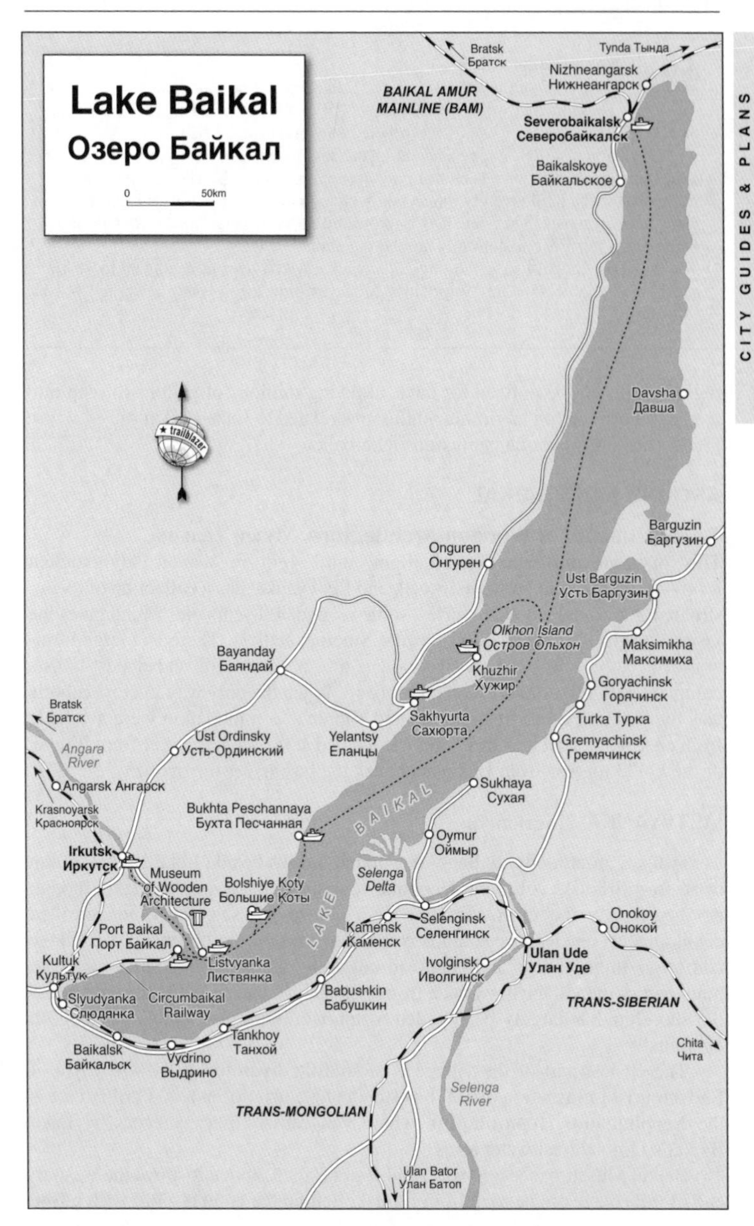
Lake Baikal
Озеро Байкал
0
50km
trailblazer
Bratsk
Братск
Tynda Тында
Nizhneangarsk
Нижнеангарск
BAIKAL AMUR
MAINLINE (BAM)
Severobaikalsk
Северобайкалск
Baikalskoye
Байкальское
Davsha
Давша
Barguzin
Баргузин
Onguren
Онгурен
Ust Barguzin
Усть Баргузин
Olkhon Island
Остров Ольхон
Maksimikha
Максимиха
Bayanday
Баяндай
Khuzhir
Хужир
Goryachinsk
Горячинск
Sakhyurta
Сахюрта
Turka Турка
Bratsk
Братск
Ust Ordinsky
Усть-Ординский
Yelantsy
Еланцы
Gremyachinsk
Гремячинск
Angara
River
Angarsk Ангарск
Sukhaya
Сухая
Krasnoyarsk
Красноярск
Bukhta Peschannaya
Бухта Песчанная
BAIKAL
Oymur
Оймыр
Irkutsk
Иркутск
Museum
of Wooden
Architecture
Selenga
Delta
Bolshiye Koty
Большие Коты
LAKE
Port Baikal
Порт Байкал
Kamensk
Каменск
Selenginsk
Селенгинск
Onokoy
Онокой
Ulan Ude
Улан Уде
Kultuk
Култук
Listvyanka
Листвянка
Ivolginsk
Иволгинск
Slyudyanka
Слюдянка
Circumbaikal
Railway
Babushkin
Бабушкин
TRANS-SIBERIAN
Tankhoy
Танхой
Baikalsk
Байкальск
Vydrino
Выдрино
Chita
Чита
Selenga
River
TRANS-MONGOLIAN
Ulan Bator
Улан Батор

Lake Baikal wildlife

Over 80% of the species in Lake Baikal cannot be found anywhere else in the world. These include 1085 types of algae, 250 mosses, 450 lichens, 1500 vascular plants, 255 small crustaceans, 83 gastropods, 86 worms and 52 fish.

Exceptionally high oxygen levels in the lake create an ideal environment for many creatures which have become or are becoming extinct elsewhere. These include freshwater seals, until recently threatened with extinction by the Buryats who turned them into overcoats. They are now a protected species, listed in the *Red Book of Endangered Species* and currently numbering about 60,000.

A unique Baikal fish is the tiny *golomyanka*, which lives at depths up to 1.5km and is made up of 35% fat. Surprisingly, it gives birth to its young alive and fully formed.

region might not be noticed for days, allowing millions of gallons to seep into the lake. For more on environmental issues related to Lake Baikal see 💻 www.greenpeace.org/russia/en/campaigns/lake-baikal.

AROUND LAKE BAIKAL

Taltsy Museum of Wooden Architecture Музей Тальцы

This open-air museum (9am-5.30pm, until 4pm in winter, adult/student R140/70) on the road between Irkutsk and Listvyanka, has a collection of reconstructed traditional wooden houses, some around 300 years old, which gives the visitor insight into the lives of the first Siberian settlers. There is a large farmhouse, a bathroom with a vast wooden tub, a water-mill and a post-house, complete with Imperial crest on its roof-top. When the only way to cross Siberia was by road and river, fresh horses and simple accommodation were available from post-houses such as this. Taltsy is located at the km47 marker from Irkutsk or the km23 marker from Listvyanka; ask the bus driver for 'moozay'.

LISTVYANKA Листвянка

Listvyanka, an attractive village of wooden houses beside Lake Baikal, 60km or so from Irkutsk, is the most popular tourist destination on the lake, though not necessarily the most attractive one, due to the seemingly uncontrolled development, reckless weekend drivers, and litter on the beaches. The village comprises three valleys and is spread out along the shore for 6km or so. The main part of the village is set back from the lake in a valley, while the strip along the shoreline has largely been ceded to tourism, with new hotels popping up continually.

The busiest part of the village is around the hydrofoil quay where you'll find a tourist information office, bus stop and a cluster of hotels. Further east is the **Nerpinarium Нерпинарий**, where you can see performances by Lake Baikal's famous freshwater seals.

Baikal Museum (see opposite) and Hotel Baikal, above it, are at the western end of the village on the road from Irkutsk. Behind the hotel is a **hill with a fine**

view over the water to the Khamar-Daban Mountains. The half-hour hike up is well worth it. At the top there's a little shelter and a tree decorated with paper ribbons that people have tied to it for good luck – an old Siberian custom.

What to see and do

Baikal Museum Музей Байкала This museum (ul Akademicheskaya 1, 9am-7pm, R250) has a number of fascinating displays on the unique marine life and animals in the Baikal area, though most of the captioning is in Russian. It also contains a model of the *Angara* and a collection of the sponges which keep the water so clean. Colonists' wives discovered that they were also very useful for polishing the samovar.

The best parts of the museum are the aquariums featuring numerous species of fish from Lake Baikal, as well as the tiny crayfish-like creatures that are unique to the lake. There are also two large tanks housing two adorable nerpas, (Baikal seals) who are zeppelin-like and unwieldy on land, but extremely fast and graceful in the water.

There's a new attraction – the submarine room – that simulates submersion into Baikal's depths in a special Mir submarine. You look at fish and wildlife swimming past the 'portholes' as the guide explains which creatures you get to see at different depths (in Russian only).

St Nicholas Church Церковь Святого Николая A pleasant 10-minute walk up the main valley – Krestovka – takes you to the tiny Svyato-Nikolskaya

Riding the Circumbaikal Railway

Rail enthusiasts and anyone seeking extended views of the lake can hop on a train running twice a week along the old Circumbaikal Railway (see p428), from Irkutsk to Port Baikal via Slyudyanka. You have two options. You can take the train that the locals use, the ***matanya***, which is slow, poorly ventilated, with grubby windows, but very cheap. You can also persuade the train driver to let you ride up front for an added fee so that you can take photos. Alternatively, you can opt for the far more comfortable tourist train package, which is more expensive, but which includes meals, a bilingual guide who'll describe to you what you are seeing, and which can easily be arranged either by yourself or with travel agents listed on p280. With the latter option, you can choose whether to travel from Port Baikal to Slyudyanka or vice versa, whereas the matanya travels between Slyudyanka and Port Baikal during the day, but does the reverse journey overnight.

To catch the matanya, you have to take the suburban train from Irkutsk to Slyudynka II, departing at 9.40am and arriving at 12.33pm. The matanya leaves Slyudyanka II at 1.52pm on Mondays, Thursdays, Fridays and Sundays, arriving in Port Baikal at 8.14pm, too late for the ferry to Listvyanka, so you have to arrange accommodation in Port Baikal in advance. A trip on the matanya costs around R180.

The tourist train departs from Irkutsk on Saturdays at 8.05am, arriving in Port Baikal at 8pm. The train then returns to Irkutsk on Sunday, leaving Port Baikal at 11.30am and arriving in Irkutsk at 9.53pm. Either way, you'll have to arrange accommodation at Port Baikal unless you have arranged alternative transport through a tour agency in Irkutsk. The tourist train package costs R2000-2500.

Confirm departure and arrival times at 💻 http://kbrz.irk.ru.

church, built in 1846 and originally situated in the nearby Nikola village, though it had to be relocated when the Angara Dam raised the water levels.

Retro Park Ретропарк A short walk back along the Krestovka stream brings you to this sculpture park resembling a scrap yard, where the different works of art are made from parts of old Soviet cars.

Lake Baikal activities Besides sunning yourself on a pebble beach beside the lake, Listvyanka is also home to a host of winter activities, which include dog sledding, hovercraft rides on the frozen lake, snowmobiling and even ice-cycling on the lake, involving bikes fitted with special tyres. 'Jack' Sheremetoff (see Baikaler Hostel, p281) can help you arrange all of the above and you can contact **Baikal Dog Sledding centre** Байкальский Центр Ездового Спорта (ul Kulikova 136a, Krestovka valley, ☎ 908 660 5098, 💻 www.baikalsled.ru – in Russian) to arrange dogsled runs through the winter forest – an unforgettable experience (run by Oleg and Natalia whose sons speak English).

Shaman Rock In the stretch of water between Baikal Museum and Port Baikal it's possible to discern a rock sticking out of the water. According to local legend, Old Man Baikal had 336 sons (the number of rivers which flow into the lake) and one daughter, the beautiful but headstrong Angara. She enraged him by refusing to marry the feeble Irkut, preferring the mighty Yenisey (Russia's longest river). The old man chained her up but one stormy night she slipped her bonds and fled north to her lover. As she ran her furious father hurled a huge boulder after her. She got away but the rock remains to this day. The level of the lake has since risen and very little of Shaman Rock is now visible.

WHERE TO STAY
1 Hotel Yakhont Гостиница Яхонт
7 Derevenka Деревенька
8 Krestovaya Pad Hotel Гостиница Крестовая Падь
12 Baikal Dream
16 Hotel Mayak Гостиница Маяк

WHERE TO EAT & DRINK
6 Proshli Vek Прошлый Век
15 Pyaty Okean Пятый Океан
21 Shury Mury Шуры-Муры
22 Chinese restaurant Китайский ресторан
24 Market Рынок
14 Café Podlemore Кафе Подлеморе

PLACES OF INTEREST
3 Hilltop Lookout Point
5 Baikal Museum Музей Байкала
10 St Nicholas Church Церковь Святого Николая
11 Retro Park Ретропарк
13 Gallery & Art Shop
18 War memorial Памятник Великой Отечественной Войне
23 Nerpinarium Нерпинарий

OTHER
2 Railway Station Железнодорожная Станция
4 Hotel Baikal Гостиница Байкал
9 Baikal Dog Sledding Centre Байкальский Центр Ездового Спорта
17 Post Office Почта
19 Tourist Information Centre/Bus station Туристическая Информация/ Автобусная остановка
20 Hydrofoil Quay Причал

Where to stay

Listvyanka has no shortage of places to stay and new places are springing up every year, though book in advance if coming in July and August.

By the time this book is published there should be an **offshoot of Baikaler Hostel** along the central Malaya Cheremshanka Valley (ask at Baikaler Hostel, p281), ideal for budget travellers.

Baikal Dream (ул Чапаева 69, Малая Черемшанка, ul Chapaeva 69, Malaya Cheremshanka, ☎ 3952 496 758, sgl/dbl from R1700/2300) is a brick guesthouse with spartan but comfortable rooms, a cosy common room and guest kitchen. Nikolai, the effusive owner, offers pickup from the bus stop and can cook meals on request. There's an excellent banya for guest use.

***Derevenka* Деревенька** (ул Горная 1, ul Gornaya 1, ☎ 3952 250 459, 🖳 www.baikal-derevenka.ru, sgl/dbl R2000/3000) consists of a family-run log cabin complex, each compact cabin equipped with toilet; in the summer you can use the shared shower cabin, whereas in the winter the banya is your only means of getting clean. The price includes breakfast; the owners can organise dog sledding, snowmobiling and diving in the Baikal. In the summer, backpackers can put up their own tents (R350/tent) and pay to make use of the showers (R50).

Fittingly shaped like a lighthouse, ***Hotel Mayak* Гостиница Маяк** (ул

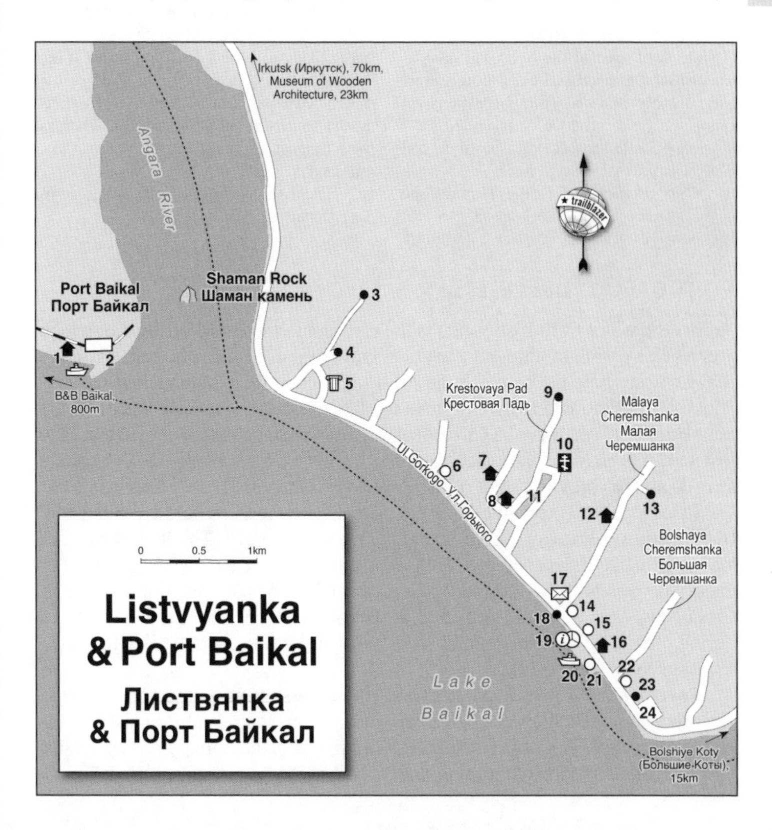

Горького 85, ul Gorkogo 85, ☎ 3952 496 910, 💻 www.mayakhotel.ru, sgl/dbl/suite R3200/3500/10,900) has a winning location with great views of the lake. The price for its modern, wi-fi equipped rooms includes buffet breakfast. Restaurant Mayak specialises in fish dishes that use local fish. The light and bright ***Krestovaya Pad Hotel*** **Гостиница Крестовая Падь** (ул Горная 14а, ul Gornaya 14a, ☎ 3952 496 863, 💻 www.krestovayapad.ru, dbl from R2600) consists of two modern curvy buildings and two VIP cottages. The restaurant serves a mélange of Russian and European dishes; the summer terrace is perfect for shashlyk. The rooms come equipped with air-con.

Where to eat and drink

A short walk east of the hydrofoil quay is the **outdoor market** рынок, selling souvenirs, freshly smoked (though expensive) omul and fresh produce, surrounded by a cluster of eateries serving shashlyk and plov (Central Asian-style rice).

Café Podlemore **Кафе Подлеморе** (ул Горького 31, ul Gorkogo 31) serves inexpensive Russian dishes, including warming porridge and pastries. ***Shury Mury*** **Шуры-Муры**, by the tourist information centre, is a lively summer terrace, while ***Pyaty Okean*** **Пятый Океан** (ул Горького 59а, ul Gorkogo 59a) and ***Proshli Vek*** **Прошлый Век** (ул Лазло 1, ul Lazlo 1) both specialise in fish dishes, many of which involve omul. There's also a **Chinese restaurant** Китайский ресторан next to the Nerpinarium.

Getting there and moving on

There are at least four buses daily in summer, as well as numerous *marshrutkas* (minibuses) travelling between Irkutsk's bus station and Listvyanka's hydrofoil quay, also stopping to pick up passengers in front of the Baikal Museum. If heading to Irkutsk towards the end of the day, you're more likely to get a seat if you board at the hydrofoil quay. Bear in mind that for the scheduled buses, you'll need to buy tickets at the tourist information centre, whereas with the rest of the minibuses, you can just pile in.

There are hydrofoils to Irkutsk in summer, departing 1-3 times daily.

PORT BAIKAL Порт Байкал

Across the water from Listvyanka is the spreadout village of Port Baikal, which you reach by walking through a nautical graveyard of rusted ship hulks. You are likely to stay here if you catch the local train along the Circumbaikal railway, which arrives too late for you to take the last ferry across to Listvyanka on the mainland, or if you hike the Circumbaikal railway. Since the village is relatively isolated, this may be the place to come if you wish to avoid the Listvyanka crowds and to enjoy the sight of the Baikal from the village's viewpoints.

Prior to 1904 Trans-Siberian passengers had to stop here and cross the lake by steamer to Mysovaya, from where the trains continued. The largest steamer was a 90m ice-breaker, the *Baikal*, which transported train carriages on her deck. She was built by the British firm of Sir WG Armstrong, Whitworth and Co in Newcastle, UK, and delivered in sections by train. She was sunk in 1919 during the Civil War. Her smaller sister ship, the *Angara*, supplied by the same firm, survived (see p277).

Several homestays operate here now, though some are quite a hike from the ferry quay, up the valley. ***B&B Baikal*** (ул Байкальская 11, ul Baikalskaya 11, ☎ 3952 607 450, 💻 www.baikal.tk, R1000pp) has plain, homely rooms; a pool table; small, spotless bathrooms and a banya. The hostess cooks delicious homemade food if you ask her in advance. There is also ***Hotel Yakhont* Гостиница Яхонт** (ул Набережная 3, ul Naberezhnaya 3, ☎ 3952 250 496, 💻 yahont@baikalrest.ru, twin R3700), an attractive timber-and-stone guesthouse by the ferry quay. The rooms are comfortable, guests have use of the lakeside terrace and banya and there's even a restaurant on the premises – the only one in the village. You can also buy basic groceries from a couple of little stores.

Three **ferries** a day run between Port Baikal and Listvyanka from May to December. Departures from Port Baikal at the time of writing were at 7.10am, 3.50pm and 5.15pm, while departures from Listvyanka were at 8.15am, 4.15pm and 6.15pm. There may be an extra ferry on Saturday evenings to pick up passengers arriving on the Circumbaikal Railway, but check that in advance. The **hydrofoil** to Listvyanka and Bolshie Koty stops at Port Baikal on Wednesdays and Saturdays.

BOLSHIYE KOTY Болшие Коты

Bolshiye Koty is a small village north of Listvyanka. Its main attraction is the peace and quiet and the picturesque 18km hiking trail that runs between the village and Listvyanka. Irkutsk University's Limnological Institute is here, where students do their practical work. Given that it's now home to less than fifty people, it's hard to believe that in the late 19th century, the village was the epicentre of a gold rush. Gold used to be extracted from the Bolshiye Koty River and the rusting dredges can still be seen 1km beyond the village. Baikal Complex (see p280) organises trips here, and also offers **homestays** (R1500). There are several other accommodation options there, which you can book through 💻 www.baikalnature.com.

From Bolshiye Koty there are hydrofoils to Irkutsk's Raketa Terminal (1½hrs, R280) via Listvyanka, 1-3 times a day (once on Monday).

HIKES AROUND LAKE BAIKAL

Surrounded by spectacular mountain chains and rugged coastline, Lake Baikal presents possibilities for outdoor adventure that are virtually unlimited. Camping gear is available for rent in Irkutsk, and travel agents there are prepared to help, supplying guides or simply organising transportation. Two treks that are easy to arrange independently, and are popular with Russians and foreigners alike, include a hike along the **Circumbaikal Railway** and camping on beautiful **Olkhon Island**.

Hiking the Circumbaikal Railway

Stretching along the shore between Port Baikal and Slyudyanka, the Circumbaikal Railway automatically defeats one problem often encountered by hikers in Russia: the lack of marked trails. There's a good path along the tracks for much of the way, and when it fades out, you simply walk the ties. Drinking water and a cold bath are always available from the lake, and there's no lack of camping spots on the shore and in the woods, many of them used (and abused) by local fishermen.

The 95km from Slyudyanka to Port Baikal, or vice versa, is an easy five- to seven-day hike over flat ground; or simply walk as far as you want and then head back. Each kilometre is marked, starting at km72 in Port Baikal (or km166 at Slyudyanka), so it's easy to tell where you are. Good topographical maps of the route are available at Hotel Baikal in Irkutsk.

There are 53 tunnels along the track; these can be a bit eerie without a flashlight. Along the way you pass through five villages as well as some smaller settlements: Shuminka is at km102, Ponamarevka at km107, Polovinniy at km110, Marituy at km120, and Kultuk is just before Slyudyanka at km156. Food and other supplies are available for purchase in basic grocery stores in villages, though it's best to bring what you need with you.

OLKHON ISLAND

Set midway up Lake Baikal's western shore, Olkhon has a dry climate and the same banana shape as the lake itself; the island is some 70km long and 15km at its widest point. Inhabited since the 5th century AD by Turkic Kurystan tribes, which were absorbed into Buryat culture in the 12th and 13th centuries, when the latter arrived at the height of Genghis Khan's empire, the island was finally colonised by Russians in the early 20th century. During the Soviet years, Olkhon has been the setting for a fish-processing factory, as well as one of the country's nicer (one imagines) Gulags. The largest island on Lake Baikal, Olkhon offers hikers a chance to roam across grassy steppe or dense taiga, making camp on sandy beaches or on majestic clifftops over the water. Sparsely inhabited by native Buryats and Russians, the island celebrated getting its first electric powerlines in summer 2005. Though tourism has certainly made inroads here, Olkhon remains a unique gem, with ample opportunity to lose yourself amidst its graceful hills and stunning bays, and the most beautiful setting from which to see the world's most impressive lake.

Khuzhir and around

There are several settlements on the island, the largest being the centrally located village of **Khuzhir**, a collection of wooden houses and dirt roads on the western shore, which is where you are likely to base yourself. There are beautiful views of the lake from the steep cliffs behind Nikita's Homestead (see opposite) and if you walk further north along the shore, you will come to the distinctive Shaman's Rock sticking out into the lake – two boulder mountains which are a sacred site to the shamanism-practising Buryat. You'll often see people trying to scramble to the top for the views. Even further along is an attractive sand-and-pebble beach that's good for sunbathing.

The stretch of water between Olkhon's north-western shore and the mainland is known as **Maloye Morye** ('Small Sea'); it is the shallower part of the lake that becomes relatively warm in the summer, and it's also the part that freezes over the quickest in winter, enabling vehicles to cross over to the island on the ice. Legend has it that swimming in the Baikal adds five years to your life; see how long you can tolerate the cold – even in the height of summer, the lake can be a cool 9°C.

Exploring the island

Tours of the island tend to focus on either the northern half or the southern half, the northern half being the more popular one. On a typical day trip you would be picked up from your guesthouse in a Soviet off-road vehicle and driven on the island's dirt road along the north-west coast, which takes in the splendid sandy Long Beach, the 'Crocodile' rock formation, the remains of the fish factory and the Gulag, and various cliff formations until you reach the Khoboy Peninsula – the most sacred part of the island for Buryats with an impressive *obo* at the tip of it with offerings scattered around. There is a 'window' in the rock along the southern part of the peninsula; if you're lucky, you might see nerpas sunbathing on the rocky beach far below.

Your driver/guide fixes up a picnic which involves cooking *ukha* (fish soup) and you then return to Khuzhir via the village of Uzury – the only east coast settlement – where all the houses have only solar power. On the way back, you will pass Mount Zhima (1274m) on your left – the highest point on the island, taboo to the Buryat, who consider it sacred.

The southern half of the island is more popular with hikers and mountain bikers than off-road vehicle tours, though it's possible to arrange trips to Shara-Nuur (Yellow Lake). Its water is said to have medicinal properties and to turn your skin red if you bathe too long. You can also visit the remnants of the earliest human settlements on the island.

If guided tours do not appeal, you can lose yourself for days on the island, camping on deserted beaches and eating by a campfire. Since there is an absence of marked trails, it's best to **head north-east from Khuzhir along the coast**. The route passes one scenic bay and clifftop promontory after another, along beaches and open hills where trails aren't needed to find your way. There are plenty of campsites on beaches or hilltops (though firewood can be hard to find). Russian families park along the shore and set up camp for days, often bringing noise and litter, but they can be avoided.

It's possible to follow this route for 40km (3-4 days) to the Khoboy peninsula, a stunning clifftop at the far northern tip of the island. Access to the lake ends about two-thirds of the way, with steep cliffs dropping to the shore from there onward. Bring food with you, as only Khuzir has grocery stores, and stock up on water at your last opportunity – at the end of the long, forested Nyurdanskaya Guba Bay. From Khoboy you can catch a ride back to Khuzhir from the many jeeps that run there. If hiking independently, make sure you're armed with a good map of the island.

Where to stay, eat and drink

More and more guesthouses are springing up in Khuzhir and around, but the most popular place to stay on the island is still ***Nikita's Homestead*** **Усадьба Никиты Гончарова** (ул Кирпичная 8, ul Kirpichnaya 8, ☎ 3952 708 885, 💻 www.olkhon.info, rooms from R650), a complex consisting of log cabins, timber houses and yurts, with its own bar and restaurant on-site (most guests opt for full board), as well as two banyas and showers. Nikita Bencharov is almost singlehandedly responsible for making the island so accessible to visitors; the staff are multilingual and the Homestead runs a reliable variety of tours. If they are full (as they frequently are in summer), you will be housed in a neighbouring spillover place.

More upmarket than Nikita's but far less lively is ***Hotel Olkhon* Гостиница Ольхон** (ул Байкальская 64, ul Baikalskaya 64, ☎ 3952 708 885, 💻 www.alphatour.ru, huts from R1200, sgl/dbl from R1300/1500), a brick hotel off Khuzhir's main square, with en suite rooms and flushing loos for those not keen on the rustic latrines popular at Nikita's and elsewhere. Rooms have lake views.

Another place to try in Khuzhir is ***Solnechnaya* Солнечная** (ул Солнечная 14, ul Solnechnaya 14, ☎ 3952 683 216, 💻 www.olkhon.com) with accommodation in small chalets, also offering full board, with meals served in a yurt. A variety of tours arranged daily. With meals, charges range from R600 to R1000pp.

Locals often rent spare rooms in summer; look for 'сдаются комнаты' signs.

Nikita's and other places offer **full board**; menus tend to be fish-heavy, with omul being prepared in a variety of different ways. In summer, informal **cafés** spring up along the main ul Baikalskaya, where you can have shashlyk, *buuzy*, grilled fish and beer.

Moving on

In summer, there are around four buses per day from Olkhon to Irkutsk and vice versa, all departing before noon (6-7hrs, R350 one way). Nikita's Homestead runs additional minibuses; book your passage in advance. The ticket price includes the short ferry ride. It's also possible to arrange a private car transfer in advance; expect to pay around R4500.

There are also two hydrofoils weekly from Irkutsk, which drop passengers off near the ferry terminal, from where you could hitch a lift to Khuzhir.

Ulan-Ude
Улан-Удэ

[Moscow Time +5] Ulan-Ude, the capital of the Buryat Republic, is a relaxed and pleasant Siberian city with quite a few traditional Siberian wooden buildings still standing in the midst of the usual concrete monstrosities, an attractive pedestrianised section, friendly and hospitable people and the world's largest Lenin head overlooking the main square. The city feels quite Asian, even though the Buryats are a minority in their own capital, and it makes a particularly worthwhile stopover if you visit **Ivolginsky Datsan** (see pp300-1), a spectacular temple complex and the centre of Buddhism in Russia.

HISTORY

In 1668 a military outpost was founded here, in a valley between the Khamar-Daban and Tsaga-Daban ranges. Strategically located beside the Selenga and Ude rivers, it was named Verkhneudinsk. A cathedral was built in 1745 and the town became a key centre on the route of tea caravans from China. The railway reached the town in 1900 and in 1949 the branch line to Mongolia was opened.

Ulan-Ude is now a pleasant city of some 386,000 (only about a fifth of whom are Buryats, the rest being mainly Russians). Local industries include the large railway repair workshop and locomotive plant, food processing, helicopter assembly and glass-making.

Buildings here require firm foundations since the city is in an earthquake zone. The most recent major tremor, measuring 9.5 on the Richter scale, was in 1959 but because its epicentre was directly beneath Lake Baikal there were no fatalities in Ulan-Ude. Military bases in the area meant that Ulan-Ude was off-limits to foreigners until the thaw in East–West relations. In 1990 Princess Anne led the tourists in with the first royal visit to Russia since the Tsar's execution. A local official declared that her visit was probably the most exciting thing to have happened since Genghis Khan swept through on his way to Moscow in 1239.

While the city today is noticeably poorer than others along the Trans-Siberian line, Ulan-Ude is going through a renaissance of another sort. Its Buryat residents are regaining pride in their national origins and reconnecting with their Buddhist roots, which were harshly suppressed under communism. This has been actively encouraged by the Dalai Lama, who has made five trips to the region since the fall of the Soviet Union.

WHAT TO SEE AND DO

Giant Lenin Head **Памятник Ленину**

Ploshchad Sovietov is dominated by the sinister bulk of the world's biggest Lenin head, 7.7 metres tall and weighing a whopping 42 tonnes. Standing in front of it you feel like Dorothy meeting the Wizard of Oz. Local Buryats believe it was put there as revenge after they resisted Sovietisation; but they say they got the last laugh. If you look closely, Lenin's eyes seem curiously Asian. The square itself is still used for military parades.

Buryat History Museum **Бурятский Исторический Музей**

The collection at the excellent Buryat History Museum (ul Profsoyuznaya 29, 10am-6pm Tue-Sun, combined ticket R180 or R80 for each of the three exhibitions) has been greatly enriched by the transfer from the Virgin Hodegetria Cathedral of a fantastic collection of items relating to Lamaism (Tibetan Buddhism) and the spiritual culture of the Buryats. Assembled from monasteries closed after the Revolution, the collection includes Buddha figures; the robes of a Buryat shaman; musical instruments (conches and horns and a beautiful guitar with a carved horse's head); a large collection of masks used in Buddhist mystery plays; and a valuable collection of Tibetan *thangkas* (devotional paintings).

In addition to thangkas used by monks practising traditional medicine, there's a unique *Atlas of Tibetan Medicine*. The history of Buryatiya is also covered, from the migration of Buryats into this area, to shamanism, the arrival of the Circumbaikal Railway, and national costume and jewelry. There is also a section dedicated to Old Believers and Buddhist ceremonial costume.

Open-Air Ethnographic Museum **Этнографический Музей**

One of Ulan-Ude's most popular attractions, this collection of reconstructed buildings (9am-5pm Tue-Sun, R80) is about 7km north of Ulan-Ude. Exhibits include a Bronze Age stone circle, an Evenki camp with birchwood wigwam, and a shaman's hut and wooden carvings.

The Buryat area contains *gers* (yurts) of felt and wood and a log cabin stocked with day-to-day items. You can also see reconstructed Kazakh, Cossack and Old Believer settlements. This place is not for animal lovers due to the dreadful zoo on-site, with camels standing in the mud, bears and tigers in tiny cages and disconsolate reindeer (the more people who complain to the guides about this the better).

Except in mid-summer it gets very cold out here; bring warm clothing. There's a good café near the entrance, selling shashlik and other inexpensive Russian staples. Marshrutka No 37 leaves from the main square for the Verkhnyaya Berezovka area; if you tell the driver in advance, he'll take a short detour from the T-junction up to the museum; otherwise, it's a 20-minute walk from the main road.

Other sights

It's worth spending some time wandering around the town as there are quite a few interesting buildings. These include several handsome mansions built by pre-Revolutionary merchants along ul Lenina, including an early 20th-century home with statues near ul Kalandarishvili.

Virgin Hodegetria Cathedral Одегитриевский Собор, at the southern end of the attractive, partially pedestrianised ul Lenina, built 1745-85, has been fully renovated and reopened. The streets around the cathedral are lined with picturesque old wooden buildings, some now being restored. The attractive **Trinity Church** Церковь Святой Троицы, built in 1798, was closed during the Communist era but has now been reopened and renovated; new bells were added in 1993. As at many Russian churches, begging babushkas crowd around the entrance.

The **City Museum** Музей Истории Города (ul Lenina 26, 10am-1pm & 2-7pm, R45) features exhibits on the fur and tea trade which impacted on the town, as well as a collection of old maps and samovars. Attached is a small art gallery featuring local works. The **Geological Museum** Геологический Музей (ul Lenina 57, 11am-5pm Mon-Fri, free entry) has a collection of Baikal region ores, rocks and crystals, as well as local works of art made of different coloured sand, many of which are for sale.

The **Opera and Ballet Theatre** Театр Оперы и Балета has splendid socialist-realist paintings and murals inside, but the doorman won't be keen to let you wander round without a ticket for a performance. The theatre was built by some of the 18,000 Japanese prisoners of war interned in Buryatia between 1945 and 1948.

PRACTICAL INFORMATION

Orientation and services

To reach the town centre from the railway station cross the lines via the pedestrian bridge. It takes about 10 minutes to walk to the main pl Sovietov. The main hotels are in this area. Even if you're not staying at **Baikal Ethnic Hostel** (see Where to stay), it's still the best place to contact for any manner of local tour, including trips to Ivolginsky Datsan.

There's a **Mongolian Consulate** (ul Profsoyuznaya 6, ☎ 211 078, 10am-12.30pm on Mon, Wed and Fri); for information on Mongolian visas see pp26-7.

There's a smoky basement **internet café** next to Baikal Plaza and a far better one inside Siberia Tour on the corner of ul Lenina and pr Pobedy.

There are **ATMs** along ul Lenina and inside Hotel Buryatia. You can change money at the central Baikal Bank (pl Sovietov 1).

Local transport

Most places, except the Datsan and the Open-Air Museum, are within walking distance. Bus No 77 runs from pl Sovietov to the airport. Buses No 7 and 10 from in front of the railway station run beside pl Sovietov and past Hotel Baikal; No 7 terminates at the central bus station and No 10 continues to the airport.

Taxis congregate by the railway and bus stations, and by pl Sovietov.

Where to stay

Even though it's not in Ulan-Ude itself, the best budget place to stay by far is the fantastic ***Baikal Ethnic Hostel*** (ул Флотская 12, Поселье, ul Flotskaya 12a, Poselye, ☎ 220 442, 🖳 www.baikalhostel.com, dorm R550), a large wooden house with guest kitchen and bar that encourage socialising, and internet. Run by the energetic Vladimir, a Buryat guide really passionate about his part of Russia and extremely knowledgeable with it, this is the place to organise anything from tours of the Ivolginsky Datsan to trips to the Old Believers' villages or even door-to-door transport between Ulan-Ude and Ulaanbaatar. Vladimir is brimming with excellent ideas and his popular winter ventures include setting up yurts on the ice of Lake Baikal so that those hiking from the shore to Olkhon Island would have somewhere to break the journey and enjoy a hot meal. The hostel is 4km west of Ulan-Ude in the nearby village of Poselye, which is served by marshrutka no 4 and other minibuses.

You could also try the decent ***railway station rest rooms*** **комнаты отдыха** (*komnaty otdykha*; sgl 'lux'/4-person R2500/750pp for 24hrs). The 'lux' rooms are worth splashing out for, as they come with TV, shower and sitting room.

Hotel Buryatia **Гостиница Бурятия** (ул Коммунистическая 47a, ul Kommunisticheskaya 47a, ☎ 211 505, sgl/dbl R2100/2700) is a Soviet throwback with rooms of different sizes and different standards, though most have been renovated by now. Some of the pluses include ATMs, an internet centre, several tour companies and even its own Buddhist temple.

Hotel Ayan **Гостиница Аян** (ул Бабушкина 164, ul Babushkina 164, ☎ 415 141, sgl/twin from R1800/2300) is inconveniently located a 20-minute walk south of the city centre, but the high standard of its modern rooms makes up for it. The pricier rooms have air-con and you can get wi-fi access on floors 1-3.

Baikal Plaza **Гостиница Байкал Плаза** (ул Ербанова 12, ul Yerbanova 12, ☎ 210 838, 🖳 www.baikalplaza.com, sgl/dbl/suite R3000/4500/7000) has been completely renovated and its super-central location and rooms equipped with all mod cons make it a popular choice.

Rooms are small but comfy in the well-run ***Sagaan Morin Hotel*** **Гостиница Сагаан Морин** (ул Гагарина 25, ul Gagarina 25, ☎ 443 647, 🖳 www.morin-tour.com, sgl/dbl R1600/2700), one stop by bus or a 10-minute walk over the bridge on ul Yerbanova from pl Sovietov. Particularly popular with Trans-Siberian travellers, it also has a café, sauna, an ATM, exchange office, and air and train ticket desks. The name means 'white horse' in Buryat.

Hotel Geser **Гостиница Гезер** (ул Ранжурова 11, ul Ranzhurova 11, ☎ 215 383, 🖳 www.geser-hotel.ru, sgl/dbl/suite R3300/3700/7300) is rather overpriced for what it is: a former hotel for the Party elite with somewhat modern rooms and prehistoric plumbing. The staff are friendly and helpful, though.

The Ulan-Ude area code is ☎ 3012. From outside Russia dial +7-3012.

WHERE TO STAY
1 Resting rooms Комнаты отдыха
3 Hotel Geser Гостиница Гэсэр
10 Baikal Plaza Hotel Гостиница Байкал Плаза
13 Hotel Buryatia Гостиница Бурятия

WHERE TO EAT AND DRINK
2 Fresh Food Market Рынок
7 Supermarket Sputnik Супермаркет Спутник
9 Safari Café
12 Bochka Бочка
18 Modern Nomads Mongolian Restaurant and Pub
25 Makarych Макарыч

PLACES OF INTEREST
5 Geological Museum Геологический Музей
6 Giant Head of Lenin Памятник Ленину
8 Buryat History Museum Бурятский Исторический Музей
15 Triumphal Arch Триумфальная Арка
17 Opera and Ballet Theatre Театр Оперы и Балета
20 City Museum Музей Истории Города
21 Shopping Arcade Гостиный Двор
22 T-34 Tank Monument Памятник-монумент «Танк Т-34»
23 Trinity Church Церковь Святой Троицы
24 Buryat Drama Theatre Бурятский Драматический Театр
27 Virgin Hodegetria Cathedral Одегитриевский Собор

OTHER
1 Railway Station Железнодорожный Вокзал
4 Central Post Office Почтамт
11 Internet Café Интернет кафе
14 Siberia Tour/internet Сибирь Тур/Интернет
16 Mongolian Consulate Кунсульство Монголии
19 Bus Station Автовокзал
26 Buses to Ivolginsky Datsan Автобусы в Датсан
28 River Station Речной Вокзал

By the end of 2011 the Ulan-Ude branch of ***Sayen Hotel***, 10 minutes' drive from the city centre, should be completed, giving the area its first hotel of that standard (see p281).

Where to eat and drink

One of the best places is ***Modern Nomads Mongolian Restaurant and Pub*** (ул Ранжурова 1, ul Randzhurova 1, mains R350), serving a good variety of Mongolian and Buryat dishes, as well as tasty salads. Unlike the Irkutsk branch, which seems to be for visitors only, this one is popular with tourists and locals alike. Friendly service and English menus with pictures make it particularly visitor-friendly.

It's difficult to miss ***Bochka*** **Бочка** ('Barrel', ул Почтамтская 1, ul Pochtamtskaya 1, mains R350), housed inside a giant barrel. They specialise in grilled meats and hearty Siberian staples, and in the summer, their beer garden is the place to be with a tankard of (expensive) brew. ***Baataray Urgöö*** **Баатарай Ургуу** ('Yurt', Verkhnyaya Berezovka, marshrutka stop 'Yurt' Юрта, mains R300) is justifiably considered to be one of the best restaurants in town. It serves Buryat cuisine in a delightful setting consisting of several interconnected yurts, lavishly decorated with Buryat national costume and rugs. This is a place for a leisurely meal but it's not the easiest to reach, being located further along the highway than the Ethnographic Museum; take marshrutka No 37 from pl Sovietov or grab a cab.

A worthy splurge, ***Chingis Khan*** **Чингис Хан** (Солнечная Башня, бул Карла Маркса 25а, Sun Tower, bul Karla Marksa 25a, mains R550) also specialises in Buryat cuisine; they also serve delicious Russian and Chinese dishes in an atmospheric setting. It's around 4km south of the Uda river, so you'll need to grab a cab; look for the Mongol warriors by the entrance.

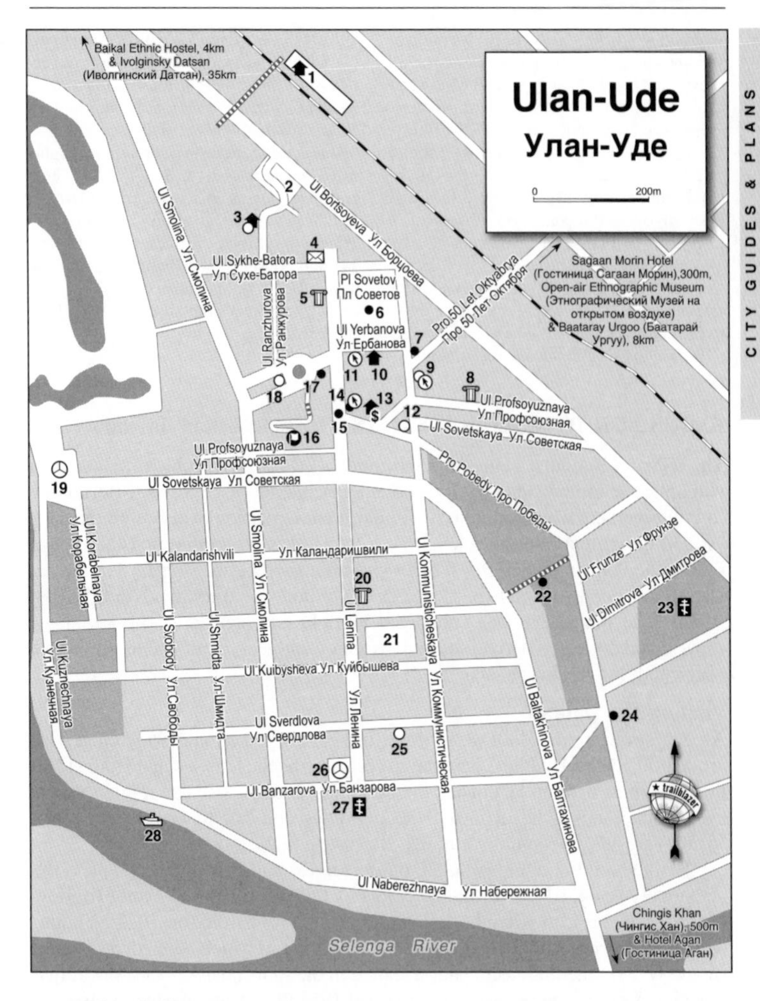

Makarych **Макарыч** (ул Свердлова 28, ul Sverdlova 28) is a no-frills *buuzy* joint, serving giant steamed dumplings and other quick eats. The large indoor **market** off ul Baltakhinova – a bustling place with every sort of food on offer – is a good spot for self-caterers, as is the 24-hour ***Sputnik supermarket*** **Супермаркет Спутник** (ул Коммунистическая 48, ul Kommunisticheskaya 48), which stocks a pricey array of local and imported groceries. ***Safari Café***, next to Sputnik, is a popular spot serving good coffee and there's wi-fi.

Moving on

By rail Ulan-Ude has frequent departures to all points along the Trans-Siberian, as well as Mongolia and China. You can buy international tickets at the railway station in the upstairs Service Centre; Baikal Ethnic Hostel and hotels such as Saagan Morin can also help you book onward tickets. Departures include Irkutsk (8-9/day, 6½-10hrs), Moscow (up to 4/day, 83-140hrs, trains No 001 and No 339 being the quickest), Chita (3/day, 9-11hrs, No 339 is the best for overnight journeys), Vladivostok (2-3/day, 63-66hrs), Ulaanbaatar (daily, 17-23hrs, No 362 at 7.02am, as well as the fast trains No 62 and 009, on Sun and Mon respectively). There are two trains a week to Beijing (Tue & Sat, 49hrs), which need to be booked well in advance in summer.

By air From Ulan-Ude's upgraded airport (🖳 www.airportbaikal.ru) there are connections to Moscow (at least 2/day, 6hrs) Irkutsk (3/week, 45mins) and Nizhneangarsk (near Severobaikalsk (daily except Sat, 1½hrs). There are also international flights to Ulaanbaatar (Tue & Sat, 1½hrs). There are fewer flights in winter, particularly to Nizhneangarsk. The airport is served by Transaero, Buryat Airlines (ul Yerbanova 14) and S7 (ul Sukhe-Batora 63, near the post office), among others. You can also buy plane tickets from hotels such as Hotel Buryatiya.

EXCURSION TO IVOLGINSKY DATSAN Иволгинский Датсан

This Tibetan Buddhist monastery, the centre of Russian Buddhism, stands on a wide plain 35km outside the city, and is a fascinating place to visit. Before the Revolution there were hundreds of similar monasteries in the area with the largest and most important at Selenginsk. Almost all were closed and the monks sent to the Gulags in the 1930s. In 1945, Stalin gave permission for Ivolginsky Datsan to be constructed here as a mark of gratitude for Buryatiya's help during WWII. The monastery was completed in 1946 and there are now 40 lamas, some of them very elderly, but novices join each year; most spend up to five years studying in Ulaanbaatar.

Visiting the Datsan

As you stroll around the Datsan don't forget that you should walk clockwise around objects of Buddhist veneration (prayer wheels, temples and stupas) and that hats must be removed inside the buildings. Guides will also remind you to keep your hands clasped inside the buildings and not to cross your arms. Visitors are shown round by a monk. Be sure to make a donation.

Work should now be complete on the largest building in the complex, the elaborately designed and brilliantly coloured **Temple of Hambo Lama Itigilov**. Itigilov was the 12th Khambo Lama and just before he died in 1927 he stipulated that his body should be buried in the position in which he died, and that it should be exhumed 30 years later. He died in the lotus position and was buried in a pine chest; when monks dug him up in 1955 they were amazed to discover his body miraculously preserved. In 2002 his body was exhumed again, still looking as if he'd only recently died. He has been declared a sacred object of Buddhism and his body is brought out four times a year; touching it allegedly heals the sick.

The **central temple**, a three-storey building constructed in 1971, burnt down four months after completion with the loss of numerous valuable *thangkas*. It was rebuilt in just seven months. Its joyous technicolour interior seems rather incongruous in grey Russia: golden dragons slide down the 16 wooden columns supporting the upper galleries (where there is a library of Tantric texts), and hundreds of incarnations of the Buddha line one wall. Easy to recognise is Manla, the Buddha of Tibetan medicine, with the dark blue face. The largest *thangka* hanging above the incarnations is of the founder of the Gelugpa (Yellow Hat) sect of Tibetan Buddhism. Juniper wood is burnt and food and money offered to the incarnations.

Beside this is a smaller stupa, and the **green temple** behind it is the oldest building in the complex, constructed in 1946. The octagonal white building houses a model of **Paradise** (*Devashin*) and a library of several hundred Tibetan and Mongolian texts, each wrapped in silk. In the big **white stupa** nearby are the ashes of the most famous of the Datsan's head lamas, Sherapov, who died in 1961. There is even a **Bo tree** (sacred fig tree) growing very successfully in its own greenhouse from seeds brought in 1956 from Delhi. Students now come from all over the region to study Buddhism here. Don't miss the incredible **mandala** inside the Tantric temple, at the far right side as you enter the complex or a prayer session with the monks in their maroon robes chanting in Tibetan amidst incense smoke and the sound of clashing cymbals.

You might be surprised at the number of non-Buddhist worshippers here, but in Ulan-Ude it's fairly common to attend Buddhist temples, Orthodox churches and Shamanist ceremonies. Given the hardship and uncertainty of Russian life, the non-Buddhists come here for the peaceful atmosphere and for respite.

Getting there

Marshrutka No 130 (R30) runs frequently from Banzarova bus station near Virgin Hodegetria Cathedral to the village of Ivolga. It sometimes continues to the Datsan but if not shared taxis (R20 per seat) will be waiting to take you on from Ivolga.

Chita
Чита

[Moscow Time +6] Chita is at the junction of the Trans-Siberian and Trans-Manchurian railway lines. The city was closed to foreigners until the late 1980s, as it was the army headquarters for Eastern Siberia and guarded the sometimes-tense Russian/Chinese border. There's just about enough to keep you occupied for a day here, including a Decembrists museum, a museum full of military hardware and a brand new golden-domed cathedral.

Founded in 1653, Chita became a *sloboda* (tax-exempt settlement) in 1690, populated by Cossacks and trappers. It was famous in the 19th century as a place of exile for many revolutionary Decembrists. George Kennan was here in 1887 and wrote: 'Among the exiles of Chita were some of the brightest, most cultivated, most sympathetic men and women we had met in Eastern Siberia.'

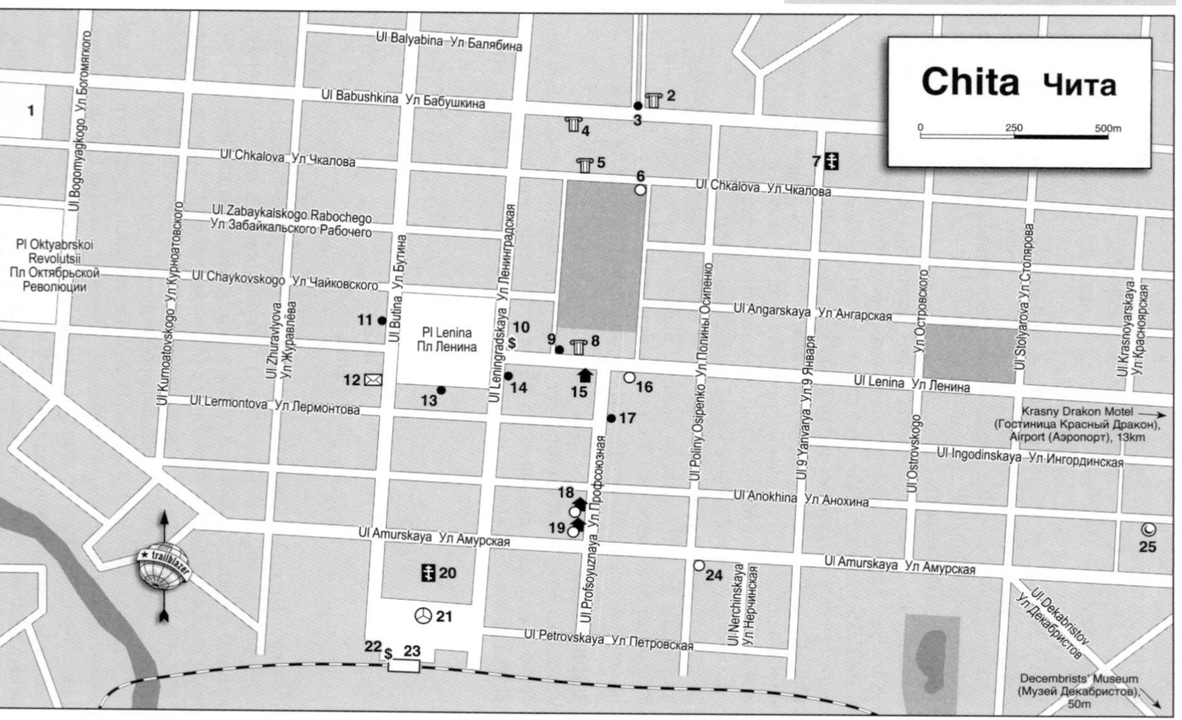

Chita Чита
0
250
500m
Ul Balyabina Ул Балябина
Ul Babushkina Ул Бабушкина
Ul Chkalova Ул Чкалова
Ul Zabaykalskogo Rabochego Ул Забайкальского Рабочего
Ul Chaykovskogo Ул Чайковского
Ul Lermontova Ул Лермонтова
Ul Bogomyagkogo Ул Богомягкого
Ul Kurnoatovskogo Ул Курноатовского
Ul Zhuravlyova Ул Журавлёва
Ul Butina Ул Бутина
Ul Leningradskaya Ул Ленинградская
Pl Oktyabrskoi Revolutsii Пл Октябрьской Революции
Pl Lenina Пл Ленина
Ul Angarskaya Ул Ангарская
Ul Lenina Ул Ленина
Ul Poliny Osipenko Ул Полины Осипенко
Ul 9 Yanvarya Ул 9 Января
Ul Ostrovskogo Ул Островского
Ul Stolyarova Ул Столярова
Ul Krasnoyarskaya Ул Красноярская
Krasny Drakon Motel (Гостиница Красный Дракон), Airport (Аэропорт), 13km
Ul Ingodinskaya Ул Ингординская
Ul Anokhina Ул Анохина
Ul Profsoyuznaya Ул Профсоюзная
Ul Amurskaya Ул Амурская
Ul Nerchinskaya Ул Нерчинская
Ul Petrovskaya Ул Петровская
Ul Dekabristov Ул Декабристов
Decembrists' Museum (Музей Декабристов), 50m
1
2
3
4
5
6
7
8
9
10
11
12
13
14
15
16
17
18
19
20
21
22
23
24
25
trailblazer

By 1900 more than 11,000 people lived here. There were nine churches, a cathedral, a nunnery, a synagogue, thirteen schools and even a telephone system. Soviet power was established in the city on 16 February 1918 but on 26 August the city was captured by the White Army. On 22 October, however, it was firmly back in Soviet hands.

Though Chita, now a city of about 380,000 and Eastern Siberia's major industrial and cultural centre, is still dominated by a large military presence, with numerous army buildings scattered around the city, trade with China has really taken off. Still, it feels well off the typical tourist trail. In fact, you'll probably feel like the first foreigner to visit if you stop here, which can make it all the more interesting and enjoyable.

WHAT TO SEE AND DO

On Chita's main square, pl Lenina, the requisite statue of the former leader is overshadowed by the scale of the square itself and several of its buildings. To the east is the **Post-Baikal Railway Management Office** Управление

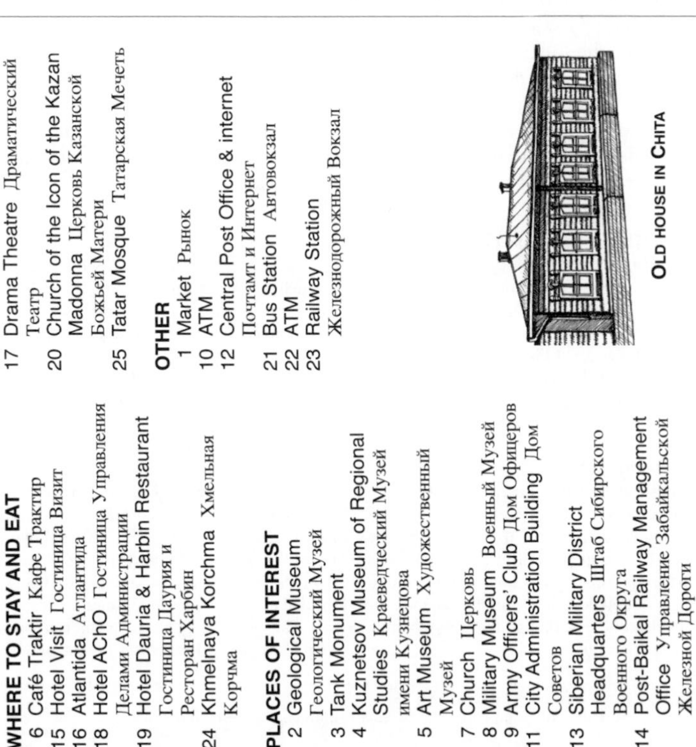

OLD HOUSE IN CHITA

Забайкальской Железной Дороги, which controls lucrative cross-border trade, including oil shipments. To the south is the massive yellow **Headquarters of the Siberian Military District** Штаб Сибирского Военного Округа, commanding troops from Omsk to Chita. And to the west is the aquamarine **City Administration Building** Дом Советов. Around the corner is the **Army Officers' Club** Дом Офицеров (ul Lenina 80). The **Military Museum** Военный Музей (ul Lenina 86, 9am-1pm & 2-5pm, R50), next door to the Club has exhibits on the Soviet military operation in Afghanistan, Beketov's Cossacks, Communist-era repressions, and military equipment. Captions are in Russian only. Out at the back is a collection of tanks and artillery.

The small **Decembrists' Museum** Музей Декабристов (10am-6pm Tue-Sun, R50) is housed in the former Archangel Michael Church on ul Dekabristov 3b, a 20-minute walk from the railway station.

Kuznetsov Museum of Regional Studies Краеведческий Музей имени Кузнецова (ul Babushkina 113, 10am-6pm Tue-Sun, R90) has an array of stuffed local fauna in the Natural History Section, as well as some beautiful photographs of winter woodlands on the lower floor, a regional archaeology exhibition and exhibits on the Evenki and other native inhabitants of the area from the 17th to the 20th centuries. Upstairs it seems as if every aspect of life in Chita and the region has been scrutinised and put on display; you can learn about anything from dentistry to dog shows.

Across from the railway station is the enormous blue and gold **Church of the Icon of the Kazan Madonna** Церковь Казанской Божьей Матери, rebuilt in 2004 after being destroyed in the 1930s.

PRACTICAL INFORMATION

Orientation and services

The main **railway station**, Chita II, is three blocks south-west of pl Lenina, a short walk from the centre of the town and most hotels. There are **ATMs** in the station.

There is **internet access** at the post office on ul Lenina 2 (8am-8pm Mon-Fri, until 7pm Sat, until 6pm Sun, R50/hour).

Where to stay

Almost all Chita's hotels operate on a strange price system; if you ask for a single or double room, you'll most likely be quoted a higher price. But if you ask for a 'space' *(miesto),* you'll be given a bed in a single or double, whichever is available, for considerably less, though these rooms may be of poorer quality.

Budget accommodation is difficult to come by, as it's mostly taken up by soldiers and Chinese traders.

Hotel AChO **Гостиница АЧО** (ул Профсоюзная 19, ul Profsoyuznaya 19, ☎ 351 968, sgl/twin from R2600/4200), inside a brick mansion that was used as a hospital during WWI, has decent en suite rooms equipped with fridges. Cheaper shared rooms with shared facilities are available.

Next door, ***Hotel Dauria*** **Гостиница Даурия** (ул Профсоюзная 17, ul Profosyuznaya 17, ☎ 262 350, sgl/twin from R3600) has fully renovated rooms with the added plus (or minus) of being located above a Chinese restaurant.

The plushest place in town is ***Hotel Visit*** **Гостиница Визит** (ул Ленина 93, ul

The Chita area code is ☎ 3022. From outside Russia dial +7-3022.

Lenina 93, ☎ 356 945, sgl/twin R3600/ 5800), with extremely comfortable, air-conditioned rooms on the 5th floor of a tower. You can stay for 12 hours or less for half the price.

Where to eat and drink

Due to the abundance of trade with China, you'll find a lot of places serving (or at least claiming to serve) good Chinese food. ***Harbin Restaurant* Ресторан Харбин**, below Hotel Dauria, serves a good range of Chinese food and is popular with businessmen; come hungry or bring a friend, as the portions are sizeable.

The young and trendy hang out at ***Atlantida* Атлантида** (ул Ленина 77а, ul Lenina 77a, mains R350) behind the Drama Theatre. There's a fancy international dining room upstairs done up in faux-Grecian style, serving a good mix of Mediterranean and Italian cuisine, while downstairs is a good pizzeria popular with students.

***Khmelnaya Korchma* Хмельная Корчма** (ул Амурская 69, ul Amurskaya 69, mains R250), decked out in chirpy folksy style, is a great local favourite for hearty Ukrainian dishes, accompanied by live music in the evenings. The *golubtsy* (cabbage leaves stuffed with meat and rice) and *vareniki* (cherry dumplings) are particularly tasty. The inexpensive business lunch is a good deal.

For good Russian food, head for ***Café Traktir* Кафе Трактир** (ул Чкалова 93, ul Chkalova 93, mains R250-400), an attractive wooden lace cottage serving a good range of salads and meat and fish dishes. In summer, there's a popular beer tent outside where you can get some great shashlyk.

Moving on

By rail The 001 stops in Chita on the way to Moscow on odd days; other good and cheaper alternatives include the 339 and the 043, both passing through on even days (105hrs). The 002 heads to Vladivostok on odd days, while a good alternative is the 008, leaving on even days (53hrs). The Beijing-bound 020 passes through in the wee hours of Wednesday morning, but if there are no tickets for that, you may consider taking the 650 in the evening to Zabaikalsk on the border and then catching a bus into China from there.

The **service centre** on the left side of the railway station (enter from outside, 8am-noon & 1-7.30pm) is your best bet for purchasing tickets.

Birobidzhan

Биробиджан

[Moscow Time +7] Birobidzhan, a sedate town of 80,000 people, is the capital of the so-called Jewish Autonomous Region, a remote site selected in 1928 as a 'homeland' for Soviet Jews. An effective propaganda campaign, as well as starvation in Eastern Europe, encouraged 41,000 Soviet Jews to move here in the 1930s. Jewish schools and synagogues were established and a considerable effort was made to give the city a Jewish feel. This included Hebrew street signs, designation of Hebrew as the region's official language and the founding of Russia's only Hebrew-language newspaper, *Birbobidzhaner Stern*.

It soon became obvious, however, that 'Stalin's Zion' was no Promised Land. Conditions were extremely harsh with winter lows of minus 40°C and vicious mosquitoes in summer, and things were made worse in 1937 by a resurgence of religious repression, including closure of the synagogues and the banning of Hebrew and Yiddish. By 1938 60% of the Jewish population had left.

In the 1950s the town developed into an agricultural and industrial centre. Birobidzhan's most famous export was rice combine harvesters from the Dalselmash factory on the western outskirts of town. The factory recently restarted after a two-year closure. Since 1991, many Jewish people have moved to Israel and today less than 6% of the population has Jewish ancestry.

WHAT TO SEE AND DO

Note the giant **menorah** in front of the railway station building and the Hebrew characters inscribed on its façade.

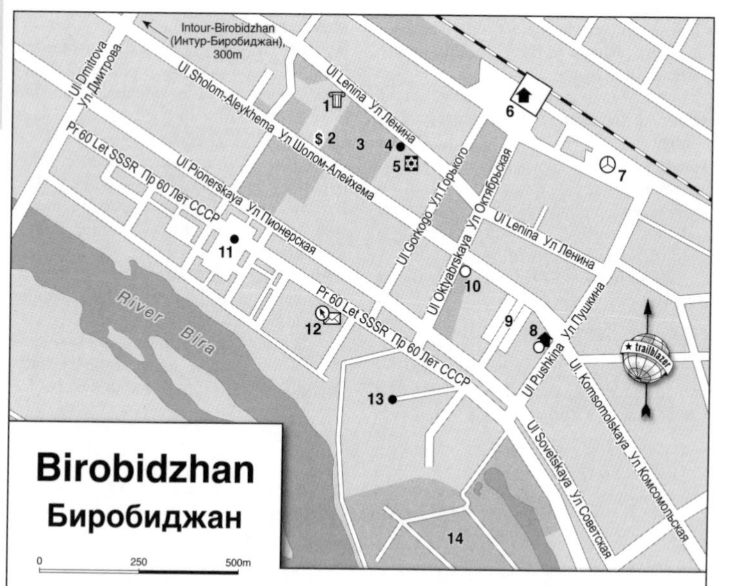

WHERE TO STAY, EAT & DRINK
- 6 Resting rooms Комнаты Отдыха
- 8 Hotel & Restaurant Vostok Гостиница и Ресторан Восток
- 9 Market Рынок
- 10 Café Kakadu Кафе Какаду

PLACES OF INTEREST
- 1 Museum of Regional Studies Краеведческий Музей
- 3 Park Pobedy Парк Победы
- 4 Freid Фрейд
- 5 Synagogue Синагога
- 11 Lenin Statue Памятник Ленину
- 13 Philharmonic Hall Филармония
- 14 Park Kultury Парк Культуры

OTHER
- 2 Sberbank Сбербанк
- 6 Railway Station Железнодорожный Вокзал
- 7 Bus Station Автовокзал
- 12 Post Office & Internet Почтамт и интернет

The **Museum of Regional Studies** Краеведческий Музей (ul Lenina 24, 10am-6pm Wed & Thur, until 5pm Fri, 9am-5pm Sat & Sun, R130) has a few exhibits on local Jewish history and a diorama of the Volochaevska Civil War battle, as well as the ubiquitous stuffed animals.

Off ul Sholom-Aleykhema, attractive **Park Pobedy** Парк Победы has a modern art sculpture in the centre. On ul Lenina 19 you'll find **Freid** Фрейд (10am-6pm Mon-Fri), Birobidzhan's Jewish cultural centre with unhelpful staff. Next door is the working **synagogue** (синагога).

The **beach** on River Bira is packed on summer weekends; walk down ul Gorkogo to the river and you'll see it on the left beside the Park Kultury. There's also an attractive promenade along the river, abloom with flowers in spring and summer.

PRACTICAL INFORMATION

Orientation and services

Everything is within walking distance of the railway and bus stations. The main streets are ul Lenina and the partially pedestrianised ul Sholom-Aleykhema.

There is intermittent **internet access** at the main post office at pr 60 Let SSSR.

Where to stay and eat

The standard ***Hotel Vostok*** **Гостиница Восток** (ул Шолом-Алейхема 1, ul Sholom-Aleykhema 1, ☎ 42162 65 330, sgl/dbl R2000/2500) is still the only hotel in town. Its stuffy restaurant with unhurried staff is one of the few places to eat out.

For another sleeping option try the ***resting rooms*** **комнаты отдыха** at the railway station (sgl 'lux'/twin/trpl R1820/750/550pp; showers R80).

Busy ***Café Kakadu*** **Кафе Какаду** near Hotel Vostok serves *draniki* (potato fritters), blini, pelmeni and hot dogs in a cafeteria setting and there is a fresh **produce market** Рынок nearby.

Moving on

All Trans-Siberian trains pass through Birobidzhan and there are several local trains daily to Khabarovsk (R236, 3hrs), so you could do this as a day trip, hopping off at Birobidzhan in the morning, storing your luggage, and then catching a suburban train to Khabarovsk when you've finished sightseeing.

Another option to/from Khabarovsk is to take a local bus (R250, 3hrs), leaving frequently throughout the day from the bus station.

Khabarovsk

Хабаровск

[Moscow Time +7] Khabarovsk is a relaxed provincial city of 582,000, picturesquely situated on three hills above the junction of the Amur River and its tributary, the Ussuri, and recent winner of the 'most comfortable city in Russia' title. In summer, holiday crowds flock to the sandy river banks, giving the place the atmosphere of a friendly seaside resort; there's an attractive riverside promenade and the heart of the city seems to have been made for strolling. It's bitterly cold in winter and when the river freezes, people drive their cars onto it and fish through holes chopped in the half-metre-thick ice.

Apart from the river, Khabarovsk boasts several interesting museums and monuments and visitors shouldn't miss the opportunity to take a boat trip along the father of all Russian rivers – the Amur.

HISTORY

In 1858 a military settlement was founded here by Count Muravyev-Amursky, the Governor-General of East Siberia who did much to advance Russia's interests in the Far East. It was named Khabarovka, in honour of the Cossack explorer who conquered the Amur region in the 17th century, and whose statue now stands in the square in front of the railway station.

By 1883 the town was known as Khabarovsk and the following year, when the Far Eastern Territories were made a region separate from Eastern Siberia, it became the administrative capital and home of the governor-general of the area.

Until the railway arrived the town was just a trading and military post, and a junction for passengers arriving by steamer along the Shilka and Amur rivers from Western Siberia. Here they would transfer to another ship for the voyage down the Amur and Ussuri to Vladivostok.

From 1875 onwards several plans were submitted for the building of the Ussuri Railway, which now runs along the great river between Khabarovsk and Vladivostok. Work began in 1893 and on 3 September 1897 a train completed the first journey between these two towns.

Early visitors

As more sections of the Trans-Siberian Railway were built, greater numbers of foreign travellers arrived in Khabarovsk. The *1900 Guide to the Great Siberian Railway* did not encourage them to stay long, reporting that: 'The conditions of life in Khabarovsk are not attractive, on account of the absence of comfortable dwellings, and the expensiveness of some products and of most necessary articles ... Imported colonial goods are sold at a high price and only fish is very cheap.' Tourists were also advised against trying Mr Khlebnikov's locally produced wine, made from the area's wild vines, because 'it is of inferior quality and without any flavour'.

Recommended sights included the wooden triumphal arch (now demolished) erected in commemoration of the visit of Tsarevich Nicholas in 1891, and the bronze statue of Count Muravyev-Amursky on the promontory above the river. After the Revolution the Count was traded in for an image from the Lenin Statue Factory, but he has since reappeared.

The city today

The railway brought more trade than tourists, and though it suffered during the Civil War, the town quickly grew into the modern city it is today. Few of its old wooden cabins remain but there are some attractive stone buildings from Imperial times. It is the capital of Khabarovsk Territory, surrounded by some of the richest mineral deposits in Russia, although the land is little more than a gigantic swampy forest. Khabarovsk is now a major industrial centre involved in engineering, petroleum refining and timber-working.

In the last few years Japanese and South Koreans have moved in, opening factories and businesses. Most of the city's foreign visitors now come from these two countries.

WHAT TO SEE AND DO

Museum of Regional Studies Краеведческий Музей

This excellent museum, based on the extensive collection of Baron Korff, a former governor-general of the Amur region, was opened in 1894 and is housed in two attractive buildings next to each other (ul Shevchenko 11, 10am-6pm Tue-Sun, R200), one being the Amur River Museum wing. With donations from hunters and explorers over the last century, the collection has grown into an impressive display of local history, flora and fauna. In the first few rooms labels are in Cyrillic, English and Latin but after that it's only Cyrillic and Latin (see pp484-5).

Among the stuffed animals in the ground-floor galleries are four Amur tigers. Also known as the Siberian or Manchurian tiger (*Felis/Panthera tigris altaica*), this is the largest member of the cat family and can weigh up to 350kg, about twice the average weight of an African lion. In the same gallery are various fur-bearing animals including the large sea-otter or Kamchatka beaver (*Enhydra lutris*) from which come the highest-priced pelts in the world. Before this animal came under official protection in the early 20th century its pelts were selling for over US$2000 each.

The upper galleries are devoted to local history and ethnography. The area was inhabited by several tribes at the time of the Revolution. The Goldi and Orochi lived near the mouth of the Ussuri, and Olchi and Giliak beside the Amur. Each tribe had its *shaman*, and some of their robes and equipment are on display as well as a suit made entirely of fish-skins (the skin of a common fish, the *keta*, was used not only for clothing but also for tents, sails and boots). There's also a display of early settlers' furniture, samovars and other utensils, including some bread baked by the original colonists.

Far Eastern Art Museum Дальневосточный Художественный Музей

Next to the Museum of Regional Studies is the Far Eastern Art Museum (10am-5pm Tue-Sun, R270), featuring a mix of permanent and temporary exhibitions. Permanent exhibits include art and craftwork, mainly carpets and footwear, of the Nanai, Nivkh, Udeghe, Evenki and Negidal peoples. There are also carved walrus tusks by Chukchi and Eskimos. On the 2nd floor there is a selection of exquisite 17th- and 18th-century religious icons. The galleries have paintings by German and Italian as well as Russian artists, and there is one work by Titian.

Military Museum Музей Истории Краснознаменного Дальневосточного Военного Округа (ДВО)

This worthwhile museum (ul Shevchenko 20, 10am-5pm Tue-Sun, R180), opposite the Far Eastern Art Museum, provides a record of military activity here since the city was founded. There are numerous pictures of Russian soldiers, as well as photographs of British, French, Italians and Americans in Vladivostok in

1918. The walls are decorated with medals and old weapons, including a weather-beaten Winchester rifle and a few Smith & Wesson pistols. There's a small display on Mongolia including a photo of Lenin and Sukhe Bator sharing a joke. Upstairs you'll find WWII memorabilia and an interesting display on the war in Afghanistan, as well as an extensive collection of WWII propaganda posters. Behind the building there's a row of armoured vehicles including a tiny MC-1 two-man tank, as well as a MiG fighter plane and a train carriage (usually locked) once used by the commander of the Russian Far East military forces.

Arboretum Питомник Деревьев

Founded long before the railway arrived, and originally set up to provide trees and shrubs for the new town's parks, the arboretum (ul Volochayevskaya, 9am-6pm Mon-Fri) claims to have a specimen of every plant species found in the Far Eastern Territories. Take bus No 1 to the corner of ul Volochayevskaya and ul Lenina, then bus No 25 to the Ussurisky stop.

Other sights and things to do

The **Amur River** is a focus of interest in winter or summer. In winter when it freezes, locals drill holes through the ice and set up little tents from which they fish. In summer the banks are crowded with sun-worshippers and swimmers. However, the city has repeatedly warned bathers to stay out because of pollution: the effects of the chemical disaster in Harbin in 2005 reached as far as Khabarovsk. A safer way to enjoy the Amur is to take one of the hour-long party boat cruises (R200) that leave regularly from the river station in summer, or to stroll along the attractive riverfront promenade, popular with strolling locals and skaters.

Looming over the riverbank, on Komsomolskaya pl, is the new **Assumption Cathedral** Успенский Собор, rebuilt in 2001 after being torn down in the 1930s. There are also regular services at the church near the railway station on Leningradskaya ul, the interior of which is beautifully decorated.

It's worth the walk uphill to view **Glory Square**, including a **Victory Monument** Монумент Победы commemorating local soldiers fallen in WWII, and the very photogenic **Cathedral of the Transfiguration** Преображенская Церковь with its five golden domes. There are also fine views of the river, especially at sunset, which is when locals like to come here.

PRACTICAL INFORMATION

Orientation and services

Khabarovsk is a large city: the railway station and the waterfront, where many of the attractions are, are almost 3km apart, a half-hour walk.

The main street, ul Karla Marksa, is to the east of the city's central square, pl Lenina, and ul Muravyeva-Amurskogo to the west of it.

Knizhny Mir Bookshop (ul Pushkina 56, 9am-7pm) has an excellent range of maps of Khabarovsk and surrounding oblasts and cities.

Banks There are **ATMs** scattered liberally around the city centre, including at most hotels, and particularly along ul Muravyeva-Amurskogo.

Communications There's internet access in the **central post office** at ul Muravyeva-Amurskogo 28 (8am-9pm,

R80/hour). Another internet café is Portal.ru, on the corner of ul Moskovskaya and ul Kim Yu Chena.

Consulates The **Chinese Consulate** (Lenin Stadium 1, ☎ 302 353) is open for visa appointments 10.30am-1pm Mon, Wed and Fri. See p27 for details about Chinese visas. There is also a **Japanese Consulate** (ul Pushkina 38a, ☎ 326 418).

Travel agents Numerous travel agencies can book city and regional tours and help you organise your train and plane tickets, as well as assisting you with getting a Chinese visa. The better agents include **Dalgeo Tours** (ul Turgeneva 78, ☎ 318 829, 🖳 www.dalgeo.com, 10am-7pm Mon-Fri), whose English-speaking staff offer a wide range of tours, including Khabarovsk day and night city tours, multi-day trips to Komsomolsk-na-Amure and winter crossings of the Amur River.

Local transport

There are regular **bus**, **trolley-bus** and **tram** services (R16). From the railway station, trams No 1 and 2 run near pl Lenina, while bus No 4 runs to pl Komsomolskaya and bus No 1 runs down ul Karla Marksa and ul Muravyeva-Amurskogo, returning to the station along ul Lenina. To get to the airport, take trolleybus No 1 from pl Komsomolskaya or bus No 35 from the railway station.

Where to stay

HOFA (see p153) can organise **homestays** in Khabarovsk.

The ***resting rooms*** **комнаты отдыха** *(komnaty otdykha)* in the railway station (sgl/4-person R1200/450 for 12hrs, or R2000/650 for 24hrs) are clean and tidy, and the single room even has a desk and a TV. Toilets are shared, and a cold shower costs R80 extra.

A short walk from the river, ***Hotel Express Vostok*** **Гостиница Экспресс Восток** (ул Комсомольская 67, ul Komsomolskaya 67, ☎ 384 797, sgl/dbl R2300/3000) is an excellent budget choice due to its central location. The rooms may be small but they're wi-fi enabled. Breakfast is not included.

The old ***Hotel Turist*** **Гостиница Турист** (ул Карла Маркса 67, ul Karla Marksa 67, ☎ 439 674, 🖳 www.habtour.ru – in Russian, dbl with/without air-con R2800/2400) had its rooms revamped a couple of years ago, though it hasn't lost its slightly rundown charm. Some rooms have balconies and breakfast is included.

Most centrally located and possibly the best value is ***Hotel Tsentralnaya*** **Гостиница Центральная** (ул Пушкина 52, ul Pushkina 52, ☎ 324 759, sgl/dbl R1900/2400), with its comfortable, air-conditioned rooms. Its main claim to fame is that Paul Theroux stayed here while researching *The Great Railway Bazaar*.

The renovated ***Hotel Zarya*** **Гостиница Заря** (ул Ким Ю Чена 81/16, ul Kim Yu Chena 81/16, ☎ 310 101, sgl/dbl from R2550/2850) sports compact rooms and the hotel has an excellent banya downstairs (R1000/hour). The staff are friendly and helpful; the price includes a good buffet breakfast.

Close to the railway station, comfortable ***Hotel Versailles*** **Гостиница Версаль** (Амурский Буль 46а, Amursky bul 46a, ☎ 659 222, sgl/dbl R2400/3350) offers cheerful rooms with all mod cons. Staff are friendly and speak English; even the free breakfast is better than normal. There is a 24-hour café here as well.

The monolithic Soviet ***Hotel Intourist*** **Гостиница Интурист** (Амурский Буль 2, Amursky bul 2, ☎ 312 313, 🖳 www.intour.khv.ru, rooms from R3700) still draws the tour groups. The rooms are nothing special, the internet is intermittent, and the lifts are prone to breaking down, just like in Soviet times, but if you get a room on one of the upper floors, you at least get great views of the Amur. The service

The Khabarovsk area code is ☎ 4212. From outside Russia dial +7-4212.

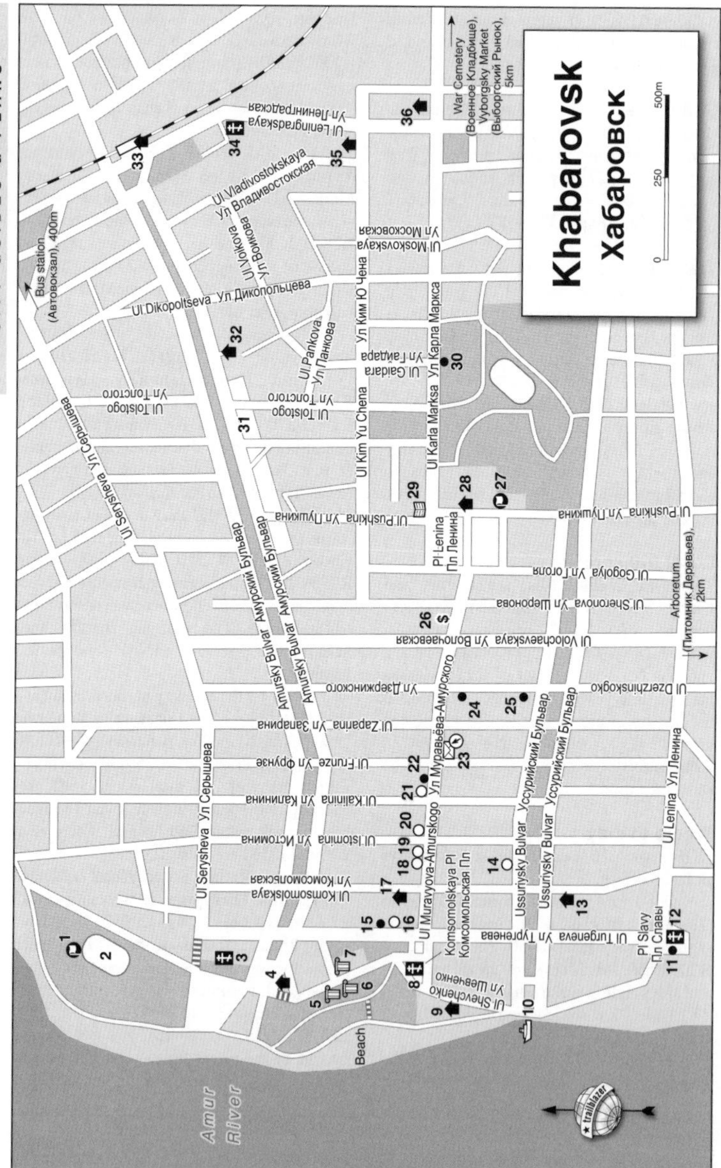

Khabarovsk
Хабаровск
0
250
500m
Amur River
Beach
Bus station (Автовокзал), 400m
War Cemetery (Военное Кладбище), Vyborgsky Market (Выборгский Рынок), 5km
Arboretum (Питомник Деревьев), 2km
Ul Serysheva Ул Серышева
Ul Tolstogo Ул Толстого
Ul Dikopoltseva Ул Дикопольцева
Ul Vladivostokskaya Ул Владивостокская
Ul Voikova Ул Воикова
Ul Leningradskaya Ул Ленинградская
Ul Moskovskaya Ул Московская
Ul Pankova Ул Панкова
Ul Kim Yu Chena Ул Ким Ю Чена
Ul Gaidara Ул Гайдара
Ul Karla Marksa Ул Карла Маркса
Ul Pushkina Ул Пушкина
Pl Lenina Пл Ленина
Ul Gogolya Ул Гоголя
Ul Sheronova Ул Шеронова
Ul Volochaevskaya Ул Волочаевская
Ul Dzerzhinskogo Ул Дзержинского
Ul Zaparina Ул Запарина
Ul Frunze Ул Фрунзе
Ul Kalinina Ул Калинина
Ul Istomina Ул Истомина
Ul Komsomolskaya Ул Комсомольская
Amursky Bulvar Амурский Бульвар
Ul Muravyova-Amurskogo Ул Муравьёва-Амурского
Komsomolskaya Pl Комсомольская Пл
Ussuriysky Bulvar Уссурийский Бульвар
Ul Lenina Ул Ленина
Ul Turgeneva Ул Тургенева
Pl Slavy Пл Славы
Ul Shevchenko Ул Шевченко
trailblazer

WHERE TO STAY

4 Hotel Intourist Гостиница Интурист
9 Hotel Parus Гостиница Парус
13 Hotel Express Vostok Гостиница Експресс Восток
17 Hotel Sapporo Гостиница Саппоро
28 Hotel Tsentralnaya Гостиница Центральная
32 Hotel Versailles Гостиница Версаль
33 Resting rooms Комнаты Отдыха
35 Hotel Zarya Гостиница Заря
36 Hotel Turist Гостиница Турист

WHERE TO EAT AND DRINK

14 Russky Restaurant Русский Ресторан
16 Café Chocolate Кафе Шоколад
18 Tsentralny Gastronom Центральный Гастроном
19 Café Blin! Кафе Блин!
20 Teppan-Yaki Теппан-Яки
21 Pelmennaya Пельменная

PLACES OF INTEREST

3 Church of St Innokent Церковь Святого Иннокентия
5 Museum of Regional Studies Краеведческий Музей
6 Far Eastern Art Museum Дальневосточный Художественный Музей
7 Military Museum Музей Истории Краснознаменного Дальневосточного Военного Округа (ДВО)
8 Assumption Cathedral Успенский Собор
11 Glory Square Victory Monument Монумент Победы
12 Church of the Transfiguration Преображенская Церковь
24 Drama Theatre Театр Драмы
30 Musical Comedy Theatre Театр музыкальной комедии
34 Church of Christ's Birth Церковь Рождества Христова

WHERE TO SHOP

22 Tayny Remesla Art Store Магазин Тайны Ремесла
31 Market Рынок

OTHER

1 Chinese Consulate Китайское Консульство
2 Lenin Stadium Стадион Ленина
10 River Station Речной Вокзал
15 Dalgeo Tours Далгео Тур
23 Central Post Office & internet Почтамт и интернет
25 InterVizit ИнтерВизит
26 ATM
27 Japanese Consulate Японское Консульство
29 Knizhny Mir Bookshop Книжный Мир
33 Railway Station Железнодорожный Вокзал

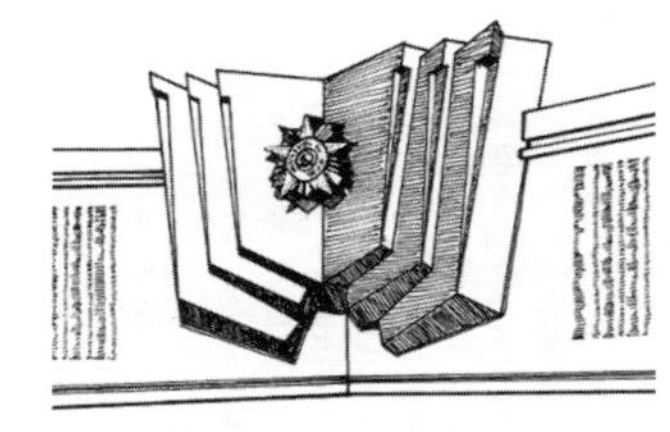

THE MEMORIAL OF GLORY
KHABAROVSK

bureau, Intour-Khabarovsk, offers a wide range of excursions.

In a historical building a block from the river, ***Hotel Parus*** **Гостиница Парус** (ул Шевченко 5, ul Shevchenko 5, ☎ 260 060, 🖳 www.hotel-parus.com, sgl/dbl R5000/6300) is one of the top hotels in town, popular with businessmen. The rooms are comfortable, though they don't quite match the grandeur of the lobby, with its chandeliers and reading room for guests. There's an excellent restaurant on-site, specialising in European dishes.

Another good top end option, ***Hotel Sapporo*** **Гостиница Саппоро** (ул Комсомольская 79, ul Komsomolskaya 79, ☎ 304 290, 🖳 www.sapporo-hotel.ru, sgl/dbl R5000/5300) is particularly popular with Japanese business people and tour groups, which is reflected in its semi-Japanese décor. The air-conditioned, wi-fi enabled rooms are decorated with bamboo and breakfast is included.

Where to eat and drink

In the summer, the best places to eat are the inexpensive riverside cafés.

Café Chocolate **Кафе Шоколад** (ул Тургенева 74, ul Turgeneva 74, meals R750) is a hip café populated by laptop-wielding residents, thanks to the free wi-fi. The menu is international – from fajitas to salads – and while not cheap, it's high quality.

The décor at ***Russky Restaurant*** **Русский Ресторан** (Уссурийский Бульвар 9, Ussuriysky bul 9, meals R1500) is beyond kitsch; you come here for the experience as much as the food. Expect tables crowded with discerning diners who appreciate the best Russian food in town, accompanied by traditional folk music. Big portions, great atmosphere.

On the corner of ul Volochayevskaya and ul Muravyeva-Amurskogo (ул Волочаевская и ул Мурвьёва-Амурского), ***Café Blin!*** **Кафе Блин!** serves just that – blini and more blini with numerous sweet and savoury fillings. Cheap and cheerful.

In the basement on the corner of ul Muravyeva-Amurskogo and ul Kalinina (ул Муравьёва-Амурского и ул Калинина) is a ***pelmennaya*** **Пельменная** serving delicious and filling pelmeni from 9am to 9pm.

Another good cheapie choice is ***Tsentralny Gastronom*** **Центральный Гастроном** (ул Муравьёва-Амурского 9, ul Muravyeva-Amurskogo 9, meals R350), where you pick up a tray and help yourself to the array of salads, soups and hot dishes, paying the cashier at the end.

Teppan-Yaki **Теппан-Яки** (ул Муравьёва-Амурского 11, ul Muravyeva-Amurskogo 11, meals R1200) is an upmarket Japanese restaurant, specialising in sushi, which they do very well indeed. Add a chilled-out interior, where you're isolated from the street noise, some minimalist bamboo decorations, and you've got one of the city's top spots.

Where to shop

Interesting local products include ginseng and a special blend of vodka and herbs known as *aralyevaya vodka*.

Attractive ul Muravyeva-Amurskogo is the place to shop. The best souvenir shop is **Tayny Remesla** art store Магазин Тайны Ремесла, ul Muravyeva-Amurskogo 17.

The best clothing and electronics market is the open-air **Vyborgsky Market** Выборгский Рынок, otherwise known as the Oriental Bazaar. As the name suggests, pretty much everything for sale here has come over the river from China. Trolleybus No 1 runs to ul Vyborgskaya, where you catch a cab for 3km to the market.

Moving on

By rail From Khabarovsk, the best service for Vladivostok is the overnight 006 (12hrs).

Heading west, the Moscow-bound 001 stops in Chita (37hrs), Irkutsk (56½hrs) and other major cities before reaching Moscow (133½hrs), another good alternative being the 043, originating in Khabarovsk (147hrs).

Other convenient options include the Novosibirsk-bound 007 and the slightly slower 133. There are also daily links to Tynda with the 325 (28hrs) and daily services to Vanino/SovGavan on the 943

❑ Excursions from Khabarovsk

Khabarovsk is an ideal base for trips into the Siberian outback. Dalgeo Tours (see p311) and Intour-Khabarovsk (see Where to stay, opposite) offer special-interest tours and excursions to many distant and not-so-distant regions.

Sakhalin is an island off the East Siberian coast. Its main attraction is the great variety of wildlife which foreigners may photograph, study, ride amongst or hunt. Most popular are fishing trips and bird-watching trips. Vanino, from where you catch a ferry to Sakhalin Island, is on the **BAM Railway**.

Other destinations in Eastern Siberia and the Far Eastern Territories that can be visited from Khabarovsk include **Yakutsk** (see pp385-7), **Kamchatka** (for fishing, hunting and adventure tours), **Perelk** in the Arctic Circle (to see the Northern Lights) and **Magadan** (a former Gulag centre).

(25½hrs), handy if you're catching a ferry to Sakhalin Island.

The only place at the station to buy international tickets is at window No 7. There is a service centre on the right-hand side of the station that sells domestic tickets (8am-8pm; enter from outside).

In town, **InterVizit** (ul Dzerzhinskogo 39, 10am-6pm Mon-Fri for train tickets, see By air for air tickets) specialise in train and air tickets. There's also the **air and rail ticket office** at ul P Komarova 8, 9am-6pm Mon-Fri, 10am-4pm Sat).

By bus Buses leave frequently from the bus station for Birobidzhan. They take about three hours and cost R250.

By boat **Boats** operate along the Amur River from June to October. Local ferries and long-distance hydrofoils all depart from the **river station** at ul Shevchenko 1.

Hydrofoils run between Khabarovsk and Nikolayevsk-na-Amure via Komsomolsk-na-Amure between May and October (daily at 7am, 17hrs to Nikolayevsk-na-Amure and 6hrs to Komsomolsk-na-Amure).

There are also several daily boats from Khabarovsk to Fuyuan in China, departing around 8am and returning around 10pm (around R3000 return, 1½hrs). Customs procedures are straightforward. Tickets are sold from kiosks prominently signposted 'Fuyuan', near the river station. You must show a Chinese visa to buy a boat ticket. From Fuyuan it's a 15-hour bus ride on to Harbin, or a shorter one to Jiamusi from where there are trains to Harbin.

By air Khabarovsk Novy Airport (☎ 263 268, 🖳 http://airkhv.ru – in Russian) – the largest airport in Russia's Far East – is 10km east of the city centre. Domestic flights include: Moscow (several daily, 8½hrs), Vladivostok (daily, 1¾hrs), Irkutsk (daily, 3hrs) and Yekaterinburg via Novosibirsk (4/week, 5hrs and 4hrs, respectively), among other major cities.

International departures include Beijing (1/week, 2hrs), Harbin (3/week, 1½hrs), Seoul (daily, 2hrs) and Niigata (2/week, 1¾hrs). All airlines have ticket booths at the airport. Alternatively, book your plane tickets at Intervizit (ul Dzerzhinskogo 39, 9am-8pm Mon-Fri, to 6pm Sat & Sun) or at the **air and rail ticket office** at ul P Komarova 8, 9am-6pm Mon-Fri, 10am-4pm Sat).

Vladivostok

Владивосток

Vladivostok is a robust city of some 600,000 people, the eastern terminus of the Trans-Siberian line and home of Russia's Pacific Fleet. Whether you're heading east or west, it's well worth stopping off to explore one of the country's biggest Cold War secrets and to enjoy the seaside town atmosphere. Be warned, the summer weather here is never very good. Locals joke that it only rains twice in June: once for 13 days, then for 14. September and October are often sunny and warm, though.

Vladivostok's dramatic setting along the hills around the Golden Horn Bay makes it quite attractive, in a busy industrial way, not unlike Chile's Valparaíso. The port is a hub of activity, with new buildings going up and an enormous bridge to Russky Ostrov (Russky Island) under construction, which will make it easier to access what will be Russia's largest aquarium and new university campus. In 2012 Vladivostok is due to host the Asia-Pacific Economic Conference, which accounts for the new hotels being built.

Until 1990 Vladivostok was off-limits to all visitors because of its military and strategic importance as one of Russia's key naval ports. Even Soviet citizens needed special permits, and foreigners, with a few notable exceptions (such as US President Gerald Ford in 1975), required nothing short of divine intervention. Now ferries link Vladivostok with ports in Japan and Korea, and although Asian tourists have arrived in droves, the city still has a somewhat cloistered feel to it.

HISTORY

This region has been occupied for many thousands of years, certainly back at least to the 2nd millennium BC; but inhabitants were largely nomadic so few relics remain. Eastern chronicles reveal that this was considered part of the Chinese empire at a very early stage but also that it was so remote and conditions so harsh that it was left well alone.

The Russians arrive

In the mid-19th century the Russians were concentrating on expanding their territory eastwards at China's expense. At the head of the exploratory missions was Count Muravyev-Amursky, who from his steamer, the *Amerika*, chose this site for a harbour in 1859. A year later a party of 40 soldiers landed to secure the region. The port was named Vladivostok ('Rule the East').

In 1861 more soldiers arrived to protect Russia's new eastern frontier, with settlers not far behind. It soon became apparent just how important a find this settlement was: Vladivostok's harbour, one of the few deep-water ports on the east coast, remains unfrozen for longer than any other in Siberia, being inaccessible for an average of just 72 days per year, compared with Nakhodka's 98.

This and Vladivostok's strategic location resulted in the shift to here of Russia's eastern naval base in 1872 from Nikolaevsk-na-Amure (frozen for an inconvenient 190 days per year).

Conflict in the east

In 1904 the Russo-Japanese war broke out. Vladivostok was heavily bombarded and trade virtually ceased but while large parts of the port were destroyed, the war was ultimately to prove beneficial: peace settlements with Japan left Vladivostok as Russia's prime east coast port although Japan gained Port Arthur and parts of Sakhalin Island.

During WWI the city served as the chief entry point for supplies and ammunition from the USA, and British, Japanese, American, Canadian and Italian troops streamed in to support the White Russians' struggle against the Bolsheviks. The most notorious foreign 'visitors' were Czech legions who had fought their way east all the way from the Ukraine in a desperate bid for freedom (see p106). The graves of many of them, and of other foreigners, can still be found in the cemetery here.

As it became clear that the Bolsheviks were gaining the upper hand, many White Russians fled abroad, and the foreign forces departed. Most had left by 1920 although some Japanese stayed on until October 1922. Finally, on 25 October, the city was 'liberated' and Soviet power established, prompting Lenin's famous comment about Vladivostok: 'It's a long way away. But it's ours'.

The Soviet period

The Soviet period meant considerable investment in the city's development. Money poured in, along with orders to develop the port and build more ships. In the last days of WWII Vladivostok assumed a key role as the centre of operations for the fight against the Japanese in Manchuria. In the space of four years 25 ships were sunk here and some 30,000 sailors perished. During the Stalin years, the port lost much of its cosmopolitan character as most of the city's foreign population were shot or deported. As the Cold War set in, the city was sealed off from the outside world and the Pacific Fleet expanded fast. The West heard little more of this protected port until 1986 when Gorbachev made his 'Vladivostok Initiative' speech, highlighting a grand new plan for Soviet economic and military commitments in the Far East. Echoing Peter the Great, he announced that Vladivostok was to become 'a wide open window to the East'.

Vladivostok today

The city is keen to establish itself as a major player on the Pacific Rim. There are periodic murmurs of a movement to make the entire Primorsky region an independent economic zone. Undoubtedly it is an area of enormous potential and, not surprisingly, it has attracted mafia gangs from all over Russia who deal in every commodity imaginable, though it doesn't affect tourists.

VLADIVOSTOK RAILWAY STATION

WHAT TO SEE AND DO

The Pacific Fleet and lookout point

Don't miss this unique opportunity to see some of the world's finest naval technology, although owing to a lack of funds it's beginning to look a little weatherbeaten now. Locals will tell you it's all right to take photographs, but telephoto lenses and too many pictures of radar sites might arouse suspicion; caution is advised. A good place to watch the ships is from **Orlinoye Gnezdo** Орлиное Гнездо (Eagle's Nest Hill), the city's top lookout spot on a hill overlooking the port. To get to the top take the **funicular railway** (R10; 7.30am-8pm) from ul Pushkinskaya, go through the less-than-salubrious underpass under ul Sukhanova and then climb up to your left. Under the memorial there are some expensive souvenir stalls.

I M Arsenyev Regional Museum Краеведческий Музей И М Арсенева

This is the biggest and best of Vladivostok's museums (ul Svetlanskaya 20, 10am-6pm Tue-Sun; R120), recalling the history of the city and the region, and named after a local writer. The impressive wildlife display has labels in English: local sea life, an Ussuri leopard, a large Amur tiger and a couple of moose locking antlers. Rarer specimens include a goral (a small goat-like antelope), a Steller's albatross, an Amursky leopard and a Chinese soft-shelled turtle.

There's a display of early settlers' belongings, the robes of a Tungus shaman and the safe from the first bank here, stuffed with old rouble notes. Upstairs there's a small exhibition about actor Yul Brynner (whose family lived here before the Revolution), naval memorabilia and local art (the wood carvings are particularly attractive).

Pacific Fleet Military Museum & Border Guard Museum Музей Тихоокеанского Флота и Музей Пограничников

Displays at the **Pacific Fleet Military Museum** (ul Semyononvskaya 18, 9am-5pm Tue-Sat, R100) include model ships and miscellaneous items from various conflicts: muskets, propaganda posters, a flame-thrower, an ejector seat and the twisted propeller and gun from a ditched fighter plane. The **Border Guard Museum** collection details the history of protecting the nearby frontier with China and has some interesting recent photos showing patrolling activities.

Submarine Museum Мемориальный Комплекс «Боевая Слава Краснознаменного Тихоокеанского Флота»

On the waterfront next to the eternal flame on the WWII memorial is an old S56 submarine (10am-7pm, R70), housing a display on the history of submarines in Vladivostok. There are early uniforms, ships' instruments, pictures of the earliest submarine (1865) and the first flotillas (1906). Much of it consists of old photographs, although you can also see some gifts to submarine commanders from foreign hosts including, strangely enough, a ceremonial key to the City of San Diego and (Tom Cruise fans, take note) a US Navy Fighter Weapons School Top Gun shield, and you can also clamber into the back section of the submarine to look at the periscope and the controls. No English captioning.

***Krasny Vympel* «Красный Вымпел»**
The Soviet Pacific Fleet's first ship, launched on 24 January 1923, is moored just opposite the Submarine Museum. Displays include photographs of early crew members, medals, uniforms and other salty memorabilia. Some of the machinery is preserved down below. However, at the time of writing, the museum was closed indefinitely for 'repairs.'

Vladivostok Fortress Museum Музей Владивостоская Крепость
Up on the hill behind the Oceanarium, reached from ul Zapadnaya, this place is well worth a visit for its large array of military hardware and the museum (10am-6pm, until 5pm in winter, R120) is housed inside the fortress, used from 1882 to 1923. Outside you can see sea mines, torpedoes and supersonic missiles, and join the school children clambering over the tanks and guns. There is also a well-camouflaged toilet amongst the hardware. Inside, exhibits with English captioning show the region's many fortresses and some of the history of the Russian-Japanese struggle for control of the Kurile Islands.

The fortress itself is one of sixteen that encircle the city, some of which are linked to underground tunnels.

Russky Island
Of the several islands that lie offshore in Zolotoy Rog (Golden Horn) Bay, Russky Island is the most important, having been of strategic military importance for over 150 years. It has only been open to foreigners over the past 10 years or so, and by the time this guide is published, the enormous bridge that is currently being built to link the island to the mainland may be completed. At the time of writing, the island was served by frequent boats from the smaller Local Ferry terminal, near to the main Marine Terminal

There are plans to move the university campus from the mainland to the island due to the extra room it would give, and Russia's largest aquarium/ marine research facility is currently being constructed on the island. Once it's completed, it will take over four hours to walk around all the exhibits.

Other sights
Primorsky Art Gallery Приморская Картинная Галерея (pr Partizansky 12, 9am-6pm Tue-Sun) has had much of its west wing art donated by the Tretyakov Gallery in Moscow. The east wing (R60) hosts temporary exhibitions by local artists, while the west wing (R70) features 19th- and 20th-century oil paintings. To get there, take buses 12, 17, 23, 40, 41 or 102 from the bus terminal on pl Semyonovskaya two stops to the 'Kartinnaya Galereya' stop.

At ul Aleutskaya 15 is the **House of the Brynner Family** Бывший Дом Бреннеров. You can't enter the former residence of Yul Brynner's family, but it's a real pilgrimage for some. In the well-tended **Naval Cemetery** are graves of Russians and foreigners who died fighting the Communists in 1919-20. It's a fair distance, on a hill overlooking Zolotoy Rog Bay, so you would be wise to take a car. The city's **Oceanarium** Океанариум (ul Batareynaya, by the seafront, 10am-8pm Tue-Sun, 11am-8pm Mon, R200) features stuffed birds and marine life and many species of live fish. There are also daily dolphin shows.

PRACTICAL INFORMATION

Orientation and services

Vladivostok is built along the Muravyev Peninsula, which stretches south-west into the Sea of Japan. Scattered around it is a series of islands, of which Russky Island (Russky Ostrov) remains the most important. The city's focal point is **Zolotoy Rog** (Golden Horn) **Bay**, so called because of its resemblance to Istanbul's Golden Horn. It's here that most ferries, warships and fishing boats dock.

The **railway station** is conveniently located on the waterfront, ideal if you're transferring directly to the **marine terminal** (*morskoy vokzal*). The railway station faces pl Lenina and ul Aleutskaya. Central hotels are within walking distance of the station; indeed almost everything is within walking distance but Vladivostok is a hilly place so distances can seem longer.

Note that the **Central Bus Station** is not at all central, being near Vtoraya Rechka suburban railway station (see Local transport, opposite).

Information *Vladivostok News*, 🖳 http://vladivostoktoday.com, is a good source of local information. *Vladivostok Times* 🖳 www.vladivostoktimes.com is also useful.

Banks There are **ATMs** at a business centre in the same building as the post office and at major banks, including **Sberbank**, ul Aleutskaya 12, which can also do currency exchange, and cash travellers' cheques.

Communications The **central post office** is on ul Aleutskaya opposite the railway station. The adjacent business centre is also a convenient place for **internet access**. **Dalsvyaz Telephone Office** (ul Svetlanskaya 57, 9am-7pm Mon-Fri, 10am-5pm Sat) is the place to make international phone calls.

Travel agents Helpful **Dalintourist** (ul Admirala Fokina 8, ☎ 490 905, 🖳 www.dalintourist.ru) offers inexpensive home-stays, city tours, and adventure and ecological excursions. Also recommended is

Discovery Travel Club (Zheleznodorozhny per 3, ☎ 777 679, 🖳 www.discoveryclub.info), run by the effusive, English-speaking Julia, who can organise anything from Chinese visas to travels in Primorsky Region, trips to Kamchatka, as well as train and ferry tickets.

Tours All the sights are within easy walking distance, but the travel agents listed above do offer city tours.

The region around Vladivostok, known as Primorye, offers plenty of opportunity for outdoor adventure. Dalintourist and Discovery Travel Club (see above) offer such trips, but they are pricey (R10,000 and up) so it's best to go with lots of people. Options include a visit to two tiger parks in the area; the 350,000-hectare Sikhote-Alin Nature Reserve, centre of a Russian-American effort to save the Amur tiger; Lake Khanka, ideal for bird-watching and site of a famous lotus bloom the first two weeks of August; and river rafting, including the wild Kema River.

Boat trips around the harbour are enjoyable, especially with the chance to see the Pacific Fleet. There is no regular cruise service, so your best bet is to pay one of the fishing boats around the marine station to take you around. They can be talked down to around R2500 for a one-hour cruise.

There are also several **islands** that can be visited independently. See Local transport, opposite.

Diplomatic representation **Australia** (ul Krasnogo Znameni 42, ☎ 427 464); **China** (Hotel Gavan, ul Krygina 3, ☎ 495 037), visa applications 9am-12.30pm on Mon, Wed and Fri; **Japan** (ul Verkhneportovaya 46, ☎ 267 481); **Korea** (ul Pologaya 19, ☎ 402 222); **UK** (ul Svetlanskaya 5, ☎ 411 312); **USA** (ul Pushkinskaya 32, ☎ 300 070); **Vietnam** (ul Pushkinskaya 107/1, ☎ 226 927).

Local transport

The **airport** is 40km outside Vladivostok. A taxi from the airport to Vladivostok railway station costs about R2000, or else take bus No 107 (R75, 1½hrs, hourly between 6.40am and 5.45pm).

Vladivostok is served by an extensive network of buses, trolleybuses and trams.

There are numerous daily ferries from the **local ferry terminal** opposite the Submarine Museum. Destinations include the popular swimming spots of Russky Island, Popov Island (where you can camp or stay in a guesthouse), Reyniky Island and Cape Peshanaya.

Where to stay

Vladivostok has a shortage of beds in summer and budget accommodation is increasingly rare as prices are pushed up by the influx of Asian tour groups.

HOFA (see p153) can arrange **homestays** in Vladivostok; as can Dalintourist (see Travel Agents).

See You Hostel (ул Крыгина 42а, кв 133 ul Krygina 42a, apt 133, ☎ 487 779, 💻 www.mixmix-hostels.com, dorm R450) is the only youth hostel in town; it consists of an apartment with guest lounge and kitchen. Aleksei, the well-travelled owner, is happy to give sightseeing tips. The website gives detailed instructions on how to reach the hostel.

Centrally located ***Hotel Renaissance*** **Гостиница Ренесанс** (ул Суханова 3, ul Sukhanova 3, ☎ 406 865, 💻 www.renaissancehotel.ru, sgl/dbl/suite from R3000/4000/7000) has somewhat haphazard décor, which includes a stuffed bear in the lobby, but the rooms are comfortable and equipped with satellite TV.

Very popular with Chinese visitors, ***Hotel Moryak*** **Гостиница Моряк** (ул Посетская 38, ul Posteskaya 38, ☎ 499 499, dbl from R2500) has quite small and basic rooms, but it's cheaper than most hotels in the area. Perks include a sauna.

Far from the hustle and bustle of Vladivostok, in a pretty forested area near the sea, ***Vlad Motor Inn*** (ул 8-я 35, Санаторная, ul 8-ya 35, Sanatornaya, ☎ 388 888, 💻 www.vlad-inn.ru, dbl R4600-5450) is an attractive retreat popular with expats. Rooms are spacious and light, the restaurant dishes are a mix of European and American, and staff speak English. Take a suburban train to Sanatornaya.

Near the station, ***Hotel Primorye*** **Гостиница Приморье** (ул Посетская 20, ul Posetskaya 20, ☎ 411 422, 💻 www.hotelprimorye.ru, sgl/dbl/suite from R3000/4200/6200) is one of the best hotels in town, with friendly English-speaking staff, sauna, wi-fi throughout, and attractive, spotless rooms, the pricier ones with views of the Golden Horn Bay.

Azimut Hotel Vladivostok **Азимут Отель Владивосток** (ул Набережная 10, ul Naberezhnaya 10, ☎ 411 941, 💻 www.azimuthotels.ru, dbl from R2200), with views of the bay from its hill location, consists of two buildings near each other: 'Vladivostok' and 'Amursky Zaliv'. The two offer revamped, wi-fi enabled rooms decorated in pastel colours and the price includes a good buffet breakfast. There's a café and a 24-hour bar for night owls.

In an attractive historical building, the Japanese-owned ***Hotel Versailles*** **Гостиница Версаль** (ул Светланская 10, ul Svetlanskaya 10, ☎ 264 201, 💻 www.versailles.vl.ru, sgl/dbl from R6500/7500), has luxurious rooms, along with a health centre and Eurocentric Restaurant Versailles.

Popular with Asian tour groups, the monolithic ***Hotel Hyundai*** **Гостиница Хюндай** (ул Семёновская 29, ul Semenovskaya 29, ☎ 402 233, 💻 www.hotelhyundai.ru, dbl/suite R6000/from 12,000) is central and plush. Wi-fi is everywhere and the range of services includes a health club, swimming-pool, sauna and two very good restaurants – European

The Vladivostok area code is ☎ 4232. From outside Russia dial +7-4232.

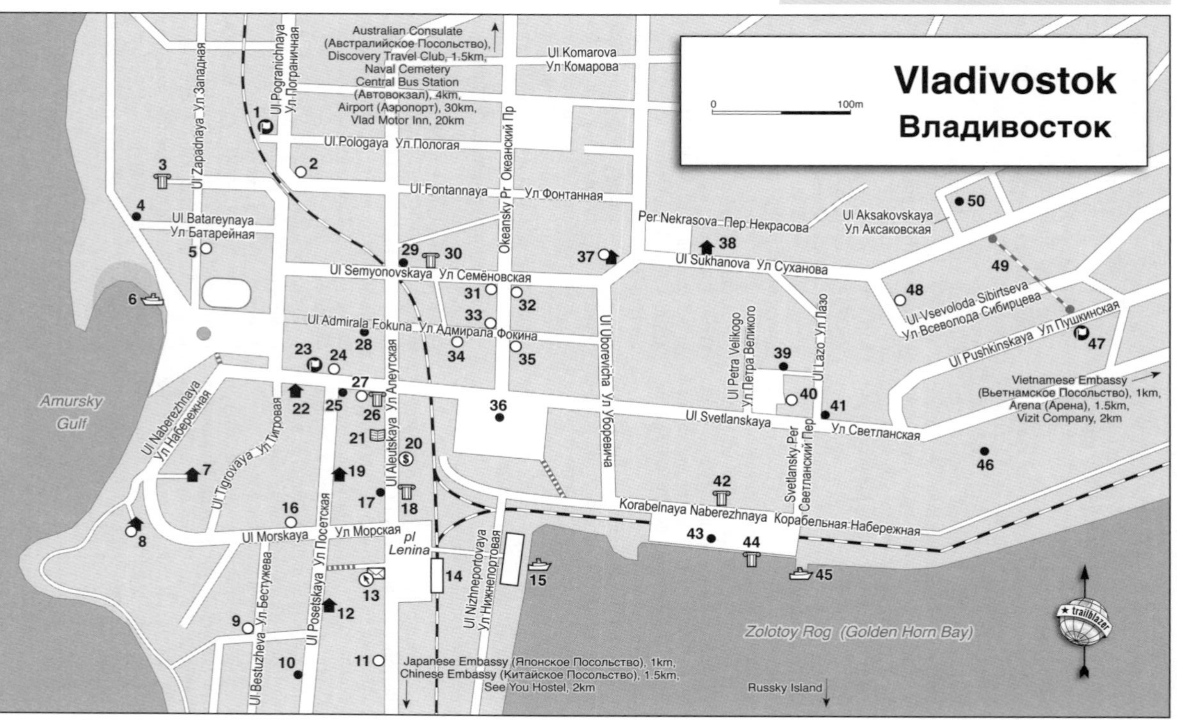
Vladivostok
Владивосток
0
100m
Amursky Gulf
Zolotoy Rog (Golden Horn Bay)
Russky Island
Australian Consulate (Австралийское Посольство), Discovery Travel Club, 1.5km, Naval Cemetery
Central Bus Station (Автовокзал), 4km, Airport (Аэропорт), 30km, Vlad Motor Inn, 20km
Japanese Embassy (Японское Посольство), 1km, Chinese Embassy (Китайское Посольство), 1.5km, See You Hostel, 2km
Vietnamese Embassy (Вьетнамское Посольство), 1km, Arena (Арена), 1.5km, Vizit Company, 2km
Ul Pogranichnaya Ул Пограничная
Ul Zapadnaya Ул Западная
Ul Batareynaya Ул Батарейная
Ul Pologaya Ул Пологая
Ul Fontannaya Ул Фонтанная
Ul Komarova Ул Комарова
Okeansky Pr Океанский Пр
Ul Semyonovskaya Ул Семёновская
Ul Admirala Fokuna Ул Адмирала Фокина
Ul Uborevicha Ул Уборевича
Ul Sukhanova Ул Суханова
Per Nekrasova Пер Некрасова
Ul Aksakovskaya Ул Аксаковская
Ul Vsevoloda Sibirtseva Ул Всеволода Сибирцева
Ul Pushkinskaya Ул Пушкинская
Ul Lazo Ул Лазо
Ul Petra Velikogo Ул Петра Великого
Ul Svetlanskaya Ул Светланская
Svetlansky Per Светланский Пер
Korabelnaya Naberezhnaya Корабельная Набережная
Ul Nizhneportovaya Ул Нижнепортовая
Ul Aleutskaya Ул Алеутская
pl Lenina
Ul Morskaya Ул Морская
Ul Posetskaya Ул Посетская
Ul Bestuzheva Ул Бестужева
Ul Tigrovaya Ул Тигровая
Ul Naberezhnaya Ул Набережная
trailblazer

WHERE TO STAY

7 & 8 Azimut Hotel Vladivostok Азимут Отель Владивосток
12 Hotel Primorye Гостиница Приморье
19 Hotel Moryak Гостиница Моряк
22 Hotel Versailles Гостиница Версаль
37 Hotel Hyundai Гостиница Хундай
38 Hotel Renaissance Гостиница Ренесанс

WHERE TO EAT AND DRINK

2 Bombay 1 Бомбей 1
5 Hanuri Ханури
8 Zabriskie Point Забриский Поинт
9 Café Nostalgia Art Shop
11 Republic Республика
16 Café Nostalgia Кафе Ностальгия
24 Rock's Cocktail Bar
27 Studio Coffee Студио Кофе
29 Clover Leaf Supermarket
31 Brauhaus Hans
32 Hare Krishna Харе Кришна
33 Italian Café Mauro Gianvanni Кафе Мауро Джанванни
34 Blinnaya Блинная
35 Edem Эдем
37 Sky Bar
40 Pizza M Grill Пицца М Гриль
48 Krestovy Pereval Крестовый Перевал

PLACES OF INTEREST

3 Vladivostok Fortress Museum Музей Владивостоская Крепость
4 Oceanarium Океанариум
17 Former House of the Brynner Family Бывший Дом Бреннеров
18 Primorsky Art Gallery Приморская Картинная Галерея
26 I M Arsenyev Regional Museum Краеведческий Музей И М Арсенева
30 Pacific Fleet Military Museum/Border Guard Museum Музей Тихоокеанского Флота и Музей Пограничников
36 Victory of Soviet Power Monument Памятник «Борцам за Власть Советов»
39 Drama Theatre Драматический Театр
42 Submarine Museum Мемориальный Комплекс «Боевая Слава Краснознаменного Тихоокеанского Флота»
43 125th Anniversary of Vladivostok Monument Обелиск в честь 125-летия Основания Города Владивостока
44 *Krasny Vympel* «Красный Вымпел»
46 Admiral Nevelsky Monument Памятник Адмиралу Невельскому
49 Funicular Railway Фуникулёр
50 Eagle's Nest Орлиное Гнездо

WHERE TO SHOP

9 Café Nostalgia Art Shop
21 Dom Knigi Bookshop Дом Книги
25 Flotsky Univermag Флотский Универмаг

OTHER

1 Korean Consulate Консульство Корея
6 Sportivnaya Gavan Pier Причал Спортивная Гаван
10 Biletur Билетур
13 Central Post Office & internet Почтамт и интернет
14 Railway Station Железнодорожный Вокзал
15 Marine Terminal Морской Вокзал
20 Sberbank Сбербанк
23 British Consulate Консульство Британии
28 Dalintourist Далинтурист
41 Dalsvyaz Telephone Office Дальсвяз Интернет Центр
45 Local Ferry Terminal Морской Вокзал Прибрежных Сообщений
47 US Consulate Консульство США

cuisine at the ***Pacific***, and Korean dishes at ***Khekimgang***.

Where to eat

Down by the popular beach at Sportivnaya there are several **cafés** serving drinks and snacks all day. Some hotels, such as Hotel Hyundai (see p321) have excellent restaurants.

A good restaurant within easy reach of the railway station is the wonderful ***Café Nostalgia*** **Кафе Ностальгия** (ул Морская 6/25, ul Morskaya 6/25, mains R350-600) which serves genuinely good coffee. The tiny restaurant is stylish and offers good Russian dishes.

Italian Café Mauro Gianvanni **Кафе Мауро Джанванни** (ул Адмирала Фокина 16, ul Admirala Fokina 16) is set in a trendy lounge with pumping music, giant video screens and a curvaceous, fully stocked bar. They charge around R350 for a thin and crispy pizza, and appetisers and salads cost just as much. ***Studio Coffee*** **Студио Кофе** (ул Светланская 18, ul Svetlanskaya 18) is where the young elite pack in for drinks and snacks.

Go to ***Blinnaya*** (Блинная at ул Адмирала Фокина 18, ul Admirala Fokina 18) for a blini craving quick-fix.

Bombay 1 **Бомбей 1** (ул Фонтанная 17, ul Fontannaya 17, [V]) does decent Northern Indian dishes and has good business lunches (noon-3pm; R400).

Republic **Республика** (ул Верхнепортовая 2, ul Verkhneportovaya 2) is a good chain for quick and inexpensive Russian dishes.

For excellent sushi, try ***Edem*** **Эдем** (ул Адмирала Фокина 22, ul Admirala Fokina 22, sushi/sashimi combos from R2000), a venerated cellar restaurant that rates among the best in town.

At ***Hare Krishna*** **Харе Кришна** (Океанский пр 10/12, Okeansky pr 10/12, closed Sun, [V]), you get three filling veggie courses for R300 in a serene atmosphere, which may include drumming and chanting or scripture-reading in the evening.

Krestovy Pereval **Крестовый Перевал** (ул Лютского 12, ul Lutskogo 12, meals R800, [V]) is a Georgian restaurant serving tasty *satsvivi* (chicken in walnut sauce), *khinkali* (giant meat-filled dumplings), *lobio* (spiced vegetable paste) and other traditional delights amidst 'Caucasian' décor. For upscale, well-prepared Korean dishes, try ***Hanuri*** **Ханури** (ул Батарейная 3a, ul Batareynaya 3a, mains R400), with elegant, minimalist décor. The noodles with seafood and sweet pumpkin porridge are particularly tasty. ***Pizza M Grill*** **Пицца М Гриль** (ул Светланская 51, ul Svetlanskaya 51, mains from R300), is an upscale establishment specialising in good pizza, as well as tasty pasta dishes, risotto and grilled meat and fish.

Self-caterers can head for **Clover Leaf** on the corner of ul Aleutskaya and ul Semenovskaya – a shopping mall with a **24-hour supermarket**.

Bars and entertainment

For a good selection of German beer and a lively ambience, head for ***Brauhaus Hans*** (ул Адмирала Фокина 25a, ul Admirala Fokina 25a), a beer house with live music most nights. ***Rock's Cocktail Bar*** (ул Светланская 7, ul Svetlanskaya 7) hosts varied live music, from ska to jazz to rock and there's a full dinner and snack menu. Tuesday is 'beer day' and Thursday is 'cocktail day', with corresponding discounts.

To enjoy the best night (and day) views of the city while sipping your expensive cocktail, go to the ***Sky Bar*** (Hotel Hyundai, see p321).

The lively ***Zabriskie Point*** **Забриский Поинт** (ул Набережная 9a, ul Naberezhnaya 9a), behind Hotel Amursky, plays nightly rock and jazz (except Mondays).

Arena **Арена** (ул Светланская 147, ul Svetlanskaya 147, 💻 www.arenavlad.ru) is Vladivostok's premier concert/entertainment venue, which hosts anything from rock gigs to all-women freestyle fighting.

Where to shop

The best souvenirs in town are sold at **Café Nostalgia Art Shop** (ul Pervaya Morskaya 6/25); take your pick from intricate wooden boat models, paintings of Vladivostok and

Asian art. **Flotsky Univermag** (ul Svetlanskaya 11) stocks all sorts of navy-related goodies. **Dom Knigi** bookshop (ul Aleutskaya 19) stocks a few classics, plus Stephen King, in English.

Moving on

By rail To buy international tickets go to window No 1 at the railway station, or else buy your ticket from the station's **Service Centre** (8am-noon & 1-5.45pm, R250 commission) at the southern end of the main building. From Vladivostok, the best way to get to Moscow is on the firmenny 001 Rossiya (odd days only, 6 days 3hrs). The 001 stops at Khabarovsk (12hrs), Irkutsk (80hrs), Novosibirsk (4 days and 4hrs) and all other major cities along the Trans-Siberian. On even days, the only Moscow-bound trains are the ultra-slow 903 and 945. The best train to Khabarovsk (5/day, 11-18hrs) is the overnight firmenny 005 Okean, though the 351 is cheaper. The 351 continues to Komsomlsk-na-Amure (26hrs) and Vanino/Sovetskaya Gavan (42hrs). For Harbin (China), the Khabarovsk-bound 351 stops at Ussuriysk on Mondays and Thursdays, one carriage detaches and continues on to Harbin (40hrs).

By bus The bus station (ul Russkaya) is 3km north of the centre. If you're heading into China, you can take a bus or share a taxi to the border at Grodekovo, four hours from Vladivostok. On the other side you catch a local bus or taxi to Suifenhe (5km), where buses to Harbin run twice a day and trains three times a day. This is a hassle to do yourself and the border crossing can be confusing, with individual travellers sometimes ignored in favour of Russian tour groups. There is also a weekly bus from Vladivostok to Harbin, China (8hrs). Agencies such as Dalintourist run Russians to Suifenhe for shopping trips; it's possible to get a ride on one of these buses for

❑ Vladivostok–Harbin border crossing

If you decide to take the train from Vladivostok to Harbin, you should have plenty of time on your hands. The train leaves Vladivostok in the evening. Two hours later it stops at **Ussurisk**, where your Harbin-bound carriage is detached. After sitting in a siding for eight hours, it is then attached to a new engine and you begin the next stage of the journey; a three-hour jaunt to the border at **Grodekovo**. So far it has taken you 13 hours to travel just 225km. Now you realise why the carriage is nearly empty: everyone else has taken the four-hour bus journey from Vladivostok to the border.

You disembark with your bags. In the customs and immigration building there is a kassa selling train tickets to Harbin. Customs and immigration officials here won't be working yet, but you can fill out your declaration form and wait upstairs. Three hours on the officials arrive and it's time to leave Russia. Bags are searched with varying degrees of enthusiasm. My visa wasn't registered with the company that issued it, and four French tourists had all overstayed their visas by a day, but none of this caused a problem. The train finally leaves Grodekovo, filled to capacity with all those sensible Russians who took the bus from Vladivostok. During the two-hour journey from Grodekovo to the Chinese border town of **Suifenhe**, Chinese customs and immigration officials enter your compartment and do their job efficiently and politely. The train is then taken off to have the bogies changed and for 3½ hours you are free to explore the delights of Suifenhe: an OK place, better than most border towns. You can change money in a hotel and get a decent meal.

You set off again in the evening, and arrive in Harbin very early the next morning, but this is Harbin North station. Even though everyone else gets off here, you should wait until the train arrives at the main railway station about 15 minutes later.

Congratulations: you have travelled a grand total of 783km in 31 hours at an average speed of 25km per hour.

Nick Hill

around R3000, which includes all the border fees; book several days in advance. Travel agencies can also help you book a bus to Harbin.

By air Vladivistok is served by several major airlines, for which you can buy tickets at **Biletur** (ul Posteskaya 17, ☎ 407 700, 🖳 www.airagency.ru): Aeroflot, Transaero, Korean Air, S7, Vladivostok Air (🖳 www.vladavia.ru) and China Southern.

Domestic departures include: Moscow (several daily, 8hrs), Irkutsk (daily except Tue and Sat, 4hrs), Yekaterinburg (4/week, 7hrs), Khabarovsk (daily, 1¼hrs), Novosibirsk (daily except Tue & Sun, 6hrs), St Petersburg (daily except Wed and Sun, 9hrs), Petropavlovsk-Kamchatsky (daily except Sun, 3hrs), Yuzhno-Sakhalinsk (several daily, 2hrs) and Yakutsk (2/week, 2hrs).

International destinations include Beijing (2/week, 2½hrs), Harbin (2/week, 2hrs), Seoul (daily except Thur, 1½hrs), Niigata (2/week, 1¾hrs), Toyama (2/week, 2¾hrs) and Hanoi (1/week, 6hrs).

❑ Ferries from Vladivostok to Japan and Korea

A ferry plies between Vladivostok and Fushiki-Toyama (**Japan**) weekly throughout the year. The two-night crossing takes about 38 hours. At the time of writing ferries depart Vladivostok at 6pm on Monday, reaching Fushiki-Toyama at 9am on Wednesday; and depart Fushiki at 6pm on Friday, arriving in Vladivostok at 9.30am on Sunday. The ships are fairly modern and comfortable, though the crossing itself is often rough.

There is now a new 'Eastern Dream' ferry operating between Vladivostok and Sakaiminato, Japan, via Donghae, Korea, departing on Wednesdays at 10am, arriving in Donghae on Thursday morning at 9am, departing at 6pm, and arriving in Sakaiminato at 8am. The ferry then departs for Vladivostok at 7pm on Friday evening.

See also box p35.

Dong Chun Ferry (Vladivostok Marine Terminal, 2nd floor ☎ 302 660, 🖳 www.dongchunferry.co.kr – in Russian/Korean) goes to Sokcho in **Korea** three times a week in summer (from Vladivostok on Sat and Zarubino, 5hrs' drive from Vladivostok, on Mon, Wed and Sat) and twice a week in winter (no Monday departures from Zarubino). For more information and bookings contact: Dong Chun Ferry Co or a travel agent, such as the one at Hotel Hyundai (see p321).

The voyage: 'A unique and memorable experience – bumping down a dirt road from Vladivostok to Zarubino in a bus with a psychotic driver, and then being the only foreigner on a boat with lots of holes in it (if I'd had a supply of duct tape I would probably have amused myself by sticking the ferry back together) and a serious and increasing list to starboard so that the people in 3rd class, myself included, spent the night sliding back and forth across the floor crashing into all and sundry. Travelling down the North Korean coast (for a while, so close you could easily take pictures of North Korea) in the middle of a typhoon takes some beating!' (**Rich Perkins**, UK)

Ulaanbaatar (Ulan Bator)

Улаанбаатар

The world's coldest capital is a fascinating place to visit even if it is, at first sight, a jumble of Soviet-style housing, ancient temples, old palaces and Dubai-style glass skyscrapers jostling each other for space amidst chaotic traffic snarls. Things are changing fast here, and the capital is filled with fascinating incongruities. Nomadic herders from the countryside have filled the city's outskirts with their *ger* tents; they retain their traditional dress and practices, and today they share the sidewalks of downtown Ulaanbaatar with young, professional urbanites.

Mongolia is a haven for adventure-seeking backpackers, with Ulaanbaatar's guesthouses serving as their base. The relatively free and democratic political system, compared with other nations in the region, has made Mongolia a darling of the international donor community. In bars and restaurants you'll likely run into UN officials, US Peace Corps volunteers or staffers from international NGOs, who make up much of the city's expat community.

With a population close to one million, Ulaanbaatar sits in a basin surrounded by four mountains: Bogd Uul, Songino Khairkhan, Chingeltei and Bayanzurkh, all part of the beautiful Khentii range, the southernmost boundary of the great Siberian taiga. The city experiences great climatic extremes; the temperature ranges from -49°C (-46°F) in winter to 38°C (93°F) in summer. There's little rainfall and on average 283 sunny days in the year. Ulaanbaatar is 1350m above sea level.

The best time to visit Ulaanbaatar is during the **Naadam Festival**, usually held between 11 and 13 July (although you'll find many other travellers heading there too, and demand for accommodation and Trans-Mongolian train tickets outstrips supply). The festival involves the three traditional Mongolian sports of horse-riding, wrestling and archery (see box pp332-3).

HISTORY

Home of the Living Buddha

For much of its 350-year existence the town was little more than a semi-nomadic settlement. From 1639 to 1778 it moved some 30 times, like a migrating *ger* (yurt) city. Da Khure Lamasery, built here in 1639, was the abode of one of the three most important lines of 'Living Buddhas', the others being the Dalai Lama in Tibet and the Panchen Lama in Peking. The one at Da Khure was usually a child who died, or rather was murdered, shortly before reaching puberty, since it was believed that the soul of a deity could dwell only in the body of a child. Between 1639 and 1706 the town was known as Örgöö, from the Mongolian word for 'palace'. From 1706 to 1911 it was Ikh Khuree or Da Khure to Mongolians, or Urga to foreigners.

Independence

When Mongolia declared itself independent of China in 1911 the city was renamed Niislel Khurehe. By this time it had become a large trading centre on the route between China and Russia. There were, in fact, three separate cities here: the Chinese, the Russian and the Mongolian. The Chinese and Russian cities were engaged in the tea and silk trades but the Mongolian city's concern was the salvation (or rather the liberation) of souls. There was a population of some 30,000 Buddhist monks in the lamaseries here.

Soviet Mongolia

After the Communist Party came to power in 1921 the capital was renamed Ulaanbaatar, meaning 'Red Hero'. With considerable help from the USSR, the city was redesigned; the architectural origins of its austere tower blocks and municipal buildings are recognisably Soviet. Besides the hideous multi-storey buildings, close ties to the Communist giant led to the destruction of private enterprise, redistribution of wealth, and the creation of cooperatives which led to famine, just as it had done in the Soviet Union. Political repressions and persecution of religious figures led to the deaths and disappearances of 27,000 people in 1937 alone, almost two-thirds of whom were monks. When Sino-Soviet relations soured in the 1960s, Mongolia sided with the latter, resulting in a disastrous loss of trade with China and increased economic dependence on the Soviet Union.

From totalitarianism to democracy

When the Soviet Union fell apart, the resulting shockwaves led to pro-democracy protests and hunger strikes. In May 1990, an amendment to the constitution allowed multi-party elections and the resulting coalition government included the old Communists rather than expelling them completely. The first few post-communism years were a difficult time for the Mongolian economy, as it collapsed without the Soviet subsidies. Nevertheless, the country recovered by building relationships with European countries, Japan, South Korea and the United States. In the mid-1990s the city experienced a private-sector boom, with new buildings springing up everywhere and shops and restaurants opening. As in Russia, most of the money for this came from Communist-era power brokers who quickly took control of privatised state assets.

In 1999-2000 Mongolia was hit by severe weather conditions: a serious drought followed by an extremely cold winter. Massive loss of livestock caused food shortages and forced many nomadic herders to flee to the city, though the Communist era's social support system no longer exists to help them. Ulaanbaatar continues to develop with speed, but it's still easy to see that under this surface layer of development the people and traditions remain largely unchanged.

WHAT TO SEE AND DO

Sühbaatariin Talbai (Sukhe Bator Square) Сухбаатарын Талбай

At the heart of the city is this large square, the scene of the pro-democracy demonstrations in 1990 that led to the first free elections. Today it's the site of patriotic celebrations and a popular meeting place. At the centre is a mounted statue of the Mongolian revolutionary leader Damdinii Sühbaatar in heroic pose; newlyweds queue up to have their photos taken here, more out of tradition than inclination. The square is dominated by the Parliament House on the north, with a massive bronze statue of the seated Genghis Khan in the centre, flanked by equally large statues of his son, Ögedei, and grandson Kublai, and a ceremonial *ger* inside for receiving guests of honour.

On the north-east side of the square is the modernistic Palace of Culture, housing the **Mongolian National Modern Art Gallery** (10am-6pm, T2000), which features fascinating depictions of Mongolian nomadic life through painting and sculpture. Next to it is the **Opera and Ballet Theatre**.

National Museum of Mongolian History
Монголын Туухийн Үндэсний Музей

This excellent museum (💻 www.nationalmuseum.mn, 9.30am-6pm mid-May to August, rest of the year 9.30am-5.30pm Tue-Sat, adult/student T2500/1200) is found in the concrete structure on the north-east side of the square. The detailed exhibits (with English captioning) trace the history of the country from the Stone Age to the post-1990 transition from communism to democracy. Highlights include the superb section featuring national costume from different parts of the country, as well as traditional jewelry and headgear, musical instruments and a collection of ornate snuff boxes. Mongol Horde fans shouldn't miss the outstanding collection on the third floor which includes 12th-century armour and weaponry and a huge scale model of ancient Karakorum.

Gandan Khiid (Gandantegchenling Khiid) Гандантэгчэнлин Хиид

This **monastery** complex (9am-9pm, T3500), the name of which translates as 'the great place of complete joy', is home to the spiritual head of Mongolia, the Khamba Lama, and is the largest and most important of its kind in the country. Mongolia once had 700 monasteries but virtually all were destroyed in the Communist crackdown at the end of the 1930s. More than 14,000 monks were killed and tens of thousands forced to give up their vows. Following the pro-democracy movement in 1990, restrictions were eased allowing some monasteries to reopen and Gandan to operate as something more than a tourist showpiece.

The original monastery on this site was built in 1785. The first group of new buildings was put up in 1938; along with the main temple there are stupas, a library and accommodation for the monks. Powdered juniper, to be thrown into the big burner outside the temple as an offering, is dispensed in a side building. Many of the buildings have been renovated. The monastery is home to over 800 monks and in the main temple, the Migjed Janraisig, you can marvel at the 26.5m tall Buddha statue, covered in gold.

It's best to visit the monastery during morning prayers between 9 and 11am to observe the intricate ceremony at the Vajradhara Temple.

GANDAN MONASTERY

You can also join in the popular pastime of feeding the pigeons by purchasing birdseed from the ladies by the gate of Gandan complex.

Bogd Khan Palace Богд Хааны Өвлийн Ордон

The palace of the last Bogd Khan ('holy king') of Mongolia (Chingisiin Örgön Chölöö, 9am-5.30pm daily May-Sept, until 4.30pm and closed Wed & Thur Oct-Apr, T2500) is a wonderful old place, full of ghosts and somewhat like Beijing's Forbidden City on a much smaller scale.

Exploring the palace you get the impression that the owners walked out just a few years ago, leaving it in the hands of rather relaxed caretakers who have forgotten to mow the lawn. Entered through a gateway guarded by four fierce-looking incarnations, the palace comprises two courtyards with small pavilions on each side. There are extensively labelled exhibits of *thangkas* (Buddhist devotional paintings), musical instruments and Buddha figures, as well as the day-to-day furnishings of the buildings.

The Bogd Khan winter palace is the white building beside the summer palace complex. Inside, the museum's exhibits include Bogd Khan's throne, fur-lined robes and crown, and his luxurious ger (the exterior covered with the skins of 150 snow leopards, and containing a stove and portable altar). His collection of stuffed animals, some of which were part of his personal zoo, is displayed somewhat haphazardly: a moth-eaten lion sharing the same quarters as a grubby polar bear. To get here, take bus No 7 heading south along Chingisiin Örgön Chölöö and get off after you've crossed the overpass.

Choijin Lama Temple Museum Чойжин Ламын Хийд-Музей

Preserved under communism as a museum of religion, this temple complex (10am-6pm May-Sept, 10am-5pm Oct-April, closed Mon & Tue, T2500), which hasn't been in operation since 1938, was the former home of Luvsan Haidav Choijin Lama, the brother of the 8th Bogdo Gegen (Bogd Khan). They were both born Tibetans.

The brightly coloured temple buildings house some beautiful and fascinating exhibits, including a large collection of *tsam* (ornate masks for Buddhist mystery plays) and graphic depictions of suffering in the underworld. Take a close look at the golden seated Buddha figure, not a statue but the mummified body of a lama, encased in gold. In the northern pavilion you may also want to check out the statues, which depict Tantric sexual positions. Immediately to the south of the museum is a statue of the Mongolian writer Natsagorj.

Natural History Museum Байгалийн Түүхийн Музей

Mongolia is well known for its dinosaur graveyards; some of the fascinating discoveries are on display in this museum (corner of Sükhbaataryn Gudamj &

❑ Entry charges

You'll find that most museums charge up to five times as much as the entry fee for the privilege of taking photos or shooting a video. Expect to pay T6000-10,000 for photos and T12,000 for video.

❑ **Crime in Ulaanbaatar**
Theft is on the increase and there have been some reports of foreigners being mugged late at night. Hassle from drunks can also be a problem. Don't wander the streets alone after dark and take particular care during Naadam time, and also at the railway station, on buses and in the market, where **pickpockets** and **bag-slitters** are rampant.

Sambugiin Örgön Chölöö, 10am-5.30pm daily May-Sept, closed Mon & Tue Oct-Apr, adult/student T2500/1000) including a tyrannnosaurus rex, the fossilised bones of a velociraptor and a protoceratops locked in mortal combat, and petrified dinosaur eggs. Also worth seeing are the stuffed animals arranged in imaginative panoramas of the Gobi desert and the mountains in the west, though thanks to the dodgy taxidermy the animals have rather dopey looks on their faces. Many endangered species are here, including the snow leopard, wild Bactrian camel, Gobi bear, khulan (wild ass), red wolf, northern otter and snow griffon.

International Intellectual Museum
By far the most original exhibition in the city, the Intellectual Museum (10am-6pm Mon-Sat, T4000) displays the life work of Tumen-Ulzii Zandraa, a genius who from the age of 11 has been designing and building incredibly complex, three-dimensional Mongolian wood puzzles. Boggling to the mind and dazzling to the eye with their ornate workmanship, these come in endless shapes and sizes, from cubes to animals to copies of world-famous buildings to puzzle chess sets, decorated with gemstones. Visitors are challenged to try their hand at the puzzles; there are even cash prizes for the most difficult ones, including US$10,000 for assembling a king piece for a particular chess set and US$100,000 for dismantling and assembling a silver turtle in 10 minutes (hundreds have tried and failed). To arrange an English-language tour, call ☎ 461 470 in advance.

Zaisan Memorial
Perched atop a hill at the southern edge of town is the remarkable Zaisan Memorial, built by the Soviets, with panoramic views of the city. The colourful murals and gigantic statue of a soldier celebrate Russian-Mongolian cooperation in WWII and the Soviet space programme. Nearby is a large golden Buddha statue, erected in 2005. To get there take bus No 7 from the front of Bayangol Hotel and get off at the end-stop, 'Zaisan'.

Zanabazar Fine Arts Museum **Занабазарын Уран Зургийн Музей**
This fascinating art museum (Juulchin Gudamj, 9am-5pm, adult/student T2500/1000) includes a comprehensive display of *thangkas* (scroll paintings), one more than 15m long, as well as other religious exhibits, such as fine Buddha statues. You also find a number of paintings, carvings and sculptures, including numerous works by Mongolia's most-celebrated sculptor and artist after whom the museum is named. There are copies of prehistoric cave paintings, robes and masks from Buddhist Tsan dances and even a gallery of modern paper-cutting art. The Red Ger Gallery on the 1st floor features some fine examples of contemporary Mongolian art.

PRACTICAL INFORMATION

Orientation and services

The city's main thoroughfare is Enkhtaivanii Örgön Chölöö (Peace Ave), lined with eateries, businesses, travel agencies and hotels. The heart of the city is Sühbaatariin Talbai (Sukhe Bator Sq), with most attractions, embassies, restaurants and hotels located within walking distance of it.

From Ulaanbaatar railway station to Sühbaatariin Talbai is about 2km. Trolleybus No 4 runs from the station to the square every half-hour, or else it's a 20-minute walk to Peace Ave.

Long-distance buses depart from the 'Dragon' bus terminal, on the main street, about 8km west of the centre. Taxis there cost around T2700, or take bus No 26 heading west from the southern side of Sühbaatariin Talbai.

Street addresses and building numbers are rarely used, making many places hard to locate.

To complicate matters further, many buildings are set back in no-man's land between streets, entrances to guesthouses are usually in the back of the building, and

❑ NAADAM FESTIVAL

Naadam is the biggest and most important Mongolian festival and is held between 11 and 13 July. In the ethnically Mongolian region of Tuva, in southern Siberia, the Tuvans of Russia celebrate the similar Naadym on 15 August. In Mongolia, even though since between the 1921 revolution and the fall of communism the festival has been organised in honour of the Mongolian People's Revolutionary Party, its roots go back several thousand years and it comprises three manly games: wrestling, archery and horse-racing – skills considered essential in ancient times.

In the capital, the festival kicks off with parades and carnivals and an opening ceremony at the **stadium** (see map p335), which lasts for around two hours on the morning of the first day. Check out the events programme in the English-language newspapers to find out what events are taking place during and even in the lead-up to the festival.

While admission to the events themselves is free, you need tickets for the opening and closing ceremonies, as well as the final round of wrestling. You can purchase tickets from tour operators and hotels, with the best seats in the stadium (protected from the elements and with the best view of the action) going for as much as T35,000. You can pick up cheap but marked-up tickets for as little as T3500 from the scalpers who hang around the stadium, though that way you're not guaranteed a seat.

Smaller Naadams take place all over the country, and can be a better way of getting really close to the action (or even participating in it!)

Wrestling

The national sport begins with either 512 or 1024 wrestlers competing in a single-elimination tournament that lasts nine rounds. The final round, which takes place before the closing ceremony, is the most exciting. Rounds are untimed and a wrestler only loses if he touches the ground with any part of his body except hands and feet. Competitors wear traditional boots, *zodog* (open-chest vest) and *shuudag* (tight-fitting shorts).

The style of a wrestler's movements depends on which bird he is representing, be it a falcon or a hawk, and before each faceoff, the two wrestlers will slap their thighs twice, meaning: 'Whether I win or lose, I will have no complaints.' The loser will untie his *zodog* as a mark of respect to the winner and all contestants perform the 'eagle dance' before the start of the tournament, imitating the bird's flight.

many businesses, especially travel offices, have no signs!

Information The excellent **tourist information centre** (9am-8pm) in the central post office on Peace Ave provides help with accommodation and general information about the city and country.

They sell maps, including topographical ones, and the Ulaanbaatar City Map, updated annually, which is also available at various hotels and kiosks. The best place for maps for other parts of Mongolia is the **Map Shop** (Ikh Toiruu, 9am-1pm & 2-6pm Mon-Fri, 10am-4pm Sat). There are also **information booths** at the railway station and airport.

English-language weeklies include the *Mongol Messenger* (💻 www.mongolia-web.com/messenger/), available from Ulaanbaatar Hotel among other places. There's also the *UB Post* (💻 http://ubpost.mongolnews.mn), and the free *UB Guide*, containing local news and entertainment info.

Mongolia's tourism department website is 💻 www.mongoliatourism.gov.mn.

(continued on p336)

Horse-racing

Mongolian horse-racing, unlike Western horse-racing, is a cross-county race of between 15km and 30km, which takes place on the open steppe and is divided into six categories in accordance with the horse's age: the two-year olds do 15km, while the six-year olds and the stallions do 30km; the rest fall in between. The jockeys are children, some of them as young as five years old.

The winning horse of each race is given the title 'The Winner of Ten Thousand', while the last horse is given the title of 'Complete Happiness'. It is the herders' tradition to praise the last horse rather than blame it to encourage it and its young rider to win the next race. The winning riders are given *airag* to drink and are then anointed with it, along with their steeds. It's believed that a winning horse's sweat brings luck, so don't be surprised if you see spectators scraping the horse's sides. The races kick off at Hui Doloon Kutag, 28km west of the city, and you can either take a bus or minivan there from outside the stadium (T2500) or grab a taxi (T25,000 return).

Archery

The nomadic tribes have been using a bow and arrow for over 3000 years, first for hunting and then in battle and as a sport. The Huns had a multitude of different arrows for different purposes and used archery contests to test their warriors' strength, eyesight and ability to shoot.

There are all kinds of traditional archery competitions, ranging from shooting a sheep's skin from a distance of 40 bows or shooting at balls made of hide while galloping on a horse. The Naadam event, however, consists of shooting 40 arrows at targets that are walls of leather rings, 4m long and 50cm high, from a distance of either 75m (men) or 60m (women). Women only shoot 20 arrows. The judges emit one of three kinds of calls (*uukhai*) after each shot, indicating its quality, and the person to hit the targets the most times is proclaimed the best *mergen*.

The archery competition is held in an open stadium next to the main stadium. The bows are sightless and made of layered horn, wood and bark, while the arrows are made from young willow branches and vulture feathers.

Ankle bone shooting

A lesser event, this takes place in a smaller tent next to the archery stadium. The event consists of flicking a sheep's anklebone at a target (also made of anklebones), around 3m away, amidst much excited shouting and yodelling.

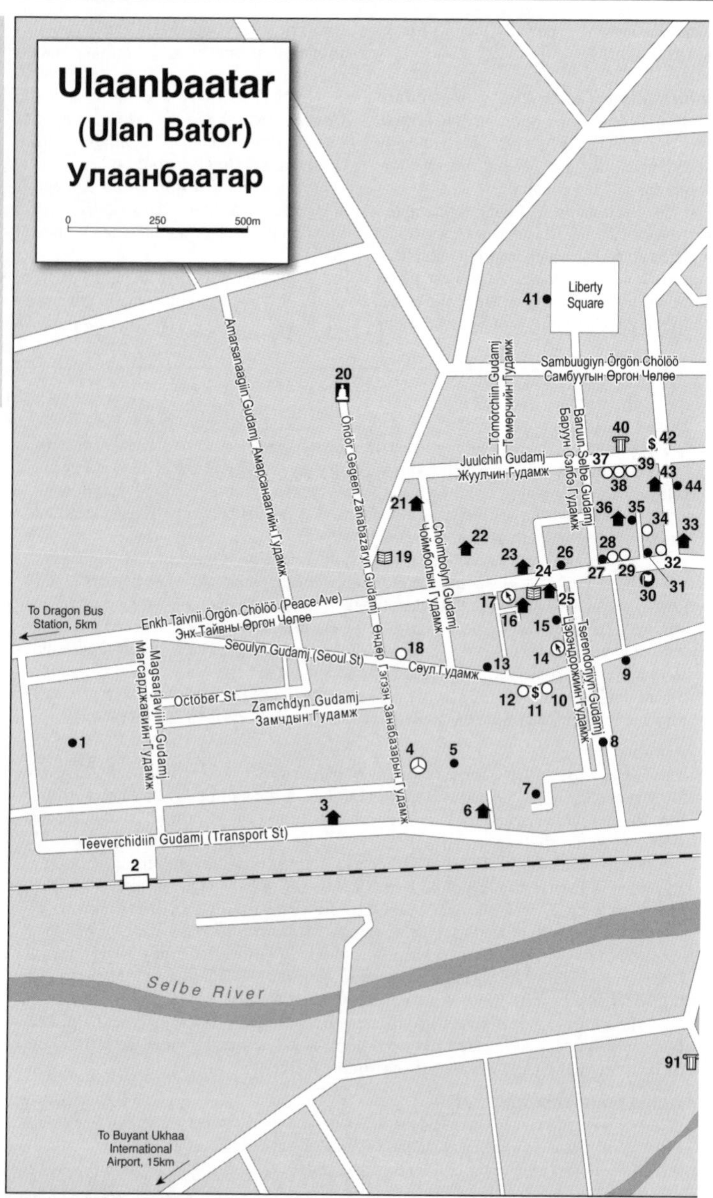

Ulaanbaatar
(Ulan Bator)
Улаанбаатар
0
250
500m
Liberty Square
Sambuugiyn Örgön Chölöö
Самбуугын Өргөн Чөлөө
Tömörchiin Gudamj
Төмөрчийн Гудамж
Baruun Selbe Gudamj
Баруун Сэлбэ Гудамж
Juulchin Gudamj
Жуулчин Гудамж
Amarsanaagiin Gudamj
Амарсанаагийн Гудамж
Öndör Gegeen Zanabazaryn Gudamj
Өндөр Гэгээн Занабазарын Гудамж
Choimbolyn Gudamj
Чойбалын Гудамж
Enkh Taivnii Örgön Chölöö (Peace Ave)
Энх Тайвны Өргөн Чөлөө
To Dragon Bus Station, 5km
Seoulyn Gudamj (Seoul St)
Сөул Гудамж
Tserendorjiyn Gudamj
Цэрэндоржийн Гудамж
Magsarjavjiin Gudamj
Магсаржавийн Гудамж
October St
Zamchdyn Gudamj
Замчдын Гудамж
Teeverchidiin Gudamj (Transport St)
Selbe River
To Buyant Ukhaa International Airport, 15km

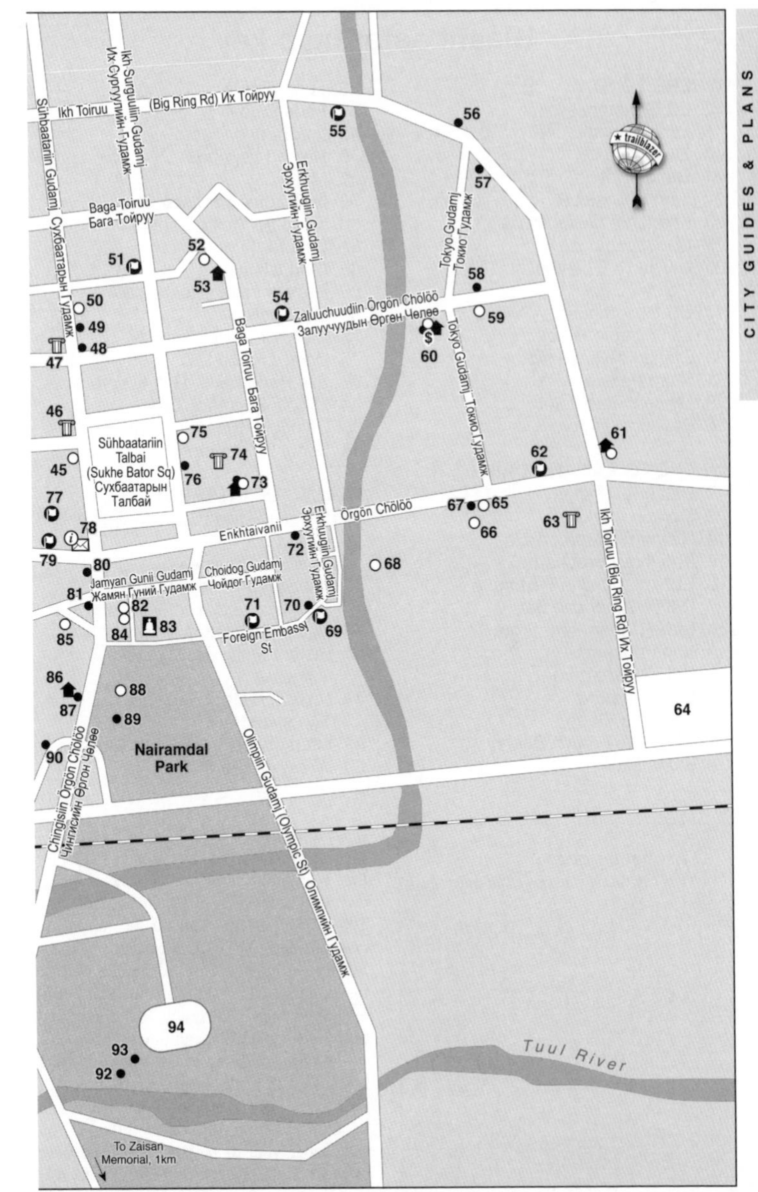

Ikh Toiruu (Big Ring Rd) Их Тойруу
Ikh Surguuliin Gudamj
Их Сургуулийн Гудамж
Sühbaatariin Gudamj Сухбаатарын Гудамж
Baga Toiruu
Бага Тойруу
Erkhuugiin Gudamj
Эрхуугийн Гудамж
Tokyo Gudamj
Токио Гудамж
Zaluuchuudiin Örgön Chölöö
Залуучуудын Өргөн Чөлөө
Baga Toiruu Бага Тойруу
Sühbaatariin Talbai (Sukhe Bator Sq) Сухбаатарын Талбай
Tokyo Gudamj Токио Гудамж
Enkhtaivanii Örgön Chölöö
Erkhuugiin Gudamj Эрхуугийн Гудамж
Jamyan Gunii Gudamj
Жамян Гуний Гудамж
Choidog Gudamj
Чойдог Гудамж
Foreign Embassy St
Ikh Toiruu (Big Ring Rd) Их Тойруу
Nairamdal Park
Chingisiin Örgön Chölöö
Чингисийн Өргөн Чөлөө
Olimpiin Gudamj (Olympic St) Олимпийн Гудамж
Tuul River
To Zaisan Memorial, 1km
trailblazer
45
46
47
48
49
50
51
52
53
54
55
56
57
58
59
60
61
62
63
64
65
66
67
68
69
70
71
72
73
74
75
76
77
78
79
80
81
82
83
84
85
86
87
88
89
90
92
93
94

Ulaanbaatar map key

WHERE TO STAY
3 LG Guesthouse A
6 Idre's Guesthouse
16 Zaya's Hostel 1
21 Genex Hotel
22 Zaya's Hostel 2
23 Khonghor Guesthouse
25 LG Guesthouse B
33 Nassan's Guesthouse
36 Golden Gobi
43 UB Guesthouse
53 Zaluuchuud Hotel
60 Chinggis Khaan Hotel
61 Khan Palace
73 Ulaanbaatar Hotel
86 Bayangol Hotel

WHERE TO EAT AND DRINK
7 Dalai Eej Market
7 Merkuri Market
10 Ristorante Marco Polo
12 Khanbrau Brauhaus
18 BD's Mongolian Barbeque & Detroit American Bar
26 State Department Store Supermarket
28 Café Amsterdam
29 Chez Bernard
32 Chinggis Club
34 Michele's French Bakery
37 Stupa Café
38 Luna Blanca
39 Face Club
45 Indra Food Planet
50 Nomad Legends
52 Muse
59 New Tornado Disco Club
60 Temuujin Restaurant
61 Sakura
65 Club Isimuss
66 Hazara Indian Restaurant
68 Metropolice
73 Da Khuree Restaurant
75 Dave's Place
82 Silk Road Bar & Grill & Veranda
84 Millie's Espresso Café
85 Chinggis Khan Irish Pub
88 Seoul Restaurant

PLACES OF INTEREST
20 Gandan Khiid (Gandantegchenling Khiid) Гандантэгчэнлин Хиид
40 Zanabazar Fine Arts Museum Занабазарын Уран Зургийн Музей
46 National Museum of Mongolian History Монголын Түүхийн Үндэсний Музей
47 Natural History Museum Байгалийн Түүхийн Музей
63 International Intellectual Museum
67 Wrestling Stadium

❑ Exchange rates

To get the latest rates of exchange see 💻 www.xe.com/ucc.

	Tughrik
US$1	T1232.50
UK£1	T1987.30
Euro€1	T1744.21
Aus$1	T1321.66
Can$1	T1297.09
China Y10	T1906.55
Japan ¥100	T1557.06
NZ$1	T1054.02
Sing$1	T1013.85
S Africa R10	T1778.34

(continued from p333)

Money and banks The *tughrik* (MNT) is the Mongolian unit of currency and it comes in notes of 1, 5, 10, 20 50, 100, 500, 1000, 5000, 10,000 and 20,000; coins are now obsolete. Mongolian currency is notoriously difficult to find or change outside the country. Many hotels and banks will exchange hard currency or travellers' cheques for tughriks, and buy tughriks.

ATMs are found in the more upmarket hotels as well as the bigger banks; note that they tend to be located inside the banks and 24-hour ATMs are thin on the ground. You can change your money on the ground floor of the State Department Store (Peace Ave

PLACES OF INTEREST *(cont'd)*
74 Mongolian National Modern Art Gallery
76 State Opera and Ballet Theatre
81 National Academic Drama Theatre
83 Choijin Lama Temple Museum Чойжин Ламын Хийд-Музей
91 Bogd Khan Palace Богд Хааны Өвлийн Ордон
92 Anklebone Shooting Area
93 Archery Stadium
94 Naadam Stadium

EMBASSIES AND CONSULATES
30 Russian Embassy
51 German Embassy
54 Chinese Embassy
55 US Embassy
62 British Embassy
69 South Korean Embassy
71 Japanese Embassy
77 Canadian Consulate
79 French Embassy

OTHER
1 International railway ticket booking office
2 Railway station and domestic ticket-booking office
5 Wind of Mongolia
8 Karakorum Expeditions
9 Legend Tour
11 Golomt Bank
13 Aeroflot
14 Internet Center
15 Tsagaan Alt Wool Shop
17 Za Internet Café
19 Map Shop
24 Books in English
26 State Department Store
27 Mary & Martha Mongolia
31 Gobi Cashmere Shop
35 Ger to Ger
41 Tengis
42 Golomt Bank
44 Mongolian Airlines
48 Nomadic Journeys
49 Egshiglen Magnai National Musical Instrument Shop
56 Air China
57 SOS Medica Mongolia Clinic
58 Flower Hotel
60 Korean Air
64 Narantuul Market
70 Shuren Travel
72 Yonsei Friendship Hospital
73 MongolCom International Calling Office
78 Central Post Office & Tourist Information Centre
80 Blue Bandana Expeditions
87 Bus to the airport
89 Tumen Ekh Song & Dance Ensemble
90 Office of Immigration, Naturalization & Foreign Citizens

44), where there's an ATM on the 5th floor. **Golomt Bank** (several branches around town including Seoul St and the corner of Juulchin Gudamj & Baga Toiruu) can change travellers' cheques and has 24-hour ATMs.

Post and telecommunications The **Central Post Office** is on the corner of Peace Ave and Sühbaatariin Talbai (8am-9pm Mon-Fri, 9am-8pm Sat & Sun). Mongolian stamps are wonderful but it's better to buy them from the hotels since they often have a greater range. The most reliable **courier company** is DHL, with representatives at the more expensive hotels including Ulaanbaatar Hotel. Parcels to the US or Europe take three to five days. **International telephone calls** are expensive but can be made from card phones in many hotels, as well as from the post office. You can purchase a card or pay per call at **MongolCom International Calling Office** (9am-7pm) next to Ulaanbaatar Hotel. Alternatively, if you have access to a landline, prepaid phone cards (US$3, 5, 10, 15 and 20) are sold at the State Department Store. There are four **mobile phone** service providers and inexpensive pay-as-you-go SIM cards are widely available.

There are scores of **internet cafés** in town, though connection can be slow. Most charge T800-1000 per hour. One of the largest is **Internet Center** (Tserendorjiyn Gudamj 65, 9am-2am, T900/hr). **Za Internet Café** (Peace Ave 62, T700/hr) is open 24 hours. There is also 24-hour internet at the Central Post Office. Numerous **free wi-fi** hotspots are appearing about town, so you can get online in some hotels and hostels and cafés such as Millie's Espresso Café (see p342).

Diplomatic representation **Canada** (Seoul St, 2nd floor, ☎ 328 285); **China** (5 Zaluuchuudiin Örgön Chölöö, ☎ 323 940, 🖳 http://mn.chineseembassy.org/eng, visa section: 9.30am-noon Mon, Wed & Fri); **France** (Enkhtaivanii Örgön Chölöö 3, ☎ 324 519); **Germany** (Negdsen Undestnii Gudamj 7, ☎ 323 325); **Japan** (Olimpiin Gudamj, ☎ 320 777); **Russia** (Enkhtaivanii Örgön Chölöö A-6, ☎ 327 191, 🖳 www.russianembassy.net, 9am-noon & 2-3pm for transit visas); **South Korea** (Olimpiin Gudamj 10, ☎ 321 548); **UK** (Enkhtaivanii Örgön Chölöö 30, ☎ 458 133); **USA** (Ikh Toiruu 59, ☎ 329 095).

Visa extensions and registration See pp26-7 for details.

Medical **SOS Medica Mongolia Clinic** (4a Bldg, Ikh Toiruu, ☎ 464 325, 9am-6pm Mon-Fri, 24-hour on-call doctors ☎ 9911 0335), staffed by Western doctors, is the best place for an emergency, though its rates are high. Otherwise, **Yonsei Friendship Hospital** (Peace Ave, ☎ 310 945, 9am-4.30pm Mon-Fri, 10am-2pm Sat), supported by the South Korean government, has more basic facilities but is cheaper.

❑ Emergency numbers

Medical emergency ☎ 103
Police ☎ 102

Local transport

While you can reach most attractions in the city on foot, Ulaanbaatar is not a comfortably walkable city; dodging the crazy traffic can be quite exhausting. To get to outlying attractions, you can use the extensive **bus** and **trolleybus** system (tickets cost T300) that covers the city, with bus route maps displayed at most bus stops. Bus 11 runs to Buyant-Ukhaa International Airport from Bayangol Hotel (3/hr, 25mins, T500), while a taxi will cost around T12,000. It takes 20 minutes to walk from the railway station to Peace Ave.

Official taxis cost T400 per kilometre, though rigged meters can be a problem. Expect to pay about T3000 for a ride from the railway station, though it may be cheaper

❑ Visas for onward travel

Getting a **Chinese visa** is fairly straightforward. The Chinese embassy issues single-/double-entry transit visas (US$30/60, valid for seven days from date of entry) and single-/double-entry tourist visas (valid for 30 days, which cost the same). Visas take four working days to process or you can pay US$20/30 extra to get it done in 2-3 days/same day. US citizens pay US$140 for all visas You must provide your passport, a passport photo and a completed application form.

Obtaining a **Russian visa** is a far more tricky process, because the antiquated Soviet rules require you to have an 'invitation' and hotel vouchers for a hotel you'll most likely not be staying at, as well as three passport-sized photos in order to get your 21-day visa (costs vary depending on your nationality; check their website for more details). The visa itself can be issued in a day or two, depending on how much you're willing to pay, but the vouchers take up to 10 days to obtain, so contact **Legend Tour** (Seoul St, Sant Asar Trading Centre, ☎ 315 158, 🖳 www.legendtour.ru, 9am-1pm & 2-6pm Mon-Fri) in advance. Some travellers have had a less than wonderful experience with them, but they may be your only way of getting that visa if you hadn't already obtained one in your home country.

❑ **Street names**

Finding your way around Ulaanbaatar is tricky: Russian street names have been abandoned wholesale for Mongolian ones in the last few years, and the script is now Mongolian Cyrillic, which has a few more characters than Russian Cyrillic. There is no single accepted way for names to be transliterated into Latin letters: Ulaanbaatar, for example, is often written Ulaanbaatar.

The Mongolian word for 'street' is *gudamj*, 'avenue' is *örgön chölöö* (meaning 'wide space') and 'square' is *talbai*.

Some examples:

Sühbaatariin Talbai	Sukhe Bator Sq
Olimpiin Örgön Chölöö	Olympic Ave
Chinggis Khaan Örgön Chölöö	Ghengis Khan Ave
Enkhtaivanii Örgön Chölöö	Peace Ave
Ikh Toiruu	Big Ring Rd
Baga Toiruu	Small Ring Rd
Zaluuchuudiin Örgön Chölöö	Youth Ave

if you hail a taxi a little way down the street and not directly at the station.

Where to stay

Most of the prices in this section are listed in US$, since many guesthouses and hotels set their rates in dollars and then collect the equivalent in *tughriks*.

Budget accommodation The city's guesthouses are good places to arrange trips to the countryside. Many also provide visa services, sell rail tickets and offer free railway station pickup.

Golden Gobi (☎ 322 632, 🖳 www.goldengobi.com, dorm/dbl US$6/19). Perpetually buzzing with backpackers, this hostel efficiently organises multi-day stays with nomads. Breakfast is included and there's intermittent wi-fi and internet in the downstairs lounge. No-frills doubles have shared baths and are in the apartment building next door.

Centrally located ***UB Guesthouse*** (corner of Baga Toiruu and Jullchin Gudamj, ☎ 311 037, 🖳 www.ubguest.com, dorm/sgl/twin/dbl US$6/15/16/18), in an apartment block opposite Golomt Bank, is a popular choice. Not only do the staff organise all manner of trips – both for guests and non-guests – but they also book train tickets. A continental breakfast is included, as well as free internet and wi-fi, guest kitchen and a comfy lounge.

A five-minute walk from the railway station behind Panorama Hotel, ***LG Guesthouse A*** (Narny Gudamj, ☎ 328 572, 🖳 www.lghostel.com, dorm/dbl US$6-8/16) is one of the largest in town, highly recommended by readers for its friendly and helpful proprietor, Bimba, and the spacious, clean, warm rooms with good beds and little touches like reading lights and free wi-fi. There's a restaurant on the premises serving Mongolian hotpot and a guest kitchen for self-caterers. ***LG Guesthouse B*** is on Peace Ave, in front of the State Department Store – very central but with fewer facilities.

Centrally located behind the Turkish Embassy, ***Nassan's Guesthouse*** (Baga Toiruu West, ☎ 321 078, 🖳 www.nassantours.com, dorm/sgl/dbl US$6/12/18) is one of the oldest hostels and tour agencies in the city, with big, bright rooms, all manner of services and very helpful, efficient staff. Enter from Baga Toiruu by going around the back of the second building up from Peace Ave. It's building A4, second entrance, third floor.

Highly recommended ***Khonghor Guesthouse*** (Peace Ave 15, Apt 6, ☎ 316 415, 🖳 http://get.to/khongor, dorm/sgl/dbl US$5/10/14) is a bit cramped and dingy,

The Ulaanbaatar area code is 011. From outside Mongolia dial +976-11.

but it's always busy and the welcoming hosts, Toroo and Degi, run anything from day trips into the nearby countryside to multi-week stays with nomads.

Idre's Guesthouse (Bldg 22, 1st Micro District, Bayangol District, ☎ 325 241, 🖳 www.idretour.com, dorm/dbl US$5/18), a busy hostel near the railway station, draws a lively backpacker crowd. Run by Idre the guide, it specialises in one-week-plus adventures all over the country, but can organise shorter trips to suit. Perks include internet access, guest kitchen, and a small book exchange.

Perfectly central, ***Zaya's Hostel*** (Tserendorj St Building 63, apt 10, 11, 12) and ***Zaya's Hostel 2*** (Peace Ave Building 25/4, 3rd floor, apt 5, ☎ 316 696, 🖳 www.zayahostel.com, dorm/sgl/dbl US$12/15/30) are efficiently run by the knowledgeable Zaya and her daughters. Both branches are luxurious apartments with light, spacious rooms, kitchen, internet and wi-fi, and attract the less rowdy budget travellers. Often fully booked, so make reservations in advance.

Mid-range and upmarket hotels

Breakfast and free internet access is included unless stated otherwise.

A good mid-range choice is ***Genex Hotel*** (Choimbolyn Gudamj 10, ☎ 328 755, 🖳 www.generalimpex.mn, sgl/dbl from US$50/80, rooms with shared bath US$35/60), not far from Gandan Khiid, a well-run and modern place with only 16 rooms, most equipped with bath, TV and fan.

Zaluuchuud Hotel (Baga Toiruu 43, ☎ 324 594, 🖳 www.zh.mn, sgl/dbl from US$40/70) has a range of refurbished spacious rooms, equipped with TVs, fridges and kettles. There's a small business centre, a sauna, and a restaurant serving European and Chinese cuisine.

The Soviet-era ***Ulaanbaatar Hotel*** (just off Sühbaatariin Talbai, ☎ 320 620, 🖳 www.ubhotel.mn, sgl/dbl from US$120/143), the city's first five-star hotel, boasts an excellent central location and a host of amenities including a sauna, billiards room and a travel office on the 4th floor. There are three plush restaurants – one serving true Mongolian specialities – and even a café serving decent coffee.

The 400-bed ***Bayangol Hotel*** (5 Chinggis Khaan Örgön Chölöö, ☎ 312 255, 🖳 www.bayangolhotel.mn, sgl/dbl from US$145/180, suites from US$316) is one of the top business hotels in the city, with a wine bar, sauna, fitness centre, travel bureau and no fewer than four restaurants, serving a combination of Mongolian and European cuisine. Most rooms have air-con, which is a blessing in summer.

One of the smartest places to stay, ***Chinggis Khaan Hotel*** (Tokyo Gudamj 5, ☎ 313 380, 🖳 www.chinggis-hotel.com, rooms from US$120, suites US$175-650) offers top-class air-conditioned rooms, with even the singles featuring king-size beds, two excellent restaurants – a Mongolian and a Chinese/Korean – an indoor swimming pool, a fitness centre, and a business centre and travel bureau.

The luxurious, Kempinski-managed ***Khan Palace*** (East Cross Rd, ☎ 463 463, 🖳 www.khanpalace.com, sgl/dbl from US$98/120) is a little way east of the centre, but its facilities more than make up for the inconvenience. The staff are helpful, the plusher rooms have luxurious bathrooms, the fitness centre boats a Japanese-style hot tub, and there's an excellent Japanese restaurant, Sakura (see p342), on site.

Where to eat and drink

It's possible to eat very cheaply (around T2500 a plate) in the city's many ***cafés***. These often have menus with pictures. Ubiquitous *buuz* (see box opposite) joints are also found all over the city. Look out for the Khaan Buuz (Хаан Бууз) and Zochin Buuz (Зочин Бууз) branches. Ulaanbaatar has some excellent international restaurants as well, and there are no McDonald's or KFCs in the city ... yet.

Restaurants For more upmarket Mongolian fare try ***Temuujin Restaurant*** at Chinggis Khaan Hotel (see above). Alternatively, ***Da Khuree Restaurant*** at Ulaanbaatar Hotel (see column opposite) dishes up some adventurous alternatives to *buuz*, such as smoked horse meat, boiled sheep intestines and grilled sheep's head, which you can wash down with *airag*, the traditional alcoholic beverage made from fermented mare's milk.

Another recommended Mongolian restaurant, serving a mix of traditional dishes and more modern alternatives, is ***Nomad Legends*** (Sühbaatariin Gudamj), popular with locals and travellers alike and perpetually packed on summer evenings.

The best pizza in town is at ***Ristorante Marco Polo*** (Seoulyn Gudamj, [V]), with pizzas for T6000-8000 and excellent pasta dishes for around T8000. The atmosphere is tasteful and cosy in the downstairs dining room, but the outdoor terrace is more pleasant in summer.

One of the best restaurants in town is ***Hazara Indian Restaurant*** (16 Enkhtaivanii Örgön Chölöö behind the Wrestling Stadium, meals around T17,000, [V]), with large portions of delicious North Indian cuisine served under colourful hangings. The garlic naan and the mango lassi are absolutely superb.

Indra Food Planet ([V]), just off Sühbaatariin Talbai, has decent Western and Mongolian fast food as well as pasta, noodle and curry dishes for under T5000. The portions are ample and there's a good number of vegan and vegetarian dishes.

For vegetarians, ***Luna Blanca*** (Juulchin Gudamj, [V]) serves excellent kebabs, wraps, salads and veggie alternatives to Mongolian dishes, such as the faux-mutton dumplings (now available in some supermarkets). ***Silk Road Bar & Grill*** (Jamiyan Guunii Gudamj), across the street

❑ Eating and drinking the Mongolian way

You may have heard horror stories about Mongolian food: namely, that it all involves boiled mutton. While mutton does indeed feature on nearly every menu, there is more to Mongolian cuisine than that. You are likely to encounter delicious **dairy products**, such as *süü* (cow, goat, sheep or yak milk), *öröm* or *üürag* (sweet cream made from cow's milk), *tarag* (yogurt), *aarts* (soft fermented cheese) and *aaruul* (dried milk curds).

Meat comes in many guises; some is either preserved for the winter through smoking or drying, such as *bortz* (dried beef), or cooked using stones preheated in the fire, a technique perfected over the centuries. One such dish is *boodog*, where the hot stones are placed inside the animal, cooking it from the inside, while the fur is singed off in a fire or with a blowtorch. Another dish is *khorkhog*, with meat and vegetables placed in a container alongside the hot stones, with some water or *airag* added; the container is then sealed. Other meaty delights include *kazy* (salted horse-meat sausages), boiled sheep's head and *khavchaakai* (slices of meat seasoned with salt and onion, put between two thin stones and placed on hot ashes). In towns you're likely come across *buuz* (steamed mutton dumplings) and *khuushuur* (fried mutton-filled pastries and pancakes). Another common dish is *shölte khuul* (hearty soup with meat, pasta and potato).

Vegetables are not widely eaten; Mongolians have never thought much of vegetarians, as some identify vegetable-eating with Chinese culture, while others are convinced that eating vegetables is just not healthy, though wild herbs, aromatic roots and onion-like greens are widely used for seasoning, as is yogurt, sour milk and dried curds. However, vegetarianism is getting a tentative foothold in the capital, as demonstrated by the highly successful ***Luna Blanca*** (see above).

Talkh (**bread**) or *bortzig* (unleavened bread) form part of most meals.

Since **milk** is such an integral part of the Mongolian diet, you are likely to come across *süütei tsai* (salty, milky tea) and *airag* (a clear spirit with a milky smell, made of fermented mare's milk).

Mongolian **beer** is strong and quite good: Khanbraü is brewed in Ulaanbaatar under a German licence. Another local brand is Chinggis Khan.

from Lama Temple, serves an ambitious mix of Asian, European and Mongolian food to a mostly foreign crowd. The salads are good, and the barbecued lamb comes highly recommended. Upstairs at the *Veranda* you can enjoy views of the Lama Temple while feasting on excellent pasta dishes. This is the businessman's and foreigner's favourite and their spicy ragout is particularly good.

BD's Mongolian Barbeque (Seoul St) has made the American concept of Mongolian barbecue popular with locals and foreigners alike. Choose your own ingredients and watch the chefs cook your food and throw it up in the air before dispensing it onto your plate. The all-you-can-eat buffet is particularly great after days on the train. (V)

Though it's out of the centre, ***Sakura*** is well worth seeking out for the excellent Japanese food prepared by the resident chef at Khan Palace Hotel (see p340). The sushi sets are expertly prepared and beautifully presented, making them a welcome antidote to the ubiquitous boiled mutton.

Korean food abounds in Ulaanbaatar, and ***Seoul Restaurant*** (in the middle of the National Children's Park, opposite the Bayangol Hotel) features an excellent buffet. There are nightly live shows and a shabu-shabu barbecue on the balcony.

Cafés and light meals ***Millie's Espresso Café*** (Marco Polo Bldg) is a bustling café opposite Lama Temple, specialising in a mix of Mongolian and European dishes and expensive imported coffee (T6000). Free wi-fi access.

At ***Café Amsterdam*** (Peace Ave), the tasty soups and sandwiches attract an interesting clientele of writers and journalists. Lunch menu T6500.

While the European-style dishes and overpriced cakes (T4000) at the Belgian-owned ***Chez Bernard*** (Peace Ave) won't win culinary prizes, they are palatable enough, and the café is a gathering point for backpackers, who use its noticeboard as a means of finding travelling companions.

If you're hankering after pizza, burgers, fries and other feel-good food look no further than ***Detroit American Bar*** (beneath BD's Mongolian Barbeque, see Restaurants). Perpetually popular with travellers, it even has an outdoor pub garden in summer.

Michele's French Bakery ([V]) is a particular favourite of the expat community and rightly so: you can enjoy their fabulous chocolate croissants (T1000) and apple strudel, as well as the paninis (T2700) and crêpes with a multitude of fillings, while chilling out to mellow music.

With its orange *ger* furniture, the small and cosy ***Stupa Café*** (Juulchin Gudamj, part of the FPTM Buddhist Centre, [V]) is an excellent spot for a sandwich or a cup of tea. You can peruse the English-language books and magazines while you eat.

Self-caterers can pick up a wide range of groceries at the supermarkets at the **State Department Store** (Peace Ave), **Dalai Eej Market** (otherwise known as Minii Delguur, off Tserendorjiin Gudamj) or **Merkuri Market**, behind Dalai Eej, where you can bargain for imported food products.

Drinking ***Dave's Place***, in the corner of the Palace of Culture on Sühbaatariin Talbai, is popular with expats. The terrace is open in summer with live music on Friday and Saturday, the menu includes burgers and other British pub delights and there's a quiz night on Thursdays at 9.30pm. It's also the headquarters of the UB Yaks rugby team.

Chinggis Club (Sühbaatariin Gudamj 10), a German-run microbrewery, stays open past midnight and is a popular backpacker watering hole. The menu is also German-inspired and the dishes are hearty; ask your Mongolian waitress in a Bavarian barmaid outfit for the delicious sausages.

If you're not expecting authentic Irishness you won't be disappointed by the popular ***Chinggis Khan Irish Pub*** (Seoul St), which draws a large and lively crowd of expats and locals alike and serves up Guinness and pub grub.

The large, airy ***Khanbrau Brauhaus*** on Seoulyn Gudamj brews its lager on the premises, and while the food is overpriced, it's particularly good for a beer on Wednesday and Saturday nights when they implement a 'stock exchange' system: if no one is buying beer, its price falls by half. Live music on Friday nights.

Nightlife

Check the English-language publications for listings. The **Arts Council of Mongolia** (🖳 www.artscouncil.mn) produces a monthly calendar that covers events, exhibitions and goings-on at most museums, galleries and theatres.

Clubs UB has a lively club scene pretty much every night of the week. **Metropolice** (inside Sky Shopping Centre, T5000) is the most stylish of them all, with the DJ playing an eclectic mix of salsa, rock, disco, techno and pop. Monday and Tuesday are electronic nights. **Face Club** (opposite Zanabazar Fine Arts Museum, T5000-6000) is a small, lively joint with a Tahiti theme and live band, while at the multilevel **Club Isimuss** (Peave Ave) patrons dance around a giant statue of Stalin, which once stood proudly outside the National Library. **Muse** (Baga Toiruu) caters to a yuppie crowd, while **New Tornado Disco Club** (opposite Flower Hotel) is the place of choice for young expats, English teachers and travellers.

Traditional music and dance Not to be missed is a nightly summer performance of traditional song, dance and *khöömii* (throat singing) by **Tumen Ekh Song & Dance Ensemble** (State Youth & Children's Theatre, Naraimdal Park, T8000). Love it or loathe it, it's guaranteed to be a unique and memorable evening. The Song and Dance Show which is on several times a week at the **National Academic Drama Theatre** (corner of Seoul St & Chingisiin Örgön Chölöö, May-Sept, T8000) is another good venue for seeing excellent traditional song and dance.

More traditional pursuits include ballet or opera at the **State Opera and Ballet Theatre** (Sühbaatariin Talbai, T6000-9000), which stages a mix of works by Mongolia's most famous playwright – Natsagdorj – as well as classics (in Mongolian).

Cinema Tengis (Liberty Square, 🖳 www.tengis.mn) has screenings of Hollywood blockbusters in English with Mongolian subtitles.

Where to shop

Things to buy include cashmere shawls and sweaters, sheepskin, woollen goods, and representations of Mongolian deities, the latter sold in many museums. Mongolia is also known for its wonderfully bizarre, oversized **postage stamps** with naïve representations of cars and trains; you can pick those up at the Central Post Office. Many shops sell 'art' and 'antiques', but most of it is tat, made in China. Though Mongolia is known for its dinosaur remains, it is forbidden to purchase fossils or take them out of the country.

The shops following come highly recommended; most are closed on Sundays.

The fascinating **Narantuul Market** (Naaran Tuul Zakh, 10am-7pm), formerly known as the 'black market', at the corner of Ikh Toiruu and Teeverchidiin Gudamj, is a good spot for anything from counterfeit designer goods to food to ger furniture. Not only is it a black market no longer, but you have to pay a T50 entrance fee, and some goods are more expensive than at other markets. It's worth the trip for the Communist memorabilia, traditional coats and boots, horse saddles and the chaotic atmosphere. To get there, take bus No 4 heading east from the southern side of Sühbaatariin Talbai and then walk along the main road south to the corner of Ikh Toiruu and Teeverchidiin Gudamj. At the market watch out for the unbelievably dextrous, and sometimes aggressive, bag-slitters and pickpockets.

High-quality cashmere goods are sold at **Gobi Cashmere Shop** (Peace Ave, opposite the Russian embassy). For all sorts of felt and woollen goodies, such as hats and quality clothing, check out **Tsagaan Alt Wool Shop** (Tserendorjiin Gudamj, opposite the State Department Store). It's a Fair Trade store that supports craftsmen who come from disadvantaged backgrounds.

Mary & Martha Mongolia (next to Café Amsterdam and the State Department

Store, www.just-perfect.co.uk) is another excellent place for woollen ponchos, shawls and scarves, felt slippers and silk goods and, like the Tsagaan Alt Wool Shop, it supports traditional Mongolian crafts by paying local artisans a fair wage.

The **State Department Store** sells standard souvenirs, but you can also pick up a bag of sheep's ankle bones, used for traditional games in the countryside.

Traditional Mongolian musical instruments, such as the morin khuur (horsehead fiddle) can be purchased at **Egshiglen Magnai National Musical Instrument Shop** (Sühbaatariin Gudamj).

You can stock up on reading material for the train trip at **Books in English** (Peace Ave, next to Za Internet Café). They have a small collection of second-hand classics and a few good contemporary novels.

Moving on

By rail Tickets for **rail travel within Mongolia** can be booked at an office on the east side of the station, though no English is spoken.

Tickets for **international trains to Beijing, Irkutsk and Moscow** can be booked at the Railway Ticket Booking Office 200m north-west of the station on Zamchydn Gudamj (8am-8pm). Some English is spoken at the foreigners' booking office upstairs in Room 212. For a few dollars extra just about any guesthouse or

❑ Mongolia – individual travel vs package tours

If you're visiting only Ulaanbaatar you can get by fine on your own, but it's not so easy outside the capital. Potential problems with language, accommodation, food and transport make joining or assembling a group a popular option, especially if time is limited. Every guesthouse in Ulaanbaatar organises budget tours, and the ones listed in this book are all recommended. These are also the best places to hook up with fellow travellers, cutting your costs significantly, as they tend to depend on the number of people in your group. Standard three-day, two-night tours that include accommodation in a *ger*, all meals and transportation, camel and horseback riding and an opportunity to see the Przewalsky horses costs around US$220 per person.

Travel companies in Ulaanbaatar

- **Shuren Travel** (Olimpiin Gudamj 8/4, Shuren Building, 5th floor, ☎ 310 869, www.shuren-travel.com) is an established operator that arranges group trekking, riding and jeep trips all over Mongolia, as well as trips to Karakorum, the Naadam festival experience and winter adventures.
- **Nomadic Journeys** (Sühbaatariin Gudamj 1, ☎ 328 737, www.nomadicjourneys.com) is the company of choice for the eco-conscious traveller. This Swedish-Mongolian outfit focuses on low-impact tourism and runs trekking, horseback, camel and yak trips, as well as rafting.
- **Wind of Mongolia** (off Seoul St, Bldg 9, apt 57, ☎ 9909 0593, www.windofmongolia.mn) is a French outfit that does both summer and winter multi-day trips, as well as rock climbing and dog-sledding adventures.
- **Karakorum Expeditions** (Gandaryn Gurav Bldg, behind the State Circus, ☎ 320 182, www.gomongolia.com) specialises in hiking and biking tours in western Mongolia as well as wildlife tours and snow leopard research tours.
- **Ger to Ger** Socially conscious operator (see box p348).
- **Blue Bandana Expeditions** (opposite the Central Post Office, ☎ 329 456, www.activemongolia.com), in The Seven Summits outdoor shop, organises individual and group hiking, biking, horse-riding and jeep tours off the beaten track in the far west and north of Mongolia. Multi-day stays with the eagle hunters and the 'winter Naadam' festival on the frozen Lake Khovsgol come highly recommended.

tourist agency will do the legwork for you. Booking office ticket allocations dry up in peak season, in which case try Nomadic Journeys (see box opposite) or UB Travel in Ulaanbaatar Hotel (see p340). You cannot buy tickets for the Moscow–Beijing trains more than a day in advance because the staff don't know how many free seats there are, so you might want to consider taking a train originating in Ulaanbaatar instead. If you buy your ticket directly at the Ulaanbaatar railway station, you will avoid the 50% markup that booking agencies place on tickets.

Going **north**, there are nightly departures of train 361 from Ulaanbaatar to Irkutsk via Ulan-Ude (daily, 33hrs); there is no 1st class – only kupé berths are available. For Russian travel beyond Irkutsk take the 005 Ulaanbaatar–Moscow (Tue 1.50pm, Apr to mid-Oct; every other Mon the rest of the year, 4 days 5hrs to Moscow), or get aboard the once-weekly Trans-Mongolian 003 from Beijing to Moscow (Thur 1.20pm). If northbound tickets are sold out or you're in a hurry, you may wish to consider taking a bus to Ulan-Ude instead; it takes 10 hours rather than 24 because border formalities take less time, and costs less. Contact Vladimir at Baikal Ethnic Hostel in Ulan-Ude (see p297 for door-to-door Ulaanbaatar–Ulan-Ude transfers).

Heading **south**, the 004 Moscow–Beijing departs Ulaanbaatar (Sun at 7.57am, 30hrs). Unless you booked your ticket weeks in advance, it's almost impossible to get seats on the direct Moscow–Beijing train in peak season, so you can also take the somewhat cheaper 024 Ulaanbaatar–Beijing (Tue 8.05am); the 024 has an additional departure at the same time on Saturdays in summer only. If you happen to be in Ulaanbaatar during Naadam when all tickets for direct trains to Beijing tend to be sold out, it's possible to take either the Ulaanbaatar to Hohhot train (Mon & Fri 8.15pm), booking your ticket as far as Jining on the main line and switching there to a nightly train to Beijing, or the Ulaanbaatar to Erlian train (Thur & Sun 8.25pm) and change to a Beijing-bound train or bus when already in China. CC Inter Tour Company, on the ground floor of Ulaanbaatar's International Railway Ticketing Office, can help you make arrangements.

By air Ulaanbaatar's **Buyant Ukhaa International Airport** has been upgraded in recent years. A taxi between the city centre and the airport costs around T8000 and takes about half an hour.

Mongolian Airlines (MIAT, Baga Toiruu West, ☎ 322 686, 💻 www.miat.com) flies to Beijing, Tokyo, Osaka, Seoul, Moscow, Irkutsk and Berlin. **Air China** (Ikh Toiruu, Bldg 47, ☎ 452 548, 💻 www.airchina.com) has frequent flights to Beijing. **Aeroflot** (Seoul St 15, ☎ 320 720, 💻 www.aeroflot.ru) has flights to Moscow, Irkutsk and Ulan-Ude. **Korean Air** (Chinggis Khaan Hotel, 2nd floor, ☎ 326 643, 💻 www.koreanair.com) has several flights a week to Seoul.

Excursions from Ulaanbaatar

ULAANBAATAR AREA

Mongolia's real draw is its countryside – vast grass plains stretching as far as the eye can see, with tiny *ger* encampments dwarfed by the vast craggy mountains and sand dunes. This is a nomadic land, where many people still lead traditional lives, herding cattle and hunting with eagles. There's no better antidote to the polluted capital than a night or two camping in a *ger* and a few days trekking or riding.

If you're using the services of a **travel agency** (see box p344) for an excursion make absolutely sure what the tour will entail so you know what you'll be getting for your money. Ask travellers who've just been on excursions for the latest recommendations. If you're renting a **jeep** for an out of town expedition for several days it's recommended that you check the odometer reading at stops as well as at the beginning and end of the trip: some operators are not above altering it in order to charge you more.

Entry to all **national parks** in Mongolia costs T3500 per foreigner and there is also a charge per vehicle.

Terelj Тэрэлж

One of the most popular places for travellers is **Gorkhi-Terelj National Park**, 80km from Ulaanbaatar. You can sleep out under the stars, drink mare's milk for breakfast and sit around campfires lulled by the sound of gently sizzling mutton kebabs. The scenery is spectacularly alpine, with icy streams crisscrossing forested mountainous terrain. Many guesthouses and tour agencies do Terelj as a day trip, which includes horse-riding, a traditional meal and a hike up to the appropriately named Turtle Rock, from where you can do an hour's climb to the Aryapala Buddhist meditation retreat to admire the view of the valley below.

Most companies make a stop at the 40-metre tall **statue of Genghis Khan** on horseback in the southern part of Terelj. Entry is US$10 and from the horse's head you get incredible views of the valley.

If travelling on your own and planning on staying overnight, a daily bus for **Turtle Rock** leaves at 4pm from the corner of Enkhtaivanii Örgön Chölöö and Zanabazaryn Gudamj (the road leading to Gandan Monastery), returning from Terelj at 7pm (T2000). A taxi costs around T35,000 each way.

There are two types of accommodation here: ***gers*** and ***hotels***. The smaller *ger* encampments are less touristy, although the atmosphere often depends as

❑ A stay at the Khot Ail camp

Some travellers who come to stay in *ger* camps around the country are disappointed to find that modern life has not left the nomadic communities untouched; they may find that their *ger* has an electric generator, solar panels or even a television. Khot Ail camp, 60km south-east of the capital, located on the banks of the Tuul River, still maintains a traditional way of life. Here, when your guide picks you up at the railway station, you get to choose whether you'd like a car or a horse. At the camp, you stay with Sara's welcoming family, and partake in daily activities, such as milking cows, learning to cook traditional Mongolian dishes, being taught Mongolian songs and how to shoot a bow and arrow. Horse and camel riding is also included, as is the opportunity to try on Mongolian dress.

Yes, most *ger* stays are now touristy, but this one is up there with the very best, and the family goes out of their way to make you feel included. Two-day, three-night stays costs around US$190 per person.

Tireless Sara can also arrange tours of Ulaanbaatar for you, which take in traditional dance and throat singing. Contact her on ☎ 9822 9832 or 8885 1035 or email her at 💻 mmunxzul@yahoo.com.sg.

much on your fellow visitors as on the place itself. Each is usually linked to a single travel agency in Ulaanbaatar, through which you must book (see box, p344). **Jalnan Meadows/Khan Khentii Ger Camp** (Nomadic Journeys) and **Elstei Ger Camp** (Shuren Travel) are two such places. You can rent horses from locals here.

Stars Observatory

A few kilometres west of Ulaanbaatar is a delightful place called Stars Observatory. It can be reached on a day trip or with an overnight stay. At the observatory there are two attractive old buildings, one a cheap ***hotel*** and the other the observatory. The observatory is open weekdays and at night the staff will let you look through the telescope. The view of the city is also worth the trip. The best way to get to the observatory is to take a taxi (around T8000).

Bogdhan Uul Nature Reserve Богдхан Уул

This unique mountain region directly south of Ulaanbaatar was proclaimed a protected area back in 1778, although conservation of Bogd Uul (which means 'Holy Mountain') actually began in the 12th century when Khan Turil declared the mountains sacred and prohibited logging and hunting in them.

A total of 65,000 hectares of Bogd Uul is a biosphere reserve. The area contains 116 species of birds, including 20 identified as endangered. Other animals in the area include musk deer, ibex, roe-deer, hare and native sable. Most of the trees are larch. Rolling, hilly, steppe grasslands stretch to the south. Clouds hang over the mountains in summer, and there are frequent thunderstorms. Snow is abundant in winter.

Bogdhan Uul's highest peak is Tsetsee Gun (2268m). It is possible to hike over the ridge to the ruins of the ancient **Manzshir Monastery** (Мандшир Хийд) and the museum (T6000) on the southern slope of Bogd Uul, overlooking a forested valley studded with boulders. The monastery was constructed in 1733 and was once home to 350 monks. The monastery complex was destroyed in 1937 during the Communist crackdown, though the main temple has since been rebuilt. A German photographer visited in 1926 and took some amazing photos of the monastery which are now on display in the museum. Spot the Buddhist rock paintings along the rocks behind the main temple.

Most hostels and hotels run day trips to the monastery. Alternatively, you can catch one of the hourly minibuses to the town of **Zuunmod** (Зуунмод, T2000, 1hr) and then take a taxi the remaining 5km.

FURTHER AFIELD

Hustain Nuruu National Park Хустайн Нуруу

About 110km west of Ulaanbaatar is this reserve dedicated to the reintroduction and preservation of the last truly wild horse, known in the West as Przewalski's horse and in Mongolia as the *takhi*. Desertification, hunting, cross breeding and competition with domestic livestock resulted in its extinction in the wild by 1969. At that time the world population was down to 161 animals in zoos. A carefully monitored breeding programme has resulted in the wild population increasing to several hundred. Accommodation is in guest *gers*. Most travel agencies and guesthouses can arrange trips to the reserve.

Karakorum (Harhorin) Каракорум (Хархорин)

This ruined city, now scattered round the modern town of Harhorin, 370km from Ulaanbaatar, was the capital of the Mongolian Empire in the 13th century. Today its centrepiece is the **Erdene Zuu Monastery** (9am-6pm summer; 10am-5pm the rest of the year; entry US$3) which was built in 1586 and was the first Buddhist centre in Mongolia. At its height the monastery housed about 1000 monks in 100 temples. During the Stalinist purges of the 1930s the monastery was badly damaged but it is once again functioning and open to visitors.

Travel agents offer three-day package trips which are the easiest way to get here. To do the trip yourself by bus you will need to book in advance at the Dragon bus station in Ulaanbaatar. The trip takes eight hours (T11,000) and the halfway stop is at the little village of Sansar. Remember to take your own food and water. In Harhorin you can stay in ***Tavan Erdene*** guesthouse (☎ 9919 4452, room US$10) on the outskirts of town, where the proprietor speaks English. There are also numerous tourist ***ger camps*** in and around Harhorin, the nicest one being Dreamland (☎ 9191 1931, *ger* for two US$85, sgl/dbl from US$60/95) which comprises luxury *gers*, a log cabin lodge and an excellent restaurant in a dining *ger*.

The Gobi

The Gobi stretches for almost 4000km along the border between Mongolia and China. It's said to contain some 33 different ecosystems as well as gazelles, the rare Argali sheep, Asiatic wild ass, wild Bactrian camel, snow leopard and ibex. The site of an ancient inland sea, the Gobi is also a treasure-chest of fossilised dinosaur bones and eggs. Only about 3% of the Gobi is true desert, so if you're expecting to see massive sand dunes everywhere, you might be disappointed. Much of the Gobi is made up of rolling steppe, though if it is dunes you want, **Khongoryn Els** (Хонгорын Элс) in the eastern part of the **Gurvan Saikhan**

❑ Ger to Ger

An innovative and socially conscious tour company, **Ger to Ger** (Arizona Plaza, Baruun Selbe Gudamj 5/3, ☎ 313 336, 🖳 www.gertoger.org) aims to introduce travellers to traditional Mongolian culture while supporting local communities in a constructive way. Ger to Ger specialises in multi-day trips, which take travellers through different parts of the country; you decide on either steppe, mountains or desert, as well as the duration and difficulty of the journey and stay with a different nomadic family each night. During the day, the families lead you to the next destination on horseback or by ox and yak carts. Accommodation is in tents, which you provide yourself, pitched outside the *gers*. A basic breakfast and dinner is provided by each family. You can take part in the nomads' daily routine, learn skills such as archery and horse-riding, and so witness what may soon be a vanished way of life.

The project is funded by the Swiss government and a Mongolian NGO, and more than half the proceeds go directly to the communities.

National Park (Гурван Сайхан) are the largest in Mongolia, up to 300m high and perfect for organising camel rides.

Nestled between the beautiful peaks of the Gurvan Saikhan (Three Beauties) Mountains, which tower 3km above the surrounding steppe, is **Yol Am Valley**. The canyon shelters glaciers which remain frozen in its shadow even through the hottest summers. Camping is not allowed in the national park but there are plenty of tourist ***ger camps*** nearby. Most travel companies organise three-day trips to the Gobi from Ulaanbaatar.

Harbin 哈尔滨

A sprawling city of 10 million, Harbin straddles two worlds. Though it's a thriving Chinese city, Harbin prides itself on its European flair, thanks to the stately architecture of its early Russian builders. With a relaxed and affluent air along the riverfront and on pedestrianised Zhongyang Dajie, Harbin makes an ideal transition point on your way into or out of China.

Lying on the Songhua River, over 1000km north-east of Beijing, this was just another small Manchurian fishing village until the construction of the East Chinese Railway in 1897-1901. The new Russian-built railway passed through Harbin, and this was also the junction for the southern spur to Port Arthur. The former village grew rapidly into a major trading centre, albeit with a wild reputation. The Hon Maurice Baring visited in 1904, expecting to find a modern industrial metropolis, but he was not impressed: 'Harbin is now called the Chicago of the East. This is not a compliment to Chicago'. Harbin continued to grow under Japanese control during the Russo-Japanese War as it served as a supply base for Japanese troops. A great many White Russian refugees settled here following the 1917 Revolution, and the Russian influence remained strong, despite the Japanese presence, until after WWII when Manchuria was officially handed over to the Kuomintang.

After the reform of the late 1970s, Harbin, along with the rest of China, experienced enormous growth and economic progress. The city became a major river port and has sponsored eight international trade fairs and the Asian Winter Games.

In 1996, the government incorporated the Songhua River region into Harbin, tripling the city's population and making it the largest city in north-east China. The goal now is to make Harbin the major international economic and trade centre of north-east China. The area hit the international news in late 2005 when a major chemical accident led to vast quantities of benzene escaping into the Songhua River, poisoning the city's water supplies.

Most foreign visitors to the city nowadays are Russians on shopping trips, and you may well be mistaken for one of them. In January and February the frozen city puts on the **Ice Lantern Festival** (see box p352) in Zhaolin Park, with a large collection of beautifully illuminated ice sculptures to draw tourists.

WHAT TO SEE AND DO

It's particularly rewarding to stroll around the **Daoliqu** area – the historical heart of the city where you are likely to be staying – especially along the pedestrianised, cobbled Zhongyang Dajie. Here you will see good examples of Imperial Russian architecture, with its turrets and cupolas, and pass three lively food markets – the more adventurous places to eat.

Church of St Sophia 圣索菲亚大教堂

Built in 1907, the **Russian Orthodox Church of St Sophia** (corner of Zhaolin Jie & Toulong Jie), is a five-minute walk east of Zhongyang Dajie facing a square with snack stalls, a popular place for locals to sit and relax. The church's exterior has been heavily restored since being damaged during the Cultural Revolution, and looks particularly beautiful when lit up at night. Inside you can see original murals and a huge, ornate chandelier.

The Church of St Sophia is also the home of **Harbin Architecture Centre** (9.30am-5.30pm, adult/student Y40/20), which consists mainly of photographs of the city dating back to the turn of the 20th century and some architectural models. In a passage at the back of the church is a selection of religious icons.

With your ticket you can also visit what appears to be a nearby annexe of the museum: walk around to a courtyard at the back of the church, where you will see steps leading underground. Down here are more Harbin photographs, including of its annual Ice Festival, but the main attraction is an enormous and impressive scale model of the city. See if you can figure out where your hotel is.

CHURCH OF ST SOPHIA

Sun Island Park 太阳岛公园

This **park**, on an island in the middle of the Songhua River, is a pleasant and (except at weekends) quiet place to stroll for a few hours. There are boating lakes, water slides and other amusements. Entry is free, though some attractions, such as the Russian Village and the Scenic Gardens, charge admission.

To get there you can take a boat (Y15) from below the Flood Control Monument, or a cable car (one way/round trip Y60/120) a few hundred metres to the west.

Siberia Tiger Park 东北虎林园

Fifteen kilometres north of Harbin is the Siberia Tiger Park (9am-4pm, adult/child Y65/30), a breeding centre for the Amur/Siberian/Manchurian tiger (see box p447), whose goal is allegedly to prepare and then release the tigers into the wild, thus saving them from extinction.

The park is home to around 500 tigers, and visitors will see some of them during the 'safari' experience, along with white tigers, lions, leopards, jaguars and pumas. You're taken around in minibuses protected with wire mesh and visitors may purchase chickens, ducks and even cows which are let loose among the tigers who then hunt them, though it is unclear how that's preparing the tigers for independent existence. Furthermore, a recent BBC report stated that this very park sells 'tiger bone wine', which contains small tiger bones. Still, you're guaranteed a sighting of these magnificent creatures, only 50 of which are left in the wild.

To get here, take bus No 85 to its final stop and then either walk for 15 minutes or take a pedicab to the park entrance (Y15).

Unit 731 Japanese Germ Warfare Base 侵华日军第731部队遗址

To experience the full horror of Japanese military activity during WWII, take a trip to the germ warfare base (8.30-11.30am & 1-4pm; Y10), run by Unit 731. The Japanese military captured Harbin in 1932 and conducted experiments on prisoners-of-war here between 1939 and 1945, to test the endurance of the human body. Over 4000 prisoners, mostly Chinese but also Soviet, Korean, British and Mongolian were killed in the most horrific ways: frozen to death, roasted alive, injected with syphilis and infected with the bubonic plague. Just before Harbin was retaken by the Soviets in 1945, the Japanese tried to cover their tracks by blowing up the base, and the story did not come to light until the 1980s, when a Japanese journalist published his findings. Little is left of the base, but the main building contains a two-room museum featuring the equipment used by the Japanese, as well as photos and some sculptures.

Take bus No 343 or 338 from the railway station and get off at the Xin Jiang Da Jie (新疆大街) stop (45mins).

Other parks

One of the most popular places to relax in is **Stalin Park (斯大林公园)** at the northern end of Zhongyang Dajie; people stroll here, fly kites and sit on giant stairways leading down to the river and it's lit up with neon colours at night. There are ice-cream stands and a café inside the historic **Russian wooden chalet**, which sits halfway between the cable car that runs to the Sun Island Park (one-way/return Y60/120) and the 1958 **Flood Control Monument** that commemorates the victims of floods up to that point in time.

The **Children's Park** (儿童公园, adult/child Y4/2), on the corner of Guogeli Dajie and Hegou Dajie, south-east of the city centre, has a small railway with a miniature diesel train; it is run by children dressed as engineers and ticket collectors but is big enough to carry adults around the park (Y8). There is also table tennis in the middle of the park if you fancy challenging anyone from the world's greatest ping-pong playing nation. To get here, take bus No 8 from the southern end of Zhongyang Dajie.

Zhaolin Park (兆麟公园), a block east of Zhongyang Dajie, is good for a bit of peace and quiet. If you're here early enough in the morning you can watch groups of locals go through their Tai Chi exercises.

WHERE TO STAY

5 Gloria Inn 凯莱商务酒店
6 Songhuajiang Gloria Plaza Hotel 松花江凯莱花园大酒店
13 Modern Hotel 马迭尔宾馆
15 Kazy International Youth Hostel 卡兹国际青年旅社
16 Zhong Da Hotel 中大大酒店
25 Bei Bei Hotel 北北快捷宾馆
27 Kunlun Hotel 昆仑饭店

WHERE TO EAT AND DRINK

9 Bi Feng Tang 避风塘
10 Food market
12 Portman
14 Food market
17 Dongfang Jiaozi Wang 东方饺子王
19 California Beef Noodle King USA
20 Ding Ding Xiang 鼎鼎香
28 California Beef Noodle King USA

PLACES OF INTEREST

1 Cable Car 缆车
2 Stalin Park 斯大林公园
3 Ferries to Sun Island Park 太阳岛游览船
4 Flood Control Monument 防洪胜利纪念塔
8 Zhaolin Park 兆麟公园
18 Church of St Sophia 圣索菲亚大教堂 & Harbin Architecture Centre
31 Children's Park 儿童公园

OTHER

7 Bank of China/ATM 自动取款机
11 Internet Bar 网吧
22 Railway Station 火车站
23 Internet Café 网吧
24 Post Office 邮局
26 Bus Station 公共汽车站
29 China International Travel Service (CITS) 中国国际旅行社
30 China Telecom 中国电信

PRACTICAL INFORMATION

Orientation and services

The area around Zhongyang Dajie, 2km north of the city centre, has most of the city's attractions in and around it, and its historical streets also have the most character. This is also where most hotels and shopping malls are.

The main **railway station** is located in the centre of the city, with the long-distance **bus station** opposite it.

The main shopping streets, Dongdazhi Jie and Guogeli Dajie, lie several blocks south-east of the railway station.

There's a convenient **post office** (8.30am-5pm) on Tielu Jie by the railway station. **Internet access** is available at the railway station, at an internet bar on Xiliu Dajie, off Zhongyang Dajie (24hrs; Y4/hour), and at a couple more places along Songhuajiang Jie, near the railway station.

Ice Lantern Festival 冰灯节

The bleak midwinter is the liveliest time to be in Harbin because it coincides with an absolutely magical spectacle. The festival takes place in Zhaolin Park, Sun Island Park and along the banks of the Songhua River, with incredible snow and ice sculptures springing up, ranging from the likes of the Forbidden City to fantastical creatures from legends. They are created either using modern technology (lasers) or traditional ice lanterns and when lit up from inside at night, take your breath away.

The festival also includes a number of winter sports, including ice skating shows, and the frozen Songhua River becomes a hive of activity, with people tobogganing, ice sailing and even swimming in the frigid water using specially cut holes in the ice. The festival officially lasts between January 5 and mid-February, though if weather conditions are right, it runs into March. Entry to the main sculpture area is Y180.

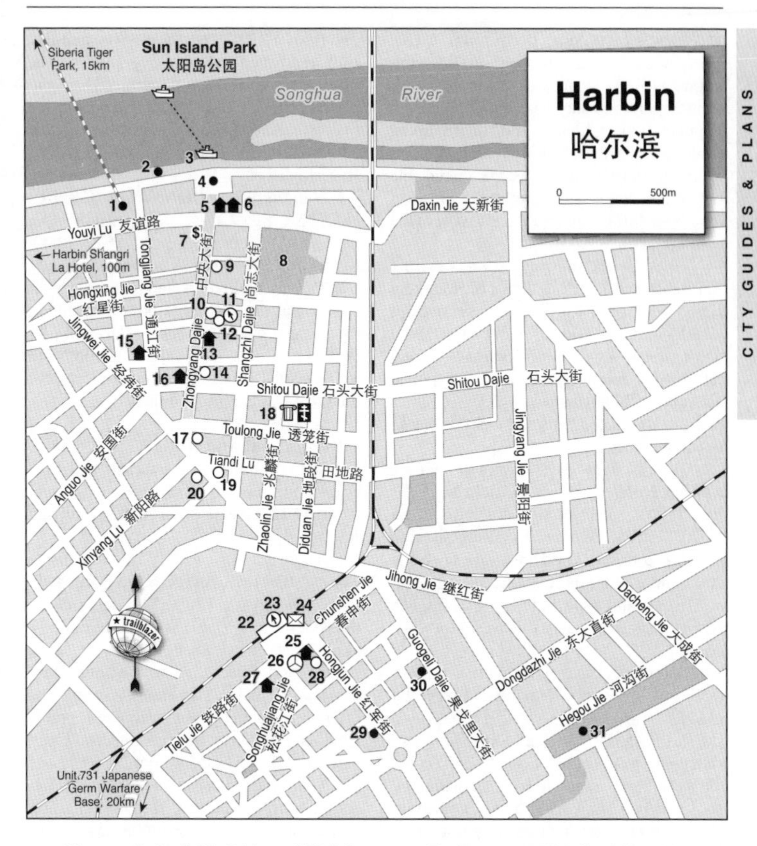

You can find reliable 24-hour **ATMs** in the Bank of China, with a handy branch at 37 Zhaolin Jie, off Zhongyang Dajie, and another at 19 Hongjun Jie. You can also cash travellers' cheques here.

International phone calls can be made from the **China Telecom** office at 420 Guogeli Dajie and also on the 2nd floor of the railway station.

China International Travel Service (CITS; ☎ 5363 3171), inside the hotel at 68 Hongjun Jie, four blocks south-east of the railway station, has helpful English-speaking staff that can assist with rail tickets and flights, even though the markup is quite hefty.

Taxis start at Y10 flagfall, with most trips around town under Y15. Watch the meter: some of them are fixed and will run up very quickly. To get to the Daoliqu area from the railway or bus station, catch bus No 13 (Y1) from the bus stop across the square from the railway station, where Guogeli Dajie meets Chunshen Jie; it runs towards Stalin Park along Tongjiang Jie.

Where to stay

Prices go up by around 20% during the Ice Lantern Festival.

Kazy International Youth Hostel 卡兹国际青年旅社 (82 Tongjiang Jie, 通江街82号, ☎ 8765 4211, no website in English;

🖳 www.hostels.com, dorm/room Y120/160), housed inside the old **main synagogue** (1909), is one of the more atmospheric places to stay. The rambling hostel, popular with Chinese and international students, has basic dorms and spotless rooms upstairs. Bathrooms are shared, the bar that doubles as reception is presided over by helpful staff, and there's wi-fi in the common area.

Opposite the railway station is the big ***Bei Bei Hotel*** 北北快捷宾馆 (10 Hongxing Jie, 红星街10号, ☎ 8785 2222, sgl/dbl/trpl Y180/270/350), with friendly staff (who don't speak English, unfortunately) and refurbished rooms which have computers and glass-walled bathrooms. The doubles boast heart-shaped beds and a buffet breakfast is included.

To the right of the railway station, ***Kunlun Hotel*** 昆仑饭店 (8 Tielu Jie, 铁路街8号 ☎ 5361 6688, dbl/suite from Y570/1350) is favoured by Trans-Siberian package tourists. The rooms are spacious and comfortable, there's a Chinese restaurant, a café and a spa, but very little English is spoken and the service leaves a lot to be desired.

A few blocks away from the action for much of the year, ***Harbin Shangri-La Hotel*** 哈尔滨香格里拉大饭店 (555 Yuyui Lu, 友谊路555号, ☎ 8485 8888, 🖳 www.shangri-la.com, sgl/dbl US$210/250) is the plushest hotel in town with a swimming pool and non-smoking rooms – a rarity in China. In the winter, there are great views of the Ice Lantern Festival.

The cheapest place to stay in the nicest part of town is ***Zhong Da Hotel*** 中大大酒店 (Zhongyang Dajie 32, 中央大街32号, ☎ 8463 8888), where the large and bright en suite rooms with attached bath start at Y220. Broadband access and Chinese breakfast are included.

Up the street and way upmarket is the misnamed ***Modern Hotel*** 马迭尔宾馆 (89 Zhongyang Dajie, 中央大街89号, ☎ 8461 4997, 🖳 http://hotel.hrbmodern.com, sgl/dbl from Y830/1150), in a 1906 building fully renovated but retaining some of the original art nouveau and marble. The light, plush rooms all have broadband access and the restaurants serve a combination of fine Chinese cuisine along with European and Russian dishes.

Songhuajiang Gloria Plaza Hotel 松花江凯莱花园大酒店 (257 Zhongyang Dajie, 中央大街257号, ☎ 8677 0000, rooms from Y700) has a prime location overlooking Stalin Park and luxurious bathrooms, but the service is poor. Next door, the cheaper and more basic ***Gloria Inn*** 凯莱商务酒店 (☎ 8463 8855, sgl/dbl/suite Y378/628/818) has comfortable rooms but the breakfast is disappointing.

Where to eat and drink

You'll find numerous restaurants and bakeries along and off Zhongyang Dajie and plenty of cheap eateries around the railway station.

There's a huge variety of inexpensive eats at the two **covered food markets** along Zhongyang Dajie. The stalls along the sides serve fine noodles, dumplings, rice dishes, fried meat, lamb and squid kebabs, and desserts, as well as nuts, pastries, and candy. The more adventurous offerings include black armoured grubs, fried grasshoppers and centipedes. Open daily in summer 8.30am-8pm.

California Beef Noodle King USA, across from the railway station and along Tiandi Lu, is a popular chain serving heaped bowls of noodles for Y12.

Bi Feng Tang 避风塘 (185 Zhongyang Dajie), a Shanghai restaurant that's always packed with locals, serves myriad kinds of steamed dumplings, as well as noodle and rice dishes. The pork belly is excellent and the picture menus have English translations.

During the sub-zero winter cold, nothing warms you up like hotpot, as evidenced by the patrons who pack ***Ding Ding Xiang*** 鼎鼎香 (Hotpot Heaven, 58 Jingwei Jie,

The Harbin area code is ☎ 0451. From outside China dial +86-451.

hotpots from Y15) in colder months. Pick your own ingredients and a special sauce, but be careful what you order, as some of the elements are quite pricey.

Portman, at Xi 7 Dao Jie 53, also just off Zhongyang Dajie, serves Russian-style food for Y50-100, fried rice dishes for Y30 and American steaks for Y190. The dining room is elegant but comfortable.

The popular ***Dongfang Jiaozi Wang*** 东方饺子王 chain (Kingdom of Eastern Dumplings, 35 Zhongyang Dajie and Hongjun Jie, next to the Overseas Chinese Hotel, [V]) has an English menu and is the place to fill up on cheap *jiaozi* (dumplings), including many vegetarian ones.

Moving on

By rail There are three trains a day to Beijing (12-13hrs). The Trans-Manchurian *Vostok* 019/020 passes through on Thursday on the way to Beijing and Moscow-bound on Sunday. The most comfortable train to Beijing is the Z16 overnighter (8.27pm departure, soft sleeper only).

There are two daily overnight trains (9hrs) to Suifenhe on the China–Russia border, from where buses run to Vladivostok. Alternatively, you can take the 023 that runs to Vladivostok every Wednesday via Suifenhe, departing at 9pm and arriving at 8am on Friday. It sits overnight at Ussuriysk, awaiting the arrival of the morning train from Khabarovsk, making the 40-hour journey the slowest means of getting to Vladivostok, though you are very likely to have your sleeping compartment all to yourself.

You can buy your own ticket at the station if you don't mind the queues or the confusion of the massive railway station, or alternatively get it through your hotel for about Y50 commission. For Trans-Siberian tickets contact Harbin Railway International Tourist Agency on the 7th floor of Kunlun Hotel, or alternatively try CITS (see p353).

You wait for the train in the assigned waiting room, not on the platform.

By bus If travelling in peak times, such as late August, when students are heading back to their respective universities and there's a shortage of train tickets to and from Beijing, you can take a daily overnight bus instead (12-16hrs). There is also one bus weekly to Vladivostok; ask at the long-distance bus station for details.

By air Flight destinations from Harbin's airport include Beijing (several daily, 2hrs), and other domestic destinations, as well as Khabarovsk (2/week, 1½hrs) and Vladivostok (2/week, 1¼hrs). You can book tickets at China International Travel Service (see p353).

Beijing 北京

Both the Trans-Manchurian and Trans-Mongolian routes, by far the most popular with travellers crossing Siberia, start or finish in Beijing, so you'll probably be spending some time in China's bustling, vibrant capital. Stepping off the Trans-Siberian at Beijing's futuristic railway station feels like stepping into a new world – a world of neon, pollution, incredible crowds of people, convoys of bicycles and silent scooters at every traffic light and strange but delicious smells. The city has been transformed by the 2008 Olympic Games, making it greener and more visitor-friendly. Beijing feels like an affluent international city, with streets and subway stations signposted in English as well as Mandarin, slick shopping malls and gleaming skyscrapers everywhere, and world-class eating, shopping and nightlife. At the same time it maintains its heritage and sports world-class historical attractions, such as the Forbidden City and the nearby Great Wall of China, as well as a multitude of parks and traditional neighbourhoods consisting of *hutong* (narrow alleyways) – the best places to observe daily life with all its quirks.

Most visitors stay for at least three days, but it's easy to spend a week here and still feel as if you've seen only a fraction of what Beijing has to offer.

HISTORY

Early history

Remains of China's oldest known inhabitant, Peking Man, were unearthed some 50km south of present-day Beijing in 1921, proving that life in this region dates back at least to 500,000BC. Chinese records go back only as far as the Zhou dynasty (12th century BC to 771BC) but indicate that by this period this region was acknowledged as the country's capital.

The city and its environs were to remain at the heart of Chinese culture and politics, although the role of capital was often lost to other cities, including Xi'an (where the 'Terracotta Army' now draws the tourists) and Luoyang. Beijing's strength, however, lay in its proximity to China's northern frontiers: by ruling from here emperors could keep a close eye on military developments to the north, where 'barbarians' were constantly threatening invasion.

Despite the construction of the Great Wall (a continuous process dating from the 2nd century BC) Genghis Khan marched through in 1215, sacked the city and then proceeded to rebuild it as his capital; the Mongols called this Khanbalik (City of the Khan). It was at this stage that the first Westerners visited, including Marco Polo, who liked the place so much that he stayed for 17 years.

The Mongol collapse and further developments

The Mongol empire fell in 1368 and the Chinese shifted their capital to Nanjing. Following a coup led by the son of the first Ming emperor, the government was moved back here and the city renamed Beijing (Northern Capital). The Manchurian invasion in 1644 established the final Chinese dynasty, the Qing, which was to rule from here until the abdication of Pu Yi, the 'Last Emperor', in 1912. Although the early years of Qing dynasty rule were successful, corruption, opium and foreign intervention soon undermined Chinese authority, and there were major rebellions in the city in the late 19th century.

From the Civil War to the present day

Under Chiang Kai-Shek the Kuomintang relocated China's capital to Nanjing in 1928, although following the Communist victory in 1949 it was moved back to Beijing. The People's Liberation Army (PLA) took over the city in January 1949, and in October, Chairman Mao declared the foundation of the People's Republic of China in Beijing. As the emperors had done before them, the Communists reshaped Beijing's architecture to further their own ends, knocking down the city's outer walls to make room for motor traffic. The city has hardly been quiet since then: every major movement in the country has had its roots here, notably the mass conventions of the Cultural Revolution and the democracy rallies (culminating in the Tiananmen Square Incident of 1989, when over 2000 civilians were killed).

As the capital (now with a population of some 22 million) roars through the second decade of the 21st century, the economy is booming, the country is changing fast and Beijing is the face that China wants to present to the world.

WHAT TO SEE AND DO

Tiananmen Square 天安门广场

Lying at the centre of the city, Tiananmen Square (**M** Tiananmen Xi/Tiananmen Dong) is the world's biggest square – three times the size of Moscow's Red Square. A political focal point since 1919 and notorious for the violence of 1989, when tanks were used against dissidents, it is the first stop for most visitors, and you'll find it teeming with people most of the time. At its centre is **Chairman Mao's Mausoleum** 毛主席纪念堂 (8am-noon Tue-Sun) where, after joining a long but surprisingly fast-moving queue, you can catch a brief glimpse of Mao's mummified body. The official party line now is that 'Mao was 70% right', but he is still revered by the enormous crowds who come to pay their respects to him. Entry is free, but you must leave your bags and cameras at one of the nearby kiosks.

North of the mausoleum, the 10,000-tonne, 36m-tall marble and granite obelisk is the **Monument to the People's Heroes** 人民英雄纪念碑. It was erected in 1958 and depicts the people's revolts against oppressors and the 1949 'liberation' by the PLA.

Tiananmen means 'Gate of Heaven', and at the northern end of the square is the gate for which the square is named. **The Gate of Heaven** 天安门 (8.30am-4.30pm, Y15), adorned with an enormous portrait of Mao, is the best place from which to observe the square.

The southern end of the square is defined by the **Main Gate** 前门 (8.30am-4pm), consisting of the Arrow Tower to the south and the actual Main Gate to the north. It dates back to the 15th century, when a wall had been in place to guard the Inner City.

Tiananmen Square
天安门广场

To the east is the **National Museum of China** 中国国家博物馆 (9am-5pm Tue-Sun; free admission; 💻 www.chnmuseum.cn) which became the largest of its kind in the world after the massive expansion effort was completed in March 2011. Not to be missed, this huge building contains 620,000 priceless relics from every period of China's history, including much about the post-WWII period, all with English labels. Pick up your free ticket at the ticket office by the West Gate by showing photo ID. On the other side of the square is the **Great Hall of the People** 人民大会堂 (8.30am-3pm, Y30), used for meetings of the National People's Congress and featuring an impressive 10,000-seat auditorium. It's open to the public whenever the Congress isn't in session.

The Forbidden City 紫禁城

To the north of the square is the **Imperial Palace** (8.30am-4pm Apr-Oct, 8.30am-3.30pm Nov-Mar, adult/student Y60/20, 💻 www.dpm.org.cn), better known as the Forbidden City, entered through the **front gate**, not to be confused with the Gate of Heaven.

The palace, which is the largest and best-preserved surviving complex of ancient buildings in China, took 14 years to complete. It was erected by the Ming emperor, Yong Le, in the early 15th century and was thereafter the home of 24 more emperors, up until the overthrow of the Qing dynasty in 1911, although following his abdication Emperor Pu Yi remained in the inner courts until 1924. The palace was off-limits to everyone except the emperors and their servants, and the emperors rarely ventured out of this enormous complex, comprising over 70 hectares and over 8700 rooms. The sheer size and opulence of its many buildings was designed to dwarf and humble the mere humans who stepped inside. The grandiose main palace buildings are located along the centre of the palace complex, with the more intimate living quarters of the emperor and his family, consisting of smaller palaces and gardens, found at the northern end.

It's impossible to see all of the palace's attractions in one go, but do set time aside for the vast palace **museum collections**, found in exhibition rooms alongside the main buildings, with exhibits on calligraphy, emperors' weddings and other subjects. Likewise, the **Gallery of Treasures** (Y10) in the north-eastern corner of the palace features jewelry, statuettes made of precious stones, and gives you access to the splendid **Nine Dragon Screen**.

It's worthwhile getting an audio guide (Y40), and have everything explained to you by Roger Moore, or else get to the palace early and see the main attractions before the crowds arrive, before making a beeline for the more secluded parts of the palace which you'll have largely to yourself.

Jingshan Park 景山公园

Rising directly to the north of the Forbidden City, the park (6am-8pm, to 9pm in the summer months, Y2) comprises sculpted gardens and a hill created in 1420 using the dirt from the moat, which serves the purpose of sheltering the palace from the bitter northern winds and spring dust storms. The last emperor of the Ming dynasty allegedly hanged himself here while the Manchu troops stormed the city and the last thing he would have seen was an incredible panoramic view of the Forbidden City below. You can enjoy that same view (the viewing platform becomes particularly crowded at sunset) or come here in the early morning to observe groups of Beijingers do their Tai-Chi exercises or walk their caged birds.

Temple of Heaven 天坛

Set inside the enormous, 267-hectare park, the Temple of Heaven (Tiantan Donglu, **M** Tiantandongmen, park 6am-9pm, sights 8am-4.30pm, entry to park Y15, entry to all sights Y35) is the site from which China's emperors conducted the country's most important religious rituals, upon which depended the well-being of the population. Natural disasters such as poor harvests were seen as a sign of the emperor losing Heaven's favour, so the Son of Heaven would come here three times a year to fulfill his spiritual duty.

The emperor would have entered the park through the **west entrance** (which is far more attractive than the east one, which teems with tourists) and spent the night inside the **Hall of Abstinence**, which is by the West Celestial Gate, east of the entrance. The most striking building in the park is the circular **Hall of Prayer for Good Harvest**, where the emperor came on the tenth day of the first lunar month. It was built entirely without the use of glue or nails, with a triple roof tiled in cobalt blue, which symbolises heaven, and decorated with dragon motifs. To the south lies the **Imperial Vault of Heaven**, where ancestral tablets were stored, surrounded by **Echo Wall** (where a whisper towards the surface on one side is perfectly audible around the opposite side – though you'd have to get here early to put it to the test without competing with other tourists).

Even further south you'll find the **Round Altar**, where great attention is paid to the heavenly number nine and its multiples – nine altar steps, nine rings of stone, and so on. Here the emperor communicated with the heavens and an entire bullock was burnt as an offering.

The park is at its best early in the morning, when you get to witness the more bizarre of the Beijing morning rituals and have the attractions to yourself for an hour or so before the hordes arrive.

TIAN TAN
THE TEMPLE OF HEAVEN

Summer Palace 故宫

This **palace** (8km north of the city, Yiheyuan Lu, **M** Beigongmen, 6.30am-8.30pm Apr-Oct, 7am-7pm Nov-Mar, entry to the park adult/student Y30/15, entry to all sections Y60/30), the summer retreat of the Imperial family since 1750, covers an area about four times the size of the Forbidden City, and is dominated by Kunming Lake, a Yuan dynasty reservoir. The entire area was razed by the English and French in 1860 as retribution for the Opium Wars, and then again in 1900 after the Boxer Rebellion, and rebuilt by Empress Dowager Cixi. Yuanmingyuan, the **Old Summer Palace** (圆明园) which lies to the north-east, was less fortunate: the Anglo-French forces wilfully destroyed the largest collection of Chinese artistic and architectural treasures outside the Forbidden City and it still lies in ruins.

The Summer Palace is a great place to explore slowly and highlights include the Long Corridor, with its 10,000 different painted scenes, Empress Cixi's personal three-level Peking opera theatre in the Garden of Harmonious Virtue, and, of course, the lake with its stunning marble footbridges. On the north shore you'll find a marble boat – the Empress's tribute to the Chinese navy, though the navy may have preferred a real boat, having been decimated by the Japanese in 1894. You can get away from the crowds either by strolling along the west side of the lake or by renting a boat near the North Palace Gate.

Lama Temple (Yonghegong) 雍和宫

The huge and superbly colourful **Lama Temple** (12 Yonghegong Dajie, **M** Yonghegong, 9am-4.30pm, Y25, audio guide Y20 with Y200 deposit) – the most important Tibetan Buddhist temple outside Tibet – is usually teeming with monks, tourists and worshippers, and awash with the scent and smoke of burning incense, which makes for an incredible spectacle. This was originally the home of Qing dynasty Prince Yong before he became Emperor Yongzheng and moved to the Forbidden City. Many of the temples and halls were completed in 1694, though it wasn't a lamasery for Tibetan monks until 1744 and the entire temple survived the Cultural Revolution unharmed, some say due to direct orders from Zhou Enlai (the first Premier of the People's Republic of China).

The worshippers crowd around the incense burners, which are centuries old, and the buildings are brightly painted both inside and out, with lots of dragon motifs, all leading you to the centrepiece, a stunning 18m statue of the Buddha carved from a single piece of sandalwood. It looks slightly shorter than its actual height because part of it is underground to prevent it from falling over. The most exciting time to be here is the Spring Festival and the last day of the lunar month when the monks perform 'Devil Dances' dressed in huge masks made to look like animal heads.

Confucius Temple 孔庙

Near Lama Temple, the peaceful **Confucius Temple** (13 Guozijian Jie, **M** Yonghegong, 8.30am-5pm, adult/student Y20/10) provides respite from the

❑ Beijing Museum Pass

This is a great deal if you're planning on extensive sightseeing in Beijing as, for Y80, this pass gives you free entry to 17 of Beijing's museums and discounted entry (typically 50% off) to nearly 30 more. There is only a limited number of passes, issued between late December and the end of January, and they are valid for the entire calendar year. You can pick up a pass at participating sights, which include Confucius Temple and the Ancient Observatory.

❑ A stroll through the *hutong* 胡同

An integral part of the city's history, the historical *hutong* neigbourhoods originally came into being during the Zhou Dynasty (1027-526BC), when Beijing was divided into residential areas according to one's social class. During the Ming Dynasty (early 15th century), the heart of the city became the Imperial Palace, with those of higher social standing permitted to live closer to the centre. *Hutong* are narrow alleyways, lined with *siheyuan* (traditional residences centered around a courtyard), with gates traditionally facing south for more light and in accordance with feng shui principles; hence most *hutong* run east to west, connected by tiny north–south alleys. The *siheyuan* belonging to nobility and wealthy merchants were particularly spacious and grand, whereas the *hutong* further away from the centre tended to be simpler and narrower. A typical *siheyuan* will have a pair of grand red doors, guarded by a pair of stone lions.

Between 1911 and 1948, the *hutong* became overcrowded, as residences previously belonging to a single family suddenly had to be subdivided to accommodate four, while in the second half of the 20th century, many traditional neighbourhoods were demolished to make way for wide streets and high-rise buildings. Still, numerous ancient *hutong* survive; they are designated protected areas and give Beijing character that other Chinese cities lack.

Though pedicab tours of the *hutong* are widely offered, it is actually more rewarding to explore them on foot by yourself, the best-preserved neighbourhoods being around the Drum Tower and Bell Tower area. You may find that some of your fondest memories of Beijing revolve around getting lost in the alleyways, accompanied by the delicious and unfamiliar smells of a multitude of food stalls, peering into courtyards and observing the bizarre daily life. The streets really come to life in the evening with residents playing *mah jong*, eating, bursting into impromptu musical recitals, having their hair cut, or simply strolling to the communal bathrooms at the end of the street in their pyjamas.

bustle and clamour of the city. In warmer months you'll find art students sketching the attractive grounds, or reading on benches in tranquil corners. In the main courtyard, beside the statue of the great man himself, there are 198 stone tablets with the names of *jinshi* scholars who passed a civil service examination during the Qing, Ming and Yuan dynasties.

Just west of the temple, **Guozijian Imperial College** (国子监) is where China's brightest students were educated in Confucianism for centuries.

Ancient Observatory 古观象台

If the weather is good you can easily spend an hour or so looking at the bizarre astronomical instruments, designed by Jesuit missionaries in the 17th and 18th centuries, and a reproduction of a Ming dynasty star map, in the largely open-air Ancient Observatory (2 Dongbiaobeng Hutong, **M** Jianguomen, Tue-Sun 9am-4pm, adult/student Y10/5). It's hard to figure out what most of them were for but they are fantastic pieces of engineering and artistry which wouldn't look out of place in a Harry Potter film. The observatory is located in a watchtower which was part of the Ming city wall, its predecessors having stood just north of the present spot since Yuan dynasty.

❑ Beijing's Olympic legacy

Hosting the planet's biggest sporting event in 2008 has left Beijing with the **world's largest airport**, designed by Lord Norman Foster, world-class sporting facilities and daring architecture that has forever altered the city's skyline.

Affectionately known as the 'Bird's Nest' (鸟巢), the Swiss-designed **National Stadium** (北京国家体育场; 9am-5pm, adult/student Y50/25) is the largest steel structure in the world, accommodating 91,000 people and currently hosting concerts and international football games. It looks spectacular when lit up at night.

Next door, the curvy, LED-lit bubble-wrapped exterior of the energy-efficient **National Aquatic Centre** (北京国家游泳中心; 9am-4.30pm Mon-Thur, 9am-6.30pm Fri-Sun, adult/student Y30/15) or 'Water Cube' (水立方) contrasts with the stadium's rigid lines. No fewer than 25 world records were set here, and the main pool remains intact, while the warm-up pool is now open for public use and there are plans to create a water theme park. Both the **Bird's Nest** and the **Water Cube** are at **M** Olympic Green.

Just west of Tiananmen Square, the 6500-seat **National Centre for Performing Arts** (国家大剧院; 2 Xichangan Jie, **M** Tiananmen Xi, 💻 www.chncpa.org, 9am-5pm, Y30), otherwise known as 'The Egg' for its distinctive titanium-and-glass dome, and designed by French architect Paul Andreu, has won great praise for its excellent acoustics. The entrance lies through the tunnel under the moat.

Perhaps the strangest of them all is the **CCTV Headquarters** (中央电视台总部大楼; 32 Dongsanhuan Zhonglu, **M** Gongzhufen, 8.30am-10pm, Y70), created by Rem Koolhaas, which has acquired the bizarre moniker of 'big underpants', though 'twisted doughnut' would be a more accurate description of the two skyscrapers melded together in a kind of angular loop. If you take a tour of the tower you can enjoy incredible panoramic views of Beijing from the open-air observation deck on Floor 22, or stay for lunch or dinner at the revolving restaurant.

Drum Tower 鼓楼 and Bell Tower 钟楼

Rebuilt in 1800 on the same spot where similar towers have stood for over 700 years, the **Drum Tower** (Gulou Dongdajie, **M** Guloudajie, 9am-5pm, adult/student Y20/10) has always been used for timekeeping: from the Song dynasty clepsydras (water clocks) to the convoluted system of the Qing dynasty, which involved beating the drum 13 times at 7pm and then once every two hours afterwards. Today it's home to 25 drums that are beaten for visitors every half hour from 9am to 11.30am and 2pm to 5pm, and besides the impressive drum performances, it's worth climbing the incredibly steep steps for the view over some of Beijing's nicest hutong.

The nearby **Bell Tower** (Dianmen Dajie, 9am-5pm, adult/student Y15/8) also dates back to the Yuan dynasty (though the current one is only 300 years old) and is named after the 500-year-old bronze bell that weighs 63 tonnes. Visitors can ring that bell for a princely sum of Y100 during the Spring Festival.

798 Art District 798 艺术新区

Modern art enthusiasts should not miss this incredible collection of **galleries** (Jiuxianqiao Beilu and Jiuxianqiao Lu), housed in abandoned factory spaces 4km north of the city centre. While several years ago this became an artists' enclave, it is now government sponsored but no less worthwhile. Wander through the narrow alleys, stop at the little cafés and check out the highlights, which include the **798 Photo Gallery** (4 Jiuxianqiao Lu, 💻 www.798photogallery.cn, 10am-6pm) with interesting photographic exhibitions by Chinese and international photographers, **Beijing Art Now Gallery** (BANG, Red Yard No 1, 💻 www.beijingartnow.com, noon-6pm), dedicated to quality exhibitions by some of the best local contemporary artists, and **Beijing Tokyo Art Projects** (4 Jiuxianqiao Lu, 💻 www.tokyo-gallery.com, 10.30am-6.30pm), featuring consistently cutting-edge work by Japanese and other international artists.

To get here, take bus 915, 918 or 934 (Y1, 25 min) from Dongzhimen Long-Distance Bus Station along the Airport Expressway to Dashanzi Lukounan.

PRACTICAL INFORMATION

Arriving in Beijing

By train Trans-Siberian trains arrive at the central railway station, **Beijing Zhan**, 3km south-east of the Forbidden City and handily located next to the subway station on Line 2.

Many other trains arrive and depart from Beijing's smart West (**Xikezhan**) station, which will be accessible by subway Line 9 in 2011.

The new Beijing South Railway station (**Nanzhan**), said to be the biggest in Asia and accessible by Subway Line 4 (and Line 14), is a massive transportation hub which will be home to the high-speed Beijing–Shanghai railway, launched in June 2011.

Beijing North station (**Beizhan**) is accessible by subway lines 2 and 13 and this is where you catch the high-speed suburban trains to Badaling.

By air Beijing's futuristic **Capital International Airport** (💻 http://en.bcia.com.cn) is 27km away from the city centre.

A convenient new **light rail line** which runs every 15 minutes links it to subway lines 2, 10 and 13 (first/last train to airport 6.30am/10.30pm, first/last train from airport 6.30am/11pm, 30mins, Y25 one way).

The cheapest way into town is by **express bus** (40-90 mins depending on traffic; Y16); there are nine lines, the most popular with travellers being Line 3 that runs to and from Beijing Railway Station (7am-midnight from the airport, 5.30am-9pm from the railway station).

Taxis cost around Y100 (including Y15 road toll); grab one from the taxi ranks and ignore approaches from drivers as scams are common.

Local transport

The **subway system**, consisting of 14 lines with five more to be constructed by 2015, is the best way of getting around much of the city. Stations are marked with a blue 'D' sign outside and station names are in English. Trains are frequent and cheap (Y2 per ride, 5am-10.30pm); however, single ride cards purchased at stations are valid only from that station on the same day. Many travellers end up joining the rest of the city's population on two wheels: there are many places that rent out **bikes**, particularly hostels and budget hotels. Even though it might be daunting at first to join the city's cycling hordes, it's a great way of covering distances between attractions that are not comfortably walkable.

Taxis are easy to flag down anywhere and inexpensive. They're metered: Y10 flagfall (Y11 at night) plus Y2/km and are great value when shared. A taxi from Beijing Zhan railway station to Sanlitun in the north of the city is about Y25. If you can't speak Chinese, get your destination written down in Chinese script and show it to the driver.

Orientation and services

The biggest problem Beijing poses for visitors is its sheer size, about the same as a small European country. *(cont'd on p368)*

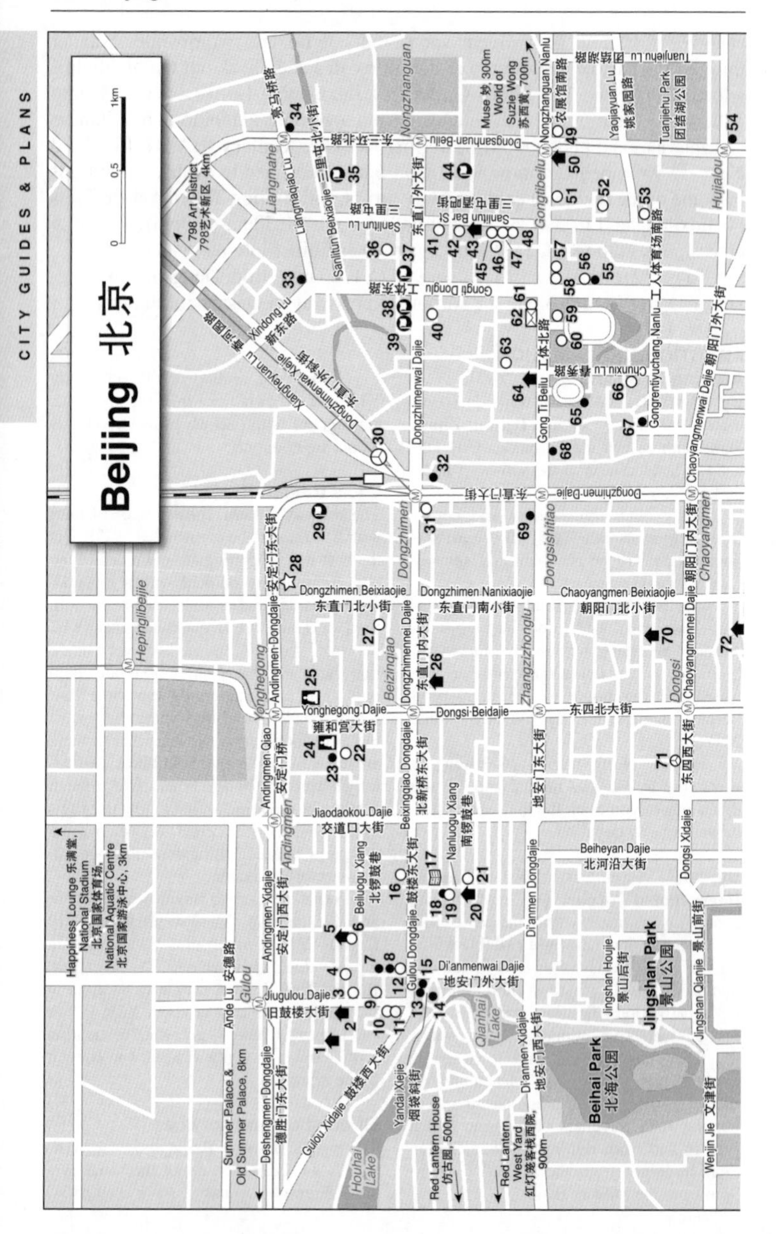
Beijing 北京
0
0.5
1km
798 Art District
798艺术新区, 4km
Happiness Lounge 乐满堂,
National Stadium
北京国家体育场,
National Aquatic Centre
北京国家游泳中心, 3km
Summer Palace &
Old Summer Palace, 8km
Red Lantern House
仿古园, 500m
Red Lantern
West Yard
红灯笼客栈西院,
900m
Muse 魅, 300m
World of
Suzie Wong
苏西黄, 700m
Beihai Park
北海公园
Jingshan Park
景山公园
Houhai
Lake
Qianhai
Lake
Tuanjiehu Park
团结湖公园
Dongzhimen Beixiaojie
东直门北小街
Dongzhimen Nanxiaojie
东直门南小街
Chaoyangmen Beixiaojie
朝阳门北小街
Jiaodaokou Dajie
交道口大街
Beiheyan Dajie
北河沿大街
Di'anmenwai Dajie
地安门外大街
Jiugulou Dajie
旧鼓楼大街
Yonghegong Dajie
雍和宫大街
Dongsi Beidajie
东四北大街
Dongzhimenwai Dajie
东直门外大街
Gong Ti Beilu
工体北路
Gongrentiyuchang Nanlu
工人体育场南路
Chaoyangmenwai Dajie
朝阳门外大街
Sanlitun Bar St
Sanlitun Lu
Xindong Lu
新东路
Liangmaqiao Lu
Nongzhanguan Nanlu
农展馆南路
Yaojiayuan Lu
姚家园路
Tuanjiehu Lu
Gongti Donglu
Chunxiu Lu
Dongsanhuan Beilu
Andingmen Qiao
安定门桥
Ande Lu
安德路
Gulou
Andingmen
Yonghegong
Hepinglibeijie
Beixinqiao
Dongzhimen
Dongsishitiao
Zhangzizhonglu
Dongsi
Chaoyangmen
Liangmahe
Nongzhanguan
Gongtibeilu
Hujialou
Wenjin Jie 文津街
Jingshan Houjie
景山后街
Jingshan Qianjie 景山前街
Dongsi Xidajie
东四西大街
Gulou Xidajie 鼓楼西大街
Yandai Xiejie
烟袋斜街
Nanluogu Xiang
南锣鼓巷
Beiluogu Xiang
北锣鼓巷

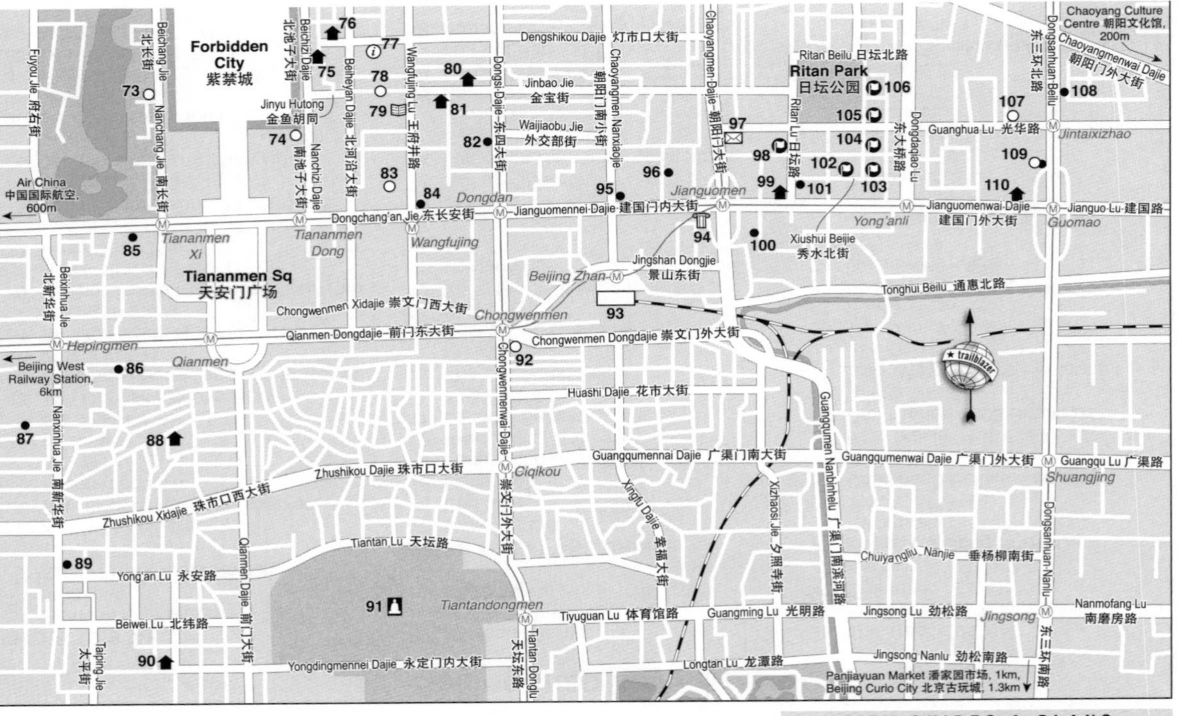
Forbidden City
紫禁城
Fuyou Jie 府右街
Beichang Jie
北长街
73
Nanchang Jie 南长街
Beichizi Dajie
北池子大街
76
75
77
78
79
Jinyu Hutong
金鱼胡同
74
Nanchizi Dajie
南池子大街
Beiheyan Dajie 北河沿大街
Wangfujing Lu 王府井路
80
81
Dengshikou Dajie 灯市口大街
Jinbao Jie
金宝街
Waijiaobu Jie
外交部街
82
83
84
Dongsi Dajie 东四大街
Chaoyangmen Nanxiaojie
朝阳门南小街
Chaoyangmen Dajie 朝阳门大街
97
Ritan Beilu 日坛北路
Ritan Park
日坛公园
106
105
104
102
103
98
99
101
Ritan Lu 日坛路
Dongdaqiao Lu
东大桥路
Guanghua Lu 光华路
107
108
109
110
Jintaixizhao
Dongsanhuan Beilu
东三环北路
Chaoyang Culture Centre 朝阳文化馆, 200m
Chaoyangmenwai Dajie
朝阳门外大街
96
95
Jianguomen
Dongdan
Air China
中国国际航空,
600m
Dongchang'an Jie 东长安街
Jianguomennei Dajie 建国门内大街
Jianguomenwai Dajie
建国门外大街
Jianguo Lu 建国路
Yong'anli
Guomao
85
Tiananmen Xi
Tiananmen Dong
Wangfujing
94
100
Xiushui Beijie
秀水北街
Tiananmen Sq
天安门广场
Jingshan Dongjie
景山东街
Beijing Zhan
93
Tonghui Beilu 通惠北路
Beixinhua Jie
北新华街
Chongwenmen Xidajie 崇文门西大街
Chongwenmen
Qianmen Dongdajie 前门东大街
Chongwenmen Dongdajie 崇文门外大街
Hepingmen
Qianmen
92
trailblazer
Beijing West
Railway Station,
6km
86
Huashi Dajie 花市大街
87
88
Chongwenmenwai Dajie 崇文门外大街
Guangqumennai Dajie 广渠门南大街
Guangqumenwai Dajie 广渠门外大街
Guangqu Lu 广渠路
Shuangjing
Nanxinhua Jie 南新华街
Zhushikou Dajie 珠市口大街
Ciqikou
Zhushikou Xidajie 珠市口西大街
Xingfu Dajie 幸福大街
Xizhaosi Jie 夕照寺街
Guangqumen Nanbinhelu 广渠门南滨河路
Dongsanhuan Nanlu
东三环南路
Tiantan Lu 天坛路
Chuiyangliu Nanjie 垂杨柳南街
89
Yong'an Lu 永安路
Qianmen Dajie 前门大街
91
Tiantandongmen
Beiwei Lu 北纬路
Tiyuguan Lu 体育馆路
Guangming Lu 光明路
Jingsong Lu 劲松路
Jingsong
Nanmofang Lu
南磨房路
Taiping Jie
太平街
90
Yongdingmennei Dajie 永定门内大街
Tiantan Donglu
天坛东路
Longtan Lu 龙潭路
Jingsong Nanlu 劲松南路
Panjiayuan Market 潘家园市场, 1km,
Beijing Curio City 北京古玩城, 1.3km

Beijing map key 北京

WHERE TO STAY

1 Bamboo Garden Hotel 竹园宾馆
2 Drum Tower Youth Hostel 古韵青年酒店
5 3 plus 1 精品酒店
20 Beijing Downtown Backpackers Accommodation 东堂客栈
26 4 Banqiao 板桥胡同4号
43 The Opposite House 瑜舍
50 Zhaolong International Youth Hostel 兆龙青年旅社
64 Sanlitun Youth Hostel 三里屯青年旅社
70 Beijing Double Happiness Courtyard Hotel 北京阅微庄宾馆
72 Hotel Côté Cour S L 演乐酒店
75 Peking International Youth Hostel 北平国际青年旅社
76 Jade International Youth Hostel 西华智德宾馆
80 Novotel Peace Hotel 诺福特和平宾馆
81 Peninsula Beijing 王府饭店
88 Leo Hostel 广聚元宾馆
90 Home Inn 如家快捷酒店
99 St Regis Beijing 北京国际俱乐部饭店
110 China World Hotel 中国大饭店

WHERE TO EAT AND DRINK

3 Café Sambal
4 Bed 床吧
6 Contempio
9 Fenghuang Zhu 凤凰竹
10 Kuan Dian 宽店
11 Le Little Saigon 西贡在巴黎
12 The Drum and Bell 鼓钟咖啡馆
19 Saveurs du Corée 韩香馆
21 Salud 老伍
22 Xu Xiang Zhai Vegetarian Restaurant 叙香斋
27 Lily Vegetarian 百合素食香草园
31 Awfully Chocolate
34 Lufthansa Center Youyi Shopping City 燕莎友谊商城
36 April Gourmet 绿叶子食品店
40 Paddy O'Shea's 爱尔兰酒吧
41 Le Petit Paris 小巴黎
42 Super 24
46 The Tree 隐藏的树
Poachers Inn 友谊青年酒吧
47 Crepanini 可百尼尼
48 Kokomo
49 Beijing Da Dong Roast Duck Restaurant 北京大董烤鸭店
51 Cantonese Deluxe Restaurant 凯悦酒家
53 Beer Mania 麦霓啤酒吧
56 Drei Kronen 1308 Brauhaus 皇冠自酿啤酒坊
57 Xiao Wang's Home Restaurant 小王府
58 The Den 敦煌
61 Purple Haze 紫苏亭
63 Feiteng Yuxiang 沸腾鱼乡
74 Grandma's Kitchen 祖母的厨房
78 Donghuamen Night Market 东华门夜市
83 Wangfujing Snack Street 王府井小吃街
92 Bian Yi Fang Roast Duck Restaurant 便宜坊北京烤鸭
107 Centro 炫酷
109 The Taj Pavillion (in China World Trade Center)

NIGHTCLUBS AND LIVE MUSIC

16 Mao Livehouse 光芒酒吧
45 Kai Club 开
52 Salsa Caribe 卡利宾拉丁舞俱乐部
59 Vics 威克斯
60 Mix 密克斯俱乐部
66 Destination 目的地
73 What 什么酒吧

ENTERTAINMENT

54 Beijing Chaoyang Theatre 北京朝阳剧院
69 Tiandi Theatre 天地剧院
86 Zhengyici Theatre 正乙祠戏楼
89 Li Yuan Theatre 梨园剧场
96 Chang An Grand Theatre 长安大戏院

SHOPPING

13 SQY-T
14 Yandai Xiejie 烟袋斜街
15 In
17 The Bookworm 书虫
18 Plastered T-shirts
55 Hong Ying 红英
79 Foreign Languages Bookstore 外文书店
84 Oriental Plaza 东方广场
87 Liulichang Lu 琉璃厂路

PLACES OF INTEREST

7 Bell Tower 钟楼
8 Drum Tower 鼓楼
23 Guozijian Imperial College 国子监
24 Confucius Temple 孔庙
25 Lama Temple (Yonghegong) 雍和宫
85 National Centre for Performing Arts 国家大剧院
91 Temple of Heaven 天坛
94 Ancient Observatory 古观象台
108 CCTV Headquarters 中央电视台总部大楼

EMBASSIES

29 Russian Embassy 俄罗斯大使馆
35 Netherlands Embassy 荷兰大使馆
37 German Embassy 德国大使馆
38 Canadian Embassy 加拿大大使馆
39 Australian Embassy 澳大利亚大使馆
44 French Embassy 法国大使馆
98 Japanese Embassy 日本大使馆
102 Mongolian Embassy 蒙古大使馆
103 Irish Embassy 爱尔兰大使馆
104 US Embassy 美国大使馆
105 British Embassy 英国大使馆
106 New Zealand Embassy 新西兰大使馆

OTHER

28 Public Security Bureau (PSB) 公安局
30 Dongzhimen Long Distance Bus Station 东直门长途汽车站
32 Mercury International Travel 和平国旅
33 Beijing International SOS Clinic 北京国际救援中心
46 Monkey Business
62 Beijing International Post Office 北京国际邮电局
65 Aeroflot 俄罗斯航空
67 Beijing Baosheng Air Service 北京保盛航空服务
68 S7 airlines *S7* 航空
71 Airport Bus Stop 机场大巴站
77 Beijing Tourist Information Center 北京旅游咨询服务中心
82 Peking Union Medical College Hospital 北京协和医院
93 Beijing Zhan (central railway station) 北京站
95 China International Travel Service (CITS) 中国国际旅行社
97 Beijing International Post Office 北京国际邮电局
100 Beijing Tourism Group (BTG) 首旅集团
101 Mongolian Airlines 蒙古航空
109 China World Trade Center 中国国际贸易中心

❑ The IC transportation smartcard 一卡通

The IC card, or the Yikatong (one card pass), is a multi-purpose travel card that can be topped up; it is similar to London's Oyster Card, only much more useful. Though primarily used to pay subway and bus fares, it can also be used with some taxi companies, restaurants, supermarkets and cinemas, saving you from queuing up and also saving you money due to discounted fares. You will most likely be using it for transportation only; if staying in Beijing for a few days, it's a good idea to get an IC card valid for 3, 7 or 15 days (these cannot be topped up; Y10/20/40, plus Y20 deposit).

IC cards can be purchased at most central subway stations. To get your deposit back, return your card to any of the central stations that issue them.

(cont'd from p363) A walking tour, taking in three or more sights in one day, is simply not possible. You'll mainly find yourself hitting one major sight (such as the Forbidden City or Summer Palace) each day, with lots of time spent on public transport.

Cycling is a good way of getting around, as many locals will testify, but braving Beijing's main streets on a bike is not for everyone. Fortunately, most streets are laid out in a neat grid with the Forbidden City and Tiananmen Square at the centre and five ring roads circling the city centre, so it's difficult to get lost.

You will have to get used to the crowded streets and packed underground, though.

China visa extensions Visa extensions are done at the Foreign Affairs branch of the **Public Security Bureau** (PSB; 2 Andingmendong Dajie, **M** Yonghegong, ☎ 8402 0101, 8.30am-4.30pm Mon-Sat), on the north-east corner of the second ring road in a huge building by the flyover.

It's relatively straightforward to extend a tourist visa by 30 days, which takes 4-5 working days to process, but it's more difficult to obtain more than one extension. The price for an extension depends on your nationality and is subject to change at short notice.

Diplomatic representation In Beijing, embassies are located in two main areas: Sanlitun and Jianguomenwai. Standard embassy opening hours are 9am to noon and then from 1.30pm to 4 or 5pm, though consular sections tend to be open only in the morning. If you can't find the embassy you need on the lists here, try 💻 www.travelchinaguide.com/embassy/foreign/beijing for an up-to-date list.

Sanlitun: Australia (21 Dongzhimenwai Dajie, Sanlitun, ☎ 5140 4111); **Canada** (19 Dongzhimenwai Dajie, Sanlitun, ☎ 5139 4000); **France** (3 Sanlitun Dongsanjie, Sanlitun, ☎ 8532 8080); **Germany** (17 Dongzhimenwai Dajie, Sanlitun, ☎ 6532 9000); **Netherlands** (4 Liangmahe Nanlu, ☎ 8532 0200); **Russia** (4 Dongzhimen Beizhongjie, ☎ 6532 1381).

Jianguomenwai: Ireland (3 Ritan Donglu, ☎ 6532 2691); **Japan** (7 Ritan Lu, ☎ 6532 2361); **Mongolia** (2 Xiushui Beijie, ☎ 6532 1203); **New Zealand** (1 Ritan Lu Dong Erjie, ☎ 6532 7000); **UK** (11 Guanghua Lu, ☎ 5192 4000); **USA** (55 Anjialou Lu, entrance on Tianze Lu, ☎ 8531 3000).

Information You can easily visit the Forbidden City, the Temple of Heaven and other attractions independently. Some sections of the Great Wall are more easily reached if you take a tour – most hotels and hostels offer them and can also book tickets for performances of Chinese acrobatics, kung fu and Beijing opera.

❑ Emergency numbers

Ambulance ☎ 120
Ambulance Beijing ☎ 999
Fire ☎ 119
Police ☎ 110

The **Beijing Tourist Information Centre outlets** at the airport (9am-5pm) and at the main railway station have a plethora of leaflets about the city and the staff speak basic English. You can also buy detailed maps of the city (Y15) in the underpass as you come off the train at Beijing Zhan station. If you're planning on spending a few days in the city, consider buying the excellent *Insider's Guide to Beijing*, updated annually and sold at the café in The Bookworm (see p376).

Free English-language **listings magazines**, the monthly *Beijinger* (💻 www.thebeijinger.com), and the bi-weekly *City Weekend* (💻 www.cityweekend.com.cn) and *Agenda* (💻 www.agendabeijing.com), are found in expat bars and restaurants, particularly in Sanlitun and also in the Qianhai Lake area.

You can find information on the city's attractions, hotel and restaurant listings and travel bargains on 💻 www.beijing-visitor.com which is a good catch-all site, while 💻 www.tour-beijing.com offers all manner of city tours, including themed ones.

Medical Beijing has excellent medical facilities.

The leading hospital is **Peking Union Medical College Hospital** (PUMCH; 1 Shuaifuyuan, **M** Wangfujing, emergency ☎ 6529 5269, 8am-4.30pm Mon-Fri, 24-hour emergency service), which covers medical and dental emergency treatment. Most doctors speak good English and there's a large foreigners' wing south of the inpatient building.

There's also **Beijing International SOS Clinic** (Suite 105, Wing 1, Kunsha Building, 16 Xinyanli, **M** Lingmahe, daily 24hrs, ☎ 6462 9100, 💻 www.internationalsos.com), offering all manner of medical services, with multi-lingual staff.

❑ **Chinese street names**

jie / dajie	街 / 大街	avenue / street
lu / xiang	路 / 巷	road / lane
hutong	胡同	narrow alleyway

❑ **Exchange rates**

To get the latest rates of exchange see 💻 www.xe.com/ucc

	Yuan
US$1	Y6.47
UK£1	Y10.43
Euro€1	Y9.15
Aus$1	Y6.94
Can$1	Y6.81
Japan ¥100	Y8.16
Mong T100	Y0.52
NZ$1	Y5.53
Sing$1	Y5.32
S Africa R10	Y9.33

Money The unit of currency is the *yuan* (Y; also called *renminbi* or RMB), which is divided into 10 *jiao* or 100 *fen* and comes in denominations of 1, 2, 5, 10, 20, 50 and 100 yuan.

ATMs are easy to find around the city, particularly along the main shopping streets, inside shopping malls and international hotels. Good places to change travellers' cheques and foreign currency are the **Industrial and Commercial Bank of China (ICBC)** branches and the **Bank of China**; you'll find a branch in the Arrival Hall at the airport as well as at Oriental Plaza (see p376).

Post and Telecommunications **Beijing International Post Office** is at Jianguomenwai Dajie, **M** Jianguomen, with other branches on Gongretiyuchang Beilu, opposite the Workers' Stadium, and opposite Beijing International Hotel. Post offices tend to be open between 9am and 5pm and you can send letters and postcards from most hotels, though packages need to be sent from post office branches. Don't seal the packages because they'll need to inspected.

There are fewer **internet cafés** now that most hotels and hostels offer free internet and/or wi-fi. If the place where you're staying by some chance doesn't have internet access, you'll find a 24-hour internet café just east of Bookworm's café (see p376), on the 2nd floor (Y5/hour), or keep an eye out for a *wangba* (网吧) sign. **Free wi-fi** spots dot the city now; many cafés and restaurants in trendy parts of town will give you a password along with your coffee.

To make phone calls you can either go to a telecommunications office or use a **pre-paid IC card** (for local and long-distance calls) or an **IP card** (for international calls) from a landline or mobile. You can buy both at China Telecom offices, newsstands and kiosks; you should never pay the face value for an IP card, as a Y100 card typically sells for around Y40, while the IC cards, used at the yellow pay phones, do sell at face value.

Different IP cards have different long-distance rates and some may only be used locally, while others can be used throughout the country.

China Mobile **SIM cards** are relatively inexpensive, setting you back Y70-120, and coming with Y50 worth of credit, which can be topped up using a credit-charging card of Y50 or Y100. Calls to local numbers are inexpensive, but calling abroad will set you back around Y6/minute.

Travel agencies These agencies can help you organise your onward travel.

Trans-Siberian specialist **Monkey Business** (Room 201, Poachers Inn, South 43 Sanlitun Beijie; entrance from The Tree courtyard, **M** Gongtibeilu, ☎ 6591 6519, 🖳 www.monkeyshrine.com, 10am-6pm Mon-Sat) can help you book your Trans-Siberian train tickets, including stopovers in Russia and Mongolia, as well as providing visa support and arranging tailor-made trips.

CITS (China International Travel Service; Beijing International Hotel, 2nd floor, 9 Jianguomenwai Dajie, **M** Beijingzhan, ☎ 6512 0507, 🖳 www.citsbj.com, 8.30am-noon & 1.30-5pm) also sells Trans-Siberian tickets, as does the **Beijing Tourism Group** (BTG; 28 Jianguomenwai Dajie, **M** Jianguomen, ☎ 6515 8010, 8.30-11.30am & 1.30-5pm Mon-Fri).

Mercury International Travel (48 Dongzhimenwai Dajie, Tower C, Oriental Kenzo Plaza, **M** Dongzhimen, ☎ 8454 9420, 🖳 www.mercury-travel.com.cn) can help you book train, bus and plane tickets, while **Beijing Baosheng Air Service** (Room 901, Block B, Jia Hui International Centre, ☎ 400 888 0589, 🖳 www.baosheng-air.com) is China's largest air ticket wholesaler specialising in both domestic and international tickets.

Where to stay

Beijing has plenty of accommodation to suit every budget.

Budget accommodation Beijing's hostels tend to be of very good quality and the ones listed here, unless stated otherwise, have kitchen facilities or on-site cafés, laundry, lockers, free internet and/or wi-fi and air-conditioning, essential in summer.

Jade International Youth Hostel 西华智德宾馆 (5 Zhide Beixiang, off Beiheyan Dajie, 东城区智德北巷5号, **M** Tiananmen Dong, ☎ 6526 9966, no independent website but can be found at 🖳 www.hostels.com, dorm/dbl Y60/280) is ideally located just a few minutes' walk from the Forbidden City. The dorms are on the ground floor of this smart two-star hotel, most rooms are en suite, and the large restaurant serves inexpensive Western and Chinese dishes.

Nearby, ***Peking International Youth Hostel*** 北平国际青年旅社 (5 Beichizi Ertiao, Beichizi Dajie, 东城区北池子二条5号, **M** Tiananmen Dong, ☎ 6526 8855, 🖳 www.peking.hostel.com, dorm/sgl/dbl Y80-90/300/390-480), located in a traditional *siheyuan* residence with an attractive flowering courtyard and very popular with backpackers, comes highly recommended for its trips to the Great Wall, the tasty café food, excellent showers and book exchange. The staff can also help you get tickets to acrobatics and kung fu shows.

Conveniently located on one of the most popular *hutong* streets, the perpetually full ***Beijing Downtown Backpackers Accommodation*** 东堂客栈 (85 Nanluogu Xiang, 东城区南锣鼓巷85号, **M** Andingmen, ☎ 8400 2429, 🖳 www.backpackingchina.com, dorm/sgl/dbl Y70-90/150/200-300) is an established backpacker favourite. Great Wall trips, an excellent restaurant and bar, private bathrooms in all rooms, handy bike rental and proximity to great nightlife make this one of the top budget choices. Free airport pickup for those staying in doubles for more than four consecutive nights.

Zhaolong International Youth Hostel 兆龙青年旅社 (2 Gongti Beilu, behind the Zhaolong Hotel, 朝阳区工体北路2号, **M** Gongtibeilu, ☎ 6597 2299, 💻 www.zhaolonghotel.com.cn, dorm/dbl Y70/180, en suite dbl Y300) attracts a lively backpacker crowd and is ideally located for Sanlitun nightlife. Extra perks include a games room, reading lounge and a hot tub. Y10 discount for HI members.

Another Sanlitun favourite, the large ***Sanlitun Youth Hostel*** 三里屯青年旅社 (1 Chunxiu Lu, off Gongti Beilu, 朝阳区春秀路1号, **M** Gongtibeilu, ☎ 5190 9288, 💻 www.sanlitun.hostel.com, dorm/sgl/dbl Y45-80/200/220) stands out thanks to the efforts of its warm and helpful staff. The dorms are spacious and clean and the bar is a great place to mingle with fellow travellers.

Located on a *hutong* market street, the popular, family-run ***Leo Hostel*** 广聚元宾馆 (52 Dashilan Xijie, 宣武区大栅栏西街52号, **M** Qianmen, ☎ 6303 1595, 💻 www.leohostel.com, dorm/dbl Y50-60/240) organises recommended 'Secret Wall' trips which include a traditional village meal, and the regular movie nights and lively bar keep guests entertained. The owner can help arrange trips to Tibet. There's a Leo Hostel 2 nearby.

Drum Tower Youth Hostel 古韵青年酒店 (51 Jiugulou Dajie, 西城区旧鼓楼大街51号, **M** Guloudajie, ☎ 6403 7702, 💻 www.drumtowerhostel.com, dorm/sgl/dbl Y40-60/170/150-240) offers superb views of the nearby *hutong* and the Drum Tower from its rooftop bar and patio, and if that weren't enough, the street it's on is teeming with bars and eateries. On-site perks include a lounge with big-screen TV and the staff can help you book your train tickets as well as organising Great Wall trips and lively nights out.

Tucked back in a *hutong* near the hopping Houhai-area nightlife, ***Red Lantern House*** 仿古园 (500m west of city, 5 Zhengjue Hutong, 西城区正觉胡同5号, **M** Xinjekou, ☎ 6611 5771, 💻 www.redlanternhouse.com, dorm/sgl/dbl Y60/160-180/200, en suite sgl/dbl Y200/280), has a high-ceilinged lobby done up like an old Beijing alley, which doubles as a canteen and bar. Staff are very friendly and speak excellent English and there's a travel desk for all your ticket needs as well as trips to the Great Wall.

If the main Red Lantern House is full the staff can find a place for you at the nearby courtyard residence of ***Red Lantern West Yard*** 红灯笼客栈西院 (111 Xinjekou Nandajie, 西城区新街口南大街111号, **M** Ping'anli) with an attractive covered common area with a tiny bridge over a carp pond.

Mid-range hotels The most attractive of the mid-range options are those in *hutong* neighbourhoods. At mid-range and top hotels it's always worth asking what discounted rates (*zhekou*) they do outside the holiday seasons.

If you're after efficient, no-frills rooms with air-con and internet access, ***Home Inn*** 如家快捷酒店 (2A Xinzhong Jie, 东城区新中街甲2号, **M** Dongsishitiao, ☎ 400 820 3333, 💻 www.homeinns.com, room Y299-399) fits the bill perfectly. There are over 70 branches of the motel around the city.

Shiny, efficient and within walking distance of the Forbidden City, ***Novotel Peace Hotel*** 诺福特和平宾馆 (3 Jinyu Hutong, 东城区金鱼胡同3号, **M** Dengshikou, ☎ 6512 8833, 💻 www.novotel.com, dbl/suite Y430-580/716) has large, light rooms with satellite TV, wi-fi that you pay for and 24-hour room service.

Hiding behind a nondescript gate, ***3 Plus 1*** 精品酒店 is a tiny boutique hotel (17 Zhangwang Hutong, Jiugulou Dajie, 东城区旧鼓楼大街张旺胡同17号, **M** Guloudajie, ☎ 6404 7030, 💻 www.3plus1bed

The Beijing area code is ☎ 010. From outside China dial +86-10 rooms.com, rooms Y1360-1600, suite Y2380) consisting of just four luxurious rooms each with custom-designed furniture and its own private courtyard. You can make use of the library, TV room and wi-fi, and the afternoon fruit and tea is a nice touch. Why not '4 bedrooms'? Because the Chinese word for 'four' is very similar to the Chinese word for 'death'.

Staying in the former home of the Qing scholar and dignitary Ji Xiaolan, ***Beijing Double Happiness Courtyard Hotel*** 北京阅微庄宾馆 (37 Dongsi Sitiao, 东城区东四四条37号, **M** Dongsishitiao, ☎ 6400 7762, 🖳 www.hotel37.com, sgl/dbl/family room Y680/1180/1680) makes for a memorable experience. Beautifully situated around two shaded courtyards inside a *hutong*, its rooms feature traditional ornate wooden furniture as well as the modern touches – flat screen TVs and wi-fi. The Happy Restaurant and Bar attract a mostly international crowd.

Hidden behind large doors is another *hutong* gem. A mix of traditional and contemporary, ***4 Banqiao*** 板桥胡同4号 (4 Banqiao Hutong, 东城区北新桥板桥胡同4号, **M** Beixingqiao, ☎ 8403 0968, 🖳 www.4banqiaocourtyard.com, sgl/dbl/suite Y518/768/1238) has attractive rooms around a pleasant courtyard, with free internet in the guest lounge. The rooftop patio is a great spot to retreat to after sight-seeing all day.

The pick of the traditional courtyard hotels is ***Bamboo Garden Hotel*** 竹园宾馆 (24 Xiaoshiqiao Hutong, Jiugulou Dajie, 西城区旧鼓楼大街小石桥胡同24号, **M** Guloudajie, ☎ 5852 0088, 🖳 www.bbgh.com.cn, sgl/twin/dbl/suite Y526/760/880/990-1760), its former owners including Empress Cixi's head eunuch and Kang Sheng, one of the masterminds behind the Cultural Revolution.

The rooms are decorated with reproduction Ming furniture, the bamboo grove and the pavilions are a delight and the restaurant serves elaborate Chinese dishes fit for aristocracy.

Upmarket hotels The rates at upmarket hotels don't tend to include a 15% tax which is added to your bill. It's common for some five-star places to set their rates in US$, but collect in yuan.

Japanese-designed, minimalist ***The Opposite House*** 瑜舍 (11 Sanlitun Lu, 朝阳区三里屯路11号院1号楼, **M** Gongtibeilu, ☎ 6417 6688, 🖳 www.theoppositehouse.com, studio Y2500-5100, suite Y25,000) is all wood and light; the sumptuous spa-style bathrooms have rain showers and there's a swimming pool. The on-site restaurants serve imaginative Mediterranean and North Asian cuisine and by night you can relax in the Mesh cocktail lounge or check out the international DJs in the basement Punk club.

Hotel Côté Cour S L 演乐酒店 (70 Yanyue Hutong, 东城区演乐胡同70号, **M** Dongsi, ☎ 6512 8020, 🖳 www.hotelcotecoursl.com, dbl/suite Y1068-1768/2168-2668) is a luxurious boutique hotel with all the charm of a 500-year-old *hutong* residence. There's incredible attention to detail, from the emerald mosaic tiles in the bathroom to the handmade Chinese silk beds, and the suites have views of the tranquil garden. There's broadband in the rooms and a reading lounge stocked with English books.

All marble and wood, ***St Regis Beijing*** 北京国际俱乐部饭店 (21 Jianguomenwai Dajie, 朝阳区建国门外大街21号, **M** Jianguomen, ☎ 6460 6688, 🖳 www.stregis.com/beijing, dbl from Y2075; Presidential Suite Y51,200) is one of the city's most luxurious hotels. Your personal butler and professional masseurs are available around the clock, there's a spa to pamper you and a swimming pool so that you can stay in shape after dining at the on-site Astor Grill.

Also excellent is the award-winning ***Peninsula Beijing*** 王府饭店 (8 Jinyu Hutong, 东城区王府井金鱼胡同8号, **M** Wangfujing, ☎ 8516 2888, 🖳 www.peninsula.com, dbl/suite Y1288-1488/2800-3500), its elegant rooms furnished with Chinese rugs and big-screen plasma TVs. You can feast on fusion cuisine at the Jing Restaurant and shop for designer gear in the Peninsula shopping arcade.

The first super-luxury hotel in Beijing, ***China World Hotel*** 中国大饭店 (1

Jianguomenwai Dajie, 朝阳区建国门外大街1号, M Guomao, ☎ 6505 2266, 🖳 www.shangri-la.com, dbl from Y2050, suites Y5000-45,000) with its opulent marble lobby, offers superb service, extensive leisure and business facilities, access to the luxury retailers at the China World Trade Center and superb dining – seafood at Aria or classic Chinese cuisine at the Summer Palace. Airport transfers are included in the price.

Where to eat and drink

The city has no shortage of places where you can eat; the best thing to do is to simply give yourself time to wander around and see what you come across, you'll never go hungry.

Budget food is easy to find: if you wander through the *hutong*, you'll come across numerous family-run eateries serving cheap, filling noodles or dumplings, or else the evening food stalls often have things on sticks for Y1 each. Fast-food chains such as McDonald's and KFC abound in the city. Inexpensive Chinese and international food is found in the food courts of every Beijing shopping mall (the **Oriental Plaza** has a good one), where the menus are more likely to have English translations or pictures of food.

Donghuamen Night Market, (Donganmen Dajie, M Dengshikou, from 6pm) is a row of stalls lining the street, serving assorted seafood and meat kebabs, noodles, fruit on sticks, flatbread with lamb and a selection of giant centipedes, scorpions and armoured black grubs on skewers for the more adventurous. Yes, it's touristy and not very cheap anymore (Y3-7 per skewer/Y15 upwards per dish), but it's worth it just to join in the clamour.

Wangfujing Snack Street (off Wangfujing Dajie, M Wangfujing) has a better selection and is more for Chinese tourists, though the prices are the same and there are places to sit and eat your noodles. Jiugulou Dajie, leading up to the Drum Tower, is lined with inexpensive eateries specialising in barbecued meat skewers, as well as restaurants serving international cuisine.

Dongzhimennai Dajie (M Beixinqiao) is lined with Chinese restaurants festooned with red lanterns (the more lanterns, the better the food quality), serving a huge variety of authentic dishes.

Beijing duck is, of course, the local speciality and the best places to try it are: ***Beijing Da Dong Roast Duck Restaurant*** (Bldg 3, Tuanjiehu Beikou, Dongsanhuan Lu, M Gongtibeilu, half-duck Y99 with pancakes), with white linen service and chefs who train for years to carve the duck just so; and ***Bian Yi Fang*** (3F, Bldg 3, New World Shopping Mall, 3 Chongwenmenwai Dajie, M Cikikou, whole duck Y150) has perfected its own slow roast technique over 150 years.

An excellent choice for a wide range of Chinese dishes is ***Xiao Wang's Home Restaurant*** (2 Guanghua Donglu, M Yong'anli, meals Y80). Their spare ribs with pepper salt are outstanding, as are their hot and spicy chicken wings and Beijing duck. There's another location nearby at the Ritan Park.

Le Little Saigon (141 Jiugulou Dajie, M Guloudajie) has a standard menu of Vietnamese dishes, but the rooftop terrace is a great place for a drink.

Muse (300m east of city, 1 Chaoyang Gongyuan Xilu, M Nonzhanguan) makes far better Vietnamese food, its pho and spring rolls drawing the crowds.

For superb Korean food, try the multi-dish taster platter at ***Saveurs du Corée*** (29 Nanluogu Xiang, M Beixinkiao, [V]); the fiery kimchi is perfect and the sweet potato noodles divine.

Café Sambal (43 Jiugulou Dajie, M Guloudajie, meals Y80) serves delicious, authentic Malaysian food in a delightful courtyard, their curry dishes and their Kumar lamb being particularly worthy of a mention.

For fiery Sichuan food, try the ***Feiteng Yuxiang*** branch (1-1 Gongti Beilu, M Gongtibeilu) for its superb *shuizhu yu* (fish chunks poached in a Sichuan peppercorn broth) or *lazi ji* (bits of fried chicken buried in a mound of dried chillies).

Kuan Dian (135 Jiugulou Dajie, M Guloudajie) serves some of Beijing's best spicy chicken wings (*yuanwei*) to a young crowd; have it with their mashed potato and try some of their barbecued scallops as an extra treat.

Fenghuang Zhu (25 Lindgan Hutong, off Jiugulou Dajie, **M** Gulousdajie, meals Y80, [V]) is an excellent place to immerse yourself in the sweet, sour and spicy flavours of Yunnan cuisine. Their tofu dishes are very flavourful, there are plenty of exotic vegetarian dishes that utilise vegetables and blossoms unheard of in the West, the spicy chicken is tender and beautifully flavoured, and the pineapple rice comes in a hollowed-out pineapple.

The dim sum at ***Cantonese Deluxe Restaurant*** (Comfort Inn, 6 Gongti Beilu, **M** Gongtibeilu) may not be the cheapest but the superb selection of fragrant, tender dumplings, attracting local crowds, is nothing short of perfection.

Grandma's Kitchen (47-2 Nanchizi Dajie, **M** Tiananmen Dong), originally started by an American grandma in China, serves comfort food that you may have been hankering after, such as burgers and fries, milkshakes, Caesar salad and apple pie.

The Tree (43 Sanlitun Beijie, behind Poachers Inn, **M** Gongtibeilu) serves arguably the best pizzas in the city from a wood-fired oven for Y55 and up, which you can wash down with some fine Belgian beers (Y40 and up).

For superbly prepared Thai food, head to ***Purple Haze*** (opposite the Workers' Stadium's north gate, in an alley behind the ICBC bank, **M** Dongsishitiao, [V]), where you can also chill out over a coffee.

If it's curry you want, ***The Taj Pavillion*** (300m north-east of city, West Wing, China World Shopping Mall, **M** Guomao, [V]) serves some of the city's best Indian/Pakistani food in an attractive setting.

Interesting choices for **vegetarians** include ***Xu Xiang Zhai Vegetarian Restaurant*** (26-1 Guozijian Dajie, **M** Beixinqiao, buffet Y70) with its superb lunch and dinner all-you-can-eat buffet featuring veggie versions of dumplings and sushi as well as a multitude of mock-meat and mock-fish dishes prepared from soy and gluten products. ***Lily Vegetarian*** (23 Caoyuan Hutong, Dongzhimennei Beixiaojie, **M** Beixinqiao) serves tasty vegetarian dishes, as well as herbal teas; the English menu is helpful, as are the staff.

For sweet and savoury crêpes, head to French-run ***Crepanini*** (81 Sanlitun Beilu, **M** Gongtibeilu), a cute café also specialising in paninis and waffles, while ***Le Petit Paris*** (29 Sanlitun Lu, **M** Gongtibeilu) does reasonably priced sandwiches.

All your chocolate cravings can be sated at ***Awfully Chocolate*** (1 Dongzhimen Nandajie, **M** Dongzhimen), their light cakes coming in three delicious flavours: chocolate, banana chocolate and rum and cherry chocolate.

To stock up for your Trans-Siberian journey, check out ***Super 24*** (24-hour supermarket, Sanlitun Lu, **M** Gongtibeilu). ***Lufthansa Center Youyi Shopping City*** (50 Liangmaqiao Lu, **M** Dongzhimen) also has a wide selection of food. If you're missing Marmite and Tetley tea, try ***April Gourmet*** (1 Sanlitun Beixiaojie, **M** Gongtibeilu), a small store specialising in those hard-to-find imported foods.

Drinking Around Sanlitun you can start at ***The Den*** (4 Gongti Donglu, next to City Hotel's entrance, **M** Gongtibeilu) one of Beijing's oldest bars where expats gather for pre-party drinking in the evening and post-party feeding in the early morning. Another long-running expat favourite is ***Poachers Inn*** (43 Sanlitun Beilu, **M** Gongtibeilu), a raucous bar with live acts at the weekend.

At ***Paddy O'Shea's***, (28 Dongzhimenwai Dajie, **M** Guomao), a genuine Irish pub and sports bar, you can enjoy the pub quiz on Wednesday nights along with your Guinness.

For superb German beers made from a 700-year-old Bavarian recipe, head to the ***Drei Kronen 1308 Brauhaus*** microbrewery (1F Bldg 5, China View, Gonti Donglu, **M** Dongsishitiao), while the bustling ***Beer Mania*** (Taiyue Fang, Nansanlitun Lu, **M** Gongtibeilu) dispenses the best selection of Belgian beers in town. ***The Drum and Bell*** (41 Zhongluowan Hutong, **M** Guloudajie) has an attractive rooftop patio where you can drink your beer and watch the sun set over the *hutong*, while at nearby ***Bed*** (17 Zhongwang Hutong), you can recline like a Roman and enjoy Asian finger food at one of the best-loved chill-out spots in the city.

Contempio (4 Zhangwang Hutong, Jiugulou Dajie, **M** Guloudajie) is an ultra-cool café by day and bar by night, its low lighting, mellow soundtrack, comfy seats and great service adding to the atmosphere.

Salud (66 Nanluogu Xiang, **M** Beixinqiao), one of the liveliest bars in Sanlitun, serves great sangria and home-made infused rums, and hosts live acts.

The pick of the hotel bars includes the classy ***Happiness Lounge*** (Pangu 7 Star Hotel, 27 Beisihuan Zhonglu, **M** Huixinxijiebeikou), 3km to the north overlooking the Bird's Nest and the Water Cube (see box p362), and ***Centro*** (Kerry Centre Hotel, 1 Guanghua Lu, **M** Guomao), with its huge, comfortable lounge and great wine selection, while the best summer terraces include ***Kokomo*** (Tongli Studios, Sanlitun Houjie, **M** Gongtibeilu) with its beachy décor and Caribbean nibbles.

Nightlife

Beijing nightlife is alive and kicking every night of the week, while weekend nights get going around midnight and carry on until dawn. Check listings for the latest happenings (see p369).

Clubs To window-shop for your party venue, good areas to head are **Sanlitun** ('Bar Street') and the **Houhai** lake district, both filled to bursting with bars and clubs that carry on late. They include the gritty student-chic ***Kai Club*** where a young crowd bounces around to break beats, house and indie, fuelled by cheap drinks.

One of the best clubs in the city is the ***World of Suzie Wong*** (700m east of the map, 1A Nongzhanguan Nanlu, west gate of Chaoyang Park, **M** Gongtibeilu), where you can chill out on one of the Ming dynasty beds if you get there early enough, join the dancers on the second floor, or mix with the hipsters on the rooftop terrace.

At ***Salsa Caribe*** (Area 4, Gongti Beilu, **M** Gongtibeilu) you can strut your stuff to great live Latin music on their sweaty, packed dancefloor.

Destination (7 Gongti Xilu, **M** Dongsishitiao) is Beijing's premier gay club which is perpetually packed at weekends. ***Mix*** (inside the north gate of the Workers' Stadium, **M** Dongsishitiao) heaves with hip-hop clubbers at the weekend and hosts quality international DJs. Nearby ***Vics*** is another dance giant, playing reggae, hip-hop, R&B and soul, with a separate chillout zone playing trance.

Live music The ever-popular ***What*** bar (72 Beichang Jie, north of the west Forbidden City gate) hosts up-and-coming musicians and bands and the music ranges from rock to psychedelic to ska.

Mao Livehouse (111 Gulou Dongdajie, **M** Guloudajie) is another popular live music venue, with a large stage and separate bar area. The bands can be hit-and-miss, but on occasion international acts play here.

Acrobatics & martial arts These two arts have been practised in China for over two millennia and your visit to Beijing is not complete without seeing one (or both!).

One of the best places to catch an acrobatics show is **Beijing Chaoyang Theatre** (36 Donsanhuan Beilu, **M** Hujialou, Y180-380, performances daily at 7.15pm), which combines hoop jumping, tumbling, bicycle tricks and plate spinning with impressive feats of strength, contortion and balance. At **Tiandi Theatre** (10 Dongzhimen Nandajie, **M** Dongsishitiao, Y120-350, performances at 7.15pm) you'll witness some of the same acts, but with one crucial difference – they are all performed by children and teenagers and are all the more moving since you sense that there's a greater potential of things going wrong. To observe the punishing stage show of the Shaolin Warriors, head to **Chaoyang Culture Centre** (200m east of the map, 17 Jintaili, **M** Guanghualu, Y200-400, performances at 7.20pm). For matinée kung fu routines, try **Li Yuan Theatre** (in Qianmen Hotel, 175 Yonganlu, **M** Qianmen Xidajie), which also stages opera performances.

❑ It's opera, but not as you know it...

Forget the mellifluous voices and stilted tragedies of the European stage and instead prepare yourself for an epic spectacle with a soap opera plot that may involve ghosts, cross-dressing nuns, clowns, kung fu fights, acrobatics, low-brow humour and even live animals.

Beijing opera is far older than its tamer European cousin; its roots reach back to the 10th century when popular legends were acted out in teahouses by travelling performers to entertain working-class folk. Since then it has evolved into an elaborate and distinctive art form – as much a visual spectacle as aural – with costumes, makeup and colours used to define a character. You can tell the importance of a character by how elaborate their headgear is, the sound of the gong and the reaction of your fellow opera-goers alerts you to important scenes coming up, and the supertitles in English and Chinese allow you to follow the convoluted plot.

Even though Beijing opera was originally intended to be watched outdoors, you could do worse than catch it either at the **Chang An Grand Theatre** (Chang An Bldg, 7 Jianguomennai Dajie, **M** Jianguomen, ☎ 6510 1309, tickets Y60-400) or the venerable **Zhengyici Theatre** (220 Xiheyan Dajie **M** Qianmen, ☎ 6503 3104, tickets Y380-700), one of the oldest wooden theatres in China.

Where to shop

For the best selection of English-language books in town, head for **The Bookworm** (Bldg 4, Nansanlitun Lu, **M** Dongsishitiao); there's a terrace ***café*** here with wi-fi. The **Foreign Languages Bookstore** (235 Wangfujing Dajie, **M** Wangfujing) is a great place for books (including the superb *Insider's Guide to Beijing* – see p369), maps and postcards about China, and has extensive English-, German- and Spanish-language sections.

Swish shopping malls stocking Mango, Zara and other usual suspects abound in the city, but **Oriental Plaza** (1 Dongchang An Jie, **M** Wangfujing) is one of the best, both for shopping and for eating (p373). Also consider China World Shopping Mall. If, however, you're looking for something more unique, check out some local designers: **Feng Ling**, at 4 Jiuxianqiao Lu, 4km north-east in the 798 Art District (see pp362-3) stocks dresses and jackets with Mao's face and propaganda slogans; **Plastered T-shirts** (61 Nanluogu Xiang, **M** Beixinqiao) is the place to come for unusual T-shirts featuring Beijing icons; **SQY-T** (7 Yandai Xiejie, **M** Guloudajie) designs limited edition concept T-shirts, such as the 'Skin of The City', with new designs each month; **In** (11 Yandai Xiejie, **M** Guloudajie) sells beautiful silk dresses, while **Hong Ying** (11 Gongti Donglu, **M** Dongsishitiao) combines hippy chic with traditional style, resulting in very affordable Mandarin-collar tops and colourful skirts and bags.

For souvenirs such as porcelain, tea sets, Buddhist statues and jewelry, try the four floors of **Beijing Curio City** (1.3km south of city, 21 Dongsanhuan Nanlu, **M** Maizizhanxilou). Avoid the tourist trap of the Friendship Store on Jianguomen Dajie and the pedestrian Qianmen Dajie, just south of Tiananmen Square, where prices are laughably high.

One of the best pedestrian shopping areas is **Yandai Xiejie** (just south of the Drum Tower, off Di'anmenwai Dajie), where you can find clothes, tea, porcelain and other gifts.

Shops along **Liulichang Lu** (**M** Hepingmen) have sold artists' materials, calligraphy and paintings for centuries, and even now you can buy calligraphy materials, scroll paintings, antique maps, art books and ceramics.

Antiques can also be found at **Panjiayuan Market** (1km south of city, **M** Guomao, 8.30am-6pm Mon-Fri, 4.30am-6pm Sat & Sun) where you can

❑ The three golden rules of shopping

• **Haggle** Even in some shopping centres, and particularly at markets. Figure out how much you're prepared to pay, ask the seller 'Can you go cheaper?' (*Neng zai pianyi yidian'r ma?*) and then if the price is too high look suitably shocked and kick off the haggling by offering no more than half of the seller's suggested price, then working your way up to the price that you're prepared to pay.
• **Don't make your interest obvious** If you're salivating over a particular item, it'll make haggling all the more difficult.
• **Walk away** If you're still not getting the price you want, shake your head sadly and pretend to be walking away in disappointment. Be convincing, though; there's no use looking at the item longingly and repeatedly saying, 'Okay, I'm going to leave now' without moving from the spot. If you execute the walk-away correctly, odds are, the seller will chase after you or call you back and you'll get the price you wanted.

find anything from Cultural Revolution memorabilia to life-size terracotta warriors; for the best bargains go early on weekend mornings.

Moving on

By rail **Domestic tickets** can be bought from Beijing Zhan station, in the Foreigners' Ticket Office (daily 5.30-7.30am, 8am-6.30pm & 7-11pm) in the north-west corner of the chaotic 1st floor, which you access through a plush waiting room.

Beijing West Railway Station (6km west of Tiananmen Square) also has a Foreigners' Ticket Office on the 2nd floor. Alternatively, CITS (see p370) will book a ticket for you for a small fee, saving you the queuing.

The T97 train to Hong Kong goes every other day from Beijing West station (24hrs). There are three daily departures for Harbin (13hrs), and frequent departures to Xian, Tianjin, Shanghai and other major Chinese cities. There are also departures to Hanoi, Vietnam (Sun & Thur afternoons, two days).

International tickets (see also pp124-8) must be booked with CITS, BTG, or another registered ticket agency such as Monkey Business (see p370 for all). BTG specialises in Trans-Mongolian and Trans-Manchurian trains, while Monkey Business specialises in Trans-Siberian journeys. Trains to Ulaanbaatar leave Tuesday morning (30hrs). There's an extra service on Monday morning in summer. The Chinese Trans-Mongolian train 003 to Moscow (six days) leaves Wednesday morning, while the Russian Trans-Manchurian train to Moscow 019 (six days) departs on Saturday night.

• **At the station** You will have to put your luggage through an X-ray machine and walk through a metal detector at the entrance to a railway station. The electronic departure board in the main hall states the train's type (ie Z or T), number, and time of departure, and you can use that information to find the correct departure lounge (there are several) from which to board your train. Tickets are checked upon entering so you know that you're in the correct lounge. In the departure lounge the board shows all departures from that lounge; most trains are shown as 'on time', immediate departures are shown as 'waiting', and when a train is ready for boarding (30mins before departure), it is shown as 'check in'. Departure announcements at the big railway stations are made in English as well as Chinese.

By air Many major airlines, including British Airways, Air France, Continental Airlines, Japan Airlines, KLM, Korean Air, Lufthansa, Qantas Airlines, SAS, Singapore Airlines, Swiss Air and United Airlines maintain offices in Beijing, and there are direct flights from Beijing to most major cities in the world, so it's usually not hard to find a seat. It can be expensive, though the situation has improved with the advent of budget pan-Asian airlines. You can buy tickets directly from airlines or from one of the recommended travel agents (see p370).

If you'd like to fly the first leg of your Trans-Siberian journey, **Mongolian Airlines** (MIAT; 7th floor, Sunjoy Mansion, Jianguomenwai, Ritan Lu 6, ☎ 6507 9297), has direct Beijing–Ulaanbaatar flights (4-5/week). **Air China** (600m west of Tiananmen Square, Civil Aviation Building, 15 Xi Changan Jie, ☎ 400 810 0999, 🖳 www.airchina.com.cn) also flies to Ulaanbaatar (5/week), as well as to Irkutsk, Khabarovsk, Vladivostok, Novosibirsk and Moscow. **Aeroflot** (Swissotel, 2 Chaoyangmen Beidajie, ☎ 6500 2412, 🖳 www.aeroflot.com) has daily Beijing–Moscow flights, while **S7** (Asia Hotel, office 202, 8 Xinzhong Xijie, Gonti Beilu, **M** Gongtibeilu, ☎ 6552 9672) has twice-weekly flights to Novosibirsk, Krasnoyarsk, Irkutsk and Vladivostok.

THE GREAT WALL OF CHINA 长城

China's most famous attraction makes an ideal day trip from Beijing. The Wall itself was not built in one massive construction project as many believe; in fact the original scheme under Emperor Shih Huang (1st century BC) was simply to join extant stretches of individual defensive walls together.

It was hoped that the resulting fortification would protect China from marauding foreigners but this was not the case. The Wall – an awe-inspiring construction feat that stretches for 6200km, starting in Jiayuguan in Gansu and ending at the Bahai Sea at Shanhaiguan, is currently responsible for drawing more visitors than ever, as those who visit at Badaling or Mutianyu will see. Those expecting an easy stroll along the wall may be surprised because different sections of the Wall are in various states of repair; the Wall comprises crumbling battlements, steep climbs and descents as it snakes up and down the hills.

Wear good shoes and be prepared for persistent refreshment and souvenir sellers, even on the less touristy sections of the Wall. Many hotels and hostels offer day tours to different sections of the Wall, though each is also reachable by public transport. Though it's possible to appreciate the beauty and sheer magnitude of the Wall at the locations near to the city, if you have time, it's well worth travelling further out, in order to see the Wall away from the crowds.

Badaling 八达岭

(7am-7pm, adult/student Y45/25, cable car one-way/return Y35/60) Closest to the city (72km from Beijing), this attractive section has been completely restored. It now has a cable car, museum and theatre and is usually overrun with tourists, though the views of the wall snaking over the surrounding hills are impressive. Go here if you don't have much time and on a weekday or in colder months to avoid the crush of humanity. Take bus 919 from Deshengmen, Tourist Bus 1 from Qianmen or Tourist Bus 2 from Beijing Railway Station. Alternatively, take a high-speed suburban train, S2, from Beijing North Railway Station (Y14-17, every hour). The Wall is a 10- to 15-minute walk from Badaling station.

Mutianyu 慕田峪

(6.30am-6.30pm, adult/student Y40/20, chairlift one-way/return Y35/50) Popular alternative to Badaling, this 2250m-long section, 90km north-east of Beijing, boasts stunning views and numerous Ming dynasty guard towers. Either take Tourist Bus 6 from outside South Cathedral at Xuanwumen at the weekend and on public holidays April to October, or Bus 916 from Dongzhimen long-distance bus station to Huairou International Conference Centre and then change for a minibus or taxi to Mutianyu (Y25-30).

Simatai 司马台

(8am-5pm, adult/student Y40/20, cable car one-way/return Y30/50) Perhaps the most picturesque section of the Wall, the 19km stretch between Simatai and **Jinshanling** 金山岭 (8am-5pm, adult/student Y50/30) is a less-developed section featuring 24 watch-towers, which lies 108km north-east of Beijing. The four-hour hike between the two is the highlight of many a visit to Beijing.

The Simatai section is particularly steep, with crumbling battlements and watchtowers; you'll need both your hands for uphill/downhill scrambles, so bring a day pack for your belongings. Make sure you're wearing sturdy shoes, and don't underestimate the strenuousness of the hike, especially on a hot summer's day. You'll be able to buy refreshments from vendors along the way. This section features walls-within-walls – obstacle walls used for defence against enemies who'd already infiltrated the Great Wall, and a zipline for thrill-seekers which descends from the halfway point to the car park (Y35).

The Jinshanling section is not as steep as Simatai and it's the only section where it's possible to camp overnight in a designated camping ground.

Many hostels operate tours which start in Jinshanling and end in Simatai, but if you're travelling out there independently, it's easier to catch public transport back from Jinshanling, so do the hike in reverse.

To get to Simatai independently, catch Tourist Bus 12 from in front of the Xuanwumen Cathedral (Sat & Sun, May-Oct, Y60) or bus 980 to Miyun (1½hrs, Y15) from Dongzhimen long-distance bus station and then switch to a Simatai-bound bus (1hr, Y15).

To reach Jinshanling, take a Chengde-bound bus from Dongzhimen long-distance bus station, get off at Jinshanling and then take a taxi to the entrance (Y10).

Huanghuacheng 黄花城

(8am-5.30pm Mon-Fri, 7am-6pm Sat & Sun, Y25) is a beautifully preserved and relatively 'untouristy' section of the wall stretching high above a natural spring lake and overgrown with wild flowers in the summer.

Some sections of the wall are quite steep, and you may have to pay a small fee (Y2) to peasants who guard the gates to reach some sections of the wall. Take a bus from Dongzhimen long-distance bus station to Huairou (1hr) and then a minibus from Huairou to Huanghua.

The Baikal Amur Mainline (BAM) region

BRATSK Братск

About 470km north of Irkutsk on the BAM line lies one of the world's largest dams. The hydroelectric power station at Bratsk, Russia's second largest after the one at Krasnoyarsk, is the chief attraction of the town. Founded in 1631, Bratsk remained a tiny village until dam construction started in 1955. The station is reputedly capable of generating 4500 MW (the world's biggest hydroelectric project is the 12,600 MW Itaipu Dam on the Brazil–Paraguay border), although lack of customers means it has never run at full capacity. Though it's one of Russia's ten most polluted cities, Bratsk is awe-inspiring considering the achievement of constructing a modern city, a giant dam and massive industrial enterprises in just two decades. But unless you're riding the BAM anyway, or are especially interested in power stations, it's probably not worth the effort.

What to see and do

The top sight is the impressive **Bratsk Hydroelectric Station** and dam. The BAM runs right alongside the dam anyway, the reservoir known as 'Bratskoye More' (Bratsk Sea), and it's certainly an impressive sight; however, if you especially want to get up close and personal with it, you can contact **Taiga Tours** (ul Mira 35, ☎ 3953 416 513, 🖳 www.taiga-tours.ru), in Bratsk, or ***Hotel Taiga*** (2nd floor; ☎ 3953 350 444), in Energetik, in advance to arrange a tour.

Between Energetik and Tsentralny, at Angara village, you'll find an open-air **ethnographic museum** (10am-5pm Tue-Sun, until 7pm in summer, R150) containing a reconstructed Evenki camp, a wooden watchtower and a fort, as well as other buildings rescued from the original Bratsk, drowned by the dam. In the forest there are several shaman sites and examples of Evenki teepees. Since the museum is off the public transportation route, at an out-of-the-way lakeside site, it's best to take a taxi.

PRACTICAL INFORMATION

Orientation Bratsk is not one town but a ring of connected settlements around the so-called Bratsk Sea, the reservoir created by the hydroelectric dam. From the south in a counter-clockwise direction, the towns are Port Novobratsk, Bratskoye Morye, Bratsk Tsentralny (the administration centre), Padun, Energetik on the dam's west bank and Gidrostroitel on the east bank.

Padunskie Porogi railway station, which serves the suburbs of Padun and Energetik, is the closest to Hotel Turist (see opposite). Padun is the most attractive part of Bratsk as it has a pleasant promenade with an old log watchtower and the city's only church. Bratsk airport is to the north of Padunskie Porogi and can be reached by a 40-minute bus trip from the station.

Where to stay

Best Eastern Taiga (ул Мира 35, Центральный, ul Mira 35, Tsentralny, ☎ 3953 414 710, sgl/dbl R2500/3000) has basic but clean rooms, rather overpriced for what they are, though there is a good on-site sauna and a passable **café-restaurant**. Some English is spoken.

Another option would be ***Hotel Turist*** **Гостиница Турист** (ул Наймушина 28, Энергетик, ul Naymushina 28, Energetik, ☎ 3953 378 743, sgl/dbl R1000/2000), a 15-minute walk away from the dam. Its cheaper, no-frills rooms are pretty good value, compared to the overpriced 'lux' rooms. ***Hotel Bratsk*** **Гостиница Братск** (ул Депутатская 32, Центральный, ul Deputatskaya 32, Tsentralny, ☎ 3953 438 436, sgl/twin from R800/1000) is a good budget option, with basic Soviet rooms.

Moving on

In summer, you can take one of the three hydrofoils a week to Irkutsk from the river station in southern Tsentralny (8am departure, arriving in Irkutsk at 9pm; the return journey is at 8.30am, arriving in Bratsk at 9pm), though the departures are weather-dependent and subject to cancellation.

The 087 train runs daily (17hrs) between Bratsk and Irkutsk, while the 291 runs to Novosibirsk (27hrs) and the 347 goes to Krasnoyarsk (20hrs). Eastbound destinations include Severobaikalsk (2/day, 14-17hrs), while the 097 runs to Tynda (41hrs) on alternate days.

SEVEROBAIKALSK Северобайкальск

Severobaikalsk, on the BAM railway, is the 'capital' of the northern end of Lake Baikal. The town provides excellent access to north Baikal attractions, which include trekking and mountaineering in the Baikal Mountains, the northern parts of the Great Baikal Trail (see box p284), downhill skiing, sailing, seal-watching and visits to indigenous villages and a Stalin-era Gulag.

The town itself is lined with multi-storey apartment buildings that may not look particularly appealing, but their foundations are specifically designed to work on permafrost and they are built to withstand the constant seismic activity in the Baikal area.

What to see and do

If you turn left out of the railway station and head west along pr 60 Let SSSR, you'll shortly come across a **P36 locomotive** Паровоз П-36 on a plinth on your left-hand side, with a star at the front and marked with the letters 'CCCP'. Other railway-related attractions include **BAM Museum** Музей БАМа (per Proletarsky 2, 10am-6pm Tue-Sat, lunch break 1-2pm, R60), with memorabilia relating to the town's creation. Adjoining it is the excellent **BAM Art Museum** Художественный Музей БАМа (same opening hours, R60), which recently hosted a wonderful exhibition by a local, internationally acclaimed artist from Nizhneangarsk, whose works drew on traditional Evenk culture for inspiration and consisted of intriguing wooden sculptures and intricate woven works incorporating Evenki kilim (rugs).

The staff at both museums are wonderfully enthusiastic, though it helps to speak at least a little Russian to get the most out of the experience, or to go with an interpreter.

To reach the northern shore of Lake Baikal, relatively unspoiled by tourism, with its steep, forest-covered mountains and pebble beaches, walk south along ul Studencheskaya, cross the bridge and then descend to the shore along the dirt road. Alternatively, you can cross the railway bridge directly behind the main railway station building and take the road leading to the lake from there.

PRACTICAL INFORMATION

Orientation and services

Everything in Severobaikalsk is within walking distance with the exception of the hydrofoil port. Bus No 1 runs between the port and the central bus station, which is in front of the railway station. Buses and marshrutkas to other destinations, such as Nizhneangarsk and Goudzhekit, also run from in front of the railway station.

A helpful **website** on the region is 💻 www.sbaikal.ru and there's a tourist information booth in front of the railway station in summer (9am-7pm) where you can get plenty of information on the area.

The **post office** is at Leningradsky pr 6 (10am-2pm & 3-7pm Mon-Fri, until 5pm Sat), and there's a handy Sberbank with **ATM** by the Torgovy Tsentr (shopping centre) next to the central market. There's good, inexpensive **internet access** both at the post office and at the public library (Leningradsky Pr 5, 10am-6pm Mon-Thur & Sat, 10am-2pm Fri).

Anya at Baikal Trail Hostel (see below) is an indispensable contact when it comes to arranging Baikal adventures. Alternatively, **BAMTour** (ul Oktyabrya 16/2, ☎ 30139 21 560, 💻 www.gobaikal.com), run by Rashit Yakhin who worked on the railway in the early 1970s but was partially disabled by a stroke, can help you arrange multi-day boat cruises, trekking, rafting and horse-riding.

Where to stay and eat

The best place for budget travellers is undoubtedly the 8-bed ***Baikal Trail Hostel*** (ул Студенческая 12, ul Studencheskaya 12, ☎ 30139 23 860, 💻 www.baikaltrailhostel.com, dorm R500), run by the ultra-helpful, English-speaking Anya. She can help organise trips to the Great Baikal Trail and other local places of interest, there's a guest kitchen and wi-fi, and you tend to get an interesting mix of Baikal Trail volunteers and adventurous travellers there.

A good choice if you're travelling in a group, the friendly ***Zolotaya Rybka*** **Золотая Рыбка** (ул Сибирская 14, ul Sibirskaya 14, ☎ 30139 21 134, 💻 www.baikalgoldenfish.ru, room from R1600) consists of three cottages with views of Lake Baikal, each with three rooms that share a bathroom with a good shower, two toilets, a mini-lounge and a kitchen.

In a central location, ***Hotel Olymp*** **Гостиница Олимп** (ул Полиграфистов 26/1, ul Poligrafistov 26/1, ☎ 30130 23 980, 💻 www.hotelolymp.ru, rooms R1500-2200) offers comfortable rooms with wi-fi and cable TV and a host of other services, including plane and train ticket booking.

A short walk from the lake, ***Dom u Baikala*** **Дом у Байкала** (пер Нептунский 3, per Neptunsky 3, ☎ 30130 23 950, 💻 www.baikal-kruiz.narod.ru, twin/summer cabin R1600/1400) consists of cosy en suite rooms in the house and some summer timber huts which share bathrooms. Guests have use of a kitchen.

Severobaikalsk's eating options are rather limited. The **central market** is a good place for fresh produce, including smoked *omul*, which costs far less here than in southern Baikal. ***Chudo-Blyodo*** **Чудо-Блюдо**, an informal café next to the market, does inexpensive Russian dishes and is popular with locals at lunchtime.

Anyuta **Анюта** (ul Poligrafistov 3a) is a small supermarket/café combo where you can dine on Russian dishes. In summer, you'll find **shashlyk** шашлык stands near the beach at the end of ul Studenchaskaya.

The best **supermarket** for self-caterers is Supermarket Vist Супермаркет Вист (Leningradsky pr 5, Ленинградский пр 5).

Moving on

By boat Between mid-June and late August hydrofoil *Kometa* departs Nizhneangarsk for Port Baikal on Wednesdays and Saturdays at 7.40am; in Port Baikal you change for the hydrofoil *Raketa* to Irkutsk, arriving at 8pm. From Irkutsk the hydrofoil makes the return trip on Tuesdays and Fridays at 8.50am. The journey costs R4200 and the timetable is subject to change and cancellation.

By train Westbound, the 091 runs to Moscow (even days, 95hrs), while the 291 serves Novosibirsk (41hrs) and the 347 runs to Krasnoyarsk (34hrs). The 071 runs to Irkutsk via Bratsk and Tayshet (odd days, 32hrs). Heading east, the 076 runs to Tynda (odd days, 27hrs), with additional services to Tynda with 098 (Sat only) and 138 (Tue only).

By air There are flights from nearby Nizhneangarsk to Ulan-Ude (5/week) and Irkutsk (3/week) in summer, though they are weather-dependent and thus subject to delays and cancellations.

AROUND SEVEROBAIKALSK

Nizhneangarsk Нижнеангарск

Nizhneangarsk, 40km east of Severobaikalsk, is wedged on a narrow strip between Lake Baikal and steep mountains. The 20km-long town has a large port for a small fishing fleet. The harbour was built for construction of the BAM to the east but the railway arrived from the west before the harbour was completed. Although the regional airport is located here, Nizhneangarsk is smaller than neighbouring Severobaikalsk.

The town is pleasant to stroll around with its mainly wooden buildings. Despite being built mostly since the mid-1970s it's not dominated by multistorey concrete flats and prefabricated buildings. Even the two-storey City

Council building is wooden. An architectural oddity is the wooden boat-rental and water-rescue station on the lake's edge. The fish-processing factory can be visited and gives an interesting insight into Russian methods and working conditions. The plant makes delicious smoked or salted *omul*.

Nizhneangarsk is linked to Irkutsk by hydrofoil (see p283). Regular buses run from Severobaikalsk to Nizhneangarsk.

Baikalskoye Байкальское

On Baikal's shore, 45km south of Severobaikalsk, is the picturesque fishing village of Baikalskoye, which makes for a pleasant day trip from Severobaikalsk. This is also the starting point of an 18km section of the Great Baikal Trail, that heads north from the village towards the radio mast along a cliffside path, from where you get amazing views of the village below. The trail runs through cedar and spruce forest, ending at Lake Slyudyanskoye, where you can stay at the basic ***Echo turbaza*** (R500), though you need to arrange that in advance with Baikal Trail Hostel (see p382).

There are two buses daily to Baikalskoye at 8am and 5pm (45mins), returning at 9am and 6pm. To get back from the Echo turbaza, you have to prearrange transport, or else take the dirt track that runs through the forest to the Baikalskoye/Severobaikalsk road and hitch a lift.

Goudzhekit Гуджекит

Goudzhekit is famous for its hot springs, which were discovered during the course of the construction of the BAM. The little spa, 300m from the tiny railway station, is very popular with locals, particularly when the weather gets cold. It's far cheaper to take the local Kirenga-bound *elektrichka* (80mins) than the westbound BAM trains; the only drawback is that they run just twice a day at 6.45am and 5.25pm, returning at 10.15am and 8.45pm. There are also three marshrutkas a day from Severobaikalsk (45mins). If you get stuck in Goudzhekit, however, there are a couple of places to stay by the spa.

Dzelinda Дзелинда

With waters believed to have curative properties, tiny Dzelinda has an even more attractive spa than Goudzhekit, set in a beautiful forest location, though it's further away (92km from Severobaikalsk). The waters, a constant 44°C, are best enjoyed in cold weather, as in summer the mosquitoes are a nightmare. You can stay overnight in a basic ***timber cabin*** with shared facilities (☎ 30130 321 42, R900), meals included, or else take the daily Novy Uoyan-bound elektrichka (6.03am, 2hrs) to the Km1155 stop and then walk for 1km along the paved road to the hot springs. The elektrichka heads back to Severobaikalsk at 7pm, so be prepared to spend the whole day at the spring unless you come as part of a tour.

Akikan Gulag Акикан Гулаг

Akikan Gulag was a mica mining camp in the late 1930s. The residue of those terrible years consists of several collapsed wooden and stone buildings, towers and barbed wire fences, as well as a mini railway with little bucket wagons, abandoned by the entrance of a collapsed mineshaft. The camp is a two-hour walk from Kholodnoye (itself an hour by bus or train from Severobaikalsk); BAMTour (see p382) can provide a guide.

YAKUTSK Якутск

Though not on the BAM as such, Yakutsk makes for an out-of-the-way attraction for adventurous travellers.

This is the capital of Sakha, the vast Yakut Republic (see box p441). Lying only 600km south of the Arctic Circle, it is one of the world's coldest cities (average temperature in January is minus 32°C) although summers are pleasantly mild (plus 19°C in July). It is also one of Siberia's oldest settlements, founded in 1632 on the banks of the mighty Lena River as a base for exploration and a trading centre for gold and furs. There is little left of historic interest in this polluted city, but it is worth visiting for the excursions on the Lena and to see the effects of permafrost. All the buildings here have to be built on massive stilts or they would sink into the ground as their heat melts the permafrost.

Only about 30% of the people are ethnic Yakuts, most of the rest being Russians and Ukrainians. Like other minority groups in Russia the Yakuts are now making themselves heard in Moscow. In 1991 an agreement was signed between the presidents of Russia and Sakha, giving the latter a certain degree of autonomy within the Russian Federation and more control over the proceeds from gold and diamond mining in this immensely mineral-rich region.

What to see and do

The most interesting place to visit in Yakutsk is the **Permafrost Institute** Институт Вечной Мерзлоты (ul Merzlotnaya 36, ☎ 4112 334 476 or 334 338; 🖳 lans@imzran.yacc.yakutia.ru; call in advance for a tour in Russian). You are taken 12m underground to see part of the old river bed, where the temperature never varies from -5°C. Permafrost is said to affect 25% of the planet and 50% of Russia. Outside is a model of a baby mammoth found almost perfectly preserved in permafrost in 2007. The original, thought to be around 40,000 years old, is in St Petersburg's Natural History Museum.

Yakutsk Museum of the History and Culture of the Peoples of the North Музей Истории и Культуры Народов Севера (pr Lenina 5/2; 10am-5pm; free entry) is said to include over 140,000 items illustrating Yakut flora, fauna and anthropology, starting from prehistoric times and ending with the 1990s. The natural history section includes one of the world's few complete woolly mammoth skeletons.

❑ Ysyakh Festival

The best time to visit Yakutsk is during the two-day fertility festival, held on or around the Summer Solstice. The festival involves traditional Yakut sports, such as wrestling, archery and stick fighting, as well as costumed revelry, competitions to create the best national dishes and traditional folk concerts. The most important parts of it are the blessing of the harvest by the White Shaman and the sacred rites of the second day's sunrise.

For an even closer look at those great beasts, check out the **Mammoth Museum** Музей Мамонтов (ul Kulakovskogo 48, 4th floor; 10am-6pm; free entry), with its star exhibit being a cryogenically preserved head of a woolly mammoth. The museum's collection also includes a diverse collection of objects from the Ice Age. Those with an interest in the region's diverse ethnic population shouldn't miss the **Museum of Archaeology and Ethnography of Yakutsk State University** Музей Археологии и Этнографии Якутского Государственного Университета (Tue-Fri 10am-5pm; Sat 11am-4pm), located in the same building and focusing on the culture, mythology and everyday life of the Yakuts, Evenki, Sakha and other Yakutian ethnic groups.

The **National Art Museum** Национальный Художественный Музей (ul Kirova 12; 10am-6pm) is particularly worthwhile for its rich collection of Yakut arts and crafts, as well as an enormous display of art by Yakuts, Russians and international artists from the 16th century to the present day.

PRACTICAL INFORMATION

Getting to Yakutsk

Until the rail link is finished the best way to get to Yakutsk is by air. Yakutsk's international airport, **Tuimaada**, is served by regular flights from Moscow, St Petersburg, Novosibirsk, Krasnoyarsk, Irkutsk, Khabarovsk and Harbin, China.

There are plans to complete the train line from Tynda to Yakutsk by 2013, but at the moment it only stretches as far as Tommot, 453km away. You can catch a twice-weekly bus from Neryungri, but that option is for the toughest travellers only: the journey lasts 20-24 hours and you can expect constant breakdowns and reckless driving on the road that held 'the world's worst road' title in 2006.

Regular passenger boats connect Yakutsk to Lensk, Olekminsk and other riverside towns in Yakutia itself, and there are infrequent passenger boats from Ust-Kut on the BAM.

Services

Tour Service Centre (Гостиница Полярная Звезда ul Yaroslavskogo 30/1, office 66; ☎ 4112 351 144; 🖳 www.yakutiatravel.com) is a reputable tour agency that can organise a variety of excursions in the area and also provide interpreters, book accommodation, organise homestays within Yakut communities and arrange onward travel.

Where to stay and eat

Hotel Lena **Гостиница Лена** (пр Ленина 8, pr Lenina 8, ☎ 4112 242 795, rooms from R2200) is centrally located and offers comfortable en suites, a money-changing facility, a café and wi-fi. Price includes breakfast. On the same block, you'll find ***Tamerlan*** restaurant, serving up Yakut and Central Asian cuisine, with the chefs cooking their dishes on the heated table in front of you.

The plush ***Hotel Tygyn Darkhan*** **Гостиница Тыгын Дархан** (ул Аммосова 9, ul Ammosova 9, ☎ 4112 435 109 or 435 309, 🖳 www.tygyn.ru, sgl/dbl/suite from R4050/4500/9900) offers elegant accommodation, as well as a swimming pool, fitness centre, sauna and one of the city's finest restaurants, specialising in traditional Sakha dishes, such as *oiogos* (baked foal ribs).

The city's top place to stay is ***Hotel Polyarnaya Zvezda*** **Гостиница Полярная Звезда** (пр Ленина 24, pr Lenina 24, ☎ 4112 341 215, 🖳 www.alrosa-hotels.ru, sgl/dbl/suite from R14,850/20,400/24,000); as befitting a hotel of its calibre, the rooms are luxurious and tastefully decorated and a full range of facilities is included, such as a tour agency, excellent restaurant, swimming pool, sauna, fitness centre and wi-fi throughout. Cruises on the Lena River arranged on request.

Excursions from Yakutsk on the Lena River

The geological formations known as the **Lena Pillars** have fascinated travellers here since the 17th century. About 140km upriver from Yakutsk, the rock of the cliffs alongside the river has been eroded into delicate shapes of a reddish brown colour. Two-day cruises leave each Friday evening in summer. From the landing it's an hour's strenuous climb to the top, for a magnificent view of the river and the cliffs. Tour groups are sometimes brought here on hydrofoil day trips from Yakutsk, leaving early in the morning and getting back after dark.

The luxury cruise ships *M/S Demyan Bedny* and *M/S Mikhail Svetlov* do 2-3 day cruises to the Lena Pillars and back. It's also possible to make a trip down the Lena from Yakutsk to Tiksi on the Arctic Ocean. Trips can be booked at the Tour Service Centre (see opposite).

TYNDA Тында

Tynda, formerly the headquarters of the BAM, is still an important railroading town of 39,000 people, though its population is decreasing. It sits at a major junction of the BAM, and the AYaM (Amur-Yatkutsk Mainline) and Little BAM, and is a functional Soviet town with a handful of attractions.

What to see and do

In front of the railway station you'll find a **freight locomotive** on a plinth dedicated to the founders of the BAM. Both at the railway station and at Hotel Yunost you may see 2009 posters commemorating the 35th anniversary of the BAM, 'The road built with love'.

BAM museum Музей БАМа (ul Sportivnaya 22, by appointment Wed-Sun 10am-6pm, R120), a couple of blocks south-west of ul Profosyuznaya, consists of four rooms, two of them covering the early history of the railway and the Gulag prisoners used as the chief labour force, as well as a model of the railway. The other rooms house other BAM-related relics; unfortunately, there's no English captioning.

Just off ul Krasnaya Presnya, you can see the **Cathedral of the Holy Trinity** Церковь Святой Троицы, the plasticky-looking Orthodox cathedral built several years ago and the source of some controversy: some felt that the money could've been better spent elsewhere. After crossing the footbridge, turn right and follow the main road to reach the dramatic **statue of a BAM worker** памятник рабочему БАМа wielding a sledgehammer. Nearby is the excellent traditional **public banya** баня (ul Amurskaya, basic admission R300, lux R850), with separate sessions for men and women. Birch branches are available. At the intersection of ul Krasnaya Presnya and ul Profsoyuznaya, you'll find a **giant hammer and sickle** – a Soviet relic that they haven't removed.

You can also do an excursion to the nearby **Evenk village** of Zarya/Pervomaiskoye деревня Заря, where there is a large local school that teaches Evenki students from surrounding villages, thus enabling the survival of the Evenki language and culture. Buses run to Zarya from the railway station several times a day.

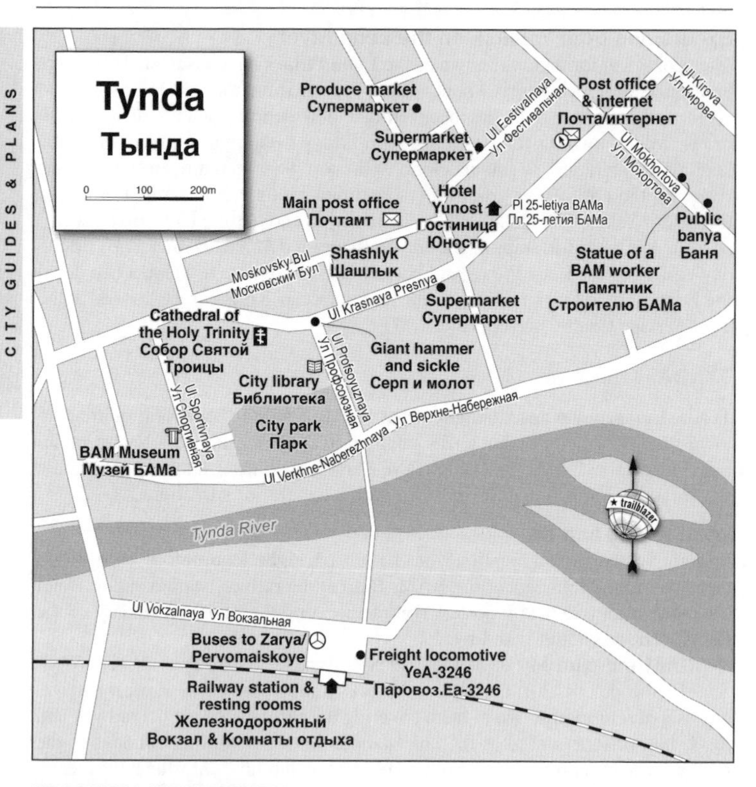

PRACTICAL INFORMATION

Orientation and services

To get to the town from the railway station, you have to cross the pedestrian bridge over the Tynda river and then keep walking straight until you hit the main ul Krasnaya Presnya, where you'll find a couple of places to eat, as well as Hotel Yunost. The **post office** (ul Krasnaya Presnya 57, 8am-noon & 1-7pm Mon-Fri, 8am-2pm weekends) has **internet** and you can find an **ATM** at the railway station.

Where to stay and eat

The railway station ***resting rooms*** **комнаты отдыха** (komnaty otdykha, sgl/twin/4-person R1500/750/450) are clean and comfortable. Otherwise, pretty much the only central option is ***Hotel Yunost*** **Гостиница Юность** (ул Красная Пресня 49, ul Krasnaya Presnya 49, ☎ 41656 43 534, sgl/dbl from R1200/1500), where *Through Siberia By Accident* author Dervla Murphy ended up staying after she'd injured her leg. The plusher rooms have very nice bathrooms.

There are a couple of **supermarkets**, one along ul Krasnaya Presnya and another on ul Festivalnaya, where you can stock up on basic staples, and a **produce market** along the street behind Hotel Yunost, with a couple of informal cheap eateries.

In summer, there's good **shashlyk** to be had at makeshift cafés in front of the main post office.

Moving on

Heading west, the 075/076 serves Moscow (even days, 120hrs) via Severobaikalsk (26hrs), and there are also slower trains to Moscow that run south via Little BAM, connecting with the Trans-Siberian and running via Irkutsk. The 963/964 runs to Komsomolsk-na-Amure (daily, 37hrs), while the daily 325/326 heads south to Khabarovsk (28hrs). There are daily trains north to Neryungri on the AYaM line (5½hrs).

KOMSOMOLSK-NA-AMURE Комсомольск-на-Амуре

Built in 1932, Komsomolsk-na-Amure was a city closed to foreigners until the end of the Soviet era. Despite the recent decline in population, it remains the largest city on the BAM, with some 250,000 inhabitants, and is relatively prosperous by Eastern Siberian standards. The city's located on a convenient railway junction, which allows for easy connection to the Trans-Siberian via Khabarovsk. Your first impression of Komsomolsk-na-Amure is likely to be coloured by the weather. If you arrive on a bleak, overcast day, bitterly cold in winter and the air thick with mosquitoes in summer, you might think that you've stepped into some ghastly time warp and ended in the Soviet Union of the '80s, the grim multi-storey buildings marginally enlivened by colourful shop signs. On a sunny day, however, the city seems transformed; you can appreciate the wide boulevards and the attractive main square, and even the deserted waterfront with the sagging river terminal building – such a contrast with the lively Khabarovsk promenade – won't seem so depressing.

What to see and do

You'll find some great **Soviet mosaics** by the river and also at Sudostroitel Park. The unusually good **Museum of Regional Studies** Краеведческий Музей (pr Mira 8, 10am-5pm Tue-Sun, R150) charts the birth and development of the modern city, which you can just about follow in spite of the lack of English captioning. Other exhibits are devoted to the native Nanai and Evenki culture, Komsomolsk's participation in WWII, as well as the Khetagurova Movement, which encouraged women to move to the Far East in the 1930s to improve the gender balance. Though 70,000 girls originally volunteered, it's not clear how many got married and stayed. There are numerous dioramas and one exhibit is devoted to Gulags in the area.

The **Fine Arts Museum** Художественный Музей (pr Mira 16, 10am-5.30pm Tue-Sun, R120) has two floors – with Western works on the ground floor and changing exhibits on the first floor consisting of mostly indigenous art – well worth visiting. The staff are enthusiastic about their work.

To the north-west of the river station, you'll find the **Great Patriotic War Memorial** Музей Великой Отечественной Войны, consisting of three stone obelisks above an eternal flame, with seven granite heads facing it and the names of the dead carved behind them. Other monuments include **Stalinist Repression Memorial Stone** Памятник Жертвам Сталинских Репрессий, next to the City Court on pr Lenina; erected by the local government after being pressured by Memorial, the NGO specialising in searching for information on repression victims to see what their fate was and whether they had been posthumously rehabilitated – which is some comfort to their relatives. There are also 16 **Japanese PoW memorials** Памятник Японским Военнопленным around the city, the most central being on pr Mira beside Hotel Amur, since it was built by the PoWs.

In the Lenin District north-east of the centre you'll find the **Yuri Gagarin Aircraft Factory** Авиационный Завод имени Юрия Гагарина, even though he never worked there. In front of it is the **Yuri Gagarin Memorial** Мемориал Юрию Гагарину, consisting of him holding a book on the Laws of the Cosmos. The book looks remarkably like a brick with a towel wrapped around it, earning it the local name of 'Brick and Towel Memorial'. Trams 4 and 5 go to the Lenin District. North-east of the city lies **Komsomolsky Nature Reserve** Комсомольский Заповедник, where you'll find several ethnic Nanai settlements, which can be visited with the assistance of Nata Tour (see below).

PRACTICAL INFORMATION

Orientation and services

Tram No 2 runs from the railway station to the waterfront past the main Sudostroitel Park. The main **post office** (pr Mira 27, 8am-7pm Mon-Fri, until 6pm Sat, until 3pm Sun) is large and modern and has good internet access (R60/hour) and there's an **ATM** at the railway station.

Nata Tour (ul Vasanina 12, room 110, ☎ 4217 201 067, 🖳 www.komsomolsknata.ru) is an experienced tour operator that does anything from 3-hour city excursions to multi-day ventures into the surrounding area, cruises on the Amur and 17-day trips to Sakhalin Island with a particular emphasis on native cultures.

Where to stay and eat

The railway station ***resting rooms*** **комнаты отдыха** (*komnaty otdykha*, sgl/3-bed R1360/690) are clean and comfortable, located on the east side of the railway station. Showers are R90 extra.

Hotel Voskhod **Гостиница Восход** (пр Первостроителей 31, pr Pervostroiteley 31, ☎ 4217 535 131, room from R2300) may not look like much from the outside, but its rooms are renovated and wi-fi equipped, and you can get an inexpensive meal at the café on the top floor.

Biznestsentr **Бизнесцентр** (ул Дзержинского 3, ul Dzerzhinskogo 3, ☎ 4217 521 522, 🖳 www.bc.kna.ru – in Russian, sgl/dbl/suite from R2200/2400/4400) is a modern hotel aimed at business travellers. Some staff speak English and the rooms are comfortable and wi-fi equipped. The café serves a combination of European and Asian dishes.

Another business traveller favourite, ***Hotel Amur*** **Гостиница Амур** (пр Мира 15, pr Mira 15, ☎ 4217 590 984) is centrally located and has clean rooms. The basic rooms with shared facilities start at R670, whereas the comfortable en suites are R1360/2800 for a single/double. The in-house restaurant serves a decent variety of Chinese dishes.

You can buy inexpensive meat-filled pastries by the bus station near the waterfront. On tiny pl Lenina you'll find ***U City*** (pr Lenina 19, meal R250), the hangout of the young and the trendy, that sells lukewarm pizza by the slice as well as Russian salads. ***Sushi City*** **Суши-сити** (corner of pr Oktyabrsky and pr Lenina, mains R350) does passable sushi, whereas ***Russkoye Zastolye*** **Русское Застолье** at the river station does inexpensive Russian dishes, such as pelmeni (mains R200). There's a ***Baskin-Robbins*** **Баскин-Роббинс** in **Singapur shopping centre** (corner of pr Lenina and ul Vasyanina).

Moving on

From Komsomolsk-na-Amure there are daily services to Khabarovsk with the 351/352 (9hrs) and to Vladivostok (27hrs). On the BAM, the 351/352 also runs a daily service to Vanino/SovGavan (11hrs). Westbound destinations include Tynda (daily, 37hrs on the 963), where you can change for a service to Severobaikalsk.

VANINO & SOVETSKAYA GAVAN Ванино и Советская Гавань

Vanino, founded in 1944, is a busy port that was originally used as a transit camp. The prisoners typically stayed here for several days, with representatives coming from various Gulags to select the strongest and fittest – a 20th-century equivalent of the slave trade. From Vanino they would be taken to Kolyma, Magadan, Sakhalin Island, Kamchatka and other parts of the inhospitable Siberian north.

Today Vanino is a commercial port, with a population of 20,000 or so, with freight ships heading for Japan, Sakhalin Island and the disputed Kuril islands.

There is little of interest in town besides the port, which you can gain access to if you have onward ferry tickets to Sakhalin Island. Vanino also has a small **History Museum** Исторический Музей (ul Matrosova, behind the big blue building to the east of the railway station, 2-7pm Tue-Fri, 10am-2pm Sat, free entry) covering Russian and Japanese history in the area.

Sovetskaya Gavan ('Soviet Harbour', often shortened to SovGavan) lies 36km further east and is the final stop for BAM completists. It was originally named Imperatorskaya Gavan ('Imperial Harbour') but its name was changed in 1926. Since the Japanese ruled the lower half of Sakhalin Island from 1905, this strategic deep-water harbour would have been the ideal place for a potential Japanese invasion and therefore had to be defended at all costs. During WWII, the Soviet Union gained control of the whole of Sakhalin Island, but the harbour continued to have great military importance during its heyday of the 1950s and 1960s as one of the three most important ports of the Pacific Fleet. Today, commercial activity has replaced military activity and the population is around 35,000. There's a good **Regional Museum** Краеведческий Музей (ul Sovetskaya 29, 10am-5pm except Mon and Sat), where you'll find information on the revolutionary and Civil War era activity in the region as well as exhibits on local native culture and a nature section where the most impressive exhibit is a giant Siberian tiger. Though the Far East was dotted with Gulags, information on them is conspicuously absent.

You can also head to the coast to check out **Krasny Partizan Lighthouse** Маяк Красных Партизан; beside the lighthouse there's a memorial dedicated to the lighthouse keepers who were tortured to death by the White Army in 1919. To get here, catch a bus from Sovetskaya Gavan to Mayachnaya and walk from there.

PRACTICAL INFORMATION

Where to stay and eat

In **Vanino** you have the choice of staying either in the station ***resting rooms*** **комнаты отдыха** (*komnaty otdykha*, sgl/3-bed R1000/600, shower R90 extra), which are perfectly comfortable and located inside the light blue railway station building, or else there's ***Hotel Vanino*** **Гостиница Ванино** (ул Чехова 1, ul Chekhova 1, ☎ 42137 51 228, rooms from R1900), with wi-fi equipped, refurbished rooms. In **SovGavan**, the newly renovated ***Hotel Sovetskaya Gavan*** **Гостиница Советская Гавань** (ул Пионерская 14, ul Pionerskaya 14, ☎ 42138 46 783, sgl/dbl from R1800/2700) has clean, comfortable rooms.

Both hotels have **restaurants** serving inexpensive Russian dishes, and SovGavan is the place to stock up on red caviar, produced by the city cannery.

Moving on

From Vanino/SovGavan, the 351/352 runs daily to Vladivostok (41hrs) via Khabarovsk (23hrs) and Komsomolsk-na-Amure (11hrs).

If SovGavan is your destination it's best to get off at Vanino and take bus 101 (R80, 1 hour, 4-5/day) to SovGavan from in front of the railway station. Even though trains may display 'SovGavan' as their final destination, they tend to arrive at Sovetskaya Gavan-Sortirovka – the marshalling yards – where you have to change to another train to Sovetskaya Gavan-Gorod (city). Even that railway station is a good 8km from the town proper and you have to walk up a hill to catch a bus from there.

ROUTE GUIDE & MAPS 5

Using this guide

This route guide has been set out to draw your attention to points of interest and to enable you to locate your position along the Trans-Siberian line. On the maps, stations are indicated in Russian and English and their distance from Moscow is given in the text.

Stations and points of interest are identified in the text by a kilometre number. In some cases these numbers are approximate so start looking out for the point of interest a few kilometres before its stated position.

Where something of interest is on only one side of the track, it is identified after its kilometre number by the approximate compass direction for those going away from Moscow; that is, on the Moscow–Vladivostok Trans-Siberian line (pp395-450) by the letter **N** (north or left-hand side of the train) or **S** (south or right-hand side), and on the Trans-Mongolian branch (pp451-60) and Trans-Manchurian branch (pp460-7) by **E** (east or left-hand side) or **W** (west or right-hand side).

The elevation of major towns and cities is given in metres and feet beside the station name. Time zones are indicated throughout the text (MT = Moscow Time). See p512 for **key map and time zones**.

Kilometre posts

These are located on the southern or western side of the track, sometimes so close to the train that they're difficult to see. The technique is to press your face close to the glass and look along the train until a post flashes by. On each post, the number on the face furthest from Moscow is larger by 1km than that on the face nearest to Moscow, suggesting that each number really refers to the entire 1km of railway towards which it 'looks'.

Points of interest and stations in this guide are identified by the nearest kilometre post visible from the train.

Railway timetables show your approximate true distance from Moscow, but unfortunately the distances painted on kilometre (km) posts generally do not:

❑ Speed calculations

Using kilometre posts and a watch you can calculate how quickly, or more usually how slowly, the train is going. Note the time that elapses between one post and the next and consult the table below. The average speed over the seven-day journey between Moscow and Vladivostok is just 69kph (43mph).

Seconds	kph	mph	Seconds	kph	mph
24	150	93	52	69	43
26	138	86	54	66	41
28	129	80	56	64	40
30	120	75	60	60	37
32	113	70	64	56	35
34	106	66	68	53	33
36	100	62	72	50	31
38	95	59	78	46	28
40	90	56	84	43	27
42	86	53	92	39	24
44	82	51	100	36	22
46	78	49	120	30	18
48	75	47	150	24	15
50	72	45	180	20	12

indeed on the Trans-Siberian they may vary by up to 40km, the result of multiple route changes over the years. Distances noted in the following route guide and in the timetables at the back of the book correspond to those on the kilometre posts. Occasionally, however, railway authorities may recalibrate and repaint these posts, thereby confusing us all! If you notice any discrepancies, please write to the author.

Station name boards

Station signs are almost as difficult to catch sight of as kilometre posts since they are usually placed only on the station building (if at all!) and not along the platform as in most other countries. Rail traffic on the line is heavy and even if your carriage does pull up opposite the station building you may have your view of it obscured by another train.

Stops

Where the train stops at a station the duration of the stop is indicated by:

● (1-6 mins) ●● (7-14 mins) ●●● (15-24 mins) ●●● + (25 mins and over)

These durations are based upon timetables for the 001/002 Moscow–Vladivostok (*Rossiya*), 003/004 Moscow–Beijing (Trans-Mongolian) and 019/020 Moscow–Beijing (*Vostok*, Trans-Manchurian) services. Actual durations may vary widely as timetables are revised, and may be reduced if a train is running late.

Only your carriage attendant knows the precise amount of time for the train you're on. Don't get off if the stop duration is less than five minutes and don't stray far from the train as it will probably move off without a whistle or other signal (except in China) and passengers can be left behind. Three of us, our carriage attendant included, were once almost left in sub-zero temperatures on the platform of a tiny Siberian station when the train left five minutes ahead of schedule.

Time zones

All trains in Russia run on Moscow Time (MT). **Siberian time zones** are listed throughout the route guide; major cities include Novosibirsk (MT+3), Irkutsk (MT+5), Khabarovsk (MT+7) and Vladivostok (MT+7). **Moscow Time** is four hours ahead of Greenwich Mean Time (GMT+4) when Russia is on Daylight Savings Time, from the last Sunday in March to the last Saturday in October; for the rest of the year MT = GMT+3 (although actual time differences with most countries of Europe, which also use DST, remain constant throughout the year). Note that **China** has a single time zone, GMT+8, for the whole country and for the whole year. **Mongolian Time** is GMT+8 year-round, as Mongolia does not observe daylight saving time.

TRANS-SIBERIAN ROUTE

Km0: Moscow Москва

Yaroslavsky Station Ярославский вокзал Most Trans-Siberian trains depart from Moscow's Yaroslavsky station, on Komsomolskaya pl (**M** Komsomolskaya). Yaroslavsky station is very distinctive, built in 1902 as a stylised reproduction of an old Russian *terem* (fort), its walls decorated with coloured tiles.

Km13: Los Лось Just after this station, the train crosses over the Moscow Ring Road. This road marks the city's metropolitan border.

Km15: Taininskaya Таининская A post-Soviet monument here, dedicated to Russia's last tsar, Nicholas II, says, 'To Tsar Nikolai II from the Russian people with repentance'.

Km18: Mytishchi Мытищи is famous for three factories. The railway carriage factory, **Metrovagonmash**, manufactured all the Soviet Union's metro cars and now builds the N5 carriages to be seen on Moscow's metro. There is a museum at the factory, although the best metro museum is in Moscow (see box p171). **Mytishchinsky monument factory**, the source of many of those

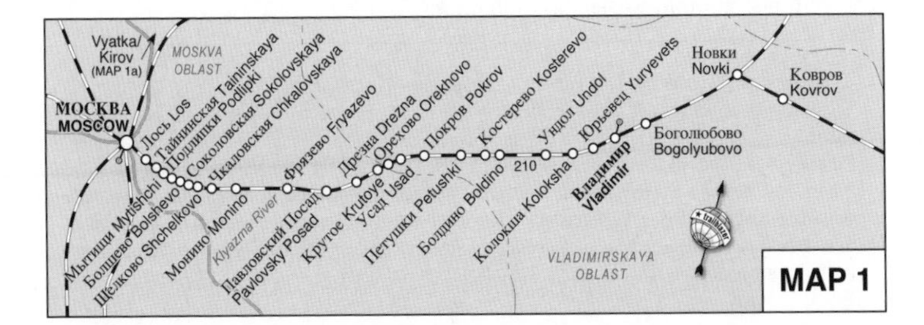

ponderous Lenin statues that once littered the country, has at last been forced to develop a new line. It now churns out the kind of 'art' banned in the Soviet era: religious statues, memorials to the victims of Stalin's purges and busts of mafia bosses. Some of its earlier achievements displayed in Moscow include the giant Lenin in front of Oktyabrskaya metro station, an equestrian statue of Moscow's founder, Yuri Dolgoruky, on Tverskaya Ploshchad, and the Karl Marx across from the Bolshoi Theatre.

Production has also slowed at the **armoured vehicle factory**, one of Russia's three major tank works, the others being in the Siberian cities of Kurgan and Omsk.

The smoking factories and suburban blocks of flats are now left behind and you roll through forests of pine, birch and oak. Amongst the trees there are picturesque wooden *dachas* where many of Moscow's residents spend their weekends. You pass through little stations with long, white-washed picket fences.

Km38: Chkalovskaya Чкаловская On your right-hand side **(S)** you'll see an aeroplane monument with the Russian inscription: 'Glory to the Soviet conquerors of the sky,' commemorating Chkalov, a famous pilot and Soviet hero (see pp225-6) who was the first man to fly nonstop from Moscow via the North Pole to Vancouver (Washington, USA, not Canada) in 1937.

Km41: Tsiolkovskaya Циолковская Close to the station lies *Zvyozdny Gorodok* (Star City), the space research centre where Russian astronauts live with their families and where they have trained for various space missions from the 1960s onwards. This part of Russia was off-limits to foreigners until 1989.

Km54: Fryazevo Фрязево This is the junction with the line to Moscow's Kursky station. Although km posts here say 54km you're actually 73km from Moscow's Yaroslavsky station. (Turn to p474 if you're travelling via Yaroslavl).

Km68: Pavlovsky Posad Павловский Посад This ancient town is a centre of textile manufacturing.

Km90: Orekhovo-Zuyevo Орехово-Зуево The town, at the junction with the line to Aleksandrov, is the centre of an important textile region. It gained its pre-revolutionary credentials in 1885 with the Morozov strike, the largest workers' demonstration in Russia up to that time.

❑ Important note on km posts – Moscow–Kotelnich

The km posts on this 900km section of the route, between Moscow and Kotelnich (near Vyatka), were originally calibrated from Kursky station. Now that most Trans-Siberian services no longer run on the line via Yaroslavl but via Vladimir and Nizhny Novgorod, there's a chance that the posts may eventually be updated and repainted with the distance from Yaroslavsky station, 19km further away than Kursky. When that happens you'll need to increase all kilometre readings from Fryazevo (Km54) up to the station before Kotelnich. At Kotelnich (Km870) you rejoin the old route.

Dacha

A dacha is much more than a country cottage or holiday home: it provides its city-dwelling owners with somewhere to grow vegetables, a base for mushroom and wild berry collecting operations as well as being a place to relax away from the urban environment. Growing fruit and vegetables and collecting mushrooms and berries are not just pastimes for Russians but provide a means of survival during lean years and a supplement to their winter diet during better times. People also pick mushrooms and berries to sell in street markets in the cities. Russians are generally very knowledgeable about preserving techniques, food value and homeopathic remedies.

As one approaches a city on the train, the dacha colonies become larger and more frequent. Each privately owned house will be set on a large wood-fenced lot. The design of the house is very eclectic: small greenhouses abound and many properties have a sauna building. The earth closet of classic design is at the foot of the garden. Electricity is supplied and there is water from a community well or tap. There may be chickens; other livestock such as a goat or milk cow would belong to permanent residents. Some of the outlying villages contain a mix of small farmsteads and old houses that have been rehabilitated into dachas. **Nancy J Scarth** (Canada)

Km110: Pokrov Покров It was in the nearby village of Novoselovo that Yuri Gagarin, the world's first astronaut, died in a plane crash in 1968. He was piloting a small aircraft when another plane flew too close. The resulting turbulence forced his aircraft into a downward spin which he was unable to correct.

Km126: Petushki Петушки If you ever see a Communist-era film with bears in it, chances are it was shot in the countryside around Petushki. The town's most famous attraction is the nearby zoo, source of many animals used in Russian movies. Petushki sits on the left bank of the Klyazma River.

Km135: Kosterevo Костерево The 19th-century painter Isaak Levitan lived near here. His house has been moved into Kosterevo and opened as a museum.

Km161: Undol Ундол The station is named after Russian bibliographer V M Undolsky, who was born near here. The town is known as Lakinsk after M I Lakin, a revolutionary killed here in 1905. But the area is probably best known for its brewery, a Soviet-era Czechoslovak joint venture. Lakinsk beer, very popular in the 1990s, is now under strong competition from Western brands.

Km191: Vladimir Владимир (●●●) **[see pp211-15]**

Vladimir was founded in 1108. In 1157 it became capital of the principality of Vladimir-Suzdal and therefore politically the most important city in Russia. It's worth visiting for its great Assumption Cathedral, its domes rising above the city as you approach, and as a stepping-stone to the more interesting town of **Suzdal** (see pp216-22), 35km away, and the wonderful Church of the Intercession on the Nerl, 10km from Vladimir.

Km202: Bogolyubovo Боголюбово **[see p216]**

Visible from the train **(N)** about 1.5km east of Bogolyubovo is the **Church of the Intercession on the Nerl**, one of Russia's loveliest and most famous churches. Built in 1165, the single-domed church sits in the middle of a field at the junction of the Nerl and Klyazma rivers. It was constructed in a single summer on the orders of Andrei Bogolyubsky, in memory of his son who died in battle against the Volga Bulgars. It was built on this prominent spot to impress visiting ambassadors. To symbolise Vladimir's inheritance of religious authority from Byzantium and Kiev the church was consecrated and a holiday declared without permission being sought.

Km240: Novki Новки This large town at the junction of the line to Ivanovo boasts one of Russia's ugliest stations. The original building is about a century old. In the 1980s, in an attempt to make it appear contemporary, it was encased in pink and fawn tiles. The result is a monumental eyesore.

About 13km eastward the train crosses the wide Klyazma River. The original bridge, built in the 1890s, was washed away in a flood. To avoid the problems of extending a new bridge across the river, engineers came up with a clever alternative. They built a bridge on dry land, on the inside of a bend in the river 1km to the west, then dug a canal beneath the bridge, detoured the river through it and filled in the old river bed. As you pass by you can see the old river course on each side of the bridge's eastern embankment.

Km255: Kovrov I Ковров I This ancient town gets its name from *kovyor*, the Russian word for 'carpet'. During the Mongol Tatar's reign in the 14th century,

The Golden Ring

You are now passing through Russia's most famous historical region, ancient birthplace of the mighty Russian state. Major Golden Ring towns on or near the current Trans-Siberian route are Vladimir, Suzdal and Nizhny Novgorod (formerly Gorky). Along the older route via Yaroslavl are Sergiev Posad (73km from Moscow; see pp195-9), Rostov-Yaroslavski (224km) and Yaroslavl (284km).

Following the collapse of Kievan Rus, the first feudal state in Eastern Europe, its capital was shifted in 1169 from Kiev to Vladimir. At that time Vladimir and the other Golden Ring towns were little more than villages but over the next two centuries all of them grew rapidly into political, religious and commercial centres.

The typical Golden Ring town of the 11th to 18th centuries consisted of *kremlin*, *posad* and *sloboda*. The Kremlin (fortress), usually in an elevated position, was ringed by earth embankments topped with wooden walls. Watch-towers were positioned strategically along the walls. Over time the earth and wooden walls were replaced by stone and brick. Inside the Kremlin were the prince's residence, plus religious and administrative buildings. Outside the Kremlin was the undefended posad, which was the merchants' and artisans' quarter. Often next to the posad was a sloboda, a tax-exempt settlement established to attract a new workforce.

After the Tatar-Mongol invasion in 1236 Moscow (Muscovy) became the invaders' centre for tax collection and its prince was granted the title of Grand Prince. Gradually Moscow's influence eclipsed that of the Golden Ring principalities and they were soon annexed, their economic and military power used to expand Moscow's own domination. By the end of the 16th century Moscow was on its way to becoming the capital of Russia. While several Golden Ring towns retained their commercial importance due to their location on major trading routes, their golden era was over.

the local tax collector accepted carpets as one of the tributes. The town's best known son was engineer Vasili Alekseyevich Degtyarev (1879-1949), father of the Soviet machine-gun. The **Degtyarev factory**, founded here in 1916, now manufactures motorcycles, scooter engines and small arms. In the town centre there is a monument to Degtyarev, holding an engineering micrometer rather than a gun. His grave is nearby and his house at ul Degtyareva 4 has been turned into a museum.

Kovrov is also famous for its excavator **factory** founded in the mid-19th century to build and maintain railway rolling stock. Its claims to fame include the world's first steam-heated passenger carriage (1866) and Russia's first hospital carriage (1877). The factory's importance is illustrated by large, colourful murals of digging machinery on the sides of Kovrov's nine-storey accommodation blocks.

Km295: Mstera Мстера The village of the same name, 14km from the station, is known for its folk handicrafts and has lent its name to particular styles of miniature painting and embroidery. Mstera miniatures, notable for their deep black background and warm, soft colours, usually depict scenes from folklore, history, literature and everyday life. They are painted in tempera (from pigments ground in water and mixed with egg yolk) onto papier-mâché boxes and lacquered to a high sheen. Mstera embroidery is characterised by two types of stitch, called white satin stitch and Vladimir stitch.

Km315: Vyazniki Вязники The name means 'little elms', after the trees on the banks of the Klyazma River among which this ancient village's first huts were sited. The town got on the map when pilgrims started flocking here after 1622 to see the miracle-working Kazan Mother of God icon. Vyazniki became famous for its icon painters, with two local masters invited in the mid-17th century to paint cathedral icons in Moscow's Kremlin.

Km363: Gorokhovets Гороховец One of the smallest of the Golden Ring towns, Gorokhovets (about 10km from the station) is worth visiting as it gives a different perspective on these ancient towns while allowing you to observe life in what is now a quiet Russian village. Gorokhovets was first mentioned in 1239 when it was burned down by the Tatar-Mongols. A fortress was built on top of the hill overlooking the town but this was destroyed in 1619 by marauding Ukrainian Cossacks under Polish command.

Architectural highlights include the Purification of the Virgin Monastery (1698) and the St Nicholas Monastery (1681-6), both of which have high, open stairways, pilasters at the corners and intricate window frames. There are also several unusual two-storey stone houses from the second half of the 17th century which were designed to imitate traditional Russian wooden mansions. Also of interest is the former *ostrog* complex, used as a stopping-point for prisoners on their way to Siberia.

Km442: Nizhny Novgorod/Gorky Нижний Новгород/Горький (●●–●●●) **[see pp222-7]** With a population of about 1.3 million, Nizhny Novgorod (still called Gorky on train timetables) is Russia's fourth-largest city after Moscow, St Petersburg and Novosibirsk. It was closed to foreigners until 1991 but tourists have now returned to this attractive Golden Ring city.

East of Nizhny Novgorod the train crosses the mighty **Volga River**, which is about 1km wide at this point. In times gone by Russians held this river in such esteem that train passengers would stand and take off their hats to Mother Volga as the train rattled onto the first spans of the long bridge. Rising in the Valdai hills, Europe's longest river meanders 3700km down to the Caspian Sea. It is to Russia what the Nile is to Egypt: a source of life and a thoroughfare.

Km509: Semyonov Семёнов Settled in the 18th century by Old Believers (see pp58-9), Semyonov still boasts many buildings from that period, identified by the five or six windows on each façade, walls covered with intricate carvings, high surrounding fences, wicket gates and large prayer rooms. In the 19th century the town became famous for rosary beads and other products of its woodworkers. It was later known for a particular form of *khokhloma* painting – fine golden patterns of flowers on a red or black background. A khokhloma school was founded here in 1925.

Km531: Ozero Озеро To the left of the station (whose name means 'lake') is shallow Svetloyar Lake, at the bottom of which, according to legend, is the invisible village of Kitezh.

Km623: Uren Урен The town was founded deep in the forests by Old Believers fleeing from persecution in the 18th century.

Km682: Shakhunya Шахунья This town near the Shakhunya River derives its name from the Russian word *shag* ('step') as the river was so narrow here

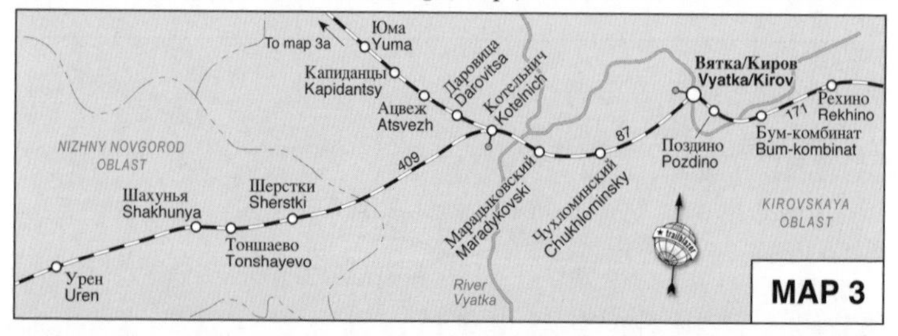

that it could be crossed in one jump. The town grew in the 1930s when the railway line between Nizhny Novgorod and Vyatka was built. Most buildings are two- and five-storey apartment blocks from the 1950s, but 1930s wooden workers' barracks can still be seen.

Km743: Sherstki Шерстки On the border between Nizhny Novgorodskaya and Kirovskaya oblasts, this station also marks the first step away from Moscow Time.

Km 743-1266 TIME ZONE MT + 1

Km870: Kotelnich Котельнич (pop: 35,700) This station sits at the junction of the Trans-Siberian (Moscow–Vladimir–Nizhny Novgorod–Vyatka) line and the Moscow–Yaroslavl–Vyatka line. For Yaroslavl this is not the place to change lines; instead go 87km east to the major city of Vyatka (Kirov) where tickets are much easier to get.

Kotelnich is an ancient commercial centre on the right bank of the Vyatka River, a major trading route between Arkhangelsk and the Volga region. Finding your way around the town is not easy as it lies in three ravines with only the town centre laid out in an orderly fashion. Here the major thoroughfare is ul Moskovskaya and along part of it are a number of buildings built in Vyatka Provincial Style from 1850 to 1880. Sights include the John the Baptist (Predtichi) Monastery and the Presentation of the Virgin (Vvedenski) Nunnery.

After leaving the station, the train crosses over the **Vyatka River**. This is the 10th longest river in European Russia, meandering for 1367km, and the Trans-Siberian crosses over it several times. When the train reaches the Vyatka River basin a few kilometres to the west of Kotelnich there is a noticeable change in the landscape as forests give way to fields and more frequent villages.

Km890: Maradykovski Марадыковский The nearby air force base has in the past been used for storage of chemical weapons' agents (mustard gas, lewisite, hydrocyanic acid and phosgene). Destruction of these chemicals was begun in 1995 and is ongoing. Ironically, the name of the settlement around the station is Mirny (Мирный) which means 'peaceful'.

Km957: Vyatka/Kirov Вятка/Киров (●●●) (pop: 501,000) Vyatka, formerly known as Kirov (and still called this on train timetables), was founded on the banks of the Vyatka River in 1181, as Klynov. It developed into a fur-trading centre entirely dependent on the river for transport and communication with the rest of the country. In the 18th century it fell under the rule of Moscow and was renamed Vyatka, soon gaining a reputation as a place of exile. In 1934 the name was changed once more, this time to Kirov, in honour of the Communist leader assassinated earlier in the same year. Sergei Kirov was at one time so close to Stalin that most people assumed he would succeed him as Party General Secretary. But he subsequently broke away, and it is more than likely that Stalin had a hand in his death, and moreover used it as an excuse for his own Great Purge in the mid-1930s, during which several million people died in labour camps.

Modern Vyatka is a large industrial and administrative centre with an attractive river front.

A branch line runs north to the Kotlas area, setting for Alexander Solzhenitsyn's *A Day in the Life of Ivan Denisovitch,* describing 24 hours in the life of a Siberian convict.

Km975: Pozdino Поздино The town around the station is called Novovyatsk and boasts one of Russia's largest ski factories. During Soviet times the factory produced 20% of the nation's skis.

Km995: Bum-kombinat Бумкомбинат This town gets its unfortunate name from its principal employer, a paper factory.

Km1052: Zuyevka Зуевка (pop: 14,300) Zuyevka was founded in 1895 during construction of the railway; during WWII hundreds of Leningraders settled here, and today their descendants manufacture swings and see-saws.

Km1127: Yar Яр About 20km before this station you leave Kirovskaya Oblast and cross the administrative frontier into the heavily industrialised **Udmurtia Republic**. Yar is the first town here and it has a number of Udmurt speakers. It also sits on a steep river bank (*yar*). There has been a metallurgical plant here for over two centuries.

Between Yar and Balyezino there are many market gardens set in rolling, open countryside. You pass vast fields of grey-green cabbages, and rows of greenhouses covered in plastic sheeting line the track in some places. There are tiny villages of log cabins with brightly painted front doors.

Km1136: Balyshur Бальшур Just before arriving at the station, you pass a steam train storage depot.

Km1165: Glazov Глазов (pop: 105,900) (•) Originally an Udmurt village, Glazov soon became infamous as a desolate and impoverished place of exile. All this was to change with the arrival of the railway and by 1900 there were over a hundred enterprises. Within a few more years the town grew into the region's largest flax, oats and oakum trading centre (oakum is a fibre used for caulking the seams of ships). There are still a few Udmurt log huts remaining. Known as *korkas*, they are positioned along an open paved courtyard. The courtyard had a massive gate which, like the hut, was often decorated with carved geometrical and plant designs.

The Udmurt homeland

The Udmurtia Republic is one of 16 republics of indigenous peoples within the Russian Federation. The population of Udmurtia is about 1.6 million, only one third of them Udmurts. They are descendants of Finno-Ugric peoples who in turn were descended from Neolithic and Bronze Age people living in the area. Udmurts started cultivation and stock raising in the 9th century AD, and from 1236 to 1552 were dominated by the Golden Horde and the Kazan khans. In 1558 Russia incorporated the entire Udmurt area and it was only in 1932 that the indigenous inhabitants were acknowledged with the declaration of an Udmurt Autonomous Oblast. Today the Udmurts are the largest Finno-Ugric language group in Russia.

Km1194: Balyezino Балезино (●●●) A change of locomotive gives you a chance to stock up from the traders on the platform.

Km1223: Cheptsa Чепца About 2km west of this station the line crosses the Cheptsa River (Km1221) which the route has been following for the last 250km. The train begins to wind its way up into the Urals. Between Cheptsa and Vereshchagino is the frontier between the Udmurt Republic and **Permskaya Oblast**. Permskaya's 160,600 sq km are, like those of Kirovskaya Oblast, lost to the swampy forests of the taiga. But Permskaya has greater prizes than its millions of pine and birch trees, for the region includes the mineral-rich Ural Mountains. The main industries include mining, logging and paper-making. Agriculture is confined to market gardening.

Km 1267-2496 TIME ZONE MT + 2

Km1310 (S): Vereshchagino Верещагино (pop: 25,000) Vereshchagino was founded at the end of the 19th century as a railway depot, and its main industry is still railways. There is a preserved FD21 steam locomotive on a plinth about 1km west of the station near the main rail depot. The town is named after Russia's greatest battlefield painter, V V Vereshchagin, who stopped here on his way to the Russo-Japanese War front in 1905. It was his final and fatal commission.

Km1340: Mendeleevo Менделеево The town is named after the chemist Dmitri Mendeleev (1834-1907), who developed the Periodic Table. He often visited this town during his inspections of the region's metallurgical plants.

Km1387: Chaykovskaya Чайковская This station is named after the composer Pyotr Ilich **Tchaikovsky** (1840-1893), who was born 180km south-east of here at a factory settlement around the Kamsko-Votkinsk industrial plant. Until recently it was believed that Tchaikovsky died of cholera but historians have now concluded that he was blackmailed into taking poison to prevent his liaison with the nephew of a St Petersburg noble being made public. The nearby town (a construction settlement for the hydroelectric dam) is called **Maiski**.

From here to Perm there are some opportunities to get photos of the train as it snakes along the winding railway.

Km1410: Overyata Оверята An 11km branch line leads south to the dirty industrial town of Krasnokamsk, which was founded in the 1930s and has a large cellulose mill. Surprisingly near the town is the popular Ust-Kachka health resort, with medicinal mud baths.

Km1429: Perm Sortirovochnaya Пермь-Сортировочная This is one of Russia's largest freight yards, handling up to 135 trains simultaneously.

Km1432: Kama River Река Кама Just before the train reaches Perm, you cross over the Kama River. From the 900m bridge which was built in 1899 you can see Perm stretching away to the left. The mighty Kama River, flowing over 2000km from the Urals to the Volga, is one of Russia's great waterways. Near the bridge the river banks are lined with cranes and warehouses.

A short distance west of Perm station (N) there's a turntable and beside it an ancient green **'O' Class locomotive** (OB 14). Engines of this type were hauling Trans-Siberian trains at the end of the 19th century.

Km1436: Perm 2 Пермь 2 (●●●) **[see pp227-31]**

Perm, now a city of just over a million inhabitants, was founded in 1723 when copper-smelting works were established here. Because of its important position on the Kama River, the Great Siberian Post Road and later the Trans-Siberian Railway, Perm quickly grew into a major trading and industrial centre.

In the days before the railway reached Perm most travellers would arrive by steamer from Nizhny Novgorod and Kazan. R L Jefferson (see pp94-5) cycled here from London in 1896 on his Siberian bike ride and was entertained by a Mr Kuznetsoff, 60-year-old president of the Perm Cycling Club, and 50 enthusiasts.

On 20 July 1907 the cyclists came out to escort an equally sensational visitor, the Italian Prince Borghese, who had just driven across Siberia from Peking in his Itala and was on his way to Paris, to win the Peking to Paris motor rally. One of the wheels of the car was damaged and after the Prince's chauffeur had replaced some of its wooden spokes he declared that the wheel must be soaked to make the wood expand before the repair could be completed. A local official suggested sending it to one of the bathing establishments along the Kama River. A bathing-machine (of the type used by Victorian swimmers at English seaside resorts) was hired and the wheel spent the night taking the waters.

Unfortunately, the centre of Old Perm is out of sight, 5km away from Perm 2 station where the Trans-Siberian train stops. This is a pity as the approaches and area around Perm 2 are dominated by dilapidated industrial enterprises.

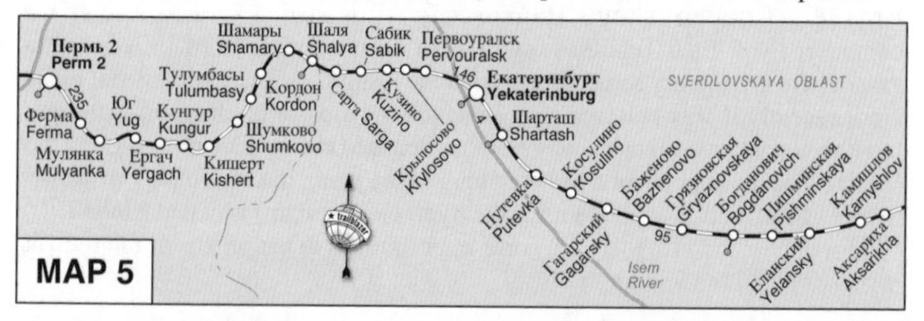

Shortly after leaving the station the train crosses a small bridge over a busy street. This street was once part of the Siberian *Trakt* (Great Post Road) which passed through Perm from 1863.

After Perm the landscape changes abruptly and forests give way to meadows and fields.

Km1460-1777 The train winds its way up to the highest point in the Urals. You might expect the mountains dividing Europe from Asia to be rather more impressive than these hills but they rise up not much more than 500m (1640ft) above sea level here. Colin Thubron (*In Siberia*) describes them as 'a faint upheaval of pine-darkened slopes'.

R L Jefferson wrote in 1896: 'The Urals certainly are not so high or majestic as the Alps or the Balkans but their wild picturesqueness is something to be seen to be appreciated.' Their wild picturesqueness is somewhat marred today by open-cast mines at Km1507 (N) and Km1509 (N). There is a large timber mill at Km1523 (N).

Km1534: Kungur Кунгур Just outside the town is a fascinating and almost unknown tourist attraction, **Kungur Ice Cave** (see pp231-2). The stockade town of Kungur was founded in 1648, 17km from its present site. By the 18th century the town was one of the largest centres in the Urals as it was a transit point on the Siberian Trakt. It had three big markets a year, numerous factories and the first technical college in the Urals, which opened in 1877. Today the town is much less important, though it is still well known in Russia for its guitar factory.

Soon after leaving Kungur you see the steep banks of the Sylva River which mark the start of the Kungur Forest Steppe. This area is characterised by rolling hills which reach 180-230m (600-750ft), a landscape pitted with troughs and sinkholes, and copses of birch, linden, oak and pine interspersed with farmland.

Km1537 (N) A picturesque church stands alone on a hill across the Sylva River. The railway line follows this river up the valley to Km1556 where it cuts across a wide plain. The trees close in again from about Km1584 but there are occasional clearings with villages and timber mills at about Km1650 (N).

Km1672: Shalya Шаля (pop: 26,900) Fifty kilometres to the west of this forestry town you enter **Sverdlovskaya Oblast**, covering 194,300 sq km, taking in parts of the Urals and extending east onto the Siberian plain. Like most of the other oblasts you have passed through, this one is composed almost entirely of taiga forest. From rich deposits in the Urals are mined iron ore, copper, platinum, gold, tungsten, cobalt, asbestos and bauxite as well as many varieties of gemstones. The soil is poor so there is very little agriculture in the region.

Km1729: Kuzino Кузино East of the large marshalling yard here the line rises once more, passing a little town built around a whitewashed church with a green dome. After about 10km the train reaches one of the Urals' most attractive rivers, the Chusavya. The line follows the course of the river for some 30km.

The U2 Affair: USSR 1, USA 0

The U2 affair represented an unprecedented Cold War embarrassment for the West. On 1 May 1960, an American U2 spyplane was shot down from a height of 20,700m (68,000ft), some 45km south of Sverdlovsk (as Yekaterinburg was then known). Its pilot, Gary Powers, baled out without activating the plane's self-destruct mechanism for fear that he would blow himself up (criticisms were later raised in Congress that he had not killed himself, either by destroying the aircraft or by pricking himself with the poisoned needle so thoughtfully provided by the CIA). He was picked up shortly after reaching the ground.

Four days later the USA announced that a U2 'meteorological aircraft' had 'gone missing' just north of Turkey after its pilot had reported problems with his oxygen mask. In a detailed press announcement it was speculated that he had fallen unconscious while the plane, automatic pilot engaged, might possibly have flown itself over Soviet territory. Shortly after this announcement, Khrushchev told the Supreme Soviet that a U2 'spyplane' had been shot down over Sverdlovsk. US presidential spokesman Lincoln White commented that 'this might be the same plane', and did his best to cool the situation by explaining the oxygen supply theory again. He concluded: 'there was absolutely no deliberate attempt to violate Soviet airspace and never has been', and he grounded all other U2s to 'check their oxygen systems'.

On 7 May Khrushchev addressed the Supreme Soviet again: 'I must tell you a secret. When I made my first report I deliberately did not say that the pilot was alive and well ... and now just look how many silly things they (the Americans) have said'. Khrushchev exploited his position, revelling in the details of the American cover-up: he was in possession of the pilot ('alive and kicking'), the 'plane, the camera, and had even had the photographs developed. He also had Powers' survival pack, including 7500 roubles, other currencies and gold rings and gifts for women. 'Why was all this necessary?' he asked, 'Maybe the pilot was to have flown still higher to Mars and was going to lead the Martian ladies astray?' He laughed at the US report that the U2 had a maximum height of 16,700m (55,000ft): 'It was hit by the rocket at 20,000m. And if they fly any higher we will also hit them'.

The U2 Affair brought the 1960 Paris Summit to a grinding halt. Following the arrival of the first U2s in England in August 1962, Moscow remarked that they ought to be 'kept far away from us'. In the USSR, Powers was sentenced to ten years but released in exchange for Rudolph Abel, a KGB spy, in 1962. The Soviet press maintained that Powers had been sent home as an 'act of clemency'. No mention was made of the exchange. A few pieces of the aircraft, plus photos of the wreckage and items from Gary Powers' survival kit are on display in Yekaterinburg's Military Museum (see p235). **Dominic Streatfeild-James** (UK)

Km1748: Krylosovo Крылосово A large factory with rows of workers' apartment blocks looks a little out of place amongst the forests up here in the Urals. From Km1764 east the area becomes quite built up.

Km1770: Pervouralsk Первоуральск (pop: 135,500) The city's name translates as First Ural City as it was here in 1727 that the Urals' first factory was opened. Following the success of its cast-iron works dozens of other factories sprang up and today the city is home to numerous heavy engineering complexes including one of Russia's largest pipeline factories. In the current economic climate many are either facing closure or have already closed.

You can see Pervouralsk's main tourist attraction, the **Europe-Asia border obelisk** from the train so there's no reason to get off.

Km1777 (S): Europe–Asia Border Obelisk People begin collecting in the corridor long before you reach the white stone obelisk which marks the continental division at this point in the Urals. The obelisk is about 15m to the east of the small Vershina (Вершина) railway platform. From nearby Yekaterinburg, tour companies run trips to the obelisk if you want to get up close and personal.

Km1816: Yekaterinburg/Sverdlovsk Екатеринбург/Свердловск (●●●+; ●●● for Trans-Mongolian, Trans-Manchurian) **[see pp232-40]**
As soon as you reach the suburbs of Yekaterinburg (pop: 1,500,000) you see a large lake on the right (Km1807-9) which feeds the Iset River running through the city. There's a **locomotive depot** west of the station. The train halts here in the largest city in the Urals, for a change of engine.

After the train leaves the station, on the right along the Iset River a mass of chimney stacks pollutes the horizon. This is Yekaterinburg's main industrial region. For about 70km east of Yekaterinburg the train winds down and out of the Urals to the West Siberian plain. You are now in Asia (though not quite in Siberia yet).

Km1912: Bogdanovich Богданович There is nothing of interest in this town unless you want to pick up some of the fireproof bricks which are its biggest product. Clay quarries and other factories make this town and region very ugly.

About 16km from Bogdanovich are the **Kurinsk mineral springs**. The *1900 Guide to the Great Siberian Railway* states, 'They are efficacious for rheumatism, paralysis, scrofula and anaemia. Furnished houses and an hotel with good rooms are situated near the baths. There is a garden and a promenade with band; theatricals and concerts take place in the casino'. Such frivolous jollities are hard to imagine in this rather gloomy region today.

Km1955: Kamyshlov Камышлов The town was founded in 1668 as a fortress and is one of the oldest settlements in the Urals. The original buildings have all gone and today the architecture of the town is predominantly late 19th and early 20th century. There is a museum here dedicated to the locally born poet S P Shchepachev and the writer P P Bazhov, who lived here on and off from 1914 to 1923.

About 6km to the west of the town, on the banks of the Pyshma River, is the Obukhov sulphur and chalybeate mineral water sanatorium, which has been famous since 1871.

Km2033: Talitsa Талица (pop: 20,100) The town is known for its Mayan (Маян) brand of bottled mineral water, believed to be good for stomach disorders. The town, which is 3km south of the station, is also known for another drink which is less beneficial: watered-down industrial alcohol which is sold as rough vodka.

Km2064: Yushala Юшала The sailors from the battleship *Potemkin* were shot here and buried at nearby Kamyshlov station.

Km2102: Siberia (Сибирь) officially begins here. The border between Sverdlovskaya and Tyumenskaya oblasts is the frontier between the Urals and Siberia. **Tyumenskaya Oblast** comprises 1.44 million sq km of flat land, tundra in the north, taiga in the south. Until oil was discovered in the region, inhabitants were engaged in reindeer herding in the north and farming in the south. Many people have been brought into the oblast in recent years to work in the petroleum and construction industries.

South of the railway line, the point where the Great Post Road crossed Siberia's frontier was marked by 'a square pillar ten or twelve feet in height, of stuccoed or plastered brick', wrote George Kennan (on his way to research *Siberia and the Exile System* in 1887). He added: 'No other spot between St Petersburg and the Pacific is more full of painful suggestions, and none has for the traveller a more melancholy interest than the little opening in the forest where stands this grief-consecrated pillar. Here hundreds of thousands of exiled human beings – men, women and children; princes, nobles and peasants – have bidden good-by (sic) forever to friends, country, and home ... The Russian peasant even when a criminal is deeply attached to his native land; and heart-rending scenes have been witnessed around the boundary pillar ... Some gave way to unrestrained grief; some comforted the weeping; some knelt and pressed their faces to the loved soil of their native country and collected a little earth to take with them into exile ... Until recently the Siberian boundary post was covered with brief inscriptions, good-byes and the names of exiles ... In one place, in a man's hand, had been written the words "Prashchai Maria" (Goodbye Mary!) Who the writer was, who Mary was, there is nothing now left to show ...' (see p85).

ROUTE GUIDE AND MAPS

Km2144: Tyumen Тюмень (●●●) (pop: 560,000) **[see pp241-4]**
Tyumen is Siberia's oldest town, founded in 1586. It was built on the banks of the Tura River, site of the former Tatar town of Chingi Tura, said to date back to the 14th century. The Russian settlement was named by Tsar Feodor Ivanovich after Tyumen Khan, who once ruled this region. It grew quickly as a trading centre, with goods arriving and being shipped on from the large port on the Tura River.

At least one million of the people who passed through this town before 1900 were convicts and exiles. Many were lodged, under the most appalling conditions, in the Tyumen Forwarding Prison. When George Kennan visited the prison in 1887, he was horrified by the overcrowded cells, the dirt and the terrible smell. He wrote: 'The air in the corridors and cells ... was laden with fever germs from the unventilated hospital wards, fetid odors from diseased human bodies and the stench arising from unemptied excrement buckets ... '. After a miserable two-week stay here, convicts were sent on prison barges to Tomsk. Conditions were not much better for the 500,000 emigrants who flooded through the town between 1883 and 1900, but they at least had their freedom. When the new railway reached Tyumen in 1888 prisoners from Russia were no longer herded over the Urals in marching parties but travelled in relative luxury in box-cars used also for the transport of cattle and horses.

Tyumen is becoming increasingly important because of oil and gas discoveries in the oblast. Other industries include shipbuilding and timber processing.

Km2214: Yalutorovsk Ялуторовск (pop: 37,500) The town sits on the bank of the wide, 1591km-long Tobol River. In 1639 it was the most easterly fortress of the Tsar's expanding empire. It later became one of the places of exile for Decembrists, who opened the first Siberian school for girls here. The school is now a museum and is next to the Decembrist museum, the latter in the house of an early and well-known exile, Sergei Muravyev-Apostol.

After crossing over the Tobol River (Km2216), you will see dozens of small, mostly salt lakes on both sides of the railway.

Km2431: Ishim Ишим (••) (pop: 62,500) The town sits on the left bank of the Ishim River which was a major trading route before the arrival of the Trans-Siberian. The town's strategic location made it a natural site for one of Western Siberia's largest trading fairs. The Nikolsk Fair was held every December and attracted more than 2000 traders, some from as far away as China. The town, founded in 1670 as Korkina, became Ishim in 1782.

North of Ishim, up the Ishim and Irtysh Rivers, lies the city of **Tobolsk** (see pp244-8), one of Siberia's oldest settlements. Yermak (see pp81-2) reached the area in 1581 and established a fort here. The Tsar hoped to develop the region by encouraging colonisation but to the Russian peasant, Siberia was as far away as the moon and no voluntary mass migration over the Urals occurred. A policy of forced migration was rather more successful.

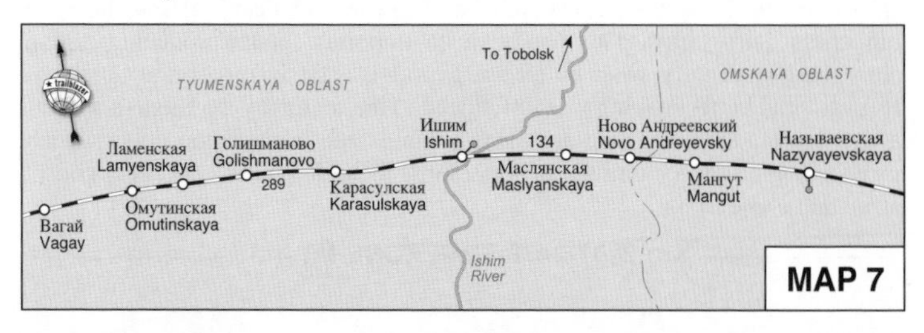

A German spy in Ishim

George Kennan recounts an amusing incident that occurred in Ishim in 1829, when Baron von Humboldt was conducting a geological survey for the Tsar. The famous explorer (who gave his name to the Humboldt Current off the west coast of South America) was growing more than a little annoyed by the petty Siberian officials who kept him from his work. He must have been rather short with the police prefect in this little town for the man took great offence and despatched an urgent letter to his governor-general in which he wrote 'A few days ago there arrived here a German of shortish stature, insignificant appearance, fussy and bearing a letter of introduction from your Excellency to me. I accordingly received him politely; but I must say I find him suspicious and even dangerous. I disliked him from the first. He talks too much ... despises my hospitality ... and associates with Poles and other political criminals ... On one occasion he proceeded with them to a hill overlooking the town. They took a box with them and got out of it a long tube which we all took for a gun. After fastening it to three feet they pointed it down on the town ... This was evidently a great danger for the town which is built entirely of wood; so I sent a detachment of troops with loaded rifles to watch the German on the hill. If the treacherous machinations of this man justify my suspicions, we shall be ready to give our lives for the Tsar and Holy Russia.' Kennan adds: 'The civilized world is to be thanked that the brilliant career of the great von Humboldt was not cut short by a Cossack bullet ... while he was taking sights with a theodolite in that little Siberian town of Ishim.'

The first exiles arriving in Tobolsk were former inhabitants of the town of Uglich who had been witnesses to the murder of Tsarevich Dmitry. With them came the **Uglich church bell** which rang the signal for the insurrection that followed the assassination. The bell was reconsecrated in Tobolsk church but, in the 1880s, Uglich Town Council decided it would like it back. Tobolsk Council refused and the case eventually went to court. The judge ruled that as the bell had been exiled for life and it was still calling the people to prayer, it had not yet completed its sentence and must therefore remain in Tobolsk. It was finally returned to Uglich during the Soviet era.

Km2497 This is the administrative frontier between Tyumenskaya and Omskaya oblasts. **Omskaya Oblast**, on a plain in the Irtysh River basin, occupies 139,700 sq km. Thick taiga forests cover the northern part of the oblast. In the south there is considerable agricultural development, the main crops being spring wheat, flax and sunflowers. As well as sheep and cattle farms, there are numerous dairy farms. This has been an important butter-producing region since the 19th century, when butter was exported as far as Turkey and Germany. It is said that butter-making was introduced to the region by the English wife of a Russian landowner. There are many swamps and lakes in the oblast which provide habitat for a multitude of water birds including duck, coot, grey goose, swan and crane.

Km 2497-3478 TIME ZONE MT + 3

Km2565: Nazyvayevskaya Называевская (pop: 14,400) **(●)** Founded in 1910 with the arrival of the railway Nazyvayevskaya grew rapidly with the influx of new agricultural workers during Khrushchev's Virgin Lands campaign. The plan was conceived following years of chronic grain shortages after WWII and involved the cultivation of 25 million hectares of land in south-western Siberia and northern Kazakhstan. To put the size of this massive undertaking into perspective, the total surface area of the UK is only 13 million hectares.

By the 1960s over-intensive farming had reduced five million of these hectares to desert. The Trans-Siberian runs through the northern part of the area; this, unlike the more fragile south, is still fertile.

The area is famous as much for its insects as for its agriculture. In 1887 Kennan found travelling through this marshy region a singularly unpleasant experience. He wrote: 'We were so tormented by huge gray mosquitoes that we were obliged to put on thick gloves, cover our heads with calico hoods and horse hair netting and defend ourselves constantly with leafy branches.' You, however, should be quite safe in your compartment.

Km2706: **Irtysh River Река Иртыш** The Irtysh rises in China and flows almost 3000km into the Ob River. It's joined here by the Om. The 650m-long bridge is built on pillars of granite from the Urals which had to be brought 1000km by river to the construction site.

Km2712: Omsk Омск (●●●+ for *Rossiya*, ●●● for Trans-Mongolian and Trans-Manchurian) (pop: 1,200,000) **[see pp248-53]**

Omsk is Siberia's second largest city, and a great deal of effort has gone into making it the greenest. The 2500 hectares of parks and gardens cannot, however, disguise the fact that Omsk is essentially an industrial city.

Just before reaching the suburbs of Omsk, you see the airport on the left. The first suburban station you pass is Karbyshevo (Карбышево) and this is where the railway from Chelyabinsk joins the Trans-Siberian railway. The train then crosses the 500m-wide Irtysh River which gives a view of Omsk to the left. The old centre of Omsk is on the right bank (eastern side). After the bridge, the train makes a left turn and on the right passes an old brick water tower, built for steam engines in the early 20th century. This has been preserved as an architectural monument.

The line between Omsk and Novosibirsk has the greatest freight traffic density of any railway line in the world.

The Kyrgyz

South of Omsk and the Baraba Steppe region lie the **Kyrgyz Steppes**, the true home of the Kyrgyz people. The area extends from the Urals in the west to the mineral-rich Altai Mountains in the south. The Kyrgyz are direct descendants of the Turkic-Mongol hordes that joined Genghis Khan's armies and invaded Europe in the 13th century. When S S Hill paid them a visit in 1854 they were nomadic herders who professed a mixture of Shamanism and Islam and survived on a diet of boiled mutton and *koumiss* (fermented mare's milk). They lived in *kibitkas* (felt tents or yurts), the doors of which were arranged to face in the direction of Mecca. Fortunately this alignment also kept out the southern winds that blew across the steppe. Of these people Hill wrote: 'The Kirgeeze have the high cheek bones ... of the Mongol Tatars, with an expression of countenance that seemed at least to us the very reverse of agreeable.' However, he warmed to his 'new half-wild friends' when they shared their 'brave mess of *stchee*' (soup) with him.

George Kennan found them equally hospitable in 1887. Inside the tent he was offered a container filled with about a litre and a half of koumiss. For fear of causing offence he swallowed the lot and to his horror, his host quickly refilled the container. Kennan wrote 'When I suggested that he reserve the second bowlful for my comrade, Mr Frost, he looked so pained and grieved that in order to restore his serenity I had to go to the *tarantas*, get my banjo and sing "There is a Tavern in the Town"'. This did not have quite the desired effect and they left shortly afterwards.

For the next 600km the train runs through the inhospitable **Baraba Steppe**. This vast expanse of greenish plains is dotted with shallow lakes and ponds, and coarse reeds and sedge grass conceal swamps, peat bogs and rare patches of firm ground. From the train it appears as if there is a continuous forest in the distance. However, what you are actually seeing are clumps of birches and aspen trees spaced several kilometres or more apart. The lack of landmarks in this area has claimed hundreds of lives.

In spring this place is hell as the air is grey with clouds of gnats and mosquitoes. The Baraba Steppe is also a vast breeding ground for ducks and geese and every year hunters bag about five million birds from this area. Below the steppe is an enormous natural reservoir of hot water, a potential geothermal energy supply currently being investigated.

The West Siberian Railway (Km2716-3343)

The original line started in Chelyabinsk, south of Yekaterinburg, and ran through Kurgan and Petropavlovsk (both south of the modern route) to Omsk. Work began in July 1892 under the direction of chief civil engineer Mikhailovsky. He was beset by problems that were also to be experienced along other sections of the line: a shortage of labour and animals, a complete lack of suitable trees for sleepers, and inhospitable working conditions (eg swamps that swarmed with insects). But in 1894 the first section from Chelyabinsk to Omsk was completed, and the Omsk to Novo-Nikolayevsk (now Novosibirsk) section opened in October 1895.

The total cost of the line was 46 million roubles, a million roubles less than the original estimate.

Km2760 (S): There is a locomotive storage depot here (mostly electric) and 3km east of it is the station of Kormilovka (Кормиловка).

Km2795: Kalachinskaya Калачинская One of the more attractive towns in Omsk Oblast, Kalachinsk (pop: 23,200) was founded in 1792 by Russian peasants who were distinct from other settlers because of their unusual dialect – *kalachon* means 'a sharp bend in a river'; *kalach* in modern Russian means 'a small padlock-shaped white bread loaf'. There's a useful bit of information.

Km2840 This is the administrative frontier between Omskaya and Novosibirskaya oblasts. The 178,200 sq km of **Novosibirskaya Oblast** extend across the Baraba Steppe region of swamps and lakes. Some of the land has been drained and is now extremely fertile. Crops include spring wheat, flax, rye, barley and sunflowers, with dairy farming in many parts of the Baraba region.

Km2885: Tatarskaya Татарская (pop: 30,000) (**•**) Tatarsk is a humdrum small town of apartment blocks and log cabins. The *1900 Guide to the Great Siberian Railway* was not enthusiastic about the place: 'The country is swampy and infested with fever. The water is bad, supplied by a pond formed by spring and bog water.' There was a church, a centre for emigrants, a school and 'the butter manufacturies of Mariupolsky, Padin, Soshovsky, Popel and Weiss, producing annually about 15,000 *puds* (250,000 kg) of cream butter'.

Km2888 (N) An attractive group of colourful log cabins. About 50km south of the line between Chany and Binsk lies Lake Chany, the centre of a local fishing industry. Catches are smaller now but in the 19th century the lake was famous for its abundant stock of large pike (weighing up to 14kg/30lbs) and carp.

Km3040: Barabinsk Барабинск (••• for *Rossiya* and Trans-Manchurian, •••+ for Trans-Mongolian) (pop: 36,100) Founded at the end of the 19th century during the construction of the Trans-Siberian. About 12km northwards is the bigger and older town of Kuybyshev (Kainsk-Barabinski).

Km3212: Chulymskaya Чулымская A large railway junction.

Km3322: Ob Обь On the left, just before reaching this station, you can see Tolmachevo airport which is one of two airports serving Novosibirsk. The city of Novosibirsk is visible to the north-east.

Km3332: The Great Ob River Bridge After nearly a century of operation, many of the steel bridges of the early Trans-Siberian are still in use today. Known as **hog-backed bridges** because of the hump in the middle of each span, they are supported by massive stone piers, each with a thick buttress that slants upstream to deflect the huge ice chunks that float down the river in the spring thaw. The 870m-long Ob Bridge is a classic hog-backed bridge made up of seven spans.

The writers of the *1900 Guide to the Great Siberian Railway* were clearly impressed by the Ob Bridge, which at the time had only just been completed. They devote almost a whole page to it, beginning: 'At the 1,328 *verst*, the line crosses the Ob by a bridge 327.50 *sazhens* long, having seven spans, the I and VII openings are 46.325 *sazhens*, the II, IV and VI, 53.65 *sazhens*, and III and V, 53.15 *sazhens*. The upper girders of the bridge are on the Herber's system.' For those unfamiliar with Russian Imperial measurement, a *verst* is 1.06km or 3500ft and a *sazhen* is 2.1m or 7ft.

Work on the bridge started in 1893 with the construction of wooden false-work which supported sections of the permanent steel structure until they could be riveted together. Bridge-building proceeded year-round and was an extremely hazardous occupation in winter. Gangs were perched 30m or more above the frozen river, bolting and riveting without safety lines or protective hoardings. More than a few dropped to their death below.

The Ob River is one of the world's longest, flowing more than 4000km north across Siberia from the Altai Mountains to the Gulf of Ob below the Arctic Ocean. As you are crossing over the Ob River, you can see Novosibirsk city centre on the left and Oktyabrsky port on the right. The passenger river station is a further 800m upstream from the port. On reaching the right bank the train turns northwards, passing the city's long-distance bus station. About 800m onwards on the right you pass a **steam locomotive** on a plinth.

Km3335: Novosibirsk Новосибирск (•••) (pop: 1,396,800) **[see pp253-9]** Novosibirsk is the capital of Western Siberia. Most trains stop long enough for you to get a good look at Siberia's largest station, an impressive glass-vaulted building that took from 1929 to 1941 to complete.

Travelling east you pass through a flat land of fields and swamps with the dachas of Novosibirskians in little groups amongst the trees. Some are particularly photogenic, like those at Km3409 (S). The line traverses an area of thin taiga to Oyash (Km3424).

Km3463: Bolotnaya Болотная The town was founded in 1805 as a stop on the Siberian Trakt, at the junction with a 250km road south to Barnaul. The town's name means 'swampy', which is certainly appropriate for this area.

Km 3479-4473 TIME ZONE MT + 4

Km3479: The **administrative frontier** between Novosibirskaya and Kemerovskaya oblasts.

Km3491: Yurga 1 Юрга 1 (pop: 80,700) The station of Yurga 2 is 7km to the south of Yurga 1. A few kilometres to the east the train crosses the Tom River, flowing an unimpressive (by Siberian standards) 700km (or twice the length of the Thames) from the Kuznetsk Basin into the Ob River.

Km3570: Tayga Тайга (•) (pop: 25,600) This town once stood in the midst of dense taiga forest. Nowadays the closest taiga is far to the east.

RL Jefferson was here in 1897 and wrote later: 'This little station was bang in the midst of the most impenetrable forest I had ever set eyes on ... in the centre of a pit it seemed, for the great black trunks of pines went up all around and left only a circular space of blue sky visible.' Annette Meakin wrote a few years later that she 'thought Taiga one of the prettiest stations in Siberia. It is only a few years old, built something after the style of a Swiss chalet.' Unfortunately it has since been replaced by a building that is rather more substantial but aesthetically less pleasing.

The station sits at the junction of a 79km branch line to the ancient city of **Tomsk** (see pp261-5), and in retrospect the site of the junction was badly chosen. The problem is that there are no rivers or large reservoirs near Taiga so water had to be carted in to feed the steam engines. Tomsk was once the most important place in Siberia. It was founded in 1604 on the Tom River and developed into a large administrative, trading and gold-smelting centre on the Great Siberian Post Road. When it was originally bypassed by the railway, Tomsk began to lose out to the stations along the main line. It is still, however, a sizeable city of half a million people, the administrative capital of Tomskaya Oblast and a large centre of industrial engineering.

Tomsk was visited by almost every 19th-century traveller to Siberia. The city was an important exile centre and had a large forwarding prison. Having almost succumbed to the stench from the overcrowded cells in 1887, Kennan wrote: 'If you visit the prison my advice to you is to breakfast heartily before starting, and to keep out of the hospital wards.' By the time Annette Meakin visited Tomsk 14 years later the railway had removed the need for forwarding prisons and she could write: 'It was not unlike a group of alms houses. We found very few prisoners.' Tomsk achieved international notoriety when at nearby Tomsk-7 on 6 April 1993 a radioactive waste-reprocessing plant blew up, contaminating an area of 120 sq km.

Near the station is a **steam engine**, P-360192, built in 1956.

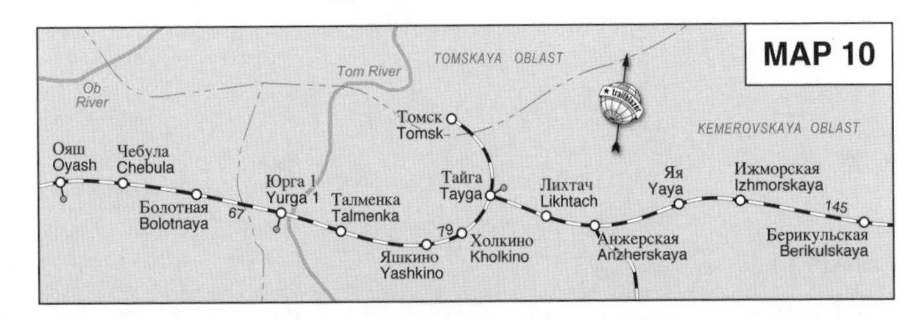

The Mid-Siberian Railway (Km3343-5191)

Work began on the Mid-Siberian Railway starting at the Ob River in the summer of 1893. Since Tomsk was to be bypassed, part of the route had to be hacked through the thick forests of the taiga regions around the station, which was aptly named Taiga. It would have been far easier to have followed the route of the Great Siberian Post Road through Tomsk but some of that city's administrators wanted nothing to do with the railway, since it would break their trade monopolies and bring down prices, damaging the economy as far as they were concerned. By the time they realised that the effect was quite the opposite it was too late to change the route. Besides, the engineers had discovered that the bypass would save 90km. The tiny village of Novo-Nikolayevsk (now Novosibirsk), situated where the railway crosses the Ob, grew quickly and soon eclipsed Tomsk as an industrial and cultural centre.

This was difficult territory to build a railway across. The swampy taiga is frozen until mid-July, so the building season was barely three months long. There was the usual labour shortage and 1500 convicts had to be brought in to help. In 1895 a branch line from Tayga reached Tomsk. Although only about 80km long, it had taken a year to build, owing to the virtually impenetrable taiga and the terrible swamps. In 1896 the line reached Krasnoyarsk and work began on the eastern section to Irkutsk. Numerous bridges were needed in this hilly country but by the beginning of 1898 the mid-Siberian was complete and the first trains rolled into Irkutsk. Total cost was about 110 million roubles.

Km3602: Anzherskaya Анжерская (pop: 92,700) This ugly coal-mining town is at the northern extremity of the giant Kuzbass (Kuznetsk Basin) coal field which contains a massive 600 billion tons of high quality, low sulphur coal. The town, formerly called Anzhero-Sudzhensk (Анжеро-Судженск), was founded in 1897 during the construction of the Trans-Siberian and in the early days of coal mining here. From the late 19th to early 20th centuries, 98% of all coal from the Kuzbass came through Anzherskaya. Most of the original miners were Tsarist prisoners, whose short and brutal lives are documented in the town's Museum of Local Studies.

A railway branch line leads south from here to **Novokuznetsk** which is the heart of the Kuzbass. In the early 1900s a plan had been put forward to link these coal fields with the Ural region where iron-ore was mined and coal was needed for the blast furnaces. The plan was not put into action until the 1930s when the so-called Ural-Kuzbass Kombinat was developed. Trains bring iron

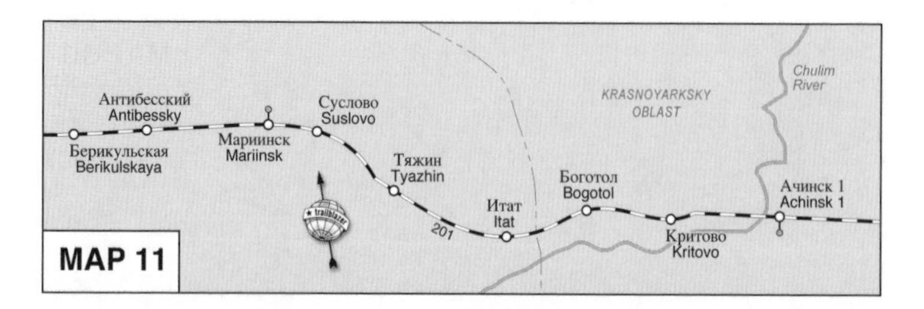

ore to Kuzbass furnaces and return with coal for the foundries of the Urals. You will have met (or will meet if you're going west) a good deal of this traffic on the line between Novosibirsk and the Urals.

Km3715: Mariinsk Мариинск (●●●) (pop: 39,100) Founded as Kisskoye in 1698, this place was nothing more than a way-station for postal riders who carried messages on the Moscow–Irkutsk postal road. In 1826, however, news of a massive gold find brought tens of thousands of fortune seekers. The gold rush lasted for decades and between 1828 and 1917 more than 50 tons of gold were extracted from the region. The town was renamed Mariinsk in 1857 after Maria Alexandrovna, the German wife of Tsar Alexander II.

Just west of the station there are large **engine repair yards** (S). Two kilometres east of the town you cross the Kiya River, a tributary of the Chulim. East of the river the line rises to cross the watershed at Km3760, where there are good views south. The line descends through the market town of **Tiazhin** (Km3779) to the river of the same name and then climbs over the next watershed, descending to **Itat**, another agricultural town.

Km3820: This is the administrative frontier between Kemerovskaya Oblast and Krasnoyarsky Kray. A *kray* is a large oblast, usually established in less developed areas of Siberia. This is also the border between Western and Eastern Siberia. **Krasnoyarsky Kray** covers 2.34 million sq km (an area the size of Saudi Arabia) between the Arctic Ocean and the Sayan Mountains in the south. Most of it is covered with taiga, although there is tundra in the region within the Arctic Circle and some agricultural land in the south. The economy is based on timber processing but there are also important mineral reserves.

Km3846: Bogotol Боготол (●) The town was founded in 1893 as a station on the Trans-Siberian although there is a much older village of the same name 8km away.

Near Bogotol are lignite (brown coal) deposits. Open cut mines can be seen from the train, scarring the landscape.

About 30km eastwards the line begins to descend, crossing the **Chulim River** at Km3917. RL Jefferson arrived here in the winter of 1897, describing the river as 'rather a small stream when compared to the Obi, Tom or Irtish but still broad enough to make two of the Thames River at London Bridge'. At the time the bridge was unfinished but engineers had the brilliant idea of freezing the rails to the thick ice, thus allowing the train to cross the river.

Km3917: Achinsk 1 Ачинск 1 (●) (214m/700ft) Achinsk was founded in 1642 as a stockaded outpost on the banks of the Chulim. It was burnt down by the Kyrgyz 40 years later but soon rebuilt. In the 18th and 19th centuries this was an important trading centre, linked by the Chulim to Tyumen and Tomsk. Tea arrived by caravan from China and was forwarded in barges. To the north, in the valleys around the Chulim basin, lay gold mines. The most valuable mines today, however, are those producing lignite. There's also a giant aluminium complex, visible from the train.

Km3932-33 (S): This is the halfway point on the line from Moscow to Beijing (via Mongolia). There's a **white obelisk** to mark it on the south side of the line but it is difficult to see. The line continues through hilly taiga, winding round sharp curves (Km4006-12) and past picturesque groups of log cabins (Km4016).

There are occasional good views, at Km4058 (N) and at Km4078 (N), after the village of **Minino** (Km4072).

Km4098: Krasnoyarsk Красноярск (●●●) (pop: 875,000) **[see pp265-71]** This major industrial city was founded in 1628 beside the Yenisey River. (*Yenisey* is also the name of the Moscow–Krasnoyarsk Express which you may see standing in the station). The original fort was named Krasny Yar. As an important trading centre on the Great Siberian Post Road and the Yenisey waterway, the town grew fast in the 18th century.

The railway reached Krasnoyarsk in 1896, some of the rails for this section having been brought from England by ship via the Kara Sea (within the Arctic Circle) and the Yenisey. Murray would not now recognise the town he described in the 1865 edition of his *Handbook for Russia, Poland and Finland* as 'pleasantly situated and sheltered by hills of moderate elevation'.

A former governor of Krasnoyarsk was the late hardline General Alexander Lebed, who stood against Boris Yeltsin in the 1996 presidential elections but finally stood down and supported Yeltsin. Yeltsin no doubt had something to do with Lebed's successful election campaign in Krasnoyarsk.

Km4100-2: Yenisey River Река Енисей Good views (N) and (S). Leaving Krasnoyarsk to the east the train crosses the great river that bisects Siberia. The Yenisey (meaning 'wide water' in the language of the local Evenki people) rises in Mongolia and flows into the Arctic Ocean, 5200km north of its source.

The river is crossed on a bridge opened only in 1999. The old bridge, almost 1km in length, dated from the 1890s and had to be built on heavy granite piers to withstand the huge icebergs which steamroller their way down the river for a few weeks each year. The cement was shipped from St Petersburg, the steel bearings from Warsaw. It took 94,000 workers three years to build it. The old bridge was awarded a gold medal at the World Fair in Paris in 1900 (the other engineering feat to win a gold medal in that year was the Eiffel Tower).

The Yenisey is the traditional border between Western and Eastern Siberia. For several kilometres after you've crossed it, lumber mills and factories blight

> **Evenki National Okrug**
> About 900km due north of here lies the town of Tura, capital of the **Evenki National Okrug**, 745,000 sq km of permanently frozen land, specially reserved for the indigenous population. The **Evenks** belong to the Tungus group of people (the names are often used interchangeably), who were originally nomadic herders and hunters. After the Buryats and the Yakuts they form the largest ethnic group in Siberia but they are scattered in small groups right across the northern regions. They once lived in wigwams or tents and survived off berries and reindeer-meat (a great delicacy being the raw marrow sucked straight from the bone, preferably while it was still warm). They discovered that Christianity fitted in well with their own Shamanistic religion and worshipped St Nicholas as deputy to the Master Spirit of the Underworld. After the Revolution they were organised into collective farms and although most of the population is now settled, there are still some reindeer-herders in the extreme north of the region.

the countryside. Opencast mining has created ugly gashes in the hills around Km4128 (N).

Km4117: Bazaikha Базаиха There is a branch line northwards from here to the closed city of Krasnoyarsk-26, a nuclear-waste reprocessing facility. The line goes through Sotsgorod station and terminates at the Gorknokhimichesky Chemical complex. Neither this line nor the city appeared on Soviet-era maps.

Between Krasnoyarsk and Nizhneudinsk the line crosses picturesque hilly countryside, with the train climbing in and out of successive valleys. There are numerous bridges on this section. There are good places for photographs along the train as it curves round bends at Km4165-4167 and Km4176-4177; then the land becomes flatter.

Km4227: Uyar Уяр At the western end of the station is a strategic reserve of working **steam locos** and also a dump of about 10 engines rusting away amongst the weeds. This town's full name is something of a tongue-twister: try saying 'Uyarspasopreobrazhenskoye' after a few glasses of vodka. In 1897 the name was changed to Olgino in honour of grand duchess Olga Nikolayevna, and in 1906 to Klyukvenaya, after the railway engineer who built this section of the line. In 1973 it again became Uyar.

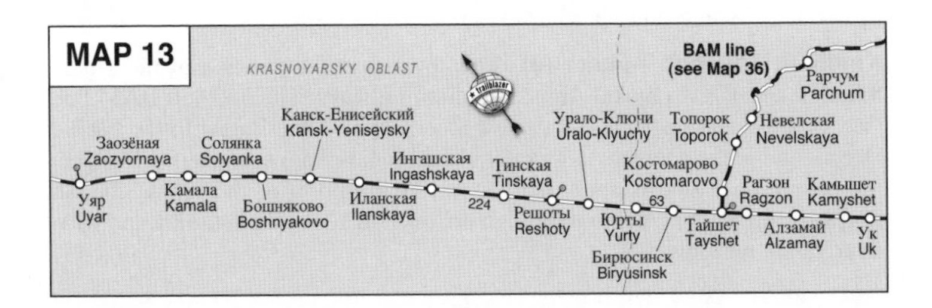

Km4262: Zaozyornaya Заозёрная (•; no stop for Trans-Mongolian) (pop: 15,600) A branch line runs northwards to the once-secret city of Krasnoyarsk-45 (also known as Zelenogorsk) where there's a space centre. East of the station there are huge opencast coal mines beside the track.

Km4343: Kansk-Yeniseysky Канск-Енисейский (•; no stop for Trans-Mongolian) (pop: 106,000) This big town, usually called Kansk, had an inglorious start. Its original wooden fortress was built in 1628, 43km from the present site. The location was badly chosen and in 1640 the fortress was moved. It was almost immediately burnt down by local Buryats, and after being rebuilt it was burnt down again in 1677. Over the following two centuries the town became a major transit point for peasants settling in Siberia. Russian author Anton Chekhov wasn't very impressed, writing that Kansk belonged among the impoverished, stagnant little towns famed only for an abundance of taverns. It's unlikely he'd change his view if he visited today.

Km4375: Ilanskaya Иланская (•••) (pop: 17,600) The site of the town of Ilansky (Иланский) was selected in 1734 by the Danish-born Russian naval explorer Vitus Bering (after whom the Bering Straits are named) during the Second Kamchatsky Expedition to explore the coast of America. It may seem strange that Bering was surveying central Siberia but he was under orders to make himself useful as he crossed to the Russian Far East. There is a **museum** of the town's history at the locomotive depot.

Km4453: Reshoty Решоты (•, *Rossiya* only) This is the junction for the line south to Abakan, an industrial centre in the foothills of the Sayan Mountains.

Km 4474-5780 TIME ZONE MT + 5

Local time is now Moscow Time + 5 hours. The line gradually swings round to the south-east as it heads towards Irkutsk. For the next 600km you will pass through one of Russia's biggest logging areas. Many of the rivers are used to transport the logs and you can often see log packs being towed down the river or piles of loose logs washed up on the banks. This section of the line is very impressive, the train constantly climbing and descending as it crosses numerous rivers and deep ravines.

Km4501-02: The river here conveniently marks the **halfway point** for the Moscow to Beijing (via Manchuria) run.

Km4516: Tayshet Тайшет (•) This town is at the junction of the Trans-Siberian and BAM (Baikal Amur Mainline) railways. The 3400km BAM line (see pp108-9 and pp467-73) traverses Siberia from Lake Baikal to the Pacific Ocean, and is the gateway to a rarely visited region known as the BAM Zone. The single-track line is about 600km to 1000km north of the Trans-Siberian Railway, running parallel to it through pristine taiga, mountain tundra and wide river valley meadows.

Before the 1970s the BAM Zone was virtually uninhabited taiga, dotted with indigenous villages. Today it has a population of about 300,000 involved in extracting natural resources from the region's enormous reserves. Only about 100 Westerners visit the region each year.

Tayshet was founded when the Trans-Siberian arrived in 1897 and is famous in Soviet 'Gulag' literature. Tayshet was a transit camp for Stalin-era prisoners heading east or west, and was a major camp of Ozerlag, the Gulag complex whose prisoners built the Tayshet–Bratsk section of the BAM. Construction of this section started in earnest after WWII. At the height of the work there were over 300 camps dotted along the line's 350km, with a total population of 100,000 prisoners. In *The Gulag Archipelago*, Alexander Solzhenitsyn writes that Tayshet had a factory for creosoting railroad ties (railway sleepers) 'where, they say, creosote penetrates the skin and bones and its vapours fill the lungs – and that is death'. The factory which makes the ties still operates.

Km4555 (S): Razgon Разгон A small, poor-looking community of log cabins. About 1km east of here the line rises and there are views across the taiga at Km4563 (S), Km4569 (N) and Km4570.

Km4631: Kamyshet Камышет It was here that George Kennan stopped in 1887 for repairs to his tarantass. While the wheel was being replaced he watched the amazing spectacle of a Siberian blacksmith shoeing a horse. 'The poor beast had been hoisted by means of two broad belly-bands and suspended from a stout frame so that he could not touch the ground', he wrote. Three of the horse's legs had been secured to the frame and 'the daring blacksmith was fearlessly putting a shoe on the only hoof that the wretched and humiliated animal could move'.

Km4640-4680: The train snakes its way through the foothills of the Eastern Sayan Mountains. The Sayan Range forms a natural frontier between Siberia and Mongolia.

At Km4648-9 you are at the **half-way point** between Moscow and Vladivostok. There are some good views and several chances for photographs of the whole train as it winds around the valleys. The best spots are around Km4657 (S), Km4660 (S), Km4662-5 and Km4667.

Km4680: Nizhneudinsk Нижнеудинск (●●●) (pop: 39,624) The area is best known for sawmills, swamps and insects. Of the mosquitoes, Kennan complained, 'I found myself blotted from head to foot as if I were suffering from some eruptive disease.'

Near Nizhneudinsk is a famous Siberian beauty spot, **Ukovsky Waterfall**; it's 18km upstream along the Ude River which flows through Nizhneudinsk. About 75km further upstream, the **Nizhneudinsky Caves** contain ancient paintings.

Siberia's smallest indigenous group, numbering less than 500, is the Tofalar (Tofy), living in and around the isolated settlement of Tofalaria, 200km from

The Tunguska Event

About 800km due north of Nizhneudinsk, on 30 June 1908, one of the largest (pre-atomic era) explosions in human history took place, in the Tunguska River region. Some 2000 sq km of forest were instantly destroyed in what came to be known as the Tunguska Event. The sound of the explosion was heard up to 350km away, the shock waves were registered on seismic equipment right around the world, and the light from the blast was seen throughout Europe. Newspapers of the time proposed all kinds of theories to explain it, from the testing of new explosives to crash-landing Martian spaceships. Scientists now believe that it was caused by a fragment of Encke's Comet, which disintegrated as it entered the Earth's atmosphere, creating a vast fireball. In September 2002 it was reported that a meteorite hit a forest area north of Lake Baikal. On a Siberian scale this was a blip compared to the Tunguska Event but it still managed to destroy an area of 65 sq km.

Nizhneudinsk. There are no roads to this village and its only regular link with the rest of the world is a helicopter service from Nizhneudinsk.

Between Nizhneudinsk and Irkutsk the country becomes flatter and the taiga thins out. The train passes through numerous timber-yards.

Km4789 (S): There is a large, well-maintained **graveyard** with a blue fence around it, standing close to the line. Some of the graves are topped with red stars, some with red crosses. Kennan wrote in 1887: 'The graveyards belonging to the Siberian settlements sometimes seemed to me much more remarkable and noteworthy than the settlements themselves ... Many graves (are) marked by three-armed wooden crosses and covered with narrow A-shaped roofs.'

Km4794: Tulun Тулун (•) (pop: 52,600) Tulun sits at the junction of the M55 Moscow–Irkutsk Highway and the main road to the city of Bratsk, 225km to the north. The town's centre, near the station, still consists mainly of wooden houses. Tulun has a **Decembrists' museum**.

The line follows the river, crossing it at Km4800 and passing a large saw-mill at Km4804 (S) which might make a good photo with the town behind it. For once there are no wires to get in the way. At Km4809 (S) there is a large opencast mine. You pass through an area of large cultivated fields.

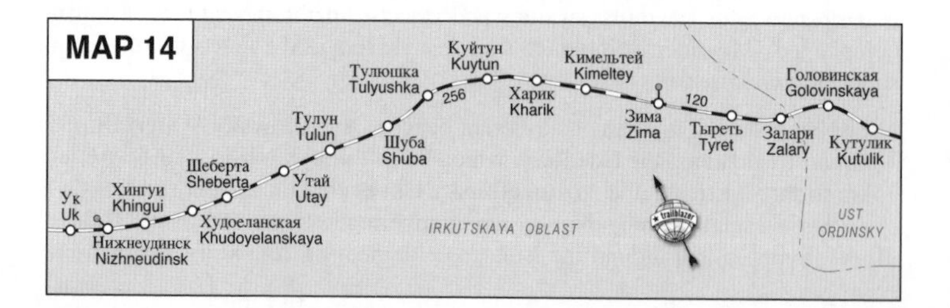

Km4875: Kuytun Куйтун The town's name means 'cold' in the language of the Buryat people (see box p426). There are cold springs in the area.

Km4940: Zima Зима (●●●) (460m/1500ft, pop: 35,900) Zima means 'winter' and at the beginning of the 19th century this was a place of exile for members of the Sectarian sect. When Tsarevich Nicholas visited Zima on 8 July 1891 the Buryats presented him with a model yurt cast in silver.

About 3km to the east of the town the railway crosses the 790km-long Oka River. The river runs brown as it cuts through seams of coal and copperas (ferrous sulphate). The mineral-rich water and earth have their benefits as the water was used to blacken tanned animal skins and, during epidemics of cholera, the copperas earth was used as a disinfectant. But it also causes goitre, which many locals suffer from today. Down the Oka near the riverside village of Burluksk are 1000-year-old petroglyphs of cattle, horses and riders.

As the line crosses the watershed you get several reasonable views: Km4958 (S), Km4972 (N), Km4977 (S) and Km4990 (S).

Km5000-40 You pass through the Ust-Ordinsky Autonomous Okrug. There's another graveyard close to the track at Km5010 (S).

Km5027: Kutulik Кутулик This station is the biggest railway town in the **Ust-Orda Buryat Nationality District**. The Ust-Orda Buryats are related to the Buryats to the east of Lake Baikal and to Mongolians but have a different language and culture. The best time to be here is during the harvest festival of Surkharban when there are races, archery competitions and the Ust-Orda's peculiar brand of wrestling. Kutulik has a museum which contains information on the Ust-Orda Buryats.

Km5061: Cheremkhovo Черемхово (●) (pop: 68,300) The town revolves around the Cheremkhovo coal deposit, and various mining and industrial complexes are dotted along 10km of the railway. The first mine can be seen from the railway about 20km east of the station.

At **Belsk** (Бельск), 31km to the south, a blackened watchtower is all that remains of a wooden Cossack fortress built in 1691.

Km5087: Polovina Половина The station, whose name means 'half', was once the halfway point on the Trans-Siberian between Moscow and Vladivostok. Today Moscow is 5090km away and Vladivostok 4212km. The reason for this discrepancy is that the station was named at a time when the Trans-Siberian ran to Moscow via Chelyabinsk and not Yekaterinburg, and to Vladivostok through Manchuria, rather than along the banks of the Amur.

Km5100: Malta Мальта It was in a house in Malta, in February 1928, that farmer Platon Brilin was helping a comrade to build a cellar. As he was digging his spade struck a white object which turned out to be a mammoth tusk carved into a female form. Excavations revealed dwellings with walls made from mammoth bones and roofs of antlers. He had discovered the remains of an ancient settlement, dating from the 13th millennium BC. A grave yielded the body

How the post was sent to Siberia

The building of the Trans-Siberian Railway revolutionised postal services across the vast Siberian steppes. By 1902 a letter could be carried from St Petersburg to Vladivostok in less than two weeks instead of several months as previously.

The first Siberian letter on record was carried to Moscow in 1582 by Yermak's Cossacks, and informed Tsar Ivan the Terrible that Siberia was now his. A regular postal system had been established in Siberia by 1600, Russian peasants being encouraged to emigrate to Siberia to work as Post House keepers and post-riders or *yamshchiki* (see p91). The post always had priority when it came to horses and to right-of-way on the new post roads. Each Post House keeper had to keep some horses permanently in reserve in case the post should arrive, and on the road a blast of the courier's horn was enough to make other road users pull over and allow the post to pass. Indeed the yamshchiki were not averse to using their whip on the drivers of carts which were slow to move out of the way.

In April 1829 the German writer Adolph Erman, travelling down the still-frozen Lena River from Irkutsk to Yakutsk, wrote that he had 'the good luck of meeting the postman from Yakutsk and Kamchatka. At my desire he waited until the frozen ink which I carried with me had time to thaw, and a few lines to friends in Berlin were written and committed to his care. The courier, or paid overseer who attended the mail from Yakutsk to Irkutsk carried, as a mark of his rank and office, a sword and a loaded pistol, hanging by a chain from his neck. In winter he obtains from the peasants the requisite supply of sledges and horses; and when the ice-road is broken up he takes boats, sometimes, to ascend the Lena' (*Travels in Siberia*).

By the time Annette Meakin travelled along the Trans-Siberian Railway in 1900 she was able to send letters home speedily by train, but she had evidently heard about dishonest postal officials and took pains to register all her letters. In *A Ribbon of Iron* she wrote 'If you do not register in Siberia there is every chance that the stamps will be taken and the letter destroyed long before it reaches the border. You cannot register after 2pm, in which case it is advisable to use a black-edged envelope. Superstition will then prevent its being tampered with'. Black-edged envelopes were used during a period of mourning.

Much of the mail still goes by train, though sadly the travelling post-office coaches formerly attached to passenger carriages are no longer widely used.

Philip Robinson (UK)

Philatelists may be interested to know that Philip Robinson is the author of *Russian Postmarks* and *Siberia – Postmarks and Postal History of the Russian Empire Period*. He has since published a collection of railway postcards, *The Trans-Siberian Railway on Early Postcards*. Many of these postcards date from the 1890s and show scenes of railway construction and tunnel building.

Enquiries to the address on p2 concerning these books will be forwarded to Philip Robinson.

of a child, still wearing a necklace and headband of bones. The child may have been a young shaman (see box p274) for the gods were thought to select their earthly representatives by branding them with some kind of deformity: the boy has two sets of teeth. Numerous figurines made of ivory have been found at Malta and also at a site in Buret, 8km from here. Many of the excavated artefacts may be seen in museums in Irkutsk. The oldest settlement so far discovered in Russia (1-2½ million years old) is at Dering Yuryakh in northern Siberia, near Yakutsk.

Km5124: Usolye-Sibirskoye Усолье-Сибирское (•) (pop: 102,600) This city on the left bank (western side) of the Angara River is the salt capital of Siberia. Don't, however, expect to find Siberian salt mines here. Until 1956 all salt was produced by pumping salty water from shallow wells into pans and leaving it to evaporate. These can still be seen on the left bank of the Angara River and on Varnichnoe Island. Nowadays the salt is produced at a **salt factory**, the biggest in Russia and source of the Extra brand of table salt, common throughout the country. The town's other big industrial plant is a 150-year-old **match factory**. Nearby, the **Usolye Health Resort** offers salt, sulphur and mud baths to cure afflictions of the limbs.

Across the river is the nearly abandoned village of **Aleksandrovskoye** which was renowned for the particularly brutal conditions of its Tsarist prison founded in 1873. In 1902 a failed revolt led by Felix Dzerzhinsky broke out here. Many of the participants in the failed 1905 Revolution were imprisoned here.

Km5130 (N) There is a large oil refinery here.

Km5133: Telma Тельма Siberia's first textile mill opened here in 1731 and it still operates today, producing work clothing.

Km5160: Angarsk Ангарск (•) (pop: 272,000) Although primarily an industrial city, Angarsk is well planned and attractive as its industrial and civic parts are separated by a wide green belt. From the station the industrial part is to the north-east (left side if you're heading away from Moscow) and the civic area on the south-west. Angarsk's major industry is oil refining; oil is pumped here by pipeline from the West Siberian, Tatarstan and Baskir oil fields. This pipeline can occasionally be spotted alongside the railway.

The city has a river port and from here hydrofoils travel downstream to Bratsk. Ferries also run between Irkutsk and Angarsk, and coming here from Irkutsk makes a pleasant day trip.

Km5170: Meget Мегет Just north of Meget there's a strategic reserve (N) of L and Ye 2-10-0s **steam engines**.

Km5178: Irkutsk Sortirovka Иркутск Сортировка (••–•••) This marshalling yard was once a small station called Innokentievskaya, in honour of St Innokent, Archbishop of Irkutsk, said to be Siberia's first miracle-worker. The nearby **St Innokent Monastery of the Ascension** was founded in 1672.

The Buryats

The largest ethnic minority group in Siberia, Buryats are of Mongolian descent. When Russian colonists first arrived at Lake Baikal the Buryats were nomads who spent their time herding their flocks between the southern shores of the lake and what is now northern Mongolia, in search of pastureland. They lived in felt-covered yurts and practised a mixture of Buddhism and Shamanism.

The Buryats lived on lake fish, bear meat and berries, although their favourite food was said to be *urme*, the thick dried layer of scum skimmed from the top of boiled milk. They hunted the Baikal seal for its fur and in winter, when the lake was frozen, they would track these animals on the ice, wearing white clothing and pushing a white sledge as a hide.

Back in their yurts the Buryats were not the tidiest of tribes, lacking even the most basic hygiene as the Soviet anthropologists Levin and Potapov point out in *The Peoples of Siberia*. Describing an after-dinner scene, they wrote: 'The vessels were not washed, as the spoons and cups were licked clean. An unwashed vessel was often passed from one member of the family to another as was the smoking pipe. Customs of this kind promoted the spread of various diseases.' It seems likely, however, that most of these diseases were brought by Russian colonists.

Although at first hostile to the Russians, the Buryats became involved in the fur trade with the Europeans and a certain amount of inter-marriage occurred. Some gave up their nomadic life and their yurts in favour of log cabins in Verkhneudinsk (now Ulan-Ude) or Irkutsk. The Buryats, who now number about 350,000, have their own **Buryat Republic** around the southern part of Lake Baikal. Its capital, Ulan-Ude (see pp294-300), was opened to tourists in 1990 and makes an interesting stopover.

The Tsar stopped here on his tour of Siberia in 1891 and the visit was thus described: 'After having listened to the singing, the Tsarevich (sic) knelt at the shrine of the Siberian Saint, kissed the relics and received the image of Innokent, presented to him by Agathangelius, Vicar of Irkutsk.

At the same time a deputation from the Shaman Buryats expressed the desire of 250 men to adopt the orthodox religion and to receive the name of Nicholas in commemoration of the Tsarevich's visit to Siberia, which was thus to be preserved in the memory of their descendants. The Imperial traveller graciously acceded to this request.'

Km5182: Irkutny Most Иркутный Мост Just east of this little station the railway crosses a bridge over the River Irkut, from which Irkutsk takes its name.

Km5185: Irkutsk Иркутск (●●●+; ●●● Trans-Mongolian, Trans-Manchurian) (440m/1450ft, pop: 594,500) **[see pp272-83]** Once known as the 'Paris of Siberia,' Irkutsk is still an interesting place and just 64km away is beautiful Lake Baikal. From the railway you cannot see much of central Irkutsk, located on the other side of the Angara River. In the distance, however, you can see the large Church of the Elevation of the Cross.

Km5214: Goncharovo Гончарово The town around the station is named **Shelekhov** (Шелехов, pop: 53,600) after a Russian merchant who led several trading expeditions to North America in the 1780s. He was made governor of the Russian settlement in America and become one of Siberia's richest merchants, with an empire based in Irkutsk.

Passing through Goncharovo you can see the town's main industry, the giant Irkutsk Aluminium Complex, founded in 1956.

The train soon begins climbing into the Primorsky Mountains. Winding through valleys of cedar and pine and crossing numerous small streams, it passes **Kultuk**, junction for the old railway line from Port Baikal. At Km5228 (N) a giant etching of Lenin waves nonchalantly from a hill. The line climbs steeply to Km5254 and then snakes downwards, providing your first glimpse of **Lake Baikal** from Km5274-8. After a tunnel at Km5290 there is a splendid view over the lake at Km5292 (N).

Km5297-8: Through another tunnel the line curves sharply round the valley and descends to the water's edge. After a junction and goods yard at **Slyudyanka 2** (Km5305) the train crawls along a part of the line that is prone to flooding from the lake.

Km5312: Slyudyanka 1 Слюдянка 1 (••; • Trans-Mongolian, Trans-Manchurian) (pop: 21,400) The station is only about 500m from the lake and the stop may give you just enough time to nip between the log cabins down to the water (see box below). Only speedy sprinters should try this (in case the train leaves early) and only if the carriage attendant confirms that the train is stopping for more than 10 minutes. Some people have been left behind doing this! ('The provodnitsas were horrified at your suggestion that it is possible to run down to Lake Baikal from Slyudyanka 1.' Howard Dymock, UK).

The station building was constructed of marble in 1904 to commemorate the building of the Circumbaikal Railway. There are usually interesting things to buy on the platform – sometimes even Baikal's own *omul* fish and boiled potatoes, or raspberries and bags of *orekha* (nuts, here meaning cedar nuts, the classic Siberian snack).

There are some photogenic log cabins near the station but Slyudyanka is otherwise a rather unattractive mining town. It does have a basic hotel should you miss your train. Slyudyanka is the starting point for hikers and rafters travelling into the Khamar-Daban Mountains to the south. Fur-trappers hunt

Time for a dip in Lake Baikal?

'Last night, I paced out the distance between **Slyudyanka-1 station** and Lake Baikal. It takes **four minutes** at normal walking pace to reach the water. There is a path leading down from the left-hand side of the main station building, before the low row of vendors' shacks. Follow it downhill (passing the church to your right) and when you reach the last road, continue on the track to the lake's edge. A handy gap has been knocked in the lakeside fence, so you can plunge in quite happily before heading back to your train. Just watch out for all the broken glass left by previous beach partygoers'. **Simon Calder (UK)**

The Circumbaikal Line

The original line from Irkutsk did not follow the route of the present railway but ran to Port Baikal. Until 1904 passengers crossed Lake Baikal on ferries which took them from Port Baikal to Mysovaya. In 1893 it had been decided that it would be impossibly expensive to build the short section of railway along the mountainous southern shore of the lake, and the idea was shelved in favour of a ferry link. From the English company Armstrong and Mitchell a specially designed combined ice-breaker and train-ferry was ordered. The 4200-ton ship, christened the *Baikal*, had three pairs of rails laid across her decks for the carriages and could smash through ice up to four feet thick. A sister ship, the *Angara*, was soon brought into service. The *Angara* has now been converted into a museum and is moored in Irkutsk (see p277).

The ferry system was not a great success, however. In mid-winter the ships were unable to break through the ice and in summer the wild storms for which the lake is notorious often delayed them. Since they could not accommodate more than 300 people between them, many passengers were subjected to long waits beside the lake. The Trans-Siberian Committee realised that, however expensive it might prove, a line had to be built to bridge the 260km gap between the Mid-Siberian and Transbaikal railways. Further surveys were ordered in 1898 and in 1901 10,000 labourers started work on the line.

This was the most difficult section to build on the entire railway. The terrain between Port Baikal and Kultuk (near Slyudyanka) was virtually one long cliff. Thirty-three tunnels and more than 200 bridges and trestles were constructed, the task made all the more difficult by the fact that in many places labourers could only reach the route by boat. Work went forward simultaneously on the Tankhoy to Mysovaya section.

The labour gangs hacked out embankments and excavated 7km of tunnels but the line was not ready at the time it was most needed. On 8 February 1904 Japan attacked the Russian Navy as it lay at anchor in Port Arthur on the Pacific. Troops were rushed by rail from European Russia but when they arrived at Port Baikal, they found the *Baikal* and *Angara* ice-bound in the severe weather. The only way across the lake was a 17-hour march over the ice. It was then that the Minister of Ways of Communication, Prince Khilkov, put into action a plan which had been successful on several of Siberia's rivers: rails were laid across the ice. The first train to set off across the frozen lake did not get far along the 45km track before the ice gave way with a crack like a cannon-shot and the locomotive sank into the icy water. From then on engines were stripped and their parts put on flatcars pulled over the ice by gangs of men and horses.

Working as fast as possible, in all weathers, labourers completed the Circumbaikal Line in September 1904 at a cost of about 70 million roubles. The first passengers found this section of the line particularly terrifying, not on account of the frequent derailments but because of the tunnels: there were none in European Russia at that time.

In the 1950s a short-cut was opened between Irkutsk and Slyudyanka, which is the route followed by the train today. The line between Irkutsk and Port Baikal is now partly flooded and no longer used. The Port Baikal to Kultuk section, however, is still operational and makes an entertaining side-trip. See box p287.

sable and ermine in the forests here. From Slyudyanka the 94km **Circumbaikal Railway** (see box above) branch line runs along the shore of Lake Baikal to Port Baikal. The train passes through a short tunnel and runs within sight of the water's edge for the next 180km. Some of the best views on the whole trip are along this section of the line.

Km5358: Baikalsk Байкальск (pop: 16,700) The skiing here is said to be among the best in the country. There are two hotels in town, one near the ski base and the other in the town centre opposite the sports centre; the latter also has a restaurant. The town also makes a good base for walks and rafting in the Khamar-Daban Mountains.

About 3km past the town on the left is the **Baikalsk Cellulose and Paper Combine**, source of a strong cellulose used in aircraft tyres. Until recently its chlorine-contaminated waste water was dumped directly into the lake, causing the number of crustacean species within a 50km radius to drop from 57 to 5. Not surprisingly the factory was the brainchild of that environmental vandal Khrushchev, who wanted to 'put Baikal to work'. This was by far Lake Baikal's biggest environmental problem, and because of the enormous cost of upgrading the plant and fitting filters, it continued its destructive operations well into the 1990s. Despite a recent upgrade, rumours persist of leaks of waste material into the lake.

Km5390: Vydrino Выдрино The river just before the station marks the border of the **Buryat Republic**. This region, which is also known as Buryatia, comprises an area of about 351,300 sq km (about the size of Italy). It was originally set aside for the Buryats (see box p426), an indigenous ethnic group once nomadic but now adapted to an agricultural or urban life. Their republic is composed of mountainous taiga, and the economy is based on fur-farming, stock-raising, food and timber-processing and the mining of gold, aluminium, manganese, iron, coal, asbestos and mica.

Km5426: Tankhoy Танхой (pop: 3000) Tankhoy sits in the middle of the 263,300-hectare **Baikalsky Nature Reserve** which was created to preserve the Siberian taiga. Occasional ferries travel from here to Listvyanka and Port Baikal.

When Prince Borghese and his team were motoring through this area in 1907 on the Peking to Paris Rally they found that since the building of the railway, the Great Siberian Post Road had fallen into disrepair. Most of the post-stations were deserted and many road bridges were rotten and dangerous. The Italians were given special permission by the governor-general to drive across the railway bridges. In fact they covered a considerable part of the journey here by driving along the railway line. Their 40-horsepower Itala was not the only unorthodox vehicle to take to the rails. On his cycling tour through south Siberia in 1896 R L Jefferson found it rather easier to pedal his Imperial Rover along the tracks than on the muddy roads.

Km5477: Mysovaya Мысовая (pop: 7200) This was the port where the *Baikal* and *Angara* (see box opposite) delivered their passengers (and their trains).

When Annette Meakin and her mother disembarked from the *Baikal* in 1900 they were horrified to discover that the waiting train was composed entirely of fourth-class carriages. The brave ladies commandeered seats in the corner of one compartment but were soon hemmed in by emigrating peasants.

When 'two dirty moujiks' climbed into the luggage rack above them, the ladies decided it might be better to wait at Mysovaya and got out. But the station-master allowed them to travel in an empty luggage-van, which gave them privacy if not comfort.

The village surrounding the town is known as **Babushkin** (Бабушкин) in honour of Lenin's friend and Irkutsk revolutionary. Ivan Babushkin was executed by Tsarist forces at this railway depot in 1906 and an obelisk marks the spot. While Mysovaya is still a major Baikal port, over 70% of the village's population works for the railways.

Between Mysovaya and Petrovsky Zavod the line skirts the lower reaches of the Khamar-Daban mountains. Around Km5536 the line enters the wide valley of the Selenga River, which it follows as far as Ulan-Ude (Km5642).

Km5504: Boyarsky Боярский The hills on the right of the station are all that remain of the ancient volcanoes of the Khamar-Daban foothills. East of the station the line leaves Lake Baikal.

Km5530: Posolskaya Посольская About 500m west of this station the train crosses over a narrow, shallow river with the odd name of Bolshaya Rechka (Big Little Stream).

About 10km downstream from here the river flows into Lake Baikal at the site of the ancient village of Posolskoye. In earlier days Russian ambassadors travelling overland to Asian capitals would rest here; the rough village got a mention in the papers of Ambassador Fyodor Baikov when he passed through in 1656. In 1681 an abbot and a monk built a walled monastery here but it has long since disappeared. Today Bolshaya Rechka hosts the Baikalsky Priboy (Baikal Surf) Holiday Camp.

Km5562: Selenginsk Селенгинск The town was founded in the 17th century as a stockaded outpost on the Selenga River. Unfortunately its wood-pulping factories are rather more in evidence today than the 16th-century monastery built for missionaries attempting the conversion of the Buryats.

The factories here and in Ulan-Ude are notorious for the industrial waste they dump into the Selenga River, which flows into Lake Baikal. Pollution from the Selenga and from the once notorious cellulose mill at Baikalsk has affected over 60% of the lake; even if the pollution were to stop tomorrow it would take 400 years for the waste to be flushed out.

The Transbaikal Railway (Km5483-6532)

In 1895 work was begun to connect Mysovaya (the port on Lake Baikal) with Sretensk, on the Shilka River near Kuenga (see p436), where passengers boarded steamers for the voyage on to Khabarovsk. Construction materials were shipped to Vladivostok and thence by boat along the Ussuri, Amur and Shilka rivers. There was a shortage of labour, for it proved impossible to get the local Buryats to work on the line. Gangs of reluctant convicts were brought in, although they became more interested in the operation after it was decided that they should receive 50 kopecks a day in return for their labour.

The terrain is mountainous and the line meanders up several valleys and over the Yablonovy Range. Owing to the dry climate, work could continue throughout the winter, although water was in short supply during these months. Workers were also faced with the problem of permafrost which necessitated the building of bonfires to thaw the ground, or dynamite to break it up.

A terrible setback occurred in July 1897 when over 300km of track and several bridges were damaged or swept away in a freak flood. The line was completed in early 1900 by which time it had cost over 60 million roubles.

Km5596: Lesovozny Лесовозный The town around the station is called Ilyinka (Ильинка). About 28km east of the station the train crosses over the Selenga River, providing an excellent photo opportunity. At Km5633-4 (N) there's an army camp with some abandoned tanks.

The train approaches Ulan-Ude along the right bank (northern side) of the Selenga River. About 1km before the station (N) is a monument to five railway workers executed by Tsarist forces in 1906 for revolutionary activities.

Km5642: Ulan-Ude Улан-Удэ (●●●–●●●+) (544m/1785ft, pop: 386,000) **[see pp294-300]** Ulan-Ude is the capital of the Buryat Republic. Stretch your legs on the platform where there is a **steam loco** (Class Su) preserved outside the locomotive workshop (N) at the western end of the station. Turn to p451 for the **Trans-Mongolian route to Beijing**.

You cross over the Uda River 2km east of the station. After a further 500m you can see the Palace of Culture (N) and a WWII memorial.

Km5655: Zaudinsky Заудинский The line to Mongolia branches off from the Trans-Siberian here.

Km5675 (N): Onokhoy Онохой There is a large number of **steam locos** at the west end of the station. From Onokhoy the train follows the valley of the River Brian. From Zaigrayevo (Km5696), the line begins to climb to Ilka, on the river of the same name. It continues to ascend the Zagon Dar range, reaching the highest point (882m/2892ft) at Kizha.

Km5734: Novoilyinsky Новоильинский About 20km past this station the train crosses the administrative frontier between the Buryat Republic and **Chitinskaya Oblast**. Chitinskaya's 431,500 sq km comprise a series of mountain ranges interspersed with wide valleys. The dominant range is the

American soldiers die defending Communists

During the Russian Civil War, American, Canadian and Japanese troops occupied parts of Eastern Siberia and the Russian Far East, helping White Russian forces battling the Communists. The undisciplined White Russians were often little more than bandits and murderers, and allied forces were often put in the awkward position of simultaneously supporting White Army soldiers and protecting the Russian population from them. An incident at Posolskaya station in January 1920 was just one of many unpleasant events that eventually undermined the allies' faith in the White Army.

White Army General Nicholas Bogomolets arrested the station master at Ulan-Ude and announced that he would execute him for Bolshevist activities. The American Colonel Morrow, based in Ulan-Ude, threatened to call out 2500 soldiers under his command unless the innocent man was released. Bogomolets retreated with the railway official to Posolskaya in his armoured train, where he opened fire in the middle of the night on the boxcar barracks of a small American garrison comprising one officer and 38 enlisted men. These soldiers swarmed out of their quarters, dropped into a skirmish line and blazed away. Sergeant Carl Robbins disabled the train's locomotive with a hand grenade before being killed. At the cost of two dead and one wounded on their side, the Americans captured the train, the general, six other officers and 48 men.

Bogomolets was released for political reasons and emigrated to Hollywood before being deported to Latvia. Sergeant Robbins and Second Lieutenant Paul Kendall posthumously received the Distinguished Service Cross.

Yablonovy (highest peak: Sokhondo, 2510m/8200ft) which is crossed by the Trans-Siberian near Amazar (Km7010). The mountains are covered in a vast forest of conifers and the climate is dry. The economy is based on mining (gold, tungsten, tin, lead, zinc, molybdenum, lithium, lignite), timber-processing and fur-farming.

Km 5781-8183 TIME ZONE MT + 6

Km5784: Petrovsky Zavod Петровский Завод (•) (pop 28,300) Local time is now Moscow Time + 6 hours. The name of the station means 'Peter's Factory', after the foundry established here in 1789 to supply iron for the region's gold mines, and still going strong today. The factory was rebuilt in 1939 next to the railway and from the train you can see the flames from its open-hearth furnaces.

On the station platform there is a **memorial** to the Decembrists that were brought here from nearby Chita in 1830, to work in the factory, and who were

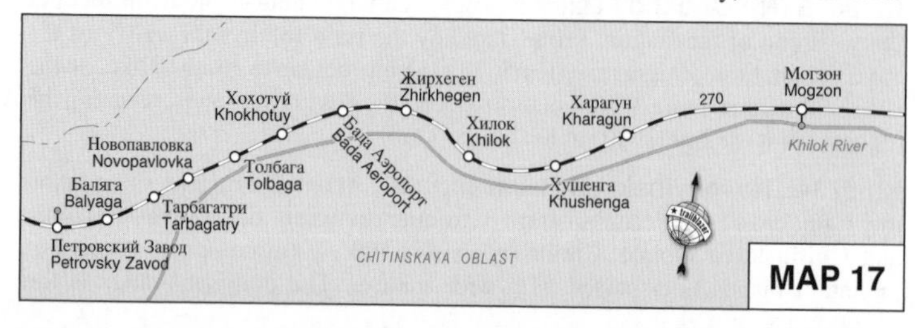

housed in the factory prison. There is also a **Decembrists' museum** in the former house of Yekaterina Trubetskaya. Princess Trubetskaya (1800-54) was the first wife of a Decembrist to voluntarily follow her husband into exile. In doing so she renounced her civil rights and noble privileges. Her name is immortalised in *Russian Women*, a poem by Nikolai Nekrasov.

East of Petrovsky Zavod the line turns north-east into the wide, picturesque valley of the Khilok River, which it follows for almost 300km to Sokhondo, crossing the Yablonovy Range between Mogzon and Chita.

Km5883: Look out for the large graveyard of old **steam locomotives**.

Km5884: Bada Aeroport Бада Аэропорт The little town is clearly a product of the aerodrome and not vice versa: it's built around a large Soviet monument, a MiG fighter plane facing skyward. The runway (N) is interesting for the large number of old aircraft there.

Km5899 (S): Here is a good place for a photo along the train as it travels on higher ground beside the river. Another is at Km5908 (S), where the train winds slowly along the water's edge.

Km5932: Khilok Хилок (●●●, *Rossiya* and Trans-Manchurian only) (805m/2640ft, pop: 13,700) East of this small industrial town you continue to climb gently up the valley beside the Khilok River. There are pleasant views over the wide plain all along the river. North of the line are the Khogoy and Shentoy mountains, part of the Tsagan Khuntei range. Near the station a granite monument topped with a star commemorates 11 Communists slain here during the Civil War.

The train now crosses the Yablonovy Mountains. The eastern escarpment is steeper than the western side and heavy freight trains travelling westwards invariably require extra engines.

Km6053: Mogzon Могзон (907m/2975ft) There's a steam locomotive dump in this dismal town, and heavily guarded prisons for several kilometres around, including one at Km6055 (N).

Km6093: Sokhondo Сохондо (944m/3095ft) This station is named after the highest peak (2510m/8230ft) in the Yablonovy Range. The line leaves the river valley and starts its climb into the range. There is a long view at Km6097 (N).

In the 1914 edition of *Russia with Teheran, Port Arthur and Peking*, Karl Baedeker drew his readers' attention to the '93 yard tunnel inscribed at its western entrance "To the Great Ocean" and at its eastern entrance "To the Atlantic Ocean" in Russian', here. The line has now been re-routed up onto a huge grassy plain. It then descends steeply through Yablonovaya, with several good views (Km6107-9).

Km6116 (S): There used to be a graveyard of steam locomotives here but now most of the engines have been dismantled. West of the town of **Ingoda** the train enters the narrow winding valley of the Ingoda River, which it follows eastwards for the next 250km. The line passes through **Chernovskaya**, where lignite is mined.

Km6125: Yablonovaya (Яблоновая) At 1040m/3412ft this is the **highest point on the line**.

Km6197: (N) About 2km west of Chita is the 16 sq km Kenon Lake. Only 6m deep, the lake is warmed by the nearby power station and at its eastern end there's a popular beach beside the railway line.

Further on the train crosses the small Chita River, and about 1km before the main station you pass through Chita 1 station where a railway factory is located.

Km6199: Chita 2 Чита 2 (●●●–●●●+) (655m/2150ft, pop: 380,000) **[see pp301-5]** Just north of the station stands the magnificent blue and gold **Church of the Icon of the Kazan Madonna**.

Founded in 1653, the capital of Chitinskaya Oblast stands beside the Chita and Ingoda rivers, surrounded by low hills. A stockaded fort was built here by Cossacks at the end of the 17th century and the town became an important centre on the Chinese trade route. In 1827 a large group of exiled Decembrists arrived here and spent the first few months building the prison that was to be their home for the following three years. Many stayed on after they had served their sentence and the town's development in the 19th century into an industrial and cultural centre was largely due to their efforts.

East of the city of Chita the train continues to follow the left bank of the Ingoda River downhill for the next 250km. The line passes through **Novaya**, whose original community and dwellings were wiped out in the great flood of 1897 (see p100). At Km6225 (S) there's a collection of log cabins which looks rather vulnerable, being built on the edge of the river flood plain.

Km6265: Darasun Дарасун (●, *Rossiya* only) Darasun is renowned for its carbonic mineral springs and the water from them has been exported to China and Korea for years. Near the station is a sanatorium where various cardiovascular and intestinal ailments are treated.

About 1km east of the station there's a good view as the train snakes along the river.

Km6270: Here you can see an army supply base surrounded by a wooden stockade.

Km6293: Karymskaya Карымская (•••) (605m/1985ft) This small industrial town was first settled by Buryats.

Km6312: Tarskaya Тарская Formerly known as Kaidalovo, this is the junction for the **railway to Beijing via Manchuria (see p460)**. A whitewashed church stands on a hill (S) above the village. You can catch good views along the river at Km6316 (S) and across the wide plains for the next 100km, especially around Km6332 (S) and Km6369 (S). The best views are all to the south, across to Mongolia.

Km6417: Onon Онон (515m/1690ft) A few kilometres east of here the clear waters of the Ingoda River are joined by those of the muddy Onon, on whose banks the great Mongol leader, Genghis Khan, was born in 1162. The Onon and Ingoda together form the Shilka River, a tributary of the mighty Amur. The railway follows the picturesque valley of the Shilka for the next 120km.

Km6446: Shilka Шилка (•) (pop: 18,200) The adjacent village of Shilka, on the Shilka River, was founded in 1897 just to serve the railway. Two years later it became a popular tourist destination with the opening of the Shivanda Health Resort (*shivanda* means royal drink in the indigenous language). Mineral water is still used to treat digestive and respiratory system disorders here. A few years later the discovery of gold nearby brought more visitors. In 1954 fluoric spar, a mineral essential in chemistry and metallurgy, was also discovered in the area.

There are several interesting-looking wooden buildings near the platform.

Crossing the Kiya River, the train continues over a great wide plain, grazing land for cattle that you may see being rounded up on horseback.

Km6496: Priiskovaya Приисковая (•) *Priisk* means mine, referring to the gold-mining town of **Nerchinsk** (Нерчинск), 10km down a branch line from here. This is where the 1689 Treaty of Nerchinsk was signed, which was to give the Manchurian emperor control over the Russian Far East and deprive the Russians of the valuable Amur region for the next 170 years.

Nerchinsk was the centre of a rich silver-, lead- and gold-mining district in Tsarist times, although the deposits were known to the Buryats long before the Russians arrived in the 17th century. In 1700 a Greek mining engineer founded the Nerchinsky Zavod works, and the first convict gangs arrived in 1722. George Kennan visited the mine in 1887 and was shown around by one of the convict

labourers. Not all the mines were the property of the Tsar, and some private owners became immensely wealthy. In one mansion he visited in Nerchinsk, Kennan could hardly believe that such opulence (tapestries, chandeliers, Oriental rugs, silk curtains and a vast ballroom) was to be found in one of the wildest parts of Siberia. From 1826 to 1917 the mines of Nerchinsk were a major Tsarist labour camp. Today Nerchinsk has 17,000 inhabitants and some worthwhile sights. These include the early 19th-century Resurrection Cathedral and a house built in the 1860s in Moorish style by a rich merchant named Butin. Next door is the Hotel Dauriya (now closed), where Chekhov stayed in 1890. Nerchinsk has a museum and a basic hotel.

On the southern side of Priiskovaya station is the small village of **Kalinino**. The 17th-century Russian explorer Yerofei Pavlovich Khabarov is buried under the walls of the old church. It is believed, however, that the corpse in the grave is actually that of his brother, Nikifor, the last resting place of Yerofei remaining unknown.

Km6511-2 (S): Standing just across the river is a large deserted church and another building beside it. In the middle of nowhere and with a thick conifer forest rising behind them, these two lonely buildings make an eminently photogenic scene.

Km6532: Kuenga Куэнга (•) This is the junction for a line which runs 52km eastwards to Sretensk (Сретенск), which was the eastern end of the Transbaikal Railway.

Sretensk (pop: 10,300) is spread over both banks of the Shilka river with the centre on the eastern bank and the railway station on the high western bank. The two were joined by a bridge across the river only in 1986. The Shilka is a tributary of the mighty Amur; the Amur forms the Chinese–Russian border for hundreds of kilometres before passing through Khabarovsk on its way north-east to the Pacific.

It was this river route that put Sretensk on Russian maps. It was a thriving river-port (considerably larger than Chita) in the 19th and early 20th centuries before the Amur Railway was opened. Passengers transferred here to ships of the Amur Steamship and Trade Company. Most of the 40 steamers that plied between Sretensk and Khabarovsk were made either in Belgium or the Glasgow yards of Armstrong and Co. Waiting here with her mother in 1900 Annette Meakin caught sight of some Chinese men with traditional pig-tails. She was not impressed and wrote, 'To me their appearance was quite girlish.'

In 1916 the Amur Railway was completed and Sretensk, bypassed, became a backwater.

The line leaves the Shilka River here, turns northwards, crosses a plain and climbs towards the eastern end of the Yablonovy Range.

Km6593: Chernyshevsk Zabaikalsky Чернышевск Забайкальский (•••) Nikolai Chernyshevsky (1828-89) was a revolutionary who toiled for years at hard-labour camps in the region.

Km6629: Bushuley Бушулей This is not the easiest area in which to build a railway, as Trans-Siberian engineers discovered. In winter it was bitterly cold and in the hot summers all surface water dried up. For most of the year the ground had to be thawed out with gigantic bonfires before track could be laid. The complex around the station is a molybdenum-ore enrichment plant. The mineral is added to steel to make it suitable for high-speed cutting tools. Scattered along the line are molybdenum and gold mines.

Km6670: Zilovo Зилово (●) The adjacent town is called Aksenovo-Zilovskoye (Аксеново-Зиловское). Southwards were the gold mines of the Kara region, also visited by Kennan, who found 2500 convicts working under appalling conditions. These mines were the property of the Tsar and from them and other Imperial mines in Eastern Siberia he could expect an average of 1630kg (3600lb) of pure gold each year.

Km6789: Ksenyevskaya Ксеньевская (●) From here the line continues across the forested southern slopes of the Eastern Yablonovy Range for 200km.

Km6906: Mogocha Могоча (●●●) (pop: 14,500) This ugly railway settlement in the Bolshoy Amazar River Valley is probably one of the harshest places on the Trans-Siberian route to live because of permafrost and summer sun. In winter the top 10cm of earth that has thawed over the summer freezes again to as low as -60°C (-87°F), killing all but the hardiest plants, while the intense summer sun singes most young shoots. The town was founded in 1910 when this section of the Trans-Siberian was being built, and later became the base for geological research expeditions seeking gold in the hills.

The town of **Olekminsk** lies on the Lena River about 700km due north of here (this being no more than a short hike for a Siberian, for, as Russian guides never tire of saying, 'In Siberia a thousand kilometres is nothing to travel and a litre of vodka is nothing to drink', although these days they rarely add the rest of the aphorism, 'and a hundred roubles is nothing to spend'). Olekminsk holds the world record for the widest annual temperature range, from minus 60°C (minus 87°F) to plus 45°C (113°F).

This was also the place of exile in the 18th century for a bizarre Christian sect whose followers were known as the Skoptsy. They saw their salvation in abstinence and castrated themselves to be sure of a place in heaven. They lived in mixed communities which they referred to as 'ships', each having a

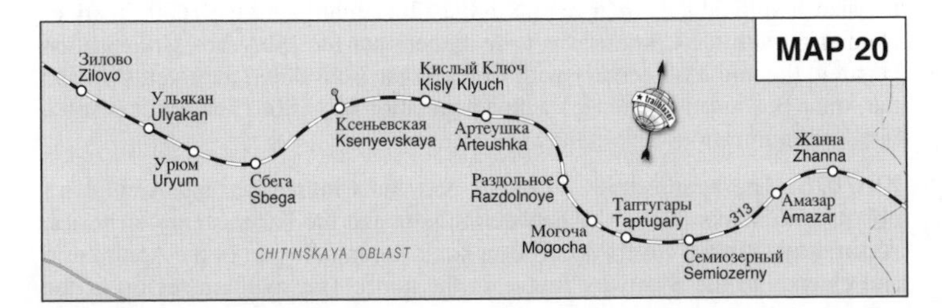

The Amur Railway (Km6532-8531)

The building of the Amur Railway was proposed in the early 1890s but surveys showed that it would prove expensive, on account of the difficult terrain. More than 100 bridges and many kilometres of embankments would be needed. Furthermore much of the region was locked in permafrost. In 1894, when the government signed the treaty with China which allowed Russian rails to be laid across Manchuria from Chita to Vladivostok, the Amur project was abandoned in favour of this considerably shorter route. The change of plan proved to be false economy, for the East Chinese line, despite a considerable saving in distance, was ultimately to cost more than the whole of the rest of the Trans-Siberian Railway.

Russia's embarrassing defeat by Japan in the 1904-5 War revealed the vulnerability of the East Chinese line. Japan was as keen as Russia to gain control of the rich lands of Manchuria and if they did decide to invade, the Russian naval base of Vladivostok would be deprived of a rail link with European Russia. A line within Russian lands was needed. The Amur project was reconsidered and, in 1907, approved.

Construction began in 1908 at Kuenga. For most of its 2000km the line would follow a route about 100km north of the Amur River, out of range of Manchuria on the southern bank of the river. Winters are particularly harsh in this region and consequently track-laying could only take place over the four warmer months; even in mid-summer considerable amounts of dynamite were needed to blast through the permafrost. There were the usual problems with insects and disease but as the rest of the railway was operating it was comparatively easy to transport workers in from west of the Urals. By 1916 the long bridge over the Amur at Khabarovsk had been completed and the railway was opened. Ironically the Japanese, as allies of the White Russians, in 1918 took over the running of the Amur Railway during the Civil War.

'helmsman' and 'crew'. They avoided drink and tobacco and were excellent farmers. Since Olekminsk is experiencing something of a baby-boom at present it must be assumed that the more unconventional practices of the Skoptsy have been abandoned.

Km7010: Amazar Амазар (●●●) The remains of a large strategic reserve of steam engines can be seen here. About 100km southwards the Shilka flows into the Amur (Heiling Chu to the Chinese). The Amur rises in Mongolia and flows 2800km along the frontier with China into the Pacific at the Sea of Okhotsk. If the Volga is the Mother River to the Russians, the Amur is the Father River. The river is exceptionally rich in fish and navigable for six months of the year. Russians explored the Amur region in the 17th century, but the 1689 Treaty of Nerchinsk with the Chinese was to lock them out for 150 years. Colonisation began in the mid-19th century with Cossack garrisons along the river. By 1860 the Amur Basin had 60 villages with a population of 11,000. The Amur is still a vital communications link in the area.

Km7075: The administrative frontier between Chitinskaya and Amurskaya oblasts also marks the border between Siberia and the Far Eastern Territories. **Amurskaya Oblast** covers 363,700 sq km in the middle part of the Amur basin and extends to the Stanovoy Range in the north. The southern region of the oblast is a fertile plain where wheat, soya-beans, flax and sunflowers are grown. Most of the area in the north is under thick forest.

Km7119: Yerofei-Pavlovich Ерофей-Павлович (●●●) The town is named in honour of the brutal explorer Yerofei Pavlovich Khabarov (see p82). At the eastern end of the station (N) is a **steam locomotive** (Em726-88) on a plinth.

The river through the town is the Urka, down which Khabarov travelled with his mercenaries in 1649 to reach the Amur. The river route opened up a shortcut to the Russian Far East from Yakutsk.

This area is particularly inhospitable, with frosts lasting from mid-October to early April and an average January temperature of -33°C. Patches of snow persist on shaded mountainsides as late as July.

Km7211: Urusha Уруша (●) Running mostly downhill for the next 100km the line passes through an area of taiga interspersed with uncultivated plains, most of it locked in permafrost.

Km7266: Takhtamygda Тахтамыгда A small settlement with a view (N) across the river valley (good views to the north continue for the next 150km). About half a kilometre east of the village (N) stands a prison, surrounded by barbed wire and patrolled by uniformed guards.

Km7273: Bamovskaya Бамовская This is a junction with the Little BAM, the line which runs north to join the Baikal-Amur Mainline (see pp108-9). It is not advisable to get off the train here without knowing when your connecting train up the Little BAM will arrive as only a few head north each day; change at Skovorodino instead.

Km7306: Skovorodino Сковородино (●) (pop: 14,100) Named after a revolutionary leader killed here in 1920 during the Russian Civil War, Skovorodino is the first stop on the Trans-Siberian line for trains travelling down the Little BAM from Tynda to Khabarovsk. If you are getting off the Trans-Siberian to go up the Little BAM, Skovorodino is the place to do it. There's also a railway depot, forestry mills and a permafrost research station.

You can see a lime-green P36-0091 **steam locomotive** by the station platform.

Km7323: Bolshoy Never Большой Невер On the left (N) side of the railway is the 800km long Amur Yakutsk Highway ('highway' being something of

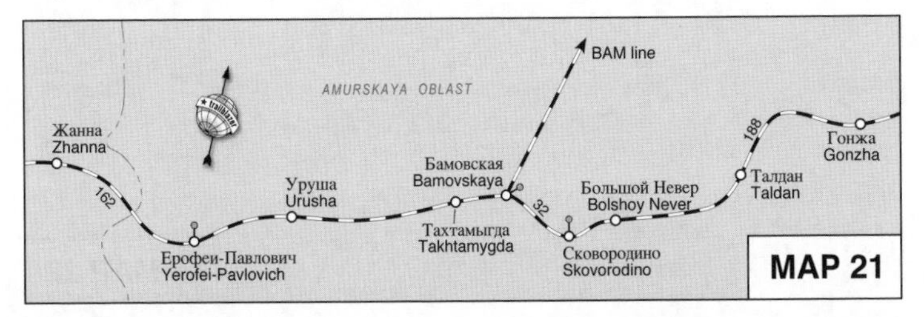

a misnomer). This terminates in **Yakutsk** (see pp385-6), capital of the Republic of Sakha, formerly known as Yakutia. This must be one of the most dismal places on the planet, for the region, which is about 13 times the size of Britain, is entirely covered with permafrost. Even in mid-summer the soil in Yakutsk is frozen solid to a depth of over 100m.

After the tunnel (Km7343-5) there's a long view (S) down a valley towards China, with more views (S) at Km7387 and Km7426-28.

Km7501: Magdagachi Магдагачи (•••) The train descends gently through Magdagachi, out of the taiga and onto a wide plain.

Km7566: Tygda Тыгда (•) There is usually a short stop here.

Km7602: Ushumun Ушумун The border with China is no more than 40km south-west of here. The train turns south-eastwards again, soon crossing an obvious climatic boundary and a not-so-obvious one marking the southern border of permafrost. From here on the larches grow much taller, reaching 35m, and birches and oaks spring up. These oaks are different from European oaks as they do not lose their leaves in winter but retain them even though they are stiff and brown. The train continues across flat lands with small clumps of trees.

Km7723: Shimanovskaya Шимановская (•) (pop: 22,000) Named after a revolutionary hero, this town played an important part in the development of both the Trans-Siberian and BAM railways. To the south the land becomes more fertile and parts of the wide plain are under cultivation.

Km7772: Ledinaya Лединая Hidden away in the trees just to the north of this station is the once-secret Svobodny-18 cosmodrome. One of the advantages of this facility over the northern Russian Plesetsk cosmodrome is said to be its lower latitude (meaning smaller rockets for the same payload). Those interested in visiting the site may not get much further than the station!

Km7815: Svobodny Свободный (•) (pop: 70,600) An attractive town on the right bank of the Zeya River, Svobodny has a proud history associated with the railways. It was founded in 1912 as Alekseyevsk, in honour of the Tsar's haemophiliac son Alexei. It expanded rapidly into a major railway town, with factories building carriages, plus a hospital, schools and an orphanage all sponsored by the railways. By the mid 1930s it was headquarters for both

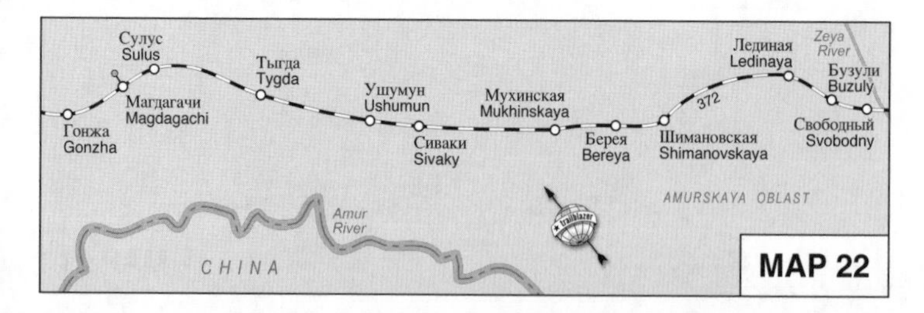

The Yakuts

Yakuts, numbering about 300,000, form the largest ethnic group in the Far Eastern Territories. They were originally semi-nomadic herders who roamed around the lands beside the Lena River. What seems to have struck 19th-century travellers most about the Yakuts was their rather squalid lifestyle. They never washed or changed their clothes, they shared their huts with their reindeer and they preferred their meat and fish once it had begun to rot. They drank a form of *koumiss* (fermented mare's milk), which they froze, sometimes into huge boulders.

To give the Yakuts their due, they were considerably more advanced than many other Siberian tribes. Although they were ignorant of the wheel (hardly much use in such a cold climate) they used iron for weapons and tools. Most Yakut clans had a blacksmith who was usually also a shaman, since metal-working was considered a gift from the gods. The Yakuts were unique among Siberian tribes in that they made pottery. Russian colonists treated them badly and demanded fur tributes for the Tsar. Yakuts have now almost completely adopted Russian culture, and although some are still involved in reindeer-herding, most work in mining and the timber industry.

the Amur section of the Trans-Siberian and the new BAM project. There's a **railway museum** here.

Beyond the town the line crosses the Zeya River, the Amur's largest Russian tributary. In the rainy season the water level may rise as fast as 30cm per hour and 10m floods have been recorded.

The area beyond the river, called the Zeysko-Bureinskaya Plain, is the main granary for the Russian Far East. This is the most highly populated area of the Amur region with villages every 10-20km separated by fields of barley, soya beans and melons. The climate and landscape are similar to parts of Ukraine and attracted many Ukrainians in the 19th century. Today over half the locals are of Ukrainian descent. You can easily spot their white-washed houses (*khatas*). The solid log constructions with overlapping log ends are Russian.

Km7873: Belogorsk Белогорск (●●●+) (pop: 67,400) Some older residents of this agricultural centre must find it difficult to remember the name of their city as it has been changed so many times. It was founded in 1860 as Aleksandrovka, which stuck until 1935 when the local council decided it should be changed to the rather more impressive Kuybyshevkavostochnaya. Just when everyone had got used to this exotic mouthful it changed again, to boring Belogorsk.

Blagoveshchensk – the New York of Siberia

Blagoveshchensk, administrative capital of Amurskaya Oblast, is a large industrial centre of 216,000 people on the left bank of the Amur River. The name means 'Good News', for it was here in 1858 that Count Muravyov-Amursky announced the signing of the treaty under which China granted Russia the Amur region. The city became a centre of colonisation, growing fast in the second half of the 19th century. Locals called it 'the New York of Siberia' because its streets were laid out in a grid pattern, American style. It became the major port on the voyage between Sretensk and Khabarovsk in the days before the Amur Railway.

In July 1900 Blagoveshchensk witnessed the cold-blooded massacre of its entire Chinese population (several thousand people) by Cossack forces, in retaliation for the murders of Europeans in China during the Boxer Rebellion. Annette Meakin wrote: 'The Cossacks, who were little better than savages, threw themselves on the helpless Chinese ... and drove them down to the water's edge. Those who could not get across on rafts were either brutally massacred on the banks or pushed into the water and drowned. The scene which followed was horrible beyond description, and the river was black with dead bodies for weeks afterwards. I have this from no less than five eye-witnesses.'

Good relations between the people of Blagoveshchensk and their Chinese neighbours across the river in the city of Heihe have been cemented in recent years with a rise in cross-border trade. Siberian lumber and machinery is ferried across the Amur to be exchanged for Chinese consumer goods. Heihe is connected by rail to Harbin (nightly departures; 12hrs), with onward links to Beijing. There is no bridge but ferries cross the river a dozen times a day (15 mins; R1200/1700 one way/return) from the Passazhirsky Port east of Hotel Druzhba. There are several daily trains from Blagoveshchensk, including the 385/386 to Vladivostok via Khabarovsk and the 81/82 to Tynda.

Decent accommodation is found at ***Hotel Druzhba*** (ul Kuznechnaya 1, ☎ 4162 37 61 40, 🖳 www.hoteldruzhba.ru; sgl/dbl/suite R1300-2000/2000-3600/5000), with facilities including wi-fi, restaurant, swimming pool and sauna. On the premises, tour agency Amur Tourist can help you arrange onward travel.

There's a branch line from Belogorsk to **Blagoveshchensk** (see box above).

You can see a P36-0091 **steam locomotive** as you leave the station.

Km7992: Zavitaya Завитая (•) (pop: 22,300) This town is famous for soya bean oil and soya flour. There is a 90km branch line to the south which terminates at Poyarkovo on the Chinese–Russian border. Only Chinese and Russian passport holders can cross there.

Km8037: Bureya Бурея (•) On the river of the same name, this town was once the centre of a large gold-mining region. It now produces tools for the coal-mining industry.

The area was once inhabited by several different tribes, most of whom were Shamanists. The **Manegres** were a nomadic people whose trademark was their shaven heads, save for one long pig-tail. The **Birars** lived in hive-shaped huts beside the Bureya and grew vegetables and fruit. North of here lived the **Tungus** (Evenki), who were hunters, and the **Orochen**, who herded reindeer.

To the east were the **Goldi**, described thus in the *1900 Guide to the Great Siberian Railway*: 'They are below average stature, and have a broad and flat face with a snub nose, thick lips, eyes shaped after the Mongolian fashion and prominent cheek-bones ... The women adorn themselves with earrings and pendants. Some of them, as a mark of particular elegance, introduce one or several small rings into the partition of the nose. The people of this tribe are characterised by great honesty, frankness and good will ... Their costume is very various and of all colours; they may at different times be seen wearing a Russian overcoat, a fish-skin suit or the Chinese dress.'

Km8088: Arkhara Архара (•) A stop at the station here is usual, with women selling snacks and fruit on the platform.

Km8118: Uril Урил On the right (S) side of the line from here to the next station, Kundur, is the Khingan Nature Reserve. The sanctuary consists of swampy lowlands dotted with Amur velvet trees and Korean cedar pine woods with a thick undergrowth of hazel trees, wild grapes and wild pepper which is related to ginseng. The sanctuary is rich in Mongol and Siberian animals seldom encountered elsewhere, including a raccoon-like dog.

Km8150-8198: There are good photo opportunities on this stretch as the train winds around the valleys.

Km8184: This is the administrative frontier between Amurskaya Oblast and Khabarovsky Kray. Like much of Russia east of the Urals, Khabarovsky Kray is composed almost entirely of swampy taiga. In the far south, however, there is an area of deciduous trees. Although the kray is extremely rich in minerals, its economy is heavily based on wood-processing, fishing and the petroleum industry.

Km8184-9289 TIME ZONE MT + 7

Local time is now Moscow Time + 7 hours. East of this frontier you enter an autonomous oblast within Khabarovsky Kray. Some stations between Obluchye and Priamurskaya are signposted in Yiddish as well as Russian, for this is part of the Yevreyskaya (Jewish) Autonomous Oblast, otherwise known as **Birobidzhan**, after its capital.

This remote region was set aside for Jewish emigration in 1928 (and the oblast established in 1934), though it never proved popular. The oblast's Jewish population today stands at about 6000 – 3% of the approximately 200,000 inhabitants of this 36,000 sq km territory.

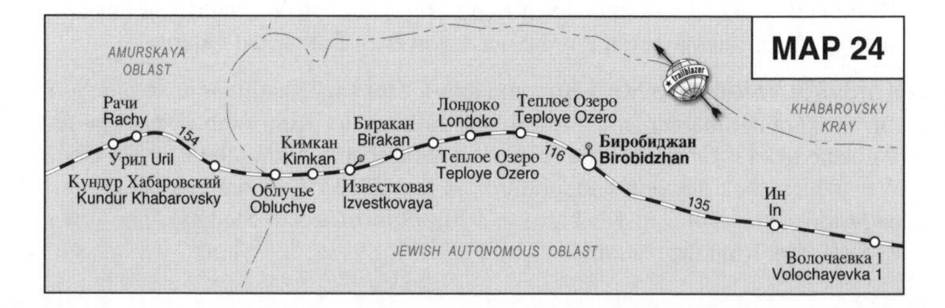

A glossy coffee-table book about Birobidzhan (written in Russian, Yiddish and English) used to be sold in the bookshops of Khabarovsk. After pages of smiling cement-factory workers, beaming miners and happy-looking milk-maids, the book ends with the following statement: 'The flourishing of the economy and culture of the Jewish Autonomous Region, the happiness of the people of labour of various nationalities inhabiting the Region, their equality, friendship and co-operation lay bare the hypocrisy (sic) of the propaganda campaign launched by the ringleaders of Israel and international Zionism, about the "disastrous situation" of Jews in the Soviet Union, about the "oppression and persecution" they are supposedly being subjected to. The working people of Jewish nationality wrathfully condemn the predatory policy of the ruling circles of Israel and give a resolute rebuff to the Zionist provocateurs.' What the book doesn't tell you is that in Stalin's anti-Jewish purges Birobidzhan's synagogue was closed and the speaking of Yiddish outlawed even here.

Km8198: Obluchye Облучье (●●●) (pop: 11,700) The town is just inside the border of the Jewish Autonomous Oblast. The tunnel just east of Obluchye was the first in the world to be bored through permafrost.

Km8234: Izvestkovaya Известковая The name means 'limestone' and there are large quarries in the area. The town sits at the junction of the Trans-Siberian and a 360km branch line to Novy Urgal (see p472) on the BAM railway. Much of this branch line was built by Japanese PoWs until their repatriation in 1949, and Japanese graves litter the area. The old part of town, with its rustic wooden buildings and household garden plots, is hidden in the trees to the west.

Km8306: Bira Бира (●, *Rossiya only*) The obelisk on the platform commemorates the good works of local philanthropist Nikolai Trofemovich and his wife. The railway runs beside the Bira River for about 100km and passes through hills rich with the ingredients of cement.

Km8351: Birobidzhan Биробиджан (●) (pop: 77,000) **[see pp305-7]**
Originally known as Tikhonkaya, the capital of the Jewish Autonomous Region was founded in 1928 on the Bira River. Once famous for the bright-red, self-propelled combine harvesters made at the Dalselmash factory and exported to Cuba, Mexico, Iraq and China, the town has been hard hit by the economic downturn.

Just east of Birobidzhan on the left (N) you pass the huge **Iyuan-Koran Memorial** which commemorates a fierce Russian Civil War battle on this site in 1922. Near the memorial are the mass graves of fallen Red Guards.

Km8480: Volochayevka 1 Волочаевка 1 This small station is just a junction for the Trans-Siberian and the 344km railway to Komsomolsk-na-Amure. Volochayevka is famous as the scene of a major battle during the Russian Civil War, which took place in temperatures as low as -35°C (there is a panoramic painting of the battle in Khabarovsk's Museum of Local Studies). The town itself is 9km from the station.

Km8512: Priamurskaya Приамурская This small town is just on the border of the Jewish Autonomous Region.

After crossing 3km of swamp and small streams you reach the 2.6km **bridge across the Amur River**, the longest bridge on the Trans-Siberian and completed in 1998. It's a combined rail and road bridge, with trains running beneath the road. Before it opened cars had to cross the Amur by ferry and trains used an old bridge, completed in 1916 and now dismantled. There is also a 7km tunnel under the Amur, built in 1937-42 for 'strategic reasons', and westbound trains sometimes use this. Khabarovsk stretches along the eastern bank of the river and the beaches here are packed with sunbathers on summer weekends. The main fishing port is 2.5km upstream.

Km8521: Khabarovsk 1 Хабаровск 1 (●●●) (pop: 690,000) **[see pp307-15]** Khabarovsk was founded in 1858 as a military outpost against the Chinese. Today it is the most pleasant of all the Russian Far East cities.

Outside the station there's an impressive statue of Yerofei Pavlovich Khabarov, the city's founder.

From Khabarovsk the line runs south to Vladivostok following the Ussuri River and the border with China. This region is a mixture of hilly country and wide flat valleys. Some 200km east of the line lies the Sikhote Alin Mountain Range, where most of the rivers you will cross have their source. In the south, firs and pines give way to a wide range of deciduous trees. There are good views across the plains to China.

Km8597: Here is the longest bridge on the Ussuri Railway. It crosses the Khor River, one of the Ussuri's widest tributaries, whose turbulent waters made its construction in 1897 extremely difficult.

Km8598: Verino Верино The town around the station is called **Pereyaslavka** (Переяславка) and was the site of a fierce Civil War battle. In front of the station there is a war memorial.

Km8621: Khor Хор The train crosses the Khor River again. The river here marks the southern boundary of the 46,000-hectare **Bolshoy-Khekhzirzky Sanctuary**.

The indigenous Udegeytsy people have a legend to explain why plants from both north and south Siberia are found here. Once two birds flying in opposite

directions collided in thick fog and dropped their loads. They'd been sent by the Good Spirit of the South and Good Spirit of the North to throw seeds on the desert plains and mountains respectively. Since then, southern wild grapevines wind around northern pine trees and the northern berry *klukva* grows side by side with the southern spiky palm *aralia,* with its metre-long leaves.

The vegetation changes considerably with elevation. At the foot of the mountains broadleaf species dominate. On the slopes are cedar, Amur velvet ash (cork is produced from its black bark) and Manchurian nut trees while on higher slopes angular pine and fir trees dominate.

Km8642: Vyazemskaya Вяземская (●●●) (pop: 16,200) This railway town was founded in 1895 and during the Russian Civil War there was fierce fighting around it. There are several memorials and a museum. To the west of the station is a plinthed **Ea series locomotive**. Some 20km to the south the countryside changes dramatically with forests of maple, alder, willow and elm.

Km8756: Bikin Бикин (●) According to the *1900 Guide to the Great Siberian Railway* the line crossed the river here and followed it south for 30km. The book states that 'this is one of the most picturesque parts of the line offering an alpine scenery. The cuttings made in basalt rocks seem to be protected by columns of cyclopean construction. Wide expanses lying amidst the cliffs are covered with a most various vegetation, shading numerous Chinese huts. The river is enlivened by the small boats of the Golds and other natives, moving swiftly on the water's surface.' Unfortunately the line does not follow exactly the same route now, instead traversing rolling hills and marshy land strewn with telegraph poles keeling over at drunken angles.

The railway crosses the Bikin River. About 200km upstream is Krasny Yar, the largest village of the indigenous **Udeghe**. Known as the Forest People for their lifestyle of fishing, hunting and gathering in the taiga, the Udeghe are facing the end of their way of life because of the voracious logging industry.

Between Bikin and Zvenyevoy is the administrative border between Khabarovsky Kray and Primorsky Kray. **Primorsky Kray** has a population of over two million people.

Km8890: Dalnerechensk 1 Дальнереченск 1 (●) (pop: 32,200) Founded by Cossacks in 1895, this town quickly became a timber centre thanks to the region's large pine and red cedar forests. A factory here is one of the few in

Decline of the Amur Tiger

Once the scourge of railway construction workers, the largest member of the cat family, also known as the Siberian tiger, is now just another zoological statistic dwindling towards extinction. The tigers' habitat once stretched as far west as Lake Baikal and to Beijing in the south but now only 350 or so Amur tigers are left in the wild in an area from Vladivostok north into the Sikhote Alin Range.

Large-scale forest clearance for timber sold to Japan and Korea forces tigers out of their territory. A male tiger can weigh up to 380kg (840lbs), almost twice the size of a lion, and requires about 400 sq km of hunting ground. A decline in their food source (deer and wild boar) has also reduced the population and forced remaining tigers to roam ever larger areas for prey.

In 1987 a train just outside Nakhodka was held up by a tiger that had strayed onto the tracks. An Amur tiger can be worth as much as US$10,000 in China, Korea and Taiwan for the medicinal value that parts of its body are believed to have, and for its skin. Poachers now slip across the Russian borders that are no longer tightly patrolled.

The animals are found in and around several nature reserves in this area: Kedrovaya Pad (near Vladivostok), Lazo and Sikhote Alin, but your chances of seeing a live Amur tiger here are close to zero. There are far more of them in zoos around the world than in the wild.

Russia which still produces wooden barrels for salted fish and seal blubber. The town has a memorial to the guards killed in the 1969 border conflict with the Chinese over Damansky Island in the Ussuri River. There were several skirmishes and each country claimed the Communist high ground as being the true Marxist revolutionary state. As both began preparing for nuclear confrontation a political solution was reached when Soviet premier Alexei Kosygin stopped in Beijing on his way home from the funeral of Ho Chi Minh. Following another round of talks in Moscow and Beijing in 1991, Damansky Island was given to China in its entirety.

Km8900: Muravyevo-Amurskaya / Lazo Муравьево-Амурская / Лазо This station is named after the explorer and governor of Eastern Siberia, Count Nikolai Muravyev-Amursky. It was formerly known as Lazo in honour of the Communist revolutionary S G Lazo (1894-1920), who was captured in 1920 by the Japanese when they invaded the Russian Far East, and executed at the station, allegedly by being thrown alive into a steam engine firebox. Two other revolutionaries, Lutsky and Sibirtsev, met a similar fate and a monument to all three stands in front of the station.

Km8941: Ruzhino Ружино (●●–●●●) A long stop for the *Rossiya* here.

Km8991: Shmakovka Шмаковка About 29km from the station is the mostly derelict **Shmakovsky Trinity-St Nicholas Monastery**, with a very curious history. Its land is now being fought over by two groups, both claiming to be its original owners. The Russian Orthodox Church maintains they built the monastery; the Russian military accept its religious past but claim that they constructed the monastery as a front for an espionage academy. It does seem more than a little coincidental that ex-army officer and Father-Superior

The Ussuri Railway (Km8531-9441)

The first plans for the Ussuri Line, as the section between Khabarovsk and Vladivostok is called, were made in 1875 and the foundation stone for the whole of the Trans-Siberian Railway was laid in Vladivostok by Tsarevich Nicholas in 1891. Priority was given to the Ussuri Line as it was seen as vital for ensuring that the strategic port of Vladivostok was not cut off by the Chinese. This was difficult territory for railway building. There was a severe shortage of labour. The local Goldi tribe, who at the time were happily existing in the Stone Age, were of no help, unable to grasp the concept of paid labour nor to understand the point of the work, never having seen a train. Prisoners recruited from the jails of Sakhalin Island were not as cooperative as convicts used on other sections of the Trans-Siberian, preferring an evening of robbery and murder in Vladivostok to the railway camps. The men here were plagued not only by vicious mosquitoes, like their fellow-workers on other sections of the line, but also by the man-eating tigers which roamed the thick forests beside the line. Siberian anthrax decimated the already small population of pack animals, and rails and equipment had to be shipped from Europe, taking up to two months to reach Vladivostok.

In spite of these difficulties the line was opened in 1897, 43 million roubles having been spent on its construction. It was double tracked in the 1930s and the branch line to Nakhodka was built after WWII.

Aleksei, who was commissioned to build the monastery, selected a site next to the remote Tikhmenevo telegraph station. This was no ordinary relay station but was classified a 'top secret military object' connected to Khabarovsk by an underground cable. And the monastery was certainly well equipped: there was even a printing press and photo lab. The military sanatorium here still operates today and the monastery is also home to 10 monks who are slowly rebuilding it.

Km9050: Spassk-Dalny Спасск-Дальний (•) (pop: 51,500) Alexander Solzhenitsyn was imprisoned in this town, where he helped build the large cement works that still operates here.

About 40km west is Lake Khanka which has a surface area of 4000 sq km but is nowhere more than 4m deep. The lake is famous for the lotus flower *eurea* which has giant buds and 2m wide leaves.

Km9109: Sibirtsevo Сибирцево (•) This area is the centre of an extremely fertile region where wheat, oats, soya beans and rice are grown. Because of labour shortages these are aerially sown and fertilised. The climate of the southern part of the Russian Far East makes most areas ideal for agriculture as the warm summer rains create a hothouse atmosphere.

A branch line runs from here through dairy-farming countryside to Lake Khanka. From Sibirtsevo south, the line winds down to Ussurisk.

Km9177: Ussurisk Уссурийск (•••) (pop: 154,500) The fertile area around Ussurisk has been inhabited for over 1000 years, first as the legendary kingdom of Bokhai and then by the Manchus. In the mid-19th century European emigrants began to settle here. At that time the town was called Nikolskoye, in honour of the Tsar.

The Vladivostok–Nakhodka Railway

Few travellers visit Nakhodka since the Japanese ferry which connects with Trans-Siberian trains now docks at Vladivostok, which is also the location of the only airport in the region. The journey of some 216km from Vladivostok to Tikhookeanskaya (Тихоокеанская), the port just south-west of Nakhodka, runs through Uglovaya (Угловая) at Km34, the mining and industrial city of Artem-Primorski (Артем-Приморский) at Km43, Novonezhino (Новонежино) at Km91, Partizansk (Партизанск) at Km170, past the vineyards of the Suchan River Valley to Nakhodka (Находка) at Km206, and on to the terminus at Tikhookeanskaya.

The town stands at the junction of the Ussuri and Chinese Eastern railways. When Tsarevich Nicholas visited in 1891 there were three wooden churches, a half-built stone cathedral and a population of 8000, many of them Chinese. Ussurisk is a now an agricultural and engineering centre, home of the Okean brand of refrigerator.

From Ussurisk there are branch lines to Harbin in China via the East Chinese Railway and to Pyongyang in North Korea. The scenery is very different from the Siberian taiga. The train winds through the hills in misty forests of deciduous trees (oak, elm, alder and maple) and across European-looking meadows filled with Friesian cows and willow trees.

Km9221: Amursky Zaliv Амурский Залив A branch line runs from here to the port of **Nakhodka**. Since most passenger ships now leave from Vladivostok there's little reason for visiting. For information on the line to Nakhodka, see box above.

Km9246: If you're heading east keep a lookout on the right (S) for your first glimpse of the Pacific Ocean.

Km9255: Uglovaya Угловая / Ugolnaya Уголная (•) The town here, called Trudovoye (Трудовое), sits at the northern edge of Uglovy Zaliv (Uglovy Bay). Pleasant beaches and clean water make it a popular swimming spot for Vladivostok's day trippers.

East of the station the railway travels down a peninsula named in honour of the famous Russian explorer, Count Nikolai Muravyev-Amursky.

Km9262: Sadgorod Садгород Near Sadgorod (which means 'garden city') was a station called Khilkovo, named in honour of Prince M I Khilkov, Minister of Ways of Communication in the Tsarist government and one of the main supporters of the Trans-Siberian. Khilkovo station has long since disappeared.

The accepted date for the start of construction of the Trans-Siberian Railway was 19 May 1891, although by that time an 18km section had already been laid from Vladivostok to Sadgorod. The Tsar's son Nicholas travelled up this line and formally inaugurated the project by tipping a barrow of ballast onto the embankment at Sadgorod, then returned by train to unveil a commemorative plaque at Vladivostok.

Km9281: Vtoraya Rechka Вторая Речка Vladivostok's main long-distance bus station is here (including buses for the airport).

Km9284: Pervaya Rechka Первая Речка According to the original 1880s plan for the Trans-Siberian this was to have been the railway's terminus, with a small branch line extending to Vladivostok. Despite the difficulties of building a multi-track railway along the steep shore, it was decided in the 1890s to extend the Trans-Siberian through to Vladivostok. Near Pervaya Rechka was a small settlement called Convicts' Hamlet, inhabited by exiled settlers who had completed their sentences.

Km9289: Vladivostok Владивосток (pop: 700,000) **[see pp316-26]**
The beginning or the end of your journey, and one of Russia's largest and most strategically important ports.

Trans-Mongolian route

The branch line to Mongolia and China leaves the main Trans-Siberian route at Zaudinsky, east of Ulan-Ude. From there it takes 5½ hours to cover the 250km to the Russia–Mongolia border. Between Ulan-Ude and the border the train travels through the heart of Buryatia, the Buryat Republic.

Note that the line turns predominantly southwards after Zaudinsky. For the entire Trans-Mongolian line we shall use (E) and (W) to show which side of the train points of interest are located. Thus if you're coming from Moscow (E) means the left side of the train and (W) the right.

Km5642: Ulan-Ude Улан-Удэ (pop: 386,000) (●●●) **[see pp294-300]**
The suburbs of Ulan-Ude extend for several kilometres and there are good views back to the city at Km5659 (W) as the train climbs high above the east bank of the Selenga River. The line follows the valley of the Selenga all the way to the Mongolian border. The scenery changes remarkably quickly to the rolling green hills which make excellent pasture for the area's many cattle. Passing through the little station of **Sayatun** (Km5677) the line crosses to the west bank of the river at Km5689-90 and continues to climb through **Ubukun** (Km5732).

Km5769: Zagustay Загустай (●) The station sits in the shadow of an ugly factory belching out thick smoke. About 6km from here is the mining town of **Gusinoozyorsk** (Гусиноозёрск), which grew from nothing to today's population of some 29,000 following the 1939 discovery of a huge coal basin.

Km5771-99: Goose Lake The line passes along the western shore of **Gusinoye Ozero** (Goose Lake). Until the Revolution the most important Buddhist *datsan* (lamasery) north of Ulaanbaatar was at **Selenginsk**, 20km to the south-east and overlooking the lake.

In 1887 George Kennan, while researching his book on Siberian prisons, arrived in Selenginsk and visited the datsan. 'We were tired of prisons and the exile system and had enough misery,' he wrote. Nevertheless he found Selenginsk 'a wretched little Buriat town'. At the datsan Kennan and his companions were

entertained by the Khamba Lama, the chief lama, who claimed through an interpreter that they were the first foreigners ever to visit his lamasery. They were treated to dinner and a special dance performance. The Khamba Lama had never heard of America, Kennan's native land; and, unaware that the earth was anything but flat, was nonplussed when Kennan explained that 'it lies nearly under our feet; and if we could go directly through the earth, this would be the shortest way to reach it'.

Today Selenginsk datsan is operating again.

Km5780: Gusinoye Ozero Гусиное Озеро (•) The line leaves the lake after this station and continues to climb from one valley to another, passing though **Selenduma** (Km5827) and still following the river.

Km5852 (W): Dzhida Джида (•) A large air-base, with bomb-proof shelters dug into hummocks in the ground.

Km5895: Naushki Наушки (•••++) At this **Russian border post** the train stops for at least three hours, usually for considerably longer; the official schedule says three hours and thirty-two minutes. Customs officials collect passports and visas, returning them (often to the carriage attendant) after about half an hour. It would be unwise to get off the train before you've got your passport back since guards may not let you back on the train without it.

The station tends to be crowded with black marketeers and some may get on the train and start selling roubles to travellers heading west; don't buy too

The old border town of Kyakhta

The border post for the railway is at the modern town of Naushki, but for the tea-caravans of old the crossing was near the large town of **Kyakhta**, 20km east of Naushki, and it is still the border crossing for cars and buses heading for Mongolia. In the 18th and 19th centuries this town, together with **Maimachen** on the Mongolian side of the border, formed one of the world's most important trading centres, based almost entirely on the tea trade. Great camel caravans brought the precious leaves here from Peking, across the Gobi Desert. Kyakhta was a bustling town of wealthy traders and tea-barons until the Trans-Siberian provided a cheaper way to move tea from China to European Russia. Maimachen is now called Altan Bulak.

On 24 June 1907 Prince Borghese and his team roared into town in their Itala and were entertained royally by local dignitaries. The morale of the tea-merchants had sunk with the recent decline in trade but was greatly boosted by the arrival of the car and they began making plans for their own motor-caravans.

An earlier visitor to these border towns was George Kennan, who attended a banquet in Maimachen where he was served dog-meat dumplings, cocks' heads in vinegar and fried lichen from birch trees, washed down by several bottles of French champagne. He was sick for the next two weeks.

In January 1920 Kyakhta witnessed a particularly appalling atrocity when the sadistic White Army General Semenov despatched 800 people suspected of being communists, using a different method of execution each day.

Today Kyakhta, with many crumbling old buildings and several vast churches hinting at prosperous times past, has a population of 18,000 and a large border-post garrison nearby.

The Trans-Mongolian Line

This route to China is an ancient one, followed for centuries by tea-caravans between Peking and Moscow. Travelling non-stop, foreigners and imperial messengers could manage the journey in 40 days of acute discomfort. This was the route of the 1907 Peking to Paris Rally, the great motor race that was won by the Italian Prince Borghese and journalist Luigi Barzini in their 40-horsepower Itala. Until the middle of the 20th century a rough track across the steppelands of northern Mongolia and the Gobi Desert in the south was the only route through this desolate country.

In 1940 a branch line was built between Ulan-Ude and the Mongolian border. After WWII work started on a line south from Naushki, and in 1949 this reached the Mongolian capital, Ulaanbaatar. The line between Ulaanbaatar and Beijing was begun in 1953 with a workforce of Russians, Mongolians and Chinese. By early 1956 it was completed and a regular rail service began between Ulan-Ude and Beijing.

many as the rate is unlikely to be favourable – and **watch your valuables** when these traders are around. There's a **bank** a long way down the platform in the Mongolia direction, signposted in English, but the exchange rate is poor. The surprisingly clean station lavatories are located in the building to the left of the station building and there's a little café in the back of the station building selling soft drinks and pastries.

Km5900: Russia–Mongolia border (●–●●●) The border, called **Dozorny** (Дозорный, meaning 'patrolled') on timetables, is marked by a menacing-looking electrified fence. The landscape is actually rather attractive, with the impressive Selenga River (prone to flooding in late summer) to the south and hills rising to the north.

MONGOLIA

Kilometre numbers below are based upon Mongolian kilometre posts. For approximate cumulative distances from Moscow see the timetables (p481).

Km21: Sühbaatar Сухбаатар (●●●++) (pop: 24,600) The customs and immigration process at this **Mongolian border town** is a rather tame affair for foreigners, although the baggage of local travellers may be thoroughly inspected. During the procedures a diesel engine is attached. The Mongolian dining-car, however, is not added until Ulaanbaatar. Black marketeers walk through the carriages offering to change your roubles for tughrik. Since Mongolian currency is almost impossible to come by outside the country, you might want to take them up on their offer, but don't forget to haggle.

The station building is an excellent example of whimsical Mongolian railway architecture. It's an incredible mélange of architectural styles: mock Gothic, Moghul and Modern topped with crenellations and painted what looks like lime green in the artificial light. You can get mutton soup at the upstairs café.

Situated at the confluence of the Selenga and Orhon rivers, Sühbaatar was founded in 1940 and named after the Mongolian revolutionary leader Damdinii

Sühbaatar (Sukhe Bator). It grew quickly, superseding the border town on the caravan route, Maimachen (now called Altan Bulak). Sühbaatar is now Mongolia's third largest industrial centre, producing matches, liquor and flour.

Km123: Darhan (Darkhan) Дархан (●●–●●●+) It takes about eight hours to cover the 380km between Sühbaatar and Ulaanbaatar. The train passes through the town of Darhan, capital of Selenga *aimak* (district). Darhan was founded in 1961 and is now the second most important industrial centre in Mongolia after Ulaanbaatar. It's a show town of planned urbanisation, and its population has increased from 1500 to over 69,000 since 1961. The main sources of employment are opencast mining, food production, construction, and the production of leather and sheepskin coats. The town is an important junction with a branch line that runs westwards to a big mining complex at **Erdenet**, and the port serves many villages along the Selenga and Orkhon rivers.

About 120km west of Darhan in the foothills of Mt Burenkhan is **Amarbayasgalant Monastery**. This vast 18th-century temple complex, which once housed 10,000 monks and drew pilgrims from many parts of Asia, was desecrated during an anti-religious movement in the 1930s but is now being restored with grants from the Mongolian government and UNESCO. Darhan is the closest train station to Amarbayasgalant. However, anyone interested in visiting the monastery would need a guide and their own vehicle, which can only be arranged easily from Ulaanbaatar.

If you'd been doing this part of the journey in the not too distant past before the railway was built, you would now be swaying back and forth in the saddle of a camel, one of many in the caravan you would have joined in Kyakhta. In the 1865 edition of his *Handbook for Russia, Poland and Finland*, Murray gives the following advice: 'It is customary for caravans to travel 16 hours a day and they come to a halt for cooking, eating and sleeping ... The Mongols are most trustworthy in their transactions, and the traveller may feel in perfect safety throughout the journey.' He also gives the following useful tips concerning local

Genghis Khan

For many decades the name of this famous Mongolian conqueror has been taboo in his home country. The Russians saw Genghis Khan as a brutal invader to be erased from the history books but with their influence rapidly fading there has been a sudden rise in Mongolian nationalism. Genghis Khan, founder of the 13th-century Mongolian Empire, is a hero once more, lending his name to the most luxurious hotel in Ulaanbaatar and also to a brand of vodka.

Along with his rehabilitation have come a number of interesting characters each claiming to be his legitimate descendant. One of the best publicised was Ganjuurijin Dschero Khan, who claimed to have been smuggled out of the country to escape the Communists when he was four years old. Mongolians were intrigued to meet him, although they didn't quite know what to make of his appearance. He arrived in a military tunic, decked out with medals inscribed 'Bazooka', 'Carbine', 'Paratroopers' and 'Special Forces', which he claimed to have won in Korea and Vietnam. Support for him waned after it became apparent that he didn't speak Mongolian.

currency: 'The use of money is as yet almost unknown in this part of the country, brick-tea cut up into slices being the token of value most recognised; but small brass buttons are highly prized.'

Mongolia

Mongolia is one of those countries that rarely makes headlines unless there's a dramatic change of leadership or policy. With just 2,791,000 people (almost a third of them below the age of 14) in an area the size of Western Europe or Alaska, it's a sparsely populated place. Mongolia is changing fast but the capital, Ulaanbaatar, is changing even faster. Nearly half the population lives in the capital, and it's estimated that over a third live below the poverty line.

Mongolia contains a surprising variety of terrain: a vast undulating plain in the east, the Gobi Desert to the south, and snow-capped mountains and extensive forests in the west. Most of the eastern plain is at an elevation of 1500m and the sun shines here for around 250 days of the year.

For many centuries the deserts and grasslands of Mongolia have been inhabited by nomadic herders living in felt tents (*yurts* or *ghers*). At certain times in world history they have come together under a powerful leader, the most famous being Genghis Khan and his grandson Kublai Khan in the 13th century. Kublai Khan introduced Tibetan Buddhism to the country although it was not until the early 17th century that most Mongolians were converted and Buddhism gained a strong grip on the country.

By the late 17th century control of Mongolia and its trade routes was in the hands of the Manchus. In 1911 the country became an independent monarchy, in effect a theocratic state since power lay with the 'Living Buddha', the chief representative of Buddhism in Mongolia, at Urga (now Ulaanbaatar). In 1921 a Communist government took power and, with considerable help from the Soviet Union, set out to modernise a country that was technologically in the Dark Ages.

In 1990 the constitution was amended to legalise opposition parties, although the first democratic elections were won by the communist Mongolian People's Revolutionary Party (MPRP). The 1996 presidential election was won by the MPRP's Natsagiin Bagabandi, but parliamentary elections the same year saw the formation of Mongolia's first non-communist government under the Democratic Union Coalition (DUC). After the DUC's pledge to introduce market reforms was stalled by former communists, the MPRP won the 2000 parliamentary election by a landslide, with Bagabandi re-elected the following year.

The 2004 parliamentary elections put in power a coalition government led by Prime Minister Tsakhiagiin Elbegdori, whose Democratic Party promised liberal market reform. President Nambaryn Enkhbayar of the MPRP was elected in 2005. Then in January 2006, crisis ensued when 10 cabinet members, all from the MPRP, stood down, citing the government's failure to curb corruption. Hundreds of protesters took to the freezing streets of Ulaanbaatar, accusing former communists in the MPRP of scuttling the government in an attempt to grab power. An uncertain truce was reached later that month when parliament approved Miyeegombyn Enkhbold, former mayor of Ulaanbaatar and head of the MPRP, as the new prime minister, though he stepped down in 2007. The MPRP, renamed the Mongolian People's Party in 2010, won the general elections in 2008, the current prime minister being Sukhbaataryn Batbold, while the presidential elections of May 2009 were won by former PM Tsakhiagiin Elbegdori of the Democratic Party.

The country is divided into 18 *aimaks* (districts). The railway line passes through three of these (Selenga, Tov and Dornogov).

Km232: Zuunhara (Dzhunkhara) Дзунхара (●●–●●●) There is a fairly long stop at this tiny station, though the town's only claim to fame is its alcohol factory.

Km381: Crossing wide open grasslands, dotted with the occasional cluster of yurts, the line begins to descend into the valley where Ulaanbaatar is situated. Looking south you catch the first glimpse (Km386) of ugly factories on the outskirts of the city (Km396).

Km404: Ulaanbaatar Улаан Баатар (●●●+) (pop: 862,800) **[see pp327-45]** (1350m/4430ft) The train spends half an hour at the Mongolian capital. Outside the locomotive shed on the eastern side of the line is a collection of **steam and diesel engines** including 2-6-2 S-116, T31-011 and T32-508 diesels, a 750mm gauge 0-8-0 469, and a 2-10-0 Ye-0266. They are beside the public road and fenced off but quite accessible. In the station building postcards (and weird Mongolian stamps which leave little room for a message on a card) can be purchased at the bar. Black marketeers may approach you to change money.

The dining-car is attached here if you're en route to Beijing and usually removed if you're Moscow-bound. For meals and souvenirs sold in the dining-car both Mongolian currency and US$ are accepted.

Km409: Ulaanbaatar extends this far west. At around Km425 the line starts to climb and for the next 50km, to Km470, snakes around giving good opportunities for photos along the train. There are good views over the rolling hills on both sides of the train.

Km507: Bagakangay Багакангай Here you can see an airfield (W) with camouflaged bunkers.

Km521: Manit Манит The blue station with its tower and weather-vane looks rather like a church.

Km560: Camels are occasionally to be seen roaming across the wide, rolling plain.

Km649: Choyr Чоыр (●●) (pop: 10,100) Just behind this pink and white wedding-cake of a station is a statue of the first Mongolian cosmonaut, VVT Ertvuntz. He's had the all-over silver paint treatment but still looks impressive. The Soviet airbase here has now closed.

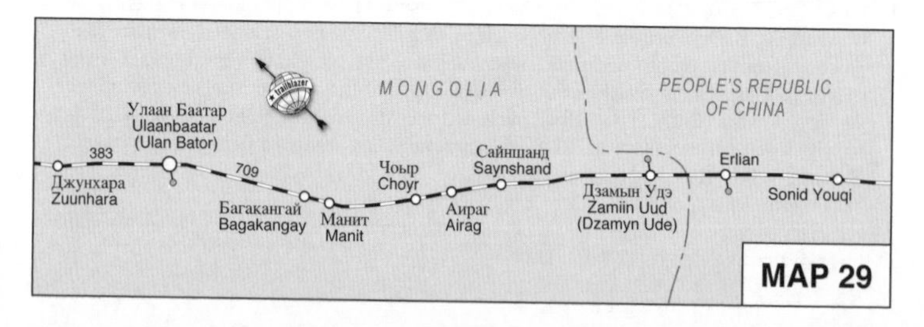

The Gobi Desert

This vast wilderness extends for 1000km north to south and 2400km west to east. Most of the part crossed by the railway is not desert of the sandy Saharan type but rolling grassy steppes. It is impressive for its emptiness: very few towns and just the occasional collection of yurts, herds of stocky Mongolian horses and small groups of camels or gazelles.

While it may not appear so, the Gobi is rich in wildlife although numbers of some species are rapidly dwindling. This is mainly the result of poaching and the destruction of habitat. There are large reserves of coal, copper, molybdenum, gold, uranium and other valuable exports. It's estimated that up to 10 billion tons of coal exist beneath the Gobi, and Japanese and Western companies are negotiating with Mongolia to extract it using strip mining techniques, which could seriously affect the delicate environmental balance. An American conservation group, Wildlife Conservation International, is helping the Mongolian Association for Conservation of Nature and Environment (MACNE) to monitor species at risk in the area. Among these are the 500 remaining wild Bactrian camels, the Gobi bear, the *kulan* (Asian wild ass) and Przewalski's wild horse, extinct in the wild although captive bred herds have now been reintroduced in parts of Mongolia.

Km733 (W): The pond here sometimes attracts groups of camels and antelope.

Km751: Airag Айраг The train doesn't usually stop at this small station, which is in the middle of nowhere and surrounded by scrap metal.

Km875 (E): There's a collection of old **steam locos** on display just to the west of Saynshand station.

Km876: Saynshand Сайншанд (●●●) (pop: 29,400) This is the largest town between the capital and Dzamyn Ude (Zamiin Uud) on the southern border. Main industries include food-processing and coal-mining. Vendors on the platform sell noodles, drinks, ice cream and paintings.

Km1113: Dzamyn Ude (Zamiin Uud) Дзамын Уде (●●●++) The station in this Mongolian border town looks like a supermarket at Christmas, with all its festive lights. There's a bank and a restaurant, both usually closed in the evening. Customs and immigration forms are collected. Customs officers inspect the luggage of Chinese and Mongolian travellers but don't seem too interested in others. This process may take 1½ hours. The scheduled stop is one hour. If it's dark you can try to spot the soldiers standing half concealed in the undergrowth by the tracks.

THE PEOPLE'S REPUBLIC OF CHINA

The kilometre numbers below show the distance to Beijing.

Km842: Erlian (Erlyan/Erenhot/Ereen) (●●●++) Chinese officials are obviously trying to outdo the evening show their Mongolian counterparts put on across the border, with a full-blown son-et-lumière. The *Vienna Waltz* blares from speakers to welcome the train and the station is decked out in red neon and

❑ Track and markers
Chinese trains ride on the left side of twin tracks (unlike right-hand-drive Russia). Kilometre markers come in a variety of sizes, usually like little grave-stones down at trackside, and there is some disagreement between them and the official kilometre locations on timetables etc. The book follows these markers where possible but for the last 70km of the journey they are not reliable, jumping at one point by 25km.

fairy lights. Chinese customs officials come on board here. If you're travelling to Beijing you must fill in health and baggage/currency declaration forms. Passports are collected.

Bogie-changing The big decision is whether to hang out at the station or stay on the train while the bogies are changed in a shed nearby. The train spends about 20 minutes at the platform and is then shunted off to the bogie-changing shed, so you have enough time to hit the loo in the station and stretch your legs, then get back on board before the train leaves for the bogie-changing. If you decide to stay at the station take something warm with you as it will be several hours before you're allowed on board again, after the train returns to the platform when the bogie-changing is complete. Most travellers stay on board the train until it gets to the shed where the bogies are changed. You could try to get out before the train is lifted off the ground and watch the bogie-changing from the ground, but the last time we made the trip this was forbidden and everyone had to stay on board once the train was in the shed. Still, it's interesting to watch the process from the window at the front or rear of your carriage.

The Chinese railway system operates on standard gauge (as do Europe and North America), which is 3½ inches narrower than the 5ft gauge in the former Soviet Union and Mongolia. Giant hydraulic lifts raise the carriages and the bogies are rolled out and replaced.

Back in the station you can change money at the bank (passport not necessary but you do need to know your passport number), or visit the Friendship Store (Chinese vodka, Chinese champagne, beer, noodles, sweets, fruit, tea, Ritz crackers and other snacks) and bar/restaurant (if open). Passports are returned and you depart shortly thereafter, the whole operation having taken anything from three to six hours.

Passing through towns with Mongolian names like **Sonid Youqi** and **Qahar Youyi Houqi**, you reach Jining in about five hours.

Km498: Jining (●●) The bulky white modernist station building is topped by a red flag. Beside it is an extensive goods yard full of working steam engines.

Travelling due south from Jining the train leaves the province of Inner Mongolia and enters Shanxi Province. This mountainous area was a great cultural and political centre over 1000 years ago. There are hills running parallel to the west and wide fields either side of the line. The train follows the course of a river which leads it into a valley and more rugged countryside after Fenezhen.

Km415: Fenezhen Between this drab town and Datong you cross the line of the **Great Wall of China** for the first time.

Km371: Datong (●●–●●●) (pop: 1,189,000) This sprawling city, founded as a military outpost by Han armies, stands in the centre of the coal-rich Datong Basin. Its major tourist attraction is **Yungang Grottoes**, a group of Buddhist cave temples in the foothills of Wuzhou Mountain (16km west of the city). These caves, dating back to 460AD, are richly decorated and renowned as one of China's three most impressive Buddhist complexes, the others being at Luoyang and Dunhuang.

If you're stopping off here, a visit to **Datong Locomotive Works** is an interesting and educational experience. This was one of the last places in the world where steam trains were made. In the 1980s they were turning them out at the rate of 240 locos per year, but the manufacture of the Class QJ 8WT/12WT 2-10-2 engine (133 tonnes; max speed 80kph) ceased in 1986 and the Class JS 2-8-2 (104 tonnes; max speed 85kph) in 1989; both are used for freight haulage and shunting work. The factory now produces parts for steam and diesel locomotives and has customers in many parts of the world. Tours are conducted twice a week and must be arranged through the Datong office of China International Travel Service (CITS).

At Datong the line swings eastwards to run parallel to the Great Wall, about 20km south of it as far as Zhangjiakou. About 100km west of Zhangjiakou you leave Shanxi and enter Hebei province. Between Km295 and Km272 (E) the Great Wall can be seen parallel to the line, on the hillside to the east. The best view is at Km284 (E).

Km193: Zhangjiakou (●●) (pop: 974,400) Founded 2000 years ago, this city used to be known by its Mongolian name, Kalgan (meaning gate or frontier). It stands at the point where the old caravan route between Peking and Russia crossed the Great Wall. Luigi Barzini described it as being like one of those 'cities one sees pictured upon Fu-kien tapestries: varied and picturesque, spreading over the bank of a wide snowy river'. He would not recognise it now; it has grown into an industrial city of just under a million people. Yet he might recall the stink he'd noticed as he drove into town on 14 June 1907, for tanning and leatherwork are still major industries here. About 15km south of the city a large factory pollutes the air with orange smoke.

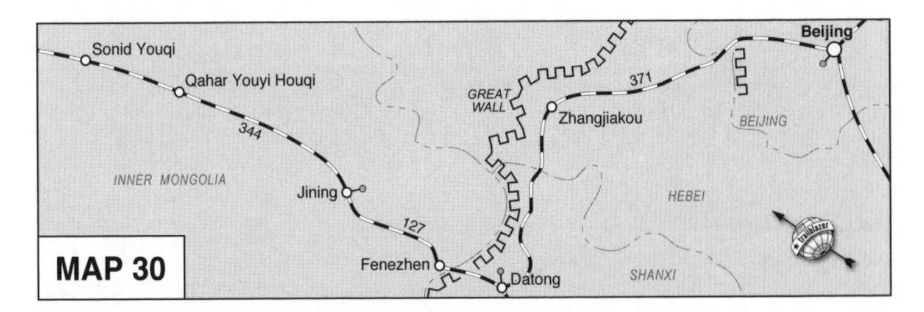

From around Km175 the scenery becomes hilly and more appealing as the line climbs the mountains north of Beijing. There are small valleys full of sunflowers, poplar groves and even apple orchards. At Km99 you cross the San Gan River, above which (E) can be seen a small isolated section of the Wall.

Km82-19: The train passes through some spectacular valley scenery, punctuated by several dozen tunnels, some several kilometres long, and bridges. In the gaps between tunnels you see mountains covered with greenery, villages and the river.

Km0: Beijing (pop: 22,011,000) **[see pp355-78]**
You arrive at the futuristic Beijing Zhan station of China's bustling capital.

Trans-Manchurian Route

For the entire Trans-Manchurian line we use (E) and (W) to show which side of the train points of interest are located. Thus if you're coming from Moscow (E) means the left side of the train, (W) the right.

Km6199: Chita Чита (●●●) **[see pp301-5]**
This is the last major Trans-Siberian station before Trans-Manchurian trains branch off to China. If you're coming from China turn to p434.

Km6293: Karymskaya Карымская (●●●) The branch line to Beijing via Manchuria leaves the main Trans-Siberian route at Tarskaya (formerly Kaidalovo), 12km east of Karymskaya. Leaving Tarskaya you cross the Ingoda River and head through open steppeland.

Some 20km further south you enter the Buryat Republic (Buryatia). The train makes brief stops at **Adrianovka** (Адриановка, Km6314), and **Mogoytuy** (Могойтуй, Km6370).

Km6444: Olovyannaya Оловянная (●–●●) The 120-flat apartment block by the station was constructed by Chinese labourers using Chinese materials. It was one of many barter deals between the Zabaikalsk (Russia) and Harbin (China) railways. Since 1988, when the first barter contract was signed, most

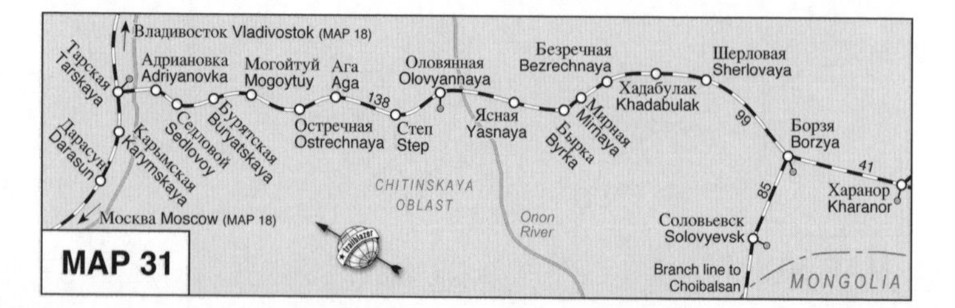

deals have involved Russia swapping fertilisers, old rails and railway wheel sets for Chinese food, clothes and shoes. As confidence has grown Harbin Railways has provided specialist services such as doctors of traditional Chinese medicine for railway staff at nearby Karpovka, uniforms for Zabaikalsk workers, and reconstruction specialists for Chita 2 and Petrovsky Zavod stations.

Leaving this picturesque town you cross the Onon River, which flows north of the main Trans-Siberian line, joining the Ingoda to form the Shilka. Genghis Khan (see box p454) was born on the banks of the muddy Onon in 1162. It might be wise to avoid taking photographs out of the windows here, as there were once said to be ballistic missile facilities in the town's outskirts.

Between Olovyannaya and Borzya you cross the Adun Chelon mountain range, passing through **Yasnaya** (Km6464) and **Byrka** (Km6477).

Km6486: Mirnaya Мирная At the western end of the station there are two small tanks whose guns appear to be aimed at the train.

Km6509: Khadabulak Хадабулак This small village is below a large hill-top telecommunications tower. There are long views northwards across the plains to the surrounding hills.

Km6543: Borzya Борзя (●●●) Founded in the 18th century, with the arrival of the railway this town became the transport hub for the south-east Zabaikalsk region. A branch line runs westwards all the way to the Mongolian city of Choibalsan. Black marketeers come aboard (if you're coming from Beijing) to tempt you with army uniforms, military watches and rabbit-fur hats. **Watch your valuables**.

There are several opportunities for photographs along the train as it snakes around the curves between Km6554 and Km6570, and especially Km6564-5 (W).

Km6590: Kharanor Харанор (●) There is a branch line from here to the east which runs to the military towns of Krasnokamensk and Priargunsk.

Km6609: Dauriya Даурия (●) This small village is surrounded by a marsh of red weeds.

Km6661: Zabaikalsk Забайкальск (●●●++) This town is within 1km of the border. Customs declarations and passports are checked on the train.

The train is shunted into the **bogie-changing sheds** at the southern end of the station. You can either stay at the station, remain in the carriage or get out and watch the bogie-changing. Taking photos in the sheds was once strictly prohibited but is now permitted. You'll have to stay at the station for 2-6 hours.

THE EAST CHINESE RAILWAY 1897-1901

The route

The original plans for the Great Siberian Railway had not included the laying of track across territories outside the Russian Empire. But when surveyors returned from the Shilka and Amur valleys in 1894 with the news that the Sretensk to Khabarovsk section of the line would prove extremely costly owing to the difficult terrain, the Siberian Railway Committee were obliged to consider an alternative. Their greedy eyes turned to the rich Chinese territory of Manchuria and they noted that a line straight across this province to Vladivostok would cut 513 *versts* (544km) off the journey to the port. Since the Chinese would obviously not be happy to have Russian railway lines extending into their territory, the Committee had to think up a scheme to win Peking over to the idea.

The Manchurian Deal

It did not take wily Russian diplomats long to work out a deal the Chinese were forced to accept. After the 1894 Sino-Japanese war the victorious Japanese concocted a peace treaty that included the payment of a heavy indemnity by the Chinese. Knowing that China was unable to pay, the Russians offered them a generous loan in exchange for the right to build and operate a railway across Manchuria. They were granted an 80-year lease on a thin strip of land 1400km long and the project was to be disguised as a Chinese enterprise financed through the Russo-Chinese Bank. The rest of the world suspected Russia of flagrant imperialism, and Russia proved them right in 1897 by annexing Port Arthur.

Work begins

Construction began in 1897 but it soon became obvious that the project faced greater problems than any that had arisen during the building of other sections. There were difficult conditions (the Greater Khingan Mountains had to be crossed); there were not enough labourers; interpreters were needed to translate the orders of Russian foremen for Chinese coolies; and the area through which the route passed was thick with *hunghutzes* (bandits). It was necessary to bring in a force of 5000 policemen to protect the workers. After the Boxer (anti-foreigner) riots began in the late 1890s it became necessary to protect the rails too, for when they were not murdering missionaries the Boxers tore up track and derailed trains.

Set-backs

After the annexation of Port Arthur another Manchurian line was begun – from Harbin south through Mukden (now Shenyang) to Dalni (now Dalian) and Port Arthur (now Lushun). Work was disrupted in 1899 by the outbreak of bubonic plague, although despite Chinese refusal to co-operate with quarantine procedures, only 1400 people died out of the total workforce of 200,000. In May 1900 Boxers destroyed 200km of track and besieged Harbin. The Russians sent in a peace-keeping force of 200,000 men but by the time the rebellion had been put down, one third of the railway had been destroyed. Despite these setbacks the line was completed in 1901. It would have been far more economical to build the Amur line from Sretensk to Khabarovsk, for in the end the East Chinese Railway cost the government more than the total spent on the entire Trans-Siberian track on Russian soil.

There's a **restaurant** across the bridge and to the left of the station with a limited menu and of dubious quality and a **bank** upstairs with predictably poor rates. The **lavatories** are bearable if you hold your breath.

THE PEOPLE'S REPUBLIC OF CHINA

Note that kilometre markers between the border and Harbin show the distance to Harbin, while those further on show the distance to Beijing.

Km935 (Bei:2323): Manzhouli (●●●++) (pop: 150,000) At this Chinese border town (once known as Manchuria Station) you must fill out currency and health declarations if you're arriving in China or, if you're leaving, fill out a departure card and present your currency declaration form. The train spends 1-3 hours here so you can visit the **bank** and the **Friendship Store** (tins of good quality peanuts, Chinese vodka, beer and other snacks). Puffing **steam locomotives** shunt carriages around the yard, a particularly impressive sight if you arrive in the early hours of a freezing winter morning.

Leaving the station you pass **Lake Dalai Nor** and roll across empty steppeland. You may see mounted herders, as did Michael Myres Shoemaker in 1902 when he passed through on his journey to Peking. Of the first Chinese person he saw, he wrote (in *The Great Siberian Railway from St Petersburg to Pekin*) 'these northern Celestials appear on the whole friendly, and are flying around in all directions swathed in furs, and mounted on shaggy horses.' European newspapers of the time had been filled with reports of atrocities committed by the xenophobic Boxer sect in Manchuria, hence his surprise at the apparent friendliness of the local population.

Km749 (Bei:2137): Hailar (●●) Rolling steppes continue from here to Haiman. If you'd been travelling in 1914 you would have the latest edition of Baedeker's *Russia with Teheran, Port Arthur and Peking* with you and would therefore be looking out for 'the fortified station buildings (sometimes adorned with apes, dragons and other Chinese ornaments), the Chinese carts with their two high wheels and the camels at pasture'. Modern Hailar is an unexotic city of 170,200 people, the economic centre of the region. Local architecture is a blend of Russian and Mongolian, including log cabins, some with yurt-style roofs. The average temperature in this area in January is a cool minus 27°C.

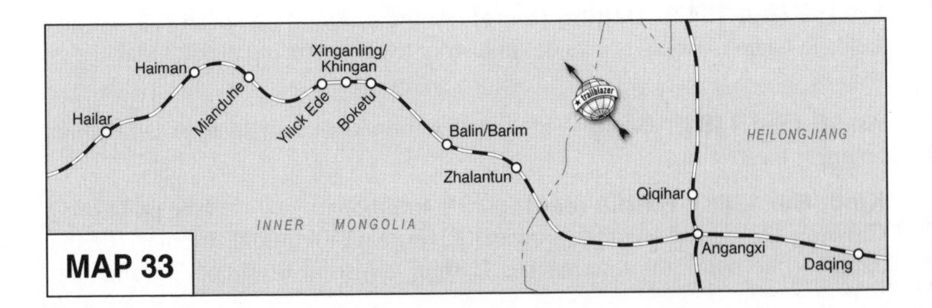

Km674 (Bei:2062): Haiman Also known as Yakoshih, this town stands near the foot of the Great Khingan Range which extends from the Russian border southwards into Inner Mongolia. The line begins to rise into the foothills of the range.

Km634 (Bei:2022): Mianduhe The train continues to climb the gently rising gradient.

Km564 (Bei:1952): Xinganling/Khingan (958m/3140ft) This station stands at the **highest point on the Trans-Manchurian line**. The 3km tunnel built here in 1901-2 was a considerable engineering achievement since most of the drilling was done during the winter, with shift workers labouring day and night.

Km539 (Bei:1927): Boketu (●●) The line winds down partly wooded slopes to the town of **Balin/Barim** (Bei: 1866) and continues over the plains, leaving Inner Mongolia and crossing into Heilongjiang Province.

Km270 (Bei:1658): Angangxi (●●–●●●) (pop: 67,900) About 40km southwards is the ancient city of **Qiqihar** (Tsitsikar). By the time he reached this point Michael Myres Shoemaker had become bored with watching 'Celestials' from the windows of the train and was tired and hungry. He writes 'In Tsitsikar, at a wretched little mud hut, we find some hot soup and a chop, also some coffee, all of which, after our days in lunch baskets, taste very pleasant.'

Over lunch they may well have discussed the nearby **Field of Death** for which the city was notorious. In this open area on the edge of Qiqihar public executions were regularly performed. Most of the criminals decapitated before the crowds were *hunghutzes* (bandits). Since the Chinese believed that entry to Heaven was denied to mortals who were missing parts of their bodies, their heads had to be sewn back in place before a decent burial could take place. However, so as not to lower the moral tone of Paradise, the government ordered that the heads be sewn on backwards.

Some 20km east of Angangxi is a large area of marshland, part of which has been designated a nature reserve. The marsh attracts a wide variety of waterfowl since it is on migration routes from the Arctic and Siberia down to southern Asia. The **Zhalong Nature Reserve**, 20km north of here, is best known for its cranes. Several of these (including the Siberian Crane) are now listed as endangered species.

Km159 (Bei:1547): Daqing (●–●●) At the centre of one of the largest oilfields in China, Daqing is a model industrial town producing plastics and gas as well as oil.

Km96 (Bei:1484): Song This small station is in an island of cultivation amongst the swamps.

Km0 (Bei:1388): Harbin (●●●) (pop: 9.4 million) **[see pp349-55]**
Crossing the wide Songhua (Sungari) River, a 1840km-long tributary of the Amur to the north, the line reaches Harbin, industrial centre of Heilongjiang

Province. It was a small fishing village until the mid 1890s when the Russians made it the headquarters of their railway building operations in Manchuria.

After Michael Myres Shoemaker visited the town in 1902 he wrote: 'The state of society seems even worse at this military post of Harbin than in Irkutsk. There were seven throats cut last night, and now, as a member of the Russo-Chinese Bank expressed it, the town hopes for a quiet season.' The *Imperial Japanese Railways Guide to East Asia* (1913) recommended 'the excellent bread and butter, which are indeed the pride of Harbin' and warned travellers away from the numerous opium dens. After the Revolution, White Russian refugees poured into the town and Russian influence on the place continued. Today there are few onion-domes or spires to be seen in what is just another Chinese city: the Russian population is now small.

The city's main tourist attraction is its **Ice Lantern Festival** (see box p352) held in January and early February each year.

At the station you can get good views along the track of the numerous steam locos, from the bridges between the platforms.

Between Harbin and Changchun you cross an immense cultivated plain, leaving Heilongjiang and entering Jilin Province.

Km1260: The line crosses a wide tributary of the Songhua River. There are numerous small lakes in the area.

Km1146: Changchun (•) (pop: 2.78 million) Changchun is the provincial capital. The station is worth a stroll, with white concrete sculptures of 'The Graces' and lots to buy from snack sellers on the platform.

Back in 1913 the *Imperial Japanese Government Railways Guide to East Asia* was reminding its readers (all of whom would have had to change at this large junction) about 'the need of adjusting their watches – the Russian railway-time being 23 minutes earlier than the Japanese'. From 1933 to 1945 Changchun was the centre of the Japanese puppet-state of Manchukuo.

It has now grown into an industrial metropolis of almost three million people. Local industries include a car factory where Red Flag limousines are assembled (guided tours possible), a rail-carriage factory and film studios. If you do get off here, local delicacies include antler broth, hedgehog hydnum stewed with orchid, and a north-eastern speciality, *qimian*, which is the nose of a moose.

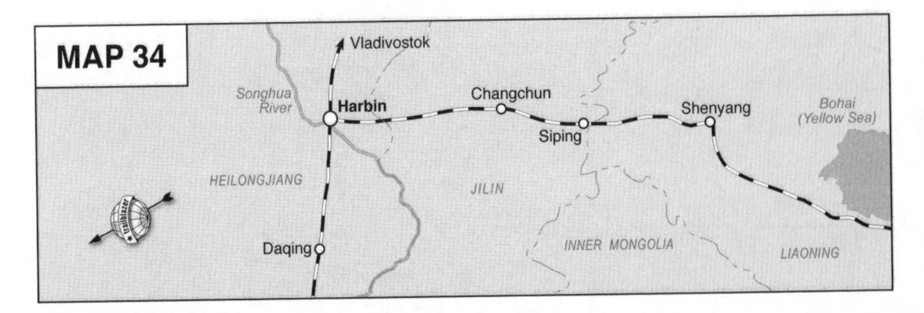

But Changchun is probably more popular with rail enthusiasts than with epicureans. RM Pacifics and QJ 2-10-2s are to be seen here and on the Changchun–Jilin line.

Km1030: Siping (•) This unattractive town does have lots of working steam locos in the station. About 10km further south the train crosses the provincial border into Liaoning Province.

Km841: Shenyang (•••) (pop: 6.73 million) An industrial giant founded 2000 years ago during the Western Han dynasty (206BC-AD24). At different times during its long history the city has been controlled by Manchus (who named it Mukden), Russians, Japanese and the Kuomintang, until it was finally taken over by Chinese communists in 1948. Shenyang is now one of the largest industrial centres in the People's Republic, but between the factories there are several interesting places to visit, including a small version of Beijing's **Imperial Palace**. There is also a **railway museum** beside the Sujiatun shed. The station has a green dome and the square outside it is dominated by a tank on a pedestal.

Km599: Jinzhou (•) From here the line runs down almost to the coast, which it follows south-west for the next 300km, crossing into Hebei Province. Beijing is just under eight hours from here.

Km415: Shanhaiguan (••) As you approach the town from the north, you pass through the **Great Wall** – at its most eastern point. This end of the Wanlichangcheng (Ten Thousand Li Long Wall) has been partially done up for the tourists. Although the views here are not as spectacular as at Badaling (70km north of Beijing, see p378), the restoration at Shanhaiguan has been carried out more sympathetically – it is restoration rather than reconstruction. The large double-roofed tower houses an interesting museum.

Km262: Tangshan (•) (pop: 1,787,000) This was the epicentre of an earthquake which demolished this industrial town on 28 July 1976. The official death toll stands at 150,000 but may have been as high as 750,000. Many of the factories have been rebuilt and the town is once again producing consumer goods. Locomotives are built here at the Tangshan Works, which until 1991 produced the SY class 2-8-2 steam engine.

Km133: Tianjin/Tientsin (••) (pop: 10.2 million) This is one of China's largest ports. In the mid-19th century the British and French marched on the

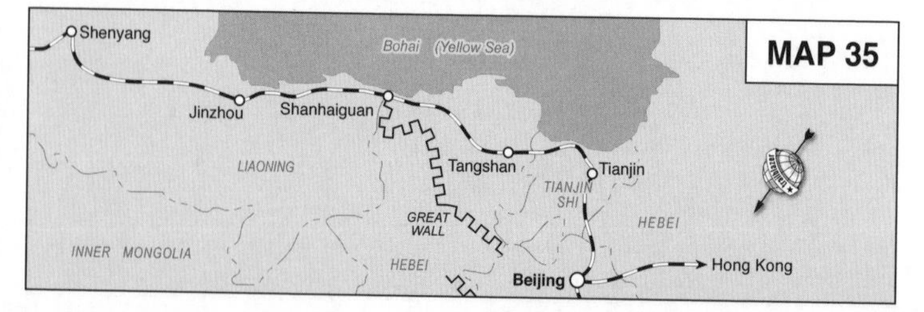

capital and 'negotiated' the Treaty of Peking which opened Tianjin to foreign trade. Concessions were granted to foreign powers just as they were in Shanghai. Britain, France, Austria, Germany, Italy, Belgium, Russia, Japan and the United States each controlled different parts of the city, which accounts for the amazing variety of architectural styles to be found here.

Chinese resentment at the foreign presence boiled over in 1870 in an incident that came to be known as the **Tientsin Massacre**, during which ten nuns, two priests and a French official were murdered. To save female babies from being killed by their parents (the Chinese have always considered it far more important to have sons than daughters) the nuns had been giving money for them. This had led more gullible members of the community to believe rumours that the nuns were eating the children or grinding up their bones for patent medicines.

One of several ferry services between China and Japan (see box p35) terminates at Tianjin.

Km0: Beijing The beginning or the end? You are now 9001km from Moscow. (See pp355-78).

The Baikal Amur Mainline (BAM)

Note: Local time is now Moscow Time + 5 hours.

Km0: Tayshet Тайшет (●●●+) (see p420) This town, population 70,000, straddles the BAM/Trans-Siberian junction and marks the start of the BAM.

Km292: Anzyobi Анзёби (●) The first of the three **Bratsk** stations. This is where you'd change trains for the Tsentralny area.

Km325: Padunskiye Porogi Падунские Пороги (●●) The second of the three Bratsk stations. This is where you'd change for a suburban train to the Energetik part of town.

Km330: The Bratsk dam At this point, the railway line crosses over the top of the gigantic dam, with great views of the 'Bratsk Sea'.

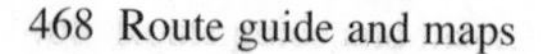

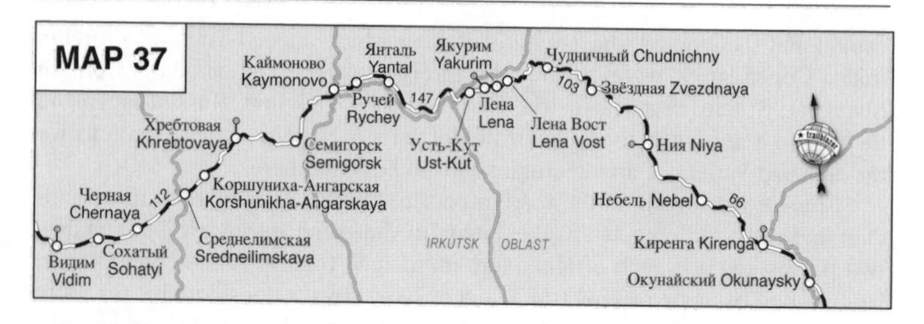

Km339: Gidrostroitel Гидростроитель (●) The final Bratsk stop serves the quiet residential area of Gidrostroitel.

Km554: Korshunikha-Angarskaya Коршуниха-Ангарская (●●●) Named after the Korshunikha creek above the town, this station serves the charmless iron-ore processing town of Zheleznogorsk-Ilimsky, founded in 1948.

Km575: Khrebtovaya Хребтовая (●) This is the junction of the BAM and the Ust-Ilimsk line.

Km715: Ust-Kut Усть-Кут One of the most vibrant little towns along the BAM.

Km722: Lena Лена (●●●+) If you're looking to take a hydrofoil up River Lena to Yakutsk, the Ust-Kut boats to the Republic of Sakha actually depart from Osetrovo River Passenger Station near Lena.

Km931: Ulkan Улькан (●) Near the town of Ulkan there are three villages whose entire male population perished at the front during WWII, turning them into ghost towns. At the eastern end of the Ulkan platform, there's a metallic Lenin relief.

Km983: Kunerma Кунерма (●) After this stop the track does a 180-degree loop before chugging along an alpine valley with mountain views on both sides and plunging into a 6km-long Daban tunnel.

Km1029: Goudzhekit Гоуджекит (●) (see p384) Some trains stop at this attractive little spot with a mini-spa built around the hot spring.

Km1064: Severobaikalsk Северобаикальск (●●●+) (see pp381-3) This town is the gateway to the beautiful northern shore of Lake Baikal and the northern sections of the Great Baikal Trail (see box p284).

Km1104: Nizhneangarsk Нижнеангарск (●) (see pp383-4) This busy fishing village makes a good day trip from Severobaikalsk.

Km1109: Nizhneangarsk II Нижнеангарск II Here you pass the little airport from which there are seasonal flights to Irkutsk.

Km1120: Kholodny Холодный A twenty-minute walk from the station is an indigenous Evenk village which is trying to keep its traditions and culture alive. Only suburban trains stop here.

Km1141: Kichera Кичера (●) You may notice the Baltic influences in the architecture of this small town as it was built by the Estonian Young Communist Party.

Km1171: Dzelinda Дзелинда (see p384) One of the newest stations along the BAM, this one was built in 1996 to accommodate the tiny hot springs spa 2km into the forest.

Km1242: Anamakit Анамакит Between here and Novy Uoyan, the railway crosses over the Upper Angara River – the largest river to flow into northern Lake Baikal.

Km1257: Novy Uoyan Новый Уоян (●●●) Built in 1976 as a support base for the railway, this small town reflects Latvian influence in its architecture. Here you're often greeted by locals selling delicious homemade food.

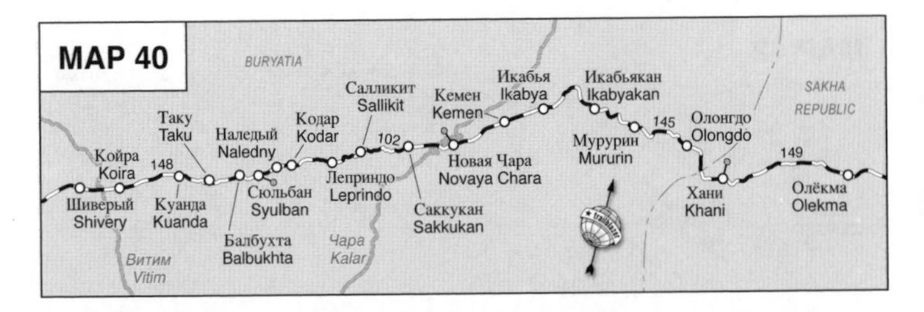

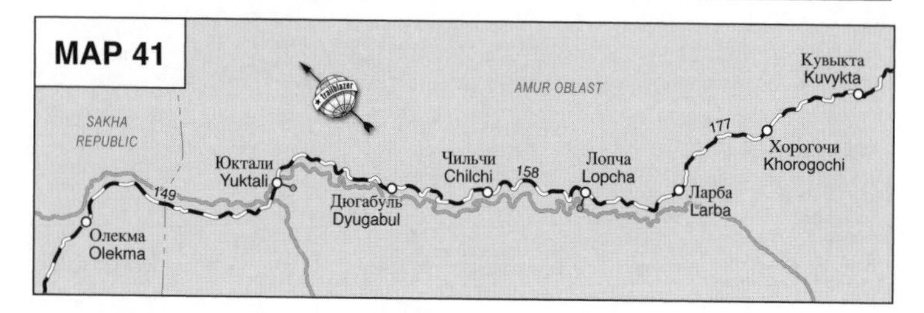

Km1330: Kyukhelbeckerskaya Кюхельбекерская (•) This station is named after the Decembrist Wilhelm Kyukhelbecker, a friend of Pushkin's who was exiled to Siberia where he eventually died. From here, the railway goes up a series of steep valleys, climbing to 1200m above sea level.

Km1400: Severomuisky Tunnel Северомуйский тоннель Here you hit the 15.3km-long tunnel – the longest in Russia – which was only completed in 2004 due to permafrost-related difficulties in the Severomuisk mountain range. The tunnel has replaced more than 50km of track which was vulnerable to avalanches.

Km1422: Ulgi Ульги This stop is named after the Buryat term for epic folk songs, in which valiant heroes battle against the forces of evil.

Km1474: Taksimo Таксимо (•••+) This little town was the refuge of White Army soldiers, priests and others who fled from the Communists after the 1917 revolution. You can stock up on limited provisions here and check out the BAM pioneer monument.

Km1559: Kuanda Куанда (••) In September 1984 this little town hosted the celebration of the BAM's completion, though the golden spike that joins the east and west sections of the BAM was actually hammered in around 15km to the east, at **Balbukhta** (Балбухта).

Km1734: Novaya Chara Новая Чара (•••) This is a large-ish town of around 10,000 inhabitants, the majority of whom work for the railway.

Km1755: Kemen Кемен The only noteworthy thing about this station is its proximity to the deepest permafrost on the BAM – 600 metres.

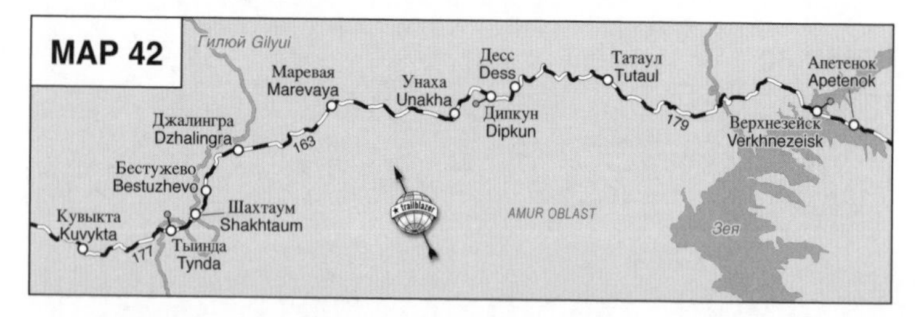

Km1851: Olongdo Олонгдо Between here and Khani lies the highest point along the BAM – 1300m above sea level.

Km1879: Khani Хани (●●●+) This is the only BAM town that's part of the Republic of Sakha.

Km2364: Tynda Тында (●●●+) (see pp387-9) One of the largest BAM towns, Tynda straddles the junction of the BAM and Little BAM that connects it to the Trans-Siberian railway at Bamovskaya. Heading north from Tynda is the AYaM, still not completed, though you can brave an arduous 24-hour bus or taxi journey up from Neryungri to **Yakutsk** (see pp385-7). Check out the train station's 1970s architecture and the freight locomotive on the plinth in front of the station.

Km2391: Bestuzhevo Бестужево (●) This station is named after a Decembrist family, where all three sons were originally sentenced to death for their participation in the 1825 anti-tsar uprising, though their sentence was eventually commuted to exile.

Km2707: Verkhnezeisk Верхнезейск (●●●+) An average BAM town with little to see.

Km3033: Fevralsk Февральск (●●●+) Here the railway line crosses the gold-bearing Selemdzha river. This little town has had problems with its infrastructure due to its unfortunate location on top of a swamp.

Km3305: Bureinsky Буреинский (●) Here the line crosses the Bureya river. Building the metal bridge across this river required remarkable sacrifices

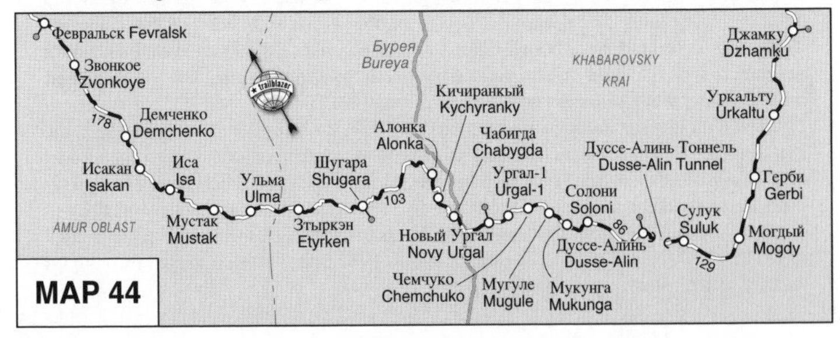

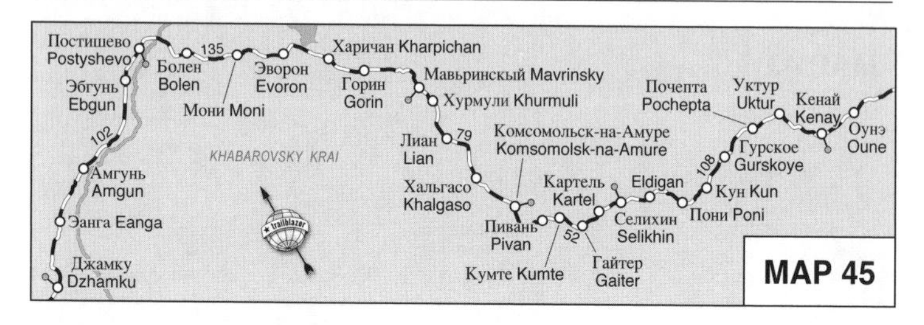

on the part of the builders, who worked in temperatures of -45°C to complete it in record time in April 1975.

Km3315: Novy Urgal Новый Ургал (●●●+) At the coal-mining town of Novy Urgal, you can switch to the north–south line and rejoin the Trans-Siberian route for a shorter trip to Khabarovsk via Birobidzhan.

Km3403: Dusse-Alin Дуссе-Алин (●) This station is at the end of the 2km-long Dusse-Alin tunnel that has a particularly tragic history (see box below).

Km3581: Amgun Амгунь (●) Between here and the station of Duki 50km away, in 1989 some hikers stumbled across the wreckage of the American-built DC-3 that crashed in this area on October 4, 1938. Its tail end is now a monument in Komsomolsk-na-Amure.

Km3633: Postyshevo Постышево (●●●) This is the station for the town of Berezovy, which is right near the Amgun river, considered to be one of the best fishing spots in eastern Siberia, rich in salmon, grayling and taimen.

The Dusse-Alin Tunnel

The Gulag prisoners who worked on the Dusse-Alin tunnel from 1939 onwards lived in atrocious conditions and scores died from starvation and overwork. When the chief engineer, Vasili Konserov, was shot in the back by the guard commander following a dispute, his death was deemed an 'accident' and he was buried with full honours as he'd previously received the Order of Lenin for his role in the construction of the Belomorski-Baltiiski Canal. Renowned Moscow Metro engineer Ratsbaum was recruited in Konserov's place to finish the job. Besides the atrocious working conditions, one of the problems faced by Ratsbaum was the lack of survey equipment, meaning that the tunnel had to be dug from both sides of the mountain using line-of-sight alone. Though there was a good chance that the two halves would not meet, which would have resulted in death by firing squad for the engineer, miraculously, they did meet and were only 20cm out!

Even though the tunnel was completed in 1950, it was only put to use in 1982, the work on the railway between here and Komsomolsk-na-Amure having been abandoned after Stalin's death. When work re-commenced in 1974, the soldiers unearthed grisly finds at the workers' camp here, including frozen corpses of the previous workers.

Backblast from aircraft jet engines had to be used to melt the 32,000 cubic metres of ice that had formed within the tunnel, and in 1982, the first train passed through on its way to Komsomolsk-na-Amure.

Km3837: Komsomolsk-na-Amure Комсомольск-на-Амуре (●●●+) (see pp389-91) This is a major industrial city, founded in 1932 and situated on the Amur river. From here, a direct railway line runs south to Khabarovsk and Vladivostok.

Km3853: Amur Bridge Straddling the Amur river, this bridge is the longest of all of the BAM's bridges at 1437 metres. The first train crossed in 1975.

Km3888: Selikhin Селихин (●●) From this large town, the railway line was supposed to run north to Cape Lazarev, where it would link the mainland to Sakhalin Island via a 9km tunnel under the strait, though this project was shelved after Stalin's death.

Km4050: Vysokogornaya Высокогорная (●●●+) Much of this town was built by Japanese PoWs, as a PoW camp was located here. The station building here resembles a Japanese temple and Japanese make pilgrimages here to visit the family graves.

Km4097: Kenada Кенада (●●) Near this stop lies the Dzigdasi village, the site of a love story between a Japanese PoW called Umoda and Marsha, a young Russian woman in exile from her native Kazakhstan. The PoW was repatriated in 1947 and never knew that Marsha gave birth to his son, who continues the search for his father.

Km4137: Tumnin Тумнин (●●) Tumnin's claim to fame is that the surrounding area is allegedly the home of the Taiga Yeti, with sightings of the creature reported on a fairly regular basis.

Km4283: Vanino Ванино (●●●) (see pp391-2) A minor port these days, Vanino originally acted as the transportation point for Gulag prisoners who were sent to the north.

Km4291: Sovetskaya Gavan-sortirovka Советская Гавань-сортировка This is the final stop for long-distance trains, though you can catch a local train from here to Sovetskaya Gavan-Gorod.

Km4309: Sovetskaya Gavan-gorod Советская Гавань-город The end of the line. Literally. This station is in the middle of nowhere and you need to catch a bus to the town proper (see p392).

APPENDIX A: ALTERNATIVE ROUTE

For travellers visiting Sergiev Posad, Rostov-Yaroslavski and Yaroslavl, the more northern rail route avoiding Nizhny Novgorod is included here. The routes follow the same track as far as Fryazevo (Km54). After Yaroslavl this route joins the main Trans-Siberian route at Kotelnich (Km870).

Km0: Moscow Москва Yaroslavsky Station Ярославский вокзал
See pp395-6 for the route as far as Fryazevo (Km54).

Km57: Abramtsevo Абрамцево About 3km from the station is the Abramtsevo estate, one of the most important centres of Russian culture in the second half of the 19th century.

Km59: Khotkovo Хотьково This town (pop: 22,000) has a well-preserved historic section on the high bank of the Pazha River which flows through its centre.

Km73 (N): Sergiev Posad Сергиев Посад **[See pp195-9]**
Have your camera ready for the stunning blue and gold domes of the cathedrals.

Km112: Aleksandrov Александров This little-known town was, for nearly two decades in the 16th century, the real capital of Russia. From 1564 to 1581 Ivan the Terrible lived here and directly ruled the half of the country which he called the *oprichnina,* having abandoned the rest to the authority of the *boyars* (nobles) and monasteries. The oprichnina was policed by *oprichniki*, mostly low-class thugs, mercenaries and foreign adventurers. Ivan the Terrible certainly deserved his soubriquet. In his dungeons here he devised and supervised some of the cruellest tortures imaginable.

Km145: Berendeyevo Берендеево There is a 21km branch line to the west from here to the Golden Ring town of Pereslavl-Zalesski.

Km200: Petrovsk Петровск About 15km east of Petrovsk you will see **Lake Nero** on the right. Rostov-Yaroslavski sits on its western shore.

Km224: Rostov-Yaroslavski Ростов-Ярославский (pop: 34,800) **[See pp200-4]**
Attractively located by Lake Nero, this is one of the most interesting Golden Ring cities.

Km240 (N): Amidst the fields and quite close to the track is a sadly neglected but **picturesque church** with five dilapidated domes and a tower.

Km284: Yaroslavl Ярославль (••) (pop: 608,600) **[See pp205-11]**
Yaroslavl was founded in 1010 by the Christian king Yaroslavl the Wise. It grew quickly into an important trading centre on the Volga shipping route. Many of the ancient cathedrals still stand in spite of the heavy fighting that went on here during the Civil War.

About five minutes after entering Yaroslavl's outskirts you pass the suburban station of **Kotorosl** (Которосль) and on the left you can see the **Church of St Peter and St Paul**.

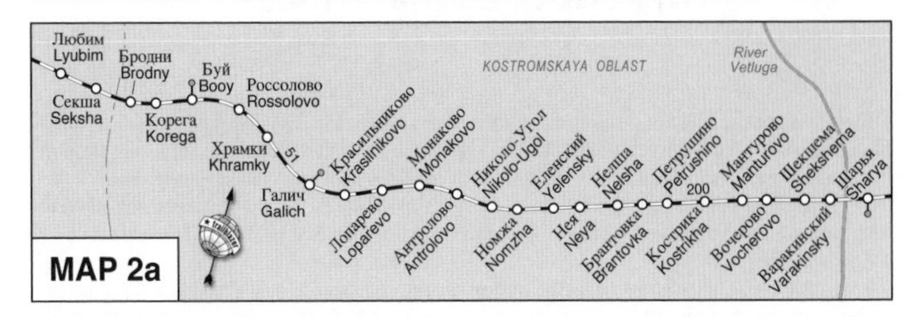

Km289: Volga River About five minutes after leaving the station, the train changes direction from north to east and crosses the mighty **Volga River**, which is about 1km wide here. In times gone by Russians held this river in such esteem that passengers would stand and take off their hats to Mother Volga as the train rattled onto the first spans of the long bridge. Rising in the Valdai hills, Europe's longest river meanders 3700km down to the Caspian Sea.

Km356: Danilov Данилов (•••) (pop: 19,000) There are often many platform traders here.

Km394: Lyubim Любим Lyubim's population is decreasing – down at least 10% since 1980 to about 6000 – typical of the Russia-wide migration trend from villages to large cities.

Km 420-1266 TIME ZONE MT + 1

Km450: Booy Буй (••) (pop: 28,700) There is nothing of interest in this industrial town specialising in cheese, flax and mineral fertilisers. Rotting silt (sapropel) is extracted from the lake and dried to be used as fuel or made into fertiliser.

Km501: Galich Галич After the station, on the right (S), you pass **Paisiev Monastery**.

Km651: Manturovo Мантурово (pop: 21,100) After leaving this industrial and forestry town the train crosses the Unzha River (Km654).

Km698: Sharya Шарья (••) (pop: 26,400) Some steam locos are stored here (L and Er classes) but numbers are dwindling. This is the region's biggest timber centre.

Km818: Svecha Свеча Roughly mid-way between Sharya and Svecha you enter **Kirovskaya Oblast**. Most of this region's 120,800 sq km are within the basin of the Vyatka River. The greater part of the oblast is taiga and the main industry here is logging.

Km870: Kotelnich Котельнич (pop: 30,700) See p401.

APPENDIX B: TIMETABLES

Timetables for the most popular trains on the Trans-Siberian, Trans-Mongolian, and Trans-Manchurian routes are given below. Unless otherwise indicated, departure times are shown; for arrival times simply subtract the number of minutes shown as the stopping time.

On the internet the best site for Russian train timetables is: 💻 www.poezda.net/en/web, with timetables searchable by station, route or train number. See box p43 for more on other useful websites.

Another useful source of information is the *Thomas Cook Overseas Timetable*, updated every two months, with single issues available from Thomas Cook Publishing (💻 www.thomascooktimetables.com).

However, timetables are subject to change, so the only completely up-to-date timetable will be the one posted in the corridor of your carriage!

Table 1 Trans-Siberian: Moscow–Vladivostok (Train Nos 001 & 002: *Rossiya*)

Departures are every other day in each direction, eastbound on odd dates and westbound on even dates. Times shown are departure times – subtract stop for arrival time.

MT = Moscow Time; **LT** = Local Time; **–** = no stop

Station		Km from Mos	Stop (mins, E/W)	Eastbound No 002 MT	LT	Westbound No 001 MT	LT	Time Zone MT+
				Day 1				
Moscow (Yaroslavsky)	Москва (Ярославский)	0	–/–	21:25	21:25	17:58	17:58	0
				Day 2				
Vladimir	Владимир	191	23/23	00:42	00:42	14:42	14:42	0
Nizhny Novgorod (Gorky)	Нижний Новгород (Горький)	442	10/10	03:45	03:45	10:59	10:59	0
Vyatka (Kirov)	Вятка (Киров)	957	15/15	10:00	11:00	05:00	06:00	1
Balyezino	Балезино	1194	23/23	13:46	14:46	01:29	02:29	1
						Day 7		
Perm 2	Пермь 2	1436	20/20	17:46	19:46	21:16	23:16	2
Yekaterinburg (Sverdlovsk)	Екатеринбург (Свердловск)	1816	23/23	23:31	01:31	15:28	17:28	2
				Day 3				
Tyumen	Тюмень	2144	20/20	04:08	06:08	10:50	12:50	2
Ishim	Ишим	2431	12/12	08:03	10:03	07:00	09:00	2
Omsk	Омск	2712	15/15	11:37	14:37	03:24	06:24	3
						Day 6		
Barabinsk	Барабинск	3040	40/30	15:54	18:54	23:33	02:33	3
Novosibirsk	Новосибирск	3335	19/19	19:35	22:35	19:53	22:53	3

❑ Kilometre-post discrepancies

Distances on official timetables do not always match those indicated by kilometre posts beside the track. Close to Moscow you may notice discrepancies of 10km or more. Beyond Kotelnich (Km870), the junction of the Trans-Siberian and Moscow–Yaroslavl–Vyatka lines, differences grow to 30-40km, largely because until a few years ago most Trans-Siberian traffic used the (longer) line via Yaroslavl.

Table 1 Trans-Siberian: Moscow–Vladivostok (Train Nos 001 & 001: *Rossiya*) cont'd

Station		Km from Mos	Stop (mins, E/W)	Eastbound No 002 MT	Eastbound LT	Westbound No 001 MT	Westbound LT	Time Zone MT+
Tayga	Тайга	3570	13/3	23:05	03:05	16:09	20:09	4
				Day 4				
Mariinsk	Мариинск	3715	25/25	01:43	05:43	13:57	17:57	4
Bogotol	Боготол	3849	2/2	03:42	07:42	11:37	15:37	4
Achinsk 1	Ачинск 1	3917	4/4	04:38	08:38	10:35	14:35	4
Krasnoyarsk	Красноярск	4098	20/20	07:42	11:42	07:37	11:37	4
Zaozyornaya	Заозёрная	4262	2/–	10:21	14:21	–	–	4
Kansk-Yeniseysky	Канск-Енисейский	4343	5/5	11:34	15:34	03:35	07:35	4
Ilanskaya	Иланская	4375	20/20	12:27	16:27	02:58	06:58	4
Reshoty	Решоты	4453	2/2	13:37	17:37	01:30	05:30	4
Tayshet	Тайшет	4516	2/2	14:39	19:39	00:25	05:25	5
						Day 5		
Nizhneudinsk	Нижнеудинск	4680	12/12	17:18	22:18	21:57	02:57	5
Tulun	Тулун	4794	2/2	18:53	23:53	20:10	01:10	5
Zima	Зима	4940	30/30	21:15	02:15	18:14	23:14	5
Cheremkhovo	Черемхово	5061	2/2	22:56	03:56	15:59	20:59	5
Usolye-Sibirskoye	Усолье-Сибирское	5124	2/2	23:53	04:53	15:03	20:03	5
				Day 5				
Angarsk	Ангарск	5160	3/3	00:19	05:19	14:37	19:37	5
Irkutsk Sortirovka	Иркутск Сортировка	5178	10/15	01:02	06:02	14:00	19:00	5
Irkutsk	Иркутск	5185	26/35	01:42	06:42	13:32	18:32	5
Slyudyanka 1	Слюдянка 1	5312	2/2	04:04	09:04	10:51	15:51	5
Ulan-Ude	Улан-Удэ	5642	30/25	09:02	14:02	06:19	11:19	5
Petrovsky Zavod	Петровский Завод	5784	2/2	11:08	17:08	03:49	09:49	6
Khilok	Хилок	5932	19/15	13:52	19:52	01:25	07:25	6
						Day 4		
Chita 2	Чита 2	6199	25/25	18:36	00:36	20:55	02:55	6
Karymskaya	Карымская	6293	18/18	20:43	02:43	18:36	00:36	6
Shilka	Шилка	6446	2/2	23:08	05:08	15:47	21:47	6
				Day 6				
Chernyshevsk-Zabaikalsk	Чернышевск-Забайкальск	6593	30/30	02:02	08:02	13:16	19:16	6
Mogocha	Могоча	6906	15/15	07:31	13:31	07:22	13:22	6
Amazar	Амазар	7010	20/20	09:28	15:28	05:33	11:33	6
Yerofei-Pavlovich	Ерофей-Павлович	7119	21/21	11:43	17:43	03:23	09:23	6
Urusha	Уруша	7211	2/1	13:27	19:27	01:23	07:23	6
						Day 3		
Skovorodino	Сковородино	7306	2/2	15:15	21:15	23:39	05:39	6
Magdagachi	Магдагачи	7501	15/15	18:31	00:31	20:40	02:40	6
Tygda	Тыгда	7576	2/2	19:32	01:32	19:27	01:27	6
Shimanovskaya	Шимановская	7723	2/2	21:50	03:50	17:10	23:10	6
Svobodny	Свободный	7815	3/2	22:59	04:59	15:58	21:58	6
Belogorsk	Белогорск	7873	30/30	00:25	06:25	15:01	21:01	6

Table 1 Trans-Siberian: Moscow–Vladivostok (Train Nos 001 & 002: *Rossiya*) cont'd

Station		Km from Mos	Stop (mins, E/W)	Eastbound No 002 MT	LT	Westbound No 001 MT	LT	Time Zone MT+
				Day 7				
Zavitaya	Завитая	7992	2/2	02:16	08:16	12:44	18:44	6
Bureya	Бурея	8037	2/2	02:59	08:59	12:03	18:03	6
Arkhara	Архара	8088	3/3	03:51	09:51	11:16	17:16	6
Obluchye	Облучье	8198	15/15	05:50	12:50	09:24	16:24	7
Bira	Бира	8306	1/–	07:48	14:48	–	–	7
Birobidzhan	Биробиджан	8351	5/3	08:34	15:34	06:35	13:35	7
Khabarovsk 1	Хабаровск 1	8521	30/30	11:07	18:07	04:29	11:29	7
Vyazemskaya	Вяземская	8642	15/15	13:14	20:14	01:55	08:55	7
Bikin	Бикин	8756	2/2	14:49	21:49	00:07	07:07	7
						Day 2		
Luchegorsk	Лучегорск	8773	1/1	15:32	22:32	23:17	06:17	7
Dalnerechensk 1	Дальнереченск 1	8890	3/3	16:31	23:31	22:19	05:19	7
Ruzhino	Ружино	8941	13/13	17:33	00:33	21:26	04:26	7
Spassk-Dalny	Спасск-Дальний	9050	1/2	19:08	02:08	19:38	02:38	7
Muchnaya	Мучная	9092	1/1	19:47	02:47	19:00	02:00	7
Sibirtsevo	Сибирцево	9109	1/1	20:07	03:07	18:39	01:39	7
Ussurisk	Уссурийск	9177	18/18	21:28	04:28	17:37	00:37	7
Ugolnaya	Угольная	9255	1/2	22:45	05:45	16:03	23:03	7
Vladivostok	Владивосток	9289		23:33	06:33	15:20	22:20	7
						Day 1		

Table 2 St Petersburg–Irkutsk (Train Nos 009 & 010 *Baikal*)

Departures are every other day in each direction, eastbound on even dates and westbound on odd dates. Times shown are departure times – subtract stop for arrival time.

MT = Moscow Time; **LT** = Local Time; **–** = no stop

Station		Km from St P/Mos*	Stop (mins, E/W)	Eastbound No 010 MT	LT	Westbound No 009 MT	LT	Time Zone MT+
St Petersburg	Санкт-Питербург			Day 1				
(Ladozhsky)	(Ладожский)		0/0	16:22	16:22	10:00	10:00	0
Volkhovsktroy 1	Волховстрой 1	*114*	5/5	18:36	18:36	07:46	07:46	0
Tikhvin	Тихвин	*192*	4/5	19:44	19:44	06:15	06:15	0
Bolshoi Dvor	Большой Двор	*218*	1/–	20:15	20:15	–	–	0
Pikalevo 1	Пикалево 1	*230*	2/–	20:35	20:35	–	–	0
Yefimovskaya	Ефимовская	*267*	–/2	–	–	04:52	04:52	0
Podbrovye	Подборовье	*288*	–/1	–	–	04:29	04:29	0
Babayevo	Бабаево	*344*	27/27	22:40	22:40	03:30	03:30	0
Kaduy	Кадуй	*420*	3/2	23:50	23:50	01:51	01:51	0
				Day 2				
Suda	Суда	*444*	2/2	00:14	00:14	01:26	01:26	0
Cherepovets 1	Череповец 1	*468*	23/18	01:13	01:13	00:52	00:52	0
						Day 5		

* Kms in italics show distance from St Petersburg as far as Svecha station, then from Kotelnich 1 station onwards shows distance from Moscow.

Table 2 St Petersburg–Irkutsk (Train Nos 009 & 010 *Baikal*) cont'd

Station		Km from St P/Mos*	Stop (mins, E/W)	Eastbound No 010		Westbound No 009		Time Zone MT+
				MT	LT	MT	LT	
Sheksna	Шексна	*506*	2/2	01:57	01:57	23:41	23:41	0
Vologda 1	Вологда 1	*592*	23/23	03:56	03:56	22:10	22:10	0
Booy	Буй	*722*	10/10	05:54	05:54	19:54	19:54	0
Galitch	Галич	*773*	4/3	06:39	06:39	18:58	18:58	0
Antropovo	Антропово	*819*	–/2	–	–	18:15	18:15	0
Nikolo-Poloma	Николо-Полома	*843*	–/2	–	–	17:51	17:51	0
Manturovo	Мантурово	*925*	2/2	08:48	08:48	16:41	16:41	0
Sharya	Шарья	*973*	13/10	09:55	09:55	15:51	15:51	0
Shabalino	Шабалино	*1067*	1/1	11:18	11:18	14:27	14:27	0
Svecha	Свеча	*1090*	–/2	–	–	14:05	14:05	0
Kotelnich 1	Котельнич 1	870	1/2	12:25	13:25	13:16	14:16	1
Vyatka (Kirov)	Вятка (Киров)	957	15/20	14:03	15:03	11:44	12:44	1
Glazov	Глазов	1165	2/2	17:21	18:21	08:20	09:20	1
Balyezino	Балезино	1194	23/23	18:16	19:16	07:50	08:50	1
Vereshchagino	Верещагино	1310	2/19	20:19	22:19	05:31	07:31	2
Meendeleevo	Менделеево	1340	–/2	–	–	04:45	06:45	2
Perm 2	Пермь 2	1436	20/20	22:24	00:24	03:11	05:11	2
				Day 3				
Kungur	Кунгур	1534	5/2	00:01	02:01	01:22	03:22	2
						Day 4		
Yekaterinburg (Sverdlovsk)	Екатеринбург (Свердловск)	1816	24/23	04:30	06:30	21:05	23:05	2
Bogdanovich	Богданович	1912	2/2	06:06	08:06	19:13	21:13	2
Tyumen	Тюмень	2144	20/21	09:38	11:38	15:25	17:25	2
Vinzili	Винзили		–/8	–	–	14:29	16:29	2
Ishim	Ишим	2431	12/15	13:29	15:29	10:41	13:41	2
Nazyvaevskaya	Называевская	2565	3/3	15:22	18:22	08:48	11:48	3
Omsk	Омск	2712	36/45	17:30	20:30	06:36	09:36	3
Kalachinskaya	Калачинская	2795	2/2	18:35	21:35	04:24	07:24	3
Tatarskaya	Татарская	2885	2/2	19:46	22:46	03:05	06:05	3
Barabinsk	Барабинск	3040	30/39	22:09	01:09	01:25	04:25	3
						Day 3		
Chulymskaya	Чулымская	3212	2/2	23:50	02:50	23:00	02:00	3
				Day 4				
Novosibirsk	Новосибирск	3335	40/40	01:59	04:59	21:09	00:09	3
Tayga	Тайга	3570	2/2	05:08	09:08	17:04	21:04	4
Mariinsk	Мариинск	3715	25/25	07:25	11:25	15:00	19:00	4
Bogotol	Боготол	3846	2/2	09:29	13:29	12:40	16:40	4
Achinsk 1	Ачинск 1	3917	4/2	10:25	14:25	11:40	15:40	4
Krasnoyarsk	Красноярск	4098	33/30	13:48	17:48	08:48	12:48	4
Zaozyornaya	Заозёрная	4262	2/2	16:28	20:28	05:41	09:41	4
Kansk-Yeniseysky	Канск-Енисейский	4343	2/2	17:38	21:38	04:29	08:29	4
Ilanskaya	Иланская	4375	20/20	18:31	22:31	03:56	07:56	4
Reshoty	Решоты	4453	5/2	20:45	00:45	02:23	06:23	4
Tayshet	Тайшет	4516	5/5	20:45	01:45	01:18	06:18	5
						Day 2		

Table 2 St Petersburg–Irkutsk (Train Nos 009 & 010 *Baikal*) cont'd

Station		Km from Mos	Stop (mins, E/W)	Eastbound No 010 MT	LT	Westbound No 009 MT	LT	Time Zone MT+
				Day 5				
Nizhneudinsk	Нижнеудинск	4680	12/12	23:29	04:29	22:42	03:42	5
Tulun	Тулун	4794	2/2	01:04	06:04	20:55	01:55	5
Kuytun	Куйтун	4875	2/2	02:09	07:09	19:48	00:48	5
Zima	Зима	4940	30/30	03:32	08:32	18:53	23:53	5
Zalari	Залари		2/2	04:24	09:24	17:31	22:31	5
Cheremkhovo	Черемхово	5061	2/2	05:21	10:21	16:33	21:33	5
Usolye-Sibirskoye	Усолье-Сибирское	5124	2/2	06:23	11:23	15:38	20:38	5
Angarsk	Ангарск	5160	4/3	06:50	11:50	15:13	20:13	5
Irkutsk Sortirovka	Иркутск Сортировка	5178	2/3	07:25	12:25	14:38	19:38	5
Irkutsk	Иркутск	5185		07:39	12:39	14:20	19:20	5
						Day 1		

Table 3 Trans-Mongolian: Moscow–Beijing (Train Nos 003* & 004*)

One per week in each direction: currently ex-Moscow on Tuesday, ex-Beijing on Wednesday. Times shown are departure times – subtract stop for arrival time.
MT = Moscow Time; **LT** = Local Time; **–** = no stop

Station		Km from Mos	Stop (mins, E/W)	Eastbound No 004 MT	LT	Westbound No 003 MT	LT	Time Zone MT+
				Day 1				
Moscow (Yaroslavsky)	Москва (Ярославский)	0		21:35	21:35	14:28	14:28	0
				Day 2				
Vladimir	Владимир	191	23/23	00:52	00:52	10:51	10:51	0
Nizhny Novgorod (Gorky)	Нижний Новгород (Горький)	442	10/10	03:55	03:55	07:11	07:11	0
Vyatka (Kirov)	Вятка (Киров)	957	15/15	10:10	11:10	01:10	02:10	1
						Day 6		
Balyezino	Балезино	1194	23/23	13:56	14:56	21:31	22:31	1
Perm 2	Пермь 2	1436	20/20	17:56	19:56	17:19	19:19	2
Yekaterinburg (Sverdlovsk)	Екатеринбург (Свердловск)	1816	23/23	23:41	01:41	11:35	13:35	2
				Day 3				
Tyumen	Тюмень	2144	20/20	04:18	06:18	06:59	08:59	2
Ishim	Ишим	2431	12/12	08:13	10:13	03:09	05:09	2
						Day 5		
Omsk	Омск	2712	15/15	11:47	14:47	23:44	02:44	3
Barabinsk	Барабинск	3040	23/23	15:46	18:46	20:03	23:03	3
Novosibirsk	Новосибирск	3335	19/22	19:23	22:23	16:15	19:15	3

* *Note that these train numbers may be listed on some timetable sources as 0033 and 0043.*

(Opposite) Clockwise from top: **1**. American-built Ea3246, Tynda station. **2**. Em730-73 at Ilanskaya. **3**. Su213-42 at the Railway Museum, Seyatel (see p260). **4**. P36-0097 at Seyatel.

ЧС2-236

Table 3 Trans-Mongolian: Moscow–Beijing (Train Nos 003* & 004*) cont'd

Station		Km from Mos	Stop (mins, E/W)	Eastbound No 004 MT	LT	Westbound No 003 MT	LT	Time Zone MT+
				Day 4				
Mariinsk	Мариинск	3715	25/25	01:09	05:09	10:20	14:20	4
Achinsk	Ачинск	3917	–/2	–	–	07:04	11:04	4
Krasnoyarsk	Красноярск	4098	20/20	06:53	10:53	04:12	08:12	4
						Day 4		
Ilanskaya	Иланская	4375	20/20	11:30	15:30	23:43	03:43	4
Nizhneudinsk	Нижнеудинск	4680	12/12	16:18	21:18	18:51	23:51	5
Zima	Зима	4940	30/30	20:11	01:11	15:12	20:12	5
Angarsk	Ангарск	5160	–/–	–	–	–	–	5
				Day 5				
Irkutsk Sortirovka	Иркутск Сортировка	5178	–/–	–	–	–	–	5
Irkutsk	Иркутск	5185	35/25	00:18	05:18	11:03	16:03	5
Slyudyanka 1	Слюдянка 1	5312	2/2	02:54	07:54	08:11	13:11	5
Ulan-Ude	Улан-Удэ	5642	30/30	08:27	13:27	03:08	08:08	5
Zagustay	Загустай	5769	–/–	–	–	–	–	5
Gusinoye Ozero	Гусиное Озеро	5800	–/–	–	–	–	–	5
						Day 3		
Dzhida	Джида	5852	2/2	12:17	17:17	23:15	04:15	5
Naushki	Наушки	5895	3hrs+	16:43	21:43	22:31	03:31	5
Dozorny	Дозорный	5900	–/–	–	–	–	–	
MONGOLIA						**RUSSIA**		
Sühbaatar	Сухбаатар	5925	1hr+	23:15		22:05		
				Day 6				
Darhan	Дархан	6023	17/5	01:05		19:20		
Zuunhara	Дзунхара	6132	25/15	03:40		17:05		
Ulaanbaatar	Улаанбаатар	6304	45/30	07:15		13:50		
Choyr	Чоыр	6551	20/15	11:53		09:19		
Saynshand	Сайншанд	7778	37/20	15:43		05:41		
Dzamyn Ude	Дзамын Удэ	7013	1hr+	20:35		01:40		
						Day 2		
CHINA				**Day 7**		**MONGOLIA**		
Erlian	二连 Эрлянь	7023	3hrs+	00:57		23:59		
Jining	济宁 Цзиннань	7356	9/6	05:56		16:09		
Datong	大同 Датун	7483	12/24	08:11		14:15		
Zhangjiakou	张家口 Цжанцзякоунань	7661	10/10	10:46		11:13		
Beijing	北京 Пекин	7865		14:04		07:45		
						Day 1		

* *Note that these train numbers may be listed on some timetable sources as 0033 and 0043.*

(Opposite) Top: ChS2 loco takes a break at Mariinsk. (Photo © Richard Mayneord).
Bottom: Changing the bogies at the Chinese border (Photo © Bryn Thomas).

Table 4 Trans-Manchurian: Moscow–Beijing (Train Nos 019 & 020: *Vostok*)

One per week in each direction; currently ex-Moscow on Friday, ex-Beijing on Saturday. Times shown are departure times – subtract stop for arrival time.
MT = Moscow Time; **LT** = Local Time; **–** = no stop

Station		Km from Mos	Stop (mins, E/W)	Eastbound No 020		Westbound No 019		Time Zone
				MT	LT	MT	LT	MT+
				Day 1				
Moscow (Yaroslavsky)	Москва (Ярославский)	0		23:55	23:55	18:13	18:13	0
				Day 2				
Vladimir	Владимир	191	23/23	03:17	03:17	14:52	14:52	0
Nizhny Nov-gorod (Gorky)	Нижний Нов-город (Горький)	442	10/10	06:10	06:10	11:09	11:09	0
Vyatka (Kirov)	Вятка (Киров)	957	15/15	12:40	13:40	05:10	06:10	1
Balyezino	Балезино	1194	23/23	16:40	17:40	01:39	02:39	1
						Day 7		
Perm 2	Пермь 2	1436	20/20	20:37	22:37	21:26	23:26	2
				Day 3				
Yekaterinburg (Sverdlovsk)	Екатеринбург (Свердловск)	1816	23/23	02:23	04:23	15:38	17:38	2
Tyumen	Тюмень	2144	30/40	07:13	09:13	11:00	13:00	2
Ishim	Ишим	2431	12/12	11:05	13:05	06:50	08:50	2
Omsk	Омск	2712	15/15	15:06	18:06	03:14	06:14	3
						Day 6		
Barabinsk	Барабинск	3040	23/22	19:17	22:17	23:08	02:08	3
Novosibirsk	Новосибирск	3335	30/30	23:12	02:12	19:37	22:37	3
				Day 4				
Mariinsk	Мариинск	3715	25/25	04:50	08:50	13:32	17:32	4
Achinsk 1	Ачинск 1	3917	2/2	07:39	11:39	10:16	14:16	4
Krasnoyarsk	Красноярск	4098	22/23	10:47	14:47	07:24	11:24	4
Zaozyornaya	Заозёрная	4262	2/2	13:32	17:32	04:30	08:30	4
Kansk-Yeniseysky	Канск-Енисейский	4343	2/2	14:42	18:42	03:17	07:17	4
Ilanskaya	Иланская	4375	22/20	15:37	19:37	02:40	06:40	4
						Day 5		
Nizhneudinsk	Нижнеудинск	4680	12/12	20:28	01:28	21:44	02:44	5
				Day 5				
Zima	Зима	4940	30/30	00:21	05:21	18:05	23:05	5
Irkutsk	Иркутск	5185	30/30	04:25	08:25	13:40	18:40	5
Slyudyanka 1	Слюдянка 1	5312	2/2	06:32	11:32	11:04	16:04	5
Ulan-Ude	Улан-Удэ	5642	30/25	11:30	16:30	06:33	11:33	5
Petrovsky Zavod	Петровский Завод	5784	2/2	13:37	19:37	04:02	10:02	6
Khilok	Хилок	5932	19/15	16:24	22:24	01:38	07:38	6
						Day 4		
Chita	Чита	6199	25/25	21:11	03:11	21:08	03:08	6
Karymskaya	Карымская	6293	30/41	23:30	05:30	18:49	00:49	6
				Day 6				
Mogoytuy	Могойтуй	6370	–/2	–	–	16:07	22:07	6
Olovyannaya	Оловянная	6444	–/2	–	–	14:19	20:19	6

Table 4 Trans-Manchurian: Moscow–Beijing (Train Nos 019 & 020: *Vostok*) cont'd

Station		Km from Mos	Stop (mins, E/W)	Eastbound No 020 MT	LT	Westbound No 019 MT	LT	Time Zone MT+
Yasnogorsk	Ясногорск	6446	–/2	–	–	13:57	19:57	6
Borzya	Борзя	6543	20/20	05:24	11:24	12:10	18:10	6
Zabaikalsk	Забайкальск	6661	5hrs+	14:06	20:06	09:13	15:13	6
CHINA				**Day 7**		**RUSSIA**		
Manzhouli	满洲里 Маньчжурия	6678	5hrs+/ 3hrs+	00:41		07:01		
Hailar	海拉尔 Хайлар	6864	8/8	02:53		01:24 **Day 3**		
Boketu	伯克图 Бокэт	7074	8/8	05:54		22:15		
Angangxi	鞍钢西 Ананси	7343	8/10	09:41		18:20		
Daqing	大庆 Дацин	7454	4/8	10:51		17:00		
Harbin	哈尔滨 Харбин	7613	24/21	13:04		15:10		
Changchun	长春 Чанчунь	7855	8/6	16:00		12:14		
Siping	四平 Сюпин	7971	6/2	17:19		10:54		
Shenyang	沈阳 Шэньян	8160	15/20	19:33		08:55		
Jinzhou	锦州 Цзиньчжоу	8402	5/4	22:16 **Day 8**		06:03		
Shanhaiguan	山海关 Шаньхэйгуань	8586	8/6	00:22		04:01		
Tangshan	唐山 Таншан	8739	3/2	02:22		02:00		
Tianjin	天津 Тяньцзинь	8868	20/6	04:00		00:38 **Day 2**		
Beijing	北京 Пекин	9001		05:32		23:00 **Day 1**		

APPENDIX C: LIST OF SIBERIAN FAUNA

There are extensive displays of local animals in the natural history museums of Novosibirsk, Irkutsk and Khabarovsk but the labelling is in Russian and Latin. The following translation is given for non-Russian-speaking readers whose Latin is rusty or non-existent. In the list below the letters given beside the animal's English name indicate its natural habitat. NS = Northern Siberia/Arctic Circle; SP = Siberian Plain; AS = Altai-Sayan Plateau/Mongolia; BI = Lake Baikal/Transbaikal region; FE = Far Eastern Territories. Where a Latin name is similar to the English (eg *Vipera* = Viper) these names have been omitted.

Accipiter gentilis goshawk (AS/SP/NS/BI/FE)
Aegoceras montanus mountain ram (AS)
Aegoceras sibiricus Siberian goat (BI)
Aegolius funereus boreal/Tengmalm's owl (BI/FE)
Aegypius monachus black vulture (AS)
Aethia cristatella crested auklet (NS/FE)
Alces alces elk/moose (SP/BI/FE)
Allactaga jaculus five-toed jerboa (SP/BI)
Alopex lagopus arctic fox (NS)
Anas acuta pintail (BI)
Anas clypeata shoveler (SP/BI/FE)
Anas crecca teal (BI/SP/FE)
Anas falcata falcated teal (SP/BI/FE)
Anas formosa Baikal teal (BI)
Anas platyrhynchos mallard (AS/SP/BI/FE)
Anas poecilorhyncha spotbill duck (AS/BI)
Anser anser greylag goose (SP/BI)
Anser erythropus white-fronted goose (AS/SP/BI/FE)
Antelope gutturosa/crispa antelope (FE)
Arctomis bobac marmot (AS/SP)
Ardea cinerea grey heron (AS/SP/BI)
Aquila clanga greater-spotted eagle (SP)
Botaurus stellaris bittern (SP/BI/FE)
Bubo bubo eagle owl (BI/FE)
Buteo lagopus rough-legged buzzard (NS/SP/FE)
Butorides striatus striated/green heron (FE)
Canis alpinus mountain wolf (AS/FE)
Canis corsac korsac/steppe fox (BI/FE)
Canis lagopus arctic fox (NS)
Canis lupus wolf (SP/BI/FE)
Canis procyonoides Amur racoon (FE)
Capra sibirica Siberian mountain goat/ibex (AS/BI)
Capreolus capreolus roe deer (SP/BI/FE)
Castor fiber beaver (SP/BI/FE)
Certhia familiaris common treecreeper (AS/BI/FE)
Cervus alces elk (AS/BI/FE)
Cervus capreolus roe-buck (BI/FE)
Cervus elephas maral deer (AS/BI/FE)
Cervus nippon sika/Japanese deer (FE)
Cervus tarandus reindeer (NS/FE)
Circus aeruginosus marsh harrier (SP/BI)
Citellus undulatus arctic ground squirrel/Siberian souslik (NS/BI/FE)
Cricetus cricetus common hamster (AS/SP/BI/FE)
Cygnus cygnus whooper swan (SP/BI)
Dicrostonyx torquatus arctic lemming (NS)
Dryocopus martius black woodpecker (SP/BI/FE)
Enhyra lutris Kamchatka beaver (FE)
Equus hemionus kulan/Asian wild ass (FE)
Eumentopias Stelleri sea-lion (NS/FE)
Eutamias sibiricus Siberian chipmunk (AS/SP/BI/FE)
Ealco columbarius merlin (NS/SP/BI/FE)
Falco peregrinus peregrine (NS/SP/BI/FE)
Falco tinnunculus kestrel (SP)
Falco vesperinus hawk (SP)
Felis irbis irbis/panther (FE)
Felis lynx lynx (SP/BI/FE)
Felis manul wild cat (AS/BI/FE)
Felis tigris altaica Amur tiger (FE)
Foetorius altaicus ermine (NS/AS/SP/BI/FE)
Foetorius altaicus sibiricus polecat (SP/BI)
Foetorius vulgaris weasel (SP/BI)
Fulica atra coot (SP/BI/FE)
Gallinago gallinago common snipe (SP/BI/FE)
Gavia arctica black-throated diver/loon (BI)
Gavia stellata red-throated diver/loon (SP/BI)
Gazella subgutturosa goitred gazelle (AS)
Grus cinerea grey crane (SP)
Grus grus common crane (SP/BI/FE)
Grus leucogeranus Siberian white crane (NS/SP/FE)

Gulo gulo wolverine/glutton (SP/BI/FE)
Gypaetus barbatus L. lammergeyer (AS)
Haematopus ostralegus oystercatcher (SP/BI/FE)
Lagomis alpinus rat hare (FE)
Lagopus lagopus willow grouse/ptarmigan (NS/SP/FE)
Larus argentatus herring gull (BI/FE)
Larus canus common gull (BI/FE)
Larus ridibundus black-headed gull (BI/FE)
Lemmus obensis Siberian lemming (NS/SP)
Lepus timidus arctic hare (NS/BI/FE)
Lepus variabilis polar hare (NS)
Lutra vulgaris otter (BI/FE)
Marmota camtschatica Kamchatka marmot (FE)
Marmota sibirica Siberian marmot (AS/SP/BI)
Martes zibellina sable (SP/BI/FE)
Melanitta deglandi American black scoter (BI)
Melanocorypha mongolica Mongolian lark (BI/FE)
Meles meles Eurasian badger (AS/BI/FE)
Microtus hyperboreus sub-arctic vole (NS/SP/FE)
Moschus moschiferus musk deer (AS/BI/FE)
Mustela erminea ermine (NS/AS/SP/ BI/FE)
Mustela eversmanni steppe polecat (AS/SP/BI/FE)
Mustela nivalis common weasel (NS/SP/BI/FE)
Mustela sibirica kolonok (FE)
Myodes torquatus/obensis Ob lemming (NS)
Nucifraga caryocatactes nutcracker (AS/SP/BI/FE)
Nyctea scandiaca snowy owl (NS)
Ochotona alpina Altai pika (AS)
Oenanthe isabellina Isabelline wheatear (AS/SP/BI)
Omul baikalensis omul (BI)
Otaria ursina sea bear (NS/FE)
Otis tarda bustard (SP/BI)
Ovis ammon argalis (sheep) (AS)
Ovis argali arkhar (AS)
Ovis nivicola Siberian bighorn/snow sheep (FE)
Panthera pardus orientalis Amur leopard (FE)
Panthera tigris altaica Siberian/Amur tiger (FE)
Panthera uncia snow leopard (AS)
Perdix perdix grey partridge (AS/SP/BI/FE)
Perisoreus infaustus Siberian jay (BI/FE)
Phalacrocorax carbo great cormorant (BI/FE)
Phoca barbata groenlandica seal (NS/FE)
Phoca baicalensis Baikal seal (BI)
Phocaena orca dolphin (NS/FE)
Picoides tridactylus three-toed woodpecker (SP/BI/FE)
Plectophenax nivalis snow bunting (NS)
Podiceps auritus Slavonian/horned grebe (AS/BI)
Podiceps cristatus great-crested grebe (AS/SP/BI)
Procapra gutturosa Mongolian gazelle (FE)
Pteromys volans Siberian flying squirrel (SP/BI/FE)
Rangifer tarandus reindeer/caribou (NS/BI/FE)
Ranodon sibiricus five-toed triton (AS/SP)
Rufibrenta ruficollis red-breasted goose (NS)
Salpingotus crassicauda pygmy jerboa (SP/AS)
Sciurus vulgaris red squirrel (SP/BI/AS/FE)
Spermophilus eversmanni Siberian marmot (BI)
Spermophilus undulatus arctic ground squirrel (FE)
Sterna hirundo common tern (BI/FE)
Strix nebulosa great grey owl (SP/BI/FE)
Surnia ulula hawk owl (SP/BI/FE)
Sus scrofa wild boar (AS/BI/FE)
Tadorna ferruginea ruddy shelduck (SP/BI/FE)
Tamias striatus striped squirrel (BI)
Tetrao urogallus capercaillie (SP/BI/FE)
Tetrao parvirostris black-billed capercaillie (BI/FE)
Tetraogallus himalayanensis Himalayan snowcock (AS)
Tetraogallus altaicus Altai snowcock (AS)
Tetrastes bonasia hazel grouse (SP/BI/FE)
Turdus sibiricus Siberian thrush (SP/BI/FE)
Uria aalge guillemot (NS/FE)
Ursus arctus bear (SP/FE)
Ursus maritimus polar bear (NS)
Ursus tibetanus Tibet bear (FE)
Vulpes vulpes red fox (AS/SP/BI/FE)

APPENDIX D: BIBLIOGRAPHY

Baedeker, Karl *Russia with Teheran, Port Arthur and Peking* (Leipzig 1914)
Barzini, Luigi *Peking to Paris. A Journey across Two Continents* (London 1907)
Byron, Robert *First Russia Then Tibet* (London 1933)
Collins, Perry McDonough *A Voyage down the Amoor* (New York 1860)
De Windt, Harry *Siberia as it is* (London 1892)
Des Cars J and Caracalla, J P *Le Transsiberien* (1986)
Dmitriev-Mamonov, A I and Zdziarski, A F *Guide to the Great Siberian Railway 1900* (St Petersburg 1900)
Fleming, H M and Price J H *Russian Steam Locomotives* (London 1960)
Gowing, L F *Five Thousand Miles in a Sledge* (London 1889)
Heywood A J & Button I D C *Soviet Locomotive Types* (London/Malmo 1994)
Hill, S S *Travels in Siberia* (London 1854)
Hollingsworth, J B *The Atlas of Train Travel* (London 1980)
An Official Guide to Eastern Asia Vol 1: Manchuria & Chosen (Tokyo 1913)
Jefferson, R L *Awheel to Moscow and Back* (London 1895)
Jefferson, R L *Roughing it in Siberia* (London 1897)
Jefferson, R L *A New Ride to Khiva* (London 1899)
Johnson, Henry *The Life of Kate Marsden* (London 1895)
Kennan, George *Siberia and the Exile System* (London 1891)
Lansdell, Henry *Through Siberia* (London 1883)
Levin, M G and Potapov, L P *The Peoples of Siberia* (Chicago 1964)
Macaulay, Lord *History of England from the Accession of James II*
Manley, Deborah *The Trans-Siberian Railway* (London 2009)
Marsden, Kate *On Sledge and Horseback to Outcast Siberian Lepers* (London 1895)
Meakin, Annette *A Ribbon of Iron* (London 1901)
Massie, R K *Nicholas and Alexandra* (London 1967)
Murray *Handbook for Russia, Poland and Finland* (London 1865)
Newby, Eric *The Big Red Train Ride* (London 1978)
Pifferi, Enzo *Le Transsiberien*
Poulsen, J and Kuranow, W *Die Transsibirische Eisenbahn* (Malmo 1986)
St George, George *Siberia: the New Frontier* (London 1969)
Shoemaker, M M *The Great Siberian Railway – St Petersburg to Peking* (London 1903)
Theroux, Paul *The Great Railway Bazaar* (London 1975)
Thubron, Colin *In Siberia* (Penguin 2000)
Tupper, Harmon *To the Great Ocean* (London 1965)

APPENDIX E: PHRASE LISTS

As with virtually every country in the world, it's possible to just about get by in Russia, Mongolia and China on a combination of English and sign language. English is spoken by tourist guides and some hotel staff but most of the local people you meet on the train will be eager to communicate with you and unable to speak English. Unless you enjoy charades it's well worth learning a few basic phrases in advance. Not only will this make communication easier but it will also earn you the respect of local people. You might even consider taking evening classes before you go, or teaching yourself with books and CDs from your local library.

The sections here highlight only a few useful words. Lonely Planet's pocket-sized phrasebooks in Russian, Mongolian and Chinese are highly recommended.

Russian

CYRILLIC ALPHABET AND PRONUNCIATION GUIDE

It's not very difficult to master the Cyrillic alphabet before you go; many letters are the same as in English and the other ones are easy enough to remember. This will enable you to decipher the names of streets, metro stations and, most importantly, the names of stations along the Trans-Siberian and Trans-Mongolian routes (Mongolian also uses a modified Cyrillic script).

The Cyrillic alphabet is derived from the Greek. It was introduced in Russia in the 10th century via a translation of the Bible made by two Greek bishops, Cyril (who gave his name to the new alphabet) and Methodius.

Cyrillic letter	Roman equiv	Pronunciation*
А а	a	f**a**ther
Б б	b	**b**et
В в	v	**v**odka
Г г	g	**g**et
Д д	d	**d**og
Е е	ye	**ye**t (unstressed: **ye**ar)
Ё ё	yo	**yo**ghurt
Ж ж	zh	trea**s**ure
З з	z	**z**ebra
И и	i, ee	s**ee**k, **ye**ar
Й й	y	bo**y**
К к	k	**k**it
Л л	l	**l**ast
М м	m	**M**oscow
Н н	n	**n**ever
О о	o	t**o**re (unstressed: t**o**p)
П п	p	**P**eter
Р р	r	**R**ussia
С с	s	**S**amarkand
Т т	t	**t**ime
У у	u, oo	f**oo**l
Ф ф	f, ph	**fa**st
Х х	kh	lo**ch**
Ц ц	ts	lo**ts**
Ч ч	ch	**ch**illy
Ш ш	sh	**sh**ow
Щ щ	shch	**s**ugar
Ы ы	y, i	d**i**d
ь	(softens preceding consonant)	
Э э	e	l**e**t
Ю ю	yu	**u**nion
Я я	ya	**ya**rd

* pronunciation shown by underlined letter/s

KEY PHRASES

The following phrases in Cyrillic script may be useful to point to if you're having problems communicating:

Please write it down for me	Напишите это для меня, пожалуйста	*Na-pi-**shi**-te e-to dlya me-nya, po-zhal-sta*
Help me, please	Помогйте мне, пожалуйста	*Po-mo-**gi**-te mne, po-**zhal**-sta*
I only speak English	Я говорю только по-английски	*Ya go-vo-**riu** **tol**-ko po an-**gli**-ski*
I need an interpreter	Мне нужен переводчик	*Mne **noo**-zhen pe-re-**vod**-chik*

CONVERSATIONAL RUSSIAN

Run the hyphenated syllables together as you speak and roll your 'R's:

General

Hello	Здравствуйте	***Zdrahz**-tvooy-tyeh*
Goodbye	До свидания	*Das-vee-**dah**-nya*
Good morning	Доброе утро	***Doh**-broyeh-**oo**tro*
Good afternoon / evening	Добрый день / вечер	***Doh**-bree-**dyen** / **vye**cher*
Please / Thank you	Пожалуйста / Спасибо	*Pa-**zhal**-sta / Spa-**see**-ba*
Do you speak English?	Говорите ли вы по-английски?	*Gava-**ree**-tyeh lee vy pa-an-**glee**-skee?*
No / Yes	Нет / да	*Nyet / da*
Excuse me (sorry)	Извините	*Eez-vee-**nee**-tyeh*
good / bad	Хорошо / плохо	*ha-ra-**sho** / **plo**-ho*
cheap / expensive	Дёшево / дорого	***dyo**-she-vo / **do**-ro-go*
Wait a minute!	Одну минуту!	*Ad-**noo** mee-**noo**-too!*
Please call a doctor	Вызовите, пожалуйста, врача	*Vy-za-**vee**-tyeh, pa-**zhal**-sta, **vra**-cha*
Is there / are there...?	Есть ли .....?	*Yest' lee ....?*
How much / many?	Сколько?	***Skol**ka?*
rouble / roubles	рубль / рубля / рублей	*roobl (1), roob**lyah** (2-4), roob**lyey** (5+)*
Please write down the price	Напишите, пожалуйста, цену	*Na-pee-**shee**-tyeh, pa-**zhal**-sta, **tseh**-noo*
ticket	билет	*beel-**yet***
1st / 2nd / 3rd class	1-й / 2-й / 3-й класс	***per**viy / fto**roy** / **treh**tiy class*
express	экспресс	*eks**pres***

Directions (see also box p79)

map	карта	***kar**-ta*
Where is ...?	Где....?	*G'dyeh...?*
hotel	гостиница	*ga-**stee**-nee-tsa*
airport / aerodrome	аэропорт / аэродром	*a-**eh**-ro-port / a-**eh**-ro-drom*
bus station	автобусная станция	*av-to-bus-na-ya stan-tsi-ya*
metro / taxi	метро / такси	*mi-**tro** / tak-**see***
tram / trolley-bus	трамвай / тролейбус	*tram-**vai** / tro-**ley**-boos*
restaurant / café	ресторан / кафе	*re-sta-**rahn** / ka-**feh***
museum / shop	булочная / гастроном	*moo-**zey** / ma-ga-**zyeen***
bakery / grocery	булочная / гастроном	***boo**-lotch-naya / gas-tra-**nom***
ticket office (theatre)	касса (театральная)	***kas**sa (te-ah-**tral**-na-ya)*

lavatory (ladies/gents)	туалет (женский / мужской)	*too-a-**lyet** (**zhen**-ski / moozh-**skoy**)*
open / closed	открыто / закрыто	*aht-**kri**-ta / za-**kri**-ta*
left / right	направо / налево	*na-**prah**-va/na-**lyeh**-va*

Numbers

1	***adeen***	один
2	*dvah*	два
3	*tree*	три
4	*che**ti**ri*	четыре
5	*pyat'*	пять
6	*shest'*	шесть
7	*sem'*	семь
8	***vo**sem'*	восемь
9	***dyeh**-vyet*	девять
10	***dyeh**-syet*	десять
11	***adeenat**sat*	одиннадцать
12	***dvenat**sat*	двенадцать
13	***treenat**sat*	тринадцать
14	*che**tir**natsat*	четырнадцать
15	*pyat**nat**sat*	пятнадцать
16	*shest**nat**sat*	шестнадцать
17	*sem**nat**sat*	семнадцать
18	*vasem**nat**sat*	восемнадцать
19	*dyevyet-**nat**sat*	девятнадцать
20	***dvad**sat*	двадцать
30	***treed**sat*	тридцать
40	***sor**ok*	сорок
50	*pidi**syat***	пятьдесят
60	*shizdi**syat***	шестьдесят
70	***syem**-deset*	семьдесят
80	***vo**syem-deset*	восемьдеся
90	*devya-**no**sta*	девяносто
100	*sto*	сто
200	***dveh**-stee*	двести
300	***tree**-sta*	тристо
400	*che**tiri**-sta*	четыресто
500	*pyat**sot***	пятьсот
600	*shest**sot***	шестьсот
700	*sem**sot***	семьсот
800	*vosem**sot***	восемьсот
900	*devet**sot***	девятьсот
1000	***teesy**acha*	тысяча

Time periods/days of the week

What time is it?	Который час?	*k**a**tori **chas**?*
hours / minutes	часа / минут	*chas**of** / mee**noot***
today	сегодня	*se**vod**nya*
yesterday / tomorrow	вчера / завтра	*fche**rah** / **zahf**tra*
Monday / Tuesday	понедельник / вторник	*pa-ni-**dyel**-nik / **ftor**-nik*
Wednesday / Thursday	среда / четверг	*sri-**da** / chit-**vehrk***
Friday / Saturday	пятница / суббота	***pyat**-nit-sah / soo-**boh**-ta*
Sunday	воскресенье	*vas-kreh-**sen**-ya*

Food and drink

menu / bill	меню / счёт	*min-**yoo** / shchot*
(mineral) water / juice	(минеральная) вода / сок	*(mee-nee-**rahl**-naya) va-**da** / sok*
vodka / whisky / beer	водка / виски / пиво	***vod**ka / **vee**skee / **pee**va*
wine / cognac	вино / коньяк	*vee**noh** / kan-**yahk***
champagne	шампанское	*sham-**pahn**-ska-yeh*
Cheers!	За Ваше здоровье!	*Zah **vah**-sheh zda-**ro**-vyeh!*
caviar / salmon / sturgeon	икра / сёмга / осётр	***eek-ra** / **syom**-ga / ah-**syo**-tr*
chicken / duck	кура / утка	***ku**-rah / **oot**-ka*
steak / roast beef	бифштекс / ростбиф	*bif**shteks** / **rost**bif*
veal	телятина	*tel**yah**tina*
pork / ham / sausage	свинина / ветчина / колбаса	*svee**nee**na / vichin**ah** / kal**bahsa***
bread / potatoes / salad	хлеб / картошка / салат	*khlyep / kar**tosh**ka / sa-**lat***
fruit / vegetables	фрукты / овощи	***froo**-kti / **o**-vo-shchi*
butter / cheese	масло / сыр	***ma**sla / syr*
eggs / omelette	яйца / омлет	*ya-**eet**-sa / ahm**let***
salt / pepper	соль / перец	*sol / **perets***
tea / coffee	чай / кофе	*chai / **koh**fyeh*
milk / sugar	молоко / сахар	*mala**ko** / **sa**khar*
I'm a vegetarian	Я вегетариянец / вегетарианка	*Ya vegeter**ya**nets / vegeter**yan**ka* (m / f)

Questions and answers

What's your name?	Как Вас зовут?	*Kahk vahs za**voot**?*
My name is ...	Меня зовут...	***Minyah** zavoot ...*
I'm from ...	Я из...	*Yah eez ...*
Britain	Великобритании	***Ve-li-ko-bree-ta-nee-ee***
USA	США	*Seh-She-**Ah***
Canada / Australia	Канады / Австралии	*Ka**na**dy / Av-**stra**-lee-ee*
New Zealand	Новой Зеландии /	***No**voy Ze-**lan**-dee-ee*
Japan	Японии	*Ya-**po**-nee-ee*
Sweden / Finland	Швеции / Финляндии	***Shve**-tsee-ee / Fin-**lyan**-dee-ee*
Norway / Denmark	Норвегии / Дании	*Nar-**ve**-gee-ee / **Da**-nee-ee*
Germany / Austria	Германии / Австрии	*Ger**ma**nee / **Av**stree*
France / Netherlands	Франции / Голандии	***Frant**see / Gol**lan**dee*
Where are you going?	Куда Вы едити?	***Kudah** viy **yeh**-di-teh?*
I'm going to ...	Я еду....	*Yah ye**doo** ...*
Are you married?	Вы женаты (m) / замужем?	*Viy zhe**nah**ty* (m) / ***zamoozhem*** (f)*?*
Do you have any children?	Есть ли у Вас дети?	*Yest-li oo vas **dyeh**-ti?*
boy / girl	мальчик / девочка	***mahl**cheek / **dyeh**vochka*
How old are you?	Сколько Вам лет?	***Skol**ka vahm lyet?*
What do you do?	Кем Вы работаете?	*Kem viy ra**boh**tayete?*
student	студент, студентка	*stu**dyent*** (m), *stu**dyent**ka* (f)
teacher	учитель, учительница	***uchee**tyel* (m), ***uchee**tyelneetsa* (f)
doctor / nurse	врачь / медсестра	*vrach / myed-sis**tra***
actor / artist	актёр / художник	*ak**tyor** / khu**dozh**neek*
engineer / lawyer	инжинер / адвокат	*eenzhen**yehr** / advo**kaht***
office worker	служащий	***slu-zhash**-chi*
Where do you live?	Где Вы живёте?	*Gdyeh viy zhiv**yo**tyeh?*

RAILWAY DICTIONARY (Словарь железнодорожных терминов)

Ticket window	**касса**
for tickets after 24 hours	предварительная продажа билетов
for tickets within 24 hours	текущая продажа билетов
working from 08.00 to 20.00	часы работы с 8 до 20
open 24 hours	круглосуточная касса
break from 13.00 to 14.00	перерыв с 13 до 14
technical break from 10.15 to 10.45	технический перерыв 10.15 до 10.45

Timetable	**расписание**
even days (ie 2, 4, 6, ... of May)	Чёт (по четным числам)
odd days (ie 1, 3, 5, ... of May)	Неч (по нечетным числам)
weekends and public holidays	вых (по выходным)
weekdays	раб (по рабочим дням)
departure / arrival	От (отправление) / Пр (прибытие)
platform / station of destination	Пл (платформа) / станция назначения

Train	**поезд**
fast train / transit train	скорый поезд / транзитный поезд
passenger train / suburban train	пассажирский поезд / пригородный поезд
de luxe express train	фирменный поезд
train is late	поезд опаздывает
train does not stop	поезд не останавливается
train does not stop at the station	поезд не оставливается на станции

Station	**вокзал, станция**
station master	начальник вокзала
station attendant	дежурный по станции
information	справка

Carriage	**вагон**
SV (1st / soft), 2-berth compartments	СВ (спальный вагон) (or) мягкий вагон
kupé (coupé / 2nd / hard), 4-berth	купейный вагон
platzkart (open sleeping)	плацкартный вагон
obshchiy (open sitting)	общий вагон
wagon which separates and joins another train part way through the journey	безпересадочный вагон (or) отцепной вагон

Ticket	**билет**
one way / return	туда / туда и обратно
adult (full) fare / child fare	полный / детский
berth number	место
upper berth / lower berth	верхнее место / нижнее место
pass such as a monthly pass	проездной билет
discount ticket (pensioners, students etc)	льготный билет
price zones	зона

Time	**время**
Moscow Time / local time	московское время / местное время

On the train	**на поезде**
Train Captain (head conductor)	начальник поезда
conductor	проводник, проводница
emergency stop handle	стоп-кран
baggage rack	багажная полка
blankets	одеяло
sheets	бельё
rolled-up mattress and pillow	постельные принадлежности

Useful railway expressions	**Полезные железнодорожные выражения**
Here is my ticket	Вот мой билет
Please show me my place	Покажите, пожалуйста, моё место
Please wake me at	Разбудите меня в ...... часов
Please wake me an hour before we arrive at	Разбудите меня, пожалуйста, за час до прибытия в ....
Where is the restaurant car or buffet car?	Где находится вагон-ресторан или буфет?
Where is the toilet?	Где находится туалет?
May I smoke here?	Здесь можно курить?
Please bring me a (another) blanket	Принесите, пожалуйста, (ещё одно) одеяло
What is the next station?	Какая следующая станция?
How many minutes will the train stop here?	Сколько минут длится стоянка поезда?
I am late for the train	Я опоздал(а) на поезд

Station signs

вход (entrance), **выход** (exit), **переход** (crossover between stations), **выход в город** (way out or exit to street level)

Mongolian

Westerners tend to have difficulty mastering the tricky pronunciation of the national language of Mongolia. Until very recently, Mongolian was written in the same script as Russian (see p462), with two additional characters: \ (pronounced 'o') and **Y** ('u'). When Mongolian is transliterated into Roman script, stress is indicated by doubling the vowels. Thus 'Ulaanbaatar' is better written this way rather than as 'Ulan Bator' as the former transliteration shows that the first 'a' in each word is stressed.

Hello	*Sayn bayna uu*
Thank you	*Bayar-lalaar*
Yes / No	*Teem / Ugu-i*
Sorry	*Ooch-laarai*
I don't understand	*Bi oilgokh-gu-i bayna*
What's your name?	*Tani ner khen beh?*
Where do you live?	*Th khaana ami-dardag beh?*
Goodbye	*Bayar-tai*
Where is ...?	*Khaana bayna veh ...?*
hotel / airport	*zochid buudal / nisyeh ongotsni buudal*
railway station / bus station	*galt teregniy buudal / avtobusni zogsool*
temple / museum	*sum / moosei*
lavatory	*zhorlon*
left / right	*zuun / baruun*
soup	*shol*
egg	*ondog*
mutton	*honini makh*
rice / noodles	*budaar / goimon*
bread / cheese	*talh / byaslag*
potato / tomato	*toms / ulaan lool*
tea / coffee	*tsai / kofee*
beer / fermented mare's milk	*peevo / airag*
How much?	*Khed?*
cheap	*khyamd*
expensive	*kheterhiy unetiy yum*

1	*neg*
2	*khoyor*
3	*gurav*
4	*doroy*
5	*tav*
6	*zurgaar*
7	*doloo*
8	*naym*
9	*ee-us*
10	*arav*
11	*arvan neg*
12	*arvan khoyor*
13	*arvan gurav*
14	*arvan dorov*
15	*arvan tav*
20	*khori*
21	*khori neg*
30	*guchin*
31	*guchin neg*
40	*doch*
50	*tavi*
60	*zhar*
70	*dal*
80	*naya*
90	*er*
100	*zuu*
200	*khoyor zuu*
1000	*neg myanga*

Chinese

The phrases below aim to give some assistance but a phrase book really is a necessity, or even a beginner's language course.

The problem with Chinese is one of pronunciation – so much depends on your tone and emphasis that if you do not get the sound exactly right you will not be understood at all. The country's main dialect is Mandarin, spoken by about three-quarters of the population. Mandarin has four tones: high tone (¯), rising (´) where the voice starts low and rises to the same level as the high tone, falling-rising (˘) where the voice starts with a middle tone, falls and then rises to just below a high tone; and falling (`) which starts at the high tone and falls to a low one.

READING PINYIN CHINESE

Pinyin is the system of transliterating Chinese into the Roman alphabet. Pronunciation is indicated by the underlined letters below:

Vowels

a as in f**a**r
e as in w**e**re
i as in tr**ee** or as in w**e**re after c, r, s, z, ch, sh, zh
o as in **o**r
u as in p**oo**h
ü as in c**ue**

Consonants

c as in ea**ts**
q as in **ch**eap
r as in t**r**ill
x as in **sh**eep
h as in lo**ch** or the **kh** in an Arabic word, with the sound from the back of the throat
z as in plo**ds**
zh as in **j**aw

KEY PHRASES

The following phrases in Chinese characters may be useful to point to if you're having problems communicating:

Please write it down for me	请为我写下来
Help me please	请帮帮我
Please call a doctor	请叫个医生来

USEFUL WORDS AND PHRASES

General

Hello	*Nĭ hăo*	你好
Goodbye	*Zài jiàn*	再见
Please	*Qĭng*	请
Do you speak English?	*Nĭ huì shuō yīng yŭ ma?*	你会说英语吗?
Yes / no	*Dùi / Bū dùi* (literally correct / incorrect)	对 / 不对

No / Sorry, but no	*Méi yǒu*	没 有
Thank you	*Xiè xie*	谢 谢
Excuse me (sorry)	*Duì bù qǐ*	对 不 起
Excuse me (may I have your attention?)	*Qǐng wèn*	请 问
Good / bad	*Hǎo / bu hǎo*	好 / 不 好
I understand / do not understand	*Wǒ dǒng le / wǒ bù dǒng*	我 懂 了/ 我 不 懂
UK / USA	*Yīng guó / Měi guó*	英 国/ 美 国
Canada / Australia	*Jīa ná dà / Aó dà lia*	加 拿 大/ 澳 大 利 亚
France / Netherlands / Germany	*Fǎ guó / Hé lán / Dé guó*	法 国/ 荷 兰/ 德 国
China	*Zhōngguó*	中 国
Foreigner	*Wai guo ren / Guilo*	外 国 人/ 鬼 佬
Translator	*Fān yì*	翻 译

Directions

Where is ...?	*Zài nǎer ...?*	在哪儿?
toilet (ladies / gents)	*cè sǔo (nu / nan)*	厕所（女 / 男)
telephone	*diàn huà*	电话
airport	*jī chǎng*	机场
bus station	*qi chē zhàn*	汽车站
train	*huǒ chē*	火车
railway station	*huǒ chē zhàn*	火车站
taxi	*chū zū qì chē*	出租汽车
museum	*bó wù guǎn*	博物馆
hotel / restaurant	*fàn-diàn*	酒店 / 饭店
guesthouse	*bīnguǎn*	宾馆
post office	*yóu jú*	邮局
PSB / CAAC office	*Gōng ān jú / Zhōng háng gǒngsi*	公安局 / 中航公司
What time will we arrive at ...?	*Liè chē shénme shí hou dào ...?*	列车什么时候到?
What station is this?	*Zhè shì nà yí zhàn?*	这是哪一站?
North	*Běi*	北
South	*Nán*	南
East	*Dōng*	东
West	*Xī*	西

Street names

Many of the street names throughout China are similar. In most of the cities you visit, for example, you will find a Renmin Lu (People's St) and Jiefang Lu (Liberation St). You will also discover that streets are named (usually) according to a system which divides them into sections: north, centre, south etc. Thus if the thoroughfare of the city is Renmin Lu, and it runs from east to west, it may well have three (or more) separate names: Renmin Rd West – Renmin Xilu, Renmin Rd Centre – Renmin Zhonglu, Renmin Rd East – Renmin Donglu. By way of an indication, the designation that is given to a particular avenue also indicates its size. Roughly the following equate to English terminology:

Street *lù* 路	Road *jiē, dàjiē* 街, 大街	Lane *xiàng* 巷	Narrow alleyway *hutong* 胡同

Numbers

1	一	*yī*	18	十八	*shí bā*
2	二	*èr*	19	十九	*shí jiŭ*
3	三	*sān*	20	二十	*èr shí*
4	四	*sì*	21	二十一	*èr shí yī*
5	五	*wŭ*	30	三十	*sān shí*
6	六	*liù*	40	四十	*sì shí*
7	七	*qī*	50	五十	*wŭ shí*
8	八	*bā*	100	一百	*yì bai*
9	九	*jiŭ*	101	一百零一	*yì băi líng yī*
10	十	*shí*	110	一百一十	*yì băi yī shí*
11	十一	*shí yī*	150	一百五十	*yì băi wŭ shí*
12	十二	*shí èr*	200	二百	*èr băi*
13	十三	*shí sān*	500	五百	*wŭ băi*
14	十四	*shí sì*	1000	一千	*yì qiān*
15	十五	*shí wŭ*	10,000	一万	*yí wàn*
16	十六	*shí liù*	100,000	十万	*shí wàn*
17	十七	*shí qī*	1 million	一百万	*yì băi wàn*

How much?	*Duō shăo qián?*	多少钱
That's too expensive	*Tài guì le*	太贵了

Time

One o'clock, two o'clock ...	*Yī diăn, èr diăn ...*	一点，二点
Ten past one (1.10)	*Yī diăn shí fēn*	一点十分
Quarter to two (1.45)	*Yī diăn sì shí wŭ fēn*	一点四十五分
Two thirty (2.30)	*Èr diăn bàn*	二点半
Monday / Tuesday / Wednesday	*Xīng qī ... yī / èr / sān*	星期一/星期二/星期三
Thursday / Friday / Saturday	*Xīng qī ... sì / wŭ / liù*	星期四/星期五/星期六
Sunday	*Xīng qī rì*	星期日
Yesterday / tomorrow / today	*zuó tiān / míng tiān / jín tiān*	昨天/明天/今天

Transport

ticket	*piào*	票
Hard seat / Soft seat	*Yìng Zuò / Ruăn Zuò*	硬座/软座
Hard sleeper / Soft sleeper	*Yìng Wò / Ruăn Wò*	硬卧/软卧
Please may I upgrade this ticket ...	*Qĭng nĭ huan gao yī ji de piào*	请你换高一级的票

Food and drink

menu	*cài dān*	菜单
mineral water / tea / beer	*kuàng quán shuĭ / chá / pí jiŭ*	矿泉水/茶/啤酒
noodles / noodle soup	*miàn / tāng miàn*	面/汤面
bread / egg	*miàn bāo / jī diàn*	面包/鸡蛋
pork / beef / lamb	*zhū ròu / níu ròu / yáng ròu*	猪肉/牛肉/羊肉
chicken / duck / fish	*jī / yā / yú*	鸡/鸭/鱼
vegetables	*shū cài*	蔬菜
Do you have any vegetarian dishes?	*Nĭ zhèr yŏu shù-cài ma?*	你这儿有蔬菜吗?
steamed rice	*mĭ fàn*	米饭
fujian fried rice	*fu jian chăo fàn*	福建炒饭
fried rice	*jī dan chăo fàn*	鸡蛋炒饭
pork in Sichuan-style sauce	*yú xiāng ròu sī*	鱼香肉丝
sweet and sour pork	*gu lao zhŭ ròu*	咕老(猪)肉
pork and onion in soy sauce	*hui guō roù*	回锅肉
pork in sweet thick sauce	*táng cù lĭjī*	糖醋里脊
beef chow mien	*niú ròu chăo miàn*	牛肉炒面
spicy beef soup with veg	*shui zhŭ niú ròu*	水煮牛肉
chicken in Sichuan sauce	*yu xian ba kuai jī*	鱼香八块鸡
chicken chow mien	*jī ròu chăo miàn*	鸡肉炒面
chicken with cashew nuts	*yao guō jī ding*	腰果鸡丁
fried tofu with meat and veg	*jia chang dòufŭ*	家常豆腐
green beanshoots	*dòu miao*	豆苗
vegetable chow mien	*su chăo miàn*	素炒面
hot and sour soup	*sūan là tāng*	酸辣汤
Delicious	*Hao chi*	好吃
Cheers!	*Gan bei!*	干杯!

INDEX

Abbreviations (M) Moscow (SP) = St Petersburg
Page references in **bold** type refer to maps

Acknowledgements

Among the many readers who have written in with advice and suggestions, thanks to Alison (NZ), Olga Belnik (Russia), Mahmood Bhutta (UK), James Boyd (Ireland), John Bradford, Jonathan Brown, Simon Calder (UK), Malcolm Carroll (UK), James Cho, Asger Christiansen (Denmark), Helen Clive, Lawrence Cotter (USA), Phil Davies (UK), Lena Davigova (Russia), Christopher Downey (Australia), Laurens den Dulk (Netherlands), Howard Dymock (UK), Col Francis and Christine Emmorey (UK), Jay Gary Finkelstein (USA), Penny Fitt (UK), Julia Fitzgerald, Claudia Gamperle (Switzerland), Emmy Gengler (USA), Yiannis Gikas (Greece), Gordon Gill (USA), Jim Gill (Australia), Jonny Googs (UK), Dmitri Gorokhov (Russia), John Gothard (UK), Tom Grant, Laura Hamelen (UK), Dr Malcolm Hannan (UK), Reijo Härkönen (Finland), Will Harrison-Cripps (UK), Alexander Hartig, Glenn Harvey (Australia), Louise Hellwig, Angela Hollingsworth (UK), Ida Holmgren, Iwan (Russia), Benedikt Jaeger (Germany), Andy Jones (HK), Oskar Karlin, Helene Karson, Ruth Kennedy, Dr Mark Krebs, Valeria Kuteeva (Russia), Rowena Lambert, Stu Lloyd (Australia), Matz Lonnedal Risberg (Norway), Karin MacArthur (Australia), Andrea Marcialis (Italy), Laurie Martin (USA), Matheu (UK) & Wieteke (Netherlands), Vicky McCarrick, Stephen McLaughlin (UK), Richard Maxey, Karen Mulders, Terry Nakazono (USA), Yuri Nemirovsky (Russia), Heather Oxley (Egypt), Oded Paporisch (Israel), John Parton, Marcus Patzig (Germany), Rich Perkins (UK), Jakub Pilch (Poland), Richard Pingree, Helen Revell, Philip Robinson (UK), Henri Julien Sandront, Nancy Scarth (Canada), Tobi Schwarzmueller (Germany), Rolf Smeds (Finland), David Soulsby (UK), Sandra Southwell, Walter Spoerle (Germany), Margaret Stack and Peter Munroe, Jonathan Streit, Duncan Taylor, Neil Taylor (UK), Mark Taylor (UK), Emmanuel du Teilhet (France), Diana Valia Chen and Andrew van der Westhuyzen (Australia), Katya Voronicheva (Russia), Julia and Chris Wallace (UK), Elizabeth Watson (UK), Ian Whitby (UK), Jan Wigsten (Mongolia), Felicity Wilcox (UK), Edward Wilson (UK), Andrew Wingham (UK), Jennie Wogan (UK), Rashit Yahin (Russia) and Andrew Young (UK).

Trans-Canada Rail Guide
Melissa Graham, 5th edn, £12.99
ISBN 978-1-905864-33-1, 256pp, 34 maps, 30 colour photos
Comprehensive guide to Canada's trans-continental railroad. Covers the entire route from coast to coast with information for all budgets. Mile-by-mile route guides. City guides and maps – ten major stops including Quebec City, Montreal, Toronto, Winnipeg, Jasper and Vancouver.

Indian Rail Handbook *Nick Hill & Royston Ellis*, 1st edn, £12.99
ISBN 978-1-873756-87-4, 256pp, 80 maps, 30 colour photos
India has the most comprehensive railway network in the world, with almost all tourist attractions accessible by rail. For most visitors travel by train is the preferred means of transport, the ideal way to see the country. This new book is a wholly inclusive guide for rail travellers in India. Foreword by Mark Tully.
- Fully-indexed rail atlas of 80 maps with all 7326 railway stations
- Rail travel for all budgets, special trains and railway history
- Timetables, suggested itineraries and how to book tickets

Japan by Rail *Ramsey Zarifeh*, 2nd edn, £13.99
ISBN 978-1-873756-97-3, 480pp, 60 maps, 30 colour photos
The real secret to travelling around Japan on a budget is the Japan Rail Pass, as explained in this guide. Includes selected routes, strip maps, where to stay and where to eat, practical information. Km-by-km route guides. '*Excellent guide*' – **The Sunday Times**

The Silk Roads *Paul Wilson*, 3rd edn, £14.99
ISBN 978-1-905864-32-4, 448pp, 60 maps, 40 colour photos
The Silk Road was never a single thread across Asia but an intricate web of shorter trade routes – Silk Roads – which together linked Asia and Europe. City guides & maps – the best sights, places to stay and restaurants for all budgets in 55 stopovers along the way. Includes Turkey, Syria, Iran, Turkmenistan, Uzbekistan, Kyrgyzstan, Pakistan, China. Plus lesser-known routes – Southern Taklamakan, Karakorum Highway, Marco Polo's route to Xanadu.

Siberian BAM Guide – Rail, Rivers & Road **[Stocks low]**
Athol Yates & Nicholas Zvegintzov, 2nd edn, £13.99
ISBN 978-1-873756-18-8, 384pp, 60 maps, 22 colour photos
Comprehensive guide to the BAM Zone in NE Siberia. Includes a km-by-km guide to the 3400km Baikal Amur Mainline (BAM) railway which traverses east Siberia from the Pacific Ocean to Lake Baikal. How to take the train and where to go in the BAM Zone.. '*An encyclopaedic companion*' – **The Independent**

Australia by Rail *Colin Taylor*, 5th edn, £12.99
ISBN 978-1-873756-81-2, 290pp, 65 maps, 30 colour photos
With 65 strip maps covering all rail routes in Australia, city guides (Sydney, Melbourne, Brisbane, Adelaide, Perth, Darwin and Canberra), and now includes the new Ghan line from Alice Springs to Darwin. '*Benefiting from Taylor's 30 years of travel on Australia's trains.*' **The Sunday Times**

TREKKING GUIDES

Europe
Corsica Trekking – GR20
Dolomites Trekking – AV1 & AV2
Scottish Highlands – Hillwalking Guide
Tour du Mont Blanc
Trekking in the Pyrenees
The Walker's Haute Route:
Mt Blanc to Matterhorn

South America
Inca Trail, Cusco & Machu Picchu

Africa
Kilimanjaro (and Mt Meru)
Moroccan Atlas – The Trekking Guide

Australasia
New Zealand – The Great Walks

Asia
Nepal Trekking & Great Himalaya Trail
Trekking in the Annapurna Region
Trekking in the Everest Region
Trekking in Ladakh

Scottish Highlands – The Hillwalking Guide *Jim Manthorpe*
ISBN 978-1-905864-21-8 2nd edn, £12.99, 320pp, 86 maps,
Covers 60 day-hikes in the following areas:

- Loch Lomond, the Trossachs and Southern Highlands
- Glen Coe and Ben Nevis
- Central Highlands ● Cairngorms and Eastern Highlands
- Western Highlands ● North-West Highlands ● The Far North
- The Islands. Plus: 3- to 4-day hikes linking some regions.

Tour du Mont Blanc
Jim Manthorpe, 1st edn, £11.99
ISBN 978-1-905864-12-6, 176pp, 50 maps, 30 colour photos

At 4807m (15,771ft), Mont Blanc is the highest mountain in western Europe, and one of the most famous mountains in the world. The trail (105 miles, 168km) that circumnavigates the massif, passing through France, Italy and Switzerland, is the most popular long distance walk in Europe. Includes Chamonix and Courmayeur guides.

Corsica Trekking – GR20 *David Abram*, 1st edn, £11.99
ISBN 978-1-873756-98-0, 208pp, 32 maps, 30 colour photos

Slicing diagonally across Corsica's jagged spine, the legendary red-and-white waymarks of the GR20 guide trekkers across a succession of snow-streaked passes, Alpine meadows, massive boulder fields and pristine forests of pine and oak – often within sight of the sea. Physically demanding from start to finish, it's a superlative 170km, two-week trek. Includes guides to gateway towns: Ajaccio, Bastia, Calvi, Corte and Porto-Vecchio.
'Indispensible'. ***The Independent***
'Excellent guide'. ***The Sunday Times***

The Walker's Haute Route – Mt Blanc to the Matterhorn
Alexander Stewart, 1st edn, £12.99
ISBN 978-1-905864-08-9, 256pp, 60 maps, 30 colour photos

From Mont Blanc to the Matterhorn, Chamonix to Zermatt, the 180km (113-mile) Walkers' Haute Route traverses one of the finest stretches of the Pennine Alps – the range between Valais in Switzerland and Piedmont and Aosta Valley in Italy. Includes Chamonix and Zermatt guides.

The Inca Trail, Cusco & Machu Picchu
Alexander Stewart, 4th edn, £12.99
ISBN 978-1-905864-15-7, 352pp, 74 maps, 40 colour photos
The Inca Trail, from Cusco to Machu Picchu, is South America's most popular trek. Practical guide including detailed trail maps, plans of Inca sites, plus guides to Cusco and Machu Picchu. Route guides to other trails in the area: the Santa Teresa Trek and the Choquequirao Trek as well as the Vilcabamba Trail plus the routes linking them. This entirely rewalked and rewritten fourth edition includes a new history of the Incas by Hugh Thomson.

New Zealand – The Great Walks *Alex Stewart*, 2nd edn, £12.99
ISBN 978-1-905864-11-9, 272pp, 60 maps, 40 colour photos
New Zealand is a wilderness paradise of incredibly beautiful landscapes. There is no better way to experience it than on one of the nine designated Great Walks, the country's premier walking tracks which provide outstanding hiking opportunities for people at all levels of fitness. Also includes detailed guides to Auckland, Wellington, Taumarunui, Nelson, Queenstown, Te Anau and Oban.

Kilimanjaro – the trekking guide to Africa's highest mountain *Henry Stedman*, 3rd edn, £12.99
ISBN 978-1-905864-24-9, 368pp, 40 maps, 30 photos
At 19,340ft the world's tallest freestanding mountain, Kilimanjaro is one of the most popular destinations for hikers visiting Africa. It's possible to walk up to the summit: no technical skills are necessary. Includes town guides to Nairobi and Dar-Es-Salaam, and a colour guide to flora and fauna. Includes Mount Meru.

Nepal Trekking and the Great Himalaya Trail
Robin Boustead, 1st edn, £14.99, ISBN 978-1-905864-31-7
256pp, 8pp colour maps, 40 colour photos
This guide includes the most popular routes in Nepal – the Everest, Annapurna and Langtang regions – as well as the newest trekking areas for true trailblazers. This is the first guide to chart The Great Himalaya Trail, the route which crosses Nepal from east to west. Extensive planning sections.

Trekking in the Everest Region
Jamie McGuinness, 5th edn, £12.99, ISBN 978-1-873756-99-7
320pp, 30 maps, 30 colour photos
Fifth edition of this popular guide to the Everest region, the world's most famous trekking region. Planning, preparation, getting to Nepal; detailed route guides with 30 route maps and 50 village plans; Kathmandu city guide: where to stay, where to eat, what to see.

Moroccan Atlas – The Trekking Guide *Alan Palmer*
ISBN 978-1-873756-77-5, 1st edn, £12.99, 268pp, 54 maps
The High Atlas in central Morocco is the most dramatic and beautiful section of the entire Atlas range. Includes 44 detailed trekking maps – showing route times, places to stay and points of interest – and 10 town and village guides with town plans (including Marrakech, Imlil, Taliouine, Ouarzazate, Azilal).

TRAILBLAZER'S BRITISH WALKING GUIDES

We've applied to destinations which are closer to home Trailblazer's proven formula for publishing definitive practical route guides for adventurous travellers. Britain's network of long-distance trails enables the walker to explore some of the finest landscapes in the country's best walking areas. These are guides that are user-friendly, practical, informative and environmentally sensitive.

- **Unique mapping features** In many walking guidebooks the reader has to read a route description then try to relate it to the map. Our guides are much easier to use because walking directions, tricky junctions, places to stay and eat, points of interest and walking times are all written onto the maps themselves in the places to which they apply. With their uncluttered clarity, these are not general-purpose maps but fully edited maps drawn by walkers for walkers.

- **Largest-scale walking maps** At a scale of just under 1:20,000 (8cm or $3^{1}/_{8}$ inches to one mile) the maps in these guides are bigger than even the most detailed British walking maps currently available in the shops.

- **Not just a trail guide – includes where to stay, where to eat and public transport** Our guidebooks cover the complete walking experience, not just the route. Accommodation options for all budgets are provided (pubs, hotels, B&Bs, campsites, bunkhouses, hostels) as well as places to eat. Detailed public transport information for all access points to each trail means that there are itineraries for all walkers, for hiking the entire route as well as for day or weekend walks.

Coast to Coast Path *Henry Stedman*, 4th edition, £11.99
ISBN 978-1-905864-30-0, 256pp, 110 maps, 40 colour photos

Cornwall Coast Path *Edith Schofield*, 3rd edition, £9.99
ISBN 978-1-905864-19-5, 256pp, 112 maps, 40 colour photos

Cotswold Way *Tricia & Bob Hayne*, 1st edition, £9.99
ISBN 978-1-905864-16-4, 192pp, 60 maps, 40 colour photos

Hadrian's Wall Path *Henry Stedman*, 3rd edition, £11.99
ISBN 978-1-905864-37-9, 224pp, 60 maps, 40 colour photos

North Downs Way *John Curtin*, 1st edition, £9.99
ISBN 978-1-873756-96-6, 192pp, 80 maps, 40 colour photos

Offa's Dyke Path *Keith Carter*, 3rd edition, £11.99
ISBN 978-1-905864-35-5, 240pp, 98 maps, 40 colour photos

Peddars Way & Norfolk Coast Path *Alexander Stewart*, £11.99
ISBN 978-1-905864-28-7, 192pp, 54 maps, 40 colour photos

Pembrokeshire Coast Path *Jim Manthorpe*, 3rd edition, £9.99
ISBN 978-1-905864-27-0, 224pp, 96 maps, 40 colour photos

Pennine Way *Keith Carter & Chris Scott*, 3rd edition, £11.99
ISBN 978-1-905864-34-8, 272pp, 138 maps, 40 colour photos

The Ridgeway *Nick Hill*, 2nd edition, £9.99
ISBN 978-1-905864-17-1, 192pp, 53 maps, 40 colour photos

South Downs Way *Jim Manthorpe*, 3rd edition, £9.99
ISBN 978-1-905864-18-8, 192pp, 60 maps, 40 colour photos

West Highland Way *Charlie Loram*, 4th edition, £9.99
ISBN 978-1-905864-29-4, 192pp, 60 maps, 40 colour photos

'The same attention to detail that distinguishes its other guides has been brought to bear here'.
THE SUNDAY TIMES

IN PREPARATION FOR PUBLICATION 2012-13:

South West Coast Path
(3 vols)

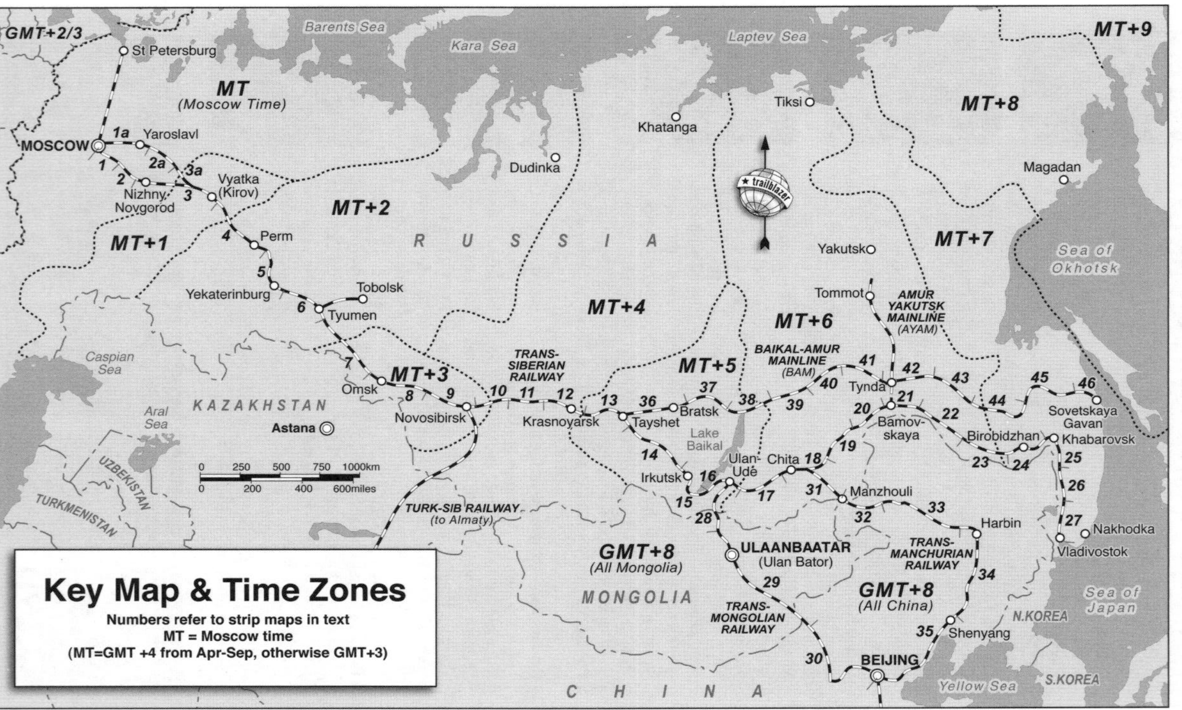
Key Map & Time Zones
Numbers refer to strip maps in text
MT = Moscow time
(MT=GMT +4 from Apr-Sep, otherwise GMT+3)
GMT+2/3
MT
(Moscow Time)
MT+1
MT+2
MT+3
MT+4
MT+5
MT+6
MT+7
MT+8
MT+9
GMT+8
(All Mongolia)
GMT+8
(All China)
R U S S I A
K A Z A K H S T A N
M O N G O L I A
C H I N A
UZBEKISTAN
TURKMENISTAN
N.KOREA
S.KOREA
Barents Sea
Kara Sea
Laptev Sea
Sea of Okhotsk
Sea of Japan
Yellow Sea
Caspian Sea
Aral Sea
Lake Baikal
MOSCOW
St Petersburg
Yaroslavl
Nizhny Novgorod
Vyatka (Kirov)
Perm
Yekaterinburg
Tyumen
Tobolsk
Omsk
Novosibirsk
Krasnoyarsk
Tayshet
Bratsk
Irkutsk
Ulan-Udė
Chita
Manzhouli
Tynda
Bamovskaya
Birobidzhan
Khabarovsk
Sovetskaya Gavan
Vladivostok
Nakhodka
Harbin
Shenyang
BEIJING
ULAANBAATAR
(Ulan Bator)
Astana
Dudinka
Khatanga
Tiksi
Yakutsk
Tommot
Magadan
TRANS-SIBERIAN RAILWAY
BAIKAL-AMUR MAINLINE (BAM)
AMUR YAKUTSK MAINLINE (AYAM)
TRANS-MONGOLIAN RAILWAY
TRANS-MANCHURIAN RAILWAY
TURK-SIB RAILWAY (to Almaty)
trailblazer
0 250 500 750 1000km
0 200 400 600miles
1 1a 2 2a 3 3a 4 5 6 7 8 9 10 11 12 13 14 15 16 17 18 19 20 21 22 23 24 25 26 27 28 29 30 31 32 33 34 35 36 37 38 39 40 41 42 43 44 45 46

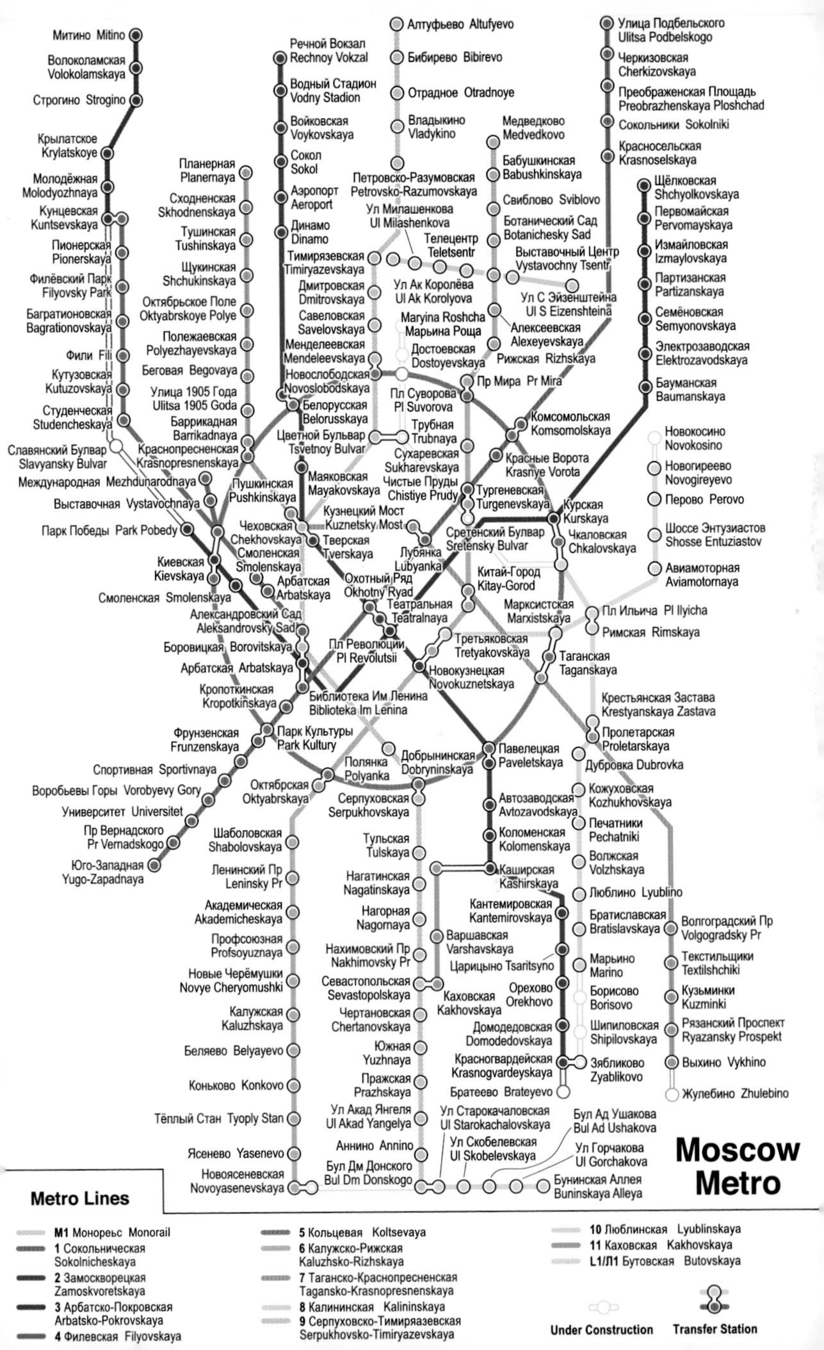
Митино Mitino
Волоколамская Volokolamskaya
Строгино Strogino
Крылатское Krylatskoye
Молодёжная Molodyozhnaya
Кунцевская Kuntsevskaya
Пионерская Pionerskaya
Филёвский Парк Filyovsky Park
Багратионовская Bagrationovskaya
Фили Fili
Кутузовская Kutuzovskaya
Студенческая Studencheskaya
Славянский Бульвар Slavyansky Bulvar
Международная Mezhdunarodnaya
Выставочная Vystavochnaya
Парк Победы Park Pobedy
Киевская Kievskaya
Смоленская Smolenskaya
Планерная Planernaya
Сходненская Skhodnenskaya
Тушинская Tushinskaya
Щукинская Shchukinskaya
Октябрьское Поле Oktyabrskoye Polye
Полежаевская Polyezhayevskaya
Беговая Begovaya
Улица 1905 Года Ulitsa 1905 Goda
Баррикадная Barrikadnaya
Краснопресненская Krasnopresnenskaya
Речной Вокзал Rechnoy Vokzal
Водный Стадион Vodny Stadion
Войковская Voykovskaya
Сокол Sokol
Аэропорт Aeroport
Динамо Dinamo
Белорусская Belorusskaya
Маяковская Mayakovskaya
Пушкинская Pushkinskaya
Чеховская Chekhovskaya
Тверская Tverskaya
Смоленская Smolenskaya
Арбатская Arbatskaya
Александровский Сад Aleksandrovsky Sad
Боровицкая Borovitskaya
Арбатская Arbatskaya
Кропоткинская Kropotkinskaya
Библиотека Им Ленина Biblioteka Im Lenina
Парк Культуры Park Kultury
Фрунзенская Frunzenskaya
Спортивная Sportivnaya
Воробьевы Горы Vorobyevy Gory
Университет Universitet
Пр Вернадского Pr Vernadskogo
Юго-Западная Yugo-Zapadnaya
Алтуфьево Altufyevo
Бибирево Bibirevo
Отрадное Otradnoye
Владыкино Vladykino
Петровско-Разумовская Petrovsko-Razumovskaya
Ул Милашенкова Ul Milashenkova
Телецентр Teletsentr
Тимирязевская Timiryazevskaya
Ул Ак Королёва Ul Ak Korolyova
Выставочный Центр Vystavochny Tsentr
Ул С Эйзенштейна Ul S Eizenshteina
Дмитровская Dmitrovskaya
Савеловская Savelovskaya
Менделеевская Mendeleevskaya
Новослободская Novoslobodskaya
Maryina Roshcha Марьина Роща
Достоевская Dostoyevskaya
Цветной Бульвар Tsvetnoy Bulvar
Пл Суворова Pl Suvorova
Трубная Trubnaya
Сухаревская Sukharevskaya
Чистые Пруды Chistiye Prudy
Кузнецкий Мост Kuznetsky Most
Лубянка Lubyanka
Охотный Ряд Okhotny Ryad
Театральная Teatralnaya
Пл Революции Pl Revolutsii
Медведково Medvedkovo
Бабушкинская Babushkinskaya
Свиблово Sviblovo
Ботанический Сад Botanichesky Sad
Алексеевская Alexeyevskaya
Рижская Rizhskaya
Пр Мира Pr Mira
Комсомольская Komsomolskaya
Красные Ворота Krasnye Vorota
Тургеневская Turgenevskaya
Сретенский Бульвар Sretensky Bulvar
Китай-Город Kitay-Gorod
Улица Подбельского Ulitsa Podbelskogo
Черкизовская Cherkizovskaya
Преображенская Площадь Preobrazhenskaya Ploshchad
Сокольники Sokolniki
Красносельская Krasnoselskaya
Щёлковская Shchyolkovskaya
Первомайская Pervomayskaya
Измайловская Izmaylovskaya
Партизанская Partizanskaya
Семёновская Semyonovskaya
Электрозаводская Elektrozavodskaya
Бауманская Baumanskaya
Курская Kurskaya
Чкаловская Chkalovskaya
Новокосино Novokosino
Новогиреево Novogireyevo
Перово Perovo
Шоссе Энтузиастов Shosse Entuziastov
Авиамоторная Aviamotornaya
Пл Ильича Pl Ilyicha
Римская Rimskaya
Марксистская Marxistskaya
Таганская Taganskaya
Третьяковская Tretyakovskaya
Новокузнецкая Novokuznetskaya
Крестьянская Застава Krestyanskaya Zastava
Пролетарская Proletarskaya
Дубровка Dubrovka
Кожуховская Kozhukhovskaya
Печатники Pechatniki
Волжская Volzhskaya
Люблино Lyublino
Братиславская Bratislavskaya
Марьино Marino
Борисово Borisovo
Шипиловская Shipilovskaya
Зябликово Zyablikovo
Волгоградский Пр Volgogradsky Pr
Текстильщики Textilshchiki
Кузьминки Kuzminki
Рязанский Проспект Ryazansky Prospekt
Выхино Vykhino
Жулебино Zhulebino
Павелецкая Paveletskaya
Автозаводская Avtozavodskaya
Коломенская Kolomenskaya
Каширская Kashirskaya
Кантемировская Kantemirovskaya
Царицыно Tsaritsyno
Орехово Orekhovo
Домодедовская Domodedovskaya
Красногвардейская Krasnogvardeyskaya
Братеево Brateyevo
Варшавская Varshavskaya
Каховская Kakhovskaya
Полянка Polyanka
Добрынинская Dobryninskaya
Октябрская Oktyabrskaya
Серпуховская Serpukhovskaya
Тульская Tulskaya
Нагатинская Nagatinskaya
Нагорная Nagornaya
Нахимовский Пр Nakhimovsky Pr
Севастопольская Sevastopolskaya
Чертановская Chertanovskaya
Южная Yuzhnaya
Пражская Prazhskaya
Ул Акад Янгеля Ul Akad Yangelya
Аннино Annino
Бул Дм Донского Bul Dm Donskogo
Шаболовская Shabolovskaya
Ленинский Пр Leninsky Pr
Академическая Akademicheskaya
Профсоюзная Profsoyuznaya
Новые Черёмушки Novye Cheryomushki
Калужская Kaluzhskaya
Беляево Belyayevo
Коньково Konkovo
Тёплый Стан Tyoply Stan
Ясенево Yasenevo
Новоясеневская Novoyasenevskaya
Ул Старокачаловская Ul Starokachalovskaya
Ул Скобелевская Ul Skobelevskaya
Бул Ад Ушакова Bul Ad Ushakova
Ул Горчакова Ul Gorchakova
Бунинская Аллея Buninskaya Alleya
Moscow Metro
Metro Lines
M1 Монорельс Monorail
1 Сокольническая Sokolnicheskaya
2 Замоскворецкая Zamoskvoretskaya
3 Арбатско-Покровская Arbatsko-Pokrovskaya
4 Филевская Filyovskaya
5 Кольцевая Koltsevaya
6 Калужско-Рижская Kaluzhsko-Rizhskaya
7 Таганско-Краснопресненская Tagansko-Krasnopresnenskaya
8 Калининская Kalininskaya
9 Серпуховско-Тимирязевская Serpukhovsko-Timiryazevskaya
10 Люблинская Lyublinskaya
11 Каховская Kakhovskaya
L1/Л1 Бутовская Butovskaya
Under Construction
Transfer Station

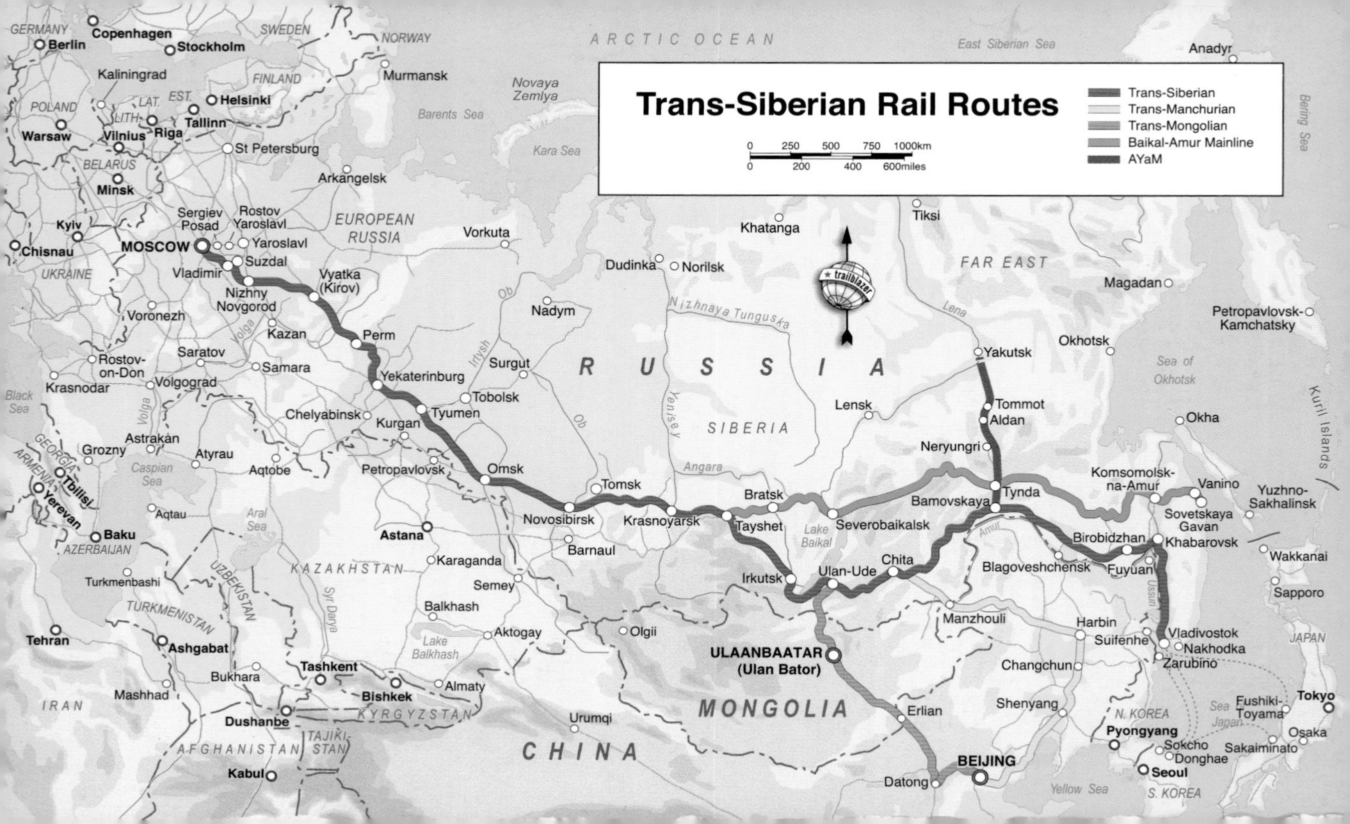

Trans-Siberian Rail Routes
Trans-Siberian
Trans-Manchurian
Trans-Mongolian
Baikal-Amur Mainline
AYaM
0 250 500 750 1000km
0 200 400 600miles
trailblazer
ARCTIC OCEAN
East Siberian Sea
Bering Sea
Barents Sea
Kara Sea
Sea of Okhotsk
Black Sea
Caspian Sea
Aral Sea
Lake Baikal
Lake Balkhash
Sea of Japan
Yellow Sea
Kuril Islands
Novaya Zemlya
RUSSIA
EUROPEAN RUSSIA
SIBERIA
FAR EAST
MONGOLIA
CHINA
KAZAKHSTAN
UZBEKISTAN
TURKMENISTAN
KYRGYZSTAN
TAJIKISTAN
AFGHANISTAN
IRAN
GEORGIA
ARMENIA
AZERBAIJAN
UKRAINE
BELARUS
POLAND
GERMANY
LITH.
LAT.
EST.
FINLAND
SWEDEN
NORWAY
JAPAN
N. KOREA
S. KOREA
Ob
Irtysh
Yenisey
Nizhnaya Tunguska
Angara
Lena
Volga
Amur
Ussuri
Syr Darya
Berlin
Copenhagen
Stockholm
Kaliningrad
Helsinki
Tallinn
Riga
Vilnius
Warsaw
Minsk
St Petersburg
Murmansk
Arkangelsk
Kyiv
Chisnau
MOSCOW
Sergiev Posad
Rostov Yaroslavl
Yaroslavl
Suzdal
Vladimir
Nizhny Novgorod
Vyatka (Kirov)
Voronezh
Kazan
Perm
Saratov
Samara
Rostov-on-Don
Krasnodar
Volgograd
Vorkuta
Yekaterinburg
Chelyabinsk
Tyumen
Tobolsk
Kurgan
Surgut
Nadym
Dudinka
Norilsk
Khatanga
Tiksi
Astrakan
Atyrau
Aqtobe
Grozny
Tbilisi
Yerevan
Aqtau
Baku
Turkmenbashi
Tehran
Ashgabat
Mashhad
Bukhara
Tashkent
Bishkek
Almaty
Dushanbe
Kabul
Petropavlovsk
Omsk
Astana
Karaganda
Semey
Balkhash
Aktogay
Urumqi
Olgii
Novosibirsk
Barnaul
Tomsk
Krasnoyarsk
Tayshet
Bratsk
Severobaikalsk
Irkutsk
Ulan-Ude
Chita
ULAANBAATAR (Ulan Bator)
Erlian
Datong
BEIJING
Manzhouli
Harbin
Changchun
Shenyang
Suifenhe
Lensk
Yakutsk
Tommot
Aldan
Neryungri
Tynda
Bamovskaya
Blagoveshchensk
Birobidzhan
Khabarovsk
Fuyuan
Vladivostok
Nakhodka
Zarubino
Komsomolsk-na-Amur
Vanino
Sovetskaya Gavan
Yuzhno-Sakhalinsk
Okha
Okhotsk
Magadan
Petropavlovsk-Kamchatsky
Anadyr
Wakkanai
Sapporo
Fushiki-Toyama
Tokyo
Osaka
Sakaiminato
Pyongyang
Sokcho
Donghae
Seoul